JAGUAR
ALL THE CARS

JAGUAR
ALL THE CARS
UPDATED PAPERBACK EDITION

NIGEL THORLEY

First published in September 2003; reprinted 2005
Second edition published in November 2009; reprinted 2011
Third edition published in February 2013
Fourth edition published in March 2016, reprinted November 2018.
This updated paperback edition published in 2024 by Veloce, an imprint of David and Charles Limited.
Nigel Thorley has asserted his right to be identified as the author of this work.

© 2024 Nigel Thorley & David and Charles
Tel +44 (0)1305 260068 / e-mail info@veloce.co.uk / web www.veloce.co.uk

All rights reserved. With the exception of quoting brief passages for the purpose of review, no part of this publication may be recorded, reproduced or transmitted by any means, including photocopying, without the written permission of David and Charles Limited.

Throughout this book, logos, model names and designations, etc, have been used for the purposes of identification, illustration and decoration. Such names are the property of the trademark holder as this is not an official publication. Readers with ideas for automotive books, or books on other transport or related hobby subjects, are invited to write to the editorial director of Veloce at the above email address. British Library Cataloguing in Publication Data – A catalogue record for this book is available from the British Library.

Design and production by Veloce, an imprint of David and Charles.
Printed in China by Asia Pacific Offset Group Ltd.

Conversion factors

	METRIC	IMPERIAL
Length (distance)		
Inches (in)	x 25.4 = Millimetres (mm)	x 0.0394 = Inches (in)
Feet (ft)	x 0.305 = Metres (m)	x 3.281 = Feet (ft)
Miles	x 1.609 = Kilometres (km)	x 0.621 = Miles
Volume (capacity)		
Cubic inches (cu in; in^3)	x 16.387 = Cubic centimetres (cc; cm^3)	x 0.061 = Cubic inches (cu in; in^3)
Imperial pints (Imp pt)	x 0.568 = Litres (l)	x 1.76 = Imperial pints (Imp pt)
Imperial gallons (Imp gal)	x 4.546 = Litres (l)	x 0.22 = Imperial gallons (Imp gal)
US gallons (US gal)	x 3.785 = Litres (l)	x 0.264 = US gallons (US gal)
Mass (weight)		
Pounds (lb)	x 0.454 = Kilograms (kg)	x 2.205 = Pounds (lb)
Hundredweight (cwt)	x 50.802 = Kilograms (kg)	x 0.020 = Hundredweight (cwt)
Torque		
Pounds-force feet (lbf ft; lb ft)	x 1.356 = Newton metres (Nm)	x 0.738 = Pounds-force ft (lbf ft; lb ft)
Pounds-force feet (lbf ft; lb ft)	x 0.138 = Kilograms-force metres (kgf m; kg m)	x 7.233 = Pounds-force feet (lbf ft; lb ft)
Power		
Horsepower (hp)	x 745.7 = Watts (W)	x 0.0013 = Horsepower (hp)
Speed		
Miles per hour (miles/hr; mph)	x 1.609 = Kilometres per hour (km/hr; kph)	x 0.621 = Miles per hour (miles/hr; mph)
Fuel consumption		
Miles per gallon (mpg)	x 0.354 = Kilometres per litre (km/l)	x 2.825 = Miles per gallon (mpg)

Contents

	Introduction	6
	Jaguar heritage	7
	Jaguar engines	12
1	**Prewar SS Jaguars** 1935 to 1940	24
2	**Postwar pushrods** 1945 to 1951	36
3	**The XK sports cars** 1948 to 1961	46
4	**The Mark VII to IX saloons** 1950 to 1961	61
5	**The Compact Jaguar saloons** 1955 to 1969	73
6	**E-type Series 1, 2 and 3 sports cars** 1961 to 1974	92
7	**The Mark X/420G saloons** 1961 to 1970	110
8	**The S-type and 420 saloons** 1963 to 1969	121
9	**The XJ Series saloons** 1968 to 1992	130
10	**Daimler DS420 limousine** 1968 to 1992	161
11	**The XJ-S** 1975 to 1996	168
12	**The XJ40 saloons** 1986 to 1994	190
13	**The New Series XJ6/12 saloons** 1994 to 1997	205
14	**XK8 sports cars** 1996 to 2005	216
15	**The XJ8 saloons** 1997 to 2002	232
16	**S-type saloons** 1999 to 2007	244
17	**X-type saloons** 2001 to 2009	260
18	**XJ6 and XJ8 saloons (X-350)** 2003 to 2009	278
19	**New XK sports cars** 2006 to 2014	292
20	**XF saloons and sportbrake** 2007 to 2015/6	310
21	**New XJ (X-351) saloons** 2010 to 2019	328
22	**F-TYPE sports cars** from 2013	343
23	**XE saloons** from 2015	362
24	**New XF saloons and sportbrakes** from 2015	377
25	**F-PACE SUV** from 2016	394
26	**E-PACE SUV** from 2018	412

Introduction

The purpose of this book is to provide a comprehensive, yet concise, guide to all the production cars that have carried the Jaguar name.

Every model is covered, from the first Jaguar (branded SS) to the current models at the time of writing. The reader will find a brief history of each car and its development changes, along with technical specifications, prices when new, years in production, numbers produced, and exterior/interior colour schemes. There is also a visual appraisal in both words and photographs covering key identification points and modifications over the production period, enabling the reader to accurately identify a particular car.

The author has tried to be as precise as possible, but individual owners could, and often did, make specific requests when ordering new cars. Consequently, some vehicles may not conform exactly to the specifications listed in this book.

Over the years Jaguar has produced 26 distinct model ranges spread across two brands, Jaguar and Daimler. Over 330 specific models have been powered by 20 engine designs, designed and/or built over time in a total of 12 factories, from the early days in Foleshill (after moving from Blackpool) to the latest developments in India, China and Austria. Jaguar worldwide sales now exceed 3.5 million vehicles at the time of writing.

More books have been written on the Jaguar marque than on any other, and the heritage of the company and its vehicles has remained of paramount importance, both to Jaguar and to the owners of their cars, past and present.

It is hoped that the reader will find much of interest here, not just as an intensive 'read' in its own right but as a handy reference guide to the company's many cars – a tribute to the British motor industry and to the name of Jaguar.

Nigel Thorley
Yorkshire, England

Jaguar heritage

The formative years of Jaguar can be traced back to humble beginnings in Blackpool, under the title of the Swallow Sidecar Company. In 1922 a partnership was formed between one William Lyons and William Walmsley, initially to produce sidecars for the motorcycle trade. Within four years the business had moved to larger premises, also in Blackpool, where stylish bodies were produced for contemporary cars like the Austin Seven. Yet more expansion resulted in the company moving to Coventry – the heart of the British motor industry – in 1928, where it gained access to unlimited supplies of raw materials and skilled labour.

In Coventry (Foleshill at this time) Swallow produced its first complete cars, the SS1 and SS2 models of 1931, though these were still very much based on another manufacturer's running gear (that of the Standard Motor Company). In 1934 SS Cars Limited was established as a

Above: *The car that started it all, the Austin Seven with unique Swallow body. Extensive use of curves, two-tone exterior paintwork, and a sporty appearance led to instant success in 1926. A saloon version plus variants on chassis as diverse as Fiat, Wolseley, and Morris followed in the 1930s. So too did a move of production from Blackpool to Coventry.*

Below: *The first car designed and built by Lyons under the SS name, the SS1, here seen in its later 1933 form with swept-back wings but still using Standard running gear.*

separate company to emphasise the ongoing importance of car production, although sidecars remained a major part of the business up to and including the Second World War.

In 1934 the partnership broke up, William Lyons taking full control of the businesses, and in 1935 the company announced its first car under the 'Jaguar' model name – the SS Jaguar 2½-litre saloon. A unique chassis using an overhead valve version of a Standard six-cylinder engine with a stylish four-door luxury body, this was supplemented by a smaller (four-cylinder) engined model and, later, by a larger 3½-litre car plus two-door drophead coupés and the SS100, a very stylish sports car based on a similar chassis and running gear. Over 20,000 SS Jaguars were produced up to the outbreak of the Second World War.

From 1939 to 1945 production was geared to the war effort, after which the sidecar business was sold off, the 'SS' insignia was dropped, and a new company name appeared – Jaguar Cars Limited. Initially postwar car production revolved around the prewar models, with some modifications and with the new Jaguar name replacing the 'SS'. The first entirely new model was the Mark V, introduced in 1948. Although using the same pushrod engine, this had an entirely new chassis with independent front suspension and a larger, stylish body, smoothing out the prewar lines.

In the same year Jaguar introduced the fabulous XK120 Super Sports, utilising the new chassis but with a sophisticated, entirely in-house designed and built twin camshaft six-cylinder engine. This was followed in 1950 by the Mark VII saloon, based on the same running gear. The XK six-cylinder unit would go on to power all subsequent Jaguars up to 1971 and would remain in production until 1992.

A move to a new factory in Allesley was completed by 1952 to expand production. Competition successes in races and rallies in the 1950s led to world recognition and major expansion, with the continued development of new models. In 1955 Jaguar introduced its first car of monocoque (chassis-less) construction, the 2.4-litre saloon, their most successful model up to that time. By 1959 the company was producing three separate model ranges from sports cars through to flagship saloons, and business was booming.

In the swinging sixties Jaguar built some of its most memorable models, like the Mark 2 saloon and E-type sports, both considered icons in the world of motoring even today. Over 90,000 Mark 2s were produced and 72,500 E-types. The company grew into a major group, purchasing other businesses like Daimler, Guy, Henry Meadows, and Coventry Climax, to become one of the most significant parts of the British motor industry, with record exports. Other new models that enhanced the range during the 1960s included the S-type and the 420, while the Daimler name was revitalised with a 2½-litre model and, later, the Sovereign.

In 1968 a merger took place between Jaguar Cars Limited and the British Motor Corporation to form British Motor Holdings, later to become

The first car to carry the Jaguar name, albeit then as a model rather than the marque – the SS Jaguar 2½-litre saloon. Offering style and 90mph-plus performance at a modest £385, this car remained in production in various forms until 1949, and set the scene for all future saloons carrying the Jaguar name.

part of the massive British Leyland organisation. During this period Jaguar introduced a one-model policy in the form of the XJ6 saloon, resulting in a total of three series covering six- and twelve-cylinder Jaguar and Daimler saloons and even coupé models – a total of over 400,000 cars produced from 1968 to 1992.

After the E-type the sporting side of the model range continued with the XJ-S grand tourer, in production from 1975 until 1996. Jaguar returned to the competition arena successfully in the 1980s and was highly accomplished in the European Touring Car Championship and at Le Mans. Finally escaping the grip of British Leyland, the company was privatised in 1984 under the helm of Sir John Egan; the original Jaguar company's founder, Sir William Lyons (knighted in 1956), died in 1985.

In 1986 the XJ40 saloon, the first completely new model since 1975, was introduced and took the company into a new era of success. Alongside the XJ-S, it became the mainstay of production in various forms, and in 1988 Jaguar established a record of building and selling more cars in a single year than ever before, a figure that the company did not better until 1998.

In 1990 Jaguar became part of the Ford Motor Company, and the first new model derived from Ford's investment was the X-300 saloon car range of 1994, followed by the XK8 (X-100) sports car in 1996. The X-300 saloons were equipped with the multi-valve straight six (AJ16) and V12 power units. With the introduction of the XK8 came a significant new engine, the AJ-V8 power

The SS100 was the first true sports car to come from the company. A choice of 2½- or 3½-litre six-cylinder engines meant speeds of up to 100mph, with an incredible 0–50mph acceleration time of 7.5 seconds. Only produced until the outbreak of the Second World War, a mere 308 were made. The SS100 was the first of an esteemed line of Jaguar sports cars, culminating in the E-type, XJ-S, XK8, and new XK.

unit, fitted to this and the later (X-308) saloon. These V8 saloons remained in production until 2002, and the XK8 sports cars have since been through further development and were produced until 2005, in both normally-aspirated and supercharged form.

From a relatively simplistic two-model base (XJ saloons and XJ-S sports) established in the 1970s, Jaguar had expanded its range to a comprehensive five-car line-up by the end of the period covered by this publication.

The last of what many would call the 'traditional' Jaguars was introduced in 2003, as the X-350 (flagship XJ) saloons, introducing new technologies of production using advanced aluminium construction. This was also the last car to be branded a Daimler model. The X-350 (later face-lifted and known as the X-358) was followed by the New XK sports cars (X-150) in 2006, also utilising aluminium architecture.

Jaguar styling has taken an entirely new direction since then, initially with the XF replacing the S-type and X-type from 2007, and the last of the XJ line (X-351) in 2009. Jaguar re-entered the two-seater sports car market with the F-TYPE in 2013. Since then, Jaguar has

Jaguar's Mark V saloon was only in production for three years from 1948 to 1951 but was a great success, particularly in overseas markets. It offered updated traditional styling and a new chassis with excellent handling capabilities. It is seen here in rare drophead coupé form.

introduced a second generation of XF saloons and a smaller saloon (XE).

For the very first time, Jaguar introduced an SUV (Sports Utility Vehicle) in 2015, the F-PACE, followed in 2018 by the smaller E-PACE.

Since the move of the original Swallow business from Blackpool in Lancashire to Coventry in Warwickshire, a significant number of cars were built there, until the re-development of the old Spitfire fighter plane/Pressed Steel body factory in Castle Bromwich, Birmingham was taken over. With the expansion of models and the take-over by the Ford Motor Company, the old Ford factory in Halewood on Merseyside was refurbished to assemble the X-type models from 2001. With the business acquisition (including Land Rover) by Tata from India, Jaguar cars are now also produced in Solihull (West Midlands), along with a new state-of-the-art engine plant in Wolverhampton. Outside the UK, plants produce cars in Austria, India and China.

At time of writing, new model styling and development was still carried out at Whitley in Coventry and administration and other activities were dealt with at Gaydon, also in Warwickshire.

Jaguar, over time, has survived the rise and fall of the British motor industry and is still regarded as one of the most respected luxury brands in the world.

Chronological order of production (SS and Jaguar models)

The following does not include Swallow sidecars or Swallow-bodied vehicles, nor specialist sports/racing cars and non-production models.

1931–33	SS1 two-light coupé
1931–33	SS2 two-light coupé
1933–36	SS1 tourer
1933–36	SS2 tourer
1934–36	SS1 two-light coupé
1934–36	SS2 four-light saloon
1934–36	SS2 tourer
1934–36	SS1 airline
1935–36	SS1 drophead coupé
1935	SS90 sports
1935–36	SS Jaguar 1½-litre saloon
1935–36	SS Jaguar 2½-litre saloon
1936–40	SS Jaguar 100 2½-litre sports
1937–40	SS Jaguar 100 3½-litre sports
1937–40	SS Jaguar 1.75-litre saloon
1937–40	SS Jaguar 2½-litre ohv saloon
1937–40	SS Jaguar 3½-litre saloon
1937–40	SS Jaguar drophead coupé (1½, 2½, 3½ litres)
1937–40	SS Jaguar 2½-litre tourer
1946–50	Jaguar 1.75-litre saloon
1946–50	Jaguar 2½-litre ohv saloon

Jaguar — All the Cars

Years	Model
1946–50	Jaguar 3½-litre saloon
1947–49	Jaguar drophead coupé (1½, 2½, 3½ litres)
1948–51	Jaguar Mark V saloon (2½, 3½ litre)
1948–51	Jaguar Mark V drophead coupé (2½, 3½ litres)
1948–54	XK120 roadster
1950–58	Mark VII saloon (including Mark VIIM)
1951–54	XK120 fixed-head coupé
1953–54	XK120 drophead coupé
1954–57	XK140 roadster
1954–57	XK140 drophead coupé
1954–57	XK140 fixed-head coupé
1955–59	2.4-litre saloon
1957	XKSS sports
1957–59	3.4-litre saloon
1957–59	Mark VIII saloon
1957–61	XK150 drophead coupé (including S models)
1957–61	XK150 fixed-head coupé (including S models)
1958–61	XK150 roadster (including S models)
1959–61	Mark IX saloon
1959–67	Mark 2 saloon (2.4, 3.4, 3.8-litres)
1960–64	Daimler SP250 sports
1960–67	Daimler DR450/DQ450 Majestic saloons and limousines
1961–64	E-type 3.8-litre sports (roadster/fixed-head coupé)
1961–64	Mark X 3.8-litre saloon
1962–67	Daimler 2.5-litre V8 saloon
1963–68	S-type saloon (3.4/3.8-litres)
1964–66	Mark X 4.2-litre saloon
1964–68	E-type 4.2-litre sports (roadster/fixed-head coupé)
1966–68	E-type 2+2 sports
1966–68	420 Saloon
1966–69	Daimler 420 Sovereign saloon
1967–68	340 saloon
1967–69	240 saloon
1967–69	Daimler V8 250 saloon
1967–70	420G saloon
1968–71	E-type 4.2-litre Series 2 sports (roadster/fixed-head coupé/2+2)
1968–73	XJ6 Series 1 saloons
1968–92	Daimler DS420 limousines
1969–73	Daimler Sovereign Series 1 saloons
1971–74	E-type Series 3 sports (roadster/fixed-head coupé)
1972–73	Jaguar XJ12 Series 1 saloon (including Daimler 66)
1972–73	Daimler Double Six Vanden Plas Series 1 saloon
1974–78	Jaguar XJ6 Series 2 saloons (including Daimlers)
1974–78	Jaguar XJ12 Series 2 saloons (including Daimlers)
1975–77	Jaguar XJ6/12 C coupés (including Daimlers)
1975–90	XJ-S V12 coupé
1978–87	Jaguar XJ6 Series 3 saloons (including Daimlers)
1978–91	Jaguar XJ12 Series 3 saloons
1978–92	Daimler Double Six Series 3 saloon
1983–87	XJ-S 3.6-litre coupé
1983–86	XJ-S 3.6-litre cabriolet
1985–87	XJ-S V12 cabriolet
1986–94	Jaguar/Daimler XJ40 AJ6 saloons
1988–90	XJ-S convertible
1991–96	XJ-S coupé/convertible
1993–94	Jaguar XJ12/Daimler Double Six (XJ40) saloons
1994–97	Jaguar/Daimler X-300 saloons
1996	Daimler Century saloon
1996–2005	XK8 sports
1997–2002	Jaguar XJ8/Daimler saloons
1998–2005	XKR sports
1999–2007	S-type saloons
2001–2009	X-type saloons
2003–2008	XJ6 and XJ8 (X-350) saloons
2004–2009	X-type estate cars
2006–2014	New XK sports cars
2007–2014	New XKR sports cars
2007–2015	XF saloons
2009 to 2019	XJ (X-351) saloons
2012-2016	XF Sportbrakes
2013-on	F-TYPE sports cars
2014-on	XE saloons
2016-on	New XF saloons
2016-on	New XF Sportbrakes
2016-on	F-PACE SUV
2018-on	E-PACE SUV

Jaguar engines

This book is not intended to be a technical publication, but it is worth spending a little time examining the ICEs (internal combution engines) designed and built by Jaguar and fitted in its cars. This section provides details of the power units installed in the various Jaguar models and their different applications.

Background

Until the introduction of the SS Jaguar 2½-litre saloon in 1935, the engines fitted to previous SS cars were taken directly from the Standard Motor Company parts bin. With the introduction of the SS Jaguar, however, the engines, although still supplied by Standard, were significantly modified to a superior overhead valve design by renowned engineer Harry Weslake.

These modified engines were subsequently fitted, in various forms, to all SS Jaguar models and postwar Jaguars, up to and including the Mark V saloons until 1951. Although, after the Second World War, William Lyons of Jaguar negotiated a deal to purchase all tooling for the six-cylinder engines from Standard, and all later production was done in-house at its Foleshill factory. During the postwar period production of the small 1.75-litre four-cylinder engine also used in the Jaguar saloon was still carried out by Standard, and this unit was subsequently used for other models like the Triumph Roadster and Renown saloon.

During the Second World War, William Lyons and his small team of engineers worked on a design for their first complete in-house engine. This was primarily designed for an entirely new saloon, later to be called the Mark VII. Lyons's specifics for the new engine were that it could comfortably power a large luxury saloon the size of a Jaguar and that it could be sufficiently advanced so as not to require major changes for subsequent models.

Coded X (for experimental), various forms and configurations of engine were tried. The XK version was the final outcome, since when this designation has remained with the engine to the present day. It was also originally intended that a four-cylinder version of the power unit would be produced, and although some examples were made – one of which, in high-compression form, powered the successful 'Goldie' Gardner MG EX135 streamlined record breaker in 1948 at over 175mph – the engine never entered production for a Jaguar motor car.

The XK engine went on to power all Jaguar production models and race cars until 1971, when it was supplemented by a very prestigious V12 power unit. Even then the XK engine remained in production, powering all manner of vehicles from Scorpion tanks to Dennis fire engines and even boats. It continued on until 1992 when the very last car powered by that engine, a Daimler DS420 limousine, left the production line.

With the purchase of the Daimler Motor Company in 1960, Jaguar inherited two of its engines for production cars, a 4.5-litre unit and a 2.5-litre V8. The larger engine remained in production until 1965, during which time it only ever powered the big Majestic Major models; thereafter production ceased with the cars. The little 2.5-litre engine, initially powering just the Daimler SP250 sports, went on to power the first Daimler models designed by Jaguar, the saloons based on the Mark 2 produced from 1962 to 1969.

It wasn't until 1971 that Jaguar introduced another engine, the celebrated V12 power unit, initially introduced in the E-type but intended for the XJ saloons. This engine never replaced the XK six but was retained for use in top-of-the-range models and remained in low volume production until 1997.

In 1983 Jaguar introduced a new six-cylinder power unit, the AJ6. Designed for a new saloon (the XJ40) it was, however, first fitted to the XJ-S sports car from that year. Later increased in capacity to 4.0 litres, it was eventually replaced by a redesigned AJ16 engine which remained in production until 1997.

Jaguar had never made a V8 engine for production until the AJ-V8 design was completed and first launched in 4.0-litre form in the 1996 XK8 sports car. It was then fitted to the equivalent XJ (X-308) saloons along with a 3.2-litre version. Variations on these engines were subsequently fitted to all XJs, XKs, S-types and XF models. They have now been replaced by new Gen III engines of 5.0-litre capacity in both normally-aspirated and supercharged forms.

Jaguar introduced a new V6 engine range (AJ-V6) in 1999, initially for the S-type in 3.0-litre form but later expanded to the XJ models and the X-type, in this case in three engine capacities.

In 2003 the first-ever diesel engine was offered in a Jaguar, then of 2.0-litre capacity, for the X-type. Since then the engine range has expanded, initially to a 2.2-litre version, then a much larger 2.7-litre diesel for the S-type and XJ, and then in 2009 with the introduction of the AJ-V6D Generation III 3.0-litre unit.

For the 2013 model year, Jaguar announced yet more new engines, this time a 3.0-litre V6 petrol unit in two performance options (both derived from the 5.0-litre V8 unit) and an updated version of the 5.0-litre petrol engine, installed for the first time in the F-TYPE sports car.

The 3.0-litre supercharged V6 engines were of 340hp and 380hp states of tune, and the 5.0-litre supercharged V8 in the F-TYPE V8 S offered 495hp and 460ft/lbs of torque. All were equipped with the new Intelligent Stop/Start system to enhance fuel economy under certain driving conditions.

The 340hp version of the supercharged V6, which debuted in the 2013 XJ and XF saloons, produced 332ft/lb of torque at 3500-5500rpm. The 380hp version, exclusive to the F-TYPE, produced 339ft/lb of torque at 3500-5500rpm. The V8 produced an even broader torque curve, with 460ft/lb produced over the 2500-5500rpm range.

Based on the Jaguar 5.0-litre V8 engine, the 3.0-litre V6 shared its all-alloy construction. The lightweight die-cast aluminium block was stiffened with cross-bolted main bearing caps, increasing rigidity and refinement. A system of counter-rotating front and rear balancer weights helped give the new supercharged V6 the smoothness and refinement characteristics of the V8 on which it was based.

The supercharged V6 and V8 engines combined high compression, direct fuel-injection, dual independent variable cam timing (DIVCT) and a supercharger to deliver their high levels of performance and efficiency. A twin vortex supercharger was mounted in the engine's 'V', and a water-cooled intercooler reduced the temperature of the intake air to optimise power and efficiency. The supercharged V6 used a higher compression ratio than the V8, 10.5:1 vs 9.5:1.

In both the V6 and V8, the aluminium cylinder heads packaged an innovative valve control system. The dual independent variable cam timing (DIVCT) system was activated by the positive and negative torques generated by the movement of the intake and exhaust valves, allowing exceptionally quick actuation rates of more than 150 degrees per second throughout the rev range.

Spray-guided direct injection delivered precisely measured quantities of fuel directly into the centre of the combustion chambers at pressures of up to 150bar (2175psi), creating a more homogeneous air–fuel mixture for cleaner and more efficient combustion. This was aided by sparkplugs that were precisely indexed both in relation to the injector and within the combustion chamber.

Despite the success of the large diesel and petrol engines, with the announcement of more new models and the need to improve fuel consumption and general efficiency/emissions, Jaguar introduced new Ingenium engines, from which a whole range of fuel-efficient smaller power units could be built. Assembled at its own Wolverhampton factory, the initial Ingenium engines cost £500m to develop. The most fuel-efficient engines yet developed by the company, they could produce up to 75mpg, with incredibly low emissions, and were designed with the future in mind to ensure they matched future requirements for low emissions and high economy.

The Ingenium units were of just 2.0-litre capacity, with 4-cylinders producing between 163 and 180PS. These all-aluminium, low-friction units had exceptionally stiff cylinder blocks and twin balance shafts to ensure low levels of vibration. Details like an acoustic sump cover, decoupled injectors, and 0.5mm ovality on the injector pump drive socket contributed to extremely quiet running.

Variable exhaust valve timing shortened the catalyst light-off phase and improved DPF regeneration, a common problem with some diesel engines. The cooled, low-pressure exhaust gas recirculation (EGR) system reduced combustion chamber temperatures, inhibiting NOx formation so the engines could meet the world's most stringent regulations.

The XK six-cylinder engine

The XK six-cylinder engine was designed with a conventional iron cylinder block fitted with a massive seven-bearing steel crankshaft. An aluminium twin-overhead-camshaft cylinder head was employed with combustion chambers of

Jaguar engines

The original Jaguar six-cylinder XK engine conceived during the Second World War. In various forms, it powered all Jaguars from the XK120 through to the XJ Series 3.

hemispherical design. A two-stage chain system was used to drive the camshafts employing separate top and bottom chains.

Initially designed as a 3.4-litre-capacity engine (3442cc), the XK was fitted with two 1.75in SU carburettors, had a bore and stroke of 83 x 106mm, and was rated at 160bhp with 195lb ft of torque at 2500rpm. Finally, great emphasis had been put on the look of the engine, with its highly polished alloy cam covers and detail finishing. As many have said in the past and today, it is as good to look at as it is to drive!

The XK power unit was first fitted to the XK120 Super Sports from 1948, and then to the Mark VII saloon in 1950, at which time production of the old in-line ex-Standard engine was stopped. Very early XK engines fitted to both these models were unique in having their polished camshaft covers secured with chromed studs only at the sides, the front sections covering the timing chains not being secured thus. This led to problems with oil leaks, and from 1951 all engines featured extra studs in these locations, an easy identification feature.

All production applications for the XK power unit from 1948 through to 1978 featured normal carburettor aspiration, either with two or three carburettors. For the majority of engines produced these were of SU manufacture, but Solex and Stromberg were also used in some models. In 1978 electronic fuel-injection became available on certain models, initially for the US market only, but later for all markets.

Another identification point for an XK engine can be found in the painted area of the cylinder heads where the spark plugs sit. Here the heads were colour coded dependent on engine compression ratio and application, eg gold for E-type and Mark X engines, various shades of blue for twin carburettor engines, etc. Also the polished alloy camshaft covers, a well-known feature of the engine's visual appeal, were replaced in 1968 by cast ribbed covers powder coated in black.

XK engines were last fitted to the Daimler DS420 limousine as late as 1992, although mainstream saloon car production ended with the Jaguar XJ6 Series 3 saloon in April 1987.

XK engine production car installations

Model	Years	Cubic capacity	Carb/Fuel injection
XK120	1948–54	3442cc	2 x SU
Mark VII/VIII	1950–8	3442cc	2 x SU
XK140	1954–7	3442cc	2 x SU
2.4 (Mark 1)	1955–9	2483cc	2 x Solex
3.4 (Mark 1)	1957–9	3442cc	2 x SU
XK150	1957–61	3442cc	2 x SU
	1958–61	3442cc	3 x SU
	1959–61	3781cc	2 x SU
	1959–61	3781cc	3 x SU
Mark IX	1958–61	3781cc	2 x SU
2.4 (Mark 2)	1959–67	2483cc	2 x Solex
3.4 (Mark 2)	1959–67	3442cc	2 x SU
3.8 (Mark 2)	1959–67	3781cc	2 x SU
E-type S1	1961–4	3781cc	3 x SU
Mark X	1961–4	3781cc	3 x SU
S-type	1963–8	3442cc	2 x SU
	1963–8	3781cc	2 x SU
E-type S1	1964–7	4235cc	3 x SU
Mark X	1964–7	4235cc	3 x SU
420/Sov	1966–9	4235cc	2 x SU† partial
340	1967–8	3442cc	2 x SU†
240	1967–9	2483cc	2 x SU†
420G	1968–70	4235cc	3 x SU†
E-type S2	1968–71	4235cc	3 x SU*†
XJ6 S1	1968–73	2782cc	2 x SU†
	1968–73	4235cc	2 x SU†
DS420	1968–92	4235cc	2 x SU†
XJ6 S2	1974–5	2782cc	2 x SU†
	1974–8	4235cc	2 x SU†
	1975–8	3442cc	2 x SU†
XJ6 S3	1979–87	3442cc	2 x SU†
	1979–87	4235cc	Fuel-injection†

* For certain markets these E-types were instead fitted with Zenith-Stromberg carburettors to reduce emissions.

† Engines featured ribbed cam covers instead of polished alloy type.

The Turner-designed Daimler 2.5-litre V8 engine, fitted to the Jaguar-designed 2.5-litre V8 and V8 250 Daimler saloons from 1962 to 1969 – the only non-Jaguar-designed engine to be used since the abandonment of the Standard-inspired units of the 1930s and 1940s.

Jaguar's legendary V12 5.3-litre engine, introduced in 1971 and discontinued in 1997, here seen in original four-carburettor form as fitted to the Series 3 E-type and XJ12 Series 1.

Daimler 2.5-litre V8 engine

Although not designed or initially built by Jaguar, this engine was inherited when the Daimler Motor Company was taken over in 1960, and was subsequently used in the new Daimler 2.5-litre V8 and V8 250 saloons up to 1969. Created by Edward Turner, it was an advanced design derived from his motorcycle experience. It was first fitted to a Daimler prototype in 1958 and, after going into production, was fitted to the SP250 glass fibre sports car introduced at the 1959 British Motor Show.

This engine was well known for its exceptional smoothness and quiet running, and after tests by Jaguar in a Mark 1 saloon following the Daimler takeover it was decided to adapt the engine for installation in the Mark 2 bodyshell, to create a new Daimler.

The V8 engine utilised a cast iron block with light alloy cylinder head and crankcase, the crankshaft being based on five main bearings. Of over-square dimensions (76.2 x 69.85mm), it developed 140bhp at 5800rpm. Its compact dimensions made it an ideal installation in the Jaguar Mark 2 bodyshell, where it was fitted with twin SU carburettors.

Daimler 2.5-litre V8 engine production car installations

Model	Years	Cubic capacity	Carb/Fuel injection
2.5-litre V8	1962–7	2548cc	2 x SU
V8 250	1967–9	2548cc	2 x SU

Later 6.0-litre version of the V12 engine, easily identifiable by the ceramic cover over the centre section of the engine, and only fitted to cars from 1993 to 1997.

V12 engine

The original concept for a V12 Jaguar engine arose with a new sports/racing car, coded XJ13, intended to race at Le Mans in the 1960s. For various reasons the project was never completed, although the only example of the XJ13 to be made still exists today. The engine designed for that car was a four-overhead-camshaft unit of complex design, far too complex for mass production. Jaguar's engineers therefore set about simplifying the concept.

The reasoning behind such a large engine was to captivate the prized North American market, at the time dominated by home-grown V8s. Jaguar's XK six-cylinder engine wasn't as powerful in many cases, and it was thought the prestige of a V12 engine in a Jaguar would open up new markets and set the company apart from both US manufacturers and other competition.

V12 engine production car installations

Model	Years	Cubic capacity	Carb/Fuel injection
E-type S3	1971–4	5343cc	4 x Stromberg
XJ12/DD6 Series 1	1972–3	5343cc	4 x Stromberg
XJ12/DD6 Series 2	1973–9 1975	5343cc	4 x Stromberg Fuel-injection
XJ12/DD6 coupé	1975–7 1975	5343cc	4 x Stromberg Fuel-injection
XJS	1975–91	5343cc	Fuel-injection
XJ12 Series 3	1979–91	5343cc	Fuel-injection
DD6 Series 3	1979–92	5343cc	Fuel-injection
XJR-S	1988–9	5343cc	Fuel-injection
XJR-S	1990–3	5991cc	Fuel-injection
XJS	1993–5	5994cc	Fuel-injection*
XJ40/DD6	1993–4	5994cc	Fuel-injection*
X-300	1994–7	5994cc	Fuel-injection*

Ribbed engine cover over the V.

The final outcome was a single overhead camshaft per bank of six cylinders, with a flat cylinder head design of alloy construction, as was the block, this time with an 'open deck' design and an aluminium crankcase. Of 5.3-litre capacity and originally fitted with no less than four Zenith-Stromberg carburettors to keep the engine height low, it also used a new advanced engine ignition system, the Lucas-based OPUS equipment.

This engine, as the XK before it, was first installed in a Jaguar sports car, the E-type. The Series 3 underwent significant redesign in order to accommodate the large V12 engine and first went into production in 1971. The engine was, however, really meant to power Jaguar's XJ saloons, the bodyshells of which were designed to take the V12. The new XJ12 model was announced in 1972, followed by Daimler models under the Double Six name.

From April 1975 the V12 engine became fuel injected by the Lucas-Bosch system, initially just for the Series 2 XJ coupé models, but later for saloons and the XJ-S sports car at its launch. Other modifications to the engine carried on throughout its life, the first being in 1981 when the May 'fireball' cylinder head design was adopted to improve engine efficiency and fuel economy. Later in the 1980s TWR Racing uprated it to 6.0-litre capacity from 5.3 litres for racing purposes, similar changes later being accommodated into mainstream production for the XJR-S sports cars, then the normal production XJSs and, from 1993, XJ40 saloons.

Low volume production of the V12 engine continued for the last of the XJSs and the X-300 saloons before finally ending in 1997, when it was replaced by the V8s.

Identification points are numerous and complex on this engine. Suffice to say that carburettor and fuel injected versions are easy to identify. The factory produced 6.0-litre V12 engines from 1993 which included many extensive and detail changes; ease of identification issues here are the ceramic ribbed cover over the top of the engine and the significantly smaller air-conditioning compressor.

AJ6/16 six-cylinder engines

The XK power unit had been in production for a long time and Jaguar desperately needed a new engine, eventually to replace it. This would be designed specifically with a saloon model – the XJ40 – in mind, but, as with other Jaguar engines, it would first see light of day in a sporting mode, in this case the XJ-S.

Two engines were designed and built under the AJ6 code name, the smaller being a 2.9-litre single camshaft canted six which effectively utilised half the V12 engine with the same bore spacings, valves and camshafts, and high compression combustion chambers. In contrast, the larger 3.6-litre engine used a four-valves-per-cylinder head arrangement, both cylinder heads made from aluminium for lightness. The camshafts were chain driven as on other Jaguar engines, with two chains for the 3.6-litre engine and one for the 2.9. Both engines shared the same basic cylinder block with seven-bearing cast iron crank, and both were fuel injected.

With a bore and stroke of 91 x 92mm, the 3.6-litre engine as installed in the XJ-S boasted 221bhp and 248lb ft of torque at 4000rpm. The 2.9-litre engine was not launched until the introduction of the XJ40 saloon in 1986, at which time, with a bore and stroke of 91 x 74.8mm it supplied 165bhp with 176lb ft of torque at 4000rpm.

The AJ6 engines were later significantly updated. The 3.6-litre was enlarged to 4.0-litre capacity in 1989, the reasoning behind this being to increase mid-range torque and enhance the feeling of effortless power and refinement. Capacity was expanded to 3980cc by increasing the stroke to 102mm. Peak torque was extended to 250lb ft at 3750rpm. Revised camshaft profiles were used with a new low-loss air cleaner system, and tappets and valve timing were also improved. The pistons were redesigned too and a forged steel crankshaft replaced the iron one. In addition an entirely new engine management

The 2.9-litre AJ6 single-cam engine, only fitted to XJ40 saloons from 1986 to 1991.

AJ16 4.0-litre engine derived for the X-300 saloon car range, but still based on the earlier AJ6 unit and first fitted to the XJS from 1993.

The 3.6-litre AJ6 engine first fitted in the XJ-S from 1983 and then into XJ40 saloons until 1990, when it was upgraded to 4.0-litre capacity.

system was adopted with digital control of fuel and ignition.

Next, in 1991, the 2.9-litre AJ6 was discontinued and replaced by a new 3.2-litre engine, derived from the larger twin-cam unit. With a capacity of 3,293cc from a reduced stroke of 83mm, power output was increased to 200bhp thanks to the four-valve head. This 3.2-litre engine was also the first produced by Jaguar to be equipped with a catalytic converter. The major advantages of the 3.2-litre unit were smoothness and better performance and fuel economy. Now with 200bhp on tap and torque increased to 220lb ft, this engine was, however, only used in the XJ40 saloons.

In early 1994 came the final development of the AJ6 engine, so modified that it was given a new name (AJ16). Power output was up again, by 7%, to 244bhp. A new cylinder head and block were employed with improved porting, cam profiles, higher compression, new pistons, and another new engine management system with sequential fuel-injection timing. Perhaps the biggest change was the adoption of individual coils over each cylinder.

The AJ16 engine, although fitted initially to the XJ-S, was really destined for the new X-300 saloons from late 1994. It only remained in production until 1997 when, as with the V12, the V8s replaced it.

As well as being fitted to the X-300 models in normal aspirated form, there was also another variant, a supercharged version of the 4.0-litre engine. An intercooled supercharger boosted inlet manifold pressure by 10.5psi, providing up to 77 extra bhp. The supercharged engines are identified by the plenum arrangement at the side of the engine finished to the same colour as the cam cover and bearing the words 'XJR6 supercharged' in red.

All the 2.9-litre, 3.2-litre, 3.6-litre, and 4.0-litre AJ6 engines had black powder coated ribbed cam covers. The 2.9-litre had a single cover of the same type as fitted to the V12 engine, the others a double-ribbed single cover incorporating the plug lead orifices. The different twin-cam engines show their litreage in the form of a sticker across the front of the cam cover. In the 1990s these covers were changed to incorporate an integrated oil filler cap.

The AJ16 engine is instantly recognisable by its silver painted, enlarged camshaft cover.

AJ6/16 engine production car installations

Model	Years	Cubic capacity (all fuel injected)
XJ-S	1983–91	3590cc
XJ40	1986–9	3590cc
XJ40	1986–91	2919cc
XJ40	1989–94	3980cc
XJ40	1991–4	3239cc
XJ-S	1991–4	3980cc
XJ-S	1994–6	3980cc (AJ16)
X-300	1994–7	3239cc (AJ16)
X-300	1994–7	3980cc (AJ16)
XJR	1994–7	3980cc (supercharged AJ16)

AJ-V8 engines

The concept of the Jaguar AJ-V8 engine came about in the early 1980s, and after much deliberation it was decided that the 'new' engine to power the next generation of Jaguars must have several attributes. Firstly, it had to achieve outstanding performance with the utmost refinement; secondly, it had to be of sound design and quality to ensure longevity in service; and thirdly, it had to be cost-effective both in production terms and in service, including its fuel economy.

Initially coded AJ26 before later becoming the AJ-V8, it was launched in the XK8 in September 1996. It was a 4.0-litre design, with a bore and stroke of 86mm and a twin-camshaft arrangement with four valves per cylinder, the largest valves of any similar-sized engine around. Of alloy design for lightness, weight was also saved in other areas like the inlet manifolding, which was plastic. The very latest electronics technology was used for engine management and ignition system, with fly-by-wire throttle control and an exceptionally efficient cooling system that permitted virtually instant warm-up of the engine. In normal 4.0-litre form it provided 290bhp, with torque of 290lb ft at 4,250rpm and exceptional smoothness, quietness, and excellent fuel economy.

After being fitted in the XK8 sports car, from 1997 it was fitted in the X-308 saloon. The unit's next development came at this time, with a new 3.2-litre version built only for the saloon, as an alternative for the lower-priced models. A supercharged version of the 4.0-litre engine was also introduced, this becoming available in the XK8 (called the XKR) from May 1998. This supercharged engine developed 370bhp and 387lb ft of torque, 10% more than the old V12 and a 27% increase over the standard 4.0-litre V8 engine. A low-maintenance Eaton supercharger was driven by a single belt to increase manifold pressure by up to 12psi. Supercharged engines are identifiable by the silvered plenum chamber on top of the engine, embossed with the words 'V8 supercharged'.

With changes, including the fitment of variable valve timing for the 3.2-litre version, this smaller engine was only fitted to the X-308 saloons until 2002. The 4.0-litre engine remained in use for S-type, XJ, and XK cars until 2002 when it was increased to 4.2-litre capacity, mated to an improved automatic transmission.

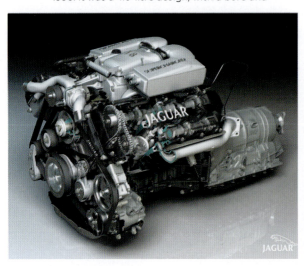

The AJ-V8 engine (seen here in its later 4.2-litre supercharged form) was, with the exception of the X-type, fitted to all Jaguar models until 2009 when it was replaced by the 5.0-litre Generation III engine.

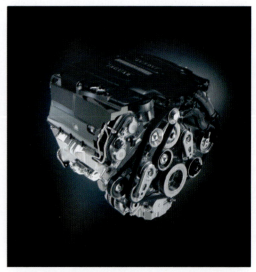

The latest petrol engine from Jaguar, the AJ-V8 Gen III 5.0-litre that replaced the 4.2-litre units in 2009.

For a brief period from 2003 a 3.5-litre version of the AJ-V8 engine was available for the XJ saloons only. The larger 4.2-litre variants ceased production in 2009 to make way for the Generation III 5.0-litre models.

The AJ-V8 Gen III engines of 5.0-litre capacity (normally aspirated and supercharged) were introduced in 2009 for the New XJ saloons, and in 2010 for the New XK sports cars and then XF saloons. These engines were of an entirely new design, and replaced the existing 3.5-litre and 4.2-litre V8 engines.

Designed and built for improved performance, fuel economy and environmental issues, for the first time recycled aluminium was used for the cylinder heads and high pressure castings for the blocks. New technology in the engines included a centrally mounted, multi-hole, spray-guided, direct fuel injection system, and a new type of variable camshaft timing system, actuated by the positive and negative torques generated by the opening and closing of the valves, instead of by oil pressure. This allowed the engine oil pump to be reduced in size, saving energy and reducing fuel consumption. Another innovation was the 'intelligent' oil pump pressure relief valve, which sensed oil pressure deep in the engine's oil galleries to control the oil pump delivery. As a result, oil pump frictional losses were reduced during the warm-up period. There was also an electronic oil level sensor feature, and servicing intervals were expanded from the traditional 10,000 miles to 15,000 miles.

Changes were also made to the supercharger, providing greater efficiency and lower noise levels.

The 5.0-litre V8 engines had a remarkable lifespan, in some form featured in every later model except the XE, New XF and E-PACE.

AJ-V6 engines

After the demise of the AJ16 engine, Jaguar was without a six-cylinder power unit until 1999, when the new medium-sized S-type saloon was introduced. Although also equipped with the AJ-V8 4.0-litre engine, this car was always designed to take the smaller V6 engine, called the AJ-V6.

The origins of the AJ-V6 lie in the Ford Duratec engine, but with significant re-engineering by Jaguar's personnel. A lightweight engine of all-aluminium construction, its basic principles follow the V8 power units. Its 2,967cc capacity offers 238bhp with excellent torque, and it has variable timing, a sophisticated engine management system, and superb smoothness.

This engine was launched in the S-type conventionally mounted, driving the rear wheels.

The first of the AJ-V6 engines of 3.0-litre capacity, as fitted to S-type saloons from 1999 on and now also fitted to X-types and the XJ6.

AJ-V8 engine production car installations

Model	Years	Cubic capacity (all fuel injected)
XK8	1996–2002	3996cc
X-308	1997–2002	3248cc
X-308	1997–2002	3996cc
XJR	1997–2002	3996cc (supercharged)
XKR	1997–2002	3996cc (supercharged)
S-type	1999–2002	3996cc
XK8	2002–9	4196cc
XKR	2002–9	4196cc (supercharged)
S-type	2002–8	4196cc
S-type	2002–8	4196cc (supercharged)
X-350	2003–5	3555cc
X-350	2003–9	4196cc
XJR	2003–9	4196cc
XF	2008–9	4196cc
XF	2009-15	5000cc
XF	2009-15	5000cc (supercharged)
XK	2009-14	5000cc
XKR	2009-14	5000cc (supercharged)
X-351	2009-19	5000cc
X-351	2009-19	5000cc (supercharged)
F-TYPE	2013-23	5000cc (supercharged)
F-PACE	2019-23	5000cc (supercharged)

However, with the launch of the smaller X-type saloon in 2001 a derivative of the engine was introduced, with a capacity of 2.5 litres. Now mounted transversely it was able to provide four-wheel drive in this mode, but only for the X-type. The 3.0-litre V6 was also fitted to the X-type and also offered four-wheel drive. The 2.5-litre engine later became available for the S-type saloon as well, although still with this model's conventional rear-wheel drive.

In 2002 another variant of the AJ-V6 engine came on the scene, of 2.0 litres capacity. This was mounted transversely, driving the front wheels only, and was fitted to a lower-priced version of the X-type for strategic markets.

The 3.0-litre petrol engine was still fitted to the XJ saloon (X-350) up to the end of its production in 2009, and to the first generation of XF saloons.

In 2012, Jaguar announced a new, highly efficient, 3.0-litre V6 petrol engine fitted to XF, XJ and F-TYPE models. Developed directly from the 5.0-litre V8 unit, it offers power outputs of 340 or 380bhp in supercharged form.

Production and installation of the engine

The 2.7-litre V6 diesel engine for the S-type saloon.

The 2.0-litre four-cylinder diesel engine for the X-type saloon.

AJ-V6 engine production car installations

Model	Years	Cubic capacity (all fuel injected)
S-type	1999–2008	2967cc
X-type	2001–9	2967cc
X-type	2001–6	2495cc
S-type	2002–7	2495cc
X-type	2002–4	2099cc
X-350	2003–9	2967cc
XF	2008–12	2967cc
XF	2012–15	2995cc
X-351	2012–19	2995cc
F-TYPE	2013–23	2995cc
XE	2015–19	2995cc
New XF	2015–19	2995cc
F-PACE	2016–19	2995cc

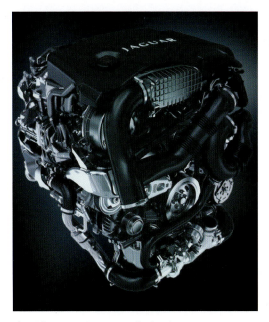

The 3.0-litre AJ-V6D Gen III Jaguar diesel engine.

continued as the top-of-the range V6 petrol engine until the introduction of next new 6-cylinder engine much later.

Diesel engines

X-404 2.0/2.2-litre

For the very first time in the history of the company, Jaguar introduced its first production diesel engine in 2003, fitted to a new version of the X-type saloon, the 2.0-litre D.

The growth and success of the diesel engine has been unprecedented in recent years and in some particular markets it is vital to have a diesel-engined car in a manufacturer's range. Jaguar, for many years, had been working on the design of such an engine, and at various times the company came close to fitting an oil-burning unit to some models. It has taken until 2003 to finally get the right engine for their application.

The origins of the Jaguar 2.0-litre diesel engine (code named X-404) lies in the Ford TDCi unit although, like the V6 petrol engines, it has been significantly enhanced to meet the demands of Jaguar owners and to uphold the characteristics required of a prestige car.

The engine was a four-cylinder unit, with a capacity of 1998cc and developed peak power of 128bhp at 3800rpm, and 243lb ft of torque at only 1800rpm. The engine was made as lightweight as possible, with a stiff cast iron block with aluminium ladder frame and alloy cylinder head. The fuel system was based on a high-pressure common-rail direct-injection system, with a variable-geometry turbocharger.

This very high-tech engine also had a system to detect and reduce combustion noise.

Installation in the X-type was transverse, transmitting power through the standard X-type five-speed manual gearbox to the front wheels only. A significant amount of sound deadening material was fitted, and a full engine cover was put in place to minimise noise.

Jaguar went a stage further with the small diesel engine in providing a 2.2-litre version with the later provision of a six-speed manual transmission for the X-type models.

These small 4-cylinder engines were fitted to the last of the X-type and first-generation XF models in 2009, as well as some export-market XJs, with the last units being produced at Ford's Bridgend factory, in readiness for Jaguar's new Ingenium units.

X-404 engine production car installation

Model	Years	Cubic capacity (all fuel injected)
X-type	2003-9	1998cc
X-type	2005-9	2198cc
XF	2014-15	2198cc
X-351	2013-19	2198cc (selected markets only)

AJD-V6 2.7-litre

In 2004, Jaguar introduced a much larger engine, suitable for the S-type and XJ saloons, of 2.7-litre capacity. A joint venture with Ford and Peugeot-

Citroën, this was an entirely different unit from the other diesel engines offered and heralded entirely new technology, like the block being made from lightweight compacted graphite iron.

It was a four-camshaft unit with twin turbochargers and 24 valves, providing over 200bhp and with torque exceeding that of the then current 4.2-litre petrol unit. Renowned for quiet running, and over 40% more fuel efficient than the equivalent petrol engine, this unit was carried over to the XF saloon in 2008, but production of this engine ceased in 2009.

AJD-V6 engine production car installation

Model	Years	Cubic capacity (all fuel injected)
X-350	2004–9	2720cc
S-type	2004–8	2720cc
XF	2008–9	2720cc

AJ-V6D 3.0-litre

The larger diesel engine was replaced in 2009 by the new AJ-V6D Gen III unit of 3.0-litre capacity, producing 240bhp or, in S form, 275bhp. Performance was therefore boosted over 30 per cent over the 2.7-litre engine, with 12% less emissions and 10% better fuel economy. A key feature of these engines was the parallel sequential turbocharger system, the first of its type to be fitted to a V-engine. A new common-rail direct-injection system was also employed and, by placing the injector crystals deeper into the engine, noise levels were dramatically reduced. Turbo lag was also reduced and service intervals were extended to 16,000 miles.

This large diesel engine remained in production until the end of X-351 production. Due to new technologies and the need for more efficient smaller engines, the big V6 diesel was not replaced.

AJ-V6D Gen III engine production car installation

Model	Years	Cubic capacity (all fuel injected)
XF	2009–15	2993cc
X-351	2009–19	2993cc

Ingenium engines

Launched with the introduction of the new small Jaguar XE models, the Ingenium engines were a new family of compact, lightweight, low-friction, low-emissions petrol and diesel engines delivering an impressive blend of performance, refinement, and, most importantly in today's world, economy.

The first of these engines were of 4-cylinder 2.0-litre capacity in two power outputs (163PS and 180PS). Clean combustion, variable exhaust valve timing and sophisticated exhaust gas after-treatment ensured the engine complied with the most up-to-date emissions legislation.

The Ingenium engines featured six key technologies that combined to reduce friction, add refinement, and improve performance/economy. These were: roller bearings on cam and balancer shafts, instead of machined-in bearing surfaces; computer-controlled variable oil pumps that saved energy by delivering the optimum amount of oil at all speeds, engine loads and temperatures; the split or twin circuit cooling system, which provided two benefits of lowering the CO_2 emissions by enabling faster warm ups, and quick cabin heat available on cold days; simplified cam drive systems designed for module application; crankshafts that were offset from the centre of the block, and finally, electronically controlled piston cooling jets, which improved efficiency in the oil pumping circuit. Jets were switched off when piston cooling was not needed. They also enabled the engine to reach its optimum operating temperature faster, further reducing CO_2 emissions.

All Ingenium engines were equipped with advanced turbochargers, centre direct high-pressure fuel injection, variable valve timing, and start-stop technology.

Petrol versions were launched in 2016, using the same architecture, initially in two versions based on direct injection 1999cc, 4-cylinder, turbo-charged configurations: 200PS and 250PS with a single turbo-charger.

In 2017 a twin turbo-charged 300PS engine with an electro-hydraulic valvetrain was launched.

A new 4-cylinder engine, badged P300, benefitted from the latest Jaguar Land Rover engine technology, including twin-scroll turbos with ceramic ball bearings to reduce friction and a high flow compressor wheel for enhanced performance.

Producing 400Nm of torque, it provided exceptional acceleration, in the XF AWD for example delivering a 0 to 60mph time of 5.8 seconds and with CO_2 emissions of just 163g/km and fuel economy of up to 40mpg.

An Ingenium 6-cylinder 3.0-litre petrol engine was launched in February 2019, for Land Rover products at that time. It featured a unique combination of an electric supercharger to deliver immediate response supported by a twin scroll turbo-charger and Continuous Variable Valve Lift, which boosted power and helped the engine to breathe with maximum efficiency.

Late in 2020 Jaguar announced a move into hybrid engines. An advanced 1.5-litre 3-cylinder

The last Ingenium engine range designed and built at Jaguar's own facility in the UK.

One of the last new 4-cylinder engines fitted to Jaguar models.

petrol engine was the latest member of the modular, flexible Ingenium engine family, with MHEV technology.

The lightweight new aluminium engine – 33kg lighter than the 4-cylinder, delivered strong performance and refinement with low levels of friction which contributed to excellent efficiency and fuel consumption. The exhaust manifold was integrated into the aluminium cylinder head, which contributed to rapid warm-up times and minimised the distance from the exhaust ports to the turbocharger's turbine wheel for improved responses.

The 3-cylinder configuration delivered a better flow of exhaust gases, ensuring the turbine wheel delivered boost pressure almost instantaneously. A highly efficient water-cooled Charge Air Cooler meant the density of air being drawn into the combustion chambers remained high, further enhancing performance and efficiency across the engine's operating range.

This was followed by a 2.0-litre 4-cylinder diesel and petrol powertrains, paired with MHEV technology, AWD and 9-speed automatic transmissions.

The 163PS 2.0-litre 4-cylinder diesel MHEV produced 380Nm, with CO_2 emissions from 167g/km and fuel economy up to 44.3mpg (6.4 litres/100km). The 204PS MHEV produced 430Nm and was capable of covering 0-60mph in 7.9 seconds (0-100km/h in 8.4 seconds) while returning up to 43.9mpg (6.4 litres/100km) with CO_2 emissions from 169g/km*.

Also available in 6-speed manual transmission, FWD-only form, was a 163PS 2.0-litre 4-cylinder diesel non-MHEV engine with CO_2 emissions from 158g/km and fuel economy up to 46.9mpg (6.0 l/100km).

The 3-cylinder engine developed for fitment to hybrid models.

All these last 3-cylinder and 4-cylinder petrol, diesel and hybrid engines were built at the Jaguar Land Rover facility in Wolverhampton.

Ingenium engine production car installation

Model	Years	Cubic capacity
XE	2015–on	most petrol/diesel variants
New XF	2016–on	most petrol/diesel variants
F-PACE	2016–on	most petrol/diesel variants

1 Prewar SS Jaguars 1935 to 1940

Background

The launch of the Jaguar name came about in September 1935 with the announcement of a new saloon model from SS Cars Limited, the manufacturers of the then current range of cars carrying that insignia, based on Standard Motor Company mechanicals. The new car, although now commonly known as a 'Jaguar', actually used the name purely as a brand model for a new car from SS, and although still based on many components supplied by Standard, the car was a major leap forward for SS and set the scene for all future models they would produce.

The main feature of the new car was an overhead valve version of the Standard six-cylinder engine that the company had already been using in their previous models. The redesign had been carried out by Harry Weslake, a formidable engineer of his day, and the end result was an engine capable of propelling the car to over 90mph. The Standard Motor Company had set up tooling specifically to build the new more powerful engine for SS Cars. The second element was the chassis, which was a revamp of the one supplied by Standard for the SS1 model, although significantly strengthened and with a new braking system incorporated. The third element of the new car was the style of its bodywork. While somewhat similar to the likes of MG, it was nevertheless a major move forward for SS, and the finished job was immediately well received.

Only two models were launched at the Mayfair Hotel in London prior to the 1935 British Motor Show, the 2½-litre straight six saloon and a 1½-litre four-cylinder version, the smaller-engined car only identifiable externally by the shorter wheelbase and bonnet area.

The only SS1 model to be retained after the introduction of the Jaguar saloons was the tourer, now also carrying the Jaguar name and using the same overhead valve engine but essentially the bodywork of the old SS1. Announced just before the SS Jaguar models was the SS90, a two-seater sports car based on the earlier SS1 model. Only very small numbers were built and it was superseded by the Jaguar SS100 sports car, announced along with the new saloons. The SS100 had the new six-cylinder overhead valve engine in a shortened version of the saloon chassis.

By the start of the Second World War, the range of models had been extended to include an even larger (3½-litre) version of the overhead valve engine in the saloons, and a range of drophead coupés. The SS100 had also gained the larger engine, while the tourer had been dropped.

Production of all models stopped with the onset of the war, as SS Cars Limited turned their attention to the war effort.

Model range and development

Models available at launch

SS Jaguar 2½-litre saloon
SS Jaguar 1½-litre saloon
SS Jaguar 2½-litre tourer
SS Jaguar 100 2½-litre sports car

A very early example of the SS Jaguar, in this case a 1½-litre model. Note the lack of front door window quarter-lights, the thick waistline trim towards the rear of the car, and the door handles situated below the waistline. Being a 1½-litre model, it has a shorter bonnet and the wing-mounted spare wheel protrudes above the bonnet line.

The 'new' SS Jaguar models were very soon upgraded, and by the end of 1936 changes had been made to improve the overall design. By 1937 two extra models had been added to the range – a 1½-litre and 2½-litre drophead coupé. These were extremely attractive, somewhat bespoke-built, two-door full hood variants of the saloons. With their introduction, the tourer model was dropped from the range.

All these cars were built around an ash framework in the traditional way, but this was a time-consuming process which proved too slow to meet the heavy sales demand for the cars. Hence, in 1938, production switched to all-steel bodies for the SS Jaguar saloons, which also meant certain changes to the design again. The drophead coupés remained virtually hand-built in the traditional manner.

With the introduction of the steel-bodied cars, SS launched another new variant to the range, a larger 3½-litre version of the straight six engine, which boosted performance considerably. A drophead coupé version of the 3½-litre model also became available, and the SS100 sports car was fitted with the bigger engine. The 1½-litre engine was enlarged to 1.75 litres in late 1937.

Production continued towards the start of the Second World War, with some changes taking effect from late 1939 and early 1940 – the 1.75-litre and the 3½-litre saloons being the last to roll off the production lines (July and December 1940 respectively).

The 1937 SS Jaguar – in this case the longer-bonnet 2½-litre version now sporting the front door window quarter-lights and the normal cover for the side-mounted spare wheel.

Exterior identification points

General points applicable to prewar SS Jaguar saloon models

Front view

- Traditional frontal aspect with separate wings flowing towards the centre and featuring individually mounted side lights on top. Integrated side light housing incorporated into the wings on 2½-litre models in 1937, standardised with all-steel production on all cars.
- Bold crested chromed radiator grille with vertical slats incorporating radiator filler cap

Frontal view of the 1½-litre saloon with separate chromed horns, smaller headlights and separate side lights on top of the front wings.

and SS Jaguar winged logo on top. The 3½-litre models had a wider and deeper radiator grille, and by 1938 the 2½-litre grille was standardised for the 1½-litre models.

- Large Lucas chromed surround, separately mounted headlamps (either side of the radiator grille), later changed to Lucas P100 type on 2½-litre models, but always fitted to 3½-litre cars. In both cases they hinge from the top.
- Twin chrome-plated horns externally mounted above bumper level. From 1940 they were changed in design and hidden out of sight beneath the wing/bumper area.
- Twin fog lamps fitted to all-steel bodied cars, except the 1½-litre models.
- Full-width, single blade, chromed front bumper.
- One-piece flat windscreen with chromed surround and twin wipers.
- Full-depth, two-piece bonnet with piano-hinged centre and chrome finisher. Bonnet lengths vary according to whether 1½- or 2½-/3½-litre models.
- Slightly wider track and longer wheelbase for all-steel models.
- All-steel models featured door, bonnet, and bonnet louvre lines all matching the rake of the front screen pillar.

Rear view
- Severe sloping rear bodywork incorporating full-width boot lid, hinged from the bottom.
- Single chromed boot lid T-handle, top centre with lock, replaced in 1940 by a vertically mounted stylised handle and lock.
- Integrated number plate mounting below boot lid with glass cover and flanked each side by single red rear lights.
- Fly-off, chromed petrol filler mounted to the left-hand side of the number plate area below boot lid area.
- Full-width, single blade, chromed rear bumper bar.
- Single exhaust tailpipe emitting from the right-hand side rear.
- Small, two-thirds-width rear screen with chromed surround.
- Steel-bodied cars included the spare wheel in a well underneath the boot, accessed by a hinged down panel incorporating the number plate housing. The bumper was hinged to aid removal of the wheel. By 1940 the spare wheel access panel was enlarged to ease the removal of the spare wheel, eliminating the need for the bumper to be hinged.

Side view
- Traditional 1930s-style full-length bodywork, incorporating flowing front wing line down to running boards and leading to curved rear wings.

The slightly later (pre-all-steel bodywork) 2½-litre saloon with wider radiator grille, integrated side lights, and the addition of the fog/driving lamps.

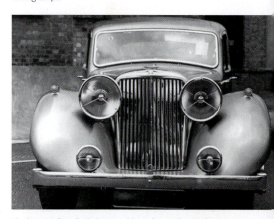

The later 3½-litre, displaying yet wider radiator grille with flatter top.

An early example of the SS Jaguar from the rear, showing the simplistic lighting treatment either side of the number plate housing, the sighting for the fuel filler, and the T-handle to open the boot lid. Also note the relationship between the bottom of the boot lid and the rear number plate housing. Finally, the 'J' emblem mounted in the centre of the bumper bar – up to the Second World War some cars carried the 'SS' insignia.

Later rear-end design with separate under-panel, accessed via T-keys, housing the spare wheel, and the revised positioning of the fuel filler. Also note the stylised boot lock and handle.

Rear compartment of a prewar SS Jaguar with the later door trim style (with pockets) and armrests above the rear wheelarches.

Early front door trim with art deco styling, with wood cappings and window surrounds.

The early 1½-litre four-cylinder Standard engine fitted to the SS Jaguar saloons.

From 1937, fitted with quarter-lights, this stylish handle wound the draught-excluder open.

The 2½-litre engine.

An example of the later all-steel bodywork, in this case a 3½-litre saloon. Note the integrated door handles into the waistline trim.

The Lucas P100 headlights, standard equipment on most 2½- and 3½-litre models and an extra cost option on the 1½-litre cars, showing the retaining clips at the bottom, as the surrounds were hinged at the top. Note also the winged badging incorporating the SS Jaguar insignia on the radiator grilles of all these models.

Comparison between the 1½- and 2½-litre models from 1937. Note the height of the spare wheel compared to the bonnet line and the length of the bonnet (the car in the foreground is the 1½-litre model.

Shown for representation only, the SS1 tourer which was effectively rebadged as an SS Jaguar, most probably to clear body stocks during the early production of the SS Jaguar saloons.

- Four-door construction with front doors and rear doors centrally hinged.
- Louvred side panels to bonnet area.
- Waistline chromed trim running from leading edge of bonnet through the doors to spears above the rear wings.
- Door handles mounted below the waistline trim. With all-steel bodies, incorporated within the waistline trim which was of a slightly different style.
- Traffic indicators mounted at the rear edge of front wings.
- Two-light glass arrangement, opening windows to front and rear doors with no quarter-lights. (Quarter-lights fitted to the front doors on post-1937 models.)
- Nearside mounting of spare wheel inset into rear section of front wing with steel cover incorporating chrome finishing, applicable to pre-all-steel models only. The 1½-litre cars more recognisable by the spare wheel height proud of the bonnet line.
- Body-coloured wire spoked wheels standard equipment on all models.
- Body length forward of bulkhead differed, 11in longer for 2½-/3½-litre models.

SS Jaguar tourer specifics

Front view
- Radiator grille similar but different from earlier SS1 models incorporating a thick centre chromed vane.
- General wing line, and standing of car from the front, much lower than the SS Jaguar saloon equivalent.

Rear view
- Squared-off sloping rear end incorporating the fuel tank and exposed spare wheel.
- Fish-eye rear-light unit, reminiscent of earlier SS models above square number plate mounting.

Side view
- Traditional line of earlier SS1 tourer with cutaway single door, hinged at the rear.
- Canvas hood arrangement with hood frame and traditional side-screens.

SS Jaguar 100 specifics

Front view
- Traditional-style lower set frontal aspect with separate wings to the saloons.
- Lower set chromed radiator surround incorporating bright mesh insert.
- P100 headlights mounted on chromed 'tripod' bracing, including the '100' insignia in the centre.
- No bumper bar fitted.

The sculptured seating, unique to the pre-Jaguar SS models, in this tourer.

The Desmo leaping Jaguar mascot. This was not fitted as standard equipment to the prewar SS Jaguar models, but was available as an accessory.

The SS Jaguar 100 sports, with a modified body from the early SS90 but fitted to a shortened version of the SS Jaguar saloon chassis and mechanicals.

The dramatic front of the SS100 with pronounced mesh grille and sweeping lines of the wings.

Rear view of an SS100 with the ungainly hood erect. The 'owl eye' rear-light unit was also used on earlier SS models like the tourer.

The drophead coupé version of the SS Jaguar saloons, with only two doors and much wider than the saloons and, in this instance, with the hood in the 'sedanca' position.

A drophead coupé with the hood fully erect. Note the Ace wheel-discs covering the wire wheels, a period option for all models.

Revised rear seating arrangement for drophead coupé models.

Rear of the drophead coupé model with the pillar-box-style rear screen.

Rear view
- Sloping rear end incorporating fuel tank and separately mounted spare wheel.
- Traditional line of earlier SS1 tourer with cut-away single door, hinged at the rear.
- Fold down front screen arrangement.
- Canvas hood arrangement with hood frame and traditional side-screens.
- Fish-eye rear-light unit, reminiscent of earlier SS models, above square number plate mounting.
- No bumper bar fitted.

Side view
- Traditional line, similar to earlier SS models with cutaway single door, hinged at the rear.
- Cut-off rear end just aft of the rear wings, emphasising the shortened wheelbase compared to other models.
- Fold-down front screen arrangement with chromed surround.
- Canvas hood arrangement with hood frame and traditional side-screens.

Drophead coupé specifics

Front view
- Lowered roof line, evident above front screen.

Rear view
- Canvas rear hood replacing steel saloon roof.
- Much smaller 'pillar-box'-style rear screen with chromed surround.

Side view
- Longer, two-door configuration.
- Single-door glass area and no rear compartment windows.
- Chromed dummy hood-irons visible at rear side of hood.

Interior identification points

General points applicable to all SS Jaguar saloon models

- Full-width wooden dashboard area with centrally mounted instruments, initially the two larger (rev counter and speedometer) flanked by smaller auxiliary gauges. Instruments set into a central black panel with switchgear. From 1937, instruments regrouped with larger rev counter/speedometer on the outside.
- Either side of instrument 'pack' wood finish continued without glove compartments. Passenger side glovebox fitted from 1937.
- Prominent dashboard top rail in wood, incorporating ashtrays and handle to open the windscreen (hinged from the top). Individual wiper controls fitted from 1937.
- Complete dashboard change in 1938 on all-steel cars. Full-width veneered dash with integrated instrumentation in the style that would follow for most other large Jaguar saloons up to the early 1960s. Inset rev counter and speedometer flanked minor gauges in the

The original dashboard layout of the SS Jaguar saloons. The large upper rail-mounted handle is to open the windscreen. Note the lack of gloveboxes on these early dashboards.

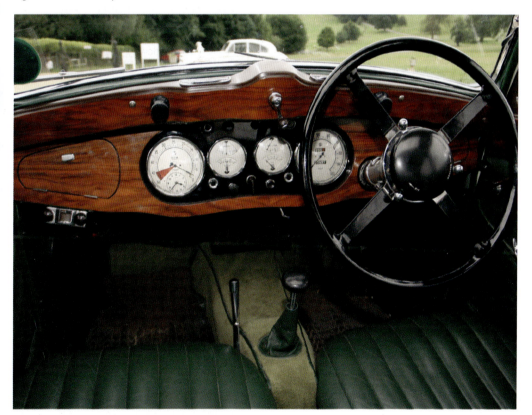

The later dashboard layout with revised instrument positions and addition of gloveboxes. Windscreen wipers are now operated by individual controls on the top rail.

centre surrounded by switchgear. Gloveboxes (with lids) now featured either side of the dashboard.
- 120mph speedometer fitted to 3½-litre models.
- A heater was added from 1940, mounted in the centre below the dash area which also included venting to the windscreen area.
- Large-diameter four-spoke steering wheel incorporating horn push and controls for throttle.
- Soft leather-finished door panels with wooden top-rails, chromed handles for door lock and window winder. Front door armrests and map pockets were included from 1937.
- Bucket-style front pleated leather seating, with better bolster support from 1937, and then also featuring cut-out areas in the seatback to aid rear-compartment legroom.
- From 1940, plain non-pleated leather seating was adopted, incorporating stuffed side-rolls to aid driver/passenger location. Also, from 1940, chromed handles at the front of each seat adjusted the height of that seat.
- From 1940, similar door trim panels fitted.
- Full-width rear bench pleated leather seat, with side armrests over each wheelarch from 1937.
- Rear footwells to allow for passenger feet areas on early cars, eliminated with sloping floor from 1937.
- From 1940, all models featured veneered picnic tables and matching ashtrays integrated into the front seat backs, and plain leather (instead of pleating) to the seating.
- Boot internal area featured plain rubber matting, and from 1940 was supplemented by ribbed rubber guide strips to support luggage.
- The boot lid incorporated a lift-up panel to reveal a fully equipped tool kit.

SS100 specifics
- Plain (unpleated) bucket seats in the front, no rear seating fitted.
- All metal, painted dashboard in kidney shape with rev counter and speedometer situated in front of the driver along with the oil pressure gauge. Other gauges spread across the passenger side of the dash with switchgear around.

The completely revised dashboard treatment for the late 1930s car, looking somewhat similar to postwar models. It has new-style instrumentation, and note the now fitted heater unit beneath the dashboard area.

The integrated tool kit into the boot lid of the SS Jaguar saloons.

Flat, plain, unpleated bucket seating for the SS100 models.

Layout of the SS100 dashboard which, was always painted to match body colour.

Technical specifications

	1.5-litre Saloon	1.75-litre Saloon
cc	1608	1776
Bore and stroke (mm)	69.5 x 106	73 x 106
Compression ratio	6.1 to 1	7.2 to 1
bhp	52	65
@ rpm	4300	4600
Fuelling	Single Solex carb	Single SU carb
Transmission	4-speed (manual)	4-speed (manual)
Wheel size (in)	18, wire	18, wire
Suspension front	Beam axle, half-elliptic leaf	Beam axle, half-elliptic leaf
Suspension rear	Live axle, half-elliptic leaf	Live axle, half-elliptic leaf
Brakes	Girling – rod operated	Girling – rod operated
Performance		
0-50mph (sec)	19.6	17
Top speed (mph)	70	72
Average mpg	25	27
Dimensions		
Length (in)	173	173
Width (in)	61.5	65.5
Height (in)	60	60
Wheelbase (in)	108	112.5
Front track (in)	48	52
Rear track (in)	48	55
Weight (cwt)	21	26.5

Optional extras

Ace wheel rimbellishers.
Unique exterior colour schemes.
Lucas chromium-plated fog lamps.
Chromium-plated badge bar.
Radio installation.
Fitted luggage for boot area.
Extra fittings to 1.5-litre models, normally standard on other cars.

Technical specifications *cont ...*

	2.5-litre Saloon	3.5-litre Saloon
cc	2663	3485
Bore and stroke (mm)	73 x 106	82 x 110
Compression ratio	7.6 to 1	7.2 to 1
bhp	105	125
@ rpm	4600	4500
Fuelling	Twin SU carbs	Twin SU carbs
Transmission	4-speed (manual)	4-speed (manual)
Wheel size (in)	18, wire	18, wire
Suspension front	Beam axle, half-elliptic leaf	Beam axle, half-elliptic leaf
Suspension rear	Beam axle, half-elliptic leaf	Live beam, half-elliptic leaf
Brakes	Girling – rod operated	Girling – rod operated
Performance		
0–50mph (sec)	10.6	9
Top speed (mph)	87	92
Average mpg	19	18
Dimensions		
Length (in)	186	186
Width (in)	66	66
Height (in)	61	61
Wheelbase (in)	120	120
Front track (in)	54	54
Rear track (in)	56	56
Weight (cwt)	32	32

Colour schemes

Exterior	Details	Seat trim colours
Olive Green		Olive Green
Maroon		Maroon
Suede Green		Red
Cream	To 1938	Suede Green
Ivory	From 1938	Dark Blue
Dark Blue		Black-Silver Grain
Black		Brown
Lavender Grey		Pigskin Grain Tan
Mountain Ash Green	From 1938	Beige
Birch Grey	From 1938	Olive
Battleship Grey	From 1938	**Hood colours**
Gunmetal	From 1938	French Grey
Honeysuckle	From 1938	Black
		Dark Sand
		Gunmetal Grey

	2.5-litre SS100	3.5-litre SS100
cc	2663	3485
Bore and stroke (mm)	73 x 106	82 x 110
Compression ratio	7.6 to 1	7.2 to 1
bhp	102	125
@ rpm	4600	4500
Fuelling	Twin SU carbs	Twin SU carbs
Transmission	4-speed (manual)	4-speed (manual)
Wheel size (in)	18, wire	18, wire
Suspension front	Beam axle, half-elliptic leaf	Beam axle, half-elliptic leaf
Suspension rear	Live axle, half-elliptic leaf	Live axle, half-elliptic leaf
Brakes	Girling – rod operated	Girling – rod operated
Performance		
0–50mph (sec)	8.8	7.1
Top speed (mph)	94	101
Average mpg	20	21
Dimensions		
Length (in)	153	153
Width (in)	63	63
Height (in)	54	54
Wheelbase (in)	104	104
Front track (in)	54	54
Rear track (in)	54	54
Weight (cwt)	23	23.3

Prices and production volumes

	Price new (£)	1935	1936	1937	1938	1939	1940	Total produced
SS Jag 2.5-litre tourer	375	■	■	■	–	–	–	105
SS Jag 1.5-litre saloon	285	■	■	■	■	–	–	2250
SS Jag 2.5-litre saloon	395	■	■	■	■	■	■	5023
SS Jag 2.5-litre dhc	415	–	–	–	■	■	■	279
SS Jag 1.75-litre saloon	298	–	–	–	■	■	■	4408
SS Jag 1.75-litre dhc	318	–	–	–	■	■	■	677
SS Jag 3.5-litre saloon	445	–	–	–	■	■	■	1067
SS Jag 3.5-litre dhc	465	–	–	–	■	■	■	241
SS Jaguar 100 2.5-litre	395	■	■	■	■	■	■	191
SS Jaguar 100 3.5-litre	445	–	–	–	■	■	■	118
Total production								**14,359**

2 Postwar pushrods 1945 to 1951

Background

With the end of the Second World War came the resumption of car production, and the company began getting back to some semblance of normality. But, having had little opportunity during the war to design new models, the prewar designs had to be resurrected and, like other manufacturers, it was vital for the company to win export sales to secure allocation of essential raw materials. SS Cars Limited had become Jaguar Cars Limited in March 1945, and thereafter the company's cars were Jaguars in their own right rather than SS Jaguars.

A major change affecting the postwar models, and one which secured Jaguar's independence from outside supply, was the acquisition of the tooling to produce the 2.5-litre and 3.5-litre pushrod engines used in the cars – although the production and rights for the smaller four-cylinder unit remained with Standard Motors.

Production started mid-year, and it was limited to the saloons. No decision seems to have been taken at the time, but it soon became apparent that the SS100 (the two-seater sports car built in small numbers before the war) would not reappear. However, the drophead coupé was reintroduced from 1947. All saloons were on offer with all three engine sizes, but drophead coupés were available only with the six-cylinder engines.

Although Jaguar had been working on an entirely new engine, this was not ready for mass production yet, nor was the bodywork for the brand new luxury saloon, to be known as the Mark VII. The latter didn't appear until 1950, while the engine was announced to the public at the 1948 British Motor Show, at the time fitted to what was intended to be a low-production sports car. However, Jaguar desperately needed a new saloon model to maintain its export drive and satisfy the demand at home for new cars. Hence, what would be destined to be called an interim model appeared at the October 1948 Motor Show – the Mark V saloon.

The designation Mark V came about merely because it was the fifth prototype of the model, and, although it very much looked like the prewar/postwar design, apart from the carryover of the engine and gearbox everything else about the car was new. A very rigid new chassis (designed for the later all-new saloon in 1950) was used, which incorporated, for the first time on an SS or Jaguar, independent front suspension and, at the rear, more suspension travel with softer springs. A hydraulic braking system was also employed for the first time, but with smaller-diameter drums because of the fitment of smaller road wheels.

The Mark V was offered only with the 2.5-litre or 3.5-litre six-cylinder overhead valve engines, with the usual Moss four-speed manual transmission.

Externally the new car was wider, taller, longer, and heavier than the outgoing models, and virtually every internal and external body panel was new, along with much more brightwork. The saloons were again accompanied by two-door drophead coupé models, but these more hand-built cars were produced in very small numbers.

The Mark V proved a very competitive car, both commercially (it represented good value for money) and in motorsport (it did well in major rallies well past the time the model was discontinued from the Jaguar range). The last Mark V left the production lines in 1951 just after the introduction of the new luxury 100mph Mark VII that the chassis had originally been intended for.

Model range and development

Models available at postwar launch
Jaguar 1.75-litre saloon
Jaguar 2.5-litre saloon
Jaguar 3.5-litre saloon

The prewar/postwar design, now badged on the radiator as a Jaguar and with slimmer waistline trims. This car also carries the Ace rimbellishers and its horns are now completely hidden.

All three Jaguar saloons (and drophead coupés) continued very much as they were before the war. Externally, identification points were thinner waistline chrome trims, new radiator grille badging, and the revised 'Jaguar' insignia (instead of 'SS') on the spinners of the wire wheels. The bonnet was also slightly shorter to make room for a deeper scuttle panel below the windscreen. One of the apparent benefits of this was that it made room to fit modern radio receiver equipment.

Mechanically, all cars now benefited from a new hypoid rear axle and revised gear ratios, and were fitted with a new Girling two-leading-shoe braking system. The Standard four-cylinder engine profited from a new water-heated inlet manifold.

Internally, the postwar cars saw a return to pleated upholstery, though without the rear seat picnic tables that were fitted to the last of the prewar models. The heater unit was improved and repositioned, hidden further under the dashboard, with new controls. The steering-wheel-mounted advance and retard controls were no longer fitted to postwar models.

The cars continued virtually unchanged until production finished in 1949, just after the launch of the replacement models – the Mark Vs.

The Mark V represented quite a leap forward for Jaguar. The smoothing out of the body style, while still retaining the previous model's 'look', the extensive use of chrome plating, and the adoption of independent front suspension and hydraulic braking brought the Jaguar range very much up to date. Another change in the running gear was the adoption of a split propeller shaft under the car, thus eliminating the need for a conventional tunnel in the rear compartment, and making for more legroom for rear-seat passengers.

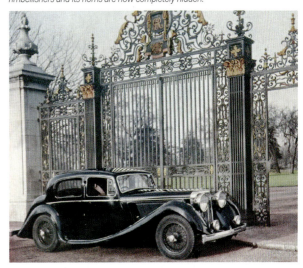

A typical advertisement picture for the postwar Jaguar saloon, in this case a 3.5-litre model. The distance between the rear of the bonnet and the windscreen indicates the slighter deeper scuttle area.

Externally, such features as the sloping bonnet, the faired-in headlights, the massive front bumper, and slimmer 'A' posts to the windscreen made the new car immediately identifiable. From the side the Mark V featured separate chrome on brass window surrounds, and wider doors with substantial push-button handles. Another 'first' was the fitment of full rear-wheel spat covers.

At the rear, similar substantial bumper bar treatment was adopted, a much deeper boot lid was fitted (allowing the spare wheel to be accommodated behind a hinged panel in the centre of the bumper), and the fuel filler was

The later postwar dashboard with hidden heater unit and large controls for it on the dashboard.

now concealed under a flush panel built into the nearside rear wing.

Internally, the Mark V was very well equipped and, with yet another change of direction, non-pleated leather seating returned yet again. The whole interior was much larger, and although the dashboard looked somewhat similar to the outgoing models it was actually quite different. A new style of four-spoke steering wheel was adopted, a design that would be used on all subsequent Jaguars, in some cases, up to 1961. Some novel features were used that were unique to the Mark V, like the trigger interior door handles.

The drophead coupé models, which were announced at the same time as the saloons, were still to be built with some aspects of traditional coachwork, like ash-framed door panels, for example. Because of the construction method, conventional door handles were also used, and the cars were built for a limited period in very small numbers, and were discontinued well before the demise of the saloons.

Subsequent changes were few on the Mark V as the production run was so small, and all attention was being given to its replacement, the Mark VII – so the Mark V slowly dropped out from the range in late 1950 to early 1951.

Compare the waistline chrome trims of this postwar car with the earlier, much thicker chrome strips used on the prewar examples.

Exterior identification points

General points applicable to postwar Jaguar saloon and drophead models

Front view
- P100 headlights with smaller clear centres.
- Headlights now hinged from the bottom instead of the top.
- Revised radiator grille badging, still incorporating the winged logo but now with chromed letters and figures, painted cream for 2.5-litre models, black for 3.5-litre models, and black infilled letters with pale lilac for the 1.5-litre models.

Prewar thicker waistline trims.

Rear view
- Rear bumper now incorporated the centrally mounted 'J' emblem, some of which were also fitted to prewar models.

Side view
- Waistline chromed trim running from leading edge of bonnet through the doors to spears above the rear wings in the same fashion as the prewar car but of much thinner section.
- Scuttle area between bottom of windscreen and bonnet now wider.
- 'SS' insignia wheel spinners replaced with those containing the word 'Jaguar'.

Postwar frontal view showing the bottom-hinged headlights and the new 'Jaguar' winged badge on the radiator grille.

Points only applicable to the Mark V models

Front view

- Lucas 'tripod' headlights faired into the front wings with chrome spears on top.
- Revised radiator grille badging, still retaining the winged emblem with the word 'Jaguar', but now incorporating either 2.5- or 3.5-litre markings.
- Pod-mounted matching chromed fog (driving) lights mounted either side of the radiator grille diagonally below the headlights.
- Traditional Jaguar-style chromed radiator grille with vertical chromed slats, and still incorporating the chromed cap screwing directly into the radiator. (Mascots remained an extra cost option with these models.)
- Traditional-styled front wings, but now with greater fairing into the main bodywork and still retaining integrated sidelight units.
- Substantial multi-component chromed bumper bar, forming two separate horizontal bumpers with quarter bumpers and vertical overriders, and number plate mounting, plus body-colour painted closing panels on top to conceal the irons.

Rear view

- Rear styling following the design of the earlier cars, but with deeper boot panel, still hinged at the bottom and including a stylised handle and lock.
- Fuel filler incorporated into the nearside wing under concealed flush body-colour painted panel.
- Substantial bumper bar treatment at the front, centre section of which folded down to access the spare-wheel compartment. Centrally mounted number plate mounting.
- Rear lighting accommodated within the rear quarter bumpers.

Side view

- Although retaining a similar style to the earlier models, body longer and taller.
- Wider doors with separate chrome-plated window surrounds, all doors featuring opening quarter-lights.
- Full-length triangular section chromed waistline trims with extended spears over the rear wings, incorporating substantial push-button door handles.
- Rear wheel spats in body colour.
- Steel wheels of smaller (16in) diameter, and chromed hubcaps with centre sections painted to match body colour, and embodying centre spinner design with 'Jaguar' name.
- Bonnet centre hinged but with separate (detachable) side panels, previously part of the whole bonnet unit.
- Ventilators fitted to the scuttle on either side of the car ahead of the front doors and behind the engine compartment side panels.

A much more modernistic approach to the prewar design in the Mark V saloon. Note the extensive chromework and the smaller 16in wheels (no longer wire wheels) with painted hubcaps to match the exterior bodywork.

Impressive frontal view of the Mark V with faired-in headlights, wing-mounted pedestal fog lamps and the substantial bumper bar arrangement with number plate mounting.

Sculptured chromed door handles operated by a push-button mechanism. Note also the retention of fresh-air ventilation in the scuttle panel.

Points only applicable to the drophead coupé Mark V models.
- Wider door incorporating conventional pull-down door handles.
- Traffic indicators mounted just to the rear of the front doors.

Interior identification points

General points applicable to postwar models
- Return to pleated upholstery in the same style of pre-1940 models.
- Centrally mounted heater unit, situated further back underneath the dashboard area.
- Heater controls now fitted to the dashboard area.
- Fitment of radio installation could now be carried out in the centre of the dash area.

Points only applicable to Mark V saloon and drophead coupé models
- Plain unpleated leather to all seating.
- Height-adjustable front seats with shaped bolsters to rear squabs.
- Full-width bench seating with raised 'wing' areas at sides to meet up with rear doors' 'D' posts.
- Flat rear floor area without a transmission tunnel intrusion.
- Plain, padded door panels incorporating trigger-style door handles with turn-buttons to instigate locking mechanism.
- Traditional style to wooden dashboard area but with rearranged switchgear and stylised instrument legends.
- Shallower dashboard top rail without individual wiper controls.
- Radio installation (where fitted) now built into the dashboard lower area, normally occupied by pull-out drawer.
- Under top dash panel 'black violet' reflected lighting for instrumentation.
- Windscreen now fixed.
- Dashboard top rail-mounted rear-view mirror.
- 18in Bluemells four-spoke steering wheel with pronounced chrome-edged box incorporating Jaguar head and indicator turn control.
- Conventional front door-mounted swivel draught excluder quarter-lights for most cars; very early examples featured the same type as at the rear.
- Rear door-mounted swivel draught excluder quarter-lights controlled by knurled sliders.

Solid brass chromed window surrounds, and here in the 'B/C' post incorporating the traffic indicator.

Rear of the Mark V with deeper boot lid and substantial bumper arrangement, behind which is a fold-down panel for access to the spare wheel.

The Mark V retained the prewar style of opening bonnet but now the side panels were separate and detachable.

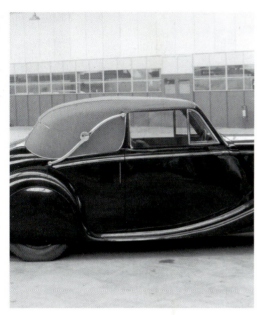

The Mark V drophead coupé with the hood erect ...

... with the hood in the 'sedanca' position ...

... with the hood down.

The dashboard layout was similar but with instruments and switches placed differently from the earlier cars. The upper rail hides the black violet lighting. Note the new-style steering wheel with prominent centre boss.

Front seating of the Mark V with stiff bolsters for added support and quite plain door panels.

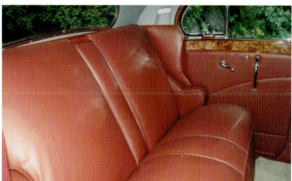

The rear compartment of the Mark V, again with unpleated upholstery. The inset rear courtesy light (one either side) in the rear quarter of the roof became a regular feature of the big Jaguar saloons into the early 1960s. Note the quite sophisticated catch to the rear door quarter-lights, new to the Mark V and which became a standard fitment on most subsequent Jaguar saloons well into the 1960s. Also note the trigger door handles with separate locking 'knob'.

41

Technical specifications

	1.75-litre	2.5-litre
cc	1776	2663
Bore and stroke (mm)	73 x 106	73 x 106
Compression ratio	7.6 to 1	7.6 to 1
bhp	65	105
@ rpm	4600	4600
Fuelling	Single SU carb	Twin SU carbs
Transmission	4-speed (manual)	4-speed (manual)
Wheel size (in)	18, wire	18, wire
Suspension front	Beam axle, half-elliptic leaf	Beam axle, half-elliptic leaf
Suspension rear	Live axle, half-elliptic leaf	Live axle, half-elliptic leaf
Brakes	Girling – rod operated	Girling – rod operated
Performance		
0–50mph (sec)	17	10.6
Top speed (mph)	72	87
Average mpg	27	16
Dimensions		
Length (in)	173	186
Width (in)	65.5	66
Height (in)	60	61
Wheelbase (in)	112.5	120
Front track (in)	52	54
Rear track (in)	55	56
Weight (cwt)	26.5	32

Optional extras

Ace wheel rimbellishers.
Unique exterior colour schemes.
Chromium-plated badge bar.
Radio installation.
Fitted luggage for boot area.
Leaper mascot for radiator grille top.
Chromium-plated wing mirrors.
Whitewall tyres.

	3.5-litre
cc	3485
Bore and stroke (mm)	82 x 110
Compression ratio	7.2 to 1
bhp	125
@ rpm	4500
Fuelling	Twin SU carbs
Transmission	4-speed (manual)
Wheel size (in)	18, wire
Suspension front	Beam axle, half-elliptic leaf
Suspension rear	Live axle, half-elliptic leaf
Brakes	Girling – rod operated
Performance	
0–50mph (sec)	9
Top speed (mph)	92
Average mpg	17
Dimensions	
Length (in)	186
Width (in)	66
Height (in)	61
Wheelbase (in)	120
Front track (in)	54
Rear track (in)	56
Weight (cwt)	32.5

Technical specifications *cont ...*

	2.5-litre (Mark V)	3.5-litre (Mark V)
cc	2663	3485
Bore and stroke	73 x 106	82 x 110
Compression ratio	7.3 to 1	6.75 to 1
bhp	102	125
@ rpm	4600	4250
Fuelling	Twin SU carbs	Twin SU carbs
Transmission	4-speed (manual)	4-speed (manual)
Wheel size (in)	16, wire	16, wire
Suspension front	Independent wishbones, torsion bar, anti-roll bar	Independent wishbones, torsion bar, anti-roll bar
Suspension rear	Live axle, half-elliptic leaf	Live axle, half-elliptic leaf
Brakes	Girling – hydraulic	Girling – hydraulic
Performance		
0–50mph (sec)	10.6	9.9
Top speed (mph)	87	92
Average mpg	16	18
Dimensions		
Length (in)	187	187
Width (in)	69	69
Height (in)	62.5	62.5
Wheelbase (in)	120	120
Front track (in)	56	56
Rear track (in)	56	56
Weight (cwt)	32.5	33

Colour schemes

Exterior	Postwar	Mark V
Olive Green	■	–
Maroon	■	–
Suede Green	■	■
Ivory	■	■
Dark Blue	■	–
Black	■	■
Lavender Grey	■	■
Mountain Ash Green	■	–
Birch Grey	■	■
Battleship Grey	■	■
Gunmetal	■	■
Honeysuckle	■	–
Dove Grey	■	–
Pastel Blue Metallic	■	–
Pastel Green Metallic	■	–

Seat trim	Post War	Mark V
Olive Green	■	–
Maroon	■	–
Red	■	■
Suede Green	■	■
Pale Blue	■	–
Dark Blue	–	–
Black	■	–
Silver Black	■	–
Brown	■	–
Pigskin Grain Tan	■	■
Beige	–	–
Biscuit	■	–
Grey	■	–
Hood		
French Grey	■	■
Black	■	■
Dark Sand	■	■
Gunmetal Grey	■	■

Prices and production volumes

	Price new (£)	1945	1946	1947	1948	1949	1950
Jaguar 1.75-litre saloon	684	■	■	■	■	■	–
Jaguar 2.5-litre saloon	889	–	■	■	■	■	–
Jaguar 2.5-litre dhc	1189	–	–	–	■	–	–
Jaguar 3.5-litre saloon	991	–	■	■	■	■	–
Jaguar 3.5-litre dhc	1263	–	–	–	■	–	–
Jaguar Mark V 2.5 saloon	1247	–	–	–	–	■	■
Jaguar Mark V 2.5 dhc	1247	–	–	–	–	–	■
Jaguar Mark V 3.5 saloon	1263	–	–	–	■	■	■
Jaguar Mark V 3.5 dhc	1263	–	–	–	■	■	■

	Price new (£)	1951	Total produced
Jaguar 1.75-litre saloon	684	–	5761
Jaguar 2.5-litre saloon	889	–	1749
Jaguar 2.5-litre dhc	1189	–	101
Jaguar 3.5-litre saloon	991	–	3860
Jaguar 3.5-litre dhc	1263	–	498
Jaguar Mark V 2.5 saloon	1247	1671	
Jaguar Mark V 2.5 dhc	1247	–	29
Jaguar Mark V 3.5 saloon	1263	7828	
Jaguar Mark V 3.5 dhc	1263	971	
Total production			**22,468**

3 The XK sports cars 1948 to 1961

Background

The XK120 was the first entirely new car produced by Jaguar after the Second World War. Announced at the British Motor Show in October 1948, it was only the second sports car ever produced by the company (the first being the SS Jaguar 100 in the 1930s) and was the first car to feature Jaguar's own in-house-designed engine, the famous XK straight six power unit.

The XK120 was not so much developed as contrived to bring publicity to Jaguar by showing off its new engine, which was actually intended for a new saloon, eventually to be called the Mark VII. Hasty work in cutting down one of the new saloon chassis and installing the XK power unit, and then hand-crafting an aluminium two-seater roadster body, led to the launch of the car at the motor show before it had ever run.

Initially intended to be sold as a very limited production car with both a 2.0-litre four-cylinder engine and the 3.4-litre six-cylinder engine, no one – least of all William Lyons – anticipated the public response to the XK120. The quantity of forward orders embarrassed Jaguar, and it soon became clear that it could not meet the demand by producing the car with an alloy body over an ash wooden frame (a typically prewar method of build). In addition the idea of a four-cylinder version (to be known as XK100) had to be dropped. Few cars (around 200 in total) actually got delivered, while the company worked towards full-scale production via an all-steel bodyshell, which began in May 1950.

Soon after the supply of XK120s got under way, they were already finding success in competition both on the race track and in road rallies. This eventually led to further development and the XK120 C-type, designed specifically for racing, which further boosted the standing of Jaguar and its XK road-going cars.

Riding on the success of the XK120 two-seater, two further production variants were produced – a fixed-head coupé from 1951, and a drophead coupé from 1953.

Production of the XK120 ceased in 1954 to make way for its replacement, by which time a total of 12,055 of all variants had been produced. That replacement was the XK140, introduced for 1954, which also came in three variants: two-seater, fixed-head, and drophead. Externally the 140s are easily identifiable, although retaining the overall style of the earlier car. Internally the changes were more subtle, except for the moving forward of the engine in the chassis to provide better legroom and, in the fixed-head version, 'occasional' rear seating. Mechanically XK140 models benefited from a more powerful version of the XK engine, improved handling, and the adoption of rack and pinion steering.

The XK140 was superseded in 1957 by the final development of the design, the XK150, a much more radical style although still retaining the styling concept of the original XK120. Externally it was a more slab-sided design with larger glass areas and more interior space. A redesign of the interior meant no veneer, while disc brakes were fitted all round. Initially the XK150 was only available in two body styles, drophead and fixed-head coupés, but in 1958 a two-seater roadster version was added followed by the 'S' high-performance versions and larger engined variants.

The XK150 left production in 1961 to make way for the all-new E-type. The total production figure for all XKs from 1948 to 1961 amounted to over 30,000.

Model range and development

Only one production model was offered of the XK120 in 1948, although subsequently three variants were produced, all based on the same chassis and basic mechanical configuration.

Models available 1948–54
XK120 open two-seater (roadster)
XK120 fixed-head coupé
XK120 drophead coupé

The principle of the three models stemmed from William Lyons's ability to produce cars catering for different markets, building on the development of an original concept and utilising as many common parts as possible, therefore keeping the cost of production down. This theme continued throughout XK production.

The original two-seater (roadster) was aimed at the true sports car market, offering minimal accommodation and equipment levels with high-performance and good handling – typical 'wind in the hair' motoring. In contrast the fixed-head coupé was a true grand tourer in its own right. Still offering the performance and handling capabilities of the two-seater, it provided virtually unheard of benefits to sports car drivers, like an integrated hard top that was part of the overall body design and made the car structurally very robust, lockable doors, wind-up windows, and even a walnut veneered dashboard.

The drophead coupé provided an amalgam of both styles. For those who wanted open-air motoring, simply releasing the windscreen catches and folding down the hood provided instant access to the sun; yet the car retained the 'comfort' elements of veneer, wind-up windows, and lockable doors.

The first 200 two-seater models were all of alloy construction, virtually hand-built and therefore very different in detail to later steel-bodied cars. The front wings formed one piece, even including the sidelight housings. Internal

In its original form the XK120 roadster was fitted with steel wheels painted to the body colour with no rimbellishers but with chromed hubcaps. Earlier cars, like this one, featured painted centres to hubcaps to match the exterior paint finish. Also on this early car are the chromed sidelight cowls on the top of the front wings. Full rear spats covered all steel-wheel cars when new.

Front view of XK120 clearly showing the slim split-bumper treatment, 'tripod' headlights and, being an early car, chromed sidelight housings. A split windscreen was common to all XK120 models.

Rear of XK120 model with just overriders fitted; this was applicable to all models. Slight changes were made to rear lighting and number plate plinths during production – see text.

floors were of plywood construction and wood was also used in the sills. Underneath the alloy structure was an ash wooden frame to support it.

When body construction changed to steel, the bonnet, doors, and boot lid remained in aluminium. Apart from the obvious feel and sound of the metal, the differences in body style between alloy and steel-bodied cars are small. There are slight curvature differences to the front wings, and at the rear the steel wings are slightly less bulbous. The early steel-bodied cars also had chromed sidelight pods on the front wings.

The majority of XK120s were fitted with conventional steel road wheels with fully enclosing rear-wheel spats. If wire wheels were specified from new, these spats were not provided and the rear wings had copper beading fitted as a finisher.

It wasn't until 1951 that the fixed-head coupé was introduced, and SE (Special Equipment) models were offered by the factory the same year. Using an improved power unit with high lift camshafts, lightened flywheel, stiffer rear springs, wire wheels, a dual exhaust system, and benefiting from Jaguar's success in racing, the XK120 SE provided an increase of 20bhp over the 'ordinary' cars.

In 1953, for the last year in production, the XK120 drophead coupé was introduced, offering the enhanced fixed-head interior with the ability to still enjoy open-air motoring.

When the XK140 was introduced in 1954 it was significantly modified, although it retained the overall style of the 120. Instantly recognisable from the outside by the fatter bumper bars, heavy cast radiator grille, and larger window areas on the fixed-head coupé, all 140 models utilised the more powerful 180bhp engine and were equipped with rack and pinion steering. In the fixed-head and drophead coupés occasional rear seating was provided. Special Equipment models were also available but now offered a boost in performance to 210bhp. The XK140 was the first Jaguar sports car to become available with the option of automatic transmission.

Models available 1954–7
XK140 two-seater (roadster)
XK140 fixed-head coupé
XK140 drophead coupé

The XK140 only stayed in production for three years, being replaced by the XK150 in 1957. Although following the basic styling features of both the earlier models the XK150 had a wider bonnet, another new grille, a flattened-out wing line, and a curved one-piece windscreen for the first time on an XK. Mechanically disc brakes were the major technological advance. Interior trim was also modified again.

Interior of XK120 roadster showing four-spoke steering wheel with prominent centre horn push and fabric-covered dashboard only applicable to roadster models. Note the cutaway doors, also found only on roadster models.

Later XK120 roadster showing the painted sidelight housings and the hood erect. Perspex side-screens were used on all XK120 roadster models. Inset is a rear view of the hood and rear screen design.

XK120 fixed-head coupé.

Models available at launch 1957
XK150 3.4-litre fixed-head coupé
XK150 3.4-litre drophead coupé

Initially there was not a two-seater (roadster) version of the XK150, this coming on line late in 1958 with a much more accentuated rear deck area compared to earlier two-seater XKs. This was also accompanied by an 'S' model with triple carburettors and a straight port cylinder head boasting an output of 250bhp. By 1959 'S' models were also available in the other two body styles. Then Jaguar introduced an extra, larger engine for the XK, of 3.8-litre capacity, either with conventional twin carburettors or with triples, the latter boosting performance again to 265bhp.

All this amounted to no less than 12 models, plus SE types; and this is where the XK150 model list becomes confusing. Early literature states that 'standard' models of the XK150 were available, supposedly with drum brakes and steel wheels (with full rear body spats) and lacking the front valance-mounted fog lamps.

XK150s were available with a choice of manual, manual with overdrive, or automatic transmission. Production of all models finally ceased in 1961.

Exterior identification points

General points applicable to all XK120s
Front view
- Twin slim-line bumper bars, between which were situated the chromed oval radiator grille containing vertical slats.
- Steel number plate mounting below the radiator on UK cars, but on the side under- or over-bumper for other markets.
- Tripod headlights.
- Growler badge to forward centre of bonnet top in bronze against a cream background, with the words 'Jaguar Cars Ltd Coventry'.
- Split windscreen with chromed surround.
- In September 1952 the front wing sidelight pods changed from chrome to body colour.

Rear view
- Twin vertical overriders to outside areas of body.
- Twin single red rear-light lenses mounted in chrome plinths.
- Full depth boot lid with operating handle to extreme base, with separate number plate surround above which incorporated a chromed reversing light/number plate illumination panel.
- Single tailpipe exhaust systems were fitted to 'standard' cars, a twin pipe arrangement to SE models.

Different interior design for fixed-head and drophead coupé XK120 models, with wood-veneered dashboard and enhanced door trim panels.

Drophead coupé XK120 model. Note revised door and hood treatment compared to that of the roadster models.

XK140 styling differed at the front from that of the 120 (behind it) by having a more prominent cast radiator grille, revised 'J' lighting, and a substantial ribbed bumper bar. Fog lights were an extra cost fitment to these cars.

Side view
- Cars with steel wheels had chromed hubcaps with centre sections painted to body colour, with wheels to match.
- Where fitted, wire wheels were of the 54-spoke type, painted either to body colour or silver and held in place by chromed eared hub spinners depicting the Jaguar name.
- Full body spats were fitted over the rear disc wheels (no covers on wire-wheel-equipped cars).
- From February 1951 front wing ventilators were added to aid intake of cool air to the cockpit.

XK120 model specifics

XK120 two-seater (alloy cars)
- Rear number plate plinth mounted on to the boot lid from the exterior.
- Wheel-arches had wired edges to add strength to the aluminium.
- Fuel filler cover lock fitted to rear bodywork.

XK120 two-seater (steel cars)
- Rear number plate plinth bolted to the boot lid from the inside with no visible fixings on the outside; this was hereafter true of all 120s, regardless of body style.
- Fuel filler cover lock fitted to the cover itself.
- From 1951 the hood extended further back, permitting the rear window to be unzipped.

XK120 fixed-head coupé
- Revised doors accommodating exterior chromed handles, locking on the driver's side, and with chromed on brass fixed window frames with quarter-lights.
- Additional quarter-lights behind the doors.

XK120 drophead coupé
- Unlike the two-seater, the front split windscreen was held within steel surrounds with a header panel, part of the main body structure, and was painted to match.
- Fuel filler moved rearwards on the body to allow room for hood retraction.
- External door handles were smaller and more rounded than fixed-head coupé models, and the window glass, frames, and quarter-lights were of a different style.
- The hood was of an alternate design, incorporating a larger rear window that unzipped to fold down.

General points applicable to all XK140s

Front view
- As XK120 except for chromed cast oval radiator grille with only seven vertical slats.
- Red circular enamel badge carrying the words 'Jaguar Cars Ltd' above a growler head, and the word 'Coventry' under it.

The fixed-head coupé XK140 was easily identifiable from the XK120 by its pronounced bumper bar treatment, heavy chromed centre boot trim, and enlarged window areas with wider doors.

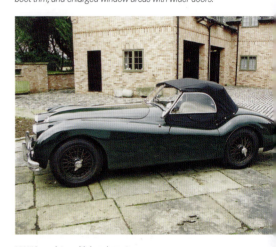

XK140 roadster with hood erect.

Above left: Interior of XK140 roadster, very similar but subtly different to the earlier XK120 model (see the picture on page 44).

Above right: Interior design for fixed- and drophead coupé XK140 models. Note the flat horn boss to the steering wheel, an easy identification point, as are the interior door handle slides.

- Deep single chromed ribbed front bumper bar with prominent chromed overriders either side of a black-painted metal number plate plinth.
- Bumper to front body distance was covered with a steel valance painted to body colour, which accommodated twin Lucas fog lamps where fitted.
- Revised headlights (not tripods) with 'J' insignia in centre.
- Separate circular indicator lenses with chromed surrounds to the lower section of the front wings.
- Chromed centre bonnet strip.

Rear view
- Deep split rear chrome bumpers with over-riders with centre section to provide metal number plate plinth and access to spare wheel.
- Number plate illumination/reversing light attached to lowermost area of boot lid (now shorter than the XK120 style).
- Vertically mounted chromed boot handle with chrome finisher running centrally up the boot lid.
- Unique chromed badge in red with silver lettering depicting the Jaguar badge, winged badge, and the 1951 win at Le Mans.
- Rear-light lenses fitted in extended chromed plinths.

Side view
- Where disc wheels were fitted, hubcaps were all chromed.
- As later XK120s except for specifics noted below.

XK140 model specifics

XK140 two-seater
- As XK120 equivalent, but look for wrap-around effect of front and rear bumpers.
- Where steel wheels were fitted, hubcaps were entirely chrome.
- At the rear the central chrome strip up the boot continues over rear deck area.

XK140 fixed-head coupé
- Raised roof line (1½in) and elongated passenger area (6½in) shows in larger window areas all round compared to XK120.
- 4in shorter in front wings and bonnet area as engine was moved forward in the chassis compared to XK120 fhc.
- Lengthened doors with new-style larger door handles mounted lower in the door.
- Steel-wheel hubcaps were chromed, not painted.

XK140 drophead coupé
- Longer hood and door window area because of occasional rear seating.
- As with other 140 models look for wrap-

XK140 drophead coupé. Note that all XK120 and XK140 dropheads feature glass side windows.

Rear view of XK140 showing the bumper bar treatment and unique badging to the boot panel, indicating appropriate Le Mans victories. Twin exhausts only applied to high-performance models.

XK150 fixed-head coupé, of a completely different styling approach to earlier models and easily identifiable by its very large side window areas and slab-sided body look.

around effect of front and rear bumper bar arrangement.

General points applicable to all XK150s

Front view
- Revised wider oval radiator grille with 16 slats incorporating a new red plastic badge depicting the growler head and the words 'Jaguar' and 'XK150' in silver.
- Similar-style bumper bar to XK140 but dished in the centre to accommodate the new radiator grille.
- Wider bonnet with raised centre section with full-length chrome finisher.
- Metal valance behind bumper bars now formed two separate panels.
- One-piece curved windscreen with slimmer surrounds.

Rear view
- Single wrap-around rear bumper bar with twin overriders.
- New boot lid-mounted number plate surround, with chromed illumination/reversing light also mounted on the boot lid. Post-1959 models with revised rake.
- Updated position of boot handle with shorter centre chromed trim and new-style badging depicting Jaguar's subsequent wins at Le Mans during the lifespan of the car (initially four wins, on later cars five).
- Rear lights initially mounted on elongated chromed plinths, later changed to significantly larger plinths and lens units incorporating separate indicator and reflector lenses.
- Rear bumper now one-piece with matching overriders. Positions of latter altered with revised lighting.

Side view
- Front wing, door, and rear wing line raised and flattened.
- On 'S' specification models, a chromed 'S' badge appeared on the doors.
- Door handles repositioned on fhc and dhc models.
- Larger window areas all round.

XK150 model specifics

XK150 two-seater
- Windscreen moved 4in rearward.
- Bonnet longer, extending rearwards towards new bulkhead and screen.
- The first XK roadster to feature glass wind-up windows.
- Curved top to door window glass structure with chrome finisher. No quarter-lights.
- Exterior door handles, a first for an XK roadster, in this case matching the style used on the XK140 fhc.
- Hood slimmer in style, with enlarged rear window and single chromed trim above.

XK150s were the only XKs to feature a one-piece wrap-around windscreen. The bumper bar treatment was similar to the XK140, but with a wider grille.

Rear view of the XK150 with one-piece bumper bar and an integrated reversing light plinth/number plate surround within the boot lid. This is a later model with larger rear-light units featuring separate indicator lenses (the colour varied according to market). Earlier XK150s featured the same lighting treatment as the XK140 (see the picture on page 47).

Revised boot badge for XK150 models with updated list of Le Mans victories.

XK150 fixed-head coupé
- Larger glass in new chromed brass window frames.
- Revised shape to front and rear quarter-lights.
- Larger rear window.

XK150 drophead coupé
- Neater hood style with chromed rain gutters and enlarged rear window (still unzippable).
- Folded hood rests higher up on rear deck area.

Interior identification points

XK120 two-seater (all models)
- Split-bench-style leather seats with ten pleats, with matching leather centre section over transmission tunnel.
- Door trim panels included a covered pocket and pull strap for door opening (early alloy cars had a knob towards the front of the trim panel).
- Leather-covered dashboard to match trim colour. Passenger side grab handle fitted to steel-bodied cars only.
- A Bluemel 18in cast black (or white in some export cars) steering wheel was fitted with four spokes that would become a standard feature on all Jaguars for many years. In the case of all XK120s this featured a protruding black horn push containing a side view of a jaguar face with chromed surround.

XK120 fixed-head coupé
- Door trims had no pockets and incorporated chromed window winding and door handles plus walnut-veneered cappings to the top section.
- Wooden cappings continued to the door frame surround securing a woollen head lining.
- Wooden cappings continued to the front screen surround and to the dashboard, which was of a totally different design to the two-seater's. Walnut veneered with lockable glove-box, pull-out drawer (also used to accommodate a radio), flip-up ashtray, and trimmed upper section incorporating demisting vents. Switchgear and some instruments changed in 1952, most noticeable from the knurled lighting switch in the centre of the dash. Switches and warning lights changed again in 1954, along with a movement of the instrument positions.
- Behind the seats a storage locker with lid was provided, trimmed to match the interior.
- Two tinted Perspex sun visors were fitted just to this model.

XK120 drophead coupé
- As fixed-head coupé but full-width map pockets to both front door trims along with hand-pulls within the wooden cappings.

This side view of a drophead coupé XK150 clearly shows the slab-sided look of the body.

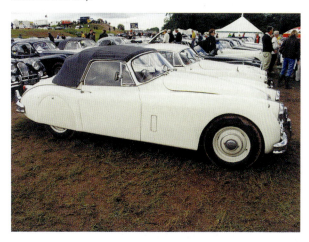

When XK150s were ordered new, wire wheels were still an extra cost option. Full rear-wheel spats applied, but are rarely seen these days if the car is fitted with steel wheels.

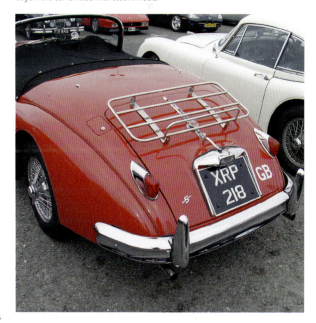

The roadster XK150 had a pronounced 'rear deck' as it was strictly a two-seater. The boot luggage rack was a period extra.

- No sun visors fitted.
- The hood mechanism was completely different to the two-seater, enabling it to be folded down quickly and easily to rest on the rear storage locker.

XK140 (all models)
- More interior accommodation due to the engine being moved forward in the chassis.
- The smaller 17in steering wheel now used a flat horn push depicting gold growler image.

XK140 two-seater
- Interior styling remained mostly as XK120 two-seater. Dashboard now moved closer to the occupants. Direction indicator stalk moved from steering wheel boss to outboard of the column.

XK140 fixed-head coupé
- Occasional rear seating in the form of two individual cushions and backrests replaced XK120's locker.
- Behind the seats a panel could fold down, giving access to the boot area for storage of larger items.
- After 1955 centre upholstered section between the front seats featured full-depth pleating.
- Revised door trims incorporating a chromed slider instead of conventional door handle.
- Slimmer seat backrests to provide more space in the rear compartment.
- Veneered dashboard now incorporated two ashtrays and chromed direction indicator switch to top centre below rear-view mirror.

XK140 drophead coupé
- As fixed-head coupé but with a fully lined hood. The shaping of this (although longer overall) was same as on the XK120.
- Larger rear window, but screen, side windows, and quarter-lights remained as on the XK120.

XK150 (all models)
- Wider, more airy interior without any veneered woodwork on any models.
- Similar seating arrangement to XK140s, and all three variants of the 150 carried the same style of trim.
- Door trim panels of different style to earlier cars, with chromed horizontal finishers and armrests and, until 1958, a trimmed pull-open ashtray to each door, changed later to a single chromed ashtray on the transmission tunnel.
- Entirely new dashboard design incorporating soft padded trim. Some instruments and switchgear also new, all in a revised layout. The passenger side glovebox had a lid, but on the driver's side it was open.

XK150 two-seater (roadster)
- Wind-down windows incorporated fixed chrome surrounds.
- A fixed tonneau cover could be pulled over the hood when down (previously a separate item on other XKs).

XK150 fixed-head coupé
- Larger window areas to previous fhc models.

See accompanying photographs for more detail.

XK150 dashboard layouts were the same regardless of model. Now without wood, they had a padded covering.

Comparison of frontal aspects: XK150 (left), XK140 (centre), and XK120 (right).

Rear comparison views of roadster models: XK120 (right), XK140 (centre), and XK150 (left).

Technical specifications

	XK120	XK140
cc	3442	3442
Bore and stroke (mm)	83 x 106	83 x 106
Compression ratio	8:1 (7:1/9:1 optional)	8:1 (7:1/9:1 optional)
bhp	160 (180 SE)	190 (210 SE)
@ rpm	5000 (5300 SE)	5500 (5750 SE)
Torque (lb ft)	195 (203 SE)	210 (213 SE)
@ rpm	2500 (4000 SE)	2500 (4000 SE)
Fuelling	2 x SU carbs	2 x SU carbs
Transmission	4-speed (3 synchro)	4-speed (3 synchro)
Wheel size (in)	16, steel or wire	16, steel or wire
Suspension front	Ind wishbone, torsion bar	Ind wishbone, torsion bar
Suspension rear	Live axle, leaf springs	Live axle, leaf springs
Brakes	4-wheel drum	4-wheel drum
Performance		
0–60mph (sec)	10	8.4
Top speed (mph)	124.6 ots (120.5 fhc; 119.5 dhc)	121.1
Average mpg	19.8 (17.2 fhc, 14.5 dhc)	16–18
Dimensions		
Length (in)	174	176
Width (in)	61.5	64.5
Height (in)	52.5 (53.5 fhc)	52.5 (55 fhc)
Wheelbase (in)	102	102
Front track (in)	51	51.5
Rear track (in)	50	51.375
Weight (cwt)	26 (27 fhc, 27.5 dhc)	28 (29 dhc)

Optional extras

XK120

Lucas fog lamps.
Fitted luggage (two suitcases to match trim).
Boot lid chromed luggage rack.
Choice of seven Radiomobile radios with fitting kits.
Auxiliary (larger) fuel tank.
Aero screens to replace full-length split screen.
Underbody steel shield for adverse road conditions.
Bucket front seats.
Dunlop racing tyres.
External (boot) spare-wheel mounting.
Heater unit (only until 1952, then standard equipment).
High-lift camshafts.
C-type cylinder head.
2in H8 SU carburettors.
Close ratio gearbox.
Wire wheels.
Dual exhaust system.
Chrome wheel rimbellishers for steel wheels.
White-finished Bluemel steering wheel.
Racing clutch.

Technical specifications *cont ...*

	XK150 3.4	XK150 3.8
cc	3442	3781
Bore and stroke (mm)	83 x 106	87 x 106
Compression ratio	8:1 (7:1/9:1 optional), 9:1 'S'	8:1 (7:1/9:1 optional), 9:1 'S'
bhp	210 (250 'S')	220 (265 'S')
@ rpm	5500	5500
Torque (lb ft)	216 (240 'S')	240 (260 'S')
@ rpm	3000 (4500 'S')	3000 (4000 'S')
Fuelling	2 x SU carbs (3 'S' models)	2 x SU carbs (3 'S' models)
Transmission	4-speed (3 synchro)	4-speed (3 synchro)
Wheel size (in)	16, steel or wire	16, steel or wire
Suspension front	Ind wishbone, torsion bar	Ind wishbone, torsion bar
Suspension rear	Live axle, leaf springs	Live axle, leaf springs
Brakes	4-wheel disc	4-wheel disc
Performance		
0–60mph (sec)	8.5 (7.8 'S')	7.6 ('S')
Top speed (mph)	123.7 (132 'S')	125 (136.3 'S')
Average mpg	20.5 (18.6 'S')	13–19
Dimensions		
Length (in)	177	177
Width (in)	64.5	64.5
Height (in)	55.5 fhc (54 two-seater)	55.5 fhc (54 two-seater)
Wheelbase (in)	102	102
Front track (in)	51.25	51.25
Rear track (in)	51.25	51.25
Weight (cwt)	28.5	29

Optional extras *cont ...*

XK140

Windscreen washers (later standard equipment).
Lucas fog lamps.
Fitted luggage (two suitcases to match trim).
Boot lid chromed luggage rack.
Choice of Radiomobile radios with fitting kits.
Aero screens to replace full-length split screen.
Underbody steel shield for adverse road conditions.
Bucket front seats.
Dunlop racing tyres.
Dunlop Road Speed whitewall tyres.
High-lift camshafts.
C-type cylinder head.
2in H8 SU carburettors.
Close ratio gearbox.
Wire wheels.
Dual exhaust system.
Chrome wheel rimbellishers for steel wheels.
White-finished Bluemel steering wheel.
Cutaway rear spats for wire-wheeled cars.

XK150

Lucas fog lamps.
Fitted luggage (two suitcases to match trim).
Boot lid chromed luggage rack.
Choice of Radiomobile radios with fitting kits.
Underbody steel shield for adverse road conditions.
Bucket front seats.
Dunlop racing tyres.
Dunlop Road Speed whitewall tyres.
Sundym tinted windscreen.
Close ratio gearbox.
Dual exhaust system.
Chrome wheel rimbellishers for steel wheels.
White-finished Bluemel steering wheel.
Jaguar leaping mascot for bonnet.
Thornton Powr-Lok differential.
Chromed badge bar.
Bluemel wood-rim steering wheel.
Weathershields sunroof (fixed-head coupé only).
Full-length tonneau cover for drophead coupé model.
Radiator blind.

Colour schemes

Exterior colour	Years	Interior Two-seater	Interior Soft top	Interior Fhc	Interior Dhc	Interior Soft top
Bronze	To 1952	Black/Tan	Fawn	Tan		
Birch Grey		Biscuit/Red	French Grey	Red	Red	
Birch Grey	1952–6	Red (140 only)	Black	Dark Blue	Dark Blue	French Grey
				Light Blue	Light Blue	Black
				Grey (140)		
Suede Green		Suede Green	French Grey	Suede Green	Suede Green	Black
			Black			
Black	To 1952	Biscuit/Pigskin	Black			
			Sand			
Black		Biscuit/Red	Black	Red		
			Sand			
Black	1952–6	Tan	Black	Tan	Tan	
Black	From 1956	Tan		Red	Red	Sand
		Red		Tan	Tan	Black
		Grey		Grey	Grey	
				Biscuit	Biscuit	
Red		Biscuit/Red	Fawn	Red	Red	Black
			Black			Fawn (140)
Red	From 1952	Red	Black	Red	Red	Black
			Fawn			Fawn
Silver	To 1952	Red	Fawn	Red		
			Black			
Silver	To 1952	Light/Dark Blue	Fawn	Light Blue		
			Black			
Pastel Blue Metallic	To 1952	Light/Dark Blue	Fawn	Light Blue		
			Black			
Pastel Green Metallic	To 1952	Suede Green	Fawn	Suede Green		
Cream	To 1952	Biscuit/Red	Fawn	Red		
Cream	To 1952	Biscuit/Pigskin	Fawn			
Pastel Blue	1952–6	Light/Dark Blue	French Grey	Light Blue	Pale Blue (140)	French Grey
			Black	Dark Blue (140)	Dark Blue (140)	Black
			Dark Blue			Blue (140)
Pastel Green	1952–6	Suede Green	Fawn	Suede Green	Suede Green	Fawn
			Black		Grey	Black
Old English White	1952–6	Biscuit/Red	Fawn	Red	Red	Fawn
	From 1952	Red	Black		Pale Blue	Black
			Blue		Dark Blue	Blue
British Racing Green	From 1952	Tan	Gunmetal	Tan	Tan	Gunmetal
		Suede Green	Black	Suede Green	Suede Green	Black
Battleship Grey	1952–6	Biscuit/Red	Gunmetal	Red	Red	Gunmetal
		Red (140 only)	Black	Grey	Grey	Black
					Biscuit	

Colour schemes *cont ...*

Exterior colour	Years	Interior Two-seater	Interior Soft top	Interior Fhc	Interior Dhc	Interior Soft top
Lavender Grey	1952–6	Red	Fawn	Red	Red	Fawn
		Suede Green	Black	Suede Green	Suede Green	Black
		Pale Blue		Pale Blue (140)	Pale Blue	
		Black Blue (140)		Dark Blue (140)	Dark Blue (140)	
Dove Grey	1952–6	Tan	Fawn	Tan	Tan	Fawn
		Biscuit	Sand	Biscuit	Biscuit	Sand
		Black		Black		
Pacific Blue	1952–6	Blue	Blue	Blue	Blue	Blue
		Grey	Black	Grey	Grey	Black
		Dark Blue (140)		Dark Blue (140)	Dark Blue (140)	
		Light Blue (140)		Light Blue (140)	Light Blue (140)	
Pearl Grey	From 1952	Red	Blue	Red	Red	Blue
		Blue	Black	Blue	Blue	Black
		Grey	French Grey	Grey	Grey	French Grey
		Light Blue		Light Blue	Light Blue	
		Dark Blue		Dark Blue	Dark Blue	
Mediterranean Blue	1952–6	Blue		Blue	Blue	
		Grey		Grey	Grey	
Maroon	1952–6	Red (140 only)	Black	Red (140 only)	Red (140 only)	Black
		Biscuit (140)	Sand	Biscuit (140)	Biscuit (140)	Sand
Arbor Green	1952–6	Suede Green		Suede Green	Suede Green	
Carmine Red	1952–6	Red		Red	Red	
Indigo Blue	From 1956	Light Blue	Blue	Light Blue	Light Blue	Blue
		Dark Blue	Black	Dark Blue	Dark Blue	Black
		Grey		Grey	Grey	
Claret (maroon)	From 1956	Red	Black	Red	Red	Black
		Maroon	Sand	Maroon	Maroon	Sand
Cotswold Blue	From 1956	Dark Blue	Blue	Dark Blue	Dark Blue	Blue
		Grey	Black	Grey	Grey	Black
Mist Grey	From 1956	Red	French Grey	Red	Red	French Grey
		Light Blue	Black	Light Blue	Light Blue	Black
		Dark Blue		Dark Blue	Dark Blue	
		Grey		Grey	Grey	
Sherwood Green	From 1956	Tan	French Grey	Tan	Tan	French Grey
		Suede Green	Black	Suede Green	Suede Green	Black
Carmen Red	From 1956	Red	Black	Red	Red	Black
Cornish Grey	From 1956	Red	French Grey	Red	Red	French Grey
		Light Blue	Black	Light Blue	Light Blue	Black
		Dark Blue		Dark Blue	Dark Blue	
		Grey		Grey	Grey	
Imperial Maroon	From 1956	Red	Sand	Red	Red	Sand
		Maroon	Black	Maroon	Maroon	Black

Prices and production volumes

	Price new (£)	1948	1949	1950	1951	1952	1953
XK120 two-seater (alloy)	1263	■	■	■	–	–	–
XK120 two-seater (steel)	–	–	–	■	■	■	■
XK120 fixed-head coupé	1694	–	–	–	■	■	■
XK120 drophead coupé	1616	–	–	–	–	–	■
XK140 two-seater	1598	–	–	–	–	–	–
XK140 fixed-head coupé	1616	–	–	–	–	–	–
XK140 drophead coupé	1644	–	–	–	–	–	–
XK150 two-seater	1666	–	–	–	–	–	–
XK150 fixed-head coupé	1763	–	–	–	–	–	–
XK150 drophead coupé	1793	–	–	–	–	–	–

	Price new (£)	1954	1955	1956	1957	1958	1959
XK120 two-seater (alloy)	1263	–	–	–	–	–	–
XK120 two-seater (steel)	–	■	–	–	–	–	–
XK120 fixed-head coupé	1694	■	–	–	–	–	–
XK120 drophead coupé	1616	■	–	–	–	–	–
XK140 two-seater	1598	■	■	■	■	–	–
XK140 fixed-head coupé	1616	■	■	■	■	–	–
XK140 drophead coupé	1644	■	■	■	■	–	–
XK150 two-seater	1666	–	–	–	■	■	■
XK150 fixed-head coupé	1763	–	–	–	■	■	■
XK150 drophead coupé	1793	–	–	–	■	■	■

	Price new (£)	1960	1961	Total produced
XK120 two-seater (alloy)	1263	–	–	240
XK120 two-seater (steel)	–	–	–	7374
XK120 fixed-head coupé	1694	–	–	2680
XK120 drophead coupé	1616	–	–	1767
XK140 two-seater	1598	–	–	3347
XK140 fixed-head coupé	1616	–	–	2798
XK140 drophead coupé	1644	–	–	2790
XK150 two-seater	1666	■	–	2264
XK150 fixed-head coupé	1763	■	–	4448
XK150 drophead coupé	1793	■	–	2673
Total production				**30,381**

Production changes

1948
XK120 two-seater launched.

1950
XK120 all-steel bodies introduced.
Curved wiper arms fitted.
Starting handle operation deleted.
Shorter dashpots fitted to SU carburettors.

1951
XK120 fixed-head coupé announced.
XK120 SE models available.
Heater became standard fitment.
Front wing ventilators added.
Chrome to body front sidelight housings.
Hood frame changed from chrome to grey paint finish.
Zipped fasteners to hood rear window added.

1952
Window-winders and door interior handles changed.
Additional studs fitted to camshaft covers at the front.
Revised instrument panel fitted.
Hood style extended further back.
Windscreen washers introduced.
Hardura boot mat fitted instead of carpet.

1953
XK120 drophead coupé announced.
(Late) Doors on dhc changed from alloy to steel.
Rear wing piping changed to body colour.

1954
XK120 dashboard style changed.
Rear reflectors added to XK120 cars for UK market.
XK140 models introduced.
(Late) Overdrive option on manual transmissions available for 140.
(Late) 140 boot lid handle changed.

1956
Auto transmission available on fhc and dhc.
Steel door skins replace alloy on fhc and dhc.
Fly-off handbrake changed to normal push-button release type.

1957
XK150 fhc and dhc models announced.

1958
XK150 two-seater announced.
XK150 two-seater 'S' launched.
Improved heating system introduced.
Fuel filler lid opening changed to rearward.
Indicator operating stalk fitted to steering column.
Larger rear-light units fitted.
Overriders on rear bumper moved inwards.
Boot badge altered to show 1957 Le Mans win.
Pull armrests added to internal door trims.

1959
XK150 fhc and dhc 'S' introduced.
XK150 3.8-litre engines available.

1961
End of XK150 sales.

Chassis numbers

Model	Right/left drive	Chassis/VIN commencing
XK120 OTS	RHD	660001
	LHD	670001
XK120 FHC	RHD	669001
	LHD	679001
XK120 DHC	RHD	667001
	LHD	677001
XK140 OTS	RHD	800001
	LHD	810001
XK140 FHC	RHD	804001
	LHD	814001
XK140 DHC	RHD	807001
	LHD	817001
XK150 OTS	RHD	820001
	LHD	830001
XK150 FHC	RHD	824001
	LHD	834001
XK150 DHC	RHD	827001
	LHD	837001

The Mark VII to IX saloons
1950 to 1961

Background

This was the first entirely new-style saloon car produced by the company after the Second World War, and the first saloon to use the still relatively new XK power unit.

After the war a change of company name to Jaguar Cars Limited (from SS) meant the re-emergence of what were basically prewar designs for the saloons, though now bearing the Jaguar name. It wasn't until 1948 that a new model – known as the Mark V – appeared, which only lasted until 1951. Although using a new chassis and suspension layout, the Mark V still utilised the straight six pushrod engine derived from Standard designs, while its bodyshell still resembled the prewar style.

The Mark V's release was a deliberate ploy by Jaguar to retain an important area of the luxury saloon market until the appearance of the 'all new' Mark VII in 1950 – the car that the XK power unit was originally designed for, with a new chassis design (temporarily used in the Mark V), independent front suspension, and an all-enveloping steel body not that far removed from the gorgeous XK120 sports car style launched in 1948.

Jaguar's Mark VII offered a new standard of luxury, refinement, style, performance, and handling to anything else on the market at the time, and at a very competitive price. Introduced at the British Motor Show in 1950, there was only one model, and at under £1000 before purchase tax it was an instant success. It would prove to be the most prolific model produced by the company up to the introduction of a smaller saloon in 1956.

Despite its size and weight the Mark VII was very successful in competition, in circuit racing, and in rallying, and in 1956 actually won the Monte Carlo Rally. It was particularly well liked in the United States, where one journalist called it 'The Prima Ballerina'. Jaguar later offered automatic transmission, and in 1954 the car was upgraded to the Mark VIIM with many significant improvements. In 1957 further development resulted in it being supplemented and renamed the Mark VIII, and then in 1958 it became the Mark IX when the engine was enlarged, and the car was equipped with power-assisted steering and all-round disc brakes to keep it abreast of newer competition.

The Mark IX remained in production until 1961, when it was eventually superseded by another all-new design, the Mark X. The Mark VII to IX models were the flagships of the Jaguar range for more than a decade and justly deserved the company's slogan of the period: 'Grace, Space and Pace'. In total over 46,000 of these cars were sold.

4 Model range and development

The first truly new saloon to carry the Jaguar name, the Mark VII was always designed to take the XK six-cylinder power unit, the earlier XK120 merely being intended as a low-production car to publicise the engine. When announced at the British Motor Show in 1950 the Mark VII was available as a simple, single model. Of 3.4-litre engine capacity, it was only available with a four-speed manual gearbox, in one trim form, and with hardly any variation to suit different markets around the world, although it was clear, from the outset, that the car was designed to 'hit' the American market.

It was certainly the most luxurious model Jaguar had produced up to that time, and there is also no doubt that it was designed to captivate a wider market, offering a higher standard of trim, performance, and value for money than any of the home-grown competition, from Lagonda to Armstrong Siddeley and even Rolls-Royce.

The underpinning of the car was a new low-slung chassis with independent front suspension, clad with a very stylish all-steel body emphasising a design style that every model from the XK120 through to the XK150 and Mark 2 would follow into the 1960s. Performance of up to 100mph was guaranteed from the 160bhp straight six engine, with sufficient room to carry five people in the utmost comfort of leather and walnut veneer plus the largest boot space of any contemporary car.

Despite the gargantuan size of the Mark VII, over 16ft in length, chrome adornment had been kept to a minimum. To provide more internal accommodation the engine was moved 5in further forward than in the previous model, and for better safety the brakes (although still drums) were servo assisted.

An instant success in America, sales boomed, and in 1952 the paint finish changed from cellulose to synthetic enamel. Jaguar had been experiencing problems in supply of the Moss four-speed gearbox and this tied in with the Americans' need for an automatic transmission version of the car. As such a Borg Warner automatic transmission became available as an option, with the quadrant and control lever fitted rather clumsily above the steering column set into the dashboard. This took effect from 1953 and where fitted a bench-type front seat could also be specified.

Numerous minor changes took place to engine and suspension and then in January 1954 a Laycock de Normanville overdrive unit was made available at extra cost for the manual transmission. Operating on top gear only it brought the ratio down to 3.54:1, allowing effortless low-speed cruising.

The Mark VII in its original 1950–4 form. Note the double ribbing to the bumper bars and the painted hubcap centres. All Mark VIIs are identified by their split windscreen and full spats covering the rear wheels. In the background is the last variant of the style, the Mark IX, dating from 1961.

Lighting treatment changes in the Mark VII design. The central picture shows an earlier car with flush-mounted fog lamps; above is the later Mark VIIM model, with separate Lucas fog lights, chromed grilles for the horns, and separate indicator lenses (orange for some markets or white, as here, for certain overseas markets).

Later in 1954 (September) a revised version of the Mark VII came on to the market. Called the Mark VIIM, although never badged as that, this model was externally recognisable by the wider-profile ribbed bumper bars (very similar to the XK140 sports car), 'J' headlights, and separate fog lamps and indicators. More prominent rear lights were also fitted, along with a wrap-around rear bumper style.

Internally, improved seating and a new steering wheel centre boss (like the XK) were other visual changes, but the most important enhancement came in the mechanics: a close-ratio gearbox, high-lift camshafts, and standardised 8:1 compression ratio boosting bhp to 190 from 160. Stiff torsion bars also helped the handling. This was a much improved car to the original Mark VII.

October 1956 saw the introduction of another new model, the Mark VIII. Visually this was easily distinguishable from the earlier models by its prominent radiator grille, leaping Jaguar mascot on the bonnet, single-piece windscreen, and chrome side trims allowing the car to be finished in a choice of two-tone paint schemes.

Internally, the Mark VIII was improved with sculptured rear seating with thicker seats all round, fitted veneered picnic tables in the rear of the front seats, and even a magazine rack where a bench seat was specified. Many other smaller trim changes were carried out and the more luxurious approach to the whole interior of the Mark VIII was epitomised by the fitting of no less than three cigar lighters. Mechanically the Mark VIII was fitted with Jaguar's B-type cylinder head, which gave a good increase in top speed and a general performance improvement which was helped by the fitting of a dual exhaust system.

Surprisingly, the Mark VIII never carried a model identification badge on the boot lid. The Mark VIIM remained in production alongside it until July 1957.

During 1956 all automatic transmission models were fitted with a new Jaguar innovation, the Intermediate Speed Hold switch, which allowed the intermediate gear to be held indefinitely by a switch mounted on the dashboard in front of the driver.

The Mark VIII was the rarest of these cars, and despite being in production until December 1959 another new model, the Mark IX, was introduced alongside it at the October 1958 British Motor Show. Externally the Mark IX looked exactly like the Mark VIII except for a discreet 'Mark IX' badge on the boot lid. Internally the differences were also very subtle. Mechanically, however, the Mark IX offered a new standard, adopting power-assisted steering as regular equipment and also becoming the first Jaguar saloon to be provided with all-round disc brakes as standard.

Mark VII and VIIM models did not feature a chromed bonnet mascot but instead had this cast head, wings, and Jaguar emblem.

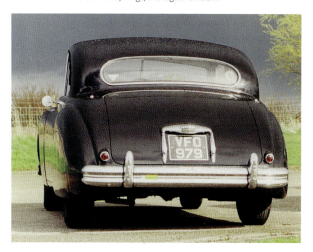

Rear view of Mark VII model with double-ribbed bumper bar. Very early cars did not feature a 'Jaguar' scripted badge on the rear and early lighting was basic (it was later revised to the Mark VIIM design – see Mark VIII lights). A single exhaust pipe also featured on Mark VII models.

Originally Mark VII models had trafficators instead of lights. Later versions with conventional indicators used a chrome finisher (see inset) until the arrival of the Mark VIIM, which was fitted with a new steel panel without finisher.

Further performance was enhanced by the fitting of a new 3.8-litre configuration (3,781cc) of the XK power unit with a new block design incorporating liners but using the existing B-type cylinder head. This boosted horse power to 220bhp with an increase in torque of over 11%. Other changes included a larger heating and ventilation system, necessitating the fitment of two six-volt batteries under the bonnet instead of one 12 volt.

Over the years a few chassis-only vehicles were supplied to outside coachbuilders, and at least one Mark IX was built into a hearse. Jaguar themselves produced a halfway house model based on the Mark VIII with some Mark IX modifications, called the Mark VIIIB. Intended for specialist work with the army and other services, including ministerial and ambassadorial work, the model looked like any conventional Mark VIII/IX but normally featured a low-compression version of the 3.4-litre engine and a revised interior with bench front seat and glass division for the rear compartment.

The well-known coachbuilding firm of Harold Radford also offered an enhanced version of the Mark VIII and IX models called the Countryman, with a centre division, seats that could be folded down to form a bed, and picnic hamper and tables, etc, in the boot. It is not known how many were actually produced.

Over 46,000 Mark VII to IX models were manufactured from 1950 through to 1961. These were the only Jaguar saloons offered between 1950 and 1956.

Exterior identification points

General points applicable to all models

Front view
- Full-width chromed bumper bar with twin vertical overriders mounted towards the centre of the body, with the number plate mounting between, fitted on the bumper.
- Vertical chromed radiator grille with vertical slats flanked by single headlights with chromed surrounds.
- Below the headlights flush-mounted fog/spot lights, or on later cars chromed horn grilles.
- Sidelight units moulded into the top of each front wing, painted in body colour.
- Chrome trim running full length of the bonnet centre.

Rear view
- Shallow rounded rear window with chromed surround.
- Severe sloping one-piece boot lid and rear wings, the former hinged at its rear.

Internal rear view of Mark VII (and VIIM) with bench-seating, plain rear coverings to the front seats, and built-in ashtrays in the door woodwork.

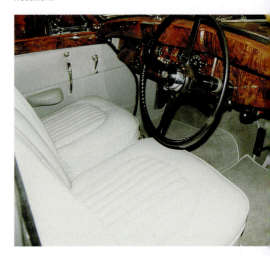
Front interior view of Mark VII. Note the pronounced horn push boss in the steering wheel and the equally pronounced area of the centre dashboard top rail.

Mark VII dashboard instrument layout remained the same throughout production of the later models, although the top rail altered in shape and style, as did the warning lights and the rear-view mirror.

- Lighting units mounted at the base of each rear wing.
- Fuel fillers (one per side) mounted at top of rear wings with lockable covers painted in body colour.
- Boot-mounted rear number plate with chrome illumination/reversing light plinth. To each side were chromed, vertically mounted lockable boot handles.
- Full-width ribbed rear bumper bar with twin vertical overriders.

Side view
- Body curvature and swage line follow XK style, sweeping down from front wing through door lines to lift again over rear wings.
- Chrome on brass window frame surrounds with quarter-lights front and rear.
- Heavy chromed horizontal trim running along entire length of bonnet sides, over bulkhead, across doors, between chromed handles, to 'spear' on rear wing.
- Rear-wheel spats fitted to all models.

Specifics
Mark VII
- Tripod headlights.
- Flush-mounted fog lamps under headlamps.
- Triple-ribbed front and rear bumper bars.
- Radiator grille with narrow surround. At the top a winged badge with Jaguar head at centre of bonnet.
- Chromed strip running full length of bonnet centre.
- Split front windscreen with chromed surround.
- Painted B/C post with trafficators.
- Hubcaps chromed with body-coloured centre sections.
- Fully enclosed rear-wheel spats.
- Single exhaust-pipe system.
- Single circular rear-light units, from 1953 fitted with additional circular reflectors above.
- Jaguar scripted badge to boot lid on all but very earliest cars.
- Earlier cars featured front wing ventilators to bring air into the footwells, later deleted.

Mark VIIM
- As above except thicker double-ribbed front and rear bumper bars (wrap-around at rear) with differing overriders.
- 'J' headlights.
- Separate Lucas fog lamps mounted on valance.
- Circular indicator lights to base of front wings.
- Vertical slatted horn grilles below headlights replaced the Mark VII's flush fog lamps.
- Apart from earliest Mark VIIMs, hubcaps were entirely in chrome.
- Larger rear-light lenses on chromed plinths.
- 'Automatic' scripted badge (where automatic

Mark VIIM interior, in this case fitted with automatic transmission with control quadrant above the steering wheel. Only when equipped with auto transmission was an umbrella-style handbrake fitted (below the dash, far right). Normally a pull-on handbrake was sited between the front seats. Note also map pockets in the front door trims.

The later Mark VIIM design is identified externally by its double-ribbed bumper bars and revised lighting/horn grilles.

Mark VIII models utilised the same rear styling as the Mark VIIM (double-ribbed wrap-around bumper bar). Mark VIIMs and Mark VIIIs also featured 'Jaguar' script to the boot lid. Swage line chromed trims enabled the use of two-tone paintwork, and Mark VIIIs (and IXs) now featured cutaway rear-wheel spats.

transmission was fitted) below the 'Jaguar' name on boot lid.
- Trafficators eliminated from the B/C post.

Mark VIII
- More prominent chromed surround to radiator grille, incorporating winged badge and Jaguar name at top leading to chrome leaping mascot at tip of bonnet and revised centre strip running the entire length of the bonnet centre.
- Single-piece windscreen with revised wiper parking.
- Side swage line chrome trims running the entire length of the body, curving down and across rear-wheel spats.
- Rear spats now cutaway at base to reveal hubcaps.
- Dual pipe exhaust system with chromed tailpipes.
- Mark VIIIs did not feature any special badging at the rear. Other aspects of rear view as Mark VIIM.

Mark IX
- Exactly as Mark VIII above except for discrete 'Mk IX' badging to bottom right-hand side of boot lid.
- Later Mark IX's featured enlarged rear-light units, similar to XK150 models though with larger chrome plinths, with individual lenses for reflectors and indicators.

Interior identification points

Mark VII
- Leather-trimmed front bucket seats with vertical pleating and chromed height adjustment handle.
- Rear bench similarly upholstered with centre fold-down armrest.
- Walnut-veneered dashboard with twin-lidded gloveboxes, that on the passenger side lockable.
- 17in Bluemels black cast steering wheel, with pronounced centre boss containing Jaguar head and circular surround (as XK120).
- Handbrake situated between front seats.
- Trimmed door panels with wooden cappings and armrests to all doors, with hidden trigger release door handles/pulls. Tool kits incorporated into both front door trims at lower level.
- Centrally mounted front ashtray to dashboard top rail also including rear-view mirror.
- Rear door trim wooden cappings with ash trays.

Mark VIIM
- As Mark VII except deeper Dunlopillo-filled

Both Mark VIII and IX models were exactly the same externally except for a unique 'Mk IX' boot badge on the latter. Frontal treatment was revised from the Mark VIIM, with prominent radiator grille surround, Jaguar leaping mascot on the bonnet, and the single-piece windscreen.

Rear view of the Mark IX saloon. This was exactly the same as the Mark VIII except for the 'Mk IX' badge on the boot lid and, where fitted, the 'automatic' script. All Mark VIIIs and IXs featured a twin exhaust-pipe system. This is a late Mark IX model, with larger rear lighting units with separate indicator lenses, never fitted to Mark VIIIs and only fitted to Mark IXs from late 1959.

Bench-seating was standard on Mark VIII/IX automatic transmission models with fold-down picnic tables and magazine rack in the rear compartment. Early Mark VIIIs featured 'open' rack. Rear seating took the form of a split-back arrangement, and ashtrays were moved to the door panel trim area.

seating all round.
- Bench front seat available for automatic transmission models with plain veneer cappings.
- Revised steering wheel with flat boss incorporating gold growler head and circular surround (as XK140).
- Map pockets included in front door trims.

Mark VIII
- Revised wooden dashboard and layout with less prominent top rail and new rear-view mirror.
- Chromed grab handle to dashboard top rail on passenger side and map holder below glove-box area, on passenger side.
- Removal of dashboard mounted ashtray.
- Two ashtrays, one in each front door trim.
- Deeper Dunlopillo-filled seating all round with revised shaped front individual seating and/or bench arrangement.
- Revised rear door wooden cappings without ashtrays, also removed to positions within door trims.
- Rear of front seats carried veneered picture tables (two) plus, on bench seat, a magazine rack in the centre with square-faced clock.
- Rear seat redesigned to simulate individual seats with revised shape to squab and centre armrest.
- Provision of nylon over-rug to rear compartment, trimmed to match interior colour.
- Boot fully Hardura covered, including spare wheel and with trimmed interior to boot lid.

Mark IX
- As Mark VIII except for removal of handbrake from between front seats, replaced by umbrella type to extreme driver's side under dash area.
- Removal of indicator switch from steering wheel to stalk on steering column.
- Slightly revised instrumentation and warning lighting.

Mark VIIIB
- As Mark VIII except bench front-seat arrangement with centre cutaway to accommodate manual gearbox lever.
- Umbrella-style handbrake as Mark IX.
- Centre division to bench seat with sliding glass panels at top, magazine rack, and picnic tables to rear.
- Revised rear bench-seating with longer centre armrest.

Manual transmission models with individual bucket front seats were available on the Mark VIII and IX, as shown here. A lambswool over-carpet was fitted to all these cars.

This is a rare Mark VIIIB model, built during the time of the Mark VIII/IX models, specifically for use as a limousine. As such a front bench seat was fitted, but with a cutaway section for the gearlever. Layout of the dashboard follows normal Mark VIII/IX practice, with less pronounced top rail and removal of the indicator switch from the steering wheel to a stalk on the column.

Rear compartment of the Mark VIIIB limousine, with centre division and longer centre armrest.

Technical specifications

	Mark VII	Mark VIIM
cc	3442	3442
Bore and stroke (mm)	83 x 106	83 x 106
Compression ratio	8:1 (7:1 optional)	8:1 (7:1/9:1 optional)
bhp	160	190
@ rpm	5200	5500
Torque (lb ft)	195	203
@ rpm	2500	3000
Fuelling	2 x SU carbs	2 x SU carbs
Transmission	4-speed (3 synchro)	4-speed (3 synchro)
		BW 3-speed auto
Wheel size (in)	16, steel	16, steel
Suspension front	Ind wishbone, torsion bar	Ind wishbone, torsion bar
Suspension rear	Live axle, leaf springs	Live axle, leaf springs
Brakes	4-wheel drum	4-wheel drum
Performance		
0–60mph (sec)	13.7	13.6
Top speed (mph)	101	102
Average mpg	17.6	17–24
Dimensions		
Length (in)	196.5	196.5
Width (in)	73	73
Height (in)	63	63
Wheelbase (in)	120	120
Front track (in)	56	56.5
Rear track (in)	57.5	58
Weight (cwt)	34.5	34.75

Optional extras

Marks VII/VIIM
Fitted luggage (available from several sources).
Choice of Radiomobile radios with fitting kits.
Underbody steel shield for adverse road conditions.
Dunlop racing tyres.
High-lift camshafts.
C-type cylinder head.
2in H8 SU carburettors.
Close-ratio gearbox.
Chrome wheel rimbellishers for wheels.
Dunlop Road Speed whitewall tyres.
Sundym tinted windscreen.
Thornton Powr-Lok differential.
Chromed badge bar.
Radiator blind.
Oil bath air cleaner system.
Straight-through exhaust system.
High-ratio steering box.
Wing mirrors.
Witter tow bar.
Cutaway rear spats to aid brake cooling.
Ace Turbo wheel trims.

	Mark VIII	Mark IX
cc	3442	3781
Bore and stroke (mm)	83 x 106	87 x 106
Compression ratio	8:1 (7:1 optional)	8:1 (7:1/9:1 optional), 9:1 'S'
bhp	210	220
@ rpm	5500	5500
Torque (lb ft)	216	240
@ rpm	3000	3000
Fuelling	2 x SU carbs	2 x SU carbs
Transmission	4-speed (3 synchro) BW 3-speed auto	4-speed (3 synchro) BW 3-speed auto
Wheel size (in)	16, steel	16, steel
Suspension front	Ind wishbone, torsion bar	Ind wishbone, torsion bar
Suspension rear	Live axle, leaf springs	Live axle, leaf springs
Brakes	4-wheel drum	4-wheel disc
Performance		
0–60mph (sec)	11.6	11.3
Top speed (mph)	106.5	114.3
Average mpg	17–22	13.5
Dimensions		
Length (in)	196.5	196.5
Width (in)	73	73
Height (in)	63	63
Wheelbase (in)	120	120
Front track (in)	56.5	56.5
Rear track (in)	58	58
Weight (cwt)	36	35.5

Marks VIII/IX

Fitted luggage (available from several sources).
Choice of Radiomobile radios with fitting kits.
Underbody steel shield for adverse road conditions.
Dunlop racing tyres.
High-lift camshafts.
C-type cylinder head.
2in H8 SU carburettors.
Close-ratio gearbox.
Chrome wheel rimbellishers for wheels.
Dunlop Road Speed whitewall tyres.
Sundym tinted windscreen.
Thornton Powr-Lok differential.
Chromed badge bar.
Radiator blind.
High-ratio steering box.
Wing mirrors.
Witter tow bar.
Ace Turbo wheel trims.

Colour schemes

Exterior colour Single	Duotone	Details	Interior trim
Suede Green			Suede Green
Ivory		To 1952	Red
			Pale Blue
Birch Grey		To 1956	Red
			Grey
			Pale Blue
Battleship Grey		To 1956	Red
			Grey
			Biscuit
Lavender Grey		To 1956	Red
			Suede Green
			Pale Blue
Gunmetal Grey		To 1952	Red
			Grey
			Pale Blue
Black			Red
			Tan
			Grey
			Biscuit
Pastel Green		To 1952	Suede Green
			Grey
Pastel Blue		To 1956	Pale Blue
Dove Grey		To 1956	Tan
			Biscuit
Twilight Blue Met		To 1952	Blue
Cream		1952–3	Red
			Red
			Biscuit
Mediterranean Blue		1953/4 only	Blue
			Grey
British Racing Green		From 1952	Tan
			Suede Green
Pacific Blue		From 1952	Light Blue
			Dark Blue
Old English White		From 1953	Red
			Pale Blue
Indigo Blue		From 1954	Light Blue
			Dark Blue
			Grey
Maroon (Imperial)		From 1956	Red
			Maroon

Exterior colour Single	Duotone	Details	Interior trim
Cornish Grey		From 1956	Red
			Light Blue
			Dark Blue
			Grey
Sherwood Green		From 1956	Tan
			Suede Green
Mist Grey		From 1956	Red
			Light Blue
			Dark Blue
			Grey
Claret		From 1956	Red
			Maroon
Cotswold Blue		From 1956	Dark Blue
			Grey
Pearl Grey		From 1956	Red
			Light Blue
			Dark Blue
			Grey
Claret	Imperial Maroon	From 1956	Red
			Maroon
Indigo Blue	Cotswold Blue	From 1956	Dark Blue
			Light Blue
			Grey
Cornish Grey	Mist Grey	From 1956	Red
			Light Blue
			Dark Blue
			Grey
British Racing Green	Forest Green	1956–8	Suede Green
			Tan
Black	Claret	From 1956	Red
			Maroon
			Grey
Black	Forest Green	1956–8	Suede Green
			Red
Carmen Red		From 1959	Red
Cotswold Blue	Mist Grey	From 1959	Red
			Light Blue
			Dark Blue
			Grey
British Racing Green	Suede Green	From 1959	Suede Green
			Tan

Prices and production volumes

	Price new (£)	1950	1951	1952	1953	1954	1955
Mark VII saloon	1276	■	■	■	■	■	–
Mark VIIM saloon	1680	–	–	–	–	■	■
Mark VIII saloon	1997	–	–	–	–	–	–
Mark IX saloon	1994	–	–	–	–	–	–

	1956	1957	1958	1959	1960	1961	Total produced
Mark VII saloon	–	–	–	–	–	–	20,937
Mark VIIM saloon	■	■	–	–	–	–	10,060
Mark VIII saloon	■	■	■	■	–	–	6247
Mark IX saloon	–	–	■	■	■	■	10,002
Total production							**47,246**

Production changes

1950
Mark VII launched.

1952
Extra studs fitted to front of cam covers.
Two-speed wipers supplied.
5.5in steel wheels replace 5in.
Moulded rubber wiper blades fitted.

1953
Automatic transmission became available.
Telescopic rear shock absorbers fitted.
Different locks fitted to boot/glovebox and to ignition.
Larger eight-bladed cooling fan attached to engine.
New horns fixed to radiator area instead of valances.

1954
Overdrive available on manual models.
Mark VIIM announced.
Trafficators eliminated from all markets.
Orange lenses fitted to all indicator lights at front.

1955
Front wing ventilators eliminated.

1956
Mark VIII introduced.
Intermediate Speed Hold added to automatic cars.

1957
(July) Mark VIIM finally discontinued.
Die-cast radiator shells replaced brass.

1958
Reutter reclining front seats available.
Power-assisted steering option for US market.
(October) Mark IX introduced.

1959
Mark VIII finally discontinued.

1960
Brake warning light added to dashboard.
Special Mark VIIIB models produced for military use.

1961
Mark IX production discontinued with just one car produced at the beginning of this year.

Chassis numbers

Model	Right/left drive	Chassis/VIN commencing
Mark VII	RHD	710001
	LHD	750001
Mark VIIM	RHD	722755
	LHD	738184
Mark VIII	RHD	760001
	RHD	780001
Mark IX	RHD	770001
		790001

The Compact Jaguar saloons
1955 to 1969

Background

Since the introduction of Jaguar's first 'in-house' engine, the XK, in 1948 – launched in the XK120 sports car – the company had grown significantly, both in size and stature, with increased sales and competition successes. From 1950, however, all saloon car sales (the backbone of the business) had concentrated on one prestigious large model: the Mark VII. If Jaguar was to make greater inroads into the car market it needed a smaller, cheaper, and higher-volume saloon. Welcome the 2.4-litre.

William Lyons at Jaguar worked on the same principle he did back in the 1930s, to capitalise on as many mechanical parts as possible from existing models in order to keep costs down and enhance profits. Hence the starting point for the new model was the XK power unit, mated to the existing Moss manual gearbox and developments of previous suspension, steering, and trim layouts. Despite this the new small Jaguar would encompass new ideas and technology far in advance of what Jaguar had used before.

It would be built around monocoque (chassis-less) construction, with the body itself providing the necessary rigidity and supporting the mechanics. A separate front subframe was designed to carry the suspension, steering, and the weight of the engine. This allowed for a much lighter structure and enabled significant strength to be built into the whole body, which was very carefully designed yet still looked like a Jaguar. Styling cues were taken from the existing XK140 sports car frontal aspect and scaled-down curves from the Mark VII saloon.

Of much smaller dimensions – only 15ft in length and just over 5ft in width – the new Jaguar saloon was still a luxurious five-seater, trimmed to the usual Jaguar standard. But it was powered by a new configuration of the XK power unit, of only 2.4-litre capacity, producing 112bhp and a top speed of just over 100mph, sufficient for a car of this size and better than the competition. This was Jaguar's particular advantage: except for a rather traditional Daimler Conquest, the avant-garde Armstrong Siddeley 234/236, and an assortment of lesser machines such as the Ford Zodiac, Vauxhall Cresta, and Humber Super Snipe, there was little competition in this area of the market.

An incredible success when launched for the 1956 model year, the Jaguar saloon was followed in 1957 by a larger 3.4-litre-engined version offering up to 120mph performance, also becoming available with all-round disc brakes. The 2.4- and 3.4-litre saloons remained in production until 1959, by which time over 35,000 had been produced, more than any other model in such a short period of time.

In 1959 the model range was significantly enhanced by the introduction of three totally revised cars, now called Mark 2s, of 2.4-litre, 3.4-litre and 3.8-litre engine capacities. These put right complaints about the earlier models, which were well known for their skittish handling resulting from a narrow rear track. More power, better handling, improved vision, and enhanced trim made the Mark 2s even more popular than their predecessors.

The top of the range 3.8-litre model was, at the time, the fastest production saloon car in the world, offering 125mph performance with acceleration to match. Available in manual, manual with overdrive, or automatic transmission form, along with the other two models this wide choice and good design meant that sales would exceed anything Jaguar had experienced before, with nearly 90,000 being produced up to 1967.

The Mark 2 was also to generate another new model in 1962, the Daimler 2.5-litre V8. With Jaguar's purchase of the Daimler Motor Company in 1960, this marque was in desperate need of a new model, and the cunning mating of Daimler's superb little V8 engine to the Jaguar Mark 2 bodyshell produced a car with an entirely different character. This was to find its own market throughout the 1960s, ending up as the most successful model produced by Daimler up to that time.

In the mid-1960s Jaguar was up against stiffer competition from other marques and was hard at work developing a new saloon car for later in the decade (the XJ6). During this same period the need to revitalise models to improve flagging sales resulted in changes being made to the entire range, not least the Mark 2s. In 1967 the range was reduced, equipment levels changed, and prices reduced to hold their market. Out went the 3.8-litre Mark 2, and the other two cars were re-badged as the 240 and 340, both having changes in trim to keep costs down. Engines were improved with straight port cylinder heads to enhance performance. Similar trim changes were made to the Daimler model. However, sales never recuperated, each model being slowly dropped from the range, the 340 first in 1968, the 240 next in 1969, and finally, later that year, the Daimler V8.

The compact Jaguar saloons of the 1950s and 1960s were the company's most successful cars up to that time, having identified an important new market for car producers which other manufacturers were eager to cater for and would eventually dominate. It would take Jaguar until 1999 to reinvent the compact luxury saloon car with the S-type.

Model range and development

First announced at the UK's 1955 Motor Show, just two models were introduced for the 1956 model year.

Frontal view of early 2.4-litre saloon. The cast radiator grille was only used on this model until 1958. For certain overseas markets the chromed leaping mascot did not feature on the bonnet.

The 2.4-litre saloon as supplied new, with steel wheels, chromed hubcaps with no rimbellishers, and full spats over the rear wheels. This is a later model with the wider radiator grille standardised with the 3.4-litre model to aid cooling and rationalise the parts bin.

Rear view of the 2.4-litre saloon, showing the small rear-light units, wrap-around bumper bar, and 'Jaguar' script on the boot lid. The cutaway spats over the rear wheels were standardised on 3.4-litre models and on 2.4s towards the end of production. This picture clearly shows the reduced-width track of the rear wheels.

Models available at launch
2.4-litre standard saloon
2.4-litre saloon

Although Jaguar initially promoted the car as a two-model line-up, there was really only one. The so-called 'standard' model never went into serious production, but was offered – as the XK100 sports car had been in 1948 – as a more economical alternative. Mechanically the same as the higher-priced model, it lacked some of the refinements expected of a Jaguar, such as a well-equipped dashboard, or even windscreen washers. The production 2.4, however, offered the usual Jaguar 'package' of leather and walnut interiors, with the XK engine mated to the usual Moss manual gearbox. At launch this model was offered with or without overdrive.

With excellent worldwide response, Jaguar soon developed the new car and in February 1957 announced the addition of a second model to the range, this time utilising the 3.4-litre XK engine taken from the XK140 sports car with the B-type cylinder head. Offering 210bhp this provided much more punch and subsequently made the model exceptionally popular on both the race circuits and rally routes of Europe.

Correspondingly in 1957 Jaguar also offered all-round disc brakes on the smaller Jaguars and most 3.4-litre cars were so equipped. The 3.4s were also identified by a wider radiator grille – to aid cooling to the larger engine – and cutaway spats over the rear wheels, also to aid cooling, this time to the brakes. Both these features were later adopted by the 2.4-litre models as well. Both models also became available with automatic transmission. They remained in production until 1959, by which time over 37,000 had been sold.

At the 1959 Motor Show Jaguar announced three new models to replace the 2.4- and 3.4-litre cars, called Mark 2s. This subsequently led to the earlier models becoming known as Mark 1s, although this title was never officially recognised by the factory, nor does it show on any badges or in any literature relating to these cars.

Using the existing 2.4-litre, 3.4-litre, and the fairly new 3.8-litre versions of the XK six-cylinder engine, the Mark 2s were a significant improvement over the earlier cars, although retaining their overall style. Widening the rear track improved handling and the inclusion of the larger engine turned the 3.8-litre Mark 2 into the fastest production saloon car in the world at that time.

Externally the Mark 2s were easily identifiable by their much larger window areas, chromed side window frames, and that wider rear-wheel track. Internally they were virtually all new, with revised seats (with picnic tables in the rear), new trim, and an entirely new dashboard layout, with the

Dashboard layout of the 2.4- and 3.4-litre (Mark 1s) followed later XK practice, but with wood surrounds. When automatic transmission was fitted the control quadrant was attached to the lower dash area, made of Bakelite, as seen here.

Above left: Front interior trim of the 2.4- and 3.4-litre models with bucket-seating and four-spoke steering wheel.

Above right: There was a choice of split-bench or bucket-seats on Mark 1 models from 1957, when automatic transmission became available. Rear seating followed normal bench practice.

Frontal styling differences between the Mark 1 (2.4- and 3.4-litre models) and the Mark 2 design from 1959 to 1967. On the left, the Mark 2 shows revised lighting treatment with flush-mounted fog lights, separate indicator lenses (different colours dependent on market), and pronounced vertical centre rib to the grille.

speedometer and rev counter directly in front of the driver and all switches and ancillary gauges grouped in the centre – a theme that would be adopted on all future Jaguar models from there on in until the 1970s.

The Jaguar Mark 2s proved an even bigger success than the 1950's 2.4 and 3.4 and, apart from minor changes, remained in production until 1967, during which time a further model was introduced in 1962. This was the Daimler 2.4-litre V8, which, as already mentioned, married Daimler's own 2.5-litre V8 engine to a Mark 2 bodyshell, initially mated to a Borg Warner Model 35 automatic transmission (later a standard manual box alternative became available). This model offered a greater degree of refinement, with performance just slightly better than the 2.4-litre Jaguar version.

Externally the Daimler benefited from a fluted radiator grille and rear boot plinth plus new badging, while internally it used a better quality of walnut veneer and split-bench type seating (without the Mark 2's picnic tables), along with other slight changes to the trim. Aimed at the more professional market place, such as solicitors, consultants, and the gentry, it never infringed on the market for the more sporty Jaguar Mark 2s.

Sales for the smaller Jaguars had proved excellent in the early 1960s and development continued throughout their years in production. All-synchromesh gearboxes were available from later in 1964, and by 1966 trim had changed in an effort to bring prices down when sales eventually started to decline. The Mark 2 spawned other medium-sized Jaguar models like the S-type and 420, which must have had some effect on sales, as did more modern machinery coming from its competitors by this time.

Because of declining sales and the need to continue the existing range until an all-new saloon could become available in 1968, Jaguar redesigned the Mark 2s in 1967, at the same time reducing the number of models on sale. First to be discontinued was the 3.8-litre, its sales already overtaken by the 420, while the two smaller-engined Mark 2s (the 2.4 and 3.4) were re-badged as the 240 and 340 and offered at reduced prices.

The 240 and 340 models now used a straight port cylinder head and the 2.4-litre model got SU carburettors instead of Solex, which improved performance somewhat, although the trim was reduced to keep prices down. Out went leather upholstery (and picnic tables) as standard, to be replaced by Ambla material (with leather as an extra-cost option). Externally the broad ribbed bumpers, so characteristic of Jaguars from the Mark VII on, were replaced by a slimline type reminiscent of the Mark X and S-type models of the period. Even items like fog lamps became an

Side view comparison between the Mark 2 (right) and the earlier Mark 1. Note the instantly identifiable larger window areas with chromed surrounds of the later car.

Rear view changes between the Mark 1 and Mark 2 models. The later car (in the foreground) shows the larger rear-light units with separate indicator lenses and revised badging. Note also the larger rear window of the later car.

This picture shows the pronounced difference in window areas between the two cars and the revised door trim treatment.

extra-cost option. The Daimler received similar treatment, being renamed the V8 250, although to keep the 'quality edge' of the Daimler marque fog lamps and leather trim remained standard features.

Although sales were boosted slightly the 'new' compact model range had a limited lifespan, the 340 being the first to meet its demise in 1968, followed in 1969 by the 240, after the introduction of the XJ6. Because there was initially no other Daimler available, the V8 250 stayed in production longer.

Apart from the standard production cars the Jaguar dealer Coombs in Surrey manufactured its own limited number of competition-modified cars, mainly Mark 2s with enhanced performance and handling characteristics. Jaguar also at one time commissioned a special estate car version called the County, which was used extensively by the factory in the 1960s and later sold off, but the model never went into production.

Near the end of production a few examples of the 340 model were made to special order with a 3.8-litre engine with the straight port cylinder head.

Exterior identification points

General points applicable to all pre-Mark 2 models

Front view
- Ribbed bumper and overrider treatment similar to XK150, with dish in centre section to accommodate radiator grille base. Steel number plate mounting in centre of bumper.
- Oval chromed radiator grille, with prominent surround and vertical slats and incorporating Jaguar growler badge with the word 'Jaguar' and the appropriate litreage of the engine.
- Oval, vertical mounted sidelight housings at the base of each front wing (also incorporating indicator bulbs).
- Two chromed, flush-mounted horn grilles with vertical slats below headlights.
- Separate Lucas fog/spot lights mounted on lip of front wings between bumper bar and wings.
- Leaping Jaguar chromed mascot atop the leading edge of the bonnet, with full-length chrome trim in the centre. (The mascot was eliminated for certain overseas markets.)

Rear view
- Severe sloping bodywork reminiscent of Mark VII to IX models.
- Shallow curved rear screen with chromed surround.

Radiator grille badging showed the size of the engine fitted to the car and was colour coded – a black background for the 2.4, red for the 3.4, and maroon for the 3.8. On the boot lid of Mark 2 models litre identification appeared, but not for the 2.4-litre model.

Close-up of Mark 2 frontal view with revised lighting and grille treatment.

Rear view of the Mark 2 shows wider track to the rear wheels, revised lighting, the use of a 'Mk 2' badge on the boot lid, and a 'disc brake' badge in the centre of the rear bumper bar.

- One-piece boot lid hinged at the rear, with centrally mounted number plate with chrome surround and chromed illumination/reversing light plinth.
- Integrated rear-light units to base of each rear wing with chromed plinth surround.
- Chromed boot lid button and escutcheon in the centre above bumper bar, below boot lid.
- Scripted 'Jaguar' name to centre of boot lid.
- Ribbed rear bumper to match front, wrapping around the curved sides of the wings and incorporating vertically mounted overriders.
- Single exhaust pipe (not chromed).

Side view
- Slab-sided but taking styling cues from both the Mark VII and XK140. Did not feature pronounced swage line as on other models.
- Chrome waistline trim ran entire length of the car, from bonnet sides, along the doors (between chromed door handles), and sweeping down the rear wings to meet the bumper bar.
- Solid window frame surrounds as part of doors without normal chrome on brass frames. Chrome edging to window frames. Quarter-lights front and rear.
- Spats covering rear wheels.
- Pronounced narrower track of rear wheels to front.
- Fuel filler mounted on left-hand side within rear wing (when looking from the rear), with cover painted to body colour.
- Wheels finished to body colour with chromed hubcaps.

Mark 1 specifics

2.4-litre (Mark 1)
- Heavy cast oval chromed radiator grille with just eight slats, incorporating plastic circular badge in black with Jaguar growler logo and words 'Jaguar 2.4 litre' surrounding it. From 1958 the grille changed to 3.4-litre style (see below and photographs).
- Rear-wheel spats completely enclosed wheels. Later changed to 3.4-litre style (see below and photographs).

3.4-litre (Mark 1)
- As above but with a wider, thinner (16) slatted radiator grille (also fitted to the 2.4-litre model from 1958), with revised red badge bearing the words 'Jaguar 3.4 litre'.
- From the side all 3.4-litre models were fitted with cutaway rear-wheel spats, later adopted for 2.4-litre cars as well.
- At the rear 3.4-litre models carried '3.4' badging below the Jaguar script on the boot lid.
- Twin exhaust-pipe system emerging from the left-hand side of the car.

Frontal treatment of the Mark 2 interior, with pronounced centre console arrangement, flatter seats, and completely revised dashboard with main instruments in front of the driver and ancillaries in the centre against a matt-black painted panel up to 1960 (black fabric-covered for later models). The steering wheel design shows that this is a pre-1964 model. See the later photograph of a Daimler interior on page 76 for the style of steering wheel used after 1964.

Above left: Rear seating arrangement for Mark 2 models, with revised flatter front seats with fold-down picnic tables.

Above right: From 1962 a Daimler model became available, identified by its pronounced fluted radiator grille and Daimler badging, with similar treatment at the rear.

Mark 2s were always available with either steel wheels or wire wheels, both chromed or painted.

General points applicable to Mark 2s, Daimlers, and subsequent models

Front view
- Bumper bar treatment very similar to Mark 1 models.
- Enlarged oval chromed radiator grille with prominent thick centre vertical vane now incorporating the growler badge at the top.
- Flush-mounted Lucas fog lamps below headlights.

Rear view
- Enlarged rear window with chromed surround.
- Enlarged rear-light units with chromed plinths, incorporating separate reflectors and indicator lenses.
- 'Disc Brake' badge to centre of rear bumper bar.
- Litreage badge (except 2.4) featured on boot lid.
- 'Jaguar' letters badge on boot lid, not scripted.

Side view
- Enlarged window areas with chrome on brass surrounds, quarter-lights front and rear.
- Chromed rain gutters along roof area.
- Sculptured door handles.
- All Mark 2s featured cutaway rear-wheel spats.
- Wider rear-wheel track.

Mark 2 and allied models specifics

2.4-litre Mark 2
- This model featured the black background badge to the radiator grille bearing the words 'Jaguar 2.4 litre'.
- At the rear there was no 2.4-litre badge on the boot lid.
- A single exhaust-pipe system exited from the left-hand side of the car.

3.4-litre Mark 2
- Red radiator grille badge bearing the words 'Jaguar 3.4 litre'.
- At the rear a '3.4' chromed badge appeared below the Jaguar emblem in the centre of the boot lid.
- Dual exhaust system.

3.8-litre Mark 2
- Maroon radiator grille badge bearing the words 'Jaguar 3.8 litre'.
- At the rear a '3.8' chromed badge appeared below the Jaguar emblem in the centre of the boot lid.
- Exhaust system as 3.4-litre Mark 2.

Daimler 2.5-litre V8
- As Mark 2 except, from the front, a closer-knit (20-slat) radiator grille incorporating a fluted surround with no badging.

From 1967 the Mark 2 models were re-badged '240' and '340', with revised slimmer bumper bars, new-style hubcaps to the steel wheels, and the replacement of the fog lamps with horn grilles (unless the former were fitted).

Rear view of the 240/340 model with revised badging and slimmer bumper bar, necessitating a deeper rear valance.

Later Daimler model, now known as the V8 250. Chromed rimbellishers with new-style hubcaps and the Daimler emblem were standard on this model, which was otherwise unidentifiable from 240/340 models from the side.

- Atop the leading edge of the bonnet a swept 'D' emblem leading to a full-width centre bonnet chrome strip of triangular section.
- From the side the only difference to Jaguar models was the use of scripted 'D' emblems on the centres of the hubcaps and the fitting of chrome rimbellishers as standard equipment to the steel wheels.
- From the rear a fluted chromed rear number plate/reversing light plinth.
- Scripted 'Daimler' badge in the centre of the boot lid.
- A chromed 'V' incorporating an '8' also on the boot lid.
- A twin exhaust system, one pipe from each side of the car at the rear with chromed tailpipes.

Daimler V8 250
- As 2.5 except at the front the adoption of the slimline bumper bars fitted to Jaguar 240/340 models.
- New-style hubcaps to steel wheels, still incorporating the 'D' emblem.
- At the rear a slimline bumper and revised 'V8 250' badging to bottom right-hand side of the boot lid.

Jaguar 240
- As Mark 2 except, at the front, replacement of fog lamps for flush-fitting dished chromed grilles.
- Slimline bumper bar front and rear with revised overriders.
- From the side a revised style of chromed hubcap with pronounced centre section incorporating growler badge on black background.
- At the rear revised badging in most cases eliminating the word 'Jaguar' and with the figure '240' sited on the right-hand side bottom area of the boot lid.
- Twin exhaust pipes as earlier 3.4- and 3.8-litre models.

Jaguar 340
- As 240 except '340' badging to boot lid.

Interior identification points

2.4-/3.4-litre
- Walnut-veneered dashboard with central layout of instruments. Passenger side lockable glovebox, driver's side open cubby.
- Bluemel black-enamelled four-spoke steering wheel with flat horn push incorporating growler badge (as per XK140).
- Separate bucket-type front seats trimmed in leather (split-bench-type arrangement for cars

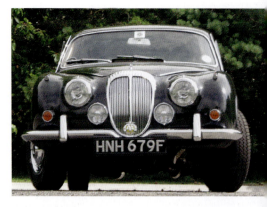

Daimler frontal treatment for the post-1967 model. The fitment of fog lights was standard on Daimler models at all times.

Different style of badging used on Daimler models, and the fluted plinth for reversing light/number plate illumination. Daimler models with the V8 engine featured a twin exhaust-pipe system emitting from either side at the rear.

Above left: Unique to Daimler models was this scripted 'D' emblem on the bonnet.

Above right: Daimler V8 250 interior showing the later style of steering wheel, also fitted to Jaguar Mark 2 models. Flatter front seats of the split-bench variety applied to Daimler, which also lacked a centre console arrangement.

equipped with automatic transmission) with rear seat bench.
- Wood surrounds to all door windows, with vinyl upholstered door trims and armrests to match interior trim colour.
- Handbrake between driver's seat and front door mounted on floor.
- Automatic transmission models with centrally mounted 'quadrant' under dashboard.

Mark 2

- Walnut-veneered dashboard with centre layout of auxiliary gauges and rocker switch gear. Speedometer and rev counter positioned in front of driver. Centre console arrangement leading down from dashboard incorporating radio speaker, radio and heater controls along with covered ashtray, console continuing rearward between the front individual seats to extractor vent for rear compartment. Lockable glovebox to passenger side of dashboard.
- Two-spoke black-coated steering wheel incorporating chromed half horn ring and centre badging depicting growler. (Design changed to Mark X style from 1964.)
- Front seats still individual but with flatter cushions (no split-bench option). Fold-down picnic tables in rear of front seats.
- Rear bench seat similar but different stitching to earlier cars.
- Door trims incorporating armrests and elasticated map pockets to the front, open pockets at the rear. Wooden cappings to all door trim tops.
- Swivel action rear quarter-light catches.

Daimler 2.5 V8

- As Mark 2s except for split-bench front seating (regardless of transmission) and replacement of centre console by revised ashtray, radio mounting in wood veneer set below centre section of dashboard incorporating heater controls.
- Scripted 'D' to centre steering wheel boss.
- No picnic tables in rear of front seats.

Daimler V8 250

- As 2.5 except for black vinyl-covered dashboard top rail.
- Vinyl trim door panel tops with simple stained wood topping.
- Aerated leather upholstery.

240/340

- As Mark 2 except majority of cars featured non-leather Ambla upholstery throughout.
- Some very late cars featured V8-style padded front dashboard top rail and simplified wooden fillets to door trim panels.

The dash layout of Daimler models followed Mark 2 practice except for the removal of the centre console in favour of this separate unit for the radio, speakers, and heater controls. This very late model shows padded dash top rail.

Rear seating on Daimler models also followed Mark 2 practice, although no picnic tables were fitted and door trims were different.

Above left: Late 240 Jaguar model. All 240/340 models normally featured Ambla upholstery instead of leather, with no picnic tables in the rear of the front seats à la Daimler.

Above right: The dash area to the side of the main instruments was used for auxiliary controls on Mark 2 and Daimler models. A brake warning light always featured, as did the slider control for the manual choke arrangement that applied to 2.4 and Daimler models. The rear window heater and switch was an option at extra cost.

5 Technical specifications

	2.4-litre	3.4-litre
cc	2483	3442
Bore and stroke (mm)	83 x 76.5	83 x 106
Compression ratio	8:1 (7:1 optional)	8:1 (7:1/9:1 optional)
bhp	112	210
@ rpm	5750	5500
Torque (lb ft)	140	216
@ rpm	2000	3000
Fuelling	2 x Solex carbs	2 x SU carbs
Transmission	4-speed (3 synchro) Later BW 3-speed auto	4-speed (3 synchro) BW 3-speed auto
Wheel size (in)	15, steel, wires optional	15, steel, wires optional
Suspension front	Ind semi-trailing wishbone, coil springs, anti-roll bar	Ind semi-trailing wishbone, coil springs, anti-roll bar
Suspension rear	Live axle, Panhard rod, leaf springs	Live axle, Panhard rod, leaf springs
Brakes	4-wheel drum, later 4-wheel disc	4-wheel drum, later 4-wheel disc
Performance		
0–60mph (sec)	14.4	9.1
Top speed (mph)	101.5	120
Average mpg	18.3	15–22
Dimensions		
Length (in)	180.75	180.75
Width (in)	66.75	66.75
Height (in)	57.5	57.5
Wheelbase (in)	107.375	107.375
Front track (in)	54.6	54.6
Rear track (in)	50.25	50.25
Weight (cwt)	27	28.5

	2.4-litre Mark 2	3.4-litre Mark 2
cc	2483	3442
Bore and stroke (mm)	83 x 76.5	83 x 106
Compression ratio	8:1 (7:1 optional)	8:1 (7:1/9:1 optional)
bhp	120	210
@ rpm	5750	5500
Torque (lb ft)	144	216
@ rpm	2000	3000
Fuelling	2 x Solex carbs	2 x SU carbs
Transmission	4-speed (3 synchro)	4-speed (3 synchro)
	Later all synchro	Later all synchro
	BW 3-speed auto	BW 3-speed auto
Wheel size (in)	15, steel, wires optional	15, steel, wires optional
Suspension front	Ind semi-trailing wishbone,	Ind semi-trailing wishbone,
	coil springs, anti-roll bar	coil springs, anti-roll bar
Suspension rear	Live axle, Panhard rod,	Live axle, Panhard rod,
	leaf springs	leaf springs
Brakes	4-wheel disc	4-wheel disc
Performance		
0–60mph (sec)	17.3	11.9
Top speed (mph)	96.3	120
Average mpg	18	16
Dimensions		
Length (in)	180.75	180.75
Width (in)	66.75	66.75
Height (in)	57.75	57.75
Wheelbase (in)	107.375	107.375
Front track (in)	55	55
Rear track (in)	53.375	53.375
Weight (cwt)	28.5	29.5

Technical specifications *cont ...*

	3.8-litre Mark 2	**240**
cc	3781	2483
Bore and stroke (mm)	87 x 106	83 x 76.5
Compression ratio	8:1 (7:1/9:1 optional)	8:1 (7:1 optional)
bhp	220	133
@ rpm	5500	5500
Torque (lb ft)	240	146
@ rpm	3000	3700
Fuelling	2 x SU carbs	2 x SU carbs
Transmission	4-speed (3 synchro) Later all synchro BW 3-speed auto	4-speed (3 synchro) Later all synchro BW 3-speed auto
Wheel size (in)	15, steel, wires optional	15, steel, wires optional
Suspension front	Ind semi-trailing wishbone, coil springs, anti-roll bar	Ind semi-trailing wishbone, coil springs, anti-roll bar
Suspension rear	Live axle, Panhard rod, leaf springs	Live axle, Panhard rod, leaf springs
Brakes	4-wheel disc	4-wheel disc
Performance		
0–60mph (sec)	8.5	12.5
Top speed (mph)	120.4	106
Average mpg	15.7	18.4
Dimensions		
Length (in)	180.75	180.75
Width (in)	66.75	66.75
Height (in)	57.75	57.75
Wheelbase (in)	107.375	107.375
Front track (in)	55	55
Rear track (in)	53.375	53.375
Weight (cwt)	30	28.5

	340	V8
cc	3442	2548
Bore and stroke (mm)	83 x 106	76.2 x 69.85
Compression ratio	8:1 (7:1 optional)	8.2:1
bhp	210	140
@ rpm	5500	5800
Torque (lb ft)	216	155
@ rpm	3000	3600
Fuelling	2 x SU carbs	2 x SU carbs
Transmission	4-speed (3 synchro) Later all synchro BW 3-speed auto	4-speed (3 synchro) Later all synchro BW 3-speed auto
Wheel size (in)	15, steel, wires optional	15, steel, wires optional
Suspension front	Ind semi-trailing wishbone, coil springs, anti-roll bar	Ind semi-trailing wishbone, coil springs, anti-roll bar
Suspension rear	Live axle, Panhard rod, leaf springs	Live axle, Panhard rod, leaf springs
Brakes	4-wheel disc	4-wheel disc
Performance		
0–60mph (sec)	8.8	13.5
Top speed (mph)	124	110
Average mpg	17–22	17
Dimensions		
Length (in)	180.75	180.75
Width (in)	66.75	66.75
Height (in)	57.75	57.75
Wheelbase (in)	107.375	107.375
Front track (in)	55	55
Rear track (in)	53.375	53.375
Weight (cwt)	30	29

Optional extras

2.4-litre saloon

Choice of three radio installations with or without rear parcel shelf-mounted speaker.
Laminated windscreen.
Chromium-plated wheel rimbellishers for steel wheels.
Ace Turbo wheel trims for steel wheels.
Witter tow bar.
Le Mans 40/45watt headlight bulbs.
Locking petrol filler cap.
Front seat belts.
Driver's seat bracket to raise seat height.
Split-style front seat arrangement (manual transmission cars).
Radiator blind.
Choice of radial, town and country, or whitewall tyres.
Borg Warner automatic transmission.
Overdrive (for non-overdrive-equipped manual transmission cars).
Cutaway rear-wheel spats for earlier cars not so fitted.
Wire wheels with conversion kit for hubs, etc.
Conversion kit to change drum-braked cars to disc-braked.
Conversion kit to change earlier disc braked cars to later 'quick change' type.
High-ratio steering box.
Lightened flywheel.
Competition clutch.
Fire extinguisher.
Chromed grab handle to passenger side of dashboard.
Powr-Lok differential.
Rear window demister.
White-finished steering wheel (export).
Gearlever extension piece.
Rheostat for dashboard lighting.
Vanity mirror for passenger sunvisor.
Stiffened shock absorbers.
Heavy-duty anti-roll bar.
Twin windtone horns.
Close-ratio gearbox.
Twin pipe exhaust system (for 2.4-litre only).
Stage 1 tuning kit, increasing bhp to 119.
Stage 2 tuning kit, increasing bhp to 131.
Stage 3 tuning kit, increasing bhp to 150.
High-lift camshafts.
Sundym tinted windscreen.
Wing mirrors.

3.4-litre saloon

Choice of three radio installations with or without rear parcel shelf-mounted speaker.
Laminated windscreen.
Chromium-plated wheel rimbellishers for steel wheels.
Ace Turbo wheel trims for steel wheels.
Witter tow bar.
Le Mans 40/45watt headlight bulbs.
Locking petrol filler cap.
Front seat belts.
Split-style front seat arrangement (manual transmission cars).
Radiator blind.
Choice of radial, town and country, or whitewall tyres.
Borg Warner automatic transmission.
Overdrive (for non-overdrive-equipped manual transmission cars).
Wire wheels with conversion kit for hubs, etc.
Conversion kit to change drum-braked cars to disc-braked.
Conversion kit to change earlier disc-braked cars to later 'quick change' type.
High-ratio steering box.
Lightened flywheel.
Competition clutch.
C-type cylinder head.
Fire extinguisher.
Chromed grab handle to passenger side of dashboard.
Powr-Lok differential.
Rear window demister.
White-finished steering wheel (export)
Rheostat for dashboard lighting.
Vanity mirror for passenger sunvisor.
Stiffened shock absorbers.
Heavy-duty anti-roll bar.
Twin windtone horns.
Close-ratio gearbox.
High-lift camshafts.
Sundym tinted windscreen.
Wing mirrors.

Mark 2 (all models)
Choice of five radio installations with or without rear parcel shelf-mounted speaker.
Laminated windscreen.
Chromium-plated wheel rimbellishers for steel wheels.
Ace Turbo wheel trims for steel wheels.
Witter tow bar.
Locking petrol filler cap.
Front seat belts.
Choice of radial, town and country, or whitewall tyres.
Borg Warner automatic transmission.
Overdrive (for non-overdrive-equipped manual transmission cars).
Wire wheels with conversion kit for hubs, etc.
High-ratio steering box.
Lightened flywheel.
Competition clutch.
C-type cylinder head.
Fire extinguisher.
Powr-Lok differential.
Rear window demister.
Heavy-duty anti-roll bar.
Close-ratio gearbox.
High-lift camshafts.
Sundym tinted windscreen and side windows.
Wing mirrors.
Childproof locks to rear doors.
Integrated ignition/starter switch to steering column.
Reclining front seats.
Steel sunroof (only offered from new from factory with differing bodyshell).
Power-assisted steering.

Daimler V8 models
Choice of five radio installations with or without rear parcel shelf-mounted speaker.
Laminated windscreen.
Ace Turbo wheel trims for steel wheels.
Witter tow bar.
Locking petrol filler cap.
Front seat belts.
Choice of radial, town and country, or whitewall tyres.
All synchromesh manual gearbox for later cars.
Overdrive (for non-overdrive-equipped manual transmission cars).
Wire wheels with conversion kit for hubs, etc.
Fire extinguisher.
Sundym tinted windscreen and side windows.
Wing mirrors.
Childproof locks to rear doors.
Integrated ignition/starter switch to steering column.
Reclining front seats.
Power-assisted steering.

240/340 models
Choice of five radio installations with or without rear parcel shelf-mounted speaker.
Laminated windscreen.
Chromium-plated wheel rimbellishers for steel wheels.
Ace Turbo wheel trims for steel wheels.
Witter tow bar.
Locking petrol filler cap.
Front seat belts.
Leather upholstery.
Choice of radial, town and country, or whitewall tyres.
Borg Warner automatic transmission.
Overdrive (for non-overdrive-equipped manual transmission cars).
Wire wheels with conversion kit for hubs, etc.
High-ratio steering box.
Fire extinguisher.
Powr-Lok differential.
Rear window demister.
Close-ratio gearbox.
Sundym tinted windscreen and side windows.
Wing mirrors.
Childproof locks to rear doors.
Integrated ignition/starter switch to steering column.
Reclining front seats.
Power-assisted steering.

5 Colour schemes

Exterior colour	Details	Interior trim
2.4- and 3.4-litre saloons		
Suede Green		Suede Green
Birch Grey	To 1957	Red
		Grey
		Pale Blue
Battleship Grey	To 1957	Red
		Grey
Lavender Grey	To 1957	Red
		Suede Green
		Pale Blue
Black		Red
		Tan
		Grey
		Biscuit
Pastel Green	To 1957	Suede Green
		Grey
Pastel Blue	To 1957	Pale Blue
		Grey
Dove Grey	To 1957	Tan
		Biscuit
British Racing Green		Tan
		Suede Green
Old English White		Red
		Pale Blue
Dark Blue	From 1958	Light Blue
		Dark Blue
		Grey
Maroon (Imperial)		Red
		Maroon
		Biscuit
Cornish Grey	From 1957	Red
		Light Blue
		Dark Blue
		Grey
Sherwood Green	From 1958	Suede Green
		Tan
Mist Grey		Red
		Light Blue
		Dark Blue
		Grey
Claret	From 1958	Red
		Maroon

Exterior colour	Details	Interior trim
Cotswold Blue	From 1958	Blue
		Grey
Pearl Grey		Red
		Light Blue
		Dark Blue
		Grey
Forest Green	1958 only	Suede Green
Carmine Red		Red
Mark 2 and Daimler 2.5 V8		
Pearl Grey	To 1966	Red
		Light Blue
		Dark Blue
		Grey
Warwick Grey	From 1964	Red
		Tan
Dove Grey	To 1966	Red
		Tan
		Grey
Mist Grey	To 1962	Red
		Grey
Carmen Red	To 1966	Red
		Black
Imperial Maroon		Red
Old English White		Red
		Tan
Primrose Yellow	From 1964	Red
		Tan
		Black
Honey Beige	From 1966	Red
		Tan
British Racing Green		Suede Green
		Tan
		Champagne
Sherwood Green	To 1966	Suede Green
		Tan
Willow Green	From 1966	Suede Green
		Black
		Champagne
Cotswold Blue	To 1965	Dark Blue
		Grey

Exterior colour	Details	Interior trim
Indigo Blue	From 1964	Light Blue
		Dark Blue
		Grey
Black		Red
		Tan
Opalescent Dark Green	From 1961	Suede Green
		Tan
		Champagne
Opalescent Blue	From 1961	Dark Blue
		Light Blue
		Grey
		Red
Opalescent Gunmetal	From 1961	Red
		Tan
Opalescent Silver Grey	From 1961	Red
		Tan
		Grey
Opalescent Silver Blue	From 1961	Dark Blue
		Light Blue
		Grey
		Red
Opalescent Bronze	From 1961	Red
		Tan
Opalescent Golden Sand	From 1966	Red
		Tan
Opalescent Maroon	From 1966	Red
		Champagne
		Tan

Exterior colour	Details	Interior trim
240, 340 and V8 250		
Willow Green		Suede Green
		Black
British Racing Green		Suede Green
		Black
		Beige
Signal Red		Black
		Red
		Beige
Regency Maroon		Red
		Beige
Old English White	Replaced by	Black
	'White' in 1968	Red
Warwick Grey		Black
		Red
		Dark Blue
Ascot Fawn		Black
		Red
Sable Brown		Beige
		Red
		Black
Indigo Blue		Black
		Red
		Dark Blue
Pale Blue		Dark Blue
		Red
		Black
Primrose Yellow		Black
Black		Red
		Dark Blue
		Beige

Prices and production volumes

	Price new (£)	1955	1956	1957	1958	1959	1960
2.4-litre saloon	1344	■	■	■	■	■	–
3.4-litre saloon	1672	–	–	■	■	■	–
2.4-litre Mark 2	1534	–	–	–	–	■	■
3.4-litre Mark 2	1669	–	–	–	–	■	■
3.8-litre Mark 2	1779	–	–	–	–	■	■
Daimler 2.5-litre V8	1568	–	–	–	–	–	–
240 saloon	1365	–	–	–	–	–	–
340 saloon	1442	–	–	–	–	–	–
Daimler V8 250	1850	–	–	–	–	–	–
Total production							

Production changes

1955
2.4-litre introduced.

1956
Rear-axle ratio changed to 4.27 on non-overdrive cars.
Shroud fitted to scuttle vent to prevent ingress of dirt.
Pressed steel sump fitted instead of alloy.

1957
3.4-litre introduced.
New radiator with revised filling neck.
(September) Wider grille fitted including revised front wings.
Automatic transmission became available.
(September) Rear-view mirror moved to roof on 3.4s.
Disc brakes introduced and later standardised.

1958
Metal toggle overdrive switch replaced plastic.
60watt brighter headlight bulbs introduced.
Cutaway rear spats fitted to 2.4s.

1959
Revised 'quick change' bridge brake calipers added.
72-spoke wire wheels replaced 60-spoke.
Vacuum reservoir tank fitted to front wing area.
(October) Mark 2s introduced.

1960
60lb oil pressure gauge replaced 100lb.
Position of steering column stalks changed over.
Oil bath air cleaners replaced by paper on 3.4/3.8.
Black-painted centre dash area substituted with Rexine.
Wider steel wheels fitted.
Organ type accelerator replaced by pendant.
Soft sun visors instead of hard type.
Strengthening added to chromed window frames.

1962
Front seatbelt anchorages fitted.
Sealed beam headlight added.
Waso steering ignition/lock available.

1963
(Late) Mark X-style revised steering wheel fitted.
Extra cutaway area in rear of front seats to increase legroom.

1964
One-piece front carpets fitted.
PVC heel pads added to carpets.
'Automatic' emblem on boot lid eliminated on all models.
Larger radiator fitted.
4.27 rear-axle ratio fitted to V8 models instead of 4.55.
D1 and D2 positions on auto box for V8 models.

1961	1962	1963	1964	1965	1966	1967	1968	1969	Total produced
–	–	–	–	–	–	–	–	–	19,705
–	–	–	–	–	–	–	–	–	17,280
■	■	■	■	■	■	■	–	–	26,322
■	■	■	■	■	■	■	–	–	29,531
■	■	■	■	■	■	■	–	–	27,848
–	■	■	■	■	■	■	–	–	13,018
–	–	–	–	–	–	■	■	■	4430
–	–	–	–	–	–	■	■	–	2804
–	–	–	–	–	■	■	■	■	4897
									145,835

1965
Hazard-light system for export models.
All-synchromesh manual gearbox fitted.
Revised clutch to fit above gearbox.
Limited-slip differential now extra cost on Daimlers.

1966
240/340/250 introduced.
Ambla upholstery standardised on Jaguars.
Rear of front seat picnic tables deleted.
S-type-style heading and visors fitted.
Fog lamps deleted as standard equipment on Jaguars.
3.8-litre Mark 2 discontinued.

1967
(February) Manual transmission available on V8 models.
(June) 2.5-litre V8 discontinued.
Reclining front seats standardised on Daimler models.
Power-steering standard on V8s.

1968
Non-earred spinners fitted to wire-wheel cars (all markets).
Revised water temperature gauge fitted with coloured segments.
(September) 340 model discontinued.

1969
(April) 240 model discontinued.
(July) V8 250 model discontinued.

Chassis numbers

Model	Right/left drive	Chassis/VIN commencing
2.4 (Mk 1)	RHD	900001
	LHD	940001
3.4 (Mk 1)	RHD	970001
	LHD	985001
2.4 (Mk 2)	RHD	100001
	LHD	125001
3.4 (Mk 2)	RHD	150001
	LHD	175001
3.8 (Mk 2)	RHD	200001
	LHD	210001
240	RHD	1J 1001
	LHD	1J 30001
340	RHD	1J 50001
	LHD	1J 80001
Daimler 2.5 V8	RHD	1A 1001
	LHD	1A 20001
Daimler V8 250	RHD	1K 1001
	LHD	1K 30001

6 E-type Series 1, 2 and 3 sports cars
1961 to 1974

Background

Jaguar had developed a well-established sports car market since 1948 with its XK range of cars, culminating in the XK150 produced from 1957 until 1961. Although offering good performance, the styling of these was still heavily based on the original XK120 of 1948, and designs were moving ahead elsewhere in the market place.

This changed with Jaguar's successes at Le Mans, won in 1955 and 1957 by its aerodynamically styled D-types. It was these cars that were to help Jaguar and its aerodynamicist Malcolm Sayer to cultivate the design that we now know as the E-type.

Launched in March 1961 at the Geneva Motor Show, the 'new' sports car, now officially known as the E-type, met the motoring world head-on and became the most talked-about car of the decade. Though offering the good old XK six-cylinder engine in XK150 3.8-litre S triple carburettor form, mated to the same old Moss gearbox, the car did herald in an entirely new independent rear suspension system that would adorn all future Jaguar models until the late 1980s. The aerodynamic body style was new but had its gestation in the D-type sports/racing car, and introduced monocoque (chassis-less) construction to Jaguar road-going sports cars for the first time. A new interior with dash layout based on the Mark 2 was also adopted and the car was available in two body styles, open and closed.

Needless to say, demand exceeded supply for some considerable time, and it wasn't until 1964 that any major changes were made to the overall design. Stylistically the car stayed the same but with better seating and, mechanically, gaining a few litres in engine capacity and a better braking system and gearbox.

In 1966 came a new addition to the range, offering an extra two occasional rear seats on a longer wheelbase bodyshell and, for the first time in the E-type, an automatic transmission, just for that model. The E-type survived substantial upgrades to meet ever more stringent safety and environmental regulations from the US, most of which appeared on the car with little ceremony. Then in 1968 came a 'new' E-type, known as the Series 2, with revised external and internal styling and many mechanical modifications. The three models, roadster, coupé, and 2+2, continued in production until 1971.

In 1971 a third generation of E-type appeared, the Series 3, for the first time showing off Jaguar's new twelve-cylinder engine in a wider bodyshell specially adapted to accept the new power unit, which also meant upgraded brakes, steering, and styling features. However, the Series 3 only remained in production until 1974, by which time the whole car was a little long in the tooth, particularly for the American market, where inevitably there was a demand for more refinement and safety.

The final E-type left the production lines in 1974 after a total production run of 72,500 vehicles over 13 years. Since that time the E-type has remained the epitome of the finest in Jaguar sports car design, a design that even current sports car producers refer back to – an icon of the 'sixties and of Jaguar sports car design for ever.

Model range and development

When it was launched the E-type was only available in one engine size with manual transmission and a choice of two body styles.

Models available at launch
E-type 3.8-litre roadster
E-type 3.8-litre fixed-head coupé

The E-type was a direct replacement for the XK150 and it was considered that just two models catered for all needs. The 3.8-litre triple carb engine pushed the performance level beyond that of the competition as, under the right conditions, the E-type genuinely could achieve 150mph, with acceleration to match.

The roadster model was a mere two-seater with a quick fold-down hood mechanism and a cover to hide the hood when down. With wind-up glass windows it offered all the accommodation found in the previous XK150 roadster. The boot space was minimal, but fitted suitcases or a chromed luggage rack were available for touring purposes.

The fixed-head coupé model was of an entirely new design, being one of the first production cars to offer a third wide opening rear door (akin to today's hatchbacks), providing a relatively flat loading area for an extensive amount of luggage. Interior accommodation was similar to the roadster, both being cars fitted out to a high specification. The fastback styling of the fixed-head coupé was particularly handsome and emphasised the styling features of the design, more so than the roadster; it was Sir William Lyons's favourite model.

Following the theme of the XK150, the E-type displayed no woodwork inside the car at all, instead relying on soft trim, and black and figured aluminium for centre areas of the dashboard and console. There were tightly gripping bucket seats, and an entirely new style of steering wheel (a drilled three-spoke design with a wood rim) that became a highly recognisable feature of the E-type over many years.

The E-type instantly became a success on the race tracks too, in the hands of well-known exponents like Graham Hill and Roy Salvadori, and demand continued to exceed supply for some time.

The only major changes in the first couple of years of production were to alter the design of the floorpan to allow for better legroom, and to fit internal locking mechanisms to the bonnet, other changes being mainly cosmetic until 1964. That year saw significant improvements in the design with less stylish but more comfortable seating and a move away from brash alloy finish

Very early E-type Series 1 roadster showing the external bonnet lock escutcheon, soon replaced by internal chromed locks. The chrome finisher to the upper section of the door was only fitted to roadster models only.

Fixed-head coupé model. All cars were fitted as standard with wire wheels, either chromed, body colour, or silver-painted. Whitewall tyres were an extra, as was the Webasto sunroof seen on this example.

Series 1 E-type frontal aspect with covered headlights, chromed centre bar to the radiator intake with growler badge, and bonnet-mounted stick-on number plate. Some US cars featured a sprung number plate mounting at low level.

of the interior to matt black. Mechanically the 3.8-litre engine was enlarged to 4.2-litre capacity, providing better mid-range torque, and with a new all-synchromesh gearbox and better brakes the E-type was an infinitely better drive overall, although some mourned the passing of the free-revving 3.8-litre engine.

The next major change came in 1966 when Jaguar added a third model to the range, this time catering for a different market by attempting to hold on to sports car drivers longer, after they had got married and had kids. The 2+2, as it became known, was a lengthened and raised version of the E-type designed to accommodate the addition of a pair of occasional seats in the rear compartment. With the lengthening of the body by 9in it was also possible to fit a Borg Warner automatic transmission so this became available at the same time, a godsend to the valuable US market.

Due to changes in US regulations the E-type needed to adapt, so during 1967 and early 1968 a special Federal model became available, features of which ended up on European cars as well. This model, now (and still unofficially) known as the Series 1½, was identifiable by the exposed headlamp treatment and, mechanically, by an adapted version of the XK engine with Zenith-Stromberg emissions carburettors instead of the British SU type, as well as by the recycling of gases across the manifold and back into the engine. It suffered somewhat in performance and to many was never as aesthetically pleasing as the earlier cars.

This model later developed into the Series 2 E-type from 1968, again to meet changes in legislation but also to bring it up to date. This was externally identifiable by its exposed headlights (different to the Series 1½ type), larger front and rear lighting units, and significantly enlarged air intake to improve cooling. Internally there was a new layout, with rocker switches, a degree of crash padding, and revised door trims. Mechanically the car was more practical, particularly so in hot climates, and with improved brakes and the availability of air-conditioning and emissions controls it proved another highly successful version of the E-type, which was still available in all three body styles.

In 1971 Jaguar announced the final phase of the E-type, the Series 3, which was originally intended to have been made available with both the existing six-cylinder XK engine and the brand new V12 unit. Designed primarily for a new upmarket saloon, the V12 engine was, as with the first XK engine, mated to a sports car initially, in this case the E-type, which had to be significantly modified to take it. The XK-engined version of the Series 3, although listed, never actually went into production.

Rear view of Series 1 roadster. The '4.2' badging on the boot only applied to post-1964 models with the larger engine. The 3.8-litre models had no such badging.

Rear view of the 4.2-litre Series 1 fixed-head coupé, showing the tailgate area.

Jaguar produced a glass fibre hardtop for the Series 1, 2 and 3 roadster models, which could be painted either black or body colour dependent on year of production. Series 3 hardtops are longer with an air extractor vent.

The Series 3 was available in just two body styles, roadster and fixed-head coupé. Both were built on the long-wheelbase 2+2 floorpan, though only the fhc offered the occasional rear seating. Widened to take bigger wheels and tyres and with another enlarged 'mouth' on the bonnet, the Series 3 was instantly recognisable from other E-types, particularly as the bonnet 'mouth' carried a chromed radiator grille as well.

Another interior redesign, now replacing the quite large wood rim steering wheel with a smaller all-leather version, the Series 3 E-type was a much more refined car all round and moved the model somewhat away from its true sports car upbringing. Quieter, softer sprung, and with power-steering, it was quicker than the Series 2 but not quite so fast as the original Series 1 models.

The fixed-head coupé design only lasted until mid-1973, when it was discontinued, followed by the roadster in 1974 when sales floundered, leaving Jaguar with no model to replace it until late in 1975, when the XJ-S appeared.

Despite the varied fortunes of the E-type, caused more than anything else by legislation, over 72,500 cars were sold, making this Jaguar sports car significantly more successful than the old XK.

In addition Jaguar hand-built 12 3.8-litre E-types for competition purposes. Now known as lightweights, these had aluminium panels and enhanced performance. The Italian coachbuilder Frua also produced a modified version of the E-type which didn't enter production; nor did a more radical design by Bertone for the Telegraph newspaper.

Exterior identification points
General points applicable to E-type Series 1s

Front view

- Aerodynamically shaped curved long bonnet sloping down at front to nose section with elongated air intake mouth, the latter with chromed splitter bar incorporating red circular growler badge.
- Twin headlight units with glass covers styled into body shape.
- Integral sidelights and indicator lenses set below headlights, above the bumper bars.
- Chromed quarter bumpers wrap-around to side of bonnet to meet wheel-arches, with small vertical overriders close to bonnet mouth at front.
- Pronounced bulge to bonnet, forward hinged and incorporating louvred panels either side of the bulge to aid cooling of the engine compartment.

Interior layout of the 3.8-litre Series 1 E-type with figured alloy brightwork on the central console and instrument panel. The traditional three-spoke wood-rim steering wheel applied to all E-types up to Series 3.

A 4.2-litre Series 1 interior showing revised seating and the replacement of figured alloy by black fabric.

Bucket seats in the 3.8-litre models were replaced by a flatter design in 4.2-litre cars.

- Majority of E-types featured 'stick-on' number plates to the leading edge of the bonnet above the mouth. Some cars, particularly in the US, were fitted with metal support plates to one side that hinged as the bonnet was raised.
- One-piece curved windscreen with chromed surround and three wiper blades.

Rear view

- Curved and tapered body areas, with indented area in the centre for number plate and illumination. Reversing light set centrally beneath. Severe curvature of under-bonnet allowed view of rear suspension and exhaust system.
- One-piece rear-hinged boot lid or side-opening door with rear screen on fixed-head coupé model.
- Fuel filler to one rear wing with cover painted to body colour.
- Twin exhaust pipes emit from centre of car under number plate area.
- Chromed quarter bumper bars to match front with overriders, wrapping around to meet rear wheel-arches.
- Integral chromed horizontal light units set above bumpers on rear wings.

Side view

- Very early 3.8-litre cars featured chromed escutcheon external bonnet locks, one per side to lower edges of rear of bonnet.
- Aerodynamic style followed through from bonnet area to rear of car with pronounced haunch over rear wing.
- Stylised chromed door handles apply to all models.
- 72-spoke wire wheels fitted to all cars, either body colour, silver enamel, or chromed, all with chromed eared hubcaps depicting 'Jaguar' name.
- Later non-'flat floor' models identifiable by view of lowered floorpan area beneath sill area of car.

E-type Series 1 specifics

E-type 3.8-/4.2-litre roadster

- Door frames incorporate chromed horizontal finisher at waist height.
- Door windows of curved glass with no support framework except at front.
- Fabric hood clipped to windscreen top rail and affixed to rear deck of bodywork.
- Perspex rear screen to hood with chromed finisher above.
- One-piece rear-hinged door lid with no external lock mechanism.
- Chromed 'Jaguar' badge to centre of boot lid.
- Chromed '4.2' badge below 'Jaguar' on boot lid. No badging on 3.8-litre models.

Coupé boot with fold-down frontal area.

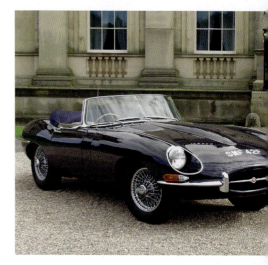

A 1967 mid-term model, now known as the Series 1½, with exposed headlights.

Series 2 E-types are identifiable from the front by the enlarged air intake area, raised bumper bar level, larger side/indicator lights, and exposed headlights with different surrounds to the Series 1½.

E-type Series 1 fixed-head coupé

- As above but doors do not have chromed waist trim.
- Chrome on brass window surround to glass accompanied by matching rear opening quarter-lights and chromed rain gutters to steel roof.
- Extended steel roof slopes back (fastback) to form a large side-opening door with glass rear screen with chromed surround. No external locks or hinges.
- Badging as roadster model.

E-type Series 1 2+2

- As fixed-head coupé but with a steeper rake and greater curvature to the windscreen.
- 3in increase in roof height.
- 9in extra length to the wheelbase, all taken up in lengthened doors and chromed window frames.
- Chromed waistline trim to doors with matching finisher on rear wing area in stepped style.

E-type Series 1½ specifics

- Front open headlights (without glass covers), necessitating a redesign of chrome trim on the bonnet side tops and around the headlamp units themselves.
- Most wire-wheel-equipped cars by this time fitted with 'easy-clean' flat centre hubs.

General points applicable to E-type Series 2s

Front view

- Redesigned nose section of bonnet with 70% larger mouth.
- Front bumper bar continued across centre of air intake, incorporating splitter bar with new oval badge depicting growler.
- Open headlights similar to Series 1½ cars but with revised chrome trim surrounds, much deeper on top.
- Sidelight/indicator units enlarged and moved to new position beneath bumper area.

Rear view

- Full-width bumper now running across the top of the rear bodywork above number plate area.
- Enlarged rear lighting units placed beneath the bumper level along with a new stainless finishing panel incorporating the reversing lights (two) and square number plate above the exhaust tailpipes.

Side view

- All Series 2 cars equipped with wire wheels used the 'easy-clean' type of flat hub accompanied by non-eared hub spinners. Some cars fitted with conventional steel road wheels, either silver

From late in 1967 the curved centre hubs of wire wheels above were changed to the 'easy-clean' style shown at the top.

Rear of Series 2 model, with full-width bumper bar treatment, alloy background panel incorporating larger lights, spread tailpipes and, usually, square number plates.

or chromed, with conventional Jaguar hubcaps depicting centrally mounted growler badge.
- Series 2s easily identifiable by open headlights and under-bumper.

E-type Series 2 specifics

E-type Series 2 2+2
- As other Series 2 models except windscreen enlarged and moved further forward, virtually eliminating a scuttle area between screen and bonnet.

General points applicable to E-type Series 3s

Front view
- Enlarged bonnet air intake mouth area now incorporating slatted grille with gold growler badge in the centre and a chromed trim scoop area below mouth. Rubber-faced overriders (or Nordel impact-absorbing units on US cars).
- Wider aspect to bonnet area with pronounced flares to bonnet sides in wheelarch areas.
- Lighting as Series 2 models.
- One-piece curved windscreen with chromed surround and two windscreen wipers.

Rear view
- Series 2 style but revised siting of reversing lights and reversal to rectangular number plates (in most markets).
- New four exhaust tailpipes in fishtail style, later replaced by twin-pipe system.
- Badging on rear depicting 'Jaguar' and 'E-type' emblems with enlarged 'V' incorporating figure '12' in chrome.

Side view
- Only built on the long-wheelbase 2+2 floorpan so recognisable by the extra length to both roadster and coupé models, particularly in the door areas.
- Flared wheel-arches front and rear.
- Chrome door finisher on both models, similar to 2+2 style but not the same.

E-type Series 3 specifics

Fixed-head coupé 2+2
- Rear tailgate incorporates chromed air extractor grille above badging.

Interior identification points

E-type Series 1 3.8-litre (all models)
- Dashboard in black finish with speedometer and rev counter directly in front of driver, with ancillary gauges and toggle switches on centre panel finished in figured alloy.
- Open glovebox to passenger side of dashboard.
- Figured alloy centre console extending down, incorporating chromed ashtray, radio, gearlever, and handbrake (fly off).

A 2+2 model, in this case a Series 2 car with US-style repeater indicator lights on the side of the bonnet. The 2+2s are instantly identifiable by the longer bodyshell, with wider doors and chromed finisher across the top of them.

Revised interior for Series 2 models, with rocker switches on the centre panel, and revised door trims and handles.

Series 3 roadster based on the longer wheelbase (2+2) floorpan. It can be identified from the side by the wider wheel-arches and chromed trim along the top of the doors (which are also wider).

- Sculptured bucket seating with wide pleating.
- Wood-rim three-spoke drilled steering wheel incorporating horn push centre boss with gold, white, and black chequered flag, laurels, and 'E-type' script.
- Upholstered door panels and sill areas with horizontal chrome trims and handles to each door.

E-type Series 1 3.8-litre roadster
- Centre chromed vertical stay rod to screen area to accommodate the sliding rear-view mirror fitted to roadster models.
- Mohair hood with beige interior lining affixed to screen via three toggle clamps.
- No sun visors fitted.
- Boot lid opened from behind driver's seat, with Hardura covering and wooden floor removable to gain access to tools and spare wheel.

E-type Series 1 3.8-litre fixed-head coupé
- Conventional roof-mounted rear-view mirror.
- Trimmed rear deck area with rails for luggage, with removable panel to access spare wheel and tools.
- Fold-down forward section to provide extra load area, chrome trimmed.
- Upholstered rear side-opening door with lock access from behind driver's seat and stay bar. Covered door hinges on later models.

E-type Series 1 4.2-litre (all models)
- Flatter front seat arrangement to 3.8-litre models with closer horizontal and vertical pleating.
- Replacement of alloy dash and console panels with black figured Rexine on centre dash panel and leather to match interior trim on centre console.
- Console now incorporated a leather-clad armrest and lidded glovebox area between seats.
- Door trims now included armrest and pulls with chrome trim.

E-type Series 1 4.2-litre roadster
- Boot locking handle behind driver's seat now incorporated a locking mechanism.
- Better-quality trim to rear compartment.

E-type Series 1 4.2-litre fixed-head coupé
- Extensive use of Rexine and Moquette to rear compartment.
- Extended trim coverings to protect luggage from catches etc, in the rear compartment.

E-type Series 1 4.2-litre 2+2 coupé
- As fixed-head coupé but at the front parcel shelves were fitted below dashboard area for storage.
- Slightly revised centre console to

All Series 3 E-types were fitted with the V12 engine necessitating a larger air intake, now with a chromed grille. Larger under-bumper lighting and wider wheel-arches also differentiate this model.

Styling cues at the rear of the Series 3 are taken from the Series 2 six-cylinder models. Prominent V12 badging on the tailgate and ventilation grille was also used on the fixed-head coupé model. The chromed steel wheels with hubcaps and black centres were used on Series 2 and 3 models except where wire wheels were specified.

Different tailpipe arrangements on the E-type Series 3. A four-pipe system was initially fitted (inset), later changed to twin pipes as seen in the main picture.

accommodate rear seating arrangement.
- Rear seating in leather with matching pleats, trimmed side panels below rear quarter-lights, and a fold-down top section of the seat for extra luggage accommodation.

E-type Series 1½ (all models)
- Front seats provided with adjustable squabs and positive locking arrangement.
- Burst-proof door locks with recessed door handles and chromed window winders incorporating black plastic knobs.
- Wider seats necessitating slightly recessed centre console sides.
- Plastic surround to rear-view mirror.
- During production of this model the centre dash layout changed to incorporate new-style rocker switches in place of toggle type.

E-type Series 2 (all models)
- Changes as the later Series 1½ models including rocker switches on dashboard, revised door trims, rear-view mirror, etc.
- Reclining front seats with fitting to accept headrests.
- Aerated perforated leather trim to seats.
- Simplified moulded centre console for radio now incorporated cigarette lighter.
- Re-siting and redesign of ashtray to centre console in front of armrest.
- Horn now operated from steering column mounted stalk and not steering wheel boss.

E-type Series 3 (all models)
- Smaller-diameter leather-covered three-spoke steering wheel fitted with black growler centre boss motif.
- Revised seating from Series 2 models but still with aerated leather seat centres.
- Vacuum-formed black centre console.
- Speaker grilles in rear compartment panelling.
- Revised door interior trims with square recessed areas for handles and squared-off armrests/pulls.

E-type Series 3 roadster
- Deeper tonneau cover fitted when hood down, extending forward to rear of front seats.
- Trimmed box area behind front seats for luggage, with hinged lid.

E-type Series 3 fixed-head coupé
- Only available as a 2+2 seating arrangement.
- Extended front seat adjustment levers to enable rear seat passengers to move the seat backs.

Interior revision of Series 3 models incorporated a small, leather-rimmed steering wheel.

Air-conditioning became available on later E-types, usually for the US market, and was fitted as shown here.

The 2+2 seating arrangement.

Technical specifications

	3.8-litre	4.2-litre Series 1
cc	3781	4235
Bore and stroke (mm)	87 x 106	92.07 x 106
Compression ratio	9:1 (8:1 optional)	9:1 (8:1 optional)
bhp	265	265
@ rpm	5500	5400
Torque (lb ft)	260	283
@ rpm	4000	4000
Fuelling	3 x SU carbs	3 x SU carbs
Transmission	4-speed (3 synchro)	4-speed all synchro 2+2 BW 3-speed auto
Wheel size (in)	15, wire	15, wire
Suspension front	Ind wishbone, torsion bar	Ind wishbone, torsion bar
Suspension rear	Ind lower wishbone, upper driveshaft link, radius arms, coil springs	Ind lower wishbone, upper driveshaft link, radius arms, coil springs
Brakes	4-wheel disc, rear inboard	4-wheel disc, rear inboard
Performance		
0–60mph (sec)	7.1	7.0 (8.9 2+2)
Top speed (mph)	149.1	150 (136.2 2+2)
Average mpg	19.7	18.5 (18.3 2+2)
Dimensions		
Length (in)	175.5	175.5 (184.5 2+2)
Width (in)	64.25	66.75
Height (in)	47 (48 fhc)	50.5 (2+2)
Wheelbase (in)	96	96 (105 2+2)
Front track (in)	50	50
Rear track (in)	50	50
Weight (cwt)	24	25.1 (27.7 2+2)

Optional extras

E-type Series 1 3.8-litre models
Choice of three radio installations with fitting kits.
Two choices of bonnet-mounted wing mirrors.
Locking petrol filler cap.
Front seat safety belts.
Clear glass rear door (fhc).
Sundym tinted glass.
Detachable glass fibre hardtop for roadster model.
Alternative choices of tyres.
Chromium-plated wire wheels.
Competition wire wheels.

E-type Series 1 and 1½ 4.2-litre models
Choice of three radio installations with fitting kits.
Two choices of bonnet-mounted wing mirrors.
Locking petrol filler cap.
Front seat safety belts.
Rear seat safety belts for 2+2 model.
Clear glass rear door (fhc).
Electrically heated rear screen for 2+2 model.
Sundym tinted glass.
Detachable glass fibre hardtop for roadster model.
Alternative choices of tyres.
Chromium-plated wire wheels.
Competition wire wheels.
Steering column lock and ignition switch.

Technical specifications cont ...

	4.2-litre Series 2	Series 3
cc	4235	5343
Bore and stroke (mm)	92.07 x 106	90 x 70
Compression ratio	9:1 (8:1 optional)	9:1
bhp	265	272
@ rpm	5400	5850
Torque (lb ft)	283	304
@ rpm	4000	5600
Fuelling	3 x SU carbs, 3 x Stromberg (US)	4 x Stromberg carbs
Transmission	4-speed all synchro	4-speed all synchro
	2+2 B/W 3-speed auto	B/W 3-speed auto
Wheel size (in)	15, wire/steel option	15, wire/steel option
Suspension front	Ind wishbone, torsion bar	Ind wishbone, torsion bar
Suspension rear	Ind lower wishbone, upper driveshaft link, radius arms, coil springs	Ind lower wishbone, upper driveshaft link, radius arms, coil springs
Brakes	4-wheel disc, rear inboard	4-wheel disc, rear inboard
Performance		
0–60mph (sec)		6.4 (6.8 2+2)
Top speed (mph)		146 (142 2+2)
Average mpg		14.5
Dimensions		
Length (in)		184
Width (in)		
Height (in)		
Wheelbase (in)		105
Front track (in)		54.5
Rear track (in)		53
Weight (cwt)		28.8 (29.5 2+2)

Optional extras cont ...

E-type Series 2 models

Choice of three radio installations with fitting kits.
Two choices of bonnet-mounted wing mirrors.
Locking petrol filler cap.
Front seat safety belts.
Rear seat safety belts for 2+2 model.
Front seat headrests.
Electrically heated rear screen.
Sundym tinted glass.
Alternative choices of tyres.
Chromium-plated wire wheels.
Competition wire wheels.
Chromium-plated steel wheels.
Air-conditioning.

E-type Series 3 models

Choice of three radio installations with fitting kits.
Electric radio aerial.
Three choices of bonnet- or door-mounted mirrors.
Locking petrol filler cap.
Front seat safety belts.
Rear seat safety belts for 2+2 model.
Front seat headrests.
Electrically heated rear screen.
Sundym tinted glass.
Alternative choices of tyres.
Wire wheels.
Chromium-plated wire wheels.
Chromium-plated steel wheels.
Detachable hardtop for roadster model.
Air-conditioning.

Colour schemes

Exterior colour Single	Details	Interior trim	Details
E-type 3.8-litre models			
Pearl Grey		Red	
		Dark Blue	
Mist Grey		Red	
Carmen Red		Red	
		Biscuit	
Imperial Maroon	1961–2 only	Tan	
Claret	1961–2 only	Beige	
Old English White		Red	
		Black	
		Cream	
Primrose Yellow	From 1963	Black	
		Beige	
British Racing Green		Suede Green	
		Tan	
		Beige	
		Light Tan	
Sherwood Green		Suede Green	
		Light Tan	
		Tan	
Cotswold Blue		Dark Blue	
Indigo Blue	1963/4 only	Light Blue	
		Red	
Black		Red	
		Grey	
		Light Tan	
		Tan	
Opalescent Dark Green		Suede Green	
		Tan	
		Beige	
		Light Tan	
Opalescent Blue		Dark Blue	
		Red	
Opalescent Gunmetal		Red	
		Light Blue	
		Dark Blue	
		Beige	
Opalescent Silver Grey		Red	
		Light Blue	
		Grey	
		Dark Blue	
Opalescent Silver Blue		Dark Blue	
		Grey	

Colour schemes *cont ...*

Exterior colour Single	Details	Interior trim	Details
Opalescent Bronze		Red	
		Beige	
		Tan	
Opalescent Golden Sand	From 1963	Black	
		Beige	
Opalescent Maroon	From 1963	Maroon	
		Beige	
E-type Series 1 4.2 and 1½ models			
Carmen Red		Red	To 1965
		Black	
		Biscuit	To 1965
Old English White		Red	
		Black	
		Cream	To 1965
Primrose Yellow		Black	
		Beige	
Sherwood Green		Suede Green	
		Light Tan	
		Tan	
Dark Blue		Light Blue	
		Grey	
		Red	
Black		Red	
		Grey	
		Light Tan	
		Tan	
Opalescent Dark Green		Suede Green	
		Tan	
		Beige	
		Light Tan	
Opalescent Blue		Dark Blue	
		Red	
Opalescent Gunmetal		Red	
		Light Blue	
		Dark Blue	
		Beige	
Opalescent Silver Grey		Red	
		Light Blue	
		Grey	
		Dark Blue	
Opalescent Silver Blue		Dark Blue	
		Grey	

Exterior colour Single	Details	Interior trim	Details
Opalescent Golden Sand		Black	To 1965
		Beige	To 1965
		Red	From 1965
		Light Tan	From 1965
Opalescent Maroon		Maroon	
		Beige	
Warwick Grey		Red	
		Light Tan	
		Dark Blue	
Willow Green	From 1967	Grey	
		Suede Green	
		Light Tan	
		Beige	
Beige	From 1967	Red	
		Suede Green	
		Tan	
		Light Tan	
British Racing Green	From 1967	Suede Green	
		Beige	
		Light Tan	
		Dark Tan	
E-type Series 2 models			
Old English White		Red	To 1969
		Black	
Primrose Yellow		Black	
		Beige	
Dark Blue		Light Blue	
		Grey	
		Red	
Black		Red	
		Grey	
		Cinnamon	
Warwick Grey		Red	
		Cinnamon	
		Dark Blue	
Willow Green		Grey	
		Suede Green	
		Cinnamon	
		Beige	
British Racing Green		Suede Green	
		Beige	
		Cinnamon	

Colour schemes cont ...

Exterior colour Single	Details	Interior trim	Details
Ascot Fawn		Red	
		Beige	
		Cinnamon	
Sable Brown		Beige	
		Grey	
		Cinnamon	
Light Blue		Dark Blue	
		Light Blue	
		Grey	
Regency Red		Beige	
		Grey	
Signal Red	To 1970	Black	
		Red	
		Beige	
E-type Series 3 models			
Old English White		Red	
		Dark Blue	
		Light Blue	
		Black	
Primrose Yellow		Black	
		Beige	To 1972
		Biscuit	From 1972
		Red	From 1972
Dark Blue		Light Blue	To 1972
		French Blue	From 1972
		Russet Red	From 1972
		Grey	To 1972
		Red	
Black	Special order from 1972	Red	
		Grey	
		Cinnamon	
Warwick Grey	To 1972	Red	
		Cinnamon	
		Dark Blue	
Willow Green	To 1972	Grey	
		Suede Green	
		Cinnamon	
		Beige	
British Racing Green		Suede Green	To 1972
		Beige	To 1972
		Biscuit	From 1972
		Moss Green	From 1972
		Cinnamon	

Exterior colour Single	Details	Interior trim	Details
Ascot Fawn	To 1972	Red	
		Beige	
		Cinnamon	
Sable Brown	To 1972	Beige	
		Grey	
		Cinnamon	
Light Blue	To 1972	Dark Blue	
		Light Blue	
		Grey	
Regency Red		Beige	To 1972
		Grey	To 1972
		Biscuit	From 1972
		Cinnamon	From 1972
		Russet Red	From 1972
Signal Red		Black	
		Red	To 1972
		Beige	To 1972
		Biscuit	From 1972
		Dark Blue	From 1972
Fern Grey	From 1972	Moss Green	
		Olive	
		Tan	
Turquoise	From 1972	Tan	
		Terracotta	
		Cinnamon	
Green Sand	From 1972	Tan	
		Olive	
		Cinnamon	
Heather	From 1972	Maroon	
		Antelope	
		Cerise	
Lavender Blue	From 1972	French Blue	
		Biscuit	
		Dark Blue	
Azure Blue	From 1972	Dark Blue	
		Biscuit	
		Cinnamon	
Silver Metallic	Special order from 1972	Black	
		Red	
		Biscuit	

Prices and production volumes

	Price new (£)	1961	1962	1963	1964	1965	1966
3.8-litre roadster	2098	■	■	■	■	–	–
3.8-litre fixed-head coupé	2197	■	■	■	■	–	–
4.2-litre roadster	1896	–	–	–	■	■	■
4.2-litre fixed-head coupé	1992	–	–	–	■	■	■
4.2-litre Series 1 2+2	2385	–	–	–	–	–	■
Series 2 roadster	2163	–	–	–	–	–	–
Series 2 fixed-head coupé	2273	–	–	–	–	–	–
Series 2 2+2	2512	–	–	–	–	–	–
Series 3 roadster	3139	–	–	–	–	–	–
Series 3 2+2	3383	–	–	–	–	–	–
Total production							

Production changes

1961
E-type 3.8-litre models introduced.
(October) Automatic handbrake pad adjustment.
Exterior bonnet fastening deleted.

1962
Revised bonnet hinges.
Steering lock/ignition switch available.
Heated rear screen available on fhc models.
(June) Heel wells fitted to floorpans.
(June) Chrome finisher added to roadster window front surround.
(November) Alloy dash finisher pattern altered.

1963
Centre armrest fitted.
One-piece luggage floor mat for fhc.
(November) Longer blades fitted to wipers.

1964
Sealed beam headlamps fitted for most countries.
E-type Series 1 4.2-litre models introduced.
Plastic screen-wash reservoir fitted.

1966
Vanity mirror fitted to passenger sunvisor.
2+2 model introduced.
Green indicator dash backlight replaced blue.
1967
Switch and warning light adopted for heated rear screen.
Series 1½ models phased in.
Ribbed cam covers phased in.

1968
Easy-clean wire-wheel hubs adopted.
Series 2 models introduced.

1967	1968	1969	1970	1971	1972	1973	1974	Total produced
–	–	–	–	–	–	–	–	7818
–	–	–	–	–	–	–	–	7663
■	■	–	–	–	–	–	–	9551
■	■	–	–	–	–	–	–	7771
■	■	–	–	–	–	–	–	5586
–	■	■	■	–	–	–	–	8641
–	■	■	■	–	–	–	–	4878
–	■	■	■	–	–	–	–	5329
–	–	–	–	■	■	■	■	7982
–	–	–	■	■	■	■	–	7310
								72,529

1970-71
First series 3 models produced; early cars included some with XK 6-cylinder engine introduced.

1972
Revised heater controls.
Remote control door mirror now available.
Waso steering lock adopted.

1973
Modified Borg Warner Model 12 auto transmission fitted.
Twin exhaust-pipe outlets replaced four-branch.
Fixed-head coupé model discontinued.

1974
Last 50 commemorative models produced.

Chassis numbers

Model	Right/left drive	Chassis/VIN commencing
E-type 3.8	RHD	850001
OTS	LHD	875001
E-type 3.8	RHD	860001
FHC	LHD	885001
E-type 4.2 S1	RHD	1E 1001
OTS	LHD	1E 10001
E-type 4.2 S1	RHD	1E 2001
FHC	LHD	1E 30001
E-type 4.2 S1	RHD	1E 50001
2+2	LHD	1E 75001
E-type S2	RHD	1R 1001
OTS	LHD	1R 7001
E-type S2	RHD	1R 20001
FHC	LHD	1R 25001
E-type S2	RHD	1R 35001
2+2	LHD	1R 4000
E-type S3	RHD	1S 1001
OTS	LHD	1S 20001
E-type S3	RHD	1S 50001
2+2	LHD	1S 70001

7. The Mark X/420G saloons
1961 to 1970

Background

Although Jaguar had expanded its saloon car range in the 1950s with the introduction of the compact models, updated to the Mark 2 from 1959, the large flagship saloon design based on the Mark VII had reigned supreme since 1950, and a replacement was badly needed. Development work on the E-type enabled Jaguar to take advantage of some of the new sports car's technology, and within a few months of the E-type's launch in March 1961 a brand new luxury saloon was announced at the British Motor Show in October.

The Mark VII having grown into the Mark VIII and then the Mark IX, it was logical that the next new model would take the name Mark X, even though it owed nothing to the earlier cars except for the by then legendary XK six-cylinder twin camshaft engine. Those who used to think the Mark VII was large were to be somewhat surprised when the Mark X was announced as an even longer and wider car – the widest production car ever produced in the UK until the introduction of Jaguar's own XJ220 supercar in the 1990s. The Mark X was a big car in every way except for its height, which emphasised the length even more, and the whole styling concept was obviously designed with the valued North American market in mind.

William Lyons had attempted to retain much of Jaguar's traditional touches but within an all-new style, although this was to have limited success. The 'old' engine and gearbox were mated to the new E-type independent rear suspension to enhance handling and ride. The extra body length and width made for interior dimensions of gargantuan size, and the Mark X was never lacking in equipment levels. The bodywork was of monocoque construction, allowing the car to sit much lower and reducing its overall height, and it was a tribute to Jaguar's engineers that it was even more structurally rigid than the outgoing Mark IX.

The styling, however, was not to meet with universal acclaim. Though aimed at the highly profitable US market, American buyers considered the Mark X to be too much like their own cars, lacking the traditional style and stature of a luxury European car. British buyers did not respond well to the new car either, because it was just too large and bulbous. Even in the early 1960s few home garages were long enough or wide enough to accommodate a vehicle of this size, and it was difficult to park and to handle in confined country lanes, leading to a substantial number of cars suffering from scratched and dented sides.

Even though the Mark X 3.8-litre model didn't sell as well as the early Mark VIIs did in the 1950s, it was updated alongside the E-type in 1964 with 4.2-litre engine and other changes, although sales continued to decline. With Jaguar's policy of revamping its whole range in 1966 the Mark X also received some minor modifications, amongst which was a change of name to 420G. Sales marginally improved, helped by the fact that the car's replacement, the XJ6, wasn't announced until September 1968 and, even then, stocks remained in short supply well into 1969, allowing production and sales of the 420G to continue into 1970.

Never considered to be one of Jaguar's better designs, the Mark X did carry its style and proportions well and was an immensely strong car overall. Many would say it was the last of the conventional Jaguars, with chrome on brass window frames and some of the traditional touches characteristic of previous models.

In total just over 25,000 Mark X/420G models were produced from 1961 to 1970, pro rata the lowest production figure per year of any Jaguar saloon style ever.

Model range and development

When introduced at the British Motor Show in 1961 there was only one model of the Mark X, with manual four-speed transmission (with or without overdrive) or Borg Warner three-speed automatic gearbox.

Model available at launch
3.8-litre Mark X saloon

The Mark X Jaguar offered a high standard of specification, incorporating the E-type's 3.8-litre XK power unit, complete with triple SU carburettors developing 265bhp, an 11% increase over the outgoing Mark IX model. Although both gearboxes were essentially the same as the Mark IX, the new independent rear suspension and the lower centre of gravity improved the handling and, to a degree, the ride.

Externally the Mark X still dripped in chrome, with the usual Jaguar leaping mascot atop the bonnet (although of smaller dimensions). Even the traditional grille was retained, cleverly adapted to fit a much lower body line by leaning it forward from the vertical position. All-new lighting adopted the latest idea of four headlamps (only really seen in the US in the previous couple of years), and due to its overall size the Mark X had a magnificent boot capable of swallowing virtually anything.

Internally the accepted Jaguar touches of veneer and leather were retained, though the dashboard took on the overall style of the Mark 2 and E-type but in a much lighter hue of walnut than before. Enormous seating in the front formed a split-bench arrangement with reclining mechanisms, and Jaguar retained the occasional picnic tables in the rear as a mark of respect to the earlier cars. However, although aimed at the executive and even chauffeur-driven markets, to enable the car to sit a lot lower the floorpan fell below the sill level, which necessitated occupants having to step over enormous sills to get in and out.

Hardly anything changed during the life of the 3.8-litre Mark X except for the adoption of an improved heating system late on. Then in 1964, after a mere 12,500 had been produced, the Mark X received the same revision treatment that the E-type got. In came the 4.2-litre version of the XK engine to improve torque, along with much improved power assistance to the brake system and a new Varamatic power-steering system to provide greater 'feel'. The by now archaic manual gearbox was improved with all-synchromesh, and even the automatic transmission was changed for the smoother Model 8 unit. The resulting 4.2-litre Mark X was virtually identical in looks to the old model except for the 4.2-litre badging on the boot lid.

At the same time, Jaguar announced a new addition to the Mark X range: the limousine model. Exactly the same mechanically and dimensionally as the standard saloon, this model did offer a centre division arrangement ideally suited to a chauffeur-driven car. A brief black and white brochure was produced on this model, which was only built to special order. In fact only 18 were made.

The next move came in October 1966 when Jaguar announced a rationalisation of its saloon models, the simplification of trim, and re-badging. The Mark X became the 420G and was only changed externally by the addition of a prominent centre vertical rib to the radiator grille, the fitting of front wing side indicator repeater lights, revised badging at the rear, and new-style hubcaps. Two-tone colour schemes also became available, accompanied by a swage coachline separating the colours. When cars were painted in a single colour chromed swage line trims were fitted. Internally 420G models were identified by the black Ambla-covered dashboard top rail incorporating a rectangular clock, a pull-out wooden tray under the centre dash panel, and aerated centre leather panels to the seats. Jaguar continued to offer a limousine model alongside the saloon but only 24 were produced, including the example used by Sir William Lyons himself as a company vehicle.

The 420G soldiered on into 1970 and a few cars were still unsold in 1971, resulting in a grand total of only 25,212 being produced since its conception back in 1961.

Exterior identification points

General points applicable to all Mark X/420G models

Front view

- Low-set frontal aspect with twin headlight arrangement (inner ones smaller than outer).
- Circular sidelights and elongated oval wrap-around indicator units inset into corners of front wings.
- Chromed horn grilles (similar to those fitted to Mark VIII/IX models) below the centre pair of headlights.

7

The Mark X/420G saloons 1961 to 1970

- Traditional but shallow version of Jaguar chromed radiator grille sloping forward from the top with vertical slats and carrying Jaguar winged badge.
- Slimline chromed bumper with matching over-riders sloping forwards, with number plate centrally mounted.
- One-piece forward-hinged bonnet incorporating grille, inner headlights, and horn grilles.
- Reduced-size Jaguar leaping mascot atop the bonnet with full-length centrally mounted chrome trim.
- One-piece wrap-around windscreen incorporating chromed surround and two wiper blades.

Rear view
- Rear wrap-around screen with chrome surround.
- Twin fuel tanks with lockable covers, one per side atop rear boot surround panel.
- One-piece boot lid incorporating chromed number plate/reversing light plinth and chromed number plate surround.
- 'Jaguar' script and, where applicable, 'automatic' script centrally mounted.
- Integrated rear-light units with chrome surround and reflectors.
- Slimline bumper wrapping around rear wings fitted with overriders to match front.
- Twin exhaust pipes emerging separately in centre of car below bumper and rear valance level.

Side view
- Elongated style very low with bulged sides incorporating swage indentation at mid-level.
- Sculptured door handles fitted sloping upwards from top of doors.
- Chrome on brass window frames with quarter-lights front and rear.
- Chromed rain gutters and horizontal thin trims at window level above door handles.
- Unique 14in steel wheels painted to body colour with chromed rimbellishers and hubcaps similar to other early 1960s models in the Jaguar range, incorporating pronounced centre section with Jaguar badge.

Mark X/420G specifics

Mark X 4.2-litre model
- Exactly as 3.8-litre except for '4.2' chrome script below Jaguar in centre of boot lid. No '3.8'-litre badging featured on previous model.

420G model
- Pronounced chromed centre rib to radiator grille.
- Revised hubcaps similar to those used on the 240/340 models, incorporating more

In 3.8-litre and 4.2-litre form the Mark X was identical externally except for a '4.2' badge on the boot lid of the latter. This body style was only used for these and the later 420G models and is instantly recognisable from any other Jaguar saloon. Pre-420G models featured the usual chromed Jaguar hubcaps containing a 'Jaguar' emblem, and chromed rimbellishers were a standard fitment.

The Mark X radiator grille featured vertical slats of equal size. For certain overseas markets the Jaguar leaper on the bonnet (of a smaller size to that used previously on other cars) was not fitted.

Up to 1964 the interior design of the Mark X was unchanged, as seen here with Mark 2/E-type layout, except for wood-veneered centre section and pull-out occasional tray below with chromed handle. The three black push-buttons on the centre console controlled the vacuum airflow/heating system.

- pronounced centre section and growler image on black badge.
- Indicator repeater lenses to forward edge of front wings.
- Painted coachline to swage area for cars in two-tone exterior paint finishes.
- Chromed trims along the entire side length of the body from front wing (behind indicator repeater) to rear wing. This trim used on single-colour models.
- Revised '420G' badging on boot lid.

NB: There were no exterior differences at all between production saloons and special order limousines.

Interior identification points

From 1964 the last of the 3.8-litre Mark Xs and all 4.2-litre Mark Xs were fitted with a revised heating system with enhanced controls as seen here.

Mark X/420G (all models)
- Dashboard layout similar to Mark 2 and E-type models with speedometer and rev counter directly in front of driver and ancillary gauges and switchgear on centre panel slightly recessed, in the case of the Mark X models finished in matching veneer to the rest of the dashboard.
- Wrap-around veneered top rail and lower panels of dashboard, meeting doors at extreme ends with chrome finishers.
- Passenger-side lockable glovebox with chromed handle.
- Under-dashboard full-length oddments shelf.
- Further shelves on front sides of the car below dashboard.
- Steering column mounted indicator stalk and, where fitted, automatic transmission quadrant (or overdrive switch).
- One-piece black plastic-coated steering wheel with two-spoke centre boss incorporating gold growler badge and surround, and half horn ring (with centre boss also operational for horn use).
- Substantial trimmed central console incorporating two chrome surround radio speakers to the side, vacuum heater control buttons, veneered ashtray and audio area and gearlever (manual models), console extending rearward between front bench-style seats to rear compartment heater extractor vents with on/off switch.
- Umbrella-style handbrake sited next to centre console speaker trim on driver's side.
- Padded door trims to match interior finish with veneered cappings and chromed door and window winder handles plus shaped armrests.
- Front seats sculptured to bench style with individual centre armrests that folded away, vertical pleating, and reclining adjustment for seat backs.

Above left: The rear compartment of Mark X/420G models did not change except for the use of aerated leather upholstery centre panels on the 420G models from 1967.

Above right: When equipped with electrically operated windows, a centre veneered panel was fitted to the console in the front of the car with separate chromed buttons in the rear doors.

With the introduction of the revised model from 1967, re-badged 420G, a prominent centre vane was added to the radiator grille, and side indicator repeater lights were incorporated into the front wings. Where single-colour exterior paint schemes were applied, a chromed swage line trim ran the entire length of the body.

The Mark X/420G saloons 1961 to 1970

- Rear compartment trimmed to match, with bench seat arrangement with central armrest.
- Rears of front seats incorporated veneered picnic tables and matching ashtrays.
- Carpeted throughout with vinyl-trimmed sill areas.
- Boot entirely Hardura covered including spare wheel with full tool box affixed to offside of boot between spare wheel and trim.

NB: Where cars were specified with electric windows the rear doors incorporated chrome window switches. The centre console included a veneered switch panel with four chromed switches to operate any of the four windows electrically.

Mark X 3.8-litre models
- Very late 3.8-litre models featured revised heater controls (see 4.2-litre below).

Mark X 4.2-litre models
- As 3.8 except for revised heater controls with four control levers in a veneered surround at the top of the centre console, above the ashtray and below the oddments shelf. These controlled airflow to each side of the car.

Mark X 4.2-litre limousine models
- As other Mark Xs except for central glass sliding division above front seats.
- Front seats have a solid bench backrest.
- Rear of backrest is fitted out with same picnic tables as saloons, and ashtrays, but with enhanced veneering along the full width.
- In the centre of the back of the front seat a solid wood (veneered) magazine rack incorporating two cigarette lighters (removed from the B/C post areas on saloons) and an auxiliary rectangular clock.
- At least one car was fitted with a cocktail cabinet arrangement instead of the above.

420G models
- Restyled dashboard top rail incorporating centrally mounted rectangular clock flanked by padded black Ambla trim on either side offering a degree of crash padding.
- Padding to top full-width oddments tray now always finished in black instead of trim colour.
- Automatic transmission quadrant control lever on steering column (where fitted) extended and with round black ball tip.
- Aerated leather centre trims to front and rear seats.
- Sill coverings now carpet instead of Ambla.

420G limousine models
- As Mark X limousines except for other 420G changes, listed previously, and revised rear magazine rack design.

Above left: With the introduction of the 420G, coinciding with other model changes within Jaguar, this new style of hubcap was fitted, now depicting a growler head emblem instead of the word 'Jaguar'.

Above right: 420G rear compartment with aerated leather panels. All Mark Xs and the 420G featured the lighter hue to woodwork.

The 420G was also available with two-tone exterior paint finishes, when a simple coachline was added to separate the two colours instead of the chromed trim.

A very small number of Mark X 4.2 and 420G limousines were produced. These had a centre division and a magazine rack or radio compartment fitted.

Technical specifications

	3.8-litre	4.2-litre
cc	3781	4235
Bore and stroke (mm)	87 x 106	92.07 x 106
Compression ratio	8:1 (7:1/9:1 optional)	8:1 (7:1/9:1 optional)
bhp	265	265
@ rpm	5500	5400
Torque (lb ft)	260	283
@ rpm	4000	4000
Fuelling	3 x SU carbs	3 x SU carbs
Transmission	4-speed (3 synchro) BW 3-speed auto	4-speed (all synchro) BW 3-speed auto
Wheel size (in)	14, steel	14, steel
Suspension front	Ind semi-trailing wishbones, coil springs, anti-roll bar	Ind semi-trailing wishbones, coil springs, anti-roll bar
Suspension rear	Ind lower wishbone/upper driveshaft link, radius arms, coil springs	Ind lower wishbone/upper driveshaft link, radius arms, coil springs
Brakes	4-wheel disc, rear inboard	4-wheel disc, rear inboard
Performance		
0–60mph (sec)	9.1	9.9
Top speed (mph)	119.5	121.5
Average mpg	14.1	14.5
Dimensions		
Length (in)	202	202
Width (in)	76	76
Height (in)	54.75	54.75
Wheelbase (in)	120	120
Front track (in)	58	58
Rear track (in)	58	58
Weight (cwt)	37	37

Optional extras

Choice of three radio installations with or without rear parcel shelf-mounted speaker.
Electric radio aerial.
Wind-up radio aerial.
Electrically operated windows (front and rear).
Laminated windscreen.
Witter tow bar.
Heated rear screen (earlier cars).
Front seat belts.
Choice of radial, town and country, or whitewall tyres.

Borg Warner automatic transmission.
Overdrive (for non-overdrive-equipped manual transmission cars).
Fire extinguisher.
Sundym tinted windscreen and side windows.
Wing mirrors.
Integrated ignition/starter switch to steering column.
Limousine appointments (only available on ordering a new car).

7 Colour schemes

Exterior colour Single	Details	Interior trim	Details
Mark X 3.8-litre models			
Pearl Grey		Red	
		Grey	To 1964
		Light Blue	To 1964
		Dark Blue	
Mist Grey		Red	
		Light Blue	To 1964
		Dark Blue	To 1964
		Grey	To 1964
Old English White		Red	To 1964
		Black	
		Light Blue	To 1964
		Dark Blue	To 1964
Carmen Red		Red	
		Beige	To 1964
		Black	1964
Sherwood Green		Suede Green	
		Light Tan	
		Tan	To 1964
		Cinnamon	1964
Cotswold Blue	To 1964	Dark Blue	
		Light Blue	
		Grey	
Black		Red	
		Grey	
		Light Tan	
		Tan	To 1964
		Cinnamon	1964
Opalescent Dark Green		Suede Green	
		Tan	
		Beige	
		Light Tan	To 1964
		Cinnamon	1964
Opalescent Blue		Dark Blue	
		Light Blue	To 1964
		Grey	To 1964
		Red	
Opalescent Gunmetal		Red	
		Light Blue	To 1964
		Dark Blue	
		Grey	To 1964
		Beige	

Exterior colour Single	Details	Interior trim	Details
Opalescent Silver Grey		Red	
		Light Blue	To 1964
		Grey	
		Dark Blue	
Opalescent Silver Blue		Dark Blue	
		Grey	
Opalescent Bronze	From late 1962	Red	
		Beige	
		Tan	
Opalescent Golden Sand	From 1963	Black	
		Beige	
Opalescent Maroon	From 1963	Maroon	
		Beige	
British Racing Green	1964	Suede Green	
		Beige	
		Light Tan	
		Cinnamon	
Mark X 4.2-litre models			
Carmen Red		Black	
Old English White		Black	
		Maroon	
Primrose Yellow		Black	
		Beige	
Sherwood Green		Suede Green	
		Light Tan	
		Cinnamon	
Dark Blue		Red	
		Grey	
Black		Red	
		Grey	
		Light Tan	
		Cinnamon	
Opalescent Dark Green		Suede Green	
		Cinnamon	
		Beige	
		Light Tan	
Opalescent Silver Grey		Red	
		Dark Blue	
		Grey	
Opalescent Silver Blue		Dark Blue	
		Grey	
Opalescent Golden Sand		Red	
		Light Tan	

Colour schemes *cont ...*

Exterior colour Single	Details	Interior trim	Details
Opalescent Maroon		Maroon	
		Beige	
Warwick Grey		Red	
		Light Tan	
		Dark Blue	
420G models			
Old English White		Red	
		Light Blue	
		Dark Blue	
Dark Blue		Light Blue	
		Grey	
		Red	
Black		Red	
		Grey	
		Light Tan	To 1968
		Cinnamon	
Warwick Grey		Red	
		Cinnamon	
		Dark Blue	
Willow Green		Beige	
		Suede Green	
		Cinnamon	
		Grey	
British Racing Green		Suede Green	
		Beige	
		Cinnamon	
Beige	To 1968	Red	
		Light Tan	
		Cinnamon	
Sable Brown	From 1968	Beige	
		Grey	
		Cinnamon	
Light Blue	From 1968	Dark Blue	
		Light Blue	
		Grey	
Regency Red	From 1968	Beige	
		Grey	
Opalescent Golden Sand	To 1968	Red	
		Light Tan	
Opalescent Silver Blue	To 1968	Dark Blue	
		Grey	

Exterior colour Single	Details	Interior trim	Details
Opalescent Silver Grey	To 1968	Red	
		Light Blue	
		Dark Blue	
		Grey	
Opalescent Maroon	To 1968	Maroon	
		Beige	
Ascot Fawn	From 1968	Red	
		Beige	
		Cinnamon	

Duotones Exterior top	Exterior bottom	Details	Interior
Black	Silver Grey	To 1968	Red
			Grey
			Light Tan
			Cinnamon
Black	Golden Sand	To 1968	Red
			Grey
			Light Tan
			Cinnamon
British Racing Green	Willow Green		Suede Green
			Beige
			Light Tan
			Cinnamon
Dark Blue	Silver Blue		Red
			Light Blue
			Grey
Black	Ascot Fawn	From 1968	Red
			Grey
			Cinnamon
Black	Warwick Grey	From 1968	Red
			Grey
			Cinnamon

Prices and production volumes

	Price new (£)	1961	1962	1963	1964	1965	1966
Mark X 3.8-litre	2392	■	■	■	■	–	–
Mark X 4.2-litre	2156	–	–	–	■	■	■
420G	2237	–	–	–	–	–	■

	Price new (£)	1967	1968	1969	1970	Total produced
Mark X 3.8-litre	2392	–	–	–	–	12,961
Mark X 4.2-litre	2156	–	–	–	–	5672
420G	2237	■	■	■	■	5542
Total production						**24,175**

Production changes

1961
Mark X 3.8-litre introduced.

1962
Oval ashtray on centre console replaced by rectangular style.
Heated rear screen provided.

1963
Larger brake pedal fitted to automatic transmission cars.
'Live' centre boss horn button fixed to steering wheel.

1964
Separate radiator header tank added.
Revised heating system fitted.
4.2-litre Mark X introduced, along with special order limousine model.

1966
Separate on/off switch added for heated rear screen.
Air-conditioning system now available.
420G model introduced.
(December) 4.2-litre Mark X discontinued.

1969
XJ6-type brake servos fitted.
Electric dash clock replaced by battery-driven type.
Military versions based on the limousine were specially produced for the military, designated 'B'.

1970
(June) 420G discontinued.

Chassis numbers

Model	Right/left drive	Chassis/VIN commencing
Mark X 3.8	RHD	300001
	LHD	350001
Mark X 4.2	RHD	1D 50001
	LHD	1D 75001
420G	RHD	GID 53720
	LHD	GID 76961

The S-type and 420 saloons
1963 to 1969

Background

Jaguar had undergone terrific expansion in the 1960s, beginning with the successful launch of the Mark 2 saloons late in 1959, then with the E-type sports car and Mark X models in 1961, plus a rebirth of the Daimler marque in the form of the 2.5-litre V8 saloon based on the Mark 2.

For 1963 William Lyons introduced another new model, this time as a 'filler' to bridge the gap between the very sporty Mark 2 saloon and the flagship Mark X, utilising as many mechanical parts as possible in order to keep the cost of production down and be able to market the new model at a reasonable price. The result – the S-type saloon.

The marketing strategy proved a good idea, for although total production numbers were far from those of the Mark 2, the S-type provided an opportunity for those who wanted something more sophisticated and upmarket, and perhaps less sporty, to stay with the Jaguar marque and avoid the big Mark X, a car not to everyone's liking, particularly if you didn't need one that size. Announced in September 1963 and only in production until 1968, 25,000 S-types were produced, effectively 25,000 more sales than Jaguar might have achieved without this model.

Though based heavily on the larger-engined Mark 2 saloons, slightly improved interiors, a better equipment level, and a bigger boot, plus the sophisticated independent rear suspension of the E-type and Mark X, allowed Jaguar to sell the S-type at a premium price.

With the reasonable success of the S-type, Jaguar looked to another interim model to boost sales further and to cater for yet another wider sector of the luxury market. Enter the 420. Substantially based on the S-type, the 420 arrived in October 1966 with the bigger 4.2-litre XK engine, further enhancements to the interior trim, and a completely revised front end treatment more in keeping with the Mark X. Costing more than the S-type, the 420 created a 'notch up' for the Jaguar driver who wanted to enhance his or her image without, again, entering the big Mark X market.

Another significant move with the 420 was the availability of a Daimler model. Like the Daimler version of the Mark 2, the Sovereign (as the 420 car was called) featured external details emulating the Daimler marque. However, for the first time this car was to be very much a badge-engineered Jaguar, and was the first Daimler to be fitted with the Jaguar XK power unit.

By this time (1966) the Jaguar saloon car range had expanded to no less than nine models, offering a wide choice to the luxury car buying public. But in line with Jaguar's later policy of model reduction, and leading up to the introduction of the XJ6, in mid-1968 the 3.8-litre S-type was dropped, and in August, just one month before the announcement of the XJ6, the 3.4-litre car was also discontinued. By September the Jaguar 420 had also disappeared from the listings, although the Daimler Sovereign version remained available well into 1969 – that is, until a Daimler XJ6 was available.

The S-type and 420 models are often overlooked by enthusiasts these days as they are not as sporty and sought-after as the Mark 2s. Nevertheless, they made an important addition to the Jaguar range in the 1960s and were actually very good cars in their own right. Over 40,000 examples were produced, which in total accounts for a significant number of saloon car sales in the 1960s.

Model range and development

When the S-type was announced in September 1963 it was based on just two versions with manual/manual with overdrive or automatic transmissions.

Models available at launch
S-type 3.4-litre saloon
S-type 3.8-litre saloon

Aimed, as it was, at another sector of the market to the Mark 2, it was only ever offered with either the 3.4-litre or 3.8-litre versions of the XK engine, in performance terms exactly the same as the Mark 2 equivalent. These were mated to the same transmissions and front suspension but with the sophisticated independent rear subframe assembly taken from the Mark X saloon. Twin fuel tanks were fitted at the rear, one in each wing instead of the single boot-mounted type in the Mark 2. The steering lock to lock was also slightly improved.

Externally the design was true to Jaguar, with an amalgamation of ideas from the Mark 2 and Mark X. The latter donated the style of the rear end – and thus an enlarged boot area to the Mark 2 – while the centre section was taken virtually exactly from the Mark 2, although with a slightly longer and flatter roof line, and at the front a smoothing out and to some little extent modernising of the Mark 2 'look' with peaked headlights, wrap-around indicators, slimline bumper treatment, and more pronounced radiator grille.

Internally the dash layout took its style from the Mark X, with the centre section in wood veneer with a similar split-bench seat arrangement yet without rear picnic tables. A prominent centre console arrangement also echoed the Mark X, with trim detail taken from that and the Mark 2. Never intended as a real sporting model, the S-type was available with wire wheels but, unlike the Mark 2, it never entered competition during its production life.

Manufacture of the S-type slowed down in 1968, resulting in the demise of the larger-engined model in June that year and the 3.4-litre model two months later. During the time of its production very little changed on the model, although later on fog lamps were replaced by

The 1960s S-type is identifiable from the Mark 2 – from which it was derived – and the later 420 by the frontal treatment seen here: slightly cowled headlights with inset fog lamps without heavy surrounds of the Mark 2 style, wrap-around indicator lights with inset sidelights, and slimline bumper bar treatment, similar to later 240/340 models. The radiator grille also has a more prominent surround.

From the side, the S-type is instantly identifiable by its elongated rear wings and larger boot area, and the absence of spats over the rear wheels. Wire wheels were an extra-cost option when new.

grilles, and Ambla upholstery became the norm instead of leather just as the Mark 2s changed over to the 240/340.

The 420 arrived mid-stream during S-type production, in October 1966, as a further enhancement to the Jaguar saloon car range. Essentially from the windscreen back the car was pure S-type externally, and even internally only benefited from minor styling changes. At the front, however, the 420 took on the styling of the Mark X, being more angular with four-headlamp treatment and a traditional grille leaning forward.

Under the skin the 420 was only available with the 4.2-litre, twin carburettor XK power unit, mated to either a manual (all-synchromesh) gearbox, with or without overdrive or automatic transmission. An improved cooling system was also adopted and the power-assisted steering (still an extra-cost option) was of the Marles Varamatic type seen on the later Mark Xs. As the basic 420 cost about £200 more than the 3.8-litre S-type, it provided another move up the ladder for Jaguar drivers aspiring to a better car.

The 420 was also the first Jaguar to get effectively badge-engineered into a Daimler model, called the Sovereign. With no mechanical changes at all, the Sovereign merely took on traditional Daimler features like the fluted grille, badging, etc, but again sold at a slightly higher price, allowing it to appeal to another market just as the V8 had done earlier in the decade. A Daimler Sovereign with automatic transmission cost £2198, very close to the price of the larger 420G.

No significant changes took place in 420 design during its relatively short lifespan, and with Jaguar's change in marketing strategy in the late 1960s it was dropped from the range in September 1968, although the Daimler Sovereign continued on into 1969. Over 15,000 420s and Sovereigns were produced in this short period, which equated to roughly the same annual sales as the S-type, both models serving to expand Jaguar's customer base using mostly the same mechanical parts.

Exterior identification points

General points applicable to all S-types
Front view
- Similar frontal aspect to Mark 2 except for removal of sidelights to lower section of wings with accompanying wrap-around indicator lenses.
- Inset fog lamps below headlights which feature 'eyebrows'.
- Radiator grille has a more prominent chrome surround than Mark 2 with the appropriate 'litre' badge centre top.
- Slimline bumper treatment as 240/340.

From the rear the S-type shows its larger boot area, similarly designed to the Mark X/420G. It also used the Mark X style of rear lights and number plate surround. Twin tailpipes emitted from underneath in the centre, as with the Mark X, rather than at the sides like the Mark 2.

Above left: Front interior layout of the S-type differed from the Mark 2, with flatter semi-split-bench seating, revised plusher door trims, and enhanced centre console area. There was also now an under-dash parcel shelf, not seen on Mark 2s but found on Mark Xs.

Above right: The S-type dashboard layout followed normal 1960s Jaguar practice, in this case with wood-veneered centre panel and oddments tray à la Mark X.

Rear compartment of the S-type, similar to but subtly different from the Mark 2, with modified seat patterning, revised door trims, and no occasional fold-down tables.

Rear view
- At the rear it was a smaller version of the Mark X/420G model design, with the same exhaust and trim treatment.
- Cars carried the usual 'Jaguar' script on the boot lid plus litreage, 'S-type', and 'automatic' badging as applicable.
- Enlarged rear window area with chromed surround.

Side view
- Quickly identifiable by the wrap-around front indicator lenses and extended rear wings.
- Elongated rear wings showing most of the rear wheels (no spats fitted).
- Each rear wing featured a lift-up panel for access to fuel filler caps.
- A flatter roof section, but otherwise all other aspects as the Mark 2.

General points applicable to all 420s

Front view
- Similar frontal aspect to the Mark X although on a smaller scale. Four-headlight treatment (no fog lamps).
- Same sidelights and indicator units as Mark X/S-type.
- Squared-off forward-leaning chrome radiator grille with vertical slats.
- Rectangular horn grilles fitted below each inner headlight.
- Slimline bumper bar with matching forward-leaning overriders but without curved centre section of the S-type. Centrally mounted number plate plinth.
- Revised front wings to accommodate outer headlights with more pronounced shaping.
- New bonnet pressing, flatter in appearance and terminating back from the grille.

Rear view
- As S-type except for the badging never showing litreage.

Side view
- As S-type except for pronounced squaring-off of front wings.
- All 420s were fitted with the later chromed hubcaps used on the 420G/240, 340, etc.

420 saloon specifics

Jaguar 420
- Mark X-style radiator grille with pronounced top section incorporating winged badge.
- Small (Mark X-sized) leaper mascot mounted on in-fill panel between radiator grille and bonnet.
- '420' badging on centre of boot lid accompanying 'Jaguar' and, where applicable, 'automatic'.

The 420 model took styling features from the Mark X, adding them to the existing S-type style. It was identifiable from the S-type by its four-headlight treatment and wider rectangular forward-leaning radiator grille, and from the Mark X by its smaller dimensions and rectangular horn grilles.

The second Jaguar design to be engineered into a Daimler, the 420 Sovereign utilised a traditional fluted radiator grille.

The rear of the 420 is visually the same as the S-type except for badging, this example being a Daimler Sovereign. This was the first Daimler model not to feature a rear number plate plinth in fluted form.

Daimler Sovereign
- Fluted radiator grille with pronounced centre chrome strip terminating at the edge of the bonnet.
- Daimler scripted 'D' in chrome featured at edge of bonnet, continuing back in the form of a centre chrome strip the full length of the bonnet.
- Scripted 'D' insignia on hubcap centres.
- At the rear a number plate light/reversing light plinth features the Daimler name.
- 'Daimler' and 'Sovereign' badging on boot lid, plus 'automatic' where applicable.

Interior identification points

S-type (all models)
- Centre dashboard section in wood veneer with pull-out veneered tray beneath legend.
- Steering wheel of the later Mark X style with active centre horn push and half horn ring.
- Full-width parcel shelf beneath dashboard with chromed heater controls in centre section.
- Mark X-style centre console with side-mounted speaker grilles, veneered ashtray and audio position, plus push-button ventilation controls (as Mark X).
- Flatter-section split-bench-style front seating with vertical pleats (aerated on later models). Reclining and fore and aft movement provided some degree of height adjustment.
- Front door trims incorporated elasticated map pockets.
- Rear compartment with more sculptured bench seat arrangement to Mark 2, with fold-down centre armrest.
- Rear of front seats plain (without pull-down picnic tables).
- Rear door trims with built-in armrests and wider pockets than Mark 2.
- Interior door locks activated by chromed 'knobs' as used on Mark VII to IX models.

420 (all models)
- As S-type except centre veneered dash panel sits flush with left- and right-hand panels.
- Dashboard woodwork surrounded by black vinyl crash padding, at the top centre a rectangular clock fitted as 420G model.
- Seats of slightly different proportions to S-type although looking very similar.
- Door trim panels feature only top cappings in wood with similar treatment at the rear.

Daimler Sovereign
- As 420 except for scripted 'D' in centre horn push boss on steering wheel.

Rear three-quarter view of the 420, demonstrating the same profile as on the S-type except for the shape at the leading edge of the front wings.

Comparison of S-type and 420 front views.

Above left: 420 and Sovereign models featured subtle changes to the interior trim, with slimmer wood cappings to the door panels and a soft padded dashboard top rail that continued around the edges of the dashboard to form a degree of crash padding. As well as other minor control changes the clock was relocated to the top centre of the dashboard.

Above right: Seat design of S-type and 420 models.

Technical specifications

	3.4-litre S-type	3.8-litre S-type
cc	3442	3781
Bore and stroke (mm)	83 x 106	87 x 106
Compression ratio	8:1 (7:1/9:1 optional)	8:1 (7:1/9:1 optional)
bhp	210	220
@ rpm	5500	5500
Torque (lb ft)	216	240
@ rpm	3000	3000
Fuelling	2 x SU carbs	2 x SU carbs
Transmission	4-speed (3 synchro), later all synchro BW 3-speed auto	4-speed (3 synchro), later all synchro BW 3-speed auto
Wheel size (in)	15, steel, wires optional	15, steel, wires optional
Suspension front	Ind semi-trailing wishbones, coil springs, anti-roll bar	Ind semi-trailing wishbones, coil springs, anti-roll bar
Suspension rear	Ind lower wishbones/upper driveshaft link, radius arms, coil springs	Ind lower wishbones/upper driveshaft link, radius arms, coil springs
Brakes	4-wheel disc, rear inboard	4-wheel disc, rear inboard
Performance		
0–60mph (sec)	13.9	10.2
Top speed (mph)	119	121
Average mpg	14–17	15.4
Dimensions		
Length (in)	187	187
Width (in)	66.25	66.25
Height (in)	55.75	55.75
Wheelbase (in)	107.5	107.5
Front track (in)	55.25	55.25
Rear track	54.25	54.25
Weight (cwt)	32	33

Optional extras

Choice of three radio installations with or without rear parcel shelf-mounted speaker.
Laminated windscreen.
Witter tow bar.
Front seat belts.

Choice of radial, town and country, or whitewall tyres.
Borg Warner automatic transmission.
Overdrive (for non-overdrive-equipped manual transmission cars).

	420/Sovereign
cc	4235
Bore and stroke (mm)	92.07 x 106
Compression ratio	8:1 (7:1/9:1 optional)
bhp	245
@ rpm	5500
Torque (lb ft)	283
@ rpm	3750
Fuelling	2 x SU carbs
Transmission	4-speed (3 synchro), later all synchro BW 3-speed auto
Wheel size (in)	15, steel, wires optional
Suspension front	Ind semi-trailing wishbones, coil springs, anti-roll bar
Suspension rear	Ind lower wishbones/upper driveshaft link, radius arms, coil springs
Brakes	4-wheel disc, rear inboard
Performance	
0–60mph (sec)	9.9
Top speed (mph)	123
Average mpg	15.7
Dimensions	
Length (in)	187.5
Width (in)	67
Height (in)	56.25
Wheelbase (in)	107.75
Front track (in)	55.25
Rear track	54.5
Weight (cwt)	33

Wire wheels with conversion kit for hubs, etc.
Fire extinguisher.
Sundym tinted windscreen and side windows.
Wing mirrors.

Integrated ignition/starter switch to steering column.
Power-assisted steering.

Colour schemes

Exterior colour	Details	Interior trim
Pearl Grey	To 1966	Red
		Light Blue
		Dark Blue
		Grey
Warwick Grey	From 1966	Red
		Tan
Dove Grey	To 1966	Red
		Tan
		Grey
Carmen Red	To 1966	Red
		Black
Imperial Maroon	To 1966	Red
Old English White		Red
		Tan
Primrose Yellow	From 1964	Red
		Tan
		Black
Honey Beige	From 1966	Red
		Tan
British Racing Green		Suede Green
		Tan
		Champagne
Sherwood Green	To 1966	Suede Green
		Tan
Willow Green	From 1966	Suede Green
		Black
		Champagne
Indigo Blue		Light Blue
		Dark Blue
		Grey
Black		Red
		Tan
Opalescent Dark Green	To 1966	Suede Green
		Tan
		Champagne
Opalescent Blue	To 1966	Dark Blue
		Light Blue
		Grey
		Red
Opalescent Gunmetal		Red
		Tan
Opalescent Silver Grey		Red
		Tan
		Grey
Opalescent Silver Blue	To 1966	Dark Blue
		Light Blue
		Grey
		Red
Opalescent Golden Sand	1966 only	Red
		Tan
Opalescent Maroon	From 1966	Red
		Champagne
		Tan
Signal Red	From 1966	Black
		Red
		Beige
Regency Maroon	From 1966	Red
		Beige
Old English White	Replaced by 'White' in 1968	Black
		Red
Ascot Fawn	From 1966	Black
		Red
Sable Brown	From 1966	Beige
		Red
		Black
Pale Blue	From 1966	Dark Blue
		Red
		Black

Prices and production volumes

	Price new (£)	1963	1964	1965	1966	1967	1968
3.4-litre S-type	1669	■	■	■	■	■	■
3.8-litre S-type	1758	■	■	■	■	■	■
420 saloon	1930	–	–	–	■	■	■
Daimler Sovereign	2121	–	–	–	■	■	■

	Price new (£)	1969	Total produced
3.4-litre S-type	1669	–	9928
3.8-litre S-type	1758	–	15,065
420 saloon	1930	–	10,236
Daimler Sovereign	2121	■	5824
Total production			**41,053**

Production changes

1963
S-type 3.4- and 3.8-litre saloons introduced.

1964
One-piece front carpets fitted.
PVC heel pads fitted to carpets.

1965
Hazard-light system for export models.
All-synchromesh manual gearbox fitted.
Revised clutch to fit above gearbox.

1966
240/340/250 introduced.
420 models introduced.
Ambla upholstery fitted to S-types.
Fog lamps deleted on S-type models.

1967
Power-assisted steering standardised on Daimler Sovereign.

1968
Non-eared spinners fitted to wire-wheel cars (all markets).
Revised water temperature gauge fitted with coloured segments.
S-types and 420 discontinued.

1969
Damiler Sovereign discontinued.

Chassis numbers

Model	Right/left drive	Chassis/VIN commencing
S-type 3.4	RHD	1B 1001
	LHD	1B 25001
S-type 3.8	RHD	1B 50001
	LHD	1B 75001
420	RHD	1F 1001
	LHD	1F 25001
Daimler Sov 420	RHD	1A 30001
	LHD	1A 70001

9 The XJ Series saloons
1968 to 1992

Background

Launched in 1968, the XJ6 was arguably the most important model ever produced by Jaguar up to that time – a car that set new standards of refinement and a car by which others would be judged for many years to come. It also brought to fruition a one-model policy, effectively replacing all other saloons produced by Jaguar at that time, namely the 240/340/V8 250, the 420/Sovereign, and the 420G. This policy could have been devastating for the company, yet proved to be an incredible success.

Surprisingly there was nothing really new about the XJ6. It still used the XK six-cylinder engine (in 420 form), linked to the same gearboxes and independent rear suspension. There was a second version with a new (2.8-litre) configuration of the XK power unit, intended to help sales in tax-/engine-size-conscious countries. At the front the XJ did feature a new suspension with anti-dive characteristics, and with new technology Jaguar was able to isolate the body from road noise significantly better than anyone else at the time. Dunlop designed new tyres for the car, which also helped.

Stylistically it was still a Jaguar, with the typical four-headlight treatment but, for the first time since the Mark VII, without a prominent, typically Jaguar radiator grille – instead a rather egg-crate design was decided upon. The car also displayed a new 'hump' in the rear quarters and a more angular rear-end style. Internally it was all new except for the layout of the dashboard, although even here new technology had been used and there was more concern for safety and crash padding.

At only £1,897 for the 2.8-litre model Jaguar had done it again, offering the ultimate in refinement and handling at a bargain basement price. Compared to the competition of the day – even the Rolls-Royce Silver Shadow – the XJ6 was quieter, faster, even more refined, and handled significantly better.

The marketing ploy of effectively offering just two cars, both virtually identical except for the engine size, paid off handsomely for Jaguar. Few people at the time missed the smaller saloons, as the XJ6 was so far ahead in driveability. It was initially envisaged that there would also be a base 'standard' model, offered without many of the by then common extras, but very few were actually made and it was never available as a production model. Even the 2.8-litre model didn't sell as well as expected, and in service problems were experienced with the engine anyway.

It wasn't until 1969 that a Daimler derivative was offered, taking the Sovereign name from the old 420. From here the range of models expanded dramatically when Jaguar announced in 1972 that there was to be a V12-engined version, the same engine seen a year earlier in the E-type sports car. Then, with XJ6 and XJ12 models in both Jaguar and Daimler guise, there were even two sizes of wheelbase available, and a top of the range Vanden Plas saloon for the ultimate in luxury and equipment. V12 Series 1 XJs were only ever available with automatic transmission.

Over 98,000 of the Series 1 XJs were produced up to 1973 when, mainly due to the ongoing demands of safety and environmental issues abroad, the car developed into the Series 2. All the models followed suit from the Series 1 cars except for the 2.8-litre engine, which was dropped in favour of another new configuration (3.4 litres). On top of this Jaguar announced another new body style, the coupé, based on the shorter wheelbase floorpan and built with only two doors, with pillarless window surrounds and a vinyl roof. Difficulties in production resulted in the coupé models appearing on the market late, and they were discontinued early on for the same reason and because of the need to expand production of the four-door models, which by this time were selling better than ever.

For the first time in their history Jaguar chose to ask an outside coachbuilder to redesign the XJ saloon to bring it more up to date, and Pininfarina did a fine job in revitalising the style to become the Series 3 from 1978. Although looking very similar to the old Series 2 design it was significantly improved, with more window space, a higher roof line, flush-mounted door handles, new trim, and a better interior. Once again it was made available in all four-door forms, from base 3.4-litre Jaguar to Daimler Vanden Plas, in both six- and twelve-cylinder variants.

Jaguar experienced many problems of poor build quality and lack of mechanical reliability in the 1970s, an image that stuck throughout the company's British Leyland period. It wasn't until Jaguar was privatised in the 1980s that matters started to improve, helped by its then new boss John Egan. The Series 3 XJs saw the company through this period and not only into profit but, with an incredibly improved product and reputation, from success to success.

The models were continually updated. The Jaguar name was taking prominence over Daimler by this time, and Jaguar lost the right to use the Vanden Plas name in the UK, although retaining it in the US. The Series 3 remained in production until 1987 for the six-cylinder models, 1991 for the V12 Jaguars, and 1992 for the V12 Daimlers – long after the appearance of a completely new replacement model (the XJ40) in 1986.

The XJ Series Jaguars must be considered a tribute not only to Sir William Lyons, who saw the car through to production in 1968, but also to the revival of the Jaguar marque in the 1980s. Even today the XJ is still considered to be one of the company's classic designs. With over 400,000 produced from 1968 to 1992, it has left a legacy that even today Jaguar refer back to.

Model range and development

All models were initially available with manual, manual with overdrive, or automatic transmission.

Models available at launch

Jaguar XJ6 2.8-litre standard saloon
Jaguar XJ6 2.8-litre saloon
Jaguar XJ6 4.2-litre saloon

The Series 1 XJ models were available in both short and long-wheelbase models, the latter being identifiable by its wider rear doors, as here. This model is the Daimler Vanden Plas version, recognisable by its vinyl roof covering (always black) and chromed swage line trim.

The Series 1 XJ6 is identified from the front by the 'egg-crate' style of radiator grille with gold growler badge. The Daimler versions featured a more pronounced fluted radiator grille with vertical slats and a chrome centre line running the entire length of the bonnet.

XJ12 Series 1 models are identified from the front by the vertical slatted grille with 'V' emblem.

Although originally listed, the 'standard' model never went into serious production and it is generally considered that only prototypes were actually made.

Perhaps not surprisingly only about a third of the Series 1 cars sold had the 2.8-litre engine, and after some time on the road they acquired a bad reputation for 'holing' a piston. This ultimately also affected resale values. In contrast the 4.2-litre model was building on previous success and offered better performance, smoother running, and improved handling than the 420G that it replaced.

Overall the Series 1 XJ6 was very well accepted, which is reflected in its sales, and apart from minor manufacturing changes little was altered during the first year of full production. In 1969 the company introduced a wider range of models, capitalising on the Daimler name at the same time by replacing the 420 Sovereign. The choice of engine size now covered both marques and production was made much easier by the effective badge-engineering of the two brands from what was ultimately the same car.

The XJ6 bodyshell had always been designed with the V12 engine in mind but, in keeping with Jaguar policy, the new engine was 'trial launched' in a lower-volume sports car first – in this case the E-type. The V12 XJ, known as the XJ12, didn't therefore appear until July 1972. It offered buyers a slightly higher specification of equipment (air-conditioning as standard, etc), all-round improved mechanics to cope with the power, and a much more attractive vertical slatted radiator grille.

Along with the XJ12 came the natural progression to Daimler, and in September 1972 the first of the long-wheelbase bodyshells appeared with another new model, the Daimler Double Six Vanden Plas, resurrecting Daimler's old Double Six model name from the 1920s. This was effectively a hand-finished car by the VDP coachworks in London, with enhanced interior and exterior trim. The long-wheelbase shell provided substantially more legroom in the rear compartment for passengers, something the shorter wheelbase model lacked compared to the old Mark X/420G design. The release of the Double Six was followed a month later by the introduction of long-wheelbase bodyshells for the other models, resulting in quite an extensive range of cars, but all still based on the one original design.

Just a year later the whole XJ range was substantially altered to become the Series 2, with an improved bodyshell with side impact bars, a virtually sealed-off front bulkhead from the passenger compartment, and new technology like fibre optic lighting and multi-pin plug connections. Externally the car benefited from a makeover, more because of changing

Rear view of the Series 1 XJ model. Apart from badging the same view applied to all Jaguar models, although this is a post-1969 model with different reflector lighting and curved tailpipes. The inset picture shows one of the earliest cars, with reflectors set into the reversing light units. Early cars also had straight pipe exhausts.

Daimler Series 1 models differed at the rear in their badging and the fluted plinth surmounting the boot lock.

Steel wheels were the norm on Series 1 XJs of all models. Basic 2.8-litre cars did not feature chromed rimbellishers, although other models did.

regulations over safety, bumper height, etc, in the United States than for aesthetic reasons. The Series 2 models are easily identifiable by their shallower radiator grille and raised bumper level at the front. The internal layout was revised and redesigned and a proper air-conditioning system was introduced for the first time.

The range announced at launch was extensive, although some of the cars didn't actually appear until much later. Short and long-wheelbase versions were offered throughout, as were 4.2 and 5.3 (V12) engines. Although originally listed the 2.8-litre wasn't made in any great numbers and was totally replaced by a new 3.4-litre-engined model in April 1975. Aimed at a possible fleet market, the specification and trim level were down and the car was only available in short wheelbase form, other short wheelbase models dropping from the range by the end of 1974.

An entirely new concept for the Series 2 was a short wheelbase two-door coupé model, also offered in both Jaguar and Daimler forms and with 4.2- or 5.3-litre engines. Although originally announced back in September 1973, it took until 1975 to get the car into viable production, which must have affected its popularity to some extent as few were actually made compared to four-door saloons. Constant problems over supply and build quality resulted in the early demise of the coupé versions in late 1977, although demand for conventional saloons held up remarkably well, even given changing circumstances at Jaguar under British Leyland ownership.

Jaguar announced the next generation of XJ saloons, known as the Series 3, at the end of 1978, although the Series 2 models were still produced until February 1979. As mentioned above, the new models were significant make-overs stylistically, with the help of Pininfarina in Italy. Only a single (long) wheelbase shell was available initially, in all three engine sizes and both Jaguar and Daimler guises, plus the Vanden Plas (now expanded to include both six- and twelve-cylinder models).

Series 3 models are easily recognisable by the raised roof line and larger window areas plus the flush-mounted door handles and rubber-faced bumper bars. The essence of the design was a lighter passenger compartment, slightly more angular approach to external styling, and general updating.

While Jaguar remained in British Leyland ownership there were problems over build quality with the Series 3, and in particular with its exterior paint finishes. With new man John Egan at the helm, however, things started to improve. The first major change came in 1981, when the V12 models were made more economical by the fitment of the May-designed cylinder head, subsequent models being called 'HE' denoting high efficiency.

Above left: For the Series 1 XJ12 and Daimler Double Six models these ventilated wheels became available, to the same specification as were fitted to E-type Series 2 and 3 models.

Above right: Chromed ventilated wheels were also available at extra cost. Both types of ventilated wheels also became the standard fitment on Series 2 XJs.

Above left: Front compartment of the Series 1 XJ6, a later model with black instrument surrounds. Daimler and XJ12 models did not feature the bright alloy finishes to the centre console, which were replaced by black fabric. A manual choke also applied to V12 models, along with different door panel trims.

Above right: Earlier Series 1 XJ6s featured chromed surrounds to the instruments as shown here.

Above left: The specially fitted rear compartment of the Daimler Double Six Vanden Plas included individualised seating, lambswool over-rugs, boxwood inlays to woodwork, and enhanced door trims.

Above right: Daimler Vanden Plas, showing revised front seating and trim.

A new five-speed manual gearbox was briefly available on the Series 3 six-cylinder cars but was never as popular as the automatic transmission variants, and was dropped later in production.

At the end of 1982 Jaguar lost its right to use the Vanden Plas name in the UK, and with the demise of the VDP Coachworks in London anyway production of these upmarket versions of the Series 3 XJ had been done on the normal assembly lines in Coventry. A move away from the Daimler marque was envisaged too, so the range of cars was reduced and the 'Sovereign' name was moved over to a new up-market Jaguar model from 1984. This was fitted with a host of extras as standard equipment, including cruise control, onboard computer, and a new-style 'pepperpot' alloy wheel.

In 1985 the 3.4-litre was revamped with tweed instead of leather upholstery, straight-grain wood veneer, and other alterations to keep the price down. Six- and twelve-cylinder models continued selling better than ever, allowing the company more time to develop their ultimate replacement saloon, the XJ40. This new car would finally arrive in late 1986, although initially production of the Series 3 saloons continued. It wasn't until April 1987 that the last XJ6 Series 3 left the line, while V12 models soldiered on considerably longer because the XJ40 was never intended to take this engine. The Series 3 12s therefore complimented the X40 range for some time, the very last Jaguar XJ12 leaving the line at the end of 1991 and the Daimler Double Six continuing in production until the end of 1992.

Over 400,000 Series XJs were produced from 1968 to 1992, a phenomenal number, making them the most successful models produced by the company up to this time. More of this basic body design have been made than any subsequent saloon at the time of writing, and it is a tribute to the Series that current models continue to reflect some of the design features from those days.

Exterior identification points

General points applicable to all Series 1 models

Front view
- Overall frontal style taken from Mark X/420G/420 models with twin headlight arrangement.
- Uniquely styled radiator grille without prominent chromed surround.
- Rectangular horn grilles below inner headlights.
- Combined rectangular wrap-around indicator/sidelight units below outer headlights.

Unique to V12-engined Series 1 models was this gold-plated emblem on the centre console.

The Series 2 XJs are identified from the front by the shallower radiator grille with enhanced surround, higher bumper bar level, and revised lighting and valance treatment. For the US market a 'federal' rubber-faced bumper bar was fitted.

Daimler models of the Series 2 design were differentiated as usual by a fluted radiator grille. The fog lamps were a period extra-cost option. Daimler models, as Series 1 variants, also featured a centre-line chromed bonnet trim.

- Slimline bumper bar with forward-leaning overriders continuing usual Jaguar design from late 1960s, with centrally mounted number plate.
- Under-bumper valance contained chromed air intake grille beneath number plate plinth and between overriders.
- One-piece forward-hinged bonnet incorporating grille and inner headlight units. Pronounced hump in centre of bonnet, no chromed adornment or leaping mascot fitted.
- One-piece curved windscreen with chromed surround and twin wipers.

Rear view
- Angular rear-end styling with tapering of rear wings.
- Combined light clusters for indicators, rear and brake lights vertically mounted in rear wings.
- Separate horizontal light clusters on boot lid for reversing lights/reflectors (reflectors later moved to other light clusters in rear wings).
- Slimline bumper treatment as front with number plate illumination panel within bumper bar.
- Twin exhaust pipes with chromed surrounds (initially straight pipes, later changed to curved), emerging through the rear under valance below bumper level.
- Chromed winged escutcheon to circular boot lock in centre of boot lid above number plate.
- One-piece boot lid with vertical section forming rear of car containing number plate, chromed surround, and badging.
- Badging initially just litreage in chrome. Later 'Jaguar' added, and other changes according to model.
- Twin fuel tanks, mounted one in each rear wing, accessed by wing-top mounted lockable chrome filler caps.
- One-piece curved rear screen with chromed surround.

Side view
- Emphasised the swage line on body with haunch over rear wing. More angular aspect of styling with higher roof line to previous (420G) model.
- Chromed window surrounds with quarter-lights at the front. Rear quarter-lights incorporated into rear doors.
- The first Jaguar to depict a leaper badge at the base of the front wings.
- Hubcaps and chrome rimbellishers followed normal Jaguar practice at the time.

Series 1 specifics

XJ6 Series 1 2.8-litre models
- Chromed radiator grille with both vertical and horizontal slats, incorporating at centre top a circular plastic growler badge in gold.

Front interior compartment of a Series 2 saloon. Note the different dashboard layout, now with all the instruments in front of the driver, and the revised steering wheel, centre console surround, and door trims.

Rear view of the Series 2 model, in this case a Daimler Vanden Plas with fluted plinth.

Above left: Jaguar models featured this style of boot plinth.

Above right: In certain markets the XJ6 Series 2 was known as the 'Executive', with appropriate badging on the radiator grille and boot lid.

- '2.8'-litre badging on boot lid.
- Standard models (few actually made) did not feature chromed rimbellishers to the steel wheels.

XJ6 Series 1 4.2-litre models
- Radiator grille as 2.8-litre model above.
- '4.2'-litre badging to boot lid.

Daimler Sovereign Series 1 models
- All models as XJ6 except for the more prominent chromed surround and fluted radiator grille incorporating vertical slats only, with wider centre slat. Scripted 'D' badge in centre of grille top.
- Chromed central trim running the entire length of the bonnet.
- 'D' emblem in centre of hubcaps.
- At the rear prominent fluted chromed plinth on boot lid above number plate area, incorporating lock mechanism.
- 'Daimler' and 'Sovereign' badges to boot lid.

Series 1 long-wheelbase models
- As normal bodyshell except for longer rear doors compared to front doors.
- On Jaguar models an 'L' chromed insignia appeared on the boot lid next to the litre size.

XJ12 Series 1 models
- Revised radiator grille with only vertical slats and prominent wider centre slat containing 'V12' emblem.
- From the side a slightly lower look to the car, due to wider-profile wheels and tyres.
- At the rear 'XJ12' badging on the boot lid.

Daimler Double Six Series 1 models
- As normal Daimler Sovereign except for 'Double Six' badging to boot lid.
- 'V12' emblem to the top of radiator grille replacing scripted 'D'.
- Wider-profile wheels and tyres gave a slightly lower look to the car.

Daimler Double Six Vanden Plas Series 1 models
- As Sovereign except for bespoke range of exterior colour schemes.
- Integrated fog/spot lights instead of horn grilles at front (also an extra on other models).
- Chromed swage line trims along entire length of body sides.
- Fitment of driver's door mirror as standard.
- Black vinyl-covered roof with chromed finisher on D post at rear.
- Ventilated steel wheels incorporating chrome rimbellishers and conventional Daimler hubcaps.
- At the rear as Sovereign except for 'Vanden Plas' badging.

Detail of the entirely new dashboard layout and design for the Series 2 XJ models.

Rear seating of Series 2 saloons, very similar to earlier cars except for the colour schemes.

The Series 2 coupé model is easily identified by its two-door configuration, with wider doors and a black vinyl roof. At various stages all the Daimlers and most of the Jaguar V12s featured the chromed swage line trim. Chromed wheels were an extra-cost item.

General points applicable to all Series 2 XJs

Front view
- Overall style of cars remained very close to Series 1 models with twin headlight units, but with new-style slimline front bumper arrangement and underriders with rubber inserts fitted.
- Bumper height raised to just below headlights, necessitating under-bumper fitment of integrated wrap-around indicator/sidelight units.
- Enlarged under-valance chrome air intake panel.
- Reduced-depth radiator grille, still with vertical and horizontal slats but with prominent chromed surround.

Rear view
- Revised rear-end treatment with chromed number plate illumination plinth also incorporating boot lock, eliminating the need for separate illumination within bumper bar.

Side view
- Although utilising, for example, different front wings, the body line followed Series 1 styling almost exactly. Series 2 quickly identifiable by raised level of front wrap-around bumper bar.
- Ventilated steel wheels now fitted, silver in colour.

XJ Series 2 specifics

XJ Series 2 six-cylinder models
- Growler badge fitted to centre top of radiator grille.
- Rear boot number plate plinth smooth finished.
- Appropriate litreage badging according to model on boot lid.

Daimler Sovereign Series 2 models
- As XJ6 except for fluted treatment to more prominent surround to reduced depth of radiator grille, featuring only vertical slats with wider centre slat. 'D' script on top centre.
- Centre bonnet chrome strip as Series 1 Sovereigns.
- 'D' emblem to hubcaps.
- Boot lid has fluted chromed plinth incorporating boot lock.
- Daimler-associated badging to boot lid.

Series 2 long-wheelbase models
- Majority of Series 2 models made on long-wheelbase bodyshell, identified by wider rear doors.

XJ12 Series 2 models
- As XJ6 models except for 'V' emblem to centre of radiator grille centre vane.

Above left: These Kent alloy wheels became available on later Series 2 cars, usually Vanden Plas and V12-engined models.

Above right: Initially all Series 2 models were equipped with these stainless steel wheel covers as standard, although the style and colour changed according to model, eg V12-engined cars had a black centre.

Series 3 XJs are identified from the side by their raised roof level, enlarged glass area, and flush-mounted door handles.

Comparison between the Series 2 front on the left and the Series 3 on the right. The latter had rubber-faced energy-absorbing bumper bars, revised radiator grilles with vertical slats only, and a new-style under-valance with improved 'mouth'. Note also the deeper windscreen.

- Similar rear badge treatment to identify as XJ12 models.

Daimler Double Six and VDP Series models
- As other Daimler Series 2 models except for 'V' emblem on radiator grille badge.
- Appropriate badging on boot lid.
- Exterior trim of VDP models (also now available with 4.2-litre engine) as Series 1 VDP model.

XJ and Daimler coupé models
- All models based on the short wheelbase Series 1 bodyshell identifiable from the side by the lack of chromed window surrounds, allowing all windows to be wound down to reveal an open side view.
- Significantly wider front doors (no rear doors). Doors incorporate no quarter-lights or window frame surrounds.
- Vinyl roof with chromed rain gutters fitted to all production coupé models.
- No coupé badging on boot lid.
- Daimler and Jaguar trim followed saloon practice.

NB: Kent five-section alloy wheels with black centres appeared during this period and were available as an extra-cost option on all models. Chromed swage line trim was at various times fitted as standard equipment to some V12 models including coupés and Vanden Plas cars. Vinyl roofs were also at one time provided as standard equipment on some V12 Jaguar models.

General points applicable to Series 3 XJs

Front view
- Retention of overall design features of previous Series 2 models except for revised bumper bar treatment with black rubber surround incorporating indicator lenses and centrally mounted number plate with full-width chrome finisher blade to the top.
- Under-valance incorporated an enlarged air intake section.
- New vertical slated chrome radiator grille with prominent surround and growler badge on top within a black background. Grille more angular and pronounced than Series 2 style.
- Twin headlight arrangement which now incorporated sidelights in outer units.
- Taller windscreen with chromed surround and twin wiper arms.

Rear view
- The same rubber bumper features as front, incorporating twin red hazard warning lights.
- New-style rear-light units incorporating reversing lights and reflectors with chrome surrounds.

Rear view of the Series 3 model, with rubber-faced bumper bar, built-in hazard warning lights, flatter boot lid plinth, revised badging, and sharper-edged rear lighting.

This comparison between V12-engined XJ saloons, Series 3 on the left and Series 1 on the right, clearly shows the differences.

Daimler treatment of the Series 3s involved the usual fluted plinths and grilles and always retained scripted badging.

This early Series 3 interior shows better-quality seating than in Series 2 models and a slightly modified dash layout, with new-style centre console and steering wheel.

- Revised flatter chrome boot plinth with hidden boot lock beneath.
- Heavy chrome/plastic script badging to boot lid according to model.
- Enlarged wrap-around rear screen with chrome surround.

Side view
- Series 3 models instantly identifiable from previous Series XJs by higher roof line, larger window areas, and wrap-around rubber-faced bumper bars.
- Side indicator repeater lenses to front corner of wings.
- Enlarged (taller) glass areas with raised and flatter roof.
- Inset flush-mounted chromed 'pull' door handles within black surrounds.
- Steel wheels completely enclosed within stainless steel ventilated trims held in position by wheel nuts. Centre of trims colour keyed according to engine size.

XJ Series 3 specifics

Jaguar XJ Series 3 six-cylinder models
- Revised boot lid badging according to litreage. Later many changes in script style according to model (see photographs).

Daimler Sovereign Series 3 models
- As Jaguar except for revised Daimler and Sovereign badging.
- New radiator grille incorporating usual fluted surround and chrome bonnet trim. Eliminated on later cars.

XJ12 Series 3 models
- As XJ6 and Daimler models except for revised badging only on boot lid.

Daimler Vanden Plas Series 3 models
- By this time produced in-house at Jaguar. Externally they were only identifiable from standard Daimler models by the swage line chrome trims running the entire length of the body sides.
- Kent alloy wheels fitted, although alternative trims could be specified.
- 'Vanden Plas' badging on the boot lid.

Later Series 3 identifiable changes

Daimler Series 3 models (post-1992)
- With the discontinuing of the VDP models the Daimler range was restricted but took on revised exterior features. Chrome swage line trims previously fitted only to VDP and some other V12 models now fitted.
- New-style stainless steel wheel trims incorporating conventional hubcaps and 'D' script in centre.
- Chrome bonnet strip discontinued.

Detail of the pre-1983 centre console area in a Series 3 saloon. Daimler models again benefited from a black-finished radio/heater control panel.

From 1984 Jaguar models took over the Sovereign name for up-market versions like this one. Otherwise very similar externally to the Daimler Sovereign, the badging changed, as did the wheel treatment.

The new pepperpot alloy wheels were designed for the Jaguar Sovereign model but could also be specified for Daimler cars.

Jaguar XJ Series 3 Sovereign models
- From 1984 up-market Jaguar model identified by silver 'pepperpot' perforated alloy wheels.
- 'Sovereign' badging on boot lid, style along with 'Jaguar' badge changed later (see photograph).

NB: Wheels for the various models altered throughout production and were also available as extra cost options (see photographs). Rear badging was also modified (see photographs).

Interior identification points

XJ6 Series 1 (all models)
- Standard dash layout with main instruments in front of driver but now within curved veneered surrounds with padding (similar to 420 saloons), with major instruments flanking central warning light unit.
- Central auxiliary gauges mounted on ribbed black plinth with rocker-type switches as Series 2/3 E-type.
- Through-flow black circular air vents to either end of fascia.
- Black vinyl surround to dash area with top-mounted central radio speaker grille and two directional air vents to screen.
- Lockable glovebox on passenger side.
- Two-spoke black plastic-covered steering wheel with half horn ring and oval central growler badge on black background.
- Column-/dash- mounted combined ignition starter switch.
- Centre console incorporating oddments shelf above, below heating/ventilation controls, radio and, if fitted, radio speaker balance control.
- Gearlever (incorporating overdrive switch on top) or automatic transmission quadrant with black surround, flanked by twin chromed flip-open ashtrays either side and cigarette lighter behind.
- Where fitted independent electric window controls mounted on console where it rises to form centre armrest and rear-hinged glovebox.
- Under-dashboard parcel shelves either side.
- Umbrella-style handbrake close to centre console as Mark X/420G.
- Door trims incorporate only thin wooden cappings on top, soft trimmed vinyl side trims with flush-mounted chromed door handles, chromed window winders, and chrome/black knurled knob to open front quarter-lights.
- Integrated armrests and door pockets, alternative design according to model.

Daimler models continued in luxury class only, normally with Kent alloy wheels though a revised stainless steel trim, incorporating a conventional hubcap, could also be specified. Chromed swage line trims appeared on all Daimler models to the end of production.

Above left: *From 1986 rear badging was revised to this embossed style except for Daimler models.*

Above right: *Later-style interior for Series 3 models incorporated a totally revised centre console with further wood veneer. Earlier Daimler-style door trim panels were also adopted for all models.*

Above left: *Daimler models continued to feature alternative seating long after the Vanden Plas name had disappeared.*

Above right: *Bench-style seating could be specified by special order for Daimler Series 3 models.*

- Individual front seating with vertical pleats and aerated upholstery centre sections. Provision for headrests from later models. Seats with adjustable recline mechanism.
- Rear compartment bench-style seating to match front style with folding centre armrest.
- Rear through-flow ventilation outlet in centre of console with on/off controls and flip-top chromed ashtray.
- Rear door trims match front.
- Where fitted electric window lift controls in chrome set into door armrests.
- Rear parcel shelf incorporated centre raised section on all but the very early cars to aid through flow of air from cabin extracted via boot surround.

Later-style seating for Jaguar saloons, here seen in a Sovereign model with enhanced woodwork.

Daimler Sovereign Series 1 models
- Wider pleating to seating without aerated sections.
- Longer diagonally mounted door pulls/armrests to front doors with separate black trimmed top section to door trim.
- Scripted 'D' badge to steering wheel centre boss.

Daimler Double Six Vanden Plas Series 1 models
- High-quality burr walnut veneer to all woodwork with boxwood inlay around edges of dashboard.
- More substantial veneered woodwork to door trims also incorporating boxwood inlays, the wood implanted in black vinyl surround.
- Centre console as Sovereign except for inclusion of gold-plated 'V12' badge to centre below gearlever quadrant. Black figured vinyl covering to console instead of alloy.
- More substantial seating with deeper backs and bolsters. Wide vertical pleating with no aeration. Fitted headrests to front seats also in better-quality leather, rear of front seats incorporating elasticated leather pockets.
- Rear of centre console revised to include cigarette lighter.
- Better-quality Wilton carpeting all round.
- Rear door trims also of amended type, both front and rear incorporating separate armrests and pockets plus built-in speaker grilles for enhanced audio equipment.
- Rear seats similar in design to front, with the appearance of being individual with pronounced centre armrest and centre in-fill.

XJ12 Series 1 models
- Revised door trims to XJ6 models, similar to but not the same as Daimlers, trimmed completely in one colour.
- Replacement of alloy centre console covering with black figured vinyl, with gold-plated 'V12' badge as Double Six.

New-style cloth upholstery could also be specified.

- Heater and allied controls have matt black surrounds instead of chrome.

XJ6 and XJ12 Series 2 (all models)
- Entirely different dashboard layout to Series 1 models, with smaller speedometer and rev counter and, although still mounted in front of the driver, now flanked either side by auxiliary gauges.
- Rectangular through-flow air vents, one to each extreme end of dashboard.
- Ignition/starter moved to opposite side of steering column flanked by combined lighting control on other side.
- New-style (flatter) steering column stalks controlling wipers, washers, main beam, etc.
- Centre of dash now occupied by large rectangular heater/air-conditioning vents in three sections, either end adjustable.
- Passenger-side lockable glovebox.
- Centre console incorporated more prominent oddments tray, below which new rectangular push-button switches operated auxiliary controls like hazard lights, fuel changeover etc. In the centre was a rectangular clock within satin surround to match instruments.
- Radio and heating/air-conditioning controls similar to Series 1 models, as were gearlever surrounds and ashtrays, although electric window lift switches now larger and black plastic instead of chrome finished.

- Two-spoke steering wheel with enlarged padded black centre section incorporating oval growler image.
- Umbrella handbrake as before.
- Front and rear seating similar to Series 1 models (dependent on model).
- Door trims revised with more complex heat-pressing design and with no wood veneer at the top at all.

Daimler Sovereign and Vanden Plas Series 2 models
- Apart from changes identified above for Jaguars, VDP followed same style as Series 1 and Sovereign cars. Still featured unique-style door trims etc.

Coupé models
- As conventional Jaguar or Daimler models except for wider door trims incorporating elongated armrest-pulls.
- Electrically operated window lifts.
- Front seats incorporated black and chrome mechanisms to release the seatback, moving it forward to gain access to the rear compartment.
- Rear seating narrower than saloons with revised side trims with armrests, pockets, and black pull-out ashtrays each side.

NB: *Specifications for interior trim changed over the production life of the Series 2. Nylon trim offered as standard on cars like the 3.4-litre base model was also available for other models. Similarly head restraints to the front seats were available as standard and/or extra-cost items, dependent on model and year produced. See accompanying photographs for more detail.*

XJ6/12 Series 3 (all models)
- Although retaining the overall style of Series 2 models, Series 3 interiors looked better quality and were. The same dash layout continued but with a different lighting switch (more pronounced black surround), uniform graphics, and with the warning lights incorporated into the major instruments.
- A new twin-spoke black steering wheel of smaller circumference with thicker rim and rectangular style soft-padded centre section incorporating the growler image.
- Steering column stalks changed over with indicators now on the left (right on all previous models).
- Although bright alloy was chosen for the centre console vertical section incorporating heater/air-conditioning controls and radio, the lower horizontal section used black figured vinyl.
- More supportive and substantial seating both front and rear without aerated panels but with wider pleating and fitted headrests at the front as well as the provision of lumber support adjustment.
- Simplified door trims similar to those featured on Series 2 models but with no heat-pressing design.
- New one-piece glass-fibre-backed head lining and, for the first time on an XJ, recessed sun visors.
- Better-quality carpeting and hidden inertia reel seat belts fitted on all front seats.

Daimler Sovereign Series 3 models
- As Jaguar except for top section above chrome strip of door trims, still finished in black instead of trim colour.
- Black surround to radio console area instead of alloy.
- 'D' badging to steering wheel centre boss.

Daimler Vanden Plas models
- As Sovereign except for flatter-type seating as previous VDP models, wider pleating, and individual rear seating as before.
- VDP-style door trims as before with wood veneer.
- No boxwood inlay to dashboard veneer.
- The last VDP Series 3 model was registered in 1983. Thereafter the same model became known simply as a Double Six, but interior spec remained the same as for the VDP.

Jaguar XJ6/12 Series 3 Sovereign models
- Only introduced in 1984, taking the Sovereign name from Daimler. As other XJs except interior better equipped as standard. Wood veneer with boxwood inlay to door trims, now taking design of trim from the VDP and later models.
- Standard equipment included on-board computer, rectangular unit crackle finished in centre of console with digital readout (see note below regarding centre console layout).

Jaguar XJ6 (post-1984) Series 3 3.4-litre models
- The intended fleet model supplied as standard, with the same style seating to XJ6 models but with Rachelle cloth covering instead of leather.
- Straight grain woodwork instead of figured walnut veneer.

NB: *Style of centre console area on all Series 3 models changed from 1983 to include a flat vacuum-formed oddments tray above, with revised veneered on to metal panelling below incorporating new controls and clock position, to accommodate the onboard computer panel where fitted. Wood veneer panelling also affixed to horizontal section of centre console.*

Technical specifications

	2.8-litre Series 1	4.2-litre Series 1
cc	2792	4235
Bore and stroke (mm)	83 x 86	92.7 x 106
Compression ratio	9:1 (7:1/8:1 optional)	9:1 (7:1/8:1 optional)
bhp	180	245
@ rpm	6000	5500
Torque (lb ft)	182	283
@ rpm	3750	3750
Fuelling	2 x SU carbs	2 x SU carbs
Transmission	4-speed all synchro, BW 3-speed auto	4-speed all synchro BW 3-speed auto
Wheel size (in)	15, steel	15, steel
Suspension front	Ind semi-trailing wishbones, coil springs, anti-roll bar	Ind semi-trailing wishbones, coil springs, anti-roll bar
Suspension rear	Ind lower wishbones/upper driveshaft link, radius arms, coil springs	Ind lower wishbones/upper driveshaft link, radius arms, coil springs
Brakes	4-wheel disc Rear inboard	4-wheel disc Rear inboard
Performance		
0–60mph (sec)	11	8.8
Top speed (mph)	117	124
Average mpg	16–20	15.3
Dimensions		
Length (in)	189.5	189.5 (194.75 long-wheelbase)
Width (in)	69.25	69.25
Height (in)	54	54
Wheelbase (in)	108.75	108.75 (112.75 long-wheelbase)
Front track (in)	58	58
Rear track (in)	58.5	58.5
Weight (cwt)	32	33 (34 long-wheelbase)

Technical specifications *cont ...*

	5.3-litre Series 1	3.4-litre Series 2
cc	5343	3442
Bore and stroke (mm)	90 x 70	83 x 106
Compression ratio	9:1	8.8:1
bhp	253	161
@ rpm	6000	5000
Torque (lb ft)	302	189
@ rpm	3500	3500
Fuelling	4 x Stromberg carbs	2 x SU carbs
Transmission	BW 3-speed auto	4-speed all synchro BW 3-speed auto
Wheel size (in)	15, steel/chrome Alloys optional	15, steel/chrome Alloys optional
Suspension front	Ind semi-trailing wishbones, coil springs, anti-roll bar	Ind semi-trailing wishbones, coil springs, anti-roll bar
Suspension rear	Ind lower wishbones/upper driveshaft link, radius arms, coil springs	Ind lower wishbones/upper driveshaft link, radius arms, coil springs
Brakes	4-wheel disc Rear inboard	4-wheel disc Rear inboard
Performance		
0–60mph (sec)	7.4	10.9
Top speed (mph)	145	117
Average mpg	15.7	16.7
Dimensions		
Length (in)	189.5 (194.75 long-wheelbase)	189.5 (194.75 long-wheelbase)
Width (in)	69.25	69.25
Height (in)	54	54
Wheelbase (in)	108.75 (112.75 long-wheelbase)	108.75 (112.75 long-wheelbase)
Front track (in)	58	58
Rear track (in)	58.5	58.5
Weight (cwt)	35 (36 long-wheelbase)	32

	4.2-litre Series 2	5.3-litre Series 2
cc	4235	5343
Bore and stroke (mm)	92.7 x 106	90 x 70
Compression ratio	8:1 (7:1/9:1 optional)	9:1
bhp	170	285
@ rpm	4500	5750
Torque (lb ft)	231	294
@ rpm	3500	3500
Fuelling	2 x SU carbs	4 x Stromberg carbs
Transmission	4-speed all synchro BW 3-speed auto	BW 3-speed auto Later GM 3-speed auto
Wheel size (in)	15, steel/chrome Alloys optional	15, steel/chrome Alloys optional
Suspension front	Ind semi-trailing wishbones, coil springs, anti-roll bar	Ind semi-trailing wishbones, coil springs, anti-roll bar
Suspension rear	Ind lower wishbones/upper driveshaft link, radius arms, coil springs	Ind lower wishbones/upper driveshaft link, radius arms, coil springs
Brakes	4-wheel disc Rear inboard	4-wheel disc Rear inboard
Performance		
0–60mph (sec)	8.9	7.8
Top speed (mph)	125	147
Average mpg	15	13.2
Dimensions		
Length (in)	189.5 (194.75 long-wheelbase)	189.5 (194.75 long-wheelbase)
Width (in)	69.25	69.25
Height (in)	54	54
Wheelbase (in)	108.75 (112.75 long-wheelbase)	108.75 (112.75 long-wheelbase)
Front track (in)	58	58
Rear track (in)	58.5	58.5
Weight (cwt)	33 (34 long-wheelbase)	35 (36 long-wheelbase)

Technical specifications *cont ...*

	5.3-litre Series 2	3.4-litre Series 3
cc	5343	3442
Bore and stroke (mm)	90 x 70	83 x 106
Compression ratio	9:1	8.8:1
bhp	285	161
@ rpm	5750	5000
Torque (lb ft)	294	189
@ rpm	3500	3500
Fuelling	4 x Stromberg carbs Later fuel-injection	2 x SU carbs Later fuel-injection
Transmission	BW 3-speed auto	5-speed all synchro
Wheel size (in)	15, steel/chrome Alloys optional	15, steel Later alloys
Suspension front	Ind semi-trailing wishbones, coil springs, anti-roll bar	Ind semi-trailing wishbones, coil springs, anti-roll bar
Suspension rear	Ind lower wishbones/upper driveshaft link, radius arms, coil springs	Ind lower wishbones/upper driveshaft link, radius arms, coil springs
Brakes	4-wheel disc, rear inboard	4 wheel disc, rear inboard
Performance		
0–60mph (sec)	7.8	10.9
Top speed (mph)	147	117
Average mpg	13.2	16.7
Dimensions		
Length (in)	189.5 (194.75 long-wheelbase)	194.75
Width (in)	69.25	69.25
Height (in)	54	54
Wheelbase (in)	108.75 (112.75 long-wheelbase)	112.75
Front track (in)	58	58
Rear track (in)	58.5	58.5
Weight (cwt)	35 (36 long-wheelbase)	34

	4.2-litre Series 3	5.3-litre Series 3
cc	4235	5343
Bore and stroke (mm)	97.07 x 106	90 x 70
Compression ratio	8:1	9:1
bhp	200	285
@ rpm	5000	5750
Torque (lb ft)	236	294
@ rpm	2750	3500
Fuelling	Fuel-injection	Fuel-injection
Transmission	5-speed all synchro BW 3-speed auto	GM 3-speed auto BW 3-speed auto
Wheel size (in)	15, steel Later alloys	15, steel or alloys
Suspension front	Ind semi-trailing wishbones, coil springs, anti-roll bar	Ind semi-trailing wishbones, coil springs, anti-roll bar
Suspension rear	Ind lower wishbones/upper driveshaft link, radius arms, coil springs	Ind lower wishbones/upper driveshaft link, radius arms, coil springs
Brakes	4-wheel disc, rear inboard	4-wheel disc, rear inboard
Performance		
0–60mph (sec)	10.5	7.8
Top speed (mph)	128	147
Average mpg	15.7	13.2
Dimensions		
Length (in)	194.75	194.75
Width (in)	69.25	69.25
Height (in)	54	54
Wheelbase (in)	112.75	112.75
Front track (in)	58	58
Rear track (in)	58.5	58.5
Weight (cwt)	35.4	36

Optional extras

Series 1 saloons

2.8-litre standard saloons
Heated rear screen.
Overdrive for manual gearbox.
Automatic transmission.
Power-assisted steering.
Electrically operated windows.
Flush-fitting fog/spot lights.
Front seat belts, or front and rear.
Laminated windscreen.
Sundym tinted glass.
Two choices of radio equipment.
Chrome wheel rimbellishers.
Wing mirrors.
Front seat headrests (from 1969).
Witter tow bar.

2.8-litre de luxe saloons
Heated rear screen.
Overdrive for manual gearbox.
Automatic transmission.
Electrically operated windows.
Flush-fitting fog/spot lights.
Front seat belts, front and/or rear.
Laminated windscreen.
Sundym tinted glass.
Two choices of radio equipment.
Chrome wheel rimbellishers.
Wing mirrors.
Front seat headrests (from 1969).
Mud flaps.
Witter tow bar.

4.2-litre saloons
Heated rear screen (standard from 1972).
Overdrive for manual gearbox.
Automatic transmission.
Electrically operated windows.
Flush-fitting fog/spot lights.
Air-conditioning.
Front seat belts, front and/or rear.
Laminated windscreen.
Sundym tinted glass.
Two choices of radio equipment or radio/cassette or cartridge unit.
Philips radio/cassette and recorder with microphone.
Electrically operated radio aerial.
Wing mirrors.
Front seat headrests (from 1969).
Mud flaps.
Witter tow bar.

V12 saloons
Flush-fitting fog/spot lights (standard on Vanden Plas).
Air-conditioning (standard on Vanden Plas).
Front seat belts (standard on Vanden Plas) and/or rear.
Laminated windscreen (standard on Vanden Plas).
Sundym tinted glass (standard on Vanden Plas).
Two choices of radio equipment or radio/cassette or cartridge unit (last standard on Vanden Plas).
Philips radio/cassette and recorder with microphone.
Electrically operated radio aerial.
Chrome-plated ventilated steel wheels.
Wing mirrors (not Vanden Plas).
Passenger-side remote door mirror (Vanden Plas only).
Front seat headrests (standard on Vanden Plas).
Mud flaps.
Witter tow bar.

Series 2 saloons

3.4-litre saloons
Heated rear screen.
Overdrive for manual gearbox.
Automatic transmission.
Electrically operated windows.
Under-bumper fog/spot lights.
Halogen headlights.
Air-conditioning.
Rear seat belts.
Laminated windscreen.
Sundym tinted glass.
Radio and/or radio/cassette system with electric aerial.
Wing mirrors.
Driver's door mirror.
Front seat headrests.
Mud flaps.
Leather upholstery.
Witter tow bar.

4.2-litre saloons
Overdrive for manual gearbox.
Automatic transmission.
Under-bumper fog/spot lights (standard on Vanden Plas).
Halogen headlights.
Air-conditioning (standard on Vanden Plas).
Rear seat belts (standard on Vanden Plas from 1975).
Sundym tinted glass (standard on Vanden Plas and all models from 1978).
Radio and/or radio/cassette system with electric aerial (standard on Vanden Plas).
Kent alloy wheels.
Whitewall tyres.
Driver's door mirror (standard on Vanden Plas).
Rear seat headrests (only on Vanden Plas).
Mud flaps.
Limited-slip differential.
Cloth upholstery.
Witter tow bar.

V12 saloons
Under-bumper fog/spot lights (standard on Vanden Plas).
Halogen headlights.

Air-conditioning (standard on Vanden Plas and on other Daimler V12s from 1975).
Rear seat belts (standard on Vanden Plas from 1975).
Sundym tinted glass (standard on Vanden Plas and all V12s from 1976).
Choice of two radio and radio/cassette systems with electric aerial (standard on Vanden Plas and from 1976 on DD6 coupé).
Kent alloy wheels.
Whitewall tyres.
Driver's door mirror (standard on Vanden Plas).
Rear seat headrests (only on Vanden Plas).
Mud flaps.
Limited-slip differential.
Cloth upholstery.
Witter tow bar.

Series 3 saloons

3.4-litre saloons
Heated rear screen (standard from 1982).
Automatic transmission (standard from 1981).
Electrically operated windows.
Under-bumper fog/spot lights.
Halogen headlights.
Air-conditioning.
Rear seat belts (standard from 1985).
Sundym tinted glass.
Premier stereo radio/cassette system.
Kent alloy wheels.
Pepperpot alloy wheels.
Electrically operated door mirrors.
Rear seat headrests (from 1983).
Mud flaps.
Cruise control (late production).
Electric front seat height adjustment.
Electric steel sunroof.
Roof rack with or without specialist fittings (from 1985).
Electric headlight wash/wipe system.
Onboard computer.
Leather upholstery.
Tailored overmats.
Witter tow bar.

4.2-litre saloons
Automatic transmission (standard from 1981).
Under-bumper fog/spot lights (standard on Daimlers from 1983).
Halogen headlights (standard from 1979).
Air-conditioning (standard on Vanden Plas and on all Daimlers from 1983 plus Jaguar Sovereigns).
Rear seat belts (standard on Daimlers and on Jaguars from 1984).
Premier stereo radio/cassette system (standard on Vanden Plas, lesser powered standard on Sovereign models from 1984).
Kent alloy wheels.
Pepperpot alloy wheels (standard on Sovereign models).
Stainless steel rimbellishers with stainless steel hubcaps (standard on some Daimlers).
Whitewall tyres.
Electrically operated door mirrors (standard on all Daimlers and Sovereigns from 1984).
Rear seat headrests (standard on Jaguar Sovereign, Vanden Plas, and later Daimlers).
Mud flaps.
Cruise control (standard on Daimlers).
Electric front seat height adjustment (standard on Daimlers and Jaguar Sovereign from 1983).
Electric steel sunroof.
Roof rack with or without specialist fittings (from 1985).
Electric headlight wash/wipe system (standard on Vanden Plas from 1979 and all Daimlers from 1985).
Onboard computer (standard on Jaguar Sovereign and Daimlers from 1983).
Cloth upholstery.
Tailored overmats.
Witter tow bar.

V12 saloons
Under-bumper fog/spot lights (standard on Daimlers from 1983).
Halogen headlights (standard from 1979).
Air-conditioning (standard on Vanden Plas and on all Daimlers from 1983 plus Jaguar Sovereigns).
Rear seat belts (standard on Daimlers and on Jaguars from 1984).
Premier stereo radio/cassette system (standard on Vanden Plas, lesser powered standard on Sovereign models from 1984).
Integrated hi-fi radio/cassette and CD player system (from 1991).
Kent alloy wheels (standard on Daimlers from 1984).
Pepperpot alloy wheels (standard on Sovereign models).
Stainless steel rimbellishers with stainless steel hubcaps (standard on some Daimlers).
Whitewall tyres.
Electrically operated door mirrors (standard on all Daimlers and Sovereigns from 1984).
Rear seat headrests (standard on Jaguar Sovereign, Vanden, Plas and later DD6).
Mud flaps.
Cruise control (standard on Daimlers and Jaguar Sovereign).
Electric front seat height adjustment (standard on Daimlers and Jaguar Sovereign from 1983).
Electric steel sunroof (standard on Daimlers from 1986).
Roof rack with or without specialist fittings (from 1985).
Electric headlight wash/wipe system (standard on Vanden Plas from 1979, Jaguar Sovereign from 1983, and all Daimlers from 1985).
Cloth upholstery.
Tailored overmats.
Witter tow bar.
Mobile phone installation (from 1988).

Colour schemes

Exterior colour	Details	Interior trim
XJ6 Series 1 2.8-litre		**Ambla**
Special order leather as 4.2-litre models below		
Old English White		Red
		Dark Blue
		Black
Warwick Grey	To 1992	Red
		Dark Blue
		Beige
Ascot Fawn	To 1992	Red
		Beige
Willow Green	To 1992	Beige
Dark Blue		Red
		Dark Blue
		Beige
Sable Brown		Beige
Light Blue	To 1992	Dark Blue
		Black
British Racing Green		Beige
Regency Red		Beige
		Red
Black		Red
		Beige
Signal Red*		Black
		Beige
		Red
Pale Primrose*		Red
		Beige
		Black
Azure Blue*		Dark Blue
		Beige
Light Silver*		Red
		Beige
		Dark Blue
Fern Grey	From 1972	Green
		Olive
		Beige
Turquoise	From 1972	Tan
		Beige
Greensand	From 1972	Tan
		Olive
		Beige

Exterior colour	Details	Interior trim
Heather Pink	From 1972	Maroon
		Antelope
		Cerise
Lavender	From 1972	Tan
		Dark Blue
XJ Series 1 4.2/5.3-litre		**Leather**
Old English White		Red
		Dark Blue
		Light Blue
Warwick Grey	To 1992	Red
		Dark Blue
		Cinnamon
Ascot Fawn	To 1992	Red
		Cinnamon
		Beige
Willow Green	To 1992	Beige
		Suede Green
		Grey
		Cinnamon
Dark Blue		Red
		Light Blue
		Grey
Sable Brown		Beige
		Grey
		Cinnamon
Light Blue	To 1992	Dark Blue
		Light Blue
		Grey
British Racing Green		Beige
		Suede Green
		Cinnamon
Regency Red		Beige
		Grey
Black	To 1992	Red
		Grey
		Cinnamon
Signal Red*		Red
		Beige
Pale Primrose*		Red
		Beige
		Black

Exterior colour	Details	Interior trim
Azure Blue*		Dark Blue
		Cinnamon
		Beige
Light Silver*		Red
		Beige
		Dark Blue
		Black
Fern Grey	From 1972	Moss Green
		Olive
		Tan
Turquoise	From 1972	Tan
		Cinnamon
Greensand	From 1972	Tan
		Olive
		Cinnamon
Heather Pink	From 1972	Maroon
		Antelope
		Cerise
Lavender	From 1972	Biscuit
		Dark Blue
		French Blue

Exterior colour	Details	Interior trim
Vanden Plas (Series 1 and 2)		**Leather**
Silver Sand		Chamois
		Tuscan
		Deep Olive
Caramel		Chamois
		Tuscan
		Deep Olive
Coral		Chamois
		Tuscan
		Deep Olive
Aegean Blue		Chamois
		Tuscan
		Deep Olive
Sage Green		Chamois
		Tuscan
		Deep Olive
Morello Cherry		Chamois
		Tuscan
		Deep Olive
Aubergine		Chamois
		Tuscan
		Deep Olive

Exterior colour	Details	Interior trim	Details	Interior trim	Details
XJ Series 2 models		**Leather**		**Cloth**	
Old English White		Red	To 1974	Garnet	
		Russet	From 1974	Sand	
		Dark Blue	To 1975	Ebony*	
		French Blue	To 1974		
		Cinnamon	From 1974		
Dark Blue		Red	To 1974	Garnet	
		Russet	From 1974	Sand	
		Dark Blue	1974–5	Ebony*	
		French Blue	To 1974		
		Biscuit			
Sable Brown	To 1975	Biscuit			
		Moss Green			
		Cinnamon			
British Racing Green		Biscuit		Sand	
		Moss Green	To 1975	Ebony*	
		Cinnamon			

Colour schemes *cont ...*

Exterior colour	Details	Interior trim	Details	Interior trim	Details
Regency Red	To 1987	Biscuit		Sand	
		Cinnamon		Ebony*	
		Red	To 1974		
		Russet	1974–5		
Black*		Red		Ebony*	
		Russet	To 1974		
		Grey	1974–5		
		Cinnamon			
Signal Red*		Red	To 1974	Ebony*	
		Russet	1974–5		
		Beige			
Pale Primrose*		Red		Ebony*	
		Beige			
		Black			
Azure Blue*	To 1975	Dark Blue		Ebony*	
		Cinnamon			
		Beige			
Light Silver*		Red	To 1974	Ebony*	
		Russet	1974–5		
		Beige			
		Dark Blue			
		Black			
Fern Grey	To 1975	Moss Green			
		Olive			
		Cinnamon	1974–5		
		Tan	To 1974		
Turquoise	To 1975	Tan			
		Cinnamon			
		Terracotta			
Greensand	To 1975	Tan	To 1974		
		Cinnamon			
		Olive			
Heather Pink	To 1975	Maroon			
		Antelope			
		Cerise			
Lavender	To 1975	Biscuit			
		Dark Blue			
		French Blue	To 1974		
		Cinnamon	1974–5		
Juniper Green	From 1975	Biscuit		Sand	
		Cinnamon			
Carriage Brown	From 1975	Biscuit		Sand	
		Cinnamon			

Exterior colour	Details	Interior trim	Details	Interior trim	Details
Moroccan Bronze	From 1975	Biscuit		Sand	
		Cinnamon			
Squadron Blue	From 1975	Dark Blue		Sand	
		Biscuit		Navy	
XJ Series 3 models		**Leather**		**Cloth**	
Tudor White	To 1986	Russet		Garnet	To 1985
		Biscuit		Sand	
Cotswold Yellow	To 1980	Cinnamon		Sand	
		Dark Blue		Navy	
Damson Red	To 1980	Russet		Garnet	
		Cinnamon		Sand	
Racing Green Metallic	To 1985	Biscuit		Sand	
Racing Green	1986–8	Cinnamon			
Silver Frost	To 1980	Russet		Garnet	
	and 1989 on	Dark Blue		Sand	
		Doeskin	From 1989		
Cobalt Blue	To 1986	Cinnamon		Sand	
		Dark Blue		Navy	
Quartz Blue	To 1980	Biscuit		Sand	
		Dark Blue		Navy	
Chestnut Brown	To 1983	Cinnamon		Sand	
		Biscuit			
Sebring Red*	To 1986	Biscuit		Sand	
Standard from 1981		Dark Blue		Navy	
Black*		Biscuit	To 1987	Garnet	
Standard from 1981		Russet	To 1981	Sand	
		Barley	From 1988		
Indigo Blue	1981–3	Biscuit†	From 1981	Beige†	From 1981
Grosvenor Brown	1984–5	County Tan†	1981 to 1983	Amber†	1981–3
Portland Beige	1981–3	Isis Blue†		Fleet Blue†	From 1981
Rhodium Silver	1981–6	Black†	1981 to 1986	Graphite†	From 1981
Sapphire Blue (light)	1981–5	Doeskin†	1981 on	Parchment†	1985 only
Coronet Gold	1981–5	Burnt Umber†	1981 to 1983		
Sable Brown	1981–3	Buckskin†	1984 on	**Wool Tweed**	From 1986
Claret	1981–6	Mulberry†	1984 on	Cheviot†	From 1986
Silversand	1981–6	Savile Grey†	1984 on	Chiltern†	From 1986
Clarendon Blue	1984–5	Barley†	1986 on	Cotswold†	From 1986
Cirrus Grey	1984–6	Magnolia†	1986 on	Pennine†	From 1986
Cranberry	1984–6	Charcoal†	1987 on		
Antelope	1984–6				
Sage Green	1984–6				
Regent Grey	1984–6				
Windsor Blue	1986				

Colour schemes *cont ...*

Exterior colour	Details	Interior trim	Details	Interior trim	Details
Steel Blue	1986				
Curlew Brown	1986				
Nimbus White	1987				
Grenadier Red	1988	Buckskin	From 1988		
Alpine Green	1987				
Arctic Blue	From 1987	Magnolia	From 1988		
Bordeaux	From 1987	Savile Grey	1988		
		Mulberry	From 1989		
Crimson	1987				
Dorchester Grey	1987–9				
Moorland Green	1987–9				
Satin Beige	1987–9	Parchment	From 1988		
Silver Birch	1987–9				
Solent Blue	From 1987	Magnolia	From 1988		
Sovereign Gold	1987				
Talisman Silver	1987–9	Doeskin	From 1988		
Tungsten Grey	From 1987	Doeskin	From 1988		
Jaguar Racing Green	From 1987	Charcoal	From 1988		
Glacier White	From 1988	Biscuit	1988		
		Charcoal	From 1989		
Westminster Blue	From 1987	Doeskin			
Savoy Grey	From 1988	Isis Blue			
Jade Green	From 1988	Savile Grey	1988		
		Parchment	From 1989		
Gunmetal	From 1988	Savile Grey	1988		
		Parchment	From 1989		
Regency Red	From 1988	Savile Grey			
Brooklands Green	From 1989	Doeskin			
Diamond Blue	From 1988	Magnolia			
Oyster	From 1989	Magnolia			
Tuscany Bronze	From 1989	Savile Grey			
			Contrast Piping		
			(available from 1988)		
			Isis Blue		
			Mulberry		
			Sage Green		
			Mid Grey		
			Buckskin		
			Barley		

† = open choice

* = special order only

Exterior colour	Details	Interior trim	Details	Interior trim	Details
Vanden Plas Series 3		**Leather**		**Cloth**	
Silversand		Chamois			
		Tan			
		Olive			
Caramel		Chamois			
		Tan			
		Olive			
Coral		Chamois			
		Tan			
		Olive			
Biascan Blue		Chamois			
		Tan			
		Olive			
Mistletoe		Chamois			
		Tan			
		Olive			
Mink		Chamois			
		Tan			
		Olive			
Amethyst		Chamois			
		Tan			
		Olive			

Prices and production volumes

Series 1

	Price new (£)	1968	1969	1970	1971	1972	1973
Jaguar XJ6 2.8-litre standard	1797	■	–	–	–	–	–
Jaguar XJ6 2.8-litre de luxe	1897	■	■	■	■	■	■
Daimler Sovereign 2.8	2336	■	–	■	■	■	■
Jaguar XJ6 4.2-litre	2254	■	■	■	■	■	■
Jaguar XJ6 4.2 L	3464	–	–	–	–	■	■
Daimler Sovereign 4.2	2713	■	–	■	■	■	■
Daimler Sovereign 4.2 L	3954	–	–	–	–	■	■
Jaguar XJ12	3725	–	–	–	–	■	■
Jaguar XJ12L	4052	–	–	–	–	■	■
Daimler Double Six swb	4398	–	–	–	–	■	–
Daimler DD6 Vanden Plas	5363	–	–	–	–	■	■
Total Series 1 production							

Series 2

	Price new (£)	1968	1969	1970	1971	1972	1973
Jaguar XJ6 2.8-litre	–	–	–	–	–	–	■
Jaguar XJ6 4.2-litre	3674	–	–	–	–	–	■
Daimler Sovereign 4.2-litre	–	–	–	–	–	–	■
Daimler Sovereign 4.2 L	4766	–	–	–	–	–	■
Jaguar XJ6 4.2 L	4124	–	–	–	–	–	■
Jaguar XJ12 L	4702	–	–	–	–	–	■
Daimler Double Six L	5612	–	–	–	–	–	■
Jaguar XJ6 coupé	4260	–	–	–	–	■	–
Daimler Sovereign 4.2 coupé	4898	–	–	–	–	–	–
Jaguar XJ12 coupé	5181	–	–	–	–	–	–
Daimler Double Six coupé	6131	–	–	–	–	–	–
Daimler DD6 Vanden Plas	7333	–	–	–	–	–	■
Daimler Sovereign 4.2 Vanden Plas	–	–	–	–	–	–	–
Jaguar XJ6 3.4-litre	4795	–	–	–	–	–	–
Daimler Sovereign 3.4-litre	–	–	–	–	–	–	–
Total Series 2 production							

1974	1975	1976	1977	1978	1979	Total produced
–	–	–	–	–	–	Not known
–	–	–	–	–	–	19,322
–	–	–	–	–	–	3233
–	–	–	–	–	–	59,077
–	–	–	–	–	–	874
–	–	–	–	–	–	11,522
–	–	–	–	–	–	386
–	–	–	–	–	–	2474
–	–	–	–	–	–	754
–	–	–	–	–	–	534
–	–	–	–	–	–	351
						98,527

1974	1975	1976	1977	1978	1979	Total produced
–	–	–	–	–	–	170
■	–	–	–	–	–	12,147
■	–	–	–	–	–	2435
■	■	■	■	■	■	14,531
■	■	■	■	■	■	57,804
■	■	■	■	■	■	16,010
■	■	■	■	■	■	2608
■	■	■	■	–	–	6487
■	■	■	■	–	–	1677
■	■	■	■	–	–	1855
■	■	■	■	–	–	407
■	■	■	■	■	■	1726
–	■	■	■	■	–	883
–	■	■	■	■	■	6880
–	■	■	■	■	–	2341
						127,961

9 Prices and production volumes cont ...

The XJ Series saloons 1968 to 1992

	Price new (£)	1978	1979	1980	1981	1982	1983
Series 3							
Jaguar XJ6 3.4-litre	11,189	■	■	■	■	■	■
Jaguar XJ6 4.2-litre	12,326	■	■	■	■	■	■
Jaguar XJ12	15,014	■	■	■	■	■	■
Daimler Sovereign 4.2-litre	12,983	–	■	■	■	■	■
Daimler Double Six swb	15,689	–	■	■	■	■	■
Daimler 4.2 Vanden Plas	17,208	–	■	■	■	■	■
Daimler DD6 Vanden Plas	20,277	■	■	■	■	■	■
Jaguar 4.2 Sovereign	18,500	–	–	–	–	–	■
Jaguar V12 Sovereign	21,000	–	–	–	–	–	■
Total Series 3 production							
Total production all series							

Production changes

1968
XJ6 2.8- and 4.2-litre models introduced.
1969
Daimler Sovereign models introduced.
Curved tailpipes introduced to exhaust system.
Front seat headrest fitments made available.
Borg Warner Model 12 auto transmission fitted to 4.0-litre models.

1970
Air intake grilles incorporated into front outer headlight surrounds.
Satin-finished scuttle ventilator replaced chrome type.
Boot spare wheel/fuel pump covers changed (tools now inside boot).
'Jaguar' treadplates fitted to sills.

1971
Rear one-piece bumper changed to three-piece.
Radio aerials no longer possible to fit on front wings.
1972
XJ12 and DD6 models introduced.
Vanden Plas Double Six introduced.
Long-wheelbase bodyshell available on most models.

1973
(September) Production of short wheelbase bodyshells ceased.

1974
Series 2 models introduced.

Last 2.8-litre engines produced.
XJ coupé models announced but not available.

1975
Coupé models became available at end of 1974.
3.4-litre XJ6 introduced.
Daimler Vanden Plas 4.2-litre model introduced.
Kent alloy wheels introduced.
Fuel-injection for V12 engines launched.
Vinyl roofs fitted to all V12 saloons.
Chrome side strips offered as option on V12 models.

1977
General Motors GM400 auto transmission fitted to V12s.
(November) Last coupés built.

1978
Fuel-injection introduced on 4.2-litre models.
Sidelights moved to outer headlights/new indicator lenses below bumper.

1979
'XJ6' badging replaced for most markets by 'XJ 4.2' etc.
(March) Series 3 models introduced.
Five-speed manual gearbox became available on six-cylinder cars.
Flat-faced headlamps fitted for cars with wash/wipe system.
Pirelli tyres offered as an alternative to Dunlop.

1980
Dunlop Supersport D7 tyres fitted to V12s.
Merlin flush-fitting rear wing radio aerials fitted.

1984	1985	1986	1987	1988	1989	1990	1991	1992	Total produced
■	■	■	–	–	–	–	–	–	5799
■	■	■	–	–	–	–	–	–	97,349
■	■	■	■	■	■	■	■	■	5408
–	–	–	–	–	–	–	–	–	11,516
■	■	■	■	■	■	■	■	■	41,497
■	■	–	–	–	–	–	–	–	1953
■	■	–	–	–	–	–	–	–	402
■	■	■	■	–	–	–	–	–	16,346
■	■	■	■	■	■	■	■	■	7235
									187,505
									413,993

1981
HE engines added to V12 models.
Cigar lighter fitted to rear compartment in Daimler models.
Door puddle lights fitted to all models.
Rear compartment reading lights included in all Daimler models.
Black vinyl covering to centre console horizontal areas.
Chrome side strips fitted to all Daimlers, optional on Jaguar V12s.
Battery cooling fan deleted from six-cylinder models.

1982
Childproof locks supplied to rear doors.
Borg Warner Model 66 auto transmission fitted to six-cylinder cars.
Minor instruments supplier changed to Veglia.
Pepperpot alloy wheels introduced.
Individual rear seating standardised on Daimler models.
Daimler marque dropped from European markets.

1983
Rachelle cloth seats introduced.
Jaguar Sovereign models introduced.
Linestone headlining standardised for all cars.
Revised style of centre console with veneer on metal, new switches, etc.
Onboard computer became available.
Revised radiator grille (no bonnet trim), new wheel trims, and hubcaps fitted to Daimler models.
New-style front wing leaper badge fitted.

1984
Acrylic paint system adopted.
From this model year the insignia Sovereign and Vanden Plas were used differently across various world markets, primarily VDP for countries where the Daimler name was not permitted.

1985
Herringbone tweed upholstery standard on 3.4, optional on other models.
Veneered door fillets provided on 3.4-litre models.
Straight-grain woodwork fitted to 3.4s.
Stainless steel treadplates fitted to all models.
'HE' script dropped from badges on V12s, and all badges now rectangular 'solid' on boot lid.
Mark III air-conditioning system fitted.

1987
Last XJ6 left factory.

1989
V12s engined from factory converted to lead-free fuel.

1990
ABS brakes introduced.

1991
Last Jaguar V12 produced.

1992
Last Daimler Double Six produced.

Chassis numbers

Model	Right/left drive	Chassis/VIN commencing	Model	Right/left drive	Chassis/VIN commencing
XJ6 S1 2.8	RHD	1G 1001	XJ12 S2 (lwb)	RHD	2R 1001
	LHD	1G 50001		LHD	2R 50001
Daimler Sov S1 2.8	RHD	1T 1001	Daimler Sov S2 DD6 (lwb)	RHD	2K 1001
	LHD	1T 50001		LHD	2K 50001
XJ6 S1 4.2 (swb)	RHD	1L 1001	Daimler S2 VDP DD6	RHD	2P 1001
	LHD	1L 50001		LHD	2P 50001
XJ6 S1 4.2 (lwb)	RHD	2E 1001	XJ6 Coupé	RHD	2J 1001
	LHD	2E 50001		LHD	2J 50001
Daimler Sov S1 4.2 (lwb)	RHD	2D 1001	XJ12 Coupé	RHD	2G 1001
	LHD	2D 50001		LHD	2G 50001
Daimler S1 VDP	RHD	2B 1001	Daimler coupé 4.2	RHD	2H 1001
	LHD	2B 50001		LHD	2H 50001
XJ12 S1 (swb)	RHD	1P 1001	Daimler coupé DD6	RHD	2F 1001
	LHD	1P 50001		LHD	2F 50001
XJ12 S1 (lwb)	RHD	2C 1001			
	LHD	2C 50001			
Daimler DD6 S1 (swb)	RHD	2A 1001			
	LHD	2A 5000			
XJ6 S2 3.4	RHD	3A 1001			
	LHD	3A 50001			
Daimler Sov S2 3.4	RHD	3B 1001			
	LHD	3B 50001			
XJ6 S2 4.2 (swb)	RHD	2N 1001			
	LHD	2N 50001			
Daimler Sov S2 4.2 (swb)	RHD	2M 1001			
	LHD	2M 50001			
Daimler Sov S2 4.2 (lwb)	RHD	2S 1001			
	LHD	2S 50001			
Daimler S2 VDP 4.2	RHD	3C 1001			
	LHD	3C 50001			
XJ6 S2 4.2 (lwb)	RHD	2T 1001			
	LHD	2T 50001			

Daimler DS420 limousine
1968 to 1992

Background

In 1960 Jaguar purchased the Daimler company and its existing model range, namely the SP250 sports car and the Majestic Major saloon, continued in low-volume production until the mid-1960s under Jaguar control. Jaguar's first improvements to the range came with the introduction of a longer wheelbase 'limousine' model based on the Majestic Major. Coded the DR450, this also remained in production until the mid-1960s, but saw a total of only 865 cars produced. None of these models fall within the bounds of this publication.

However, with the merger of Jaguar Cars and the British Motor Corporation to form British Motor Holdings, the need was identified for a new 'carriage trade' limousine to replace both the Daimler Majestic and the ageing Austin Princess (later the Vanden Plas Princess). Apart from independently produced 'stretched' models of existing saloons, the only true limousine available 'off the shelf' by that time was the Rolls-Royce Phantom, which was too expensive for many private companies, embassies, or the trade to buy.

As Jaguar owned the Daimler name and already manufactured a vast floorpan for the Mark X/420G, and the British Motor Corporation owned the Vanden Plas Coachworks in London, it was a natural progression for the company to produce a new vehicle based heavily on Jaguar parts but utilising the prestigious Daimler name and the specialist coachbuilding abilities of VDP. The resultant DS420 limousine, as it became known, came out in 1968, virtually coinciding with the amalgamation of the British motor industry into British Leyland. The Jaguar 420 engine (with twin carburettors) had been mated to other Jaguar mechanical aspects from the Mark X and the XJ6. Other Jaguar input included the 420G floorpan and many inner panels, along with much of the trim from the same model, down to instruments, brightwork, and so on.

The body, designed by Vanden Plas, was reminiscent of the halcyon days of Hooper-bodied Daimlers, and there is no doubt that the overall styling met with the approval of everyone. At 18ft 10in long and weighing in at around 42cwt it was no lightweight, but interior accommodation was what a limousine was all about and the DS420 fitted the bill remarkably well, particularly at £4425.

The DS420 was offered as either a limousine model or a chassis only, allowing individuals to have their own bodywork hand-crafted. A hearse equivalent became available which proved very popular with the carriage trade. Just a couple of chassis-only vehicles were supplied for very special bodies, which were adapted to landaulette style. A saloon model was also considered, but it was felt that there would be little demand for such a traditionally styled car in the late 1960s.

The cars were initially built at the Vanden Plas Coachworks in London and were sold through normal Daimler channels, but with the closure of VDP in 1981 production moved to a special limousine shop facility at the Jaguar Browns Lane Plant in Coventry.

The DS420 was regularly updated to meet the demands of the market and to coincide with changes to other Jaguar and Daimler models, specifically in order to keep down the cost of production, which was very high, the car still being essentially hand-built.

The limousine's peak year was 1970, when 489 were sold. Production finally ceased at the end of 1992 when it became impractical to continue making such a car, both financially and because of changing regulations. A total of 5043 cars were produced, a not insignificant figure compared to previous Daimler limousines, or indeed Rolls-Royce sales. The DS420 remained very popular in the carriage trade for many years after production had finished and is now considered a classic in its own right.

Model range and development

The DS420 was announced in April 1968 and was available initially in just two forms. On its announcement at the British Motor Show that year it received a Silver Medal for coachwork design.

Models available at launch
Daimler DS420 limousine (standard equipment)
Daimler DS420 chassis (for private coachbuilders)

There is no definitive DS420 model. The 'standard' limousine offered in 1968 amounted to a long-wheelbase bodyshell with a fixed front and rear bench seat arrangement, occasional pull-up rear seating for additional passengers, and automatic transmission. At the price you didn't get such features as air-conditioning, electrically operated windows, or even full leather upholstery.

Right from the start chassis were supplied to various outside organisations, mostly for conversion to hearses, the height of the front screen and long-wheelbase being ideally suited to this form of vehicle.

Due to a drop in demand, poorer quality control, and the final demise of the separate Vanden Plas coachbuilding facility, production moved to Jaguar's factory in 1981, when various changes took place in trim construction to cater for quicker and easier production methods. At this time the gearbox was changed to the modern and more refined General Motors unit, and the usual equipment levels were improved with air-conditioning as standard.

The basic essence of the DS420 remained unchanged throughout production, although specification and equipment levels were constantly improved and updated to meet the demands of the market, individual tastes and, of course, the Jaguar parts bin. No other models were ever produced and the last car (a chassis to be built as a hearse) left the Browns Lane works in November 1992. The next to last car went to the Jaguar Daimler Heritage Trust, where it remains to this day.

The Daimler DS420 limousine filled a gap in the market for a highly specialised vehicle which some would say still exists to this day.

Styled by Vanden Plas, built around Jaguar parts, the DS420 takes cues from the Mark X/420G models. Differences from the front amount to the enlarged radiator grille surround with Daimler flutes and the scripted 'D' emblem on the bonnet.

Side view reveals the sheer size of the DS420, which is instantly identifiable from any other Jaguar/Daimler model.

The rear of the DS420 is unique but again takes styling cues from the Mark X/420G, using the same lighting and bumper bar. However, the overriders changed throughout production. The boot-mounted number plate plinth/illumination panel initially used the Mark X plinth with Daimler badge, which was changed in the 1970s to this unique Daimler plinth.

Exterior identification points

General points applicable to early DS420s

Front view

- Frontal aspect similar to Mark X/420G with twin headlight treatment. Wrap-around indicator lenses, horn grilles, and slimline bumper bar with overriders and centrally mounted number plate plinth.
- Prominent rectangular radiator grille with vertical chrome slats and typical Daimler flutes to the upper section.
- Alligator-style opening bonnet with prominent swept 'D' mascot and full-length centrally located chrome strip along bonnet.
- Steeply raked one-piece windscreen with chromed surround and two windscreen wipers.

Rear view

- One-piece rear screen with chromed surround.
- Severe sloping rear wings and rear-hinged one-piece boot lid.
- Adapted light clusters from Mark X/420G.
- Daimler 420 Sovereign-style rear number plate/reversing light plinth mounted centrally on boot lid.
- Slimline rear bumper as Mark X/420G.
- No badging apart from scripted 'Daimler' on boot lid.
- Twin exhaust pipes emerged underneath bumper bar and rear valance as Mark X/420G.

Side view

- Softened razor-edged styling, long-wheelbase, with severe slope to rear wings and boot area.
- Significant use of chrome including waistline trim running the entire length of the body from the front wing, across the doors between the handles, and sloping down following the wing line to the rear.
- Traditional chrome on brass window surrounds with enlarged rear side windows with quarter-lights.
- Steel wheels painted either to body colour or silver with standard equipment chrome rimbellishers and conventional chromed hubcaps following later Daimler design.

General changes to DS420 during production

Front view

- Horn grilles initially amended to a horizontally slatted simpler circular design. Later changed again to rectangular style.
- Sidelight/indicator units altered to a rectangular style, affixed in the same position.

Changes to the bumper bar, overriders, and other exterior trim occurred throughout the life of the DS420. The car on the left is to the original design with Mark X bumper/overriders and 240/340 horn grilles. The car on the right is a post-1970 model with rubber-faced overriders and plainer horizontal slatted horn grilles.

Another later version of the external trim, with rubber-faced energy absorbing bumper bars, adapted from the Series 3 XJ design from the mid-1980s, which necessitated revised rectangular sidelight units and XJ Series 1 horn grilles.

Above left: Initially, up until the end of the 1980s, DS420s came as standard with steel painted wheels with conventional Jaguar hubcaps. Nearing the end of production Kent alloy wheels were used, these being adapted to take hubcaps.

Above right: Interior layout and fitments were always down to personal order requirements. A 'conventional' model would include a rear bench trimmed in either leather, cloth, or other material, with extra occasional seating as seen here. Wind-up windows were the norm, electrics, including division etc, being down to special order. In this very late model Series 3 adapted trim was used for the door panels.

- Overriders changed to smaller chromed style with rubber buffers.
- Later model bumper bar altered to adapted style from Series 3 XJ, of rubber-fronted style with chrome top finisher blade, and indicator lenses mounted within the rubber.

Rear view
- Later cars fitted with bespoke extended chrome fluted number plate/reversing light plinth.
- Mid-term bumper bar featured smaller overriders with rubber buffers. Later models featured Series 3 rubber-faced bumper bar incorporating rear fog lamps and with chrome finisher blades.

Side view
- Significant use of chrome including waistline trim running the entire length of body from the front wing, across the doors between the handles, and sloping down following the wing line to the rear. Simplified on later models.
- Steel-wheel design changed at various stages, sometimes without chromed rimbellishers. Later cars equipped with adapted Kent alloy wheels but still with chromed hubcaps.

Interior identification points

DS420 (early models)
- Mark X/420G-style dashboard layout with or without black padded top dashboard roll.
- Steering wheel and column as Mark 420G, including automatic transmission quadrant and indicator stalk.
- Door and other soft trimming adapted from Mark X/420G style.
- Initially a bench-type front seat arrangement trimmed to match Mark X style.
- Rear compartment on standard limousine has bench seat arrangement with vertical pleating and fold-away centre armrest.
- Door and other soft trimming adapted from Mark X model with wood cappings to upper sections and rear window surrounds.
- Occasional fold-away seating to centre section of the rear compartment trimmed to match.
- Conventional manual sliding glass partition between front and rear compartment trimmed in vinyl and wood.

Identifiable changes during production
- Design, layout, and type of instrumentation changed throughout production, moving away from pure 420G original.
- Very late cars featured manually operated choke control on dashboard.
- Later steering wheels and columns adapted from Series 3 Daimler model.
- Door and other soft trimming simplified to a style unique to DS420.
- Mid-term split-bench front seat arrangement, later changed to individual front seats with full adjustment.
- Automatic transmission quadrant repositioned to floor, centrally mounted within black fibre console.
- Centrally situated E-type Series 3 chromed handbrake replaced umbrella style.
- Door and other soft trimming in rear compartment simplified to match front.

NB: Most DS420 models were made to special order so interior trim will vary dramatically from car to car, including the use of non-leather upholstery, electric divisions, side curtains, etc. See accompanying photographs and other details within the production changes listing for some of these features.

More elaborate interiors were fitted, like this 'mobile office'... or a veneered and fully fitted cocktail cabinet.

Above left: Most of the trim for the driving compartment came directly from the Mark X/420G, with adaptations which included a centre console to accept the later style of automatic transmission control. Earlier cars used a steering column-mounted control as found on Mark Xs.

Above right: Front compartment seating varied from a simple vinyl-covered bench through to fully adjustable separate leather seats on the later models and, again, similarities can be seen with other Jaguar/Daimler models, like the 420 and Mark X.

Technical specification

	DS420
cc	4235
Bore and stroke (mm)	92.07 x 106
Compression ratio	7:1 (8:1 optional)
bhp	245
@ rpm	5000
Torque (lb ft)	283
@ rpm	3500
Fuelling	2 x SU carbs
Transmission	BW 3-speed auto
Wheel size (in)	15, steel, later alloy
Suspension front	Ind semi-trailing wishbones, coil springs, anti-roll bar
Suspension rear	Ind lower wishbones/upper driveshaft link, radius arms, coil springs
Brakes	4-wheel disc, rear inboard
Performance	
0–60mph (sec)	13.4
Top speed (mph)	109
Average mpg	14.8
Dimensions	
Length (in)	226
Width (in)	77.5
Height (in)	63.5
Wheelbase (in)	141
Front track (in)	58
Rear track (in)	58
Weight (cwt)	42

Optional extras

Choice of two types of radio installations for front and rear compartment.
Electric radio aerial.
Electrically operated front and rear windows.
Electrically operated rear quarter windows.
Electrically operated centre division.
Chromium-plated flag mast for bonnet.
Adjustable reading lamps in the rear compartment.
Nylon over-rugs for the rear compartment.
Rubber fitted matting for the front compartment.
Laminated windscreen.
Heated rear screen.
Front seat belts.
Rear seat belts.
Fire extinguisher.
Sundym tinted windscreen and side windows.
Wing mirrors.
Integrated ignition/starter switch to steering column (earlier cars).
Fog/spot lamps.
Electrically heated rear screen.
Rear compartment footrests.
Chromium-plated badge bar.
Sony colour TV in veneered cabinet.
Single or dual tone colour finishes and interior trims to suit individual requirements.
Equipped and veneered cocktail cabinet for rear compartment.
Media veneered cabinet to incorporate audio visual systems.
Fluorescent lighting for rear compartment.
West of England cloth upholstery for rear compartment.
Full leather trim throughout car.
Alternative wood veneers.
Curtains for rear compartment.
Fold-away veneered writing tables.
Refrigerated cool box for boot area.
Central division and rear window blinds.
Exterior colour schemes to individual requirements.

Colour schemes

Exterior colour	Single/Duotone	Interior trim
Embassy Black	Single	Bespoke
Carlton Grey	Single	
Maroon	Single	
Navy	Single	
Silver	Single	
Cream	Single	
Embassy Black	Duotone	Carlton Grey
		Silver
		Maroon
		Green
Navy	Duotone	Silver Blue

Later Coventry production: any combination of Jaguar/Daimler standard colours could be specified, as well as bespoke colours.

Prices and production volumes

	Price new (£)	1968	1969	1970	1971	1972	1973	1974
DS420 chassis	2369	■	■	■	■	■	■	■
DS420 limousine	4425	■	■	■	■	■	■	■

	1975	1976	1977	1978	1979	1980	to 1992	Total
DS420 chassis	■	■	■	■	■	■	■	903
DS420 limousine	■	■	■	■	■	■	■	4141
Total production								**5044**

Production changes

1968
DS420 model introduced.

1981
Production moved from London to Coventry.
Nylon carpeting fixed.
GM400 auto transmission fitted instead of Borg Warner.
Thermo plastic paint finish adopted.
Steering column-mounted ignition/starter switch supplied.
Series 3 XJ steering wheel adopted.

1983
Improved air-conditioning system.
Revised door locks fitted using fewer keys.

1984
Split-bench type seating for front (adjustable).
Auto gearbox quadrant moved to floor from steering column.
Pre-formed centre console fitted to accommodate gearlever.
E-type Series 3 handbrake fitted to centre, replacing umbrella type.
Chrome rimbellishers now extra-cost option for road wheels.
Revised bumper bar overriders (small, including rubber facings) introduced.
Rectangular horn grilles replaced circular type.
Rectangular sidelight/indicator lenses replaced circular type at front.
Rear number plate plinth revised to fluted design.

1985
Front sidelights incorporated in headlight units.
Manual choke system adopted.

1986
Series 3 XJ-style front and rear rubber-faced bumper bars fitted.
Reduced-depth radiator grille fitted to accommodate above.
'Daimler' scripted badge appeared on boot lid for first time.

1987
Revised siting of steering column to provide better driving position.

1989
Kent alloy wheels fitted, adapted to accept Daimler hubcaps.

1992
Daimler DS420 discontinued.

Chassis numbers

Model	Right/left drive	Chassis/VIN commencing
Daimler DS420 Limo	RHD	1M 1001
	LHD	1M 20001

11 The XJ-S 1975 to 1996

Background

With the demise of the E-type in 1974 few people realised that Jaguar would be abandoning the sports car market, for although the company had initially contemplated a direct replacement this was not to be – a situation brought about not so much by Jaguar, as by world opinion.

Most other manufacturers were casting aside the principle of an open-top two-seater with rakish styling, plenty of noise, a relatively hard ride, and all the other features associated with the true sports car that marques like Jaguar, Triumph, and MG had become famous for. Instead, changing legislation, the need for improved safety – particularly for the US market – and drivers wanting more refinement in an everyday car, forced manufacturers to think of producing coupés and grand touring cars that would cater for a wider audience and, if based on existing saloons, would be cheaper to produce and therefore more profitable.

Jaguar had, to some extent, already gone down this route with the Series 3 E-type, in that it was a much more refined car than previous Es. They had also introduced the ill-fated XJ coupé as an alternative to a four-door saloon in 1973, though it didn't actually appear until late in 1974 for 1975 delivery, and was abandoned in 1977, partly due to build problems.

This set the scene for the XJ-S or XJ 'sport', utilising the short wheelbase floorpan of the XJ saloon, essentially the same V12 engine and suspension, as well as many other mechanical and trim items, this being considered an economical way forward. Allied to this was Jaguar thinking that it would be best to move up-market with such a two-door coupé, no longer catering for a relatively small sports car audience but instead aiming at another market 'new' to Jaguar and at a much higher price. In fact the XJ-S was geared to be the most expensive production car the company had produced, so it was marketed at owners of Jensen Interceptors, Ferraris, Maseratis, and other well-known luxury super-cars.

For the exterior design two basic ideas were considered, one coming from Jaguar's in-house styling department, the other from Malcolm Sayer, already well known for his work on the E-type. His design won out and was to be a radical move for Jaguar, virtually abandoning the traditional style and features normally expected from the marque. This had a negative effect on existing customers because the car was nothing like previous Jaguars – no wood veneer inside, hardly any chrome outside, avant-garde exterior styling, and not a Jaguar leaper to be found anywhere! The effect on the 'other' market was also not encouraging; Jaguar's poor 1970s reputation didn't help, and few considered that the XJ-S had the 'street cred' of, say, a Ferrari.

When launched at £8900 it certainly wasn't cheap by Jaguar standards and was actually very close in price to competitors like the Mercedes SL and Porsche 911; and although faster than most, extreme thirst for fuel and worries over longevity proved deadly for the new car. Sales seemed reasonably encouraging for the first couple of years, but they soon started to decline, to the point where the Board at Jaguar considered dropping the whole project. This may have happened had it not been for the foresight of the new man at the helm, John Egan.

By 1981 the XJ-S had been revitalised with a more economical engine, improvements in build quality, and the restoration of some semblance of traditionalism. Sales started to rise, helped in addition by race-track success in the US initially, and later in Europe courtesy of the TWR team competing in the European Touring Car Championship. In 1984 TWR won the championship and drivers' championship outright from BMW, and the popularity of the XJ-S soared.

Other models entered the range during the 1980s, offering cheaper alternatives and, with the cabriolet, a return to semi-open-top motoring. Pressure from the US resulted in a full convertible, which appeared at the end of 1987 and gave another boost to a car and company that were now in the throes of significantly better times;

The original XJ-S cars, now known as pre-HE, are identified by the black rubber bumper bars front and rear. For the first couple of years in production they also featured this matt black boot panel and chromed finisher to the B/C post area. All pre-HF models had the Kent alloy wheels depicted here.

Frontal aspect of the pre-HE XJ-S from 1975 to 1981, with black radiator grille and rubber bumper bars.

Pre-HE XJ-Ss featured no interior wood veneer, merely alloy and black. All cars from 1975 through to 1991 carried this style of bar gauge instrument binnacle.

From 1981 the car was called the XJ-S HE, identified from the side by its twin coachlines and starfish alloy wheels.

1989 proved a record year for XJ-S sales, with over 10,000 being produced.

The model was totally rejuvenated in 1991 with a new bodyshell, yet greater improved quality, and a 4.0-litre engine (eventually a 6.0-litre was added as well). Year on year the XJ-S was improved, and even when the world became aware of a forthcoming entirely new replacement (the XK8) sales were still better than they had been in the 1970s or early 1980s.

Despite the XJ-S being considered early on as somewhat of an 'ugly duckling' it went through several revival stages, eventually earning its keep handsomely. Today it is still unique in its styling and is as instantly recognisable as the E-type. Over 115,000 were produced in its 21-year history and even its XK8 replacement is based on the same floorpan. The XJ-S turned out to be a fitting tribute to Jaguar and was perhaps the ultimate refined sporting grand tourer.

Model range and development

In simple terms there was but one model of XJ-S at its launch in September 1975, your only choices being from a very limited selection of exterior colour schemes and manual (four-speed) or three-speed automatic transmission.

Model at launch
XJ-S 5.3-litre coupé

This was the most expensive production car made by Jaguar up to that time, but for your £8900 you got quite an inclusive package. Only available with the 5.3-litre V12 engine, now fuel injected, the XJ-S also benefited from leather upholstery, electric windows, air-conditioning, and alloy wheels all as standard equipment. In terms of performance, with a 150mph-plus top speed and acceleration to go with it, it was a match for anything Jaguar had ever produced before, and pretty close to most of the competition.

The downsides to the XJ-S were the body style, with its unusual 'flying buttresses' flowing down from the roof to the rear wings, and the lack of brightwork, woodwork, or even rear seat accommodation – and the price, which also reflected in the car's abysmal fuel economy! By 1980 annual sales had dwindled to just over 1000 cars, which didn't warrant production. The manual transmission car hadn't been popular either.

Jaguar boss John Egan set about improving the concept and build quality of the XJ-S, which was effectively relaunched in 1981 as the XJ-S HE (standing for High Efficiency). The cylinder heads had been redesigned by May, and with improved combustion the V12 was now well capable of up to 20mpg if driven carefully. Jaguar also styled in some more traditional features like chrome-

HE front view, with chromed grille and revised rubber-faced impact-absorbing bumper bar treatment.

Rear view of HE model showing badging and rubber-faced bumper bar.

Above left: Revised interior from the pre-HE models, initially with burr elm woodwork, replaced from 1987 by walnut. Black fabric coverings to the centre console were also replaced by wood veneer in 1987. Steering wheel design changed to S3 XJ from S2 XJ style on pre-HE models.

Above right: Starfish alloy wheels were only ever fitted to XJ-S models, initially as standard on the HE and the 3.6-litre cabriolet and then as an option on other cars up to 1991.

topped rubber bumpers (adapted from the Series 3 saloons), a special set of Starfish alloy wheels just for this model, a swage coachline to break up the slab-sided look of the body and, inside, the return of veneer (elm). All this, accompanied by vastly improved build quality, set the XJ-S on a road to recovery and assured it of success second time around.

The next move to increase sales was by offering a wider range. A second XJ-S model was therefore launched with an alternative engine, a brand new 3.6-litre multi-valve straight six unit (AJ6) destined for a new saloon yet to appear, the XJ40. (Like Jaguar's earlier XK and V12 engines, the AJ6 was introduced in a sporting model, the XJ-S, before entering service in a saloon.) Slight changes in the standard of trim enabled the 3.6-litre XJ-S to be marked at a lower price to the top of the range V12 HE. The new model was also offered with a five-speed Getrag manual gearbox (the V12 being no longer available with any manual option) and was £2000 cheaper to buy than the V12, offering better fuel economy. The 3.6 manual could even hold its own to 60mph against the larger-engined car.

Another new model appeared at the same time in an attempt to satisfy US demand for a convertible Jaguar. The XJ-S cabriolet introduced in 1983 offered a degree of hand finishing with a rear-section fold-away hood and front targa panels. Launched as a car to special order it was later to become available with the V12 engine as well but was never as popular as anticipated, due to the time it took to open and close the impractical top compared to the fully electrically operated concealed hoods of its competitors.

Jaguar eventually totally re-engineered the XJ-S bodyshell to create a proper two-seater convertible, announced at the end of 1987. This top of the range model, initially only available with the V12 engine, was sumptuously equipped with a fully electrically operated hood and even a glass heated rear screen. At £36,000 it was again the most expensive Jaguar you could buy and it was a hit in the US.

There was lots more publicity for the XJ-S in the 1980s of course, with three years in the European Touring Car Championship and the announcement of a sportier XJR-S special edition, initially produced by TWR themselves and later under the JaguarSport name as a joint venture with Jaguar. These cars offered a sports handling kit, improved brakes and engine manifolding, enhanced interior, and an exterior bodykit if required. Jaguar also produced limited edition models specifically for different markets, like the Collection Rouge for the USA, and the Le Mans for European markets to celebrate Jaguar's 1988 and 1990 wins.

By 1989 more XJ-Ss had been produced than all the E-types ever made, and twice as many as

Cabriolet models were introduced in 1984 with targa-top arrangement and XJ-SC badging on the boot lid.

Above left: Interior of the cabriolet model, now available with manual transmission. This car also featured part-leather/part-cloth upholstery, available on all models from this time.

Above right: Rear seating was not included as standard on cabriolet models. Instead this box arrangement was fitted with luggage rails.

The XJ-S convertible from 1988, always equipped with these lattice alloy wheels as standard.

Seat design changed for the convertible, and was later fitted to other models as well. Electric seat adjustment was also available, with a generally improved trim level and walnut veneer. There were no rear seats, this new style of box arrangement being present instead, which was different to that of the cabriolet (see picture above). Note also revised steering wheel.

the XK of the 1950s. However, sales started to tumble significantly in 1991 and Jaguar, without an alternative car to offer, re-engineered the XJ-S at a cost of over £50m and renamed it the XJS. This had a virtually entirely new bodyshell, though now easier to produce, and galvanised. The overall styling was only subtly altered so as not to damage what was, after all, by now an established and accepted design. With smoothed-out lines, improved glass area, a redesigned interior, a new 4.0-litre engine (with, later, a 6.0-litre V12 form as well), the XJS was relaunched yet again. This time there was not only the 4.0-litre coupé and convertible, but a 5.3-litre coupé and convertible and a 6.0-litre XJR-S JaguarSport performance model.

After an initial dip, sales rose again in 1993 and 1994, with yet more enhancements, the new 6.0-litre 318bhp V12 engine, changed frontal and rear styling features, and finally, in 1995, the 'Celebration' models to commemorate 60 years of the Jaguar marque and the final demise of the XJS.

Even in 1996 over 3000 XJSs were delivered and at the time that its replacement, the XK8, was announced there were few new XJSs around in the dealers to sell. A total of 115,413 had been produced in 25 years, and the XJS had achieved Jaguar's dream of providing the ultimate grand tourer.

Several special editions were produced in the heyday of the XJ-S, and many companies then and now produce modified versions, most of which commenced with TWR, the racing firm, for the European Touring Car Championship. It was TWR that produced the original Jaguar XJ-S Sport model, later adapted to the JaguarSport range (see below). Jaguar also at one time envisaged producing a Daimler XJ-S but only one was produced. A longer wheelbase model was even conceived, to provide more interior space.

A limited run of bespoke convertibles was also produced in America from standard coupé models with agreement from the factory. Manufactured by the Hess and Eisenhardt coachbuilding company, they were not only sanctioned by Jaguar but sold to special order through US dealerships. This only lasted until Jaguar introduced its own in-house convertible in 1987.

Exterior identification points

General points applicable to all XJ-Ss and XJSs

Front view
- Wrap-around bumper bar incorporated indicator lenses and number plate mounting in the centre (see photographs for different style post-1981).
- Front under-valance with air intake

Lattice alloy wheels fitted from 1983, standard on V12 convertibles and as an option on all other models.

Limited edition models included the Le Mans car with US-style four-headlight treatment.

The facelift model was introduced from 1991 with most body panels replaced. This convertible model shows the revised external look of these post-1991 cars, which at this time retained the rubber-faced bumper bars.

Comparison between the pre- and post-facelift models (the latter in the foreground), with revised rake to the windscreen, pillarless side windows without quarter-lights, and…

slatted grille, below which was a full-width black rubberised spoiler, on later models incorporated into all-enveloping bumper bar.
- Single oval headlights with surrounds featured, for UK and European cars, a conventional four-headlight treatment, with chrome surround for US and Canadian models.
- Shallow radiator grille with horizontal slats, full width between headlights and central badge.
- One-piece forward-hinged bonnet, with front centrally mounted circular 'gunmetal' growler badge, swept down at front to meet radiator grille. Bonnet shaped to meet wings and headlight pods. AJ6 cars featured raised centre bonnet section to clear engine height, later adopted for all cars.
- Rear of bonnet bulkhead-mounted air intake in various finishes according to model and year.
- One-piece curved windscreen with chromed surround and twin wiper blades.

Rear view
- Rear heated screen with chromed surround following contours of roof and buttresses (coupé models).
- Flat boot panel with black-painted vertical section on early models only (see production changes).
- On boot vertical panel appropriate badging according to model and year (see photographs).
- Centre boot panel plinth contained twin reversing lights, hidden boot lock, and the name 'Jaguar' in bold lettering on a finisher surrounding boot key lock, later changed completely with facelift models (see photographs).
- Rear light units wrap around wings at base and sculptured to wing curvature at the top. Facelift models featured neutral density integrated light units (see photographs).
- Wrap-around bumper to match front, although in this case running for the entire length of rear wings to meet the rear wheel-arches.
- Twin exhaust tailpipes emerged from rear valance as on XJ saloons.

Side view
- Coupés of all ages are instantly identifiable by the flying buttress flowing down from roof panel to rear wings, on the nearside featuring concealed fuel filler cap.
- Slab-sided with waistline body crease. Later models featured swage coachlines according to model and year.
- Ford Cortina-chromed flush door handles and black powder-coated door and window surrounds with non-opening front quarter-lights. Facelift models abandoned door window frames, revised rear window treatment, and had new door handle design (see photographs).

... revised side elevation. Note the rear side window changes and boot styling.

Analogue instrumentation introduced on the XJS from 1991, initially in wood veneer, later replaced by the style seen here except for V12-engined cars.

Interior alterations affected all models with the facelift, including a new centre console, better switchgear, and revised seating.

More changes from 1993, with all-enveloping plastic bumper bars painted to body colour. This is the later 2+2 convertible model, which necessitated a shallower rear window.

173

The XJ-S 1975 to 1996

- Driver's door-only mounted mirror on early cars. Later design changed and fitted mirrors both sides.
- Alloy wheels fitted to all cars of differing types according to model and year (see accompanying photographs).

XJ-S model specifics

Pre-HE coupés
- Black rubber bumper bars front and rear with no chrome finishers.
- Headlights and radiator grille with chromed surround.
- Separate under-valance black spoiler.
- Centrally mounted radiator grille depicted 'V12' emblem.
- 'XJ-S'-only badging featured on boot panel.
- Matt black vertical boot panel only featured on very early cars.
- GKN Kent alloy wheels fitted.

XJ-S HE coupés
- New-style rubber bumper bars front and rear incorporating chromed top finishers similar to those used on Series 3 XJ saloons. Different more prominent bumper bars featured on some US models.
- Growler badge in pewter style now fitted to forward centre area of bonnet. Side indicator repeater lenses on forward edge of front wings (larger type fitted to US and Canadian models).
- Five-spoke silver/grey Starfish alloy wheels fitted.
- Double-stripe swage coachline along entire length of body.
- Larger chrome-plated door mirrors now fitted to both doors.
- 'XJ-S' badge now moved to left-hand side from right and 'HE' badging fitted to other side of boot lid panel (later changed to 'V12').

XJ-S 3.6-litre coupés
- Growler badge in centre of radiator grille.
- New bonnet with raised centre section.
- Silver finish pepperpot alloy wheels, but Starfish were available as an option.
- '3.6' badging on right-hand side of boot lid.

Cabriolet (all models)
- Side view above door height revised with 'solid' frame, black powder coated with more pronounced B/C post with chromed leaper badge at base. Door and window surround as part of main body structure with chromed rain gutters.
- No rear wing buttresses.
- Coupé roof effectively cut away and replaced with fabric-covered removable targa panels over driver and front seat passenger. Fabric-covered crossover bar from side to side of the car, and behind it a fold-down fabric hood arrangement with Perspex rear screen.

The deeper rear window of the earlier two-seater convertibles easily identifies these cars from the outside.

The 2+2 seating arrangement in the post-1992 convertibles.

Revised rear bumper bar treatment, which also included 'square' tailpipes.

Above left: Later car interior, in this case a V12 with different seat stitching and a half-wood/half-leather steering wheel, which was later also adopted for all Celebration models.

Above right: Five-spoke alloy wheels became available on XJS models from 1993.

- All cabriolets fitted with either Starfish or lattice alloy wheels.
- At the rear 'XJ-SC' badging and either '3.6' or 'V12' dependent on model. Fuel filler moved to top of nearside rear wing utilising XJ Series chromed lockable cover.

Convertible models (up to 1991)
- Side view easily identifiable by the frameless construction of the windows with no quarter-lights.
- Fitted fabric hood with small rear windows that electrically descend into the body when hood mechanism operated.
- No rear wing buttresses, and fuel filler cap positioned and of the same type as on cabriolet models.
- Rear screen of glass with impregnated heating element.
- Boot badges followed coupé practice.
- All convertibles followed later coupé practice with thinner multi-coloured swage coachlines.

XJS models (post-1991 facelift)
- All cars now featured the 3.6-litre-style bonnet panel with raised centre section.
- Revised style of under-valance air intake.
- Blackened radiator grille but with chrome horizontal top finisher.
- Recognisable from the side by the frameless door windows without quarter-lights and enlarged glass area to rear side windows (coupés only).
- Substantial chromed rain gutters curved to match frame of rear side windows (coupé models).
- Revised rake to front screen with thinner chromed surround.
- Lattice alloy wheels initially fitted to all models. Other styles and options became available later.
- Square-design indicator repeaters now fitted to rear bottom edge of front wings (replaced by badges for some export markets).
- New-style flush chromed door pulls and locks.
- More angular appearance at the rear with buttresses retained for coupé model.
- Neutral density rear lighting units now incorporate enlarged reflector units stretching across boot lid to meet centrally mounted number plate.
- Chromed surround at rear now incorporates central section for boot lock and number plate illumination.
- Stronger 'XJS' badging, also showing 'V12' badging where applicable to offside and 'Jaguar' to nearside.
- In all identification for post-facelift models, both written and badging, 'XJS' was used instead of 'XJ-S'.

XJS models (1993–6)
- An ease of identification point was the adoption of all-enveloping reinforced plastic

For a limited period in 1994 4.0-litre models gained colour-keyed brightwork around the headlights and door mirrors.

Last of the line top of the range V12 coupé with later 20-spoke alloy wheels, only fitted as standard on this model.

Last of the line 4.0-litre Celebration convertible with five-spoke alloy wheels (an alternative to the diamond-turned wheels available at this time).

Comparison frontal view of the three styles of XJ-S and XJS from the 1981 HE (centre), to facelift on the right, and Celebration on the left.

bumper bars at the front with chrome top finishers, and incorporating rectangular indicator lenses, number plate surround, under-bumper spoiler, and air intake and side reflectors at the front. Bumpers painted to body colour.
- For a period of about a year V12 models identified by chromed surrounds to headlights and wing mirrors, with 4.0-litres identified by these areas being colour-keyed. Later changed so that all models returned to chromed finish.
- At the rear same style of bumper bar treatment with integrated rear fog lights.
- Square or oval exhaust tailpipes according to model.
- Convertible rear screen altered to a smaller size to accommodate fold-down around 2+2 seating arrangement (see interior changes).
- Most cars fitted with new five-spoke alloy wheels but others available to order.
- From 1995 'Celebration' models featured Aerosport diamond-turned alloy wheels, chromed surround to rear number plate, and restyled bonnet badge.

NB: Variations in alloy wheel type occurred several times during production and were available as extra-cost options anyway. See production changes and accessories listing.

Factory special editions
- *Collection Rouge*: Only available to the US market. Finished in Signal Red with matching diamond-turned and painted lattice alloy wheels and gold coachline. US-style four-headlight treatment and revised badging, with 'Collection Rouge' on boot lid and gold-plated growler badge on bonnet.
- *Classic Collection*: Only available to the US market. Similar to Collection Rouge except limited range of exterior colours, new 'Classic' badging on boot lid, and rear spoiler fitted to most cars. Revised front badging as Rouge.
- *Le Mans*: Only available in European markets to commemorate Le Mans wins in 1988 and 1990. US four-headlight treatment at front with gold growler badge on bonnet. Front spoiler painted to body colour. Twin gold coachlines along side of car and unique 'Le Mans' badging on boot panel. Lattice wheels and sports suspension fitted. Limited range of exterior paint finishes.
- *JaguarSport XJR-S models*: Factory-build standard XJ-S shipped down to JaguarSport Bloxham works in Oxfordshire for final finishing, much of which was dependent on individual customer order. Replacement of front and rear bumpers by pre-formed plastic type painted to body colour. Front bumper incorporated indicator lighting as usual but also under-valance and air intake.

Unique to the XJ-S were the TWR JaguarSport models built as a joint venture between Jaguar and the TWR Company, offering a more sporty appeal at a premium price. This early example with a modified 6.0-litre engine shows typical JaguarSport options like the bodykit and wheels and slightly lower-set suspension.

Revised interior for JaguarSport cars included leather-covered gear knob, special steering wheel, and badging.

Rear-end treatment for JaguarSport models included bumper kit, four exhaust tailpipes, revised badging, and spoiler.

Facelift-style XJR-S by JaguarSport before production ceased at the end of 1992. Here the later style of body has been adapted to a similar specification to that of the earlier models, with new-style sports wheels.

Front radiator and light surrounds black powder coated. Door mirrors colour-keyed to exterior paint finish, as was rear bumper, which incorporated hazard lighting and under-valance with exhaust tailpipes. Brightwork again finished to either body colour or black powder coated. Speedline alloy wheels fitted with flush centre caps hiding wheel nuts. Wider wheels and tyres to suit. Over-sills to body sill areas painted to body colour. Boot lid spoiler curving down over both rear wings with hole drilled to accommodate radio aerial. Later post-1991 facelift cars adapted to same styling basis but with revised panels. Rear boot spoiler changed so as not to infringe on radio aerial. New alloy wheels with exposed wheel nuts.

NB: Models produced by outside companies, including the initial TWR car, are not covered in this book.

Interior identification points

Pre-HE models (1975–81)

- Predominantly black trim finish to dashboard and centre console area with bright alloy areas around radio/air-conditioning panel and auxiliary switch/clock panel.
- Instrumentation binnacle mounted directly in front of the driver incorporating speedometer, rev counter, and bar gauges for ancillary instruments. Row of warning lights above and below in plastic surround.
- Two-spoke steering wheel with leather surround of same design as early Series 2 saloons.
- Air-conditioning ventilator layout at each end of dashboard adjustable, and in central area following Series 2 XJ format.
- Centre console layout as Series 2 saloons but with shallower slope to mid-area leading up to armrest.
- Lockable glovebox on passenger side of dashboard.
- Bucket type seating with horizontal pleats in the leather inserts and incorporating built-in headrests. Seat adjustment to allow access to rear compartment.
- Rear sculptured seat area to match style of front.
- Door panels heat embossed with full-length armrests/door pulls and built-in pockets.
- Door handles and lock mechanisms as XJ saloons and lower panels incorporating carpet areas and speaker grilles.
- Rear side windows do not open.
- All pre-HE XJ-Ss were finished in leather trim, but cloth available to special order.
- Boot trimmed in black carpet with preformed plastic spare wheel cover.

Later-type spoiler treatment on the XJR-S model was also available for the standard cars.

Different styles of coachline were used on XJ-S models. Pre-HE models had no coachline. HE and 3.6-litre cars featured this style of double line.

Twin thin opposing colour lines used on cars from 1988 on.

After facelift a single colour line was adopted.

HE and V12 models (1981–91)
- Burr elm veneered woodwork fitted to horizontal sections of dashboard and auxiliary switch panel. From 1987 also fitted to ski-slope on centre console.
- Elm woodwork cappings also fitted to revised-style door trims without heat embossing in trim.
- Black vinyl replaced previous bright alloy finish around centre console area. Veneer on later cars changed to burr walnut (see production changes).
- Steering wheel of later XJ type with more rectangular centre boss and thicker rim, replaced again in 1987 by one incorporating finger grips. Two horn push-buttons to centre spoke.
- Rear seating now incorporated built-in seatbelt connectors.
- Boot now carpeted in grey with black soft spare wheel cover.

NB: After 1989 other changes took place according to model, such as the fitting of another (four-spoke) steering wheel, revised seating, etc. See production changes.

3.6-litre models (1983–91)
- As HE and V12 except for seats having part-leather/part tweed covering to centre sections on standard models, all-leather being an extra-cost option.
- Manual gearbox models featured black leather gaiter to gearlever on centre console, replacing auto transmission quadrant, and stitched leather gear knob.

Cabriolet models
- As above 3.6, HE, and V12 models but door trims all leather. Revised windscreen surround to accommodate catches for targa panels. Catches also located in centre strengthening bar in roof.
- Twin targa panels made from glass fibre and upholstered inside with black circular locks initially, later chromed handles.
- Rear hood section lined and manually folded back after releasing black circular lock from strengthening bar.
- Rear seating removed and replaced by carpeted box area with two lockable lids incorporating luggage rails and, in the footwells, map pockets.
- Carpeted rear section to bulkhead.
- Black fabric envelope provided in boot to accommodate targa panels when removed from the roof.
- When hood down, a matching coloured tonneau fitted by studs and Velcro covered the hood.

Convertible models (1987–91)
- As coupés except for enhanced leather interior.
- Burr walnut veneer instead of elm.
- New seat design with stiffer bolsters and electric adjustment operated from control pads on side of centre console.
- Rear compartment featured stiffened and carpeted bulkhead area and one-piece storage box with lockable lid and luggage rail.
- Hood fully lined.

All facelift models (1991–6)
- Revised dashboard layout incorporating analogue instrumentation to binnacle in front of driver with revised ignition/starter and lighting switches.
- Centre dash section also revised with touch-sensitive switchgear, new digital clock, and/or onboard computer.
- New audio/air-conditioning layout. Smoother switchgear to console area, squared-off trim areas to centre console.
- Front seating similar to previous convertible, now all with electrical adjustment on door trims.
- Frameless door windows (coupé models) with no quarter-lights.
- Rear seating amended in style to suit front, incorporating seatbelt connectors. Cloth and leather trim alternatives available on coupés.
- Occasional rear seating fitted from 1992 on convertible models, necessitating a new bodyshell and revised bulkhead area behind.
- Hood amended, with a shallower window to accommodate rear seating when hood down.
- By 1994 seating style altered again with ruched leather available on certain models and two-tone dashboard trim.
- 'Celebration' models featured half-wood/leather steering wheel, available on other cars as option.

Factory special editions
- *Collection Rouge*: Only available to the US market. Magnolia interior piped red, with red carpets and burr elm woodwork.
- *Classic Collection*: Only available to the US market. Leather interior matching to exterior colour, pale finishes with contrast colour piping. Walnut veneer and better-quality carpeting.
- *Le Mans*: Only available to European markets. Revised-type seating from the convertible in Autolux leather with contrast colour piping and carpets (better quality). Embossed 'Le Mans' name to headrests. Leather-covered steering wheel and gear knob, and door tread plates depicting car number and wins at Le Mans. Darker wood staining. Boot similarly trimmed.
- *JaguarSport XJR-S models*: Improved seating with embossed 'XJR' logos, Autolux leather, matching leather-covered steering wheel and door trims. Walnut veneer.

Technical specifications

	5.3-litre pre-HE	5.3-litre HE
cc	5343	5343
Bore and stroke (mm)	90 x 70	90 x 70
Compression ratio	9:1	11.5:1
bhp	285	299
@ rpm	5800	5800
Torque (lb ft)	294	318
@ rpm	3500	3000
Fuelling	Fuel-injection	Fuel-injection
Transmission	GM 3-speed auto 4-speed (all synchro) limited	GM 3-speed auto
Wheel size (in)	15, alloy	15, alloy
Suspension front	Ind wishbone, coils, anti-dive	Ind wishbone, coils, anti-dive
Suspension rear	Ind lower wishbone, upper drivelink, radius arms, coil springs	Ind lower wishbone, upper drivelink, radius arms, coil springs
Brakes	4-wheel disc, rear inboard	4-wheel disc, rear inboard
Performance		
0–60mph (sec)	6.9	6.5
Top speed (mph)	153	150
Average mpg	12.8	17.9
Dimensions		
Length (in)	191.75	191.75
Width (in)	70.5	70.5
Height (in)	49.6	50.4
Wheelbase (in)	102	102
Front track (in)	58.5	58.5
Rear track (in)	58	58
Weight (cwt)	33.2	35

Technical specifications *cont ...*

	6.0-litre	3.6-litre
cc	5993	3590
Bore and stroke (mm)	90 x 78.5	91 x 92
Compression ratio	11:1	9.6:1
bhp	308	221
@ rpm	5350	5100
Torque (lb ft)	355	249
@ rpm	2850	4000
Fuelling	Fuel-injection	Fuel-injection
Transmission	GM 3-speed auto	5-speed (all synchro)
		ZF 4-speed auto
Wheel size (in)	15, alloy	15, alloy
Suspension front	Ind wishbone, coils, anti-dive	Ind wishbone, coils, anti-dive
Suspension rear	Ind lower wishbone, upper drivelink, radius arms, coil springs	Ind lower wishbone, upper drivelink, radius arms, coil springs
Brakes	4-wheel disc, rear outboard	4-wheel disc, rear outboard
Performance		
0–60mph (sec)	6.6	7.2
Top speed (mph)	161	137
Average mpg	17.6	25
Dimensions		
Length (in)	189.75	191.75
Width (in)	70.5	70.5
Height (in)	48.8	50.4
Wheelbase (in)	102	102
Front track (in)	58.5	58.5
Rear track (in)	58	58
Weight (cwt)	36.6	32

	4.0-litre
cc	3980
Bore and stroke (mm)	91 x 102
Compression ratio	9.5:1
bhp	223
@ rpm	4750
Torque (lb ft)	278
@ rpm	3650
Fuelling	Fuel-injection
Transmission	5-speed (all synchro)
	ZF 4-speed auto
Wheel size (in)	15, alloy
Suspension front	Ind wishbone, coils, anti-dive
Suspension rear	Ind lower wishbone, upper drivelink, radius arms, coil springs
Brakes	4-wheel disc, rear inboard, later outboard
Performance	
0–60mph (sec)	7.4
Top speed (mph)	137
Average mpg	26
Dimensions	
Length (in)	191.75
Width (in)	70.5
Height (in)	49.2
Wheelbase (in)	102
Front track (in)	58.5
Rear track (in)	58
Weight (cwt)	32

Optional extras

Pre-HE models
Manual four-speed all synchromesh gearbox.
Fog/spot lights mounted underneath front bumper bar.
Rear seat belts.
Sundym tinted glass.
Radio/cassette or cartridge system.
Passenger-side door mirror.
Mud flaps.
US four headlights with trim and surrounds.
Cloth upholstery.
Whitewall tyres.

HE, V12, and 3.6-litre coupés up to 1991
Automatic transmission (alternative to auto on 3.6-litre engines).
Fog/spot lights mounted underneath front bumper bar.
Rear seat belts (early cars only).
Enhanced radio/cassette system.
Mud flaps.
US four headlights with trim and surrounds.
Cloth upholstery.
Whitewall tyres.
Lattice wheels of two sizes (dependent on model).
Starfish alloys (where not equipped).
Kent alloy wheels.
Cruise control.
Onboard computer.
Tailored overmats.
Headlight wash/wipe system.
Integrated hi-fi system with CD player.
Leather upholstery where cloth fitted as standard.
Boot rack with specialist fittings for skis, etc.
Wood veneer gear knob.

Cabriolets
As above plus:
Hood envelope to store hood when off the car.
Glass fibre/fabric-covered hardtop with built-in glass screen and heating element.
Wind deflector to fit on screen rail above rear-view mirror.

Post-1991 cars
Side body mouldings painted to body colour.
Black rubber/chrome side body mouldings incorporated Jaguar logo.
Fog/spot lights mounted underneath front bumper bar.
Enhanced radio/cassette system.
Mud flaps.
US four headlights with trim and surrounds.
Cloth upholstery.
Whitewall tyres.
Cruise control.
Onboard computer.
Tailored overmats.
Headlight wash/wipe system.
Integrated hi-fi system with CD player.
Leather upholstery where cloth fitted as standard.
Boot rack with specialist fittings for skis, etc.
Wood veneer gear knob.
Sheepskin over-rugs.
Child's safety seat.
Child's booster cushion.
First-aid kit for boot area.
Space-saver spare wheel.
Fire extinguisher for boot area.
Jaguar warning triangle.
Headlamp converters.
Headlamp safety covers.
Roof box (coupés only).
Mobile telephone kits.
Sports suspension option (where not standard).
Lattice wheels (two sizes).
Five-spoke wheels (alloy or chrome).
JaguarSport Speedline wheels.
Diamond-turned wheels.
20-spoke wheels.

Colour schemes

Exterior colour	Details	Interior trim	Details	Interior	Details
XJ-S pre-HE		**Leather**		**Cloth**	
Old English White	To 1977	Russet		Sand	From 1976
		Dark Blue		Garnet	From 1976
		Cinnamon		Ebony	From 1976
		Black			
Tudor White	From 1977	Russet		Sand	
		Biscuit		Garnet	
		Black		Ebony	
Dark Blue		Russet		Sand	From 1976
		Dark Blue		Ebony	From 1976
		Biscuit		Garnet	From 1976
		Black			
Cobalt Blue	From 1978	Cinnamon		Sand	
		Dark Blue		Navy	
		Black		Ebony	
British Racing Green	To 1977	Biscuit		Sand	From 1976
		Cinnamon		Ebony	From 1976
		Moss Green	1975 only		
		Black			
Racing Green Metallic	From 1977	Biscuit		Sand	
		Cinnamon		Ebony	
		Black			
Regency Red		Biscuit		Sand	From 1976
		Cinnamon		Ebony	From 1976
		Russet	1975 only		
		Black			
Damson Red	From 1977	Russet		Sand	
		Cinnamon		Garnet	
		Black		Ebony	
Black*		Russet		Sand	From 1976
		Black		Ebony	From 1976
		Cinnamon		Garnet	From 1976
		Biscuit			
Signal Red	To 1977	Biscuit		Sand	From 1976
		Russet	1975 only	Ebony	From 1976
		Black			
Sebring Red	From 1978	Biscuit		Sand	
		Dark Blue		Navy	
		Black		Ebony	
Silver*	To 1977	Russet	1975 only	Sand	From 1976
		Biscuit		Ebony	From 1976
		Dark Blue		Garnet	From 1976
		Black			
Coronet Gold	From 1978	Russet			
		Biscuit			
		Black			

183

Colour schemes cont ...

Exterior colour	Details	Interior trim	Details	Interior	Details
Silver Frost	1976–7	Russet		Navy	
		Dark Blue		Garnet	
		Black		Ebony	
Carriage Brown		Biscuit		Sand	From 1976
		Cinnamon		Ebony	From 1976
		Black			
Chestnut Brown	From 1978	Cinnamon		Sand	
		Biscuit		Ebony	
		Black			
Squadron Blue	To 1978	Biscuit		Sand	From 1976
		Dark Blue		Navy	From 1976
		Black		Ebony	From 1976
Quartz Blue	From 1978	Biscuit		Sand	
		Dark Blue		Navy	
		Black		Ebony	
Yellow Gold	1976–7	Dark Blue		Ebony	From 1976
		Black			
Cotswold Yellow	From 1978	Dark Blue		Sand	
		Cinnamon		Navy	
		Black		Ebony	
Juniper Green	From 1976	Biscuit		Sand	
		Cinnamon		Ebony	
		Black			
Moroccan Bronze	From 1976	Biscuit		Sand	
		Cinnamon		Ebony	
		Black			
XJ-S and XJS later models		**Leather**		**Cloth**	
Tudor White	To 1987	Isis Blue		Fleet Blue	
		County Tan	To 1984		
		Mulberry	From 1984		
Portland Beige	To 1984	Burnt Umber		Graphite	
		Black			
Cobalt Blue	To 1987	Doeskin		Beige	
		Biscuit			
Racing Green	To 1985	Biscuit		Beige	
		Doeskin			
Claret	To 1987	Doeskin		Beige	
		Biscuit			
Black*		Doeskin	Plus post-1987 choice		
		Isis Blue			
		Savile Grey	From 1984		
		Charcoal	From 1987		

Exterior colour	Details	Interior trim	Details	Interior	Details
Silversand	1984–6	Doeskin		Graphite	From 1984
		Burnt Umber	To 1984		
		Black	From 1984		
Sebring Red	To 1987	Biscuit		Fleet Blue	To 1984
		Isis Blue		Beige	To 1984
		Black		Graphite	From 1984
Rhodium Silver	To 1987	County Tan	To 1984	Graphite	
		Mulberry	From 1984		
		Black			
Chestnut Brown	To 1984	County Tan		Graphite	
		Biscuit			
		Black			
Sapphire Blue (light)	To 1986	Isis Blue		Fleet Blue	
		Biscuit		Beige	
Grosvenor Brown	To 1985	County Tan	To 1984	Beige	
		Buckskin	From 1984		
		Biscuit			
Sable Brown	To 1984	Doeskin		Beige	
		Biscuit			
Coronet Gold	To 1986	Buckskin		Graphite	
		Burnt Umber	To 1984		
		Black			
Indigo Blue	To 1984	Isis Blue			
		Doeskin			
Clarendon Blue	1984–6	Savile Grey			
		Doeskin			
Cirrus Grey	1984–6	Buckskin		Beige	
		Biscuit			
Cranberry	1984–7	Doeskin		Graphite	
		Black			
Regent Grey	1984–7	Savile Grey			
		Doeskin			
Sage Green	1984–6	Doeskin		Beige	
Antelope	1984–7	Buckskin			
		Mulberry			
		Doeskin	From 1986		
Windsor Blue	1986–7	Biscuit			
		Savile Grey			
Steel Blue	1986–7	Doeskin			
		Isis Blue			
Mineral Blue	To 1983	Biscuit			
Claret	To 1986	Doeskin			
		Biscuit			

Colour schemes *cont ...*

Exterior colour Single	Details	Interior trim	Details
Nimbus White	1987 only	Isis Blue†	To 1994
Westminster Blue	From 1987	Savile Grey†	To 1994
Jaguar Racing Green	To 1990	Doeskin†	To 1994
Grenadier Red	1987–91	Biscuit†	To 1992
Alpine Green	1987–90	Buckskin†	To 1994
Arctic Blue	1987–92	Mulberry†	To 1992
Bordeaux Red	1987–92	Barley†	To 1994
Crimson	1987–90	Magnolia†	To 1994
Dorchester Grey	1987–90	Cream†	From 1992
Moorland Green	1987–90	Parchment†	From 1992
Satin Beige	1987–92	Cherry Red†	1992–4
Silver Birch	1987–92	Oatmeal†	From 1994
Solent Blue	1987–94	Coffee†	From 1994
Sovereign Gold	1987 only	Nimbus Grey†	From 1994
Talisman Silver	1987–92	Regatta Blue†	From 1994
Tungsten	1987–92	Warm Charcoal†	From 1994
Glacier White	From 1988		
Signal Red	From 1988		
Savoy Grey	1990–2		
Diamond Blue	1990–4	**Tweed**	
Mica Jade Green	From 1990	Pennine Black†	1987–92
Mica Gunmetal	1990 to 1994	Chiltern Beige†	1987–92
Mica Regency Red	1990 to 1994	Cotswold†	1987–92
Brooklands Green	1991–2 only	Cheviot Grey†	1987–92
Tuscany Bronze	1991 only	**Hood**	
Meteor Red	1992 only	Blue†	
British Racing Green	From 1992	Black†	
Kingfisher Blue	From 1992	Brown†	
Platinum	From 1992	Beige†	From 1988
Silver Frost	From 1992	Burgandy†	From 1993
Oyster	From 1992	**Sculp Fabric**	
Mica Flamenco	From 1992	Doeskin†	1992–4
Mica Morocco Red	From 1992	Barley†	1992–4
Mica Rose Bronze	From 1993	Savile Grey†	1992–4
Sapphire Blue (dark)	From 1994	Isis Blue†	1992–4
Titanium	From 1994	Oatmeal†	From 1994
Ice Blue	From 1994	Coffee†	From 1994
Topaz	From 1994	Nimbus Grey†	From 1994
Steel Grey	From 1994	Regatta Blue†	From 1994

† = open choice by customer

* = special order only

Prices and production volumes

	Price new (£)	1975	1976	1977	1978	1979	1980
Pre-facelift models							
XJ-S pre-HE	8900	■	■	■	■	■	■
XJ-S HE coupé	18,950	–	–	–	–	–	–
XJ-S V12 coupé	21,700	–	–	–	–	–	–
XJ-S V12 cabriolet	26,995	–	–	–	–	–	–
XJ-S V12 convertible	36,000	–	–	–	–	–	–
XJR-S coupé	35,000	–	–	–	–	–	–
XJ-S 3.6-litre coupé	19,248	–	–	–	–	–	–
XJ-S 3.6-litre cabriolet	20,756	–	–	–	–	–	–

	Price new (£)	1981	1982	1983	1984	1985	1986
XJ-S pre-HE	8900	■	–	–	–	–	–
XJ-S HE coupé	18,950	■	■	■	■	■	■
XJ-S V12 coupé	21,700	–	–	–	–	–	–
XJ-S V12 cabriolet	26,995	–	–	–	–	■	■
XJ-S V12 convertible	36,000	–	–	–	–	–	–
XJR-S coupé	35,000	–	–	–	–	–	–
XJ-S 3.6-litre coupé	19,248	–	–	■	■	■	■
XJ-S 3.6-litre cabriolet	20,756	–	–	■	■	■	■

	Price new (£)	1987	1988	1989	1990	1991	Total produced
XJ-S pre-HE	8900	–	–	–	–	–	15,526
XJ-S HE coupé	18,950	■	–	–	–	–	29,944
XJ-S V12 coupé	21,700	■	■	■	■	■	16,159
XJ-S V12 cabriolet	26,995	■	–	–	–	–	3863
XJ-S V12 convertible	36,000	■	■	■	■	■	11,571
XJR-S coupé	35,000	–	■	■	■	■	448
XJ-S 3.6-litre coupé	19,248	■	■	■	■	■	8867
XJ-S 3.6-litre cabriolet	20,756	■	–	–	–	–	1150
Total pre-facelift production							**87,528**

Prices and production volumes *cont ...*

Facelift models	Price new (£)	1991	1992	1993	1994	1995	1996
XJS V12 5.3-litre coupé	43,500	■	■	■	–	–	–
XJS V12 5.3-litre convertible	50,600	■	■	■	–	–	–
XJS V12 6.0-litre coupé	45,100	–	–	■	■	■	■
XJS V12 6.0-litre convertible	52,900	–	–	■	■	■	■
XJR-S 6.0-litre coupé	45,500	■	■	■	–	–	–
XJR-S 6.0-litre convertible	–	■	–	–	–	–	–
XJS 4.0-litre coupé	33,400	■	■	■	■	■	■
XJS 4.0-litre convertible	39,000	■	■	■	■	■	■

	Price new (£)	Total produced
XJS V12 5.3-litre coupé	43,500	1199
XJS V12 5.3-litre convertible	50,600	3674
XJS V12 6.0-litre coupé	45,100	774
XJS V12 6.0-litre convertible	52,900	1787
XJR-S 6.0-litre coupé	45,500	787
XJR-S 6.0-litre convertible	–	50
XJS 4.0-litre coupé	33,400	5667
XJS 4.0-litre convertible	39,000	13,864
Total facelift production		**27,802**
Total XJS production		**115,330**

Chassis numbers

Model	Right/left drive	Chassis/VIN commencing
XJ-S coupé	RHD	2W 1001
	LHD	2W 50001

Production changes

1975
XJ-S pre-HE model introduced.

1976
Chromed B/C door pillar deleted.

1977
GM400 automatic transmission replaced Borg Warner unit.

1978
Chromed radiator grille fitted.
Matt black boot panel deleted.
Manual transmission model deleted from range.

1979
Larger square-type exterior door mirrors fitted.
Trim colour centre console adopted.
Radio aerial mounted to offside instead of nearside.

1980
Rear fog lamps fitted to bumper.
P-Digital fuel-injection system fitted.
Aerial now flush-fitted to rear wing.

1981
XJ-S HE model introduced.
Rear anti-roll bar deleted.
Black vinyl spare wheel cover in boot replaced solid type.

1983
XJ-S 3.6-litre coupé and cabriolet models introduced.

1984
Hard plastic front spoiler fitted.

1985
V12 cabriolet model introduced.
Sun visors colour-keyed to trim hereafter.
Cloth seat option became available.

1986
Introduction of H & E US-adapted convertibles.
Mark III air-conditioning system fitted to all models.
Three-point inertia reel seat belts fitted.

1987
Wood veneered ski slopes fitted to centre console.
Two windscreen-washer jets replaced the one previously used.
Heated door mirrors fitted.
Stainless steel sill tread plates adopted.
Revised style of steering wheel.
Locking filler cap adopted for coupé models.
Electric lumbar support fitted to V12 models.
Sports suspension pack available for six-cylinder models.
Rear anti-roll bar reintroduced.
3.6-litre cabriolet model deleted from range.

1988
V12 cabriolet model deleted from range.
TEVES ABS system available.
Side coachline stripes redesigned.
V12 convertible launched.
XJR-S model introduced.

1989
US Collection Rouge model brought out.
XJR-S 6.0-litre model introduced.
Wipers changed to park on opposite side of screen.
Tilt-action steering column introduced.
Ignition switch moved to steering column from dashboard.
Trim co-ordinated dash roll available.
Driver's side airbag fitted to US specification models.
Restyled exterior door handles.

1990
Le Mans special edition launched.
Catalytic converters standardised on all models.

1991
Facelift models introduced (XJS).

1992
4.0-litre convertible model introduced.
Driver's side airbag standardised on all cars.
Improved under-floor bracing for convertible models.

1993
Colour-keyed plastic bumper bars fitted.
2+2 seating now fitted to convertible models.
6.0-litre V12 engine fitted to V12 models.

1994
AJ16 power unit replaced AJ6 six-cylinder unit.
Passenger-side air bags fitted to all cars.

1995
Celebration models introduced.
V12-engined cars deleted from range unless to special order.

1996
XJS production terminated.

12 The XJ40 saloons 1986 to 1994

Background

The Jaguar company had gone through some trying times in the 1970s and apart from regular upgrades of their only saloons, the XJ6/12, had not produced an entirely new car since 1968. Even after the introduction of the last version of this model, the Series 3, the company was still experiencing problems in build quality, the cars being produced by outdated manufacturing methods which also made them too costly to build. At least some of these problems must be laid at the feet of British Leyland.

Jaguar had, however, been working on a new replacement saloon as far back as the Series 2 XJ – in fact, small-scale models had been produced as early as 1972. With so much energy being absorbed by the development of the existing XJs and the upcoming XJ-S, the 'new' project (code named XJ40) was not given the priority it deserved. Jaguar was also hampered by continuous interference from British Leyland, which at one time actually considered using the Rover V8 (ex-Buick) engine in the new car, which would have meant the end of engine production at Jaguar.

Just as Jaguar had approached Pininfarina regarding the restyling of the Series 3 XJ, it also encouraged them – and other Italian designers – to put in proposals for the new car, none of which proved suitable.

It wasn't until just before John Egan arrived on the scene at Jaguar that BL actually approved a £32m investment in a new engine (the AJ6, first seen in the XJ-S in 1983). It wasn't then until 1981 – more than three years after the Series 3 XJ had been announced – that the Board agreed to a further £80m investment in the XJ40 project after finally agreeing the exterior design from a glass fibre mock-up.

It appeared that speed was of the essence by this time, and the money was approved on the undertaking that the XJ40 would be ready for launch by 1983. This was never a practical deadline and in the meantime it was fortunate that Jaguar's image improved dramatically, leading to an upsurge in sales of its existing models. This gave the company more time to develop the XJ40 into a better car. Deadlines came and went and it wasn't until the British Motor Show of 1986 that the XJ40 finally arrived, with two engine sizes (2.9-litre and 3.6-litre), two styles of trim, and a Daimler-badged model.

The XJ40 brought Jaguar up to date with all-new technology, being electronically the most technically advanced car in the world at the time (bar the ill-fated Aston Martin Lagonda). It was also quicker and cheaper to produce, more economical to run, and therefore the most significant new model since the original XJ6. Despite all that was 'new' with the car, Jaguar decided to call it XJ6 again, though it was and still is widely known by its XJ40 factory code name, which conveniently distinguishes it from its forebear.

Due to demand and other practicalities the XJ40 wasn't launched in the US until 1987, by which time it was already proving to be a great success in the UK market. Some Series 3 XJ6s had trickled through until April 1987, and Jaguar ended up with a two saloon model line-up in that the V12-engined Series 3 models would continue on into the early 1990s.

The XJ40 model range was tight but effective, even if many people considered the smaller-engined 2.9-litre car to be under-powered. This was eventually replaced in 1990 by a 3.2 version of the larger unit, which itself was enlarged to 4.0 litres in 1989.

The years 1988 and 1989 proved to be momentous ones for Jaguar because it sold more cars then than it had ever done before. Most of this was down to the XJ40, which sold 39,432 units in 1988 and 32,833 in 1989, the 40's best-ever years.

As the original bodyshell of the XJ40 had never been designed to take the big V12 engine (a throwback to Jaguar personnel deliberately 'engineering out' any chance of getting the Rover V8 in!), a V12 XJ40 didn't arrive on the scene until 1993, by which time the old Series 3 models had disappeared.

Jaguars had long been regarded as 'old mens' cars', and in order to redress this situation the XJ40 tried to capture a younger market with its Sport model of 1993–4. Relatively subtle changes to exterior and interior had a slight effect, but only just over 3600 were actually sold. Jaguar also got concerned about sales late on when there was public awareness about a replacement model for the end of 1994 (the X-300). For that last year, therefore, it announced yet another model, the Gold, offering a high degree of standard equipment at a special offer price.

Along the way the joint venture with TWR, JaguarSport, produced more sporty versions of the XJ40. A very limited run of long-wheelbase Majestic models was also made to order. In the valued US market several special editions were marketed, bringing back the Vanden Plas and Majestic names.

The XJ40 was a vital model for Jaguar, coming at just the right time. It saw the company out of BL control, into private ownership, and then into the Ford empire. Although only in production from 1986 to 1994, over 208,000 cars were made, and even the replacement X-300 owes much to the XJ40.

Model range and development

When one considers that the Series 3 V12 models were still produced for much of the XJ40 period, the

Although exactly the same bodyshell was used for all XJ40 models, numerous changes differentiate each car. The standard XJ6 models all featured the four-headlight treatment and plastic hubcaps on steel wheels. XJ6 models also used powder-coated black window surrounds as depicted here.

Top of the range Sovereign and Daimler models featured rectangular headlight units and chromed window surrounds.

Daimler styling cues involved swage line chrome trims along the entire length of the body, chromed window surrounds as Sovereign, and alloy wheels.

During the first year in production the Jaguar Sovereign model featured this black-painted boot panel like the Daimler.

initial range of new models was comprehensive for Jaguar at this time.

Models available at launch (manual and auto transmission variants)

Jaguar XJ6 2.9-litre saloon
Jaguar XJ6 3.6-litre saloon
Jaguar Sovereign 2.9-litre saloon
Jaguar Sovereign 3.6-litre saloon
Daimler 3.6-litre saloon

The XJ6 models were effectively the base models of the range. Indeed, the 2.9-litre was offered at a price of just over £16,000 (cheaper than any Jaguar produced since 1983) in an attempt to enter the management fleet market. In neither engine size, these cars did not feature such luxuries as leather upholstery, air-conditioning, alloy wheels, ABS, or automatic transmission within the basic price. You did, however, get an onboard computer, the then entirely new Vehicle Condition Monitor, and a five-speed manual gearbox.

The Sovereign models were aimed fairly and squarely at traditional Jaguar customers, usually businessmen with a company-supplied vehicle. Better equipped than the outgoing Series 3 Sovereign models, you got ABS, rear ride height-adjustable suspension, eight-way electrically adjustable front seats, and six-speaker hi-fi radio/cassette system. That was on top of the usual Sovereign equipment, such as air-conditioning, headlight wash/wipe, cruise control, onboard computer, etc. The one thing you still had to pay extra for initially were alloy wheels.

The Daimler was the most expensive and therefore top of the range vehicle, built to the usual standards by Jaguar with fluted external trim treatment and different shaping to the seating. The Sovereign and Daimler models, although utilising the same bodyshell as the XJ6s, had a different frontal lighting treatment which instantly differentiates them.

Manual and automatic transmissions were offered throughout the range, the latter utilising a new 'J-gate' control quadrant, unique to Jaguar and still used to this day. This allowed a certain degree of manual control over intermediate gears.

Apart from the usual minor changes and manufacturing modifications, the range ran virtually unaltered until 1988, when a new car appeared, the XJR. Based on the 3.6-litre model, this vehicle was enhanced by the JaguarSport company at its Oxfordshire premises. According to customer requirements, the model received a new exterior paint finish, body styling kit, mechanically better brakes, stiffer suspension, and even improved engine manifolding.

From 1990 scripted badging was replaced by the embossed style shown here. XJ6 models used quite a plain rear end without much chrome adornment ...

... whereas top of the range cars from 1990 featured chrome surrounds to rear lights and enhanced boot chromes.

The 4.0-litre Sovereigns are identified by the extra chrome on the boot area and, normally, lattice-style alloy wheels.

In 1990 the conventional production models started to change when the larger-engined cars were substantially upgraded. A new 4.0-litre version of the AJ6 power unit was adopted for this model, which brought with it improved mid-range torque. Stylistically the car gained more chrome and internally the previous all-electronic dashboard was replaced by analogue instrumentation.

The same interior treatment took effect on the last of the 2.9-litre models, which were also mechanically upgraded from 1991 with the complete replacement of this engine by a 3.2 single cam unit based on the larger twin-cam engines. The later engine offered greater smoothness with enhanced performance.

Regular updates appeared each model year but it wasn't until 1993 that another new model appeared in the XJ40 range. For the first time two V12-engined cars were offered, one a Jaguar XJ12 and the other a Daimler Double Six. Equipped similarly to the Sovereign and Daimler models, there were subtle differences (see details below). The V12 engine had been significantly improved, now of 6.0 litres capacity and 318bhp. By this time the XJ40 was the only saloon model available from Jaguar, the very last Series 3 having left the factory at the end of 1992.

At the end of 1993 Jaguar announced yet another XJ40 model, the Sport, or 'S' as it became known. Trying desperately to cater for a younger market the S models (only available in six-cylinder engine form) offered colour co-ordinated exterior trim to the body, five-spoke alloy wheels, and revised interior trim, including rosewood instead of walnut veneer.

Some long-wheelbase models were produced of various engine sizes to special order and for some overseas markets Daimler variants were badged as Jaguar and/or Vanden Plas.l.

In 1994 the final new XJ40 model appeared: the Gold. Based on the standard XJ6 3.2-litre model, a special reduced exterior colour range, gold-plated badge on the boot, and a mix of interiors between standard and S, and offered at a modest price, the Gold allowed Jaguar to recapture lost sales in the XJ40's final twelve months. Sales of all XJ40 models in 1994 only accounted for just over 10,000 vehicles, less than half the previous year, mostly due to public knowledge that a replacement model (the X-300) would be arriving soon.

At various times other options for XJ40 models were considered, such as a short wheelbase two-door coupé and a five-door estate car, both of which didn't progress beyond driving prototype stages. Carriage-trade manufacturers also completed a number of stretched limousines, both four- and six-door variants, based on the XJ40 design, as well as hearse bodies.

Up to 1990 all XJ40s featured a digitised instrument binnacle as depicted here. This picture also shows the original style of steering wheel, prior to the fitment of air bags from 1992.

Analogue instruments appeared in 1990 for all models.

For the US market the Daimlers were, and still are, badged as Jaguar Vanden Plas.

Above left: Jaguar Sovereign models became equipped with boxwood inlays to the veneer, later also adopted for Daimler models.

Above right: For base models tweed-style upholstery was fitted, along with a plainer straight-grain woodwork. Air-conditioning was an extra-cost option initially.

The US range of XJ40 models also changed year by year, although it never received the base model XJ6s. The names Vanden Plas and Majestic were resurrected for special top of the range (Daimler equivalent) models at various times, also for the US market only.

Exterior identification points
General points applicable to all XJ40s

Front view
- Squared-off chromium-plated radiator grille with vertical slats and thick centre bar, atop of which is a growler badge.
- Matched pairs of twin headlights or rectangular single units dependent on model, with chromed surrounds.
- Rubber-faced full-width bumper bar incorporating sidelight and indicator lenses with reflectors within the wrap-around section and centrally mounted number plate area. Chrome-plated blade to top of bumper bar.
- Under-valance in body colour with black plastic air intake and spoiler. Design changed from 1992.
- Forward-hinged bonnet, quite flat in profile.
- Large bonded windscreen with chrome surround and centrally mounted single wiper.

Rear view
- Wrap-around bumper treatment as at the front incorporating red reflector and red high-intensity fog lights.
- Flat boot lid with pronounced lip and vertical panel incorporating number plate and badging.
- Chromed boot lock finisher with concealed number plate lighting and boot lock button.
- Rectangular rear lighting units at extremities of body, neutral density or more lenses dependent on model and age, some with chromed surrounds.
- Centre vertical boot lid section carrying make and model badges and centrally mounted number plate with chrome surround.
- Black plastic finisher between vertical portion of boot lid and rear valance. Twin exhaust pipes emit from either side of the car below bumper level through cut-outs in valance.

Side view
- Slightly more slab-sided styling to previous Jaguar XJ6 but retaining slight 'hump' over rear wheelarch. Six-light window styling (rear quarter-lights separate to rear door frames).
- All cars featured a trim finisher at the base of the D-post roof section where it meets the rear wing, either chrome or body colour dependent on age of car.

Until 1993 the solitary Daimler model used a similar rear interior treatment to previous models, with the addition of chromed cup-holders in the occasional veneered tables.

Above left: A simple 'D' emblem on the fluted radiator grille and Daimler badging at the rear separated European cars from the US Vanden Plas models.

Above right: Revised interior layout from 1990, with the analogue instruments and here, in this 1992 model, the new steering wheel with airbag.

Cloth replaced tweed for the interior of non-leather-equipped cars, along with revised door trims.

- Side indicator repeater lights to top rear section of front wings (design changed from rectangular to square in 1991). Badges featured on US spec cars.
- Chromed rain gutter surrounds.
- Chromed or black powder-coated window frames and B/C post dependent on model and year (see accompanying photographs).
- Chromed door mirrors and flush-mounted chromed door handles.
- Unusual metric-sized steel road wheels with grey plastic rimbellishers incorporating separate push-fit centre section to access wheel nuts and including growler badges (changed to non-metric wheels and ventilated rimbellishers from 1991). Alloy wheels fitted as extra-cost option initially, later standardised on some models. Type of wheel changed through production (see photographs).

XJ40 model specifics

XJ6 models

- Two pairs of single circular headlights with chrome surrounds within a body-coloured mounting.
- Radiator grille with chromed slats and grey growler badge.
- Steel wheels with plastic rimbellishers as standard equipment.
- Black powder-coated window frames.
- 'Jaguar' and 'XJ6' scripted badges on boot lid panel.

Sovereign models

- Single rectangular sealed beam headlight units with chromed surrounds. Chromed window frames.
- Early cars supplied with steel wheels and rimbellishers, later fitted with metric-sized teardrop alloy wheels with exposed wheel nuts, also an option on early cars at extra cost. Later cars also used different alloy wheel styles (see photographs and production details).
- 'Jaguar' and 'Sovereign' badges in rectangular brushed alloy finished format. Very early Sovereign examples fitted with matt black painted vertical cover to boot lid underneath badges and number plate surround.
- With the introduction of 4.0-litre models greater use of chrome at rear of car (see photographs for details).

Daimler model

- Fluted radiator grille surround with 'D' emblem badge at centre top.
- Lights and window surrounds as Sovereign.
- Scripted 'D' badging to alloy wheels. Design changed to Roulette style from 1991.
- Slim full body-length swage line chrome trims.

For the Jaguar XJ12 came a revised grille with painted slats and gold growler badge, and four-headlight treatment. The Daimler Double Six version retained a chrome grille and rectangular headlights. Until the end of 1993 chromed window surrounds also featured on the XJ12, but were then changed to black powder coating.

The S (Sport) model was introduced for the 1994 model year. This was identified from the outside by its five-spoke alloy wheels in either eggshell or silver finish, red growler badges to the wheels, painted radiator grille slats, and revised coachlines.

At the rear the S model gained a painted plinth with new badging, and a choice of colour density for rear-light units.

- Vertical boot lid panel matt black finished as earlier Sovereigns (later dropped) but incorporating 'Daimler' scripted badge to left-hand side.
- Low-density rear-light units recognisable from dark grey finish instead of red. With introduction of Daimler Double Six model in 1993 revised multi-vane alloy wheels fitted and 'Double Six' scripted badging added to rear boot area.

XJ6 3.2-litre model
- As XJ6 except fitted with ventilated silver-painted rimbellishers on new 15in steel wheels (standard equipment, alloys optional).

XJ12 model
- Frontal treatment with four headlights as XJ6 except for black centre grille vanes and gold growler badge on top.
- Wider-profile tyres fitted with 16in lattice alloy wheels.
- Initially chrome-plated window surrounds, later changed to black powder coated.
- At rear chromed surrounds to rear-light units and boot lid, with 'XJ12' rectangular brushed alloy style badging to right-hand side.

Sport models
- As XJ6 except for body-coloured centre vanes to radiator grille.
- Five-spoke alloy wheels (silver or eggshell finished) with wider-profile tyres.
- Colour-keyed door mirrors.
- Twin coachlines with 'S' logo to lower half of body sides accompanied by single gold coachline along swage.
- At the rear plastic in-fill panel to boot vertical area incorporating '3.2 S' or '4.0 S' badging.
- Contrast density rear-light units fitted without chromed surrounds of later cars.

Gold model
- As XJ6 except for gold growler badge on grille top and black centre vanes. Kiwi diamond-turned alloy wheels.
- Twin gold coachlines along entire length of swage line.
- At the rear 'Gold' badging against a black rectangular background.

XJR models
- As XJ6 except for matt black centre grille vanes (later changed to egg-crate style).
- Colour-keyed front and rear bumper bars.
- Revised front under-valance and spoiler treatment.
- Initially XJ6-style four-headlight treatment, replaced, when egg-crate grille came in, with rectangular lights from Sovereign model.

Revised seating style, rosewood woodwork, and contrast upholstery separated the S model from normal Jaguars.

Another new model for 1994 was the Gold with a limited range of exterior colours, new diamond-turned alloy wheels, and painted grille slats.

At the rear the Gold model featured new badging and the S style plinth.

Above left: The S seating with horizontal pleating.

Above right: For the last few months the top of the range Daimler versions were offered with ruched-style leather upholstery.

- Flat-design Speedline alloy wheels, later changed for ventilated type with exposed wheel nuts.
- Glass fibre sill extensions sculptured and in body colour.
- Later egg-crate grille cars featured rubbing strips along lower section of body sides.
- Chromed window surrounds or colour-keyed.
- At the rear revised under-valance.
- Plastic in-fill panel to vertical section of boot and 'XJR' badging.

Interior identification points

XJ6 models

- Straight-grain walnut veneer to upper section of dashboard and door cappings.
- Instrument binnacle in front of driver incorporating mixture of bar instruments and electronically driven analogue speedometer and rev counter, also TV Vehicle Condition Monitor with digital read-outs, all in a matt black surround. Completed revised analogue instrumentation binnacle fitted from 1990 within wood-veneered surround.
- Supplementary switch panels flank steering column containing lighting switches on one side and onboard computer controls plus cruise control (where fitted) on the other.
- Black two-spoke steering wheel with prominent centre boss containing oval growler emblem (later changed to four-spoke incorporating airbag).
- Multi-use stalks either side of steering column operating indicators, horn, main beam, wipers, and computer mode scrolling. Designs changed through production.
- Black plastic air control vents to extreme ends of dashboard and additionally a rectangular air vent system in the centre.
- Lockable passenger-side veneered glovebox incorporating vanity mirror etc. Later deleted to accommodate passenger airbag.
- Sculptured centre console area with wood veneer incorporating heater/air-conditioning controls, auxiliary switchgear, audio unit, and gearlever/automatic transmission quadrant, plus damped ashtray and armrest storage box with hinged lid.
- Handbrake sited between driver's seat and centre console, with black vinyl surround.
- Preformed solid door panels to match trim, with armrest pulls, pocket areas, and door-mounted audio speakers (design later changed). Chromed pull door handles. Electric window lifts on all models operated from black controls within armrest area (design changed several times throughout production).

Throughout Daimler production it was also possible to specify conventional bench-type rear seating.

Passive-style seat belts were made available for the US market.

Three different styles of indicator repeater lights were fitted to the front wings on European cars (not fitted to US spec models). The earliest rectangular type (see earlier pictures) was used until 1991, when this square type was adopted, only to be replaced on the very last cars by the inset flush style.

- Individual front seating in tweed, later changed to cloth (leather at extra cost) with vertical pleats at the rear incorporating rear lighting in the headrests (later moved to seat backs).
- Rear bench-type seat arrangement with centre fold-down armrest and initially no headrests.
- Boot area carpeted, with carpet cover to vertically mounted spare wheel, and black attaché case-style tool box fitted. From 1992 spare wheel position moved to accommodate carpet-covered battery area and tool kit relocated to rear inward face of valance.

Sovereign models
- As XJ6 except for full walnut veneer interior with boxwood inlays to dashboard and door cappings.
- Instrument binnacle set against mock-wood-veneer background.
- Air-conditioning standard fitment.
- Leather upholstery with vertical pleating.
- Front seats electrically adjustable from switch pack on sides of centre console.
- Rear seat headrests standard.
- Enhanced audio system fitted, initially of Clarion manufacture.

Daimler models
- As Sovereign except for 'D' badging to steering wheel centre boss.
- No boxwood inlays to walnut veneer on earlier cars.
- Flatter, wider-pleated all-leather seating of revised style, the front seats incorporating walnut-veneered picnic tables in the rear with chromed drinks coasters.
- Rear seating of individual style with enlarged centre fold-down armrest and console area over transmission tunnel incorporating veneer finishing and 'Daimler' scripted badge.
- Door trim design entirely different to Jaguar models with separate armrest arrangement and more pronounced door pockets.
- Wood-veneered surrounds to door window lift switches.
- Nylon over-rugs fitted to rear compartment.
- Electrically operated sunroof panel standard fitment.
- With introduction of the Double Six model in 1993 matched leather-clad gear knob and handbrake surround were incorporated.
- From 1994 ruched leather seating of more rounded style available.

NB: US spec cars usually of the higher-quality Sovereign or Daimler equipment levels. From 1990 passive seatbelt arrangements were also fitted to some US models.

As with the XJ-S the JaguarSport organisation adapted production XJ40s for a more youthful market. Called the XJR, these initially featured similar body treatment to the XJ-S models, later to be adapted for normal Jaguar production with a revised grille design as shown here.

The XJR came with a bodykit and rear plinth arrangement as well.

3.2-litre model
- As XJ6 but part-leather/part-cloth upholstery mix introduced still with vertical pleats.
- Fitment of rear seat headrests.
- Revised door trims, later fitted to all non-Daimler models with curved armrest pulls.
- Walnut veneer added to replace straight-grain veneer.

XJ12 model
- As Sovereign except stiffer and more sculptured front seat bolsters.
- Laser-etched 'V12' gold emblem to glovebox area.
- Later-style instrument binnacle, door trims, and four-spoke steering wheel.

Sport models
- As XJ6 except for seating incorporating horizontal wide pleating both front and rear with stiffer bolsters.
- Rosewood-stained maple woodwork instead of walnut veneer. No boxwood inlays.
- Matching rosewood gear knob.
- Dashboard top roll and door cappings colour-keyed to rest of interior trim.

Gold model
- As XJ6 except for unique wide vertical pleating to leather seating incorporating the stiffer bolsters.
- Walnut-veneer woodwork.
- Matching wooden gear knob.
- Handbrake surround and dashboard top roll/door cappings trimmed to match interior.

XJR models
- Interior trim changes dependent on individual order requirements, usually featuring magnolia leather.
- Momo four-spoke matching leather steering wheel.
- Embossed 'XJR' headrests.
- Contrast piped upholstery with contrast carpeting.
- Some later cars equipped with Daimler-style door trims, and some cars equipped with either walnut veneer or walnut with boxwood inlays.
- Leather-clad gearshift knob on all models.

1: After the earlier plastic wheel covers (see the 2.9-litre car on page 188) this style of plastic wheel cover was adopted from 1991.

2: This style of plastic wheel cover then took over in 1992.

3 and 4: Two styles of teardrop alloy wheels were fitted to the XJ40 models, one metric size.

5: Lattice style wheels adopted for sport handling kit-modified cars, XJ12s, and later most 1990 Sovereign models.

6: Five-spoke wheels for the S model, later available for other models and XJS as well.

7 and 8: Later styles of alloy wheels fitted to Sovereign models, and others as optional.

9: Multi-spoke, as fitted to the Daimler Double Six models.

10: Roulette-style wheel normally fitted to 4.0-litre Daimler models but also offered for other cars.

11 and 12: Early Speedline and later Sport wheels fitted to XJR models, the latter also being used for late model XJS cars.

Technical specifications

	2.9-litre	3.6-litre
cc	2919	3590
Bore and stroke (mm)	91 x 74.8	91 x 92
Compression ratio	12.6:1	9.61
bhp	165	221
@ rpm	5600	5000
Torque (lb ft)	176	249
@ rpm	4000	4000
Fuelling	Fuel-injection	Fuel-injection
Transmission	Getrag 5-speed synchro ZR 4-speed auto	Getrag 5-speed synchro ZR 4-speed auto
Wheel size (in)	TD Metric alloys, later 15in alloys	TD Metric alloys, later 15in alloys
Suspension front	Ind twin wishbones anti-dive, coil springs	Ind twin wishbones anti-dive, coil springs
Suspension rear	Ind lower transverse wishbones, driveshafts upper link, anti-squat, coil springs	Ind lower transverse wishbones, driveshafts upper link, anti-squat, coil springs
Brakes	4-wheel disc, ventilated front	4-wheel disc, ventilated front
Performance		
0–60mph (sec)	10.8	7.4
Top speed (mph)	118	135
Average mpg	19.8	18.7
Dimensions		
Length (in)	196.4	196.4
Width (in)	79	79
Height (in)	54.25	54.25
Wheelbase (in)	113	113
Front track (in)	59	59
Rear track (in)	59	59
Weight (lb)	2140	2190

Optional extras

Side body mouldings painted to body colour.
Black rubber/chrome side body mouldings incorporated Jaguar logo.
Fog/spot lights mounted within front valance (standard on some models).
Enhanced radio/cassette system.
Mud flaps.
Cloth/tweed upholstery alternative to leather-upholstered cars.
Leather upholstery alternative to cloth-/tweed-upholstered cars.
Whitewall tyres (post-1992 US cars only).
Cruise control (where not fitted as standard).
Tailored overmats.
Headlight wash/wipe system (where not fitted as standard).
Integrated hi-fi system with CD player.
Roof-rack system with specialist fittings for skis, luggage box, etc.
Wood veneer gear knob.
Sheepskin over-rugs for non-Daimler/Vanden Plas models.
Child's safety seat.
Child's booster cushion.
First-aid kit for boot area.
Space-saver spare wheel.
Fire extinguisher for boot area.
Jaguar warning triangle.
Headlamp converters.
Headlamp safety covers.
Roof box.
Mobile telephone kits.
Sports suspension option (where not standard).
Stainless steel door edge guards.

	4.0-litre	6.0-litre
cc	3980	5993
Bore and stroke (mm)	91 x 102	90 x 78.5
Compression ratio	9.5:1	11:1
bhp	235	318
@ rpm	4750	5400
Torque (lb ft)	285	342
@ rpm	3750	3750
Fuelling	Fuel-injection	Fuel-injection
Transmission	Getrag 5-speed synchro ZF 4-speed auto	GM 5-speed auto
Wheel size (in)	15/16	16
Suspension front	Ind twin wishbones anti-dive, coil springs	Ind twin wishbones anti-dive, coil springs
Suspension rear	Ind lower transverse wishbones, driveshafts upper link, anti-squat, coil springs	Ind lower transverse wishbones, driveshafts upper link, anti-squat, coil springs
Brakes	4-wheel disc, ventilated front	4-wheel disc, ventilated front
Performance		
0–60mph (sec)	7.1	6.8
Top speed (mph)	138	155
Average mpg	19	12.9
Dimensions		
Length (in)	196.4	196.4
Width (in)	79	79
Height (in)	54.25	54.25
Wheelbase (in)	113	113
Front track (in)	59	59
Rear track (in)	59	59
Weight (lb)	2290	2415

Electrically operated sunroof (non-Daimler/Vanden Plas models).
Wind deflector for sunroof.
Rear screen blinds.
Snow chains.
Electrically operated boot-mounted cooler box.
Luggage net for boot area.
Witter tow bar kit.
Cup-holders for forward centre console area.
Heated windscreen.
Ultrasonic intrusion security system.
Tool kit (later model cars not equipped as standard).
Sports suspension handling kit.
15in lattice alloy wheels.
16in lattice alloy wheels.
16in five-spoke eggshell or silver alloy wheels.
15in radial alloy wheels.
15in teardrop metric or later non-metric alloy wheels.
16in Speedline alloy wheels.
16in ventilated Speedline alloy wheels with exposed wheel nuts.
16in diamond-turned 20-spoke alloy wheels.
16in Aero alloy wheels.
16in Kiwi diamond-turned alloy wheels.
15in Roulette alloy wheels.
Air-conditioning (non-equipped cars).
Anti-lock braking system (non-equipped cars).
Rear seat headrests.
Heated door lock barrels.
Limited-slip differential.
Ride-height rear suspension levelling system.
Eight-way front adjustable seats.
Heated front seats.

Prices and production volumes

	Price new (£)	1986	1987	1988	1989	1990	1991
2.9 Standard/Daimler	16,495	■	■	■	■	■	–
2.9 Sovereign	22,995	■	■	■	■	■	–
3.6 Standard	18,495	■	■	■	■	–	–
3.6 Sovereign	24,995	■	■	■	■	–	–
3.6 Federal	–	■	■	■	■	–	–
3.6 Daimler	28,495	■	■	■	■	–	–
3.2 Standard	26,200	–	–	–	–	■	■
3.2 Sport	29,950	–	–	–	–	–	–
3.2 Gold	28,450	–	–	–	–	–	–
3.2 Sovereign	34,550	–	–	–	–	■	■
4.0 Standard	25,200	–	–	–	–	■	■
4.0 Sport	34,950	–	–	–	–	–	–
4.0 Gold	28,950	–	–	–	–	–	–
4.0 Sovereign	32,500	–	–	–	–	■	■
4.0 Federal	–	–	–	–	–	■	■
4.0 Daimler	36,500	–	–	–	–	■	■
XJ6 long-wheelbase	52,700	–	–	–	–	–	–
6.0 Export	–	–	–	–	–	–	–
6.0 Jaguar	46,600	–	–	–	–	–	–
Daimler Double Six	51,700	–	–	–	–	–	–
6.0 long-wheelbase	–	–	–	–	–	–	–
Majestic (various models)	–	–	–	–	–	–	–
Miscellaneous prototypes	–	–	–	–	–	–	–
Total production							

Colour schemes

Exterior	1992	1993	1994	Total produced	Details
Glacier White	–	–	–	11,191	
Oyster	–	–	–	2957	To 1993
Signal Red	–	–	–	9349	
Black	–	–	–	49,941	
Regency Red	–	–	–	13,319	To 1993
Westminster Blue	–	–	–	10,313	
British Racing Green	■	■	■	13,056	
Kingfisher Blue	–	■	■	3117	From 1991
Rose Bronze	–	–	■	1499	1994 only
Flamenco Red	■	■	■	3491	From 1991
Gunmetal Grey	■	■	■	13,585	
Morocco Red	–	–	■	500	From 1993
Dorchester Grey	–	–	■	23	
Jade Green	■	■	■	50,409	
Isis Blue	■	■	■	12,864	
Silver Frost	■	■	■	8876	
Sapphire Blue	■	■	■	67	1994 only
Diamond Blue	–	■	■	1325	From 1992
Platinum Grey	–	■	■	1565	
Regency Red (Micra)	–	■	■	1102	US Majestic only
Black Cherry	–	–	–	101	To 1993
Black Cherry (Mica)	–	–	■	50 (approximately)	US Majestic only
Meteor Red	■	–	–	33	To 1993
				208,733	

Interior (all cars)	
Doeskin	
Barley	
Savile Grey	
Isis Blue	
Cream	US Majestic only
Cherry Red	
Charcoal	
Parchment	
Magnolia	Extra cost

Piping	Dash top rolls
Blue	Grey
Sage Green	Sage Green
Cherry Red	
Buckskin	
Coffee	US Majestic only

Production changes

1986
XJ40 models introduced (2.9-litre, 3.6-litre).

1988
Integrated Clarion sound systems fitted.
Heated door mirrors standardised on all cars.
Rear screen blinds and heated door locks standardised on Daimler.

1989
Door mirror style changed.
Rear compartment reading lights standardised on Sovereign models.
Boxwood inlay to walnut veneer added to Daimler.
XJR model introduced.

1990
4.0-litre engines replaced 3.6-litre.
ZR electronically controlled auto transmission with Sport and Normal modes (4.0-litre only).
New Getrag 290 manual box fitted, lever moved forward 15mm.
Teves ABS system replaced Girling/Bosch.
Extra chrome trim added to boot area on upmarket models.
Analogue instrumentation binnacle fitted to all models.
Indicator column stalk operation changed.
Toggle fitted to driver's door window lift button.
Dashboard top roll co-ordinated option available.
XJR 4.0-litre model introduced with revised exterior styling.

1991
US Majestic Vanden Plas model introduced.
3.2-litre model replaced 2.9-litre.
TD Metric wheels and tyres replaced by 15in.
Square-style side indicator repeater lights fitted to front wings replaced rectangular type.

1992
Fuel filler cap gained lip for ease of opening.
Sports handling pack becomes available.
Revised front under-valance and spoiler.
Fog/spot lamps standardised on Daimler.
New-style rimbellisher fitted for steel-wheel-equipped cars.

Twin electric cooling fans fitted.
Auto gearshift interlock system introduced.
Boot lid liner now carpeted, replacing board.
Battery moved to boot position.
Boot side-saddle panels reduced in size to increase boot space.
Full electric front seat adjustment now fitted as standard with headrests (Sovereign and Daimler).
Electric front seat height adjustment standardised on XJ6.
Redesigned door trim panels.

1993
Driver's airbag fitted, necessitating fitment of new steering wheel (four-spoke with horn pushes).
Redesigned air-conditioning control panel.
Heated front screen available.
Full integrated security system available on all models.
Enhanced hi-fi sound system with larger speakers.
Fabric cloth material replaced tweed on non-leather-equipped seats.
XJ12 and Daimler Double Six models introduced.
3.2-litre Sport model introduced.

1994
4.0-litre Sport model introduced.
Passenger-side air bags included on all models.
Space-saver spare wheel fitted as standard on all models.
Black-painted window frames for XJ12 model replaced chrome finish.
Flush front wing side indicator repeater lights fitted.
Shaping of column-mounted control stalks changed.
Flush-fitting door lock buttons fitted.
Ruched-style leather seating available on Daimler models.
New-style six-cylinder camshaft cover fitted with integrated oil filler cap.
Gold model introduced.
All models discontinued.

The New Series XJ6/12 saloons
1994 to 1997

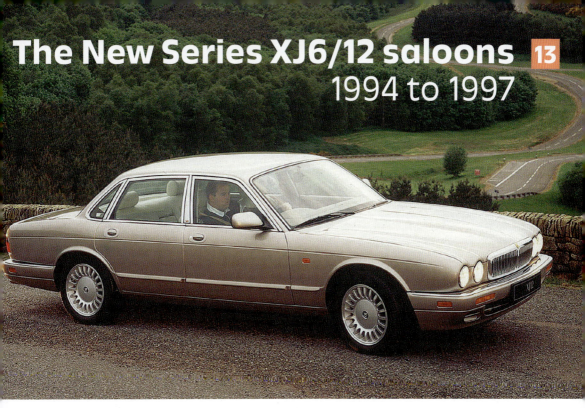

Background

The first new saloon model range to be produced by Jaguar under Ford ownership (code-named X-300) benefited from the latter's expertise and money, while at the same time building on the established good features of the outgoing XJ40 range and previous Jaguar styling touches. Its launch played heavily on the phrase 'New Series XJ', emphasising the 'new' aspect yet still retaining the old insignia XJ, first seen on a production car back in 1968.

Introduced in September 1994, these New Series cars offered superior build quality to previous models, which meant better panel fit and finish, improved protection against corrosion, and overall better quality control. It also meant a return to more curvaceous styling, Jaguar deliberately comparing the new car with the previous Series 3 XJ. And it also meant revised interiors, if not that radically different to the XJ40 range.

Mechanically these X-300 models were no major move forward either, relying on previous Jaguar practice and building on existing success with other models. Suspension, brakes, and steering, although enhanced, could be described as merely a direct development of the XJ40 design. The 6.0-litre V12 engine used in the XJ12 and Daimler Double Six was first seen in the XJ40 in 1993. The six-cylinder AJ16 engine had also made its debut in another Jaguar, the XJS, earlier in 1994, although it had been developed with the X-300 saloon in mind. Lastly, the new cars still carried the old-established 'XJ6' or XJ12' insignia or their Daimler equivalents.

In a nutshell, therefore, what the X-300 models offered was more of the same but with improved quality, a touch of retro-styling, and, perhaps more importantly, a massively improved model range. This included more sporty models to attract a younger market and, for the first time ever in a production Jaguar, a supercharged-engined.

Again building on ideas from the XJ40 range, each X-300 model carried unique styling touches and suspension geometry, since at this time these were still the only saloon cars the company produced.

The New Series saloons nevertheless had a very short production run, somewhat akin to the 2.4- and 3.4-litre compact saloons of the 1950s, and, like those models, they were replaced by similar looking, although significantly modified cars after about three years. The X-300 production ceased in 1997, initially with the V12 models quietly dropping out of production. Then, in October, the whole range was replaced by the X-308 models with V8 engines.

Model range and development

The New Series Jaguars encapsulated a whole range of models based around the 3.2-litre and 4.0-litre AJ16 six-cylinder and 6.0-litre V12 power units.

205

Models available at launch (manual and auto available for six-cylinder models)

XJ6 saloon (3.2-litre)
XJ6 Sovereign (3.2-litre and 4.0-litre)
XJ6 Sport (3.2-litre and 4.0-litre)
XJR supercharged saloon (4.0-litre)
XJ12 saloon (6.0-litre)
Daimler Six (4.0-litre)
Daimler Double Six (6.0-litre)

This made a total of nine models, the most extensive range Jaguar had ever produced around one bodyshell design, each being specifically geared to a particular sector of the anticipated market. For example, the base XJ6 was produced down to price in the hope of catering to the fleet market and those entering Jaguar ownership for the first time. As such it did not feature alloy wheels, air-conditioning, or even leather upholstery as standard equipment – in essence the same format as was offered by the lower-priced XJ40s. This was in order to maintain a competitive edge compared to the products of rival manufacturers.

In contrast Sovereign models were intended for the traditional Jaguar owner who wanted all the luxury features as standard, like air-conditioning, alloy wheels, and chromed trim, plus a compliant ride for comfort. The Sport, on the other hand, catered to a younger audience, far more so than the XJ40 S had. It had colour-keyed trim to the exterior paintwork, contrasting interior trim colours and, on the driving side of things, stiffer suspension, wider wheels, and more supportive seats – a much better combination than the XJ40 offered.

The entirely new concept of a supercharged Jaguar targeted another sector of the market, those who wanted the ultimate in performance and driving experience to match the likes of the BMW M series. The most powerful model in the range, the supercharged XJR also benefited from further enhanced suspension and steering and even wider wheels. The high-performance, harsher ride, and superb handling meant that, to a degree, luxury equipment levels were tempered.

At the top end of the price bracket were the Daimler models, designed to meet the needs of the company chairman who wanted the ultimate in luxury and, indeed, rarity, with low production numbers compared to the other models. Virtually everything was supplied as standard equipment, but with softer touring suspension. The Double Six name was retained for the V12-engined model, while the 4.0-litre was now not only a Daimler but a Daimler Six.

In 1996 long-wheelbase versions of all the cars were offered at extra cost, and later became standard for the Sovereign and Daimler versions. The extra 6in of wheelbase was accommodated in

The X-300 is clearly identifiable from the previous XJ40 models by its more rounded front and rear corners and its lower-set front. This top of the range Jaguar Sovereign model featured extra chrome (window surrounds, grille, and rear lights). It is also built on the longer wheelbase bodyshell, identified by the wider rear doors.

The XJR supercharged saloon was only built on the shorter wheelbase bodyshell, with de-chroming of exterior trim except for the bumper blades. It can also be identified not only by the badging but also by the wider Sport wheels and mesh radiator grille.

The Sport model benefited from a degree of colour-keying, revised coachline treatment at the bottom of the doors near the rubbing strip, and the Dimple alloy wheels.

Subtle frontal changes affected the models. The chromed radiator grille was reserved for Jaguar Sovereign and base XJ6 models.

the rear compartment to provide more legroom, and necessitated wider rear doors.

From their launch, the X-300 cars had never been fitted with a front passenger glovebox, a carryover from the XJ40 after the fitment of a front passenger airbag system. From 1996, however, front passenger gloveboxes were fitted under the airbag area and a kit became available to convert earlier cars to this specification. Small in size, it nevertheless met demands for more storage space.

By popular demand an extra model also entered the range in 1996, a 4.0-litre version of the standard XJ6 model becoming available. Coinciding with this, all cars received minor trim makeovers, such as revised radiator grille treatment, uprated interiors, and alternative alloy wheel options.

Also in 1996, Jaguar introduced a special limited edition Century model, to commemorate 100 years of the Daimler marque. Based on the long-wheelbase Daimlers, these featured every conceivable extra including ruched-leather upholstery, individually electrically adjustable rear seats, chromed alloy wheels, and bespoke paint finishes. The most expensive production model ever made by Jaguar at that time, only 100 were produced with the six-cylinder engine and another 100 with the V12 power unit.

Late in 1996 another new model appeared for the 1997 model year. This was the Executive, aimed at younger, middle-management owners. Based on the XJ6 model with enhanced Sport leather trim, half-wood/leather steering wheel, wider Sport wheels and tyres, and air-conditioning, the Executive helped to cultivate this new market and became the most popular model sold that year. It remained in production until the demise of the X-300.

Outside the UK the standard XJ6 was not offered, and in many markets the Daimlers were marketed under the Jaguar Vanden Plas name. Cars destined for the US also featured a revised boot lid pressing to accommodate the different style of number plate mounting and some cars were fitted with a swivel action Jaguar leaper mascot on the bonnet, illegal in the UK.

Although a concept styling exercise was produced for an X-300 estate car, this never entered production. Jaguar also produced a one-off 18ft stretched limousine based on the Daimler Six, initially used by the then Chairman, Sir Nick Scheele. This car still exists today in the Jaguar Daimler Heritage Trust. Another concept was the Daimler Corsica, utilising a short wheelbase Daimler bodyshell. Jaguar's Special Vehicle Operations department turned this into a very attractive two-door convertible as another mark of respect for the 100th anniversary of the Daimler marque in 1996, but

Colour-keyed grille slats for the Sport model.

Fluted chromed grille for the Daimlers.

Rear external treatment also changed from model to model. Apart from obvious badging variations (always in different colours) models like the Sovereign and the Daimlers featured chromed surrounds to the rear lights.

Above left: Other models did not feature the chrome trim.

Above right: There were no chromed screen surrounds for the Sport or XJR models.

it was never actually fitted with an engine. This model, too, can be found in the JDHT collection.

Worth mentioning, although strictly not of Jaguar manufacture, are the Eagle Coachworks six-door limousines and hearses produced around the X-300 models, both Jaguar and Daimler variants. Eagle, part of the Wilcox Group, purchased cars direct from Jaguar and with their approval converted them for various uses.

As mentioned above, the Daimler Double Six and XJ12 were discontinued mid-term 1997, with the other models continuing to be manufactured until the introduction of the XJ8.

Exterior identification points
General points applicable to all X-300s

Front view
- More curvaceous frontal aspect than previous models, with rounded radiator grille with growler badge top centre.
- Four headlights in two pairs with chromed bezels, the inner pair incorporating sidelights.
- All-enveloping plastic bumper bar painted in body colour with chromed top finisher. Bumper with indicator lights, central number plate surround and side reflectors. Bumper also incorporates under-valance with or without integrated fog lights according to model.
- One-piece forward-hinged bonnet with curvature to match headlights and raised centre section.
- One-piece bonded windscreen with centrally mounted single wiper arm.

Side view
- Similar profile to previous XJ40 models except for greater curvature to front and rear wing extremities.
- Removal of body finisher to base of D-post roof and rear wing (now smoothed area).
- All-enveloping bumper bar treatment easily identifies models from XJ40s.
- Lower section of body length fitted to painted rubbing strips.
- Flush-mounted indicator repeater lights on front wings (or badges for some overseas markets).
- New style of rounded flush-mounted door handles, either painted or chromed in the case of Daimlers.

Rear view
- Curved and tapered rear end totally at contrast with previous XJ40 saloons.
- All-enveloping rear bumper bar matching the front but with no integrated lighting other than side reflectors and incorporating the

Daimlers had a shorter chromed boot plinth. As with the XJ40, US-destined Daimlers were badged as Jaguar Vanden Plas and also received a totally different boot lid pressing because of the number plate style differences.

Badge colouring changed for all models and the special limited edition Century model got even better treatment.

A mix of cloth and leather was used for Sport and XJR models unless otherwise specified. Both models also used contrast colours for other trim aspects.

Sovereign models got full leather trim and traditional walnut instead of the black-stained maple of the Sport and XJR models.

under-valance with cut-outs for exhaust system.
- Twin exhaust pipes, one emerging from either side, oval-shaped chromed trims.
- Boot lid tapered vertical section with indentation for number plate, and plinth finisher incorporating concealed number plate lighting and push-button boot lid lock (chromed or body colour dependent on model).
- Wrap-around rear-light units at extreme sides of rear wings, Sovereign and Daimler models with chromed surrounds.
- Rectangular 'Jaguar' or 'Daimler' badges to left-hand side and model designation to right-hand side.

X-300 model specifics

XJ6 models
- Chrome surround and vertical slats to radiator grille.
- Chromed windscreen and rear screen surrounds.
- Chromed rain gutters.
- Black powder-coated window frames.
- Colour-coded door mirrors and door handles.
- Steel wheels with silver-painted plastic rimbellishers standard equipment (alloys at extra cost when new).
- Boot plinth chromed.
- 'Jaguar' and 'XJ6' rectangular badging on boot lid.

Sport models
- As XJ6 but with body-coloured vertical slats to the radiator grille.
- Dimple alloy wheels.
- Dual coachlines above the side rubbing strips.
- 'XJ Sport' badging to boot lid and 'Sport' badging to B/C post.
- No chromed screen surrounds.

XJR model
- As Sport except for colour co-ordinated radiator grille shell with mesh centre replacing the vanes.
- No chrome surrounds to front and rear screens.
- Matt black rain gutters.
- Sport ventilated five-spoke alloy wheels.
- Colour co-ordinated boot lid plinth.
- Larger-diameter exhaust outlets.
- 'XJR' badge to central B/C post mounting between front and rear window frames. 'XJR' badging to boot lid.

Sovereign models (including XJ12)
- Chromed radiator grille.
- Chromed windscreen and rear window surrounds.
- Chromed rain gutters.
- Chromed window frames.

Standard XJ6 models did not come equipped with air-conditioning or full leather trim.

From the introduction of the Daimler Century model, and continued on with the Double Six, separate heated and adjustable rear seating became the norm.

A new model for 1997 was the Executive, offering a high degree of standard equipment at a special price. The wheels fitted to the car in this photograph are not the originals.

Badging colours changed according to model.

- 14-spoke diamond-turned or 20-spoke alloy wheels, later changed.
- Chromed boot lid plinth.
- Chromed rear-light cluster surrounds.
- 'Sovereign' or 'V12' badging on boot lid accompanied by 'Jaguar' on other side.

Executive model
- A cross between standard XJ6 and Sport models. Chrome was strongly featured in all areas except the window frame surrounds (matt black).
- Alloy wheels of Dimple design (like the Sport), but unlike the Sport were polished alloy without the grey-finished centres.
- Chromed boot lid plinth.
- 'Executive' badging on boot lid.

Daimler models
- As Sovereign with extensive chromework around grille, glass areas, rear lights, rear plinth, etc.
- Fluted design radiator grille surround with chromed slats.
- Diamond-turned alloy wheels on Double Six, chrome on Six.
- Chromed door mirrors/door handles.
- Boot lid of shorter width to Jaguar and fluted.
- 'Daimler' badging replacing Jaguar on boot lid, and 'Six' or 'Double Six' badging.
- Sunroof standard on Double Six model.

NB: Market differences applied to some overseas cars – eg 'Vanden Plas' badging on top of range Jaguar model for the US market, using Daimler-styled fluted grille etc.

Daimler Century models
- Followed other Daimler models but were identified externally by 'Century' badging to boot lid and similar badging on some cars to bottom rear quarter of front wings.
- Chromed alloy wheels fitted unless otherwise stated by individual purchaser.

Interior identification points

General points applicable to all X-300s
- Interior layout similar to XJ40 models with more rounded seat styling.
- Bevelled-edge wood veneers.
- Rounded centre console area with smooth satin-finished switchgear.
- Four-spoke steering wheels incorporating prominent centre boss containing airbag.

In the case of these cars there were basically three distinct types of interior styling treatment,

There were chromed rear-light surrounds for top of the range models.

Analogue instrumentation was retained on the X-300 models from the XJ40, with wood surround for the XJ6, Sovereign, XJ12, and Daimler models.

The Daimler Century model was identified by badging, chromed edge to the rubbing strips, and chromed alloy wheels.

Styling cues identified the whole range of X-300 models, all based on the same bodyshell.

two on Jaguar models plus one with variations on Daimler cars. It is better here to deal with each style of interior separately, also showing the models they were applicable to.

Sport (applicable to Sport and XJR models)
- Black stained maple woodwork.
- Aerated leather steering wheel (with or without additional wood feature).
- Two-tone contrasting upholstery colour schemes.
- Stiffer bolster seating with horizontal pleating and ventilated centre panels.

Classic (applicable to XJ6, XJ12, and Sovereign models)
- Walnut-veneered woodwork.
- Smooth leather-covered steering wheel (with or without additional wood feature).
- Seating style more rounded using vertical pleats, curved cushions with, generally, more sombre trim colour schemes, in some cases with contrast coloured piping.
- Standard XJ6 models were normally equipped with cloth centre panels to the seats, unless all leather was specifically requested by an individual purchaser.

NB: Executive models differed and were a combination of both the above styles, having walnut-veneered woodwork, a smooth leather/wood steering wheel, Sport-style seating, and sombre colour scheming.

Daimler models
- Burr walnut veneer with boxwood inlays.
- Matched occasional tables built into the rear of the front seats.
- Seating style squarer with wider vertical pleats with the option of flat or ruched leather, both of a higher quality than that used on the equivalent Jaguar models.
- Century models featured ruched Autolux leather to all seats and a different style of rear seating consisting of individual seats with centre console with electrical control functions and control over the movement of the front passenger seat (when unoccupied). This type of individualised rear seating became standard equipment on all Double Six cars or an extra-cost option on Daimler Sixes.

All details of trim and specification given above relate to standard production cars. Certain owners may well have specified changes to suit their individual requirements, so it is not unusual to find some more basic models with a higher specification than that described here.

Above left: Plastic wheel covers were standard on XJ6 models.

Above right: Dimple wheels were standard equipment on the Sport models.

Above left: This wheel, adapted from the Dimple with polished finish, was fitted to the Executive model.

Above right: Chromed wheels fitted to the Daimler Century and later available as an extra-cost option.

Above left: Twenty-spoke wheels fitted to the XJ12 and available as an option.

Above right: Kiwi fitted to later Sovereign models and available as an extra-cost option.

Above left: An extra-cost option alloy available for X-300 models.

Above right: Lattice wheels also available on the X-300 as an extra-cost option.

13 Technical specifications

	3.2-litre	4.0-litre
cc	3239	3980
Bore and stroke	91 x 83mm	91 x 102mm
Compression ratio	10:1	10:1
bhp	219	249
@ rpm	5100	4800
Torque (lb ft)	232	289
@ rpm	4500	4000
Fuelling	Fuel-injection	Fuel-injection
Transmission	Getrag 5-speed synchro ZR 4-speed auto	Getrag 5-speed synchro ZF 4-speed auto
Wheel size (in)	7 x 16 (8 x 16 Sport)	7 x 16 (8 x 16 Sport)
Suspension front	Ind unequal-length wishbones, anti-dive, coil springs	Ind unequal-length wishbones, anti-dive, coil springs
Suspension rear	Ind double wishbones, driveshafts as upper link, anti-squat, coil springs	Ind double wishbones, driveshafts as upper link, anti-squat, coil springs
Brakes	4-wheel disc, all ventilated	4-wheel disc, all ventilated
Performance		
0–60mph (sec)	8.9 (7.9 manual)	7.8 (7 manual)
Top speed (mph)	139 (138 manual)	144 (143 manual)
Average mpg	26.9	26.8
Dimensions	**Short wheelbase**	
Length (in)	197	
Width (in)	70	
Height (in)	51	
Wheelbase (in)	112	
Front track (in)	57.25	
Rear track (in)	57	
Weight (lb)	3968	3968

Optional extras

Fog/spot lights mounted within front valance (standard on some models).
Enhanced radio/cassette system.
Mud flaps.
Cloth upholstery alternative to leather-upholstered cars.
Leather upholstery alternative to cloth-upholstered cars.
Cruise control (where not fitted as standard).
Tailored overmats.
Headlight wash/wipe system (where not fitted as standard).
Integrated hi-fi system with CD auto-changer in boot.
Roof-rack system with specialist fittings for skis, luggage box, etc.
Wood-veneer gear knob (where not fitted as standard).
Sheepskin over-rugs for non-Daimler models.
Child's safety seat.
Child's booster cushion.
First-aid kit for boot area.
Space-saver spare wheel.
Fire extinguisher for boot area.
Jaguar warning triangle.
Headlamp converters.
Headlamp safety covers.
Roof box.
Mobile telephone kits.
Sports suspension option (where not standard).
Electrically operated sunroof (non-Daimler/Vanden Plas models).

	Supercharged	6.0-litre
cc	3980	5993
Bore and stroke	91 x 102mm	90 x 78.5mm
Compression ratio	8.5:1	11:1
bhp	326	318
@ rpm	5000	5350
Torque (lb ft)	378	353
@ rpm	3050	2850
Fuelling	Fuel-injection	Fuel-injection
Transmission	Getrag 5-speed synchro ZF 4-speed auto	GM 5-speed auto
Wheel size (in)	8 x 17	8 x 16
Suspension front	Ind unequal-length wishbones, anti-dive, coil springs	Ind unequal-length wishbones, anti-dive, coil springs
Suspension rear	Ind double wishbones, driveshafts as upper link, anti-squat, coil springs	Ind double wishbones, driveshafts as upper link, anti-squat, coil springs
Brakes	4-wheel disc, all ventilated	4-wheel disc, all ventilated
Performance		
0–60mph (sec)	6.6 (5.9 manual)	6.8
Top speed (mph)	155 (155 manual)	155
Average mpg	23.4	18.4
Dimensions	**Long-wheelbase**	
Length (in)	201	
Width (in)	70	
Height (in)	52	
Wheelbase (in)	116	
Front track (in)	57.25	
Rear track (in)	57	
Weight (lb)	4134	4354

Rear screen blinds.
Snow chains.
Electrically operated boot-mounted cooler box.
Luggage net for boot area.
Witter tow bar kit.
Cup-holders for forward centre console area.
Heated windscreen.
Ultrasonic intrusion security system.
Tool kit (mounted in under-bonnet area).
Air-conditioning (non-equipped cars).
Eight-way front adjustable seats (where not fitted).
Heated front seats.
Jaguar 'growler' alloy wheel centre badges, various colours.
Power-folding door mirrors.
Chrome door mirror surrounds (where not fitted).

Bright rear number plate surround (chrome).
Self-dipping rear-view mirror.
Wood/leather steering wheel (where not fitted).
Passenger compartment glovebox kit (pre-1996 models).
16in Dimple anthracite infill alloy wheels.
16in Turbine chromed alloy wheels.
16in Dimple (no infill) alloy wheels.
16in Turbine alloy wheels.
16in 20-spoke alloy wheels (plastic centre cap).
16in 20-spoke alloy wheels (exposed wheel nuts).
16in Kiwi alloy wheels.
16in Aero alloy wheels.
16in lattice alloy wheels.
17in XJR five-spoke alloy wheels (exposed wheel nuts).

Colour schemes

Exterior colour	Details	Seats	Fascia	Piping
Glacier White	To 1996	Oatmeal (fabric)	Antelope	
Spindrift White		Coffee (fabric)	Coffee	
Signal Red	1997	Nimbus Grey (fabric)	Slate Grey	
Black†		Regatta Blue (fabric)	Warm Charcoal	
Anthracite (black)	To 1996	Black Marble Sport/Warm Charcoal	Warm Charcoal	
Westminster Blue†	1997	Grey Marble Sport/Oatmeal	Warm Charcoal	
British Racing Green†		Grey Marble Sport/Nimbus Grey	Warm Charcoal	
Kingfisher Blue		Parchment	Sage Green	Sage Green
Rose Bronze		Cream	Coffee	Coffee
Flamenco Red		Cream Sport	Warm Charcoal	
Carnival Red†	To 1996	Nimbus Grey	Slate Grey	Slate
Morocco Red	1997	Nimbus Grey Sport	Warm Charcoal	
Cabernet	To 1996	Coffee	Coffee	Cream
Jade Green	1997	Oatmeal	Antelope	Antelope
Sherwood Green		Oatmeal Sport	Warm Charcoal	
Silver Frost		Regatta Blue (fabric)	Warm Charcoal	Warm Charcoal
Sapphire Blue†		Warm Charcoal	Warm Charcoal	Nimbus Grey
Topaz (gold)		Mushroom‡	Coffee‡	Coffee‡
Ice Blue†		Silk White‡	Sage Green‡	Sage Green‡
Titanium Grey†				
Steel				
Turquoise*	To 1996	Schemes applicable to all cars and exteriors except where indicated.		
Aquamarine*	1997	* = only available on XJR/Sport models.		
Antigua Blue*		† = only colours for Executive models.		
Nautilus Blue		‡ = Century models only.		
Spruce Brown				

Production changes

1994
X-300 models introduced.

1995
Long-wheelbase bodyshells available.
(Late) Individual electrically operated seats included on Daimler Double Six.
XJ6 4.0-litre standard saloon introduced.

1996
Front passenger door external key lock eliminated.
Daimler Century Six and Double Six models launched.
Daimler Corsica Concept coupé produced.
Passenger-side glovebox added to all models.
XJ6 Executive model introduced.

1997
Flatter rear seat cushion featured on bench-seats.
Inertia three-point centre seatbelt fitted.

Air-conditioning standardised on 3.2-litre Sport model.
Wood/leather steering wheel standardised on all models except XJ6.
Black radiator grille vanes replaced chrome on 3.2-litre XJ6.
Long-wheelbase bodyshell standardised on 4.0-litre Sovereign model.
16in 20-spoke alloys become available, standard on 4.0-litre Sovereign.
Wooden gear knob standard fitment on 4.0-litre Sovereign/Daimler models.
Electric fold-back door mirrors standardised on all Daimler models.
CD players repositioned to nearside of boot area.
(April) Last XJ12 left the production line.
(September) Production discontinued, replaced by XJ8.

Prices and production volumes

	Price new (£)	1994	1995	1996	1997	Total produced
XJ6 3.2-litre	28,950	■	■	■	–	17,346
XJ6 3.2-litre long-wheelbase	33,750	–	–	■	■	747
XJ6 4.0-litre	–	–	■	■	■	2474
XJ6 4.0-litre long-wheelbase	–	–	–	■	■	203
XJ Sport 3.2-litre	29,950	■	■	■	■	7265
XJ Sport 4.0-litre	34,450	■	■	■	■	2534
Sovereign 3.2-litre	37,950	■	■	■	–	2377
Sovereign 3.2-litre long wheelbase	43,250	–	–	■	■	305
Sovereign 4.0-litre	42,950	■	■	■	–	28,490
Sovereign 4.0-litre long wheelbase	45,500	–	–	■	■	4973
XJR	45,450	■	■	■	■	6547
XJ12	53,450	■	■	■	■	564
XJ12 long-wheelbase	–				■	535
XJ6 Executive 3.2-litre	34,650	–	–	■	■	–
Daimler Six	49,950	■	■	–	–	1362
Daimler Six long-wheelbase	54,750	–	–	■	■	1330
Daimler Double Six	59,950	■	■	–	–	1007
Daimler Double Six long wheelbase	66,450	–	–	■	■	1230
Daimler Century Six	54,750	–	–	■	–	100
Daimler Century Double Six	–	–	–	■	–	100
Vanden Plas 4.0-litre*	–	■	■	■	■	3831
Vanden Plas 4.0-litre long wheelbase	–	–	■	■	■	7989
Sovereign XJ12*	–	■	■	■	■	673
Sovereign XJ12 long-wheelbase*	–	–	–	■	■	56
Total production						**92,038**

Overseas models

14 XK8 sports cars 1996 to 2005

Background

With the introduction of the XJ-S in 1975 Jaguar changed its policy of producing sports cars to one of making sporting grand tourers. Although not met with overall acclaim when launched, by the time the XJS went out of production in 1996 it had achieved what Jaguar had set out for it to do – to be a highly refined, effortless to drive, well-built, two-door grand tourer. It had been in production for 21 years, during which time it was constantly upgraded to meet the demands of the market and changing technology, and Jaguar needed something special to replace it. Ultimately this wouldn't become available until 1996 in the form of a car coded X-100, to be known in production as the XK8.

When Ford took Jaguar over in 1990 there was little on offer in the way of proposed new models. The XJ-S was selling better than ever, and although extensive work had been carried out on a replacement (the XJ41, also known as the F-type) the project was somewhat ill-conceived and was soon abandoned completely.

Ford had grave concerns about Jaguar's new model policy, and felt it was vital to launch new models in order to improve sales and, particularly, profitability (remembering that the XJ-S was still being built using 1970s technology). The first fruits of Ford involvement seen by the public were the replacements for the XJ40, the X-300 saloons, for although attention was turned to a replacement for the XJ-S right from the start it would take until 1996 for the car to be seen in the flesh.

The principles behind the X-100, or XK8 as we should call it now, were to build on the later success of the XJS, utilising the existing floorpan for speed and cost saving but updating the car significantly to meet the ever-increasing demands of the lucrative market for prestige sporting cars. Money for the development of the XK8 was tight, as was the schedule to bring it to production. The use of the XJS floorpan dictated the overall dimensions and interior accommodation, but the XK8 featured an entirely different body style and interior trim package plus new mechanics, not least the first use of the latest AJ-V8 4.0-litre engine developed by Jaguar and produced at the Ford plant in Bridgend, Wales.

A degree of retro styling took cues from the old E-type sports car and the XJ220 Supercar that Jaguar produced on a limited basis in the early 1990s. This decision was to create a connection between the new XK and classic Jaguar sports cars, hence the rebirth of the 'XK' insignia. The totally replanned interior also retained, if anything, more of a traditional feel than its XJS and E-type predecessors. Strategically, for marketing reasons if not practicality, the 2+2 seating arrangement remained.

Mechanically, as well as the 4.0-litre V8 engine the latest electronically controlled GM400 transmission was employed, mated to the J-gate transmission operation. An entirely new front subframe of aircraft technology design was incorporated with new front suspension and revised braking system and steering, overall a superior package to the XJS.

Enhanced creature comforts included dramatically improved rubber sealing techniques for doors and windows, particularly important for the convertible model on which, due to the constraints of the XJS floorpan, Jaguar was unable to fit an integrated metal cover over the hood when down; there was, however, a fast-action fitted hood cover. To meet the demands of the valued US market the boot was made as large as possible, promoted at the time as capable of carrying the obligatory two sets of golf clubs!

Finally launched at the British Motor Show in 1996, the XK8 found immediate success and the model range was increased thereafter. It remained in production until 2005 when it was replaced by an entirely new model.

Model range and development

When it was launched in October 1996 there were just two versions of the XK8 available.

Models available at launch (automatic transmission only)
XK8 4.0-litre coupé
XK8 4.0-litre convertible

It is perhaps significant that the opening advertising and promotional statement for the XK8 bore the words 'The Cat is Back,' confirming that Jaguar had built into the new car elements of past greats such as the E-type and, of course, the XJS.

The essentials of the XK8 design comprise a monocoque construction bodyshell built around the pre-existing XJS floorpan, offering two-door coupé and convertible coachwork with 2+2 seating arrangement. Although using the existing floorpan, with new technology the XK8 was built with 30% fewer panels than the previous model but with 25% more torsional stiffness. Polyurethane injection moulding was used for front and rear bumper bars, with projection technology for front lighting within a curvaceous front emulating the old E-type and XJ220 nose treatment. Smoothness of line was brought back into Jaguar sporting car styling, with a distinct lack of chromework or add-on trim.

A much lighter structure than previously, the smoothness of line made the car more attractive, stable, aerodynamic, and even easier to keep clean. The 17in or 18in alloy wheels were

The styling of the XK8 is unique, not being used by any other model within the Jaguar range. This 1997 example of the convertible version shows that there have been no changes in styling throughout the model's years in production. The 18in alloy wheels fitted to this example were an extra-cost option on early cars.

From 1996 to mid-1997 the rear view of XK8 models did not change, but from late 1997-on, a high-level brakelight was mounted on the boot lid of convertible models and within the rear screen of coupés.

Front view of XK8 models. The 2000 model year example on the left only differs from the earlier model on the right in its flush-mounted fog lamps (inset on the earlier car).

a standard fitment, with Pirelli P-Zero tyres. The very latest rubber technology allowed for almost perfect sealing of doors and windows, the latter electrically sensored to raise a little extra when the doors were closed to grip into the rubber seals, also releasing themselves as the doors were opened.

Internally Jaguar emphasised the traditional features of woodwork with a choice of two schemes, Classic (burr walnut) and Sports (dark-stained maple with contrasting soft trim colours). Virtually nothing internally was carried over from the XJS.

Mechanically the new XK8 was a tour de force in technology. Firstly the new AJ-V8 4.0-litre engine was seen for the first time in this model. Of alloy construction with four valves per cylinder and variable cam phasing, this engine uses a specially designed management system. It achieves a very quick warm up and is mated to the ZR 5HP24 electronically controlled five-speed automatic transmission.

Its double wishbone independent front suspension has springs mounted directly to the body, and the suspension is carried in a unique aircraft technology aluminium subframe. At the rear the fully independent rear suspension with outboard brakes takes its lead from the XJ40 and later X-300 saloons and is available with Jaguar's Computer Active Technology Suspension system (CATS).

1997 was the first full production year for the XK8, during which over 14,500 cars were sold worldwide, a record number, greater than any year of XJS production and more than Jaguar itself had anticipated. Although the majority of customers came from previous XJS owners, there were clear signs that the XK8 had had an effect on the sales of other cars, particularly Mercedes.

Little changed with the XK8 over the next couple of years until, in May 1998, two more models were added to the range. Called the XKR, in coupé and convertible forms, these featured the supercharged version of the AJ-V8 engine, first fitted to the XJR V8 at the launch of the XJ8 range in 1997, mated to a new Mercedes five-speed automatic transmission. The engine and transmission were essentially the same as fitted to the XJR. Producing 370bhp, the supercharged V8 was nearly 10% more powerful than the old V12 engine and nearly 30% more powerful than the standard XK8 normally-aspirated 4.0-litre.

The XKR package also included Computer Active Technology Suspension, a new Servotronic steering system, and improved brakes to match the higher performance, the car being governed to a 155mph safe maximum.

As a necessity to cope with the increased heat under the bonnet louvres were fitted to the

Above left: For the first three years standard production XK8s were fitted with these 17in Revolver alloy wheels, which were also available in chromed form to special order.

Above right: 18in Flute wheels were fitted as extra-cost options.

Interior of the 'classic' XK8 models (with walnut veneer) remained visually unchanged from 1996 until the introduction of the XKR model in 1998.

The Sport interior provided greater contrasts in trim colour schemes and the use of stained maple woodwork instead of walnut.

bonnet area on each side (another throwback to E-type days) and a neat spoiler was added to the boot lid to improve aerodynamics. Along with 'Supercharged' and 'XKR' badging the more powerful models featured a mesh grille insert at the front and the XKR became the first production Jaguar to be fitted with larger wheels and tyres at the rear than at the front.

Since that time the basic structure of XK8 models has remained unchanged, although the car has been regularly upgraded in virtually every model year. In 2000, in time for the British Grand Prix at Silverstone, Jaguar announced a special edition of the XKR, called the Silverstone. This was finished in Platinum Silver externally and carried 'Silverstone' bonnet and boot badging. These cars also had 20in Detroit split-rim alloy wheels as standard equipment. The interior was also treated to unique treatment and both coupés and convertibles were produced.

In 2001 the XK8 range was revamped, with slight changes to the exterior styling including flush-mounted fog/spot lights and new badging, and internally with revised seating including, for the first time, adjustable headrests. Then In 2002 the model was enhanced again, with new Xenon lighting, other minor changes to the trim package, and the adoption of a new 4.2-litre version of the AJ-V8 engine plus a supercharged version, now boasting 400bhp.

To commemorate the 100th anniversary of Sir William Lyons, the founder of the company, Jaguar introduced a limited run of XKR 100 models with unique badging, all finished in Anthracite Black paintwork.

The company also produced a one-off XKR-R with four-wheel drive, S-type rear suspension, and six-speed manual gearbox, but this did not go into production.

In 2004, further updates in exterior and interior design helped to maintain sales to the end of production. There were also other special editions for the home and US markets, like the Portfolio, Carbon Fibre and, towards the end of production, the S and Victory models.

The XK range, as covered here, came to the end of production in 2005 after an incredible lifespan. It was the most successful sporting Jaguar produced up to that time.

Exterior identification points

General points applicable to all XK models

Front view
- Identifiable from the curvaceous frontal aspect, not seen on any other Jaguar model since the E-type and XJ220.

All XKR (supercharged) models feature a mesh grille inset. This car is fitted with R-Performance split-rim alloy wheels.

All XKR models feature inset bonnet louvres.

A 'Supercharged' badge is fitted to the front nose section and boot panel of XKR models.

XK8 sports cars 1996 to 2005

- No front bumper bar treatment, instead an integrated preformed curved frontal energy-absorbing panel painted to body colour, from which front wings, bonnet, and lighting flow. Centrally mounted growler badge, separate number plate mounting, and 'mouth' either with chromed splitter bar or mesh grille, dependent on model (see pictures). From 2004, revised frontal aspect with larger 'mouth', and new-style trim and lighting.
- Integrated front fog lights incorporated into the nose section, flush-mounted on later models (see pictures).
- Sculptured combined headlamp/sidelight/indicator units using 'projector' technology or Xenon lights dependent upon model. Integrated headlamp wash system.
- One-piece forward-hinged bonnet with raised centre section.
- One-piece bonded windscreen with metal, painted surrounds.

Rear view
- Tapered and curved styling treatment not featured on other Jaguar models.
- Rear-hinged boot lid with curved lip (later with spoiler added, which varied according to model). Vertical section incorporated number plate panel and lighting, initially with painted plinth cover, and later changed to chrome and with integrated push-button boot lid opening facility.
- Rear-light clusters formed into the shape of the rear wings, later models with chrome surround, and very late models with new style.
- Preformed energy-absorbing one-piece bumper/valance painted to body colour, later models with more pronounced lip, different exhaust cut-outs, and variations in lower styling.
- Twin exhaust pipes with chromed oval trims emitting from either side below bumper/valance, larger on XKR models and later XKRs with quadruple tailpipes.
- 'Jaguar' and model badging either side of the number plate surround, the latter incorporating key lock for boot lid (earlier models only). Later cars featured solid badging, which also differed according to model.

Side view
- Unique style of car with slight wedge shape to rear and tapered frontal appearance different from any other Jaguar model.
- Distinct lack of chrome adornment to side of car (except for US models, where chromed door mirrors and handles applied).
- Oval reflectors fitted to leading edge of front and rear wing/bumper areas.

XKR models have 'Supercharged' emblems on the instrumentation and the XKR logo embossed into the steering wheel centre.

The 2004 facelift XK8 with enlarged mouth and air intake below.

Rear three-quarter view of 2000 to 2001 model year XKR coupé, depicting chromed surrounds to the rear lights and chromed boot plinth (both also applicable to XK8 models during this period).

Post-2000 to 2001 model year XKR convertible, showing the boot lid-mounted brakelight (always painted to body colour) and extra brightwork at the rear.

- Indicator repeaters fitted to rear of front wings (not US cars).
- Body-coloured rubbing strips fitted to rear of front wings, running back across doors to edge of rear wings. These were deleted from 2004 model year.
- Flush-mounted door handles and locks.
- Frameless door windows, no quarter-lights, fixed rear quarter-lights (coupé). Retracting smaller rear side windows in convertibles.
- Grey-painted rain gutters on coupé models.
- Concealed fuel filler cap incorporated into rear nearside wing under flush panel, opened from electric switch on the dashboard.
- Alloy wheels fitted to all cars, dependent on market, model, and year.
- Sill area curved to underside of car up to 2004, and thereafter an over-sill of pronounced section was fitted.

XK8 model specifics

XK8 coupé

- Front air intake incorporates horizontal chrome splitter bar with two vertical grey-painted plastic overriders on to which is normally mounted the registration plate support panel. Both the chrome splitter bar and overriders changed style from 2004 onward with deep front valance area as well.
- 'Jaguar 4.0-litre' (later '4.2-litre') growler badge fitted to nose section.
- Inset matching fog lights fitted to all models, from 2001 flush mounted.
- Bonnet without louvres.
- Roof section forms part of whole bodyshell, flowing down to meet the rear wings at the side and incorporating a large glass (heated) rear screen with surround.
- Grey-finished window surrounds up to 2003, thereafter black finished.
- Side areas fitted with body-coloured rubbing strips, later removed.
- Sculptured sill areas with protective painted finish. From 2004 with facelift, more pronounced 'add-on' sill covers fitted.
- Rear side quarter-lights bonded with flush surrounds and do not open.
- Early cars featured a choice of just two alloy wheel types, 17in Revolver or 18in Flute. Many others supplemented the model range over the years (see photographs).
- 'XK8' scripted badge to rear wing right-hand side panel with matching 'Jaguar' badge on opposite side. Originally the 'XK8' carried the key lock to the boot lid but, from 2001, badges were changed to solid chromed type, and boot lid key lock moved to the boot lid plinth.
- From 2001, the chromed boot lid plinth incorporated the boot lock, push-button, and number plate lighting.

Early style XK8 seating with combined headrests.

XKR seating from introduction through to 2000.

Post-2001 XK8 seating with separate adjustable headrests.

Post-2001 XKR seating with revised pleating and separate adjustable headrests.

- Boot spoiler fitted to post-2004 model year cars.
- Twin chromed tailpipes emerging from cut-outs in rear bumper/valance area. Enlarged pipes from 2004 model year.

XK8 convertible
- As coupé above, but without steel roof section, replaced by fabric-covered hood with frame and lining, affixed from revised windscreen surround (incorporating locking mechanism). Full-width glass rear screen with heated element. Boot lid same as coupé.
- Reduced-size rear quarter windows, retractable.

XKR models
- As XK8 models except nose splitter bar replaced by a full-nose mesh grille, enlarged on later facelift models from 2004.
- 'Jaguar Supercharged' growler badge to centre of nose section.
- Sculptured louvres painted to body colour, one per side, set into bonnet either side of raised area.
- 18in Double-Five original alloy wheel specified for this model, later updated several times according to model year (see accompanying pictures).
- Rubberised rear wheelarch extensions fitted to accommodate wider track of wheels/tyres.
- Body-colour mini-spoiler fitted to boot lid area, modified on later models.
- 'Jaguar Supercharged' growler badge fitted to centre of boot lid on early cars.
- 'XKR' scripted badges match those of XK8s above, later also changed to rectangular solid type.
- Larger bore exhaust pipe trims compared to XK8 models. Later models featured quadruple pipe system (from 2004).
- Larger rear boot spoiler fitted from 2004.

Special edition models

Silverstone
- Only finished in Platinum Silver exterior paint with appropriate re-badging.

XKR100
- Only finished in Anthracite Black exterior paint with appropriate badging and sill tread plates.

Carbon Fibre
- 2004/5 model with quad exhaust pipes and 20in split-rim alloy wheels.

Portfolio (US)
- Only finished in choice of Coronado Blue or Jupiter Red.
- 20in split-rim alloy wheels.

Above left: *Limited edition Silverstone models all featured unique badging.*

Above right: *Silverstone model interiors are all in black with contrast piping.*

Current coupé model XK8. Apart from the Gemini alloy wheels, (standard on XK8 models) the only differentiating point from earlier cars are the chromed and 'jewelled' rear-light units.

Above left: *Revised rear lighting of the modern 'jewelled' type on the current XK8 and R models, along with revised embossed badging.*

Above right: *Interior enhancements for current models include the option of contrast leather trim and R-Performance options like the alloy gear knob. When satellite navigation is fitted, a centrally mounted TV screen and controls replace auxiliary gauges on the dashboard.*

Victory (US)
- Leading up to the end of production. Available in special option colours – Black Copper, Frost Blue, Bay Blue, or Satin Silver, as well as normal Jaguar colourways.
- Chromed finish 19in Atlas alloy wheels for normally-aspirated model, 20in Victory alloys for XKR versions.

4.2 S
- The European equivalent of the Victory (above) with 4.2 S badging.
- Atlas alloy wheels, not chromed for European models.

Interior identification points

General points applicable to all models

- Full-width wood-veneered dashboard in oval shape (originally walnut or grey-stained maple, later options included birds eye maple and piano black), with primary instrumentation in front of the driver, deeply inset with auxiliary gauges in the centre of the dashboard mounted below the air-conditioning outlets. When fitted with satellite navigation, the screen replaces these gauges.
- Secondary air vents placed at either end of the dashboard, all outlets black plastic finished.
- Onboard computer control pod sited on driver's side, next to the rev counter.
- Auxiliary warning lights within main instruments.
- Four-spoke steering wheel, either entirely leather clad or half-leather/half-wood veneer. Incorporates horn push and driver's airbag, and embossed Jaguar growler head. Side controls for operation of audio system. High-spec models have similar side dials for cruise control.
- Centre console (similar design and layout to X-300 saloons), with digital air-conditioning controls and read-out, auxiliary lighting, seat heating (where fitted), traction control, headlight adjustment, and audio unit. This area around the sound system controls was modified in post-2004 models. J-gate transmission quadrant with black surround incorporating buttons for 'Sport' mode and (where fitted) cruise control. Flush-mounted ashtray with damped lid, behind which is the centre console armrest and glovebox. Cup-holders in armrest (where fitted).
- Passenger-side airbag situated under veneered dash panel, below which is the glovebox with lid, trimmed to match interior of the car.

The later facelift XKR model with enlarged mesh grille and under-valance.

Very late XKR rear, incorporating the quadruple exhaust tailpipes, revised, deeper bumper/valance and 'R' badging.

A 4.2 S model from 2005 with revised seating, alternative veneer choice and inset navigational system replacing the auxiliary gauges.

- Soft door side trims with chromed door handles. Door pulls incorporating pocket fitted with wood-veneered window switch pack.
- Front door panel audio speakers fitted behind trim panels, with tweeter speakers (Premium Sound system only) fitted in forward portion of door top window channel area.
- Reclining seats with integral headrests trimmed in leather (some part-cloth on earlier Sport spec models) with electric adjustment controlled from the side of the seat. Post 2001 models with more substantial seating incorporating separate, adjustable headrests. Different seat style options from 2004 on.
- Rear bench-style sculptured occasional seating with seat belts, flanked by speaker grilles in rear side panels. On coupé models large rear parcel shelf incorporates woofer speaker and grille.

NB: Interior variations between coupé and convertible models are restricted to the hood operation button on the centre console, shaping of the rear quarter windows, and slight differences to the trim layout to accommodate the lined hood and mechanism.

Very late 4.2-litre naturally aspirated V8 engine installation in the XK8.

XK model specifics

XKR models
- 'Supercharged' legend incorporated into main instruments in front of driver. 'XKR' logo embossed into centre steering wheel airbag boss (later changed to stylised 'R').
- Contrast seat stitching to XK8 models.
- Style of seating upholstery changed in 2001 model year, and then later from 2004 with the option of Recaro seating available in two-tone trim colourways.
- From 2004, stylised 'R' badging featured on rear of car.
- From 2002, chromed/trimmed 'R' J-gate control knob fitted.

Trim styles
- Originally there were two styles of interior trim levels, affecting all models, except special editions. These were:

Classic
- High-quality walnut-veneer woodwork.
- Complimenting upholstery trim colours.
- Matching leather or wood-veneered/leather steering wheel.
- Matching wooden gear knob.

Sport
- Dark-stained maple woodwork.
- Leather-covered steering wheel.
- Contrasting two-tone upholstery schemes.
- Leather-covered gear knob.

- From 2004 sport trim was no longer offered (and had never been offered in the US market), replaced with a wider range of trim options including veneers.

Silverstone model
- The main difference between this model and other XKR models is in the upholstery – black with red piping to leather and carpets.

XKR100 model
- Black trim only.

Carbon Fibre model
- Carbon fibre dashboard replacing veneer.
- Recaro sports seating.

Portfolio model
- High-quality burr walnut interior woodwork.
- Matching leather trim with high-quality stitching, piping, and carpet edges to match exterior blue or red of models, including steering wheels.

Victory/S models
- Elm-veneer interior for XK8s, carbon fibre interior trim on XKR versions only.
- Polished sill tread plates.

NB: There is also a range R-Performance options available for the XK models. For further information consult the options listing.

1: When 19in and 20in alloy wheels are fitted to XK models a special black rubber insert is fitted to the wheelarch.

2: 18-inch Double Five, standard fit on XKR at launch.

3: These Sport wheels were never fitted as standard but were available as an option.

4: 17in Gemini wheel, standard equipment on later model XK8s.

5: 18in Centaur wheel (later alternative to Flute and Double Five wheels).

6: 19in Apollo (2003/4 option).

7: 18in Hydra (later XKR standard wheel).

8: 20in Detroit (R-Performance split-rim wheel).

9: 20in Montreal (R-Performance split-rim wheel).

10: 20in Paris (R-Performance split-rim wheel).

11: *17in Lamina, standard for XK8s, 2004 on.*

12: 18in Impeller (later optional).

13: 19in Atlas (final fit XK8 S/Victory, and others optional).

14: 18in Aris (2004/5 standard higher spec XK8 models, others optional).

15: 20in Sepang (R-Performance split-rim wheel, only for post-2004 model year cars).

16: The Victory wheels fitted to the very last Victory special edition models destined for the US market.

225

Technical specifications

	4.0-litre	4.0-litre supercharged
cc	3996	3996
Bore and stroke (mm)	86 x 86	86 x 86
Compression ratio	10.75:1	9:1
bhp	290	370
@ rpm	6100	6150
Torque (lb ft)	290	387
@ rpm	4250	3600
Fuelling	Fuel-injection	Fuel-injection
Transmission	5-speed auto	5-speed auto
Wheel size (in)	17 or 18	18 or 19
Suspension front	Ind unequal-length wishbones, anti-dive, coil springs	Ind unequal-length wishbones, anti-dive, coil springs
Rear suspension	Ind double wishbones, driveshafts as upper links, anti-squat, coil springs, CATS optional	Ind double wishbones, driveshaft as upper links, anti-squat, coil springs
Brakes	4-wheel disc, all ventilated	4-wheel disc, all ventilated
Performance		
0–60mph (sec)	6.5	5.2
Top speed (mph)	155	155
Average mpg	23	23
Dimensions		
Length (in)	187	187
Width (in)	72	72
Height (in)	51	51
Wheelbase (in)	102	102
Front track (in)	57	57
Rear track (in)	57	57
Weight (lb)	3560 (3759 convertible)	3616 (3814 convertible)

Optional extras

Mud flaps.
Cruise control (where not fitted as standard).
Tailored overmats.
Headlight power-wash system.
Premium hi-fi system with CD auto-changer in boot.
Child's safety seat.
Child's booster cushion.
First-aid kit for boot area.
Space-saver spare wheel.
Full-size spare wheel.
Fire extinguisher for boot area.
Jaguar warning triangle.
Headlamp converters.
Headlamp safety covers.
Mobile telephone kits.
Snow chains.
Luggage net for boot area.
Witter tow bar kit.
Cup-holders for forward centre console area.
Heated windscreen.
Ultrasonic intrusion security system.
Tool kit roll.
Heated front seats.
Jaguar 'growler' alloy wheel centre badges, various colours.
Power-folding door mirrors.
Chrome door mirror surrounds (where not fitted).
Bright rear number plate surround (chrome).
Self-dipping rear-view mirror.
Wood/leather steering wheel (where not fitted).
Foglamp protective covers.
Wind deflector (convertible models only).
Tailored front seat covers.
Boot-mounted carrier.
Luggage box for boot mounting on carrier.
Boot rack ski holder.
Boot rack cycle/mountain bike holder.
Various options of fitted luggage for the boot.
Round alloy gear knob.
Satellite navigation system (later cars).
Reverse park aid.
Auxiliary power socket.
Tracker security system.
Aspheric door mirrors.

	4.2-litre	4.2-litre supercharged
cc	4196	4196
Bore and stroke (mm)	96 x 90.3	96 x 90.3
Compression ratio	11:1	9:1
bhp	300	400
@ rpm	6000	6100
Torque (lb ft)	310	408
@ rpm	4100	3500
Fuelling	Fuel-injection	Fuel-injection
Transmission	6-speed auto	6-speed auto
Wheel size (in)	17, 18, or 19	17, 18, 19, or 20
Suspension front	Ind unequal-length wishbones, anti-dive, coil springs	Ind unequal-length wishbones, anti-dive, coil springs
Rear suspension	Ind double wishbones, driveshafts as upper links, anti-squat, coil springs, CATS optional	Ind double wishbones, driveshafts as upper links, anti-squat, coil springs
Brakes	4-wheel disc, all ventilated	4-wheel disc, all ventilated
Performance		
0–60mph (sec)	6.1	5.2
Top speed (mph)	155	155
Average mpg	24.9	22.9
Dimensions		
Length (in)	187	187
Width (in)	72	72
Height (in)	51	51
Wheelbase (in)	102	102
Front track (in)	57	57
Rear track (in)	57	57
Weight (lb)	3715 (3913 convertible)	3825 (4001 convertible)

Lockable boot-mounted security box.
Adaptive cruise control.
Xenon headlight units (where not fitted).
Heated rear screen.
Rear spoiler.
Air filtration system to air-conditioning.
Cold climate pack.
Bird's eye maple veneer (2004 as alternative to walnut veneer).
Burr elm veneer (2004 as alternative to walnut veneer).
Piano black finish (2004 as alternative to walnut veneer).
Memory pack of interior trim additions.
Technology pack of Adaptive cruise control, speed limiter, Alpine sound system, and navigational system.
18in seven-spoke sports alloy wheels (exposed wheel nuts).
17in XJR five-spoke alloy wheels (exposed wheel nuts).
17in five-spoke Revolver chromed alloy wheels.
18in Apollo alloy wheels (later cars).
17in XJR-style five-spoke alloy wheels.
17in Lamina five-spoke alloy wheels (later cars).
18in Impeller alloy wheels (later cars).
18in seven-flute alloy wheels.
17in Gemini five-spoke double flute alloy wheels (post-2002).
18in Centaur seven-spoke alloy wheels (post-2002).
18in Hydra alloy wheels (standard on XKR post-2002).
18in Aris (2004/5 model year optional choice).
19in Atlas (2004/5 model year optional choice).

R-Performance specifics
18in Milan split-rim alloy wheels.
18in Winter alloy wheels.
20in Paris split-rim alloy wheels.
20in Detroit split-rim alloy wheels.
20in Montreal nine-spoke alloy wheels (post-2002).
20in Sepang (only applicable to facelift models, post-2004).
Brembo brakes.
XK handling pack (XK8 models only).

Colour schemes

Exterior colours	Details	Interior Sport	Fascia	Details
Spindrift White	To 2001	Charcoal	Charcoal	
Sherwood Green	To 1999	Ivory	Charcoal	
Antigua Blue	To 2000	Oatmeal	Charcoal	To 2002
Anthracite (black)	To 2002	Nimbus	Charcoal	2000–2
Titanium Grey	1996/7, 2000	Dove	Charcoal	From 2003
British Racing Green	To 2004	Cranberry	Charcoal	From 2003
Aquamarine*	To 1998	Cranberry/Charcoal	contrast	From 2003
Topaz (gold)	To 2004	Heritage Tan	Charcoal	From 2003
Carnival Red	To 2003	Heritage Tan/Charcoal	contrast	From 2003
Sapphire Blue	To 2002			
Ice Blue	To 1997			
Meteorite Silver	1997–2000			
Amaranth (purple)	1997–9	**Veneer**		
Phoenix Red	1999–2004	Grey Maple		
(first year XKR only)		Burr Walnut	option	2003–4
Alpine Green	1999–2000	Grey Stain		2003–4
Emerald Green	2000–2	Carbon Fibre		From 2004
Mistral	2000–2	Burr Elm		From 2004
Westminster Blue	2000–2	Piano Black	option	From 2004
Pacific Blue	2000–4			
Seafrost	2000–4			
Platinum	From 2000			
White Onyx	2001–4			
Roman Bronze	2001–2			
Zircon	2003–4			
Jaguar Racing Green	From 2003			
Quartz	From 2003			
Adriatic Blue	2003–4			
Slate	2003–4			
Ebony	2003–4			
Midnight	From 2003			
Ultraviolet Blue	2004			
Salsa Red	2004			
Radiance Red	2003–4			
Satin Silver*	2005			
Bay Blue*	2005			
Frost Blue*	2005			
Copper Black*	2005			

* = Relates to Victory and S models only for 2005 model year

All interior colour schemes optional with exterior paint finishes.

Interior Classic	Fascia	Details	Hood	Details
Teal	Dark Teal	To 1999	Black	
Cashmere	Sable	To 2004	Blue	
Ivory	Sable		Green	To 2004
Charcoal	Charcoal		Stone	To 1999
Oatmeal	Antelope	To 2002	Dark Beige	
Nimbus	Slate	2000-4	Light Beige	2000-4
Dove		From 2003	Sable or Flint	
Cranberry		2003-4		
Cranberry/Charcoal	contrast	2003-4		
Heritage Tan		2003-4		
Heritage Tan/Charcoal	contrast	2003-4		
Veneer				
Grey Maple	option	From 2003		
Burr Walnut				

Seating style	Details
Classic	Standard on XK8s to 2005
Sport	Standard on XKRs and better spec'd XK8s to 2005
Sport Luxury	New-style standard seating from 2005
Recaro	Standard on higher spec'd XKRs

Prices and production volumes

	Price New (£)	1995	1996	1997	1998	1999	2000
XK8 4.0-litre coupé	47,950	■	■	■	■	■	■
XK8 4.0-litre convertible	54,950	■	■	■	■	■	■
XKR coupé	60,105	–	–	–	–	■	■
XKR convertible	67,105	–	–	–	–	■	■
XKR Silverstone coupé	67,310	–	–	–	–	–	■
XKR Silverstone convertible	72,710	–	–	–	–	–	■

	Price New (£)	2001	2002	2003	2004	2005	Total
XK8 4.0-litre coupé	47,950	■	■	–	–	–	19,748*
XK8 4.0-litre convertible	54,950	■	■	–	–	–	46,770*
XKR coupé	60,105	■	■	–	–	–	9478*
XKR convertible	67,105	■	■	–	–	–	13,620*
XKR Silverstone coupé	67,310	–	–	–	–	–	233
XKR Silverstone convertible	72,710	–	–	–	–	–	325
XKR 100 coupé	69,950	■	–	–	–	–	100
XKR 100 convertible	74,950	■	–	–	–	–	100
XK8 4.2-litre coupé	48,700	–	■	■	■	■	–
XK8 4.2-litre convertible	55,345	–	■	■	■	■	–
XKR 4.2-litre coupé	56,695	–	■	■	■	■	–
XKR 4.2-litre convertible	63,345	–	■	■	■	■	–
XKR Carbon Fibre coupé	64,650	–	–	–	■	■	–
XKR Carbon Fibre con.	71,450	–	–	–	■	■	–
XK Portfolio convertible	66,645	–	–	–	■	–	–
XK8 Victory/S coupé	50,000	–	–	–	–	■	–
XK8 Victory/S convertible	56,800	–	–	–	–	■	–
XKR Victory/S coupé	60,000	–	–	–	–	■	–
XKR S convertible	66,800	–	–	–	–	■	–
Total production							**90,374**

Includes special editions

Production changes

1996
XK8 coupé/convertible introduced.

1997
Boot-mounted high-level brakelight fitted.

1998
XKR models became available.

1999
Stiffening pillar added to seatbelt anchorage/B post area on convertibles.
Servotronic power steering system from XKR now fitted to XK8 models.
Air-assisted fuel injectors fitted to V8 engines.
Continually variable cam timing replaced two-stage phasing on 4.0-litre engines.
Electronic cruise control actuation fitted.

2000
Adaptive cruise control fitted to XKR model.
Satellite navigation system available on XK models.
Rain sensing wipers available for XKR models only.
Enhanced Alpine 320-watt Premium Sound system for all models.
Electric seatbelt tensioners added to all models.
XJR engine enhanced with new engine management system.
CD system standardised on all XK models.
XKR Silverstone Special Edition introduced.

2001
XK8/R facelift, flush-mounted front fog lamps in revised nose section.
XK8 revised front 'splitter' bar design.
New lens-style rear-light clusters with chromed surrounds.
Chrome boot plinth now incorporating external boot lid catch.
Revised rear bumper with deeper skirt.
Towing eye now fitted behind bumper under concealed flap.
Larger chromed exhaust tailpipes.
Adaptive Restraint Technology fitted.
Reinforced front side-members in bodyshell for extra stiffness.
New front seat design with separate headrests and extra electrical adjustment.
XKR 100 introduced to commemorate 100th anniversary of founder of company.

2002
4.2-litre engines replace 4.0-litre.
ZR six-speed automatic transmission fitted to all models.
XKR standardised with larger Brembo ventilated disc brakes.
CATS suspension standardised on all XK models.
Emergency Brake Assist technology added.
Revised rear 'solid' badging.
Xenon headlights standardised on all models.
Leaping cat mascot on passenger-side airbag door.
Recaro racing seats now available as extra-cost option.

2004
Styling makeover for final production period, incorporating enlarged nose area, over-sills, and front and rear bumper/valance treatment.
Removal of side mouldings, black window surrounds, rear spoiler added to XK8, and larger spoiler for XKR models.
Revised exhaust treatment according to model.
Addition of driver-controlled Automatic Speed Limiter System.
Availability of special technology and premium packs to further enhance specification.

2005
Range rationalised with final production special editions, plus reduction of paint, interior finishes.
Production discontinued.

15 The XJ8 saloons 1997 to 2002

Background

After the success, though limited production period, of the X-300 range introduced under Ford influence, in September 1997 the next generation of XJ saloons appeared to replace it. Coded X-308, this was the first time that the designation XJ8 was seen, as the essence of the new models was the AJ-V8 engine, first seen in the XK8 a year earlier. As well as the 4.0-litre V8, both normally-aspirated and supercharged, there was a new 3.2-litre version for entry level models.

Mechanically the XJ8s were improved in other areas, with better gearbox, suspension upgrades, and improved steering areas. Stylistically they looked very similar to the X-300 but were in fact different in many areas, not least in having an entirely new interior layout. Build quality was improved yet again over the previous model.

Following on from the success of the X-300, an expansive range of cars was offered, from a base 3.2-litre V8 through to the supercharged XJR version, with a model built to suit most buyers' requirements. Just as there were two Daimler models in the X-300 range, so there were for the XJ8, only this time both would utilise V8 power units and one would be of the supercharged type, making the Daimler Super V8 the fastest production Daimler ever produced.

However, just as the X-300 range had a relatively short production run, so too did the XJ8 range, which only lasted until 2002. Even so, during this time the range was changed several times and all the cars gained a unique reputation for quality and longevity, more so than any previous Jaguar saloon models.

The last XJ8s left the production line in mid-2002 prior to the launch of their replacements, coded X-350. There would be a gap of nearly 12 months before the new cars were available to the public, during which time the last remaining examples of the XJ8 were sold through, marking the end of another Jaguar era.

The all-new technology of the replacement X-350s would see the flagship range of Jaguar models through more years than the X-308.

Model range and development

The XJ8 encapsulated a whole range of models very similar to the outgoing X-300 cars, based around the 3.2-litre and 4.0-litre V8 engines.

Models available at launch

XJ8 saloon (3.2-litre)
XJ8 Sovereign (4.0-litre)
XJ8 Sport (3.2-litre)
XJ8 4.0-litre
XJR supercharged saloon (4.0-litre)
Daimler Eight (4.0-litre)
Daimler Super V8 (supercharged 4.0-litre)

This total of seven models was one less than was available for the X-300 range, but each one was specifically geared to a particular sector of the anticipated market. The base XJ6 3.2-litre (or Executive, as it was also known and later designated) was an ideal entry level into Jaguar flagship motoring. Ideal for those who wanted the prestige of a big luxury saloon but at a bargain price, it nevertheless offered such items as air-conditioning, alloy wheels, and leather upholstery as standard equipment. The XJ8 4.0-litre was initially more or less a larger-engined version of the XJ8, though later it became equipped as a Sport model but retained the exterior chrome trim and interior veneer.

The Sport was similarly priced and roughly to the same specification but offered a slightly stiffer ride, wider tyres and wheels, colour-keying of exterior trim, and a more youthful interior, again all in leather. In contrast the Sovereign model was, as usual, intended for the traditional Jaguar owner who wanted all the luxury features as standard with the benefit of lots of chrome and detail.

The supercharged XJR took up the mantle of the six-cylinder model but offered significantly better performance and refinement and was again intended for the BMW M5 and similar market. The most powerful model in the range, it also benefited from further enhanced suspension and steering and even wider wheels. As before, the high-performance, a harsher ride, and superb handling meant that to a degree luxury equipment levels were tempered.

At the top of the range were the Daimler models, to meet the needs of the company chairman who wanted the ultimate in luxury and, once again, rarity, production numbers being low compared to the other models. It was also thought that with the demise of the V12 Jaguar, the Daimlers would cater for a slightly wider market this time. Virtually everything was supplied as standard equipment, but with softer touring suspension and slight alterations to exterior and interior trim to differentiate them from Jaguars. The Daimler Eight used the normally-aspirated 4.0-litre engine and, indeed, met and exceeded the specification of the equivalent Jaguar Sovereign. The Super V8 offered XJR performance with slightly softer suspension, the longer wheelbase bodyshell, and an enhanced interior.

Short and long-wheelbase bodyshells were still available, although the short version was earmarked for the XJ8, Sport, and XJR models, while the majority of Sovereigns and Daimlers were supplied with the longer shell.

Outside the UK the same principles applied for the XJ8 as with the X-300 models, namely the base models were not offered and the Daimler model range was called Jaguar Vanden Plas.

Little happened to the range over the next couple of years, although at one time the 3.2-litre Sport was dropped, at which time the 4.0-litre XJ8 was upgraded to become a mix of luxury saloon and sport model. Later the 3.2-litre Sport returned due to popular demand, and thereafter it stayed in production until the end.

In the last year of production (2002) Jaguar introduced a new model to the range, effectively

External styling changes from the previous XJ6/12 (X-300) models to the XJ8 range are subtle. Side views of both cars show the XJ8 model (on the right) with oval reflectors set into the front and rear bumper bars.

An unusual view of the XJ8 shows the chromed bumper blades at the front. Previous models enjoyed a single full-width blade.

Frontal differences between the 1994–7 six- and twelve-cylinder models and the V8s are shown in the more rounded valance air intake, circular fog lamps, oval indicator lenses, differing styles of headlights, and the more rounded exterior to the radiator grille.

Rear differences were the styling 'lip' to the bumper bar/valance and revised badging of the V8 (on the left).

bringing together trim aspects of the 3.2 with the Sovereign model. Called the SE (Special Equipment), a high degree of standard interior accommodation was offered, all for less than £36,000, making it a very attractive proposition in this sector of the market.

Minor changes took place to all models throughout production. Specifications were enhanced and such items as alloy wheel design changed regularly to meet fashion needs.

No other special versions of the X-308 were produced although, as with the X-300, the Eagle Coachworks produced four- and six-door limousines and hearses, both Jaguar and Daimler variants.

The XJ8 proved a vital flagship model range to Jaguar, even after the launch of the new and smaller S-type and X-type models from 1999 on. These were arguably the best cars Jaguar had built up to that time.

Exterior identification points

XJ8 model
- Chrome trim to radiator grille, screen surrounds, rain gutters, waistline trims and boot plinth.
- Matt black window frames.
- Colour co-ordinated door mirrors and handles.
- Grey plastic vertical slats to the radiator grille.
- Distinctive halogen headlights with chrome centre spot and vertical rib.
- A single contrasting swage coachline.
- 'Jaguar' and 'XJ8' badging to boot lid.
- 20-spoke alloy wheels standard equipment, with plastic centre caps to cover wheel nuts incorporating grey Jaguar growler emblems.
- For later updates on 4.0-litre models see detailed photographs.

Sport model
- As XJ8 except for:
- Black vertical slats to the radiator grille; radiator grille surround colour-keyed to exterior paint finish.
- Dual coachline above the side rubbing strips.
- Matt black-finished rain gutters and front and rear screen surrounds.
- Dimple alloy wheels.
- 'Jaguar' and 'XJ Sport' badging to boot lid and 'V8' badging to B/C post.

XJR model
- As Sport except for:
- Colour co-ordinated radiator grille shell with mesh centre replacing the vanes.
- Sport ventilated five-spoke alloy wheels.
- Larger exhaust outlets.
- 'Jaguar' and 'XJR' badging to boot lid.

Boot badge legends and backgound colours changed from the previous X-300 models. For example, most XJ8 badges are based on a grey background (Daimlers being the exception). The 'Executive' badge only applied from 2001.

The B/C pillars between the doors always show the 'V8' insignia, unlike X-300 models, which show 'V12', 'Sport', 'XJR', etc, according to model.

The XJ8's interior was 90% changed from that of the X-300, with curved dashboard, inset instruments (like the XK8), and curved centre console surround. This car is an XJ8 model (the half-wood/half-leather steering wheel was an extra-cost option). The same style applied to Executive and SE models.

Above left: XJ8 consoles are more rounded than on the X-300, and include an integrated audio/telephone pad. This is a post-1999 model, with a leather-clad gear selector surround instead of the black plastic used on earlier models.

Above right: XJ8 4.0-litre interior with revised seat cushions, as used from 2000 on. These models were available with or without dark-stained maple woodwork.

Sovereign models, like the Daimler cars, enjoyed full chroming, including window frames and radiator grille.

The supercharged model is easily identifiable by its mesh radiator grille insert and lack of chrome trim.

Sport models featured de-chroming like the XJR, but had the grille centre vane panel painted in grey.

Daimler models like the one on the left included fluted grille and chromed door handles/door mirrors. The XJ8 (later the Executive model) is on the right, with different grille treatment.

One of the last Executive models, the SE shared much of its specification with the Sovereign, and had a chromed grille but no chromed door frames.

The rear view of XJ8 Executive and SE models shows a chromed boot plinth and relevant badging but no chromed surrounds to the rear-light units. A high-level brakelight in the rear screen is fitted to all XJ V8 models.

As with the previous models, V8 Daimlers used a shorter fluted chromed boot plinth.

Rear aspect of the XJR model shows a painted boot plinth (also applicable to Sport models) and larger exhaust tailpipes.

Sovereign model
- All-chrome exterior trim including window frames, front and rear screens, and rear-light cluster surrounds.
- A choice of alloy wheels (see photographs).
- 'V8' script to B/C post, 'Jaguar' and 'Sovereign' badging to rear boot lid.

Daimler models
- As Sovereign except for:
- Fluted design radiator grille surround and boot plinth (and of shorter width to Jaguar type).
- Sunroof standard on Super V8.
- Unique alloy wheels (see photographs) and chromed door mirrors/door handles.
- 'Daimler' badging replacing Jaguar on boot lid, 'Eight' or 'Super V8' badging also on boot lid.

SE model
- As XJ8 except for 'SE' badging on boot lid and reverse park aid equipment fitted as standard to rear bumper.

NB: Market differences applied to some overseas cars: eg 'Vanden Plas' badging, use of Daimler grille to Jaguar models, etc.

A wide variety of alloy wheel designs were available throughout production, many of which could have been specified by buyers upon initial purchase. A chromed mesh radiator grille was also made available later in production for the XJR model, so some cars were fitted with this from new.

Interior identification points

General points applicable to all XK models
- Sunroof standard on Super V8.
- Curved dashboard with main instruments deeply inset in front of the driver with onboard computer control panel. Black plastic air-conditioning outlets, one either side of dashboard, plus centre vent area flanking circular clock. Centre console of similar appearance to previous models although more curved in style with integrated audio system and auxiliary switchgear for heated seats (where fitted), traction control (where fitted), headlight adjustment, and air-conditioning controls with digital temperature read-out and telephone pad controls.
- Veneered centre console containing J-gate gearshift mounted initially in black plastic surround, later changed to leather. Switches incorporated for Sport gearbox mode and cruise control (where fitted).
- Concealed trim flush-mounted damped ashtray arrangement as XK8.

Above left: *Interior view of the Sport model with dark-stained maple woodwork and high-contrast interior colour schemes. The similar style seating to X-300 Sport models was different to later 4.0-litre XJ8 cars (see the picture on page 232). All XJ8 models had leather upholstery. This early car shows the black plastic surround to the gearlever area, later changed to stitched leather.*

Above right: *Front interior of the Daimler model. All Daimlers featured better-quality, burr walnut veneering, with boxwood inlays as seen in the passenger-side fascia and door panel.*

Rear compartment of Daimler Super V8. Veneered picnic tables and boxwood inlays are standard to all models, while the split-seating arrangement is standard on the Super V8 and optional on the Eight.

Above left: *Twenty-spoke alloy wheels were fitted to XJ8 models for two years, and were optional on others.*

Above right: *Dimple alloys, previously fitted to X-300 Sport models, continued on all XJ8 Sport cars.*

Above left: *The Cosmic alloy was never fitted as standard equipment but was available as an option to other alloy wheels on XJ8 models.*

Above right: *The Crown alloy wheels normally fitted to Daimler models were also available on Jaguars, but with a growler emblem in the centre.*

- Centre armrest incorporating lid and storage area.
- Steering wheel of four-spoke design common to all Jaguars of this era, either leather-covered or wood/leather-covered incorporating airbag and horn push. Auxiliary switch packs to either side of steering wheel for audio controls, telephone, and cruise control (where fitted).
- Passenger-side glovebox of larger dimensions to previous X-300 model.
- Door trim panels incorporating full-length armrests, window lift controls, and map pockets with shaped wood-veneered cappings.
- Curved front seats, all electrically operated, with vertical pleats and integrated stitching.
- Matching rear bench arrangement with fitted headrests and fold-down centre armrest.

XJ8 model
- Initially 3.2-litre and later SE plus early 4.0-litre models. As above but with figured walnut veneer to dashboard, centre console ski-slope, and door cappings.
- Complimentary trim finishes in two-tone and normal vertically pleated seating.

Sport model
- As XJ8 except for:
- Dark-stained maple woodwork throughout.
- Contrast two-tone upholstery and squarer more supportive sports front seats with wider horizontal pleating and aerated sections. No lumbar support available.
- Rear bench-seating to match.

Sovereign model
- As XJ8 except for burr walnut-veneer woodwork throughout. Wood-veneer finish to door window lift switch packs.

Later 4.0-litre models
- A mix of Sport and Sovereign, incorporating walnut-veneer woodwork but with slightly revised sports seating with horizontal pleats (see photographs).

XJR model
- As Sport.

Daimler models
- As Sovereign except for:
- Boxwood inlay to woodwork, higher-quality burr walnut-veneer woodwork throughout.
- More rounded seating with wider pleats in higher-quality leather.
- Colour-keyed items such as handbrake surround and gear knob.
- Walnut-veneered picnic tables behind front seats.
- Only available on longer wheelbase models, primarily for Super V8, individualised rear

Above: The complete range of later alloy wheels fitted and available on XJ8 models.

Left: The Penta five-spoke fluted wheel was another alloy available on XJ models.

seating arrangement with extended centre console between seats and following on from front armrest area, incorporating wood-veneered panel and electric switchgear for electrically adjustable seating.

All details of trim and specification given above relate to standard production cars. Certain owners may well have specified changes to suit their individual requirements, so it is not unusual to find some more basic models with a higher specification than that described here.

Technical specifications

	3.2-litre	4.0-litre
cc	3248	3996
Bore and stroke (mm)	86 x 70	86 x 86
Compression ratio	10.5:1	10.75:1
bhp	240	290
@ rpm	6350	6100
Torque (lb ft)	233	290
@ rpm	4350	4250
Fuelling	Fuel-injection	Fuel-injection
Transmission	ZR 5-speed auto	ZF 5-speed auto
Wheel size (in)	16, alloy	17, alloy
Suspension front	Ind unequal-length wishbones, anti-dive, coil springs	Ind unequal-length wishbones, anti-dive, coil springs
Suspension rear	Ind double wishbones, driveshafts as upper links, anti-squat, coil springs, CATS optional	Ind double wishbones, driveshafts as upper links, anti-squat, coil springs, CATS optional
Brakes	4-wheel disc, all ventilated	4-wheel disc, all ventilated
Performance		
0–60mph (sec)	8.1	6.9
Top speed (mph)	140	150
Average mpg	23.5	23.7
Dimensions		
Length (in)	197 (201 long-wheelbase)	197 (201 long-wheelbase)
Width (in)	69	69
Height (in)	51 (52 long-wheelbase)	51 (52 long-wheelbase)
Wheelbase (in)	112 (116 long-wheelbase)	112 (116 long-wheelbase)
Front track (in)	57	57
Rear track (in)	57	57
Weight (lb)	3769	3769

Optional extras

Mud flaps.
Cruise control (where not fitted as standard).
Tailored overmats.
Headlight power-wash system.
Premium hi-fi system with CD auto-changer in boot.
Child's safety seat.
Child's booster cushion.
First-aid kit for boot area.
Space-saver spare wheel.
Full-size spare wheel.
Fire extinguisher for boot area.
Jaguar warning triangle.
Headlamp converters.
Headlamp safety covers.
Mobile telephone kits.
Snow chains.
Luggage net for boot area.
Witter tow bar kit.
Cup-holders for forward centre console area.
Heated windscreen.

Ultrasonic intrusion security system.
Additional zip-fastening tool kit.
Heated front seats (where not fitted).
Jaguar 'growler' alloy wheel centre badges, various colours.
Power-folding door mirrors.
Chrome door mirror surrounds (where not fitted).
Bright rear number plate surround (chrome).
Self-dipping rear-view mirror.
Wood/leather steering wheel (where not fitted).
Foglamp protective covers.
Tailored front seat covers.
Boot cargo net.
Boot luggage hooks.
Luggage retainer clips and/or straps.
Roof-mounted rack.
Two-bar roof-rack carrier.
Ski/cycle holders.
Luggage frame for roof rack.
Compact, Sport or large roof box.

	4.0-litre supercharged
cc	3996
Bore and stroke (mm)	86 x 86
Compression ratio	9:1
bhp	370
@ rpm	6150
Torque (lb ft)	387
@ rpm	3600
Fuelling	Fuel-injection
Transmission	ZF 5-speed auto
Wheel size (in)	18, alloy
Suspension front	Ind unequal-length wishbones, anti-dive, coil springs
Suspension rear	Ind double wishbones, driveshafts as upper links, anti-squat, coil springs, CATS
Brakes	4-wheel disc, all ventilated
Performance	
0–60mph (sec)	5.3
Top speed (mph)	155
Average mpg	21.6
Dimensions	
Length (in)	197
Width (in)	69
Height (in)	51
Wheelbase (in)	112
Front track (in)	57
Rear track (in)	57
Weight (lb)	3913

Various options of fitted luggage for the boot.
Round alloy gear knob.
Satellite navigation system (later cars).
Reverse park aid (where not fitted).
Auxiliary power socket.
Tracker security system.
Aspheric door mirrors.
Lockable boot-mounted security box.
Xenon headlight units (where not fitted).
Air filtration system to air-conditioning.
Engine block heater.
Cold climate pack.
Electric sunroof (where not fitted).
Rear window blinds.
Deflector for sunroof.
CATS suspension package (where not fitted).
Chromed grille surround (where not fitted).
Alternative woodwork veneers (according to model).
16in 20-spoke alloy wheels (plastic centre caps).
16in Dimple with anthracite infill alloy wheels.

16in Dimple alloy wheels (plain).
16in Crown alloy wheels (centre cap covers).
16in Starburst alloy wheels.
16in Cosmic five double-spoke alloy wheels.
16in Lunar seven-spoke alloy wheels (later models).
16in Eclipse five-spoke alloy wheels (later models).
16in multi-spoke Corona alloy wheels (later models).
17in XJR Sport alloy wheels (exposed wheel nuts).
17in Celtic ten-spoke alloy wheels (later models).
18in Penta five-spoke alloy wheels (later models).
18in seven-flute alloy wheels.
18in Asteroid seven-spoke alloy wheels (later standard XJR model).

R-Performance specifics
18in Milan split-rim alloy wheels.
18in Winter alloy wheels.
19in Montreal alloy wheels (later models).
Brembo brakes.
XK handling pack (XK8 models only).

15 Colour schemes

The XJ8 saloons 1997 to 2002

Exterior	Details	Models applicable	Interior Sport/XJR	Fascia	Details
Spindrift White	To 2001	Non-Sport/XJR until 2000	Charcoal	Charcoal	
Sherwood Green	To 2000	Non-Sport/XJR	Ivory	Charcoal	
Seafront		Non-Sport/XJR until 2000	Oatmeal	Charcoal	
Anthracite (black)			Nimbus	Charcoal	To 2002
Titanium Grey	To 2002	Non-Sport/XJR until 2000			
British Racing Green					
Aquamarine	To 1999	Sport/XJR			
Topaz (gold)		Non-Sport/XJR until 2000			
Carnival Red		Spot/XJR until 2000			
Sapphire Blue					
Mistral	To 2002	Non-Sport/XJR until 2000			
Meteorite Silver	To 2000				
Amaranth (purple)	To 2000	Non-Sport/XJR	**Veneer**		
Westminster Blue		Non-Sport/XJR until 2000	Grey Maple		
Madeira (maroon)	To 2000	Non-Sport/XJR	Figured Walnut	option	From 2001
Spruce Green	To 1999	Non-Sport/XJR	Burr Walnut	option	From 2001
Alpine Green	1999–2001	Non-Sport/XJR until 2000			
Emerald Green	1999–2002	Non-Sport/XJR until 2000			
Antigua Blue	1999–2000				
Platinum Grey	From 2000				
Pacific Blue	From 2000				
White Onyx	From 2001				
Roman Bronze	2001–2				
Slate Grey	2002 only				
Quartz	2002 only				
Aspen Green	2002 only				
Zircon	2002 only				

Interior colour schemes applicable to all Sport/XJR model exterior colours.

Interior XJ8/Sovereign/ Daimler	Fascia	Details	Contrast piping
Oatmeal	Antelope		Antelope
Cashmere	Sable	To 2002	Sable
Ivory	Sable		Sable
Charcoal	Charcoal		Nimbus
Nimbus	Slate	Sovereign/Daimler	Slate
Catkin	Pine	Sovereign/Daimler	Pine
Cranberry/Charcoal	contrast		
Heritage Tan			
Heritage Tan/Charcoal	contrast		
Veneer			
Figured Walnut			
Burr Walnut		Sovereign/Daimler	

Interior colour schemes applicable to all XJ, Sovereign, and Daimler exterior colours except where indicated.

Prices and production volumes

	Price new (£)	1997	1998	1999	2000
XJ8 3.2-litre	35,675	■	■	■	■
XJ8 3.2-litre long-wheelbase	–	■	■	■	■
XJ8 3.2-litre Sovereign	–	■	■	■	■
XJ8 3.2-litre Sovereign long wheelbase	–	■	■	■	■
3.2-litre Sport	34,475	■	■	■	–
XJ8 3.2-litre Executive	35,950	–	–	–	■
XJ8 3.2-litre SE	35,950	–	–	–	–
XJ8 4.0-litre	40,975	■	■	■	■
XJ8 4.0-litre long-wheelbase	–	■	■	■	■
XJ8 4.0-litre Sovereign	43,950	■	■	■	■
XJ8 4.0-litre Sovereign long wheelbase	46,575	■	■	■	■
XJ8 4.0-litre SE	40,950	–	–	–	–
XJR	50,675	■	■	■	■
XJR 100	58,935	–	–	–	–
4.0-litre Vanden Plas	–	–	–	■	■
4.0-litre Vanden Plas long wheelbase	–	■	■	■	■
4.0-litre VDP S/C long-wheelbase	–	–	■	■	■
Daimler Eight	–	■	■	■	■
Daimler Eight long-wheelbase	52,575	■	■	■	■
Daimler Super V8	–	–	–	■	■
Daimler Super V8 long-wheelbase	62,775	■	■	■	■
Total production					

NB: Use of Sovereign name varies by model and by world market.

Production changes

1997
XJ8 models introduced.

1999
Chrome external trim pack available as extra-cost option for XJR model.
Short wheelbase Sovereign model becomes available.
Improved clock graphics on dashboard.
Soft-stitched colour-keyed gearbox surround replaced plastic on centre console.
Repositioned switch pack on front passenger seat for rear adjustment.
Burr walnut option for XJR model.
Servotronic power-steering system from XKR fitted to all saloons.
Air-assisted fuel injectors fitted to all V8 engines.
Continually variable cam timing replaced two-stage phasing on 4.0-litre engines.
Electronic cruise control actuation fitted.
Larger XKR-style brake discs fitted to XJR model.

2001	2002	Total produced
■	–	20,235 Inc Exe/SE
■	■	771
■	■	2095
■	■	385
■	■	1108
■	■	
–	■	
■	■	8369
■	■	148
■	■	36,635 Inc SE
■	■	11,566
–	■	
■	■	15,203 Inc long wheelbase
■	–	100
–	–	1
■	■	21,080
■	■	788
■	■	164
■	■	2119
■	■	76
■	■	2387
		123,230

with longer cushion and improved lateral support.
XJR engine enhanced with new engine management system.
XJ8 3.2-/4.0-litre models gain 12-way electric front seat adjustment as standard equipment.
XJ8 3.2-/4.0-litre models gain all chromed window surrounds as standard equipment.
XJ8 3.2-/4.0-litre models gain rear compartment cigar lighter and boot-mounted warning triangle.
Rain sensing wipers/CD player/heated windscreen standard on Sovereign models.
XJR standard equipment now included cruise control, 12-way seat adjustment, and rain sensing wipers.
XJR standard equipment also comprised heated screen, CD, rear cigar lighter, tool kit, and warning triangle.
XJR standard equipment also included carpet mats, and new Asteroid alloy wheels.
320-watt Premium sound system standardised on Daimler Eight.
3.2-litre Sport model discontinued from range.

2001
3.2-litre Sport model reintroduced.
Standard XJ8 model now badged as 'Executive'.
'Executive' now fitted as standard with rain sensing wipers, CD, cruise control, and reverse park aid.
Sovereign model gains heated front seats and reverse park aid as standard equipment.
Reverse park aid fitted as standard to all Daimler models.
XJR 100 model introduced to commemorate 100th anniversary of founder of company.

2002
3.2-litre SE (Special Equipment) model introduced.
4.0-litre SE model replaces previous 4.0-litre XJ8.
Daimler and Sovereign models now made to special order only.
(End) Production of all XJ8 (X308s) discontinued.

Sports pack became available for Sovereign models with wider alloy wheels.

2000
Satellite navigation system becomes available as extra-cost option on any model.
Rain sensing wipers available on all models except XJ8 Executive.
Enhanced Alpine 320-watt Premium sound system for all models.
Improved sports seating for Sport and XJR saloons

16 S-type saloons 1999 to 2007

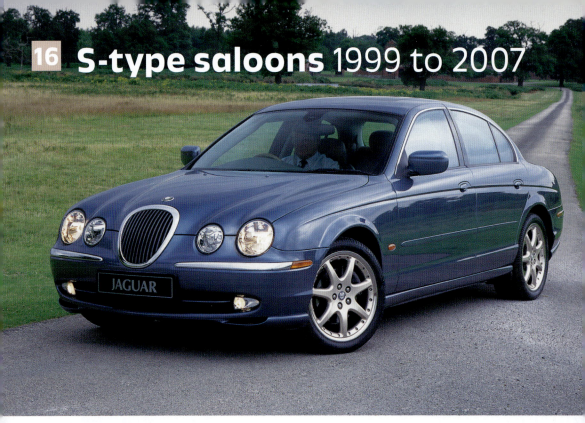

Background

It was in the mid-1950s that Jaguar recognised the potential expansion to their market if they produced a smaller luxury saloon model for those who didn't need or want a gargantuan prestige car like the Mark VII. Although there were plenty of 'medium'-sized saloons around from car makers like Ford, Humber, Riley, Wolseley and others, the only company to have successfully produced a small prestige saloon in a similar class to Jaguar was Daimler (at that time still an independent company), with its Century model. Of quality manufacture, it had the image, but was a little staid and lacked somewhat on the performance front.

At the end of 1955 Jaguar introduced its legendary 2.4-litre saloon, which marked a turning point in company policy, utilising new technology and offering the motor car buying public a smaller, cheaper, and more economical option, something Jaguar hadn't done since the old postwar 1.75-litre saloon had been dropped. This led the company to further success, widening their product range, market sector and, of course, profitability – exactly what the current S-type has achieved for Jaguar today. The 2.4-litre model led to the Mark 2, then extra models like the 1960s S-type, 420, and also Daimler models, and again as then, the new S-type range has expanded since its introduction in 1999; and, of course, the X-type stems from the same stable.

So successful was Jaguar in this 'new' market in the 1950s and 1960s that many other companies entered it, not least the likes of BMW, who stole the show from Jaguar in the 1980s. In contrast Jaguar took a different route with the introduction of the XJ6 in 1968 that led to a one-model policy which in itself was successful, although many mourned the passing of the sporting small 'compact' luxury models, particularly the Mark 2.

For many different reasons, such as the lack of resources and finance, Jaguar stayed with their one-saloon range throughout the life of the Series XJs, the XJ40, and the X-300/X-308, until 1999, when, after over 30 years without a smaller car, the company announced the launch of the S-type, revisiting a name from the 1960s.

Starting at a modest £26,000, the S-type was an all-new car, built at the Jaguar Castle Bromwich factory in Birmingham, the first complete Jaguar to be built there (the facility was normally used for building and painting bodies for other models in the Jaguar range). It used an up-to-date floorpan jointly developed with Ford (and also used by Lincoln in America), and both a new V6 engine of 3.0-litre capacity and the AJ-V8 power unit used in the XK8 and XJ. There were different gearboxes, both manual and automatic, new front and rear suspensions and steering, and an entirely updated body style built with the latest technology.

The very curvaceous body style was like nothing else on the market, with a multiplicity of shapes and body lines created by the very latest in body press techniques. A slight retro look was achieved with the radiator grille, a mix of racing C-type from the 1950s and Mark 2 from the 1960s. The very curved body line also, in other areas, echoed Jaguars of the past, particularly around the roof line. To go with this an all-new interior layout was part of the package, again with the latest electronics technology, even down to voice activation of some controls for the better-equipped models.

The S-type became Jaguar's most successful model produced in its first couple of years, and the range has developed to include more models. It has turned out to be a fabulous addition to the range of saloons offered by Jaguar. It not only provided for a new sector of the market, which normally purchased cars like the BMW 5 Series and E-class Mercedes, but also for those wishing to down-size from larger cars. It therefore found new markets that the company hadn't catered to in years, and hardly had any effect on the sales of other Jaguars.

All S-types are instantly identifiable from any other Jaguar model by the frontal treatment. This first generation car (1999–2002) shows the Mark 2/C-type radiator-style treatment. Fog lights were an extra-cost option on base models. The bonnet badge proclaimed the engine size (3.0- or 4.0-litre).

Model range and development

Models available at launch

S-type 3.0-litre saloon (manual or automatic)
S-type 3.0-litre SE (Special Equipment) (manual or automatic)
S-type 4.0-litre saloon (automatic)

The S-type was the most important new model since the introduction of the XJ6 in 1968, but despite its all-new technology and design it took a mere three years to get into production. The basis of its design and styling was carried through on all models, the only differences being in equipment specification and engine size, following established Jaguar practice.

All S-types featured the then unique swan-neck front suspension design and new rear suspension with integrated parts from the Ford part bin. The 4.0-litre model used the existing AJ-V8 power unit from the XJ and XK8, which featured the existing ZF automatic transmission mated to the J-gate operation. No manual option was available. The new 3.0-litre V6 engine was also unique to Jaguar, although it was initially built in Canada. A very refined responsive unit, this was either mated to a Ford four-speed automatic transmission, again with J-gate operation, or a brand new Ford-built five-speed manual gearbox.

Visually the S-type was all new, with very curvaceous styling that was quicker, easier,

Again, the rear view is entirely different to all other Jaguar models, with pronounced curvature to the boot surround. All cars have 'S-type' badging, 3.0-litre models without an engine size whereas later cars show the 'V8' insignia where applicable.

The only identifying features from the side, between the early S-types and the 2002 models are in the design of the door mirrors and a different choice of alloy wheels, but at the end of 2001 the side rubbing strips were removed.

and lighter to produce than any previous Jaguar bodyshell. The styling is still unique and makes the car instantly recognisable on the road compared to any other car from any manufacturer. The interior design was all new too, and although not universally liked by many Jaguar traditionalists, the whole interior would be replanned for later production.

The state of interior trim varies dramatically according to how much the S-type buyer wants to spend, even the Special Equipment models being available with a host of extra-cost options including satellite navigational systems, voice recognition operation of key controls, and so on.

Apart from minor production alterations, the S-type range remained unchanged until 2001, when a new model, the Sport, was added. Based on experience gained with the larger XJ range, the Sport offered an alternative for a younger market. It had colour co-ordinated exterior trim, a dark-stained maple interior, and the usual features such as sports seating and other minor differences in trim.

The next and most major change to the S-type range to date came in 2002, when all the models underwent a complete revamp. They received minor changes to exterior trim plus a completely new interior layout, copied from the then still new X-type and emulated in the latest X-350 models. Mechanically there were also a number of changes. Bodies were now laser welded for extra strength and higher-strength steels were used in key areas. Although the 3.0-litre models remained virtually unchanged, there was a new 2.5-litre V6-engined version at a lower price, the engine being taken from the X-type saloon although still, in the case of the S-type, in rear-wheel drive form. At the same time, following on from work done on the XK8s, the 4.0-litre engines were upgraded to 4.2-litre capacity, improving their performance.

A supercharged 4.2-litre S-type also became available. This came with a special structural 'shear ring' around the back seat area to provide a further 7% improvement in torsional strength to aid the vehicle's performance and handling characteristics. It also had all the usual supercharged Jaguar features, like mesh radiator grille, colour-keyed exterior trim, revised interior, and stiffer suspension layout. Lastly, all 4.2-litre S-types received a brand new ZF six-speed automatic transmission, offering the ultimate in gear change refinement.

The model continued to develop with enhanced equipment levels. In 2002 electrically adjustable foot pedals were fitted to all models.

In 2004 the bodywork was facelifted and featured a lighter, aluminium bonnet, revised bumper treatment, complete revised rear-end styling, and the removal of the side rubbing strips. Other changes included a wider range of

Facelift model from 2004 on. Note in particular the revised shaping to the front and rear bumper areas and blades, the slightly taller rear end, more prominent, less sculptured sills and overall cleaner lines.

Prior to 2002 the grille area looked like this (except for colour-coding for the Sport model). This particular car is equipped with a spring-loaded 'leaper' mascot instead of the conventional growler litre badge at this time. These leapers were only fitted to S-types for certain markets, not including the UK.

Cloth interior was standard on 3.0-litre models and, later, on 2.5-litre cars, although leather could be specified. The style of seating applied to all early models, although Sports seats could be specified.

alloy wheels, new styling for the door mirrors and, most important, the launch of the first diesel S-type, using the 2.7-litre engine covered in the 'Jaguar engines' chapter.

In 2005 the 2.5-litre engine S-types were dropped from the range and Jaguar started to offer limited editions like the XS from 2006, providing a degree of sportiness to the exterior design with revised bumper bar and spoiler treatment. For 2007 the Spirit became the base model but with extra equipment as standard, like leather upholstery and automatic transmission, and all models adopted similar frontal styling to the R model during the run-down in production to make way for the replacement model, the XF. The S-type finally ended production in 2007.

Above left: *Interior dashboard layout used until 2002, in this case with the optional satellite navigational system with screen. The half-wood/half-leather steering wheel was optional.*

Above right: *This console shows the manual transmission (not available on 4.0-litre models) and the alternative layout used for cars not equipped with a navigational system.*

Exterior identification points

General points applicable to all S-type models

Front view
- Curvaceous frontal aspect instantly recognisable and different from any other Jaguar model.
- Oval radiator grill with chrome or painted surround, later incorporating growler badge.
- Four separate headlight units in spherical style, outer units with side and indicator lights.
- All-enveloping preformed energy-absorbing bumper/valance arrangement mating with front wings and upper panel surround. This incorporates number plate surround, behind which is lower air intake area with splitter bar or other design according to model and year. Multi-curved one-piece rearward-hinged bonnet shaped around grille and lights, initially in steel, later changed to aluminium. Bonnet originally included growler badging with litre indication, later dropped.
- One-piece curved windscreen with twin wiper blades.

Rear view
- Bonded and curved one-piece rear screen with heated element.
- High-level brake warning light within rear screen.
- One-piece rear-hinged boot lid, differing in shape according to year model and, in some models, incorporating rear spoiler.
- Rear number plate surround in centre of boot lid with chromed finisher and lock/illumination panel.
- Oval rear-light units, changed according to model year, with jewelled lenses.
- All-enveloping rear bumper bar treatment with chromed blades to match the front, but altered dependent on model year and specification.

This rear compartment shot shows the different style and pleating of Sports seats.

Post-2004 S-type frontal appearance. The style of bumper/valance varies according to model, this one applying to the conventional saloon and diesel model.

- Twin exhaust pipes with chromed trims, differing according to engine size and type.

Side view
- Heavily swaged sides with pronounced curvature to roof section and front wing area.
- Flush-mounted, colour-keyed door handles.
- Sculptured and colour-keyed front door mirrors (different design on facelift models).
- Flush-mounted indicator repeater lights at rear of front wings, and colour-keyed rubbing strips along the side (deleted on post-2001 models).
- Sculptured sills (design changed with facelift models).
- Limousine-style door frames that curve into the roof section.
- Black side-window surrounds.
- Alloy wheels fitted to all models, size and style being dependent on model year and specification.

S-type model specifics

Standard and SE models (1999–2002)
- Radiator grille with grey plastic vertical slats.
- Chromed bumper bar blades.
- Fog lights initially standard equipment on SE model only.
- 7in x 16in Classic alloy wheels standard on 3.0-litre, 7.5in x 16in Dynamic for SE and 4.0-litre, with other options at extra cost (see photographs).

Sport model (up to 2002 model year)
- Radiator grille colour-keyed to body paint.
- Colour-keyed bumper bar blades.
- 7.5in x 17in Sport alloy wheels fitted.
- Colour-keyed boot lid plinth.
- Colour-keyed rear bumper bar blades.

S-type model changes (2002–3)
- As others above except for the following changes:
- Xenon lighting treatment at the front instantly recognisable from the smaller light units internally.
- Radiator grille surround incorporating circular growler badge at the top, eliminating the need for a badge on top of the bonnet.
- Removal of side rubbing strips (from 2002 model year).
- Rounded style of door mirrors fitted.
- Chromed window surrounds (dependent upon model).
- Revised-style badging on the boot lid.

S-type R model
- As 2002 model year styling changes except for:
- Radiator grille colour-keyed to body paint, incorporating mesh insert.
- Colour-keyed bumper blades and other colour co-ordinating as Sport model.

The introduction of the Sport model brought about de-chroming of exterior trim front and rear for ease of identification.

Sport interior with high-contrast upholstery.

Revised S-type from 2002, showing amended grille and badging, light units, door mirrors, later style wheels, additional chrome at top of doors, and the plain sides without rubbing strips.

- Zeus 18in alloy wheels as standard.
- 'R-Performance' badging on boot lid.

S-type model changes (2004–7)

- Exterior facelift incorporating slightly wider and lower radiator grille with revised vanes (where applicable).
- Simpler design to front and rear bumper/valance (design varying according to model).
- Subtle changes to the curvature of bonnet panel.
- More prominent and less sculptured sill panels.
- Revised rear lighting treatment and boot panel.
- Wider boot finisher panel with concealed lock.
- From 2006 a uniform frontal styling approach was carried out with mesh grille and R-style bumper/valance treatment.

XS model

- A later, special edition model, not available in 4.2-litre form.
- 18in Mercury alloy wheels.
- Lower front spoiler.
- Upper and lower bright mesh grilles.
- Boot lid spoiler.
- Exhaust-pipe trail trims.
- Aluminium interior trim.
- Only available in Midnight, Platinum, Quartz or Ultraviolet colours.

Interior identification points

General points applicable to all S-types

Pre-2002

- One-piece dashboard assembly with semi-circular centre console area vertically mounted in metal painted grey.
- Centre console encompassing integrated audio system, cassette holder box, damped ashtray, and auxiliary switches for air-conditioning etc, with digital readout for clock, audio, and air-conditioning temperatures. Where equipped with navigational system, TV screen and controls replace cassette box. Damped ashtray below with J-gate transmission control in veneered surround with auxiliary switches for Sport mode and cruise control (where fitted). Cup-holder with flush-mounted lid, armrest incorporating lift lid and storage area. Handbrake built into passenger side of console area.
- Complete instrument binnacle in front of driver, also featuring warning lighting and illumination.
- Air-conditioning vents in grey plastic either side of the dashboard and centrally mounted vents as well.
- Onboard computer control pack set into

S-type R models only appeared from 2002 so have the new-style front. Note the new bumper bar/under-valance style applicable to this model.

As at the front, the S-type R model had de-chromed trim at the rear, plus a boot spoiler and special badging.

A virtually new interior for all S-types from 2002 takes styling cues from X-type models. All S-types are now equipped with an electronic handbrake, operated from the chromed half-moon button between the gearlever surround and the centre console glovebox.

- dashboard beside binnacle.
- Passenger-side glovebox underneath veneered panel concealing passenger airbag.
- Maple-veneer woodwork to top of dashboard, gear surround section of centre console, and door trims.
- Four-spoke leather or leather/wood steering wheel incorporating airbag and horn push centre boss. Side of wheel controls for audio system, telephone, and cruise control (where fitted).
- Door trims sculptured with veneered inserts and wood surrounds to window lift controls. Door pulls/armrests and preformed pocket areas. Chrome-finished door handles with integrated lock mechanisms.
- Choice of seat styling dependent on model, all based on separate electrically adjustable front seats and bench-style rear with centre armrest.

Post-2002 (identifying differences from earlier cars)
- Dashboard assembly and layout similar to X-type and X-350 saloons, curved top roll with revised instrument binnacle in front of driver.
- Centre console of curved design with new upholstered areas between the seats. Centre console incorporating integrated audio system, cassette holder box, damped ashtray, and auxiliary switches for air-conditioning etc, with digital readout for clock, audio, and air-conditioning temperatures on larger screen area. Satin black-finished switch gear and no grey metal finishes like previous models. Where equipped with navigational system, large TV screen and controls replace 'manual' switches relying on touch-sensitive controls visible on TV screen. J-gate transmission control in veneered surround

Above left: New-style grille from 2002, featuring integrated growler badge. The Sport model still has a colour-keyed surround, all other models chromed except for the R model, with mesh insert.

Above right: New-style front-light units help to identify 2002 models and beyond from earlier cars.

Side view of an early S-type R with much wider and larger-diameter wheels/tyres.

Very late S-type model with sporting kit, later adopted for the XS model.

with auxiliary switches for Sport mode and cruise control (where fitted). Cup-holder with flush-mounted lid, armrest incorporating lift lid and storage area. Handbrake now merely a chromed moon-shaped pull lever in centre at rear of console (conventional handbrake on manual-transmission cars).
- Dual-zone air-conditioning system.
- Four-spoke leather or leather/wood steering wheel as X-type, incorporating airbag and horn push centre boss. Side of wheel controls for audio system, telephone, and cruise control (where fitted).
- Revised seat styling dependent on model, with stiffer bolsters.
- Electrically adjustable foot pedal arrangement from switch on steering column side.
- From 2003 a wider range of interior options became available, including later figured alloy and piano black as an alternative to wood veneer.
- Non-perforated leather trim brought in from 2006 to replace Classic style. All models thereafter supplied with leather trim (no cloth option).

Model specifics

Standard and SE models
- Bird's eye-stained maple-veneered woodwork.
- Leather or cloth seating with vertical pleats and forward-curved stitching.
- Leather or wood/leather steering wheel.

Sport model
- Bird's eye grey-stained maple-veneered woodwork.
- Leather sports steering wheel.
- Stiffer bolster aerated upholstery seating.

S-type R model
- Bird's eye grey-stained maple-veneered woodwork.
- Warm charcoal trim with another contrasting colour.
- Thick leather ribbed sports steering wheel.
- Unique R-Performance seats with horizontal pleating, contrast colour upholstery centre sections fitted with headrests using Isofix seat bracketry.
- Contrast colour upholstery door panels in warm charcoal and another colour.
- Leather and alloy-finished gear knob.
- Fitted foot mats as standard to match upholstery.

All details of trim and specification given above relate to standard production cars. Certain owners may well have specified changes to suit their individual requirements, so it is not unusual to find some more basic models with a higher specification than that described here.

Revised, clearer instrumentation from 2004 included two message centres in the main dials.

Dashboard treatment is entirely different on 2002 models from previous S-types. This particular car is equipped with satellite navigational equipment, with the large central screen, touch-sensitive controls, and voice activation.

Above left: Alternative centre console layout for cars not equipped with satellite navigation.

Above right: Alternative centre console layout for standard cars without CD player and enhanced air-conditioning system.

1: Classic alloy wheels, original standard equipment for the 3.0-litre models;
2: Dynamic alloy wheels, normally standard on SE models, but an option on other models;
3: Sport wheels, an option for all earlier models;
4: Helios, the standard 16in wheels on 2.5-litre models;
5: Herakles, the standard wheels on Sport models up to 2004.
6: Spirit alloy wheels, standard fit on SE models up to 2004;
7: 17in Kronos wheels were a standard fit on 4.2-litre SE and 2.7-litre diesel models;
8: Zeus wheels fitted to the S-type R models;
9: Juno 17in wheels, standard from 2004 on all SE models;
10: Aurora 17in wheels, standard on 2.5-litre S model;
11: Triton 18in wheels, standard from 2004 on all Sport models and on SEs in 2007;
12: Mercury 18in wheels, standard on XS models;
13: Vulcan 18in wheels, standard on post-2004 R model;
14: Indianapolis 18in wheels, extra cost option post-2004 models;
15: Monaco 18in wheels, extra-cost option post-2004 models;
16: Melbourne 18in wheels, extra-cost option post-2004 models;
17: Antares 17in wheels became standard fit on SE models in 2006;
18: Valencia 18in wheels, extra-cost option from 2006;
19: The larger 19in Barcelona wheels came in 2007, just for the R model.

Technical specifications

	2.5-litre	2.7-litre diesel
cc	2497	2720
Bore and stroke (mm)	81.65 x 79.5	81 x 86
Compression ratio	10.5:1	17:1
bhp	201	206
@ rpm	6800	4000
Torque (lb ft)	184	320
@ rpm	4000	1900
Fuelling	Fuel-injection	Fuel-injection
Transmission	ZF 5-speed auto Ford 5-speed synchro	ZF 6-speed automatic
Wheel size (in)	16 or 17, alloy	16, 17, or 18, alloy
Suspension front	Ind double wishbones, alloy control arms, anti-dive, coil springs	Ind double wishbones, alloy control arms, anti-dive, coil springs
Suspension rear	Ind double wishbones, alloy control arms, co-axial coil springs CATS optional	Ind double wishbones, alloy control arms, co-axial coil springs CATS optional
Brakes	4-wheel disc, all ventilated	4-wheel disc, all ventilated
Performance		
0–60mph (sec)	8.2	8.1
Top speed (mph)	142	143
Average mpg	25.4	36
Dimensions		
Length (in)	189	189
Width (in)	69	69
Height (in)	55	55
Wheelbase (in)	113	113
Front track (in)	60	60
Rear track (in)	60	60
Weight (lb)	3572	3947

Technical specifications *cont ...*

	3.0-litre	4.0-litre
cc	2967	3996
Bore and stroke (mm)	89 x 79.5	86 x 86
Compression ratio	10.5:1	10.75:1
bhp	240	281
@ rpm	6800	6100
Torque (lb ft)	221	287
@ rpm	4500	4300
Fuelling	Fuel-injection	Fuel-injection
Transmission	ZF 5-speed auto Ford 5-speed synchro	ZF 5-speed auto
Wheel size (in)	16 or 17, alloy	16 or 17, alloy
Suspension front	Ind double wishbones, alloy control arms, anti-dive, coil springs	Ind double wishbones, alloy control arms, anti-dive, coil springs
Suspension rear	Ind double wishbones, alloy control arms, co-axial coil springs CATS optional	Ind double wishbones, alloy control arms, co-axial coil springs CATS optional
Brakes	4-wheel disc, all ventilated	4-wheel disc, all ventilated
Performance		
0–60mph (sec)	6.9 manual, 7.6 auto	6.6
Top speed (mph)	146	150
Average mpg	22.7	24.5
Dimensions		
Length (in)	189	189
Width (in)	69	69
Height (in)	55	55
Wheelbase (in)	113	113
Front track (in)	60	60
Rear track (in)	60	60
Weight (lb)	3610	3805

	4.2-litre	4.2-litre supercharged
cc	4196	4196
Bore and stroke (mm)	86 x 90.3	86 x 90.3
Compression ratio	11:1	9:1
bhp	300	400
@ rpm	6000	6100
Torque (lb ft)	310	408
@ rpm	4100	3500
Fuelling	Fuel-injection	Fuel-injection
Transmission	ZF 6-speed auto	ZF 6-speed auto
		Ford 5-speed synchro
Wheel size (in)	17 or 18, alloy	17 or 18, alloy
Suspension front	Ind double wishbones, alloy control arms, anti-dive, coil springs	Ind double wishbones, alloy control arms, anti-dive, coil springs
Suspension rear	Ind double wishbones, alloy control arms, co-axial coil springs CATS optional	Ind double wishbones, alloy control arms, co-axial coil springs CATS optional
Brakes	4-wheel disc, all ventilated	4-wheel disc, all ventilated
Performance		
0–60mph (sec)	6.2	5.3
Top speed (mph)	155	155
Average mpg	22.5	22.5
Dimensions		
Length (in)	189	189
Width (in)	69	69
Height (in)	55	55
Wheelbase (in)	113	113
Front track (in)	60	60
Rear track (in)	60	60
Weight (lb)	3826	3969

Optional extras

Automatic transmission (where not fitted, 2.5/3.0 models only).
Manual transmission (2.5/3.0 models only).
Mud flaps.
Cruise control (where not fitted as standard).
Tailored overmats.
Lambswool overmats.
Fitted seat covers.
Headlight power-wash system.
Premium hi-fi system with CD auto-changer in boot.
Child's safety seat.
Child's booster cushion.
First-aid kit for boot area.
Space-saver spare wheel.
Full-size spare wheel.
Fire extinguisher for boot area.
Jaguar warning triangle.
Headlamp converters.
Headlamp safety covers.
Mobile telephone kits.
Snow chains.
Luggage net for boot area.
Witter tow bar kit.
Heated windscreen.
Ultrasonic intrusion security system.
Additional zip-fastening tool kit.
Heated front seats (where not fitted).
Jaguar 'growler' alloy wheel centre badges, various colours.
Power-folding door mirrors.
Sculptured rear number plate.
Self-dipping rear-view mirror.
Wood/leather steering wheel (where not fitted).
Front fog lamps (early cars only).
Foglamp protective covers.
Boot cargo net.
Boot luggage hooks.
Luggage retainer clips and/or straps.
Roof-mounted rack.
Two-bar roof-rack carrier.
Ski/cycle holders.
Luggage frame for roof rack.
Compact, Sport, or large roof box.
Various options of fitted luggage for the boot.
Round alloy gear knob.
Satellite navigation system (later cars).
Reverse park aid (where not fitted).
Auxiliary power socket.
Tracker security system.
Aspheric door mirrors.
Lockable boot-mounted security box.
Air filtration system to air-conditioning.
Engine block heater.
Cold climate pack.
Electric sunroof (where not fitted).
Rear window blind.
Deflector for sunroof.
Xenon headlights (later models only).
Rain sensing wipers.
Leather upholstery (2.5-/3.0-litre models only).
Electrically adjustable foot pedal box (where not fitted, later cars only).
Ski-hatch.
CATS suspension package (where not fitted).
16in Classic seven-spoke alloy wheels.
16in Dynamic five-spoke alloy wheels.
16in Spirit ten-spoke alloy wheels.
16in Helios ten-spoke alloy wheels (later models).
16in Artemis alloy wheels (later models).
17in Sport ten-spoke alloy wheels.
17in Kronos six double-spoke alloy wheels (later models).
17in Herakles five-spoke alloy wheels (later models).
18in Zeus five-spoke alloy wheels (later models).
Post-2004 options of dashboard treatment including Piano Black and Aluminium, along with alternative veneer finishes.
With later 'Premium' specification models, option of contrast colour piping to leather upholstery, bespoke gear knobs, and higher-quality veneering.
Polished alloy gear knobs for automatic transmission models.
Front and rear parking sensors.
Sport collection incorporating front spoiler, upper and lower bright or black mesh grilles.
Juno 17in wheels, later models.
Aurora 17in wheels, later models.
Triton 18in wheels, later models.
Mercury 18in wheels, later models.
Vulcan 18in wheels, later models.
Indianapolis wheels, later models.
Monaco 18in wheels, later models.
Melbourne 18in wheels, later models.
Antares 17in wheels, later models.
Barcelona 19in wheels, later models.
Valencia 18in wheels, later models.

R-Performance specifics
18in Monaco split-rim alloy wheels.
18in Indianapolis split-rim alloy wheels.
Brembo brakes.

Colour schemes

Exterior	Details	Interior	Fascia	Details
Spindrift White	To 2001	Almond	Mink	To 2002
Pacific Blue	From 2002		Charcoal	
Seafront		Cashmere	Sable	To 2002
Anthracite (black)	To 2002		Charcoal	
Titanium Grey	To 2002	Pewter	Granite	To 2002
British Racing Green		Charcoal	Charcoal	
Emerald Green	To 2002	Ivory (leather only)	Sable	
Topaz (gold)			Charcoal	
Carnival Red	To 2003	Sand	Sable	2003 only
Sapphire Blue	To 2002	Dove		From 2003
Mistral	To 2002	Cranberry		2003 only
Meteorite Silver	To 2000	Cranberry/Charcoal	contrast	2003 only
Alpine Green	To 2001	Heritage Tan		2003 only
Westminster Blue	To 2002	Heritage Tan/Charcoal	contrast	2003 only
Platinum Grey	From 2000	Champagne		From 2004
White Onyx	From 2001	Dove/Graphite		From 2004
Roman Bronze	2001 only	Dove/Warm Charcoal		From 2004
Slate Grey	From 2002	Light Sand/Charcoal		From 2004
Quartz	From 2003			
Aspen Green	2002 only	**Veneers**		**Details**
Zircon	From 2002	Grey Maple		To 2004
Ebony	From 2003	Bronze Maple		To 2004
Jaguar Racing Green	From 2003	Aluminium		From 2004
Adriatic Blue	2003 only	Bronze Stained Madonna		From 2004
Midnight	From 2003	Burr Walnut		From 2004
Ultraviolet Blue	From 2004	Grey Stained Bird's Eye Maple		From 2004
Radiance Red	From 2004	Satin Mahogany		From 2006
Indigo	From 2006			
Winter Gold	From 2006			

16 Prices and production volumes

S-type saloons 1999 to 2007

	Price New (£)	1998	1999	2000	2001	2002	2003
2.5-litre	24,950	–	–	–	–	■	■
2.5-litre Sport	27,450	–	–	–	–	■	■
2.5-litre SE	28,900	–	–	–	–	■	■
3.0-litre	26,700	–	■	■	■	–	–
3.0-litre Sport	30,600	–	■	■	■	■	■
3.0-litre SE	31,150	–	■	■	■	■	■
4.0-litre	35,350	■	■	■	■	–	–
4.0-litre Sport	38,400	–	–	■	■	–	–
4.2-litre	36,000	–	–	–	–	■	■
4.2-litre R	47,400	–	–	–	–	■	■
Total production		290	53,002	53,523	38,325	36,150	31,920

	Price New (£)	2004	2005	2006	2007	Total produced
2.5-litre	24,950	■	–	–	–	(1) 21,765
2.5-litre Sport	27,450	■	–	–	–	(1)
2.5-litre S	–	■	–	–	–	(1)
2.5-litre SE	28,900	■	–	–	–	(1)
3.0-litre	26,700	■	■	■	–	(2) 74,675
3.0-litre Spirit	28,995	–	–	■	■	(2)
3.0-litre S	29,277	–	■	■	–	(2)
3.0-litre Sport	30,600	■	■	–	–	(2)
3.0-litre XS	31,995	–	■	■	■	(2)
3.0-litre SE	31,150	■	■	■	■	96,116
2.7-litre D	29,347	■	■	■	–	(3) 31,119
2.7-litre Spirit	29,995	–	–	–	■	(3)
2.7-litre D S	30,697	–	■	■	–	(3)
2.7-litre D Sport	–	■	■	–	–	(3)
2.7-litre D XS	30,947	–	■	■	■	(3)
2.7-litre D SE	30,947	■	■	■	■	(3)
4.0-litre	–	–	–	–	–	(4) 40,058
4.0-litre Sport	–	–	–	–	–	(4)
4.2-litre	–	–	–	–	–	(5) 19,610
4.2-litre Sport	37,552	■	■	–	–	(5)
4.2-litre SE	36,452	■	■	■	–	(5)
4.2-litre R	–	■	■	■	■	8043
Total production		26,567	23,868	16,701	11,040	291,386

Production changes

1999
S-type 3.0-litre and 4.0-litre models introduced.

2001
Dynamic Stability Control (DSC) standardised on all models.
Improved ZF steering system fitted to all models.
Sports pack including CATS suspension available for all models.
Rear door sill tread plates added.
CD players now fitted to boot area instead of glovebox.
Boot under-floor area revised to accommodate tools and jack.
New boot lid liner with pull strap.
Side body mouldings discontinued.
Sport model introduced.

2002
Facelifted exterior with revised grille incorporating badge.
Facelifted exterior with chromed window surrounds, new door mirrors, and rear badging.
New interior layout similar to X-type.
Electrically adjustable foot-pedal box.
Enhanced seat design.
Improved Alpine 140-watt or Premium 320-watt sound systems.
Side air bags supplied.
Adaptive Restraint Technology.
ZR 6-speed automatic transmission fitted to all models.
4.2-litre V8 engines replace 4.0-litre models.
Automatic handbrake system.
New double-wishbone front suspension.
Revised rear subframe.
Larger-diameter disc brakes fitted to all models.
New 2.5-litre model introduced.
New supercharged 4.0-litre S-type R model introduced.

2004
Exterior facelift to body style with new frontal and rear-end treatment, lighting and sills.
Availability of 2.7-litre diesel engine.
Rationalisation of model range. Aluminum interior rim added as an alternative to wood veneers.

2005
Special edition XS models were introduced to replace the Sport models. All 2.5-litre production ceased. All new models now featured the R-style bumper and mesh grille treatment.

2006
Range rationalised again with Spirit model replacing standard cars but with extra specification.

2007
Production of S-type ceased, to make way for the replacement XF model.

17 X-type saloons 2001 to 2009

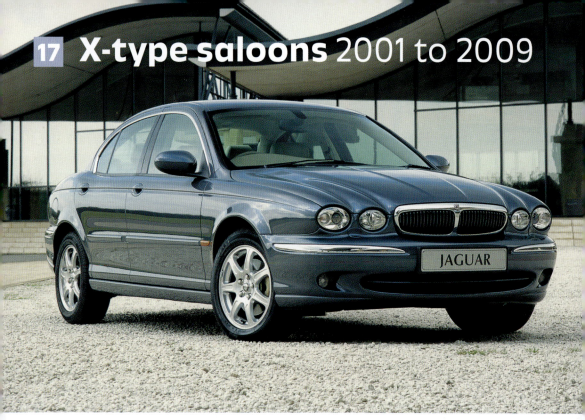

Background

As mentioned in the preceding chapter, for many years Jaguar offered just one saloon model range in different formats. Then in 1999 came the S-type, which opened up a new market for smaller cars. At the time of the S-type launch, however, an even smaller model was under development. Coded X-400, this was to become the X-type.

The X-type represented entirely new territory for Jaguar, as the smallest cars it had previously produced had been the 2.4-litre and its progeny, more akin to the current S-type in size, stature, and market sector. Jaguar's decision to enter a new market place with a smaller car was motivated by two factors: firstly, the general appeal of smaller cars to the motoring public, offering cheaper prices and better economy; and secondly, the need to develop a 'family' of cars, something competitors like BMW had been very good at.

This 'family' concept was necessary in order that Jaguar could encourage new markets for its cars – younger buyers who, hopefully, would aspire to other Jaguar models and stay loyal to the brand. Typically a young sales executive would be able to accommodate a 2.0-litre X-type within his company benefits package; then, as he progressed through the organisation and became a sales manager, he would choose an S-type. Perhaps at director level an XJ6 might be acceptable, and so on.

The X-type was therefore conceived to hit important growth areas in the market for under 40-year-olds, and to offer not only a viable but a better alternative to cars like BMW's 3 Series, the Audi A4, and others. Jaguar was targeting what it called 'The New Jag Generation', consisting for the most part of people who had never before considered buying a new Jaguar.

Launched in the 2001 model year, the X-type was the smallest car Jaguar had ever commercially produced. Starting at a modest £22,000, it was built at the ex-Ford factory in Halewood, Merseyside, the first British Jaguar not to be built in the West Midlands. Converting the workforce and its manufacturing ethos from Ford Escorts to X-types was a major feat for Jaguar. All X-type production came from Halewood and subsequently, with the bringing together of Land Rover and Jaguar, all Land Rover products have since been produced there.

Although the X-type was another all-new car, the Ford parts bin had once again been raided, and development alongside the Ford Mondeo in some key areas allowed Jaguar to achieve a quick yet successful fix. Introduced as just a four-door saloon, another entirely new innovation for Jaguar was that all original X-type models were equipped with four-wheel drive. Engine options were taken from the S-type in the form of the 3.0-litre V6 power unit, adapted for the four-wheel drive layout, and Jaguar developed a smaller 2.5-litre V6 version from the same unit. Automatic and manual gearboxes followed S-type practice.

The body style took key cues from the XJ range, with conventional Jaguar front-end treatment accompanied by a slightly wedge-shaped profile to provide more boot space, and a higher roof level to provide more interior accommodation. Features of S-type design were keyed into the X-type too, such as the all-enveloping bumper bar treatment and the very latest body pressing and assembly techniques.

The X-type provided Jaguar with a four-model line-up, and since its launch it achieved record sales. New models were added, including the Indianapolis, in both engine sizes, and in 2003 the diesel option became available in 2.0-litre form. This was also supplemented later by the 2.2-litre diesel option, available with a new six-speed manual transmission.

The body range was expanded with the introduction of the first production Jaguar estate car, available in all engine sizes and trims. Later special editions have included the Spirit and XS, and for 2008 the bodywork received a major facelift to give a more sporting appeal to the frontal aspect, as well as changes to exterior trim, the rear bumper area, and the interior.

From the 2008 model year a six-speed automatic transmission with sequential change became available on the 2.2-litre diesel engine cars, which necessitated a major rework of the floorpan and other areas of the car.

Production of X-type models finished in 2009, at which time the XF saloon replaced it.

Model range and development

The range of X-type models introduced in 2001 was quite extensive.

Models available at launch (manual and automatic transmissions)

X-type 2.5-litre saloon (Classic)
X-type 2.5-litre Sport
X-type 2.5-litre SE (Special Equipment)
X-type 3.0-litre Sport
X-type 3.0-litre SE (Special Equipment)

All X-types featured a development of the S-type suspension and steering layout, but adapted, of course, for the four-wheel drive system. The 2.5-litre engine provided good performance and smooth refinement at a lower cost, making X-type ownership available to a different category of driver, yet retaining the smoothness of a six-cylinder unit. The 3.0-litre, on the other hand, provided enhanced performance, both over the 2.5 and the equivalent S-type model, particularly so because of the smaller and lighter body.

On the pre-facelift models the only external differences in X-type models are in the radiator grille/bumper bar treatment and alloy wheels fitted. This is an early SE model which, like the standard saloon, has chromed grille, bumper blades, and window surrounds.

The Sport models have colour co-ordinated exterior trim features throughout.

An early 2.0-litre Sport model with black window surrounds and conventional alloy wheels.

Visually the X-type showed its connection with previous Jaguar heritage by its typical four headlight and curvaceous frontal aspect treatment, while the interior, although all new, also offered a degree of retro-styling in its use of typical Jaguar features.

The principles behind the X-type range were based on price, allowing the purchaser to choose between excellent performance and a relatively good turn of speed dependent on budget and, perhaps, insurance. With three choices of specification – standard (now known as Classic), SE, and Sport – this gave a wide variety of options and price. Essentially the basic X-type models were determined squarely by price. Although they included standard features like air-conditioning and four-wheel drive, owners had to pay extra for leather upholstery and other traditional details normally associated with a Jaguar. So, in 2002 you could drive your first new Jaguar for just £22,000, a very competitive price for that important advantage over the competition – four-wheel drive.

In contrast, the Sport offered something different, for the younger market or those wishing either to stand out or get away from Jaguar's previous 'old man' image. Different seating and interior trim finishes allied to de-chroming of the exterior trim made for a more sporty appearance and feel. At the other end of the scale were the Special Equipment (SE) models, offering a high degree of standard equipment, including leather upholstery, chrome, and so on. So, something for those who wanted a smaller but luxurious car and the prestige of the Jaguar name.

Right from the start Jaguar made little secret of the fact that the X-type range would be built on over a number of years, and the next phase came in 2002 with the launch of another new engine size. This 2.0-litre V6 power unit, designed by Jaguar from its existing 2.5-litre engine, was fitted to the X-type but with only front-wheel drive, as it was felt that four-wheel drive would be too much of a drag on its performance. This model, available in all three trim options, opened up yet another new market for Jaguar. Strategically priced at £19,995 it also broke new ground as, pro rata, it was the cheapest production Jaguar ever produced. This 'new' market also brought in company car ownership, where engine capacity and price are important issues.

Next came a special edition model which appeared at the 2002 British Motor Show in the form of the X-type Indianapolis. Essentially a 2.5- or 3.0-litre Sport X-type with a lot of standard features and a new colour scheme combination. This was the first of only a couple of special editions produced.

Another new engine added to the X-type range was the 2.0-litre diesel unit in 2003, and this was

The Indianapolis, one of the X-type special editions, shown in one of only three external colour schemes available and with the unique alloy wheels which could also be purchased separately for other models.

Rear view of pre-facelift model; boot spoilers only applied to the Sport and Indianapolis models at the time. The boot plinth and bumper bar blades were chromed on other models.

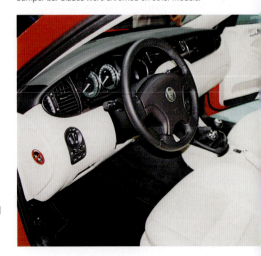

This interior view of the Sport model shows the different pleating to the seat faces and the high-contrast trim colours.

the first Jaguar production car to be fitted with an oil engine. Different from the other X-types at this time, the 2.0-litre models offered only front-wheel drive instead of AWD (all-wheel drive). An even more dramatic addition took place in 2004 with the Estate Car version of the X-types becoming available, and then in 2005 a further new engine, another diesel, this time of 2.2-litre capacity, also front-wheel drive.

As with the medium-sized S-type model, the X-type range has included some other special edition models, the Spirit and the XS. The whole range was stylistically facelifted in 2007 with a new, more aggressive style of frontal aspect, and other trim changes. By this time the 2.0-litre and 2.5-litre petrol engine models had been discontinued.

The X-type Estate Car follows all the trim specifications of the saloon models.

Exterior identification points

General points applicable to all X-types
Front view
- Frontal view initially adapted from the larger XJ saloon styling, facelifted in 2007 with more prominent grille and bumper/valance area.
- Four elliptical reflector headlamp units (with the option of Xenon units), incorporating side and indicator lights.
- Horizontal radiator grille with body colour/chromed surround and vertical slats of mesh inserts according to model and year. Initially a conventional growler badge featured, but from 2007 this changed in style.
- All-enveloping preformed plastic front bumper/valance area, incorporating number plate mounting, blades, air intake with splitter bar, and integrated fog lamps. Designs vary according to model and year.
- One-piece rear-hinged sculptured bonnet.
- One-piece bonded windscreen with surround finisher and twin wiper blades.

Rear view
- Wrap-around rear screen with surround, incorporating high-mounted rear brakelight.
- One-piece rear-hinged boot lid including spoiler. Centrally mounted Jaguar plinth, later models with lengthened 'signature' panel, featuring boot lock and number plate lighting.
- Styled rear-light units to match bodywork, with current technology lenses.
- One-piece all-enveloping rear bumper/valance unit, varying in design and finish according to model and year.
- Unique 'X-type'-style badge and scripted engine capacity according to model.

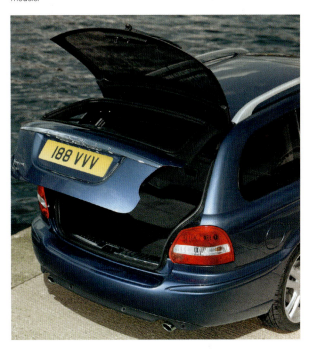
The very practical way in which the tailgate operates on the X-type estate models.

Interior of standard and SE leather-upholstered models. Note the different seat style to Sport models and the lighter-veneer finish.

Side view
- A combination of traditional Jaguar profile with slightly raised rear end, and pronounced uplift over rear wheelarch area.
- Flush-mounted door handles in body colour.
- Body-colour front door mirrors.
- Deep swage line at waist level with body-painted rubbing strip on earlier models to the lower section of front, rear wings, and door areas.
- Indicator repeaters at rear of each front wing.
- Limousine-style door frames with no rain gutters.
- Alloy wheels fitted to all models, dependent on specification and year.

X-type specifics

Unless indicated otherwise, identification points apply to cars of all engine sizes.

Standard (Classic) models
- Chromed bumper bar blades.
- Chromed radiator grille.
- 16in Calcos alloy wheels, standard original fit.

Sport models
- Body-coloured grille surround and boot lid finisher.
- Body-coloured bumper bar blades front and rear.
- Black finish to door window surrounds.
- 17in Andros or 18in Aruba alloy wheels, standard original fit.

Indianapolis model
- Only available in three exterior paint finishes.
- Body-coloured radiator grille surround with mesh insert.
- Body-coloured bumper bar blades front and rear.
- Body-coloured boot plinth/spoiler.
- 18in x 15-spoke Indianapolis alloy wheels.

SE models
- Chrome-finished radiator grille and rear boot finisher.
- 16in Tobago or 17in Cayman alloy wheels, standard original fit.
- Chromed bumper bar blades.

S models
- As Classic model except for alloy wheels.
- 17in Andros alloy wheels.

Sport Premium models
- Black mesh radiator grille insert with body-coloured surround.
- Body-coloured boot lid 'signature' finisher.
- Headlight power-wash, standard equipment.
- Heated front windscreen, standard equipment.

The centre console design varies according to specification. This car is equipped with satellite navigation, hence the screen.

Sport interior with non-leather seat facings and non-satellite navigation centre console.

Rear interior of Sport non-leather-upholstered car. Seat pleating varies from Sport to standard.

- Rear spoiler.
- 18in Aruba alloy wheels.

Sovereign models
- As SE model but with additional heated windscreen.
- 17in Cayman alloy wheels.

Spirit/XS models
- 18in Aruba alloy wheels.
- Front spoiler.
- Upper and lower black mesh grille.
- Sill appliqués.
- Boot lid spoiler.

Interior identification points

General points applicable to all X-types

- Dashboard assembly and layout similar to S-type and X-350 saloons, curved top roll with instrument binnacle in front of driver.
- Centre console of curved design with upholstered areas between the seats. Incorporates integrated audio system, damped ashtray, and auxiliary switches for air-conditioning, etc, with digital readout for clock and audio. Satin black-finished switchgear. Where equipped with automatic air-conditioning system a separate digital read-out screen features at top of centre console, replacing three rotary controls. Where navigational system fitted, large TV screen relying on touch-sensitive controls visible on screen replaces other screen read-outs. J-gate or gearlever transmission control in surround of varying finishes (see specifics). Cup-holder with flush-mounted lid, armrest incorporating lift lid, and storage area. Handbrake situated within rear of console.
- Four-spoke leather or leather/wood steering wheel as later S-type incorporating airbag and horn push centre boss with growler badge. Side of wheel controls for audio system, telephone, and cruise control (where fitted).
- Individual front seat styling dependent on model.
- Rear bench seat arrangement to match.
- Door trim panels softly upholstered with inserts, window lift switch packs, door armrests, integral pockets, and audio speakers. Chromed door locks.

Model specifics

Standard (Classic) models
- Bird's eye maple veneer until 2004, then replaced by bronze-stained sapele.
- Manually adjusted cloth seating.
- Vinyl trim coloured steering wheel.

An X-type fitted with the Sports Collection pack of trim detail showing spoilers, sill appliqués, and black mesh grilles.

The facelift X-type model showing the more pronounced front-end treatment, revised sill and rubbing strip design, and new-style door mirrors.

Rear of the facelift model showing new-style bumper area and trim on boot lid. Note from facelift, an aerodynamic radio antenna is fitted.

Example of later facelift interior trim with carbon fibre and aluminium instead of wood veneer and redesign to gear knob and surround.

- Complementary colour scheming to all interior areas.
- Manually operated rear door windows (2.0-litre models only).
- Single-slot CD player.
- Soft vinyl gear knob.

Sport models
- Bird's eye maple veneer.
- Cloth centre seat panels with leather outside panels and horizontal pleating.
- Centre armrest with cup-holders.
- Perforated leather gear knob.
- Electrically adjustable front seats (both).
- Twin rear head restraints.
- Sports leather steering wheel.

SE models
- As Classic models above plus:
- Door inserts to match facia.
- Leather gear knob.
- Rear head restraints.
- Centre armrest with cupholders.
- Trip computer with message centre.

Indianapolis model
- Mottled-effect maple veneering to woodwork on dashboard.
- Alcantara-trimmed central areas of seats with leather outside areas, and stiffer bolsters to front seats, and horizontal pleating.
- Centre armrest with cup-holders.
- Sport leather-clad aerated steering wheel.
- Driver's seat four-way seat adjustment, passenger height adjustment.
- Alcantara-trimmed centre areas of door trim panels.
- Electrically operated windows at front only.
- Automatic climate control system with digital screen.
- Single-slot CD player.
- Sports leather/alloy gear knob.
- Warm charcoal-coloured upper fascia with flint-coloured carpets.

S models
- As Classic models above plus:
- Choice of grey-stained maple or bronze sapele veneers.
- Leather gear knob.
- Rear centre armrest with cup-holders.
- Half-cloth/healf-leather seat trim.
- Electrically adjustable seats at front.
- Electrically controlled front and rear windows.

Sport Premium models
- As Sport models plus:
- Carbon fibre facia trim.
- Perforated leather grip steering wheel.
- Sport perforated leather gear knob.
- Alcantara seat trimming.

Very late model alternative soft grain leather option to seating, with needle diamond stitching pattern.

The 2.0-litre V6 S model offers a higher degree of specification to the normal car at a special price.

Interior of the Indianapolis model, with unique veneer figuring to the woodwork and Alcantara seat trimming.

- Electrically adjustable and heated front seating.
- Six-disc CD player.
- Cold climate pack.
- Trip computer with message centre.
- Aruba alloy wheels.

Sovereign models
- As SE plus the following:
- Half-leather/half-veneer steering wheel.
- Walnut veneer.
- Six-disc CD player.
- Alpine Premium sound system.
- Satellite navigational system.
- Jaguar Voice system.

All details of trim and specification given above relate to standard production cars. Certain owners may well have specified changes to suit their individual requirements, so it is not unusual to find some more basic models with a higher specification than that described here.

X-type 2004 model changes

With the introduction of the diesel-engined version in 2003 came subtle styling changes to the whole X-type.

Exterior
- Classic and Sport models now incorporate body-colour bumper bar blades (no longer chrome).
- Matt black B & C pillar window surrounds on Classic models.
- Chromed vertical radiator grille vanes on SE models.
- Rear boot lid finisher now widened.
- Boot release button moved from top centre of finisher to underneath.
- 'Crystal'-design side indicator lenses on all models.
- 'D' badging on boot lid for the diesel-engined models.

Interior
- Soft-touch material used on the parcel shelf area.
- Fore and aft tilting for front seat headrests added.
- Reshaping of front seats to allow for more space in centre console area.
- Twin cup-holders standardised on all models in centre console area.
- Two additional sound system speakers for models equipped with standard audio system.
- Enhanced 320-watt Premium sound system with ten speakers.
- Black background (instead of green) for instruments.
- Outside temperature warning light fitted to instrument binnacle.

Revised siting for the boot release button, now underneath out of sight.

The mid-term rear-end treatment (pre-facelift) with elongated boot signature plinth. Note this is a diesel model displaying less prominent exhaust tailpipes.

Another new move for Jaguar is the availability of carbon fibre instead of wood veneer in the X-type, affecting all models from 2004 model year.

X-type 2005/6 model changes

- Sports Collection Pack now available to enhance the styling of the models. This incorporated a front spoiler, black mesh grilles, de-chroming pack, sill appliqués, boot lid spoiler, revised rear valance, and exhaust tailpipe trims, much of which subsequently appeared on the XS model.

X-type 2007 model changes

- The X-type models were facelifted in 2007, providing the following changes:
- More prominent and squarer horizontal radiator grille with wide mesh grille and new-style growler badge.
- Smoother-finish bumper bar/valance area with larger air intake and inset fog lights.
- New-style, flatter side rubbing strips.
- Full-width boot lid 'signature' panel.
- Revised style to rear bumper bar/valance area and tailpipe arrangements.
- Revised seating style (according to model).

The fully enclosing cover on top of the diesel engine makes it instantly identifiable from petrol versions.

1: 16in X7 wheels, original standard equipment on 2.0-litre standard and SE models.

2: 16in X10 wheels, original standard equipment on 2.5-litre standard and SE models.

3: 17in X7 Flute wheels, original standard equipment on the 3.0-litre SE.

4: 17in X-Sport wheels, original standard equipment on all Sport models.

5: The original X5 wheels. Unique at the time to 3.0-litre cars, later replaced by X7 (see above).

6: 16in Calcos wheels, the standard wheels from 2004 for all standard (Classic) models.

7: 16in Tobago wheels, the standard fit from 2004 on 2.0-litre SE models.

8: 17in Cayman wheels, the standard fit from 2004 on 2.5-litre and 3.0-litre SE models.

9: 17in Andros wheels, the standard fit on 2.0-litre and 2.2-litre Sport models from 2004.

10: 18in Aruba wheels, the standard fit on 2.5-litre and 3.0-litre Sport models from 2004, and on the special edition XS models. (This wheel was also available in an 18in split-rim form as an extra-cost option.)

11: 18in R-Performance Melbourne split-rim wheels, available from 2004 as an extra-cost option.

12: 16in Saba wheels became the standard wheel on standard (Classic) models from 2006.

Alcantara (mock suede) trim, once only available on the Indianapolis X-type, is now available for all X-type models.

Twin cup-holders identify the interior of the 2004 model year X-types from the earlier models.

13: *17in Belize* wheels became the standard fit on S models from 2006.

14: *18in Proteus* wheels became the standard fit on Sport Premium models from 2006.

15: *16in Antares* wheels became available in 2006 replacing all other 16in wheels.

16: *17in Bermuda* alloy wheels became available in 2006 as a supplementary wheel to the only other 17in wheel available then, the Belize.

17: New R-Performance *18in Valencia* split-rim alloy wheels became available in 2006, replacing the Melbourne.

18: *17in Barbados* wheels were introduced with the facelift models from the 2008 model year, fitted as standard to all SE models.

19: *18in Abaco* wheels, were introduced with the facelift models from the 2008 model year, fitted as standard to all Sport Premium models.

269

Technical specifications

	2.0-litre	2.5-litre
cc	2099	2495
Bore and stroke (mm)	81.6 x 66.8	81.6 x 79.5
Compression ratio	10.75:1	10.3:1
bhp	157	194
@ rpm	6800	6800
Torque (lb ft)	148	180
@ rpm	4100	3000
Fuelling	Fuel-injection	Fuel-injection
Transmission	Ford 5-speed synchro Ford 5-speed auto front-wheel drive	Ford 5-speed synchro Ford 5-speed auto 6-speed manual option (from late 2005) 4-wheel drive
Wheel size (in)	16, 18 (from 2006), alloy	16 or 17, 18 (from 2006), alloy
Suspension front	Ind double wishbones, alloy control arms, anti-dive, coil springs	Ind double wishbones, alloy control arms, anti-dive, coil springs
Suspension rear	Ind double wishbones, alloy control arms, co-axial coil springs	Ind double wishbones, alloy control arms, co-axial coil springs
Brakes	4-wheel disc, all ventilated	4-wheel disc, all ventilated
Performance		
0–60mph (sec)	8.9 manual, 10.4 auto	7.9 manual, 8.5 auto
Top speed (mph)	130	140
Average mpg	30.7	29.5
Dimensions		
Length (in)	183 (186 estate)	183 (186 estate)
Width (in)	68	68
Height (in)	53 (58 estate)	53 (53 estate)
Wheelbase (in)	104	104
Front track (in)	60	60
Rear track (in)	60	60
Weight (lb)	3197	3428

	3.0-litre	2.0-litre diesel
cc	2967	1998
Bore and stroke (mm)	89 x 7.5	86.0 x 86.0
Compression ratio	10.5:1	18.2:1
bhp	231	128
@ rpm	6800	3800
Torque (lb ft)	209	243
@ rpm	3000	1800
Fuelling	Fuel-injection	Common rail fuel-injection
Transmission	Ford 5-speed synchro Ford 5-speed auto 6-speed manual option (from late 2005) 4-wheel drive	Ford 5-speed synchro 6-speed manual option (from late 2005)
Wheel size (in)	16 or 17, 18 (from 2006), alloy	16,17, 18 (from 2006), alloy
Suspension front	Ind double wishbones, alloy control arms, anti-dive, coil springs	Ind double wishbones, alloy control arms, anti-dive, coil springs
Suspension rear	Ind double wishbones, alloy control arms, co-axial coil springs	Ind double wishbones, alloy control arms, co-axial coil springs
Brakes	4-wheel disc, all ventilated	4-wheel disc, all ventilated
Performance		
0–60mph (sec)	6.6 manual, 7.1 auto	9.5
Top speed (mph)	146	125
Average mpg	27.5	50.3
Dimensions		
Length (in)	183 (186 estate)	183 (186 estate)
Width (in)	68	68
Height (in)	53 (58 estate)	53 (58 estate)
Wheelbase (in)	104	104
Front track (in)	60	60
Rear track (in)	60	60
Weight (lb)	3428	3311

Technical specifications *cont ...*

	2.2-litre diesel
cc	2198
Bore and stroke (mm)	86 x 94.6
Compression ratio	17.5:1
bhp	155
@ rpm	3500
Torque (lb ft)	360
@ rpm	1800
Fuelling	Fuel-injection
Transmission	6-speed manual gear
	6-speed automatic with sequential change (from 2008)
Wheel size	16, 17 or 18, alloy
Suspension front	Ind double wishbones, alloy control arms, anti-dive, coil springs.
Suspension rear	Ind double wishbones, alloy control arms, co-axial coil springs.
Brakes	4-wheel disc, all ventilated
Performance	
0–60mph (sec)	8.5
Top speed (mph)	137
Average mpg	47
Dimensions	
Length (in)	183 (186 estate car)
Width (in)	68
Height (in)	53 (58 estate car)
Wheelbase (in)	104
Front track (in)	60
Rear track (in)	60
Weight (lb)	3473

Colour schemes

Exterior	Details	Interior	Details
White Onyx	To 2008	Ivory	To 2004 (reintroduced in 2006)
Pacific Blue	To 2006	Sand	To 2003
Phoenix Red	To 2003	Dove	To 2003
Anthracite (black)	To 2003	Charcoal	
Titanium Grey	To 2003	Cranberry	Cloth only 2003
British Racing Green	To 2007	Heritage Tan	To 2004
Emerald Green	To 2003	Champagne	2003–7
Topaz (gold)	To 2006	Stone	2003–7
Carnival Red	To 2003	Spice (red)	From 2008
Adriatic Blue	To 2003	Barley	From 2008
Westminster Blue	To 2003	Oyster (non-seating)	From 2008
Platinum Grey	To 2007	**Veneers**	
Quartz	2003–7	Grey Maple	To 2003
Ebony	From 2003	Carbon Fibre	From 2002
Zircon	To 2007	Bird's-eye Maple	
Jaguar Racing Green	To 2008	Bronzed Stained Sapele	2003–7
Ultaviolet Blue	2003–7	Piano Black	From 2004
Radiance Red	2003–7	Burr Walnut	From 2005
Salsa Red	2003–5	Rosewood	From 2008
Midnight	2005–8	**Contrast piping**	
Indigo	From 2006	Mocha	2005–7 (only Sovereign models)
Winter Gold	From 2006	Stone	2005–7 (only Sovereign models)
Glacier Blue	From 2007	Charcoal	From 2008
Shadow Grey	From 2007	Barley	From 2008
Liquid Silver	From 2007	Oyster	From 2008
Chilli Red	From 2007	**Seat style**	
Ultimate Black	From 2008	Classic	Vertical pleating (cloth or leather, from 2008 changed to horizontal pleating)
Emerald Fire (green)	From 2008		
Tekite Grey	From 2008		
Lazuli Blue	From 2008	Sports	Horizontal pleating (cloth, leather, Alcantera or perforated)
Ionian Blue	From 2008		
Porcelain	From 2008	Sports Premium	Diamond stitching from 2008

Prices and production volumes

X-type saloons 2001 to 2009

	Price New (£)	2001	2002	2003	2004	2005	2006
2.0-litre petrol	19,995	–	■	■	■	■	–
(Estate)	20,447	–	–	–	■	■	–
2.0-litre diesel	19,995	–	–	■	■	■	■
(Estate)	20,472	–	–	–	■	■	■
2.0-litre diesel XS	22,995	–	–	–	–	–	■
2.0-litre Sport petrol	22,245	–	■	■	■	–	–
(Estate)	22,702	–	–	–	■	–	–
2.0-litre Sport D	22,245	–	–	■	■	■	■
(Estate)	22,727	–	–	–	■	■	■
2.0-litre SE petrol	22,995	–	■	■	■	■	–
(Estate)	23,347	–	–	–	■	■	–
2.0-litre SE D	22,995	–	–	■	■	■	■
(Estate)	23,372	–	–	–	■	■	■
2.0-litre V6 S	20,995	–	–	–	■	■	–
2.0-litre diesel S	20,332	–	–	–	–	■	■
(Estate)	21,472	–	–	–	–	■	■
2.0-litre S/Prem D	27,000	–	–	–	–	–	–
(Estate)	28,400	–	–	–	–	–	–
2.0-litre Sov D	28,000	–	–	–	–	–	–
(Estate)	29,400	–	–	–	–	–	–
2.2-litre Sport D	22,302	–	–	–	–	■	■
(Estate)	23,472	–	–	–	–	■	■
2.2-litre SE D	25,302	–	–	–	–	■	■
(Estate)	26,472	–	–	–	–	■	■
2.2-litre S/Prem D	27,802	–	–	–	–	■	■
(Estate)	28,972	–	–	–	–	■	■
2.2-litre Sov D	27,802	–	–	–	–	■	■
(Estate)	28,972	–	–	–	–	■	■
2.2-litre diesel S	22,500	–	–	–	–	–	–
(Estate)	23,900	–	–	–	–	–	–
2.5-litre	22,000	■	■	■	■	–	–
(Estate)	23,202	–	–	–	■	–	–
2.5-litre XS	24,770	–	–	–	–	–	■
2.5-litre Sport	24,000	■	■	■	■	■	■
(Estate)	25,552	–	–	–	■	■	■

Optional extras

2007	2008	2009	Total produced (to 2008)
–	–	–	(1) 49,762
–	–	–	(5) 1587
■	–	–	(4) 55,615
■	–	–	(8) 16,747
–	–	–	(4)
–	–	–	(1)
–	–	–	(5)
■	–	–	(4)
■	–	–	(8)
–	–	–	(1)
–	–	–	(5)
■	■	■	(4)
■	■	■	(8)
–	–	–	(1)
■	■	■	(4)
■	■	■	(8)
–	■	■	(4)
–	■	■	(8)
■	■	■	(4)
■	■	■	(8)
■	–	–	(9) 31,294
■	–	–	(9)
■	■	■	(9)
■	■	■	(9)
■	■	■	(9)
■	■	■	(9)
■	■	■	(9)
■	■	■	(9)
–	■	■	(9)
–	■	■	(9)
–	–	–	(2) 99,939
–	–	–	(6) 4306
–	–	–	(2)
–	–	–	(2)
■	–	–	(6)

Automatic transmission (where not fitted).
Manual transmission.
Mud flaps.
Cruise control.
Tailored overmats.
Lambswool overmats.
Fitted seat covers.
Headlight power-wash system.
Premium hi-fi system with CD auto-changer in boot.
Child's safety seat.
Child's booster cushion.
First-aid kit for boot area.
Space-saver spare wheel.
Full-size spare wheel.
Fire extinguisher for boot area.
Jaguar warning triangle.
Headlamp converters.
Headlamp safety covers.
Mobile telephone kits.
Snow chains.
Luggage net for boot area.
Witter tow bar kit.
Heated windscreen.
Ultrasonic intrusion security system.
Additional zip-fastening tool kit.
Heated front seats (where not fitted).
Jaguar 'growler' alloy wheel centre badges, various colours.
Power-folding door mirrors.
Self-dipping rear-view mirror.
Wood/leather steering wheel (where not fitted).
Foglamp protective covers.
Boot cargo net.
Boot luggage hooks.
Luggage retainer clips and/or straps.
Roof-mounted rack.
Two-bar roof-rack carrier.
Front parking sensors.
Alcantara upholstery.
Carbon fibre trim.
Piano black trim detail.
Ski/cycle holders.
Luggage frame for roof rack.
Compact, Sport, or large roof box.
Various options of fitted luggage for the boot.
Round alloy gear knob.
Satellite navigation system.
Reverse park aid.
Tracker security system.
Aspheric door mirrors.
Lockable boot-mounted security box.
Air filtration system to air-conditioning.
Engine block heater.
Cold climate pack.
Electric sunroof.
Rear window blind.
Deflector for sunroof.

Prices and production volumes *cont ...*

X-type saloons 2001 to 2009

	Price New (£)	2001	2002	2003	2004	2005	2006
2.5-litre SE	24,750	■	■	■	■	■	■
(Estate)	26,552	–	–	–	■	■	■
2.5-litre S	22,052	–	–	–	–	■	■
(Estate)	23,222	–	–	–	–	■	■
3.0-litre Sport	25,500	■	■	■	–	–	–
(Estate)	27,052	–	–	–	■	–	–
3.0-litre SE	26,250	■	■	■	■	–	–
(Estate)	28,052	–	–	–	■	–	–
2.5-litre Indianapolis	27,500	–	–	■	–	–	–
3.0-litre Indianapolis	29,000	–	–	■	–	–	–
3.0-litre S/Prem	29,277	–	–	–	–	■	■
(Estate)	30,447	–	–	–	–	■	■
3.0-litre Sov	29,277	–	–	–	–	■	■
(Estate)	30,447	–	–	–	–	■	■
Total production (to 2008)	Total includes 79 miscellaneous models and prototypes						

Production changes

2001
X-type 2.5-litre and 3.0-litre models introduced.

2002
2.0-litre models launched.
Indianapolis models introduced.

2003
2.0-litre diesel models available.
Last of Indianapolis special editions produced.

2004
Introduction of estate models.
Cosmetic changes to interior and exterior trim.

2005
2.0-litre petrol engine models phased out.
2.2-litre diesel engines available.
S models increased.
Launch of Sport Premium range.

2006
Spirit and XS limited editions introduced.

2007
2.5-litre and 3.0-litre petrol engines discontinued.

2008
Facelift models introduced.
General model range contraction.

2009
Production ceased.

2007	2008	2009	Total produced (to 2008)
■	–	–	(2)
■	–	–	(6)
■	–	–	(2)
■	–	–	(6)
–	–	–	(3) 91,595
–	–	–	(7) 4382
–	–	–	(3)
–	–	–	(7)
–	–	–	(2)
–	–	–	(3)
■	–	–	(3)
■	–	–	(7)
■	–	–	(3)
■	–	–	(7)
			355,227

Optional extras
cont ...

Xenon headlights.
Rain-sensing wipers.
Leather upholstery (where not fitted).
Ski-hatch.
Ten-way electrically adjustable front seats.
Rear door electric window operation (where not fitted).
Sport perforated leather seating.
Air-conditioning with pollen filters.
Front compartment cup-holder.
Dynamic stability control.
CATS suspension package (where not fitted).
16in X7 seven-spoke alloy wheels.
16in X10 ten-spoke alloy wheels.
17in X7 Flute alloy wheels.
17in X-Sport alloy wheels.
16in Calcos, Tobago, Saba or Antares alloy wheels.
17in Cayman, Andros, Belize, Bermuda or Barbados alloy wheels.
18in Aruba, Proteus and Abaco alloy wheels.

R-Performance specifics
18in Monaco split-rim alloy wheels.
18in Indianapolis split-rim alloy wheels.
Brembo brakes.
Handling pack.
R-Performance Melbourne and Valencia split-rim alloy wheels.
Sports collection trim pack.

18 XJ6 and XJ8 saloons (X-350)
2003 to 2009

Background

If Jaguar's model range has been known for two things, they are the company's superbly styled sports cars and its refined saloons, and since the introduction of the original XJ6 back in 1968 over one million saloons carrying that XJ insignia have been produced.

Just as the XJ40 saw Jaguar out of BL control, the X-300 replacement was the first car produced under Ford control, heralding better build quality, and the X-308 brought about the change from straight six and V12 power units to an all-V8 line-up. The success of the XJ's heritage cannot be overstated, particularly when one considers that until 1999 it was the only saloon body-shape available from Jaguar. It was therefore fitting that Jaguar decided to retain the XJ insignia for its current flagship saloons, and at the same time to reintroduce another XJ6.

Code-named X-350, this entirely new XJ was announced in 2003, a major leap forward for Jaguar. Although initially utilising the engine line-up from other models, for the first time in a production model the XJs were fitted with an all-aluminium body structure featuring highly sophisticated bonding and riveting methods. If that was not enough, there wasthe air suspension system, dynamic stability control, the latest development of Jaguar's Computer Active Technology suspension, adaptive cruise control, multi-media system, voice activation of some controls, additional air bags, and even a heated steering wheel!

Even the exterior styling of the X-350 warrants special appreciation. While, importantly, maintaining strong links to previous models, the overall design boasted many new features and provided for more interior space and luggage accommodation. Internally it was all new. Following a similar design style to the X-type and later S-types, it had many more features and a host of specifications and trim levels to suit what became a very lucrative and sophisticated market.

And that was the essence of the X-350. More than any previous XJ, this car had to cater for a more demanding customer – someone with a statement to make, who wanted the very best in quality and technology – and it proved a more than even match of the competition.

Instead of a Daimler model, there was a Super V8 Jaguar variant when the car was introduced in April 2003 (and models badged 'Vanden Plas' for the States), but a Daimler version was offered at the end of 2005 for a limited period. At that time XJs were offered with a choice of four engines – 3.0-litre, 3.5-litre, 4.2-litre and 4.2-litre supercharged. The 3.5-litre variant was dropped in 2008 and a 2.7-litre diesel version was offered from 2005. Then, in 2007, the model was facelifted to provide a more contemporary, aggressive look to the styling, along with other trim changes.

In 2009 the X-350 was discontinued to make way for another, entirely new XJ saloon for the 2010 model year.

Model range and development

No fewer than ten models were initially launched in the X-350 range.

Models available at launch
XJ6 saloon
XJ6 Sport
XJ6 SE (Special Equipment)
XJ8 saloon (3.5-litre V8)
XJ8 Sport (3.5-litre V8)
XJ8 SE (Special Equipment 3.5-litre V8)
XJ8 Sport (4.2-litre V8)
XJ8 SE (Special Equipment 4.2-litre V8)
XJR saloon (supercharged 4.2-litre)
Super V8 (supercharged 4.2-litre)

This is an impressive line-up, being a wider range than offered with the previous X-308 cars and, pro-rata, better value for money, given the high tech nature of the new models. It is worth spending a moment examining these new cars in some detail, as they are so significantly different to any previous XJ.

Firstly, as regards the styling, Jaguar had to take note of common criticisms levelled at previous XJs, such as lack of headroom, rear compartment legroom, or even boot space. Also, research had shown that people are now bigger overall, so more space was wanted for everyone, including the driver. The styling of the X-350 had to accommodate this without losing the very essence of 'Jaguarism' in the design.

The bodywork is all-aluminium, incorporating aircraft technology in epoxy bonding and riveting, resulting in the car being 40% lighter and 60% stiffer than the previous XJ8. Mechanically, the cars utilise very similar suspension to the S-type, but with a sophisticated air suspension system that even alters the height of the vehicle to meet the requirements of the surface being driven on. Along with other features like emergency brake assist, voice-activated controls, electronic parking brake, and bi-Xenon headlights, the X-350 is the most adventurous and lavishly equipped car Jaguar has ever produced. It is designed to create an overall air of quality, down to special features like a self-closing boot panel and one-touch bonnet closure.

Stylistically the bodywork takes its main cue from the X-type in a much larger form, yet retains touches everywhere you look from previous Jaguar models, even back to the Series saloons of the 1960s and 1970s. It is also the best-built Jaguar to date, with text-book panel gaps and finish, a tribute to the company.

This initial range was extensive, based around four engine options; the existing S-type 3.0-litre V6, a new 3.5-litre V8 configuration, and the 4.2-litre V8 in normally-aspirated and supercharged

Pre-facelift X-350 XJ6 and XJ8s are identifiable from previous X-300 and XJ8 models by the taller roof, protruding door handles (always chromed), limousine-style flush-fitting door frames, and the taller rear end. This is an XJ6 example, which uses the black centre grille slats.

Pre-facelift radiator slatted grille applied to standard models, SE, and some Sovereign models.

Mesh grille originally applied to XJR model only, later adopted for Sport and Sport Premium.

form. The 3.0-litre signified the reintroduction of the XJ6 insignia, previously used from 1968 to 1997. This model effectively took over from the previous 3.2-litre X-308 Executive, but it was now also available in Sport and SE (Special Equipment) forms. Strategically priced, it was the most popular 'entry' model in the UK at the time, sitting nicely alongside the lower-priced sector from the competition.

For those who wanted better performance, the 3.5-litre V8 was offered within the same range of models, and the larger 4.2-litre engine's models were only available in Sport form to special order. The most lavishly equipped, top of the range model at the time was the Super V8, which included many of the features normally associated with previous Daimler models.

From 2004, model designations and specification started to change. The first was an extra model, the 3.5-litre Sport Premium, offering a higher level of equipment than the Sport model. Later in the same year the 3.0-litre and 4.2-litre Sovereign models were added, and long-wheelbase versions were offered.

A new 2.7-litre diesel engine version, the TDVi, was introduced in 2005 in Executive (replacing the standard XJ models), Sovereign and Sports Premium versions, and the SE models and Sport model were discontinued.

For the 2006 model year a solitary Daimler model became available for a limited period of time in long-wheelbase Super Eight (supercharged) form. Another special model was the Portfolio, based on a concept primarily aimed at the US market. This one-off special edition saw the XJ through the final phases of production at the old Browns Lane, Coventry, factory in 2006, after which all subsequent X-350s were produced at the Castle Bromwich plant near Birmingham.

Apart from minor trim changes, the next and final stage of development came with a facelift in 2007 with a redesigned front and rear end, enhanced interiors, and model rationalisation. The facelift, although initially offered with all engine sizes, by 2008 for the 2009 model year, the 3.0-litre petrol engine was 'officially' dropped from the range, but some were still produced. As with some previous XJs, for certain overseas markets Daimlers were badged as Jaguar and/or Vanden Plas models.

Production of the X-350 range was phased out in 2009 to make way for the 2010 entirely new XJ saloons.

Exterior identification points

General points applicable to all X-350s

From whatever angle you view them, these models are significantly different to previous cars – larger

Side view of the pre-facelift X-350 standard wheelbase model, emphasising the raised haunches at the rear.

Long-wheelbase equivalent model showing the aesthetically pleasing lines eliminating the usual need to just extend the rear door area.

Rear view of typical pre-facelift X-350 showing the extra chrome applying to non-Sport and R models.

Typical boot badging on the X-350 models, common to all models; only the supercharged models have a coloured 'R' emblem.

Leather interiors apply to all models, with style varying according to model. This shows a standard/Executive XJ6 model with leather-clad steering wheel.

in overall dimensions, with less frontal over-range, a higher roof line, and a more pronounced wedge-shaped profile from front to rear.

Front view

- Four-headlamp treatment, slightly elliptical in shape, the inner pair slightly smaller.
- Traditional XJ-shaped radiator grille, surround in chrome on standard, SE, and Super V8 models, body-coloured on Sport and XJR, initially with mesh insert for Sport, Sport Premium, and XJR models, cross-slat insert in black on standard, or chrome on SE/Super V8 models. Facelift models have a more angular grille profile, all models in body colour, with bright mesh insert, also applicable to all models; the centre vane incorporated a pronounced, contemporary growler badge.
- Integrated front bumper bar/valance also forming part of upper structure around lights and radiator grille. Preformed and energy absorbing, with number plate mounting, enlarged oval air intake beneath with splitter bar, and built-in fog lights. Facelift models have a more pronounced front bumper/valance arrangement with deep mesh under-grille and circular fog lamps. Chromed bumper bar blades from earlier cars now removed.
- Individual chromed bumper bar blade finishers.
- One-piece curved and shaped rear-hinged bonnet with raised centre section.
- One-piece curved windscreen with black or chrome surround, from 2005 bonded without surround. Twin wiper arms.

Rear view

- All-enveloping rear bumper, combined valance treatment as front. Facelift bumpers have a deeper and smoother finish without chromed bumper blades.
- Reverse park sensors fitted to all rear bumpers.
- Twin exhaust pipes emitting either side of the valance, chromed trims.
- One-piece tapered boot panel, rear-hinged, with pronounced horizontal swage and wide 'Jaguar' plinth incorporating boot lock and concealed number plate lighting. Boot plinth chromed on standard, SE, Super V8, and Sovereign models; body colour on others. Rectangular chromed boot badges, vary according to model.
- Facelift models incorporate a full boot-width 'signature' panel, chromed on all models except Sport Premium and XJR. New-style boot badging.
- Triangular rear-light clusters with unique LED lighting.
- Rear curved screen with high-level brakelight, black or chromed surrounds, from 2005 bonded without surrounds.

Typical Sport interior with contrast trim and revised rectangular pleat sections in the seating.

XJR interior with dark-stained maple like the Sport, but revised seating.

Above left: XJR rear compartment showing a different style of seat treatment. The multi-media control panel is situated in the centre armrest.

Above right: Rear compartment of the Daimler model showing screens for the multi-media system and inset laptop tables. Soft grain leather trim also applied to the Super V8 Jaguar model.

Side view

- More pronounced 'wedge' shape of profile.
- Less frontal body overhang.
- Raised and curved roof area with no rain gutters and pronounced rake to front screen.
- Limousine-style door frame surrounds with black window surrounds and full roof length finishers in chrome on all models except Sport, Sport Premium, and XJR (high-gloss black).
- Protruding 'chunky' door handles.
- Waist-height swage line and, at the lower level, body-colour rubbing strips (discontinued in 2006) extending from front wing-mounted indicator repeater light to rear doors.
- No quarter-lights in front doors, non-opening quarter-lights in rear doors, no windows in rear quarters.
- Fuel filler in rear wing with flush cover.
- Alloy wheels fitted to all models, varying dependent upon model and specification.
- Facelift models all feature more sculptured sill areas, revised door mirrors incorporating indicator tell-tails and 'signature' vertical air vent at the rear of each front wing.

X-350 model specifics

The same specification applies to any engine size, the only external difference being the boot lid badging.

Pre-facelift (2007) models

XJ6 models
- Horizontal and vertical black-painted slats to radiator grille with chrome surround.
- Chromed window surrounds.
- Chromed boot plinth.
- Halogen headlights.
- 17in Elegant alloy wheels.
- 'XJ6' badge on boot lid.

Sport models
- Body-coloured radiator grille surround, initially with black slatted inner grille, in 2005 changed to black mesh finish.
- Black window surrounds.
- Body-coloured boot plinth.
- Bi-Xenon headlights.
- 18in Dynamic alloy wheels.
- 'XJ Sport' badging on boot lid.

Special Equipment models
- Horizontal and vertical chromed slats to radiator grille with chromed surround.
- Chromed window surrounds.
- Chromed boot plinth.
- Halogen headlights.
- 18in Luxury alloy wheels.
- 'SE' badging on boot lid.

The instrument display for X-350 models is entirely new compared to the previous X-308 style.

The facelifted XJ exterior with much revised frontal aspect. Note the enlarged lower grille area, more pronounced radiator grille and badge area, new fog lamps, new style to bumper/valance, cleaner-looking sides and the 'signature' vertical air vent in the front wing.

The newer smoother look of the post 2006 models without the side rubbing strips and with flush-bonding of the front and rear screens.

Above left: Centre console of XJR model showing dark-stained maple woodwork and unique R-style gearlever knob.

Above right: Walnut veneer for XJ6, SE, and Super V8 models. All X-350 models are equipped with the electronic handbrake previously seen on S-type models. It is operated by the half-moon chrome button to the rear of the gearlever.

XJR models

- Mesh insert to radiator grille with body-coloured surround.
- Black window surrounds.
- Body-coloured boot plinth.
- Bi-Xenon headlights.
- 19in Performance alloy wheels.
- New-style 'R-Performance' badging on boot lid.

Super V8 models

- Chromed grille surround with horizontal and vertical chromed slats until 2004, when changed to a bright finish mesh insert.
- Chromed window surrounds.
- Chromed boot plinth.
- Bi-Xenon headlights.
- Heated front windscreen.
- Front distance park sensors.
- 18in Prestige alloy wheels.
- 'Super V8' badging on boot lid.

Sovereign models

- As SE models except with Bi-Xenon headlights, 19in Custom alloy wheels, 'Sovereign' rear boot badging.

Sport Premium models

- As Sport models but including front headlight wash system, heated front screen, and 19in Custom alloy wheels.

Long-wheelbase models

- Amended profile to roof line to accommodate the extra length.
- Wider front and rear doors.
- Not available in some models unless by special order.
- Additional 'L' to rear badging.

Daimler models

- Built as Super V8 model with following amendments:
- Fluted chromed radiator grille surround with chromed vertical slats and 'D' emblem at centre-top.
- Rapier 18in alloy wheels.
- Chromed door mirrors.
- Fluted chromed rear boot signature panel.
- 'Daimler' badging to boot lid.

Facelift models

- All the facelift models carry many of the same features except for:
- Halogen lighting for XJ6, Xenon all other models.
- No headlamp washers, standard equipment on XJ6 models.
- Badging and alloy wheel types differ according to model.

The rare Daimler Super V8 model showing the unique fluted radiator grille treatment.

Rear view of the facelifted XJ model. Note the smoother and lower bumper/valance area, revised 'signature' panel on the boot lid.

Unique door handle style, always chromed, on X-350 models.

- Daimler facelift model retained traditional grille treatment but gained the revised bumper bar/under-valance and lower grille of the Jaguar models.

Interior identification points

General points applicable to all X-350s

- General style of dashboard follows current X-type and S-type theme with instrument binnacle in front of driver, air-conditioning vents to either side and centre of dashboard.
- Centrally mounted analogue clock in dashboard between air-conditioning vents.
- Wood-veneer features to dashboard top, door cappings, and other areas dependent on model.
- Four-spoke steering wheel with airbag centre boss, Jaguar growler badge, and fingertip controls for audio system, telephone, and cruise control (where fitted).
- Soft-trimmed centre console with auxiliary control buttons, large digital read-out screen for audio/air-conditioning information (also used for satellite navigation equipment when installed). Satin black finish.
- Damped ashtray.
- Traditional J-gate controls with different styles of gear knob dependent on model.
- One-touch chromed handbrake pull instead of conventional handbrake.
- Centre armrest with cup-holders etc.
- Door trims in soft upholstery with window switch packs, chromed door handles, armrests/pulls, and integrated door pockets plus wood cappings.
- Individually style seats of differing types and upholstery dependent on model, all electrically operated.
- Rear seat arrangement to match front, again dependent on model.

Model specifics

As with previous XJ practice there are differing types of trim, in this case four styles, which are best covered individually with appropriate models indicated.

Classic (standard) XJ6/SE and Sovereign models

- Complementary trim colour schemes with matching upper fascia area.
- Standard leather-clad steering wheel, half-wood veneer on SE/Sovereign models.
- Burr walnut-veneer woodwork on fascia, centre console area, door cappings, and gear knob.
- Leather seating with horizontal pleats (XJ6) or vertical pleats (SE and Sovereign models).
- Fixed rear bench seat with triple headrests to match front upholstery.

Sport/Sport Premium models

- Dashboard top roll, steering wheel, and door top rails always finished in charcoal.
- Leather-clad steering wheel, later changed to R-Performance style.
- Contrast colour trim schemes to door inner trim panels and seat centres or all-charcoal finish.
- Grey-stained maple-veneer woodwork.
- Perforated leather seating with 'window pane'-style panelling and stiffer bolsters.
- Wooden gear knob.

Super V8

- Complementary trim colour schemes with matching upper fascia area.
- Complementary coloured leather and burr walnut heated steering wheel.
- Navigational 'touch' screen in centre console.
- Fixed front compartment telephone.
- Burr walnut-veneer woodwork on fascia, centre console area, door cappings, and gear knob.
- Ruched-leather seating with horizontal pleated panels, with or without contrast piping.
- Rear bench seat electrically adjustable with multi-media centre in centre armrest area.

Long-wheelbase models

- As above, dependent on model variant plus:
- Electrically heated rear bench seat with electric seat adjustment and memory, standard on Super V8 and Daimler models only.
- Heated steering wheel, standard only on Super V8 and Daimler models.
- Rear multi-media centre, standard only on super V8 and Daimler models.
- Rear laptop tables set into the front seat backs, standard only on Daimler model.

Portfolio model

- This was a limited edition model based on an initial concept on the X-308 saloon. This was available, primarily for the US market, but was also available in other markets by order. All cars were finished with black interior to a totally different style from other XJ models.

All details of trim and specification given above relate to standard production cars. Certain owners may well have specified changes to suit their individual requirements, so it is not unusual to find some more basic models with a higher specification than that described here. From 2006 a wider range of interior finishes was available to replace the conventional maple or walnut veneers. Check details in pictures and colour schemes.

1: *17in Elegant wheels*, original fitment on XJ6 models, deleted in 2004.

2: *18in Dynamic wheels* were fitted as standard on Sport and SE models until 2005.

3: *18in Luxury alloys*, original fitment on SE and, in 2004, for XJ6.

4: *18in Prestige alloys* were the standard fit on Super V8 models up to 2004.

5: *19in Performance alloy wheels* were standard equipment on XJR models to 2005.

6: *20in Sepang alloy wheels* were standard on Portfolio models, optional on Daimler models, and an extra-cost option on all others.

7: *19in Custom wheels*, initially an extra-cost option became standard on Sport Premium models, and for 2004 on Sovereign model.

8: *18in Rapier wheels* became the standard fit on Sovereign and Super V8 models from 2005, and then on the Daimler model.

9: *18in Tucana wheels* became the standard fit on XJ6 models from 2005.

10: *19in Sabre wheels* became the standard fit on XJR models from 2005.

11: *19in Polaris wheels*, initially fitted to facelift Sovereign models, became an extra-cost option for 2008/9 model years.

12: *19in Carelia wheels* – the standard fit on Executive facelift models.

13: *20in Cremona wheels* were only fitted to Sport Premium and XJR models in 2008.

14: *20in Takoba wheels* were standard fit on Sovereign and Super V8 models during the last year of production.

15: *20in Callisto wheels* were original fitment on Executive, Sport Premium, Sovereign, and XJR models from 2008 up to the end of production.

16: The unique *19in Vela alloy wheels* produced for the facelift Daimler model only.

285

Technical specifications

	2.7-litre diesel	3.0-litre
cc	2722	2967
Bore and stroke (mm)	81 x 88	89 x 79.5
Compression ratio	17.3:1	10.5:1
bhp	204	240
@ rpm	4000	6800
Torque (lb ft)	321	221
@ rpm	1900	4100
Fuelling	Fuel-injection	Fuel-injection
Transmission	ZF 6-speed auto	ZF 6-speed auto
Wheel size (in)	18 (variable)	17 or 18, alloy
Suspension front	Ind double wishbones, coil springs air suspension standard	Ind unequal-length double wishbones, anti-dive, coil springs, air suspension standard
Suspension rear	Ind double wishbones, coil springs, air suspension standard	Ind double wishbones, coil springs, air suspension standard
Brakes	4-wheel disc, all ventilated	4-wheel disc, all ventilated
Performance		
0–60mph (sec)	7.8	7.8
Top speed (mph)	141	145
Average mpg	35	27
Dimensions		
Length (in)	199	199
Width (in)	73	73
Height (in)	55	55
Wheelbase (in)	117	117
Front track (in)	61	61
Rear track (in)	60	60
Weight (lb)	3657	3406

Optional extras

Air suspension (selected models only).
De-chromed exterior trim pack (selected models only).
Power fold-back mirrors (where not fitted).
Headlamp power-wash (where not fitted).
Heated front screen.
Front distance park aid (where not fitted).
Electric sunroof.
Variable heated seat cushions (where not fitted).
16-way electrically adjustable front seats (selected models only).
Wood/leather steering wheel (where not fitted).
Heated wood/leather steering wheel.
Four-zone climate control system.
Adaptive cruise control.
Lambswool over-rugs.
Ski-hatch.
Rear sunblind (electric).
Side manually operated window blinds.
Premium sound system.
Telephone installations.
Voice activation control.
Satellite navigation system.
Rear-mounted multi-media system with TV screens.
Electrochromatic rear-view mirror with compass.
Mud flaps.
Tailored overmats.
Child's safety seat.

	3.5-litre	4.2-litre
cc	3555	4196
Bore and stroke (mm)	86 x 76.5	86 x 90.3
Compression ratio	11:1	11:1
bhp	262	300
@ rpm	6250	6000
Torque (lb ft)	254	310
@ rpm	4200	4100
Fuelling	Fuel-injection	Fuel-injection
Transmission	ZF 6-speed auto	ZF 6-speed auto
Wheel size (in)	17 or 18, alloy	18, alloy
Suspension front	Ind unequal-length double wishbones, anti-dive, coil springs, air suspension standard	Ind unequal-length double wishbones, anti-dive, coil springs, air suspension standard
Suspension rear	Ind double wishbones, coil springs, air suspension standard	Ind double wishbones, coil springs, air suspension standard
Brakes	4-wheel disc, all ventilated	4-wheel disc, all ventilated
Performance		
0–60mph (sec)	7.3	6.3
Top speed (mph)	150	155
Average mpg	26.5	26
Dimensions		
Length (in)	199	199
Width (in)	73	73
Height (in)	55	55
Wheelbase (in)	117	117
Front track (in)	61	61
Rear track (in)	60	60
Weight (lb)	3560	3560

Child's booster cushion.
First-aid kit for boot area.
Space-saver spare wheel.
Full-size spare wheel.
Fire extinguisher for boot area.
Jaguar warning triangle.
Headlamp converters.
Headlamp safety covers.
Snow chains.
Luggage net for boot area.
Witter tow bar kit.
Tracker security system.
Alternative woodwork veneers (according to model).

Long-wheelbase bodyshell to special order on non-production models.
Tyre-pressure monitoring system.
Wheel options (dependent on model and standard equipment):
17in Elegant.
18in Dynamic, Luxury, Prestige, Rapier, and Tucana.
19in Performance, Custom, Sabre, Polaris, and Carelia.
20in Sepang, Cremona, Takoba, and Callisto.

R-Performance option
20in Sepang split-rim alloy wheels.

Technical specifications *cont ...*

	4.2-litre supercharged
cc	4196
Bore and stroke (mm)	86 x 90.3
Compression ratio	9:1
bhp	400
@ rpm	6100
Torque (lb ft)	408
@ rpm	3500
Fuelling	Fuel-injection
Transmission	ZF 6-speed auto
Wheel size (in)	18 or 19, alloy
Suspension front	Ind unequal-length double wishbones, anti-dive, coil springs, air suspension standard
Suspension rear	Ind double wishbones, coil springs, air suspension standard
Brakes	4-wheel disc, all ventilated
Performance	
0–60mph (sec)	5
Top speed (mph)	155
Average mpg	23
Dimensions	
Length (in)	199
Width (in)	73
Height (in)	55
Wheelbase (in)	117
Front track (in)	61
Rear track (in)	60
Weight (lb)	3671

Variances

Long-wheelbase models:

Weight (lb)	3560
Length (in)	205
Wheelbase (in)	124

Colour schemes

Exterior	Details	Interior	Details	Contrast piping	Details
White Onyx	To 2007	Ivory		Charcoal	
Jaguar Racing Green	To 2007	Sand	Until 2005	Sable	To 2007
British Racing Green	To 2007	Dove	2004–8	Granite	To 2008
Radiance Red		Charcoal		Charcoal	
Pacific Blue	To 2007	Cranberry		Mocha	From 2007
Platinum Grey	To 2007	Champagne	2004–8	Navy	From 2008
Quartz	To 2007				
Ultraviolet Blue	To 2007	**Fascias**	**Details**	**Stitching**	**Details**
Seafrost	To 2007	Mocha		Black	To 2008
Slate	To 2007	Granite	To 2008	Heritage Tan	To 2005
Topaz	To 2007	Charcoal		Cranberry	To 2006
Ebony		Navy	From 2008	Warm Charcoal	From 2008
Zircon	To 2007			Granite	From 2008
Midnight	From 2004			Dove	From 2008
Winter Gold	From 2006				
Indigo	From 2006	**Contrasts**		**Details**	
Botanical Green	From 2007	Ivory/Charcoal		To 2005	
Emerald Fire	From 2007	Heritage Tan/Charcoal		To 2005	
Vapour Grey	From 2007	Cranberry/Charcoal			To 2005
Frost Blue	From 2007				
Blue Prism	2007	**Veneers**		**Details**	
Azure Blue	From 2008	Burr Walnut			
Ultimate Black	From 2007	Grey-Stained Maple			
Pearl Grey	From 2007	Aluminium		From 2006	
Lunar Grey	From 2007	Elm		From 2007	
Liquid Silver	From 2007	Satin American Walnut		2007–8	
Porcelain	From 2007	Rich Oak		From 2008	
Garnet	From 2006*	Burr Walnut with Boxwood inlay		Only applicable to Daimler model	

* = Daimler model only

Prices and production volumes

	Price new (£)	2003	2004	2005
XJ6 3.0-litre swb	39,000	■	■	■
XJ6 3.0-litre lwb	Sp order	–	–	■
XJ6 3.0-litre Sport swb	42,250	■	■	–
XJ6 3.0-litre SE/Sov swb	42,250	■	■	■
XJ6 3.0-litre Sov lwb	45,750	–	–	■
XJ6 2.7-litre TDV swb	43,272	–	–	■
XJ6 2.7-litre TDV lwb	46,770	–	–	–
XJ6 2.7-litre S/Prem swb	49,272	–	–	■
XJ6 2.7-litre Sov swb	49,272	–	–	■
XJ6 2.7-litre Sov lwb	52,770	–	–	–
XJ8 3.5-litre swb	41,550	■	■	■
XJ8 3.5-litre lwb	Sp order	–	■	■
XJ8 3.5-litre Sport swb	44,802	■	■	■
XJ8 3.5-litre SE swb	48,000	■	■	■
XJ8 3.5-litre S/Prem	47,302	–	■	■
XJ8 4.2-litre swb	51,500	■	■	■
XJ8 4.2-litre lwb	60,375	–	■	■
XJ8 4.2-litre Sport swb	Sp order	■	–	–
XJ8 4.2-litre SE/Sov swb	57,902	■	■	■
XJ8 4.2-litre SE/Sov lwb	61,995	–	■	■
XJ8 4.2-litre VDP swb	USA	■	■	–
XJ8 4.2-litre VDP lwb	USA	–	■	■
XJ8 4.2-litre Limo S/c	–	■	–	–
XJ8 4.2-litre Super V8 swb	68,500	■	■	■
XJ8 4.2-litre Super V8 lwb	71,975	–	■	■
XJR 4.2-litre S/charged swb	58,500	■	■	■
XJR 4.2-litre S/c VDP lwb*	61,277	–	■	■
Daimler Super V8	79,277	–	–	■
Total production		**27,811**	**15,100**	**13,594**

* = this figure includes Portfolio model

2006	2007	2008	2009	Total produced
■	■	■	■	4861
■	■	■	■	476
–	–	–	–	626
■	■	■	■	4512
■	■	■	■	2233
■	■	■	■	3647
■	■	■	■	230
■	■	■	–	760
■	■	■	■	3453
■	■	■	■	696
■	■	■	–	981
■	■	■	–	225
■	–	–	–	523
■	■	■	–	3890
■	■	■	–	747
■	■	■	–	15,840
■	■	–	–	8836
–	–	–	–	190
■	■	■	■	6322
■	■	■	■	1735
–	–	–	–	4194
■	■	■	■	6872
–	–	–	–	9
■	■	■	■	1309
■	■	■	–	943
■	■	■	■	7316
■	■	■	–	1277
■	■	■	–	853
10,032	**10,270**	**5912**	**837**	**83,566**

19 New XK sports cars
2006 to 2014

Background

Jaguar's new sports car (replacing the 1996–2005 XK8 and XKR models) was announced in October 2005 ready for the 2006 model year. Taking strong cues from the ALC (Aluminium Lightweight Coupé) concept car, the New XK, as it was called, also inherited many technical features from the X-350 saloons.

Unusual for a sports car, the New XK was designed as a convertible first to ensure the maximum rigidity possible, and the all aluminium body construction followed the same processes as the big XJ saloon. The new car was, therefore, not only 20% lighter than the outgoing XK8 but was also an astonishing 50% stiffer. Despite this high-tech move forward with outstanding contemporary styling, the car was initially launched with the existing 4.2-litre AJ-V8 engine, developing 300bhp but with multi-hole injectors to the fuel-injection system, mated to the ZF six-speed automatic transmission. A limited number of cars were also produced with the X-350 3.5-litre saloon engine. Innovative features included keyless entry and start facilities, active front lighting that followed the steering, sequential gearshift operation from steering wheel-mounted paddles and, in the case of the convertible, a fully retracting hood under an aluminium tonneau closing panel.

Key safety features included automatically deploying rollover bars at the rear of the cockpit, and, unique at the time, a pyrotechnic deployable bonnet system which in the event of accidental collision with a pedestrian would instantly raise the height of the bonnet above the hard areas beneath to provide a softer impact. Larger brakes with an improved overall braking system, with modified steering and suspension, completed the new package.

Announced as both 2+2 coupé and convertible, the New XK continued to provide excellent boot accommodation (suitable for the obligatory two sets of golf clubs!). The interior was a complete redesign with clearer instruments, new layout, and many more creature comforts than previous models.

It wasn't until a year later for the 2007 model year that the XKR variants were announced, also in coupé and convertible form. Now boasting a 420bhp supercharged engine, improved brakes and suspension, subtle trim changes differentiated the XKRs from the normally-aspirated XK models.

Towards the end of 2007 the Portfolio was announced as a special edition to the XKR range, but only as a coupé model (later added to the convertible range in 2008). Then, at the Geneva Motor Show in March 2008, Jaguar announced the XKR-S, based on the XKR but with improved performance and aerodynamics. In 2008 the XK60 was announced as the replacement for the basic XK models with higher-spec equipment levels and revised trim.

Then, in 2009, for the 2010 model year the XK was effectively relaunched with an all-new 5.0-litre V8 engine in both normally-aspirated and supercharged forms, with a large degree of interior and exterior trim changes, plus other mechanical refinements.

The XK continued to develop into the XKR-S and XKR-S GT, the latter becoming one of the most powerful sports cars in the world, with mechanical aspects based on the new F-TYPE model.

Within the last couple of years of production, the artisan Special Edition model was announced, followed by similar limited editions for world markets, and finally the Signature and Dynamic R models, representing the ultimate in New XK development. These two final models saw the end of XK production in 2014, with no direct replacement produced.

Model range and development

The New XK was promoted at launch as 'the car that demands your immediate attention'.

Models available at launch

New XK 4.2-litre 2+2 coupé
New XK 4.2-litre 2+2 convertible

The principles of this virtually entirely new Jaguar sports still lay in a monocoque construction, but now of ultra-lightweight aluminium and, unlike the previous XK8, was neither designed for nor used in any other model. Here was a much lighter, more aerodynamic car, more economical to produce and maintain, and economical to run, with styling that was contemporary and 'sharp', yet retaining many of the features well known to Jaguar sports cars since the 1960s.

It was offered with a choice of 18in, 19in or 20in alloy wheels and the option of run-flat tyres and a tyre-pressure monitoring system. Standard

Direct comparison between the latest XK (top) and the previous 1996 model.

Always conceived as a convertible, this is an early example with the 20in Santa alloy wheels showing the clean lines of the hood.

Early XK frontal aspect with smoother treatment to the under-bumper area, inset fog lights, and chrome 'splitter' bar to the grille area.

Rear view of an early XK convertible with discreet spoiler with built-in brakelight.

equipment included Xenon headlights, reverse parking aid, and auto-locking system upon leaving the car. The New XK was the first Jaguar to carry the now well-known 'signature' wing vents in the front wings.

Internally the cars were fitted out to a very high standard, with a choice of wood veneer or alloy finishes, standard equipment cruise control, and a sophisticated security system.

The drivetrain followed that of the X-350 saloons (without air suspension) and some design elements from the S-type models. Incorporated was a four-channel ABS system with analogue control and Electronic Brakeforce Distribution ensuring the correct balance of braking forces spread across all four wheels.

One of the most interesting aspects of the new car was the 'sound', produced by the exhaust system and by a complex valve system which allowed a degree of noise to enter the cockpit of the car.

The first customer cars were delivered in 2006 and it wasn't until 2007 that the XKR supercharged version came to the marketplace. The new engine supplied 420bhp with 560Nm of torque, providing an incredible acceleration time of under 5sec to 60mph. Springs and shock absorbers were uprated for this model along with a recalibration of the CATS (Computer Active Technology Suspension) package.

Subtle exterior changes to differentiate the XKR from the XK included new-style bumper treatment and grille, louvres set into the bonnet, the alloy finish to the front wing side vents, and the four exhaust pipes instead of two. Internally the XKR was identifiable by its revised trim and seating.

Towards the end of 2007, the Portfolio was announced as a special edition to the XKR range, but only as a coupé model. Cosmetically, it was available in a limited colour palate, Black or Liquid Silver, but, unusually, out of ten exported to Australia, five were Black and five Shadow Grey. These cars had a unique front-end treatment with alloy-finished grille, vents, and unique bonnet louvres. Along with interior trim changes, mechanically it had an enlarged braking system.

At the Geneva Motor Show in 2008, Jaguar announced the next 'special' XK, the XKR-S. Although essentially still based on the XKR model, the engine management system was recalibrated along with tweaks to the suspension and aerodynamics, to improve performance. Jaguar claimed a top speed of 174mph, making it the fastest Jaguar production car since the XJ220 supercar in the 1990s. The massive disc brakes and six-pot callipers were a carryover from the Portfolio model mentioned above. On sale through 2008, production was limited to just 200 cars, all for the European market.

In 2008 the XK60 was announced as the replacement for the basic XK (non-supercharged

The early coupé model with sculptured rear tailgate emphasising the pronounced haunches of the car.

The distinctive interior treatment, totally different from previous XKs with great use of alloy finishes. This car is equipped with the burr walnut veneering.

With the introduction of the XKR models, came revisions to the front and rear styling and different finish to items like the side 'signature' vents. Note also the louvres added to the bonnet for XKR models only.

models), in both coupé and convertible forms. The new car offered extra equipment levels as standard, including 20in alloy wheels, alloy gear knob and surround, and enhanced exterior front, rear and side trims.

At the Geneva Motor Show in 2009 the XKs received a major boost with the replacement of the above models with the 2010 model year cars, the highlight of which was the fitment of new AJ-V8 Gen III 5.0-litre V8 engines providing a 23% increase in performance and 12% increase in torque over the previous 4.2-litre units. Other mechanical upgrades included steering and brakes and the adoption of a JaguarDrive control system for gear changes. Offered in both normally-aspirated and supercharged forms, in both convertible and coupé, there are three models now: the XK, the XKR, and the XK Portfolio (the latter with a higher trim specification), all with exterior and interior changes to the previous models.

In 2010, Jaguar announced a limited run of 75 cars carrying the insignia XKR75, all finished in a single colour of Stratus Grey, some with an optional grey signature striping. Revised aerodynamic trim was carried out to match the 174mph performance from its enhanced drivetrain, suspension and exhaust system. There was also a commemorative plaque signed by Ian Callum and Mike Cross inside the car. A similar model, the XKR 175, was produced for the US and Canadian markets.

With the new engine in 2011 Jaguar took the XK a stage further and produced a new coupé variant retaining the XKR-S insignia but with what Jaguar dubbed, 'the most extreme expression yet of Jaguar's passion'. With revised fuel mapping, modified suspension and brakes, an aggressive new exterior and changes to the interior, the XKR-S became the fastest of the XK variants. The XKR-S was available as a convertible by 2012.

Still with 2011, Jaguar introduced some enhanced 'packs' for owners to personalise the XKs. The Speed Pack allowed customers to extend the car's top speed up to an electronically limited 174mph with unique engine and transmission recalibration, along with necessary aerodynamic amendments to suit. Alternatively, a Black Pack created a more visual impact to the car with revised wheels and exterior detailing. Finally, there was the Dynamic Pack, for the XKR models. This included all the enhancements of the Speed Pack, with added revisions to the suspension and steering for a more dramatic driving experience. Coinciding with these packs was the Jaguar Designers' Choice Programme, offering a wide range of bespoke interior finishes for customers.

In 2012 an artisan Special Edition model (SE) was added to the range of cars in both coupé and

The most powerful regularly available XK: the XKR-S.

With the introduction of the 5.0-litre, all XKs now featured the unique JaguarDrive control for gear selection.

Side view of the 2008 Portfolio coupé, with 20in Cremona alloy wheels and enlarged braking system.

Revised XK frontal view for 2008 models.

The very latest XKR, equipped with the 5.0-litre engine and, in this case, with Nevis 20in wheels.

convertible form, offering unique trim features with extra equipment levels.

At the 2013 Geneva Motor Show, Jaguar announced their very limited production run of just thirty XKR-S GTs, designed by their Engineered to Order (ETO) division. This was a track-focused but road-going iteration of the XK, with extensive aerodynamic, suspension, brakes and steering changes, some aspects of which came directly from the new F-TYPE sports car.

In 2014, a limited edition Portfolio model called the XK66 was released for the German market. Only 66 examples were built. Also in 2014, the last year of XK production, Jaguar announced their final mainstream models, the XK Signature and Dynamic R, replacing all the previous models (except the XKR-S).

The luxury focused XK Signature with the normally aspirated 5.0-litre engine was fitted with a host of additional features as standard. The Dynamic R replaced the XKR, and cost £10,000 less than a similarly specified car would have cost just months before, and was only £27,500 less to buy than the range-topping XKR-S.

The essence of the Dynamic R was that it took the XKR's supercharged engine and 6-speed gearbox and matched them to the Speed, Black, Dynamic and Aerodynamic packs as standard. That provided the better balanced suspension for performance, exhaust, spoilers, etc, plus a useful increase in top speed to 174mph. The car also showed off revised interior trim and specification.

That still didn't represent the end of the XK, because a limited edition Final Fifty XKR model was announced for the US market. This car incorporated some panels taken from the XKR-S GT and had the Dynamic Pack fitted.

These models saw out production of the XK in 2014.

Exterior identification points

General points applicable to XK models (up to 2010 model range)

Front view

- Curvaceous frontal aspect emulating previous XK but with more pronounced nose and lower under-bumper incorporating spoiler and lower grille area.
- Nose includes mesh insert, in front of which is a chromed splitter bar with centrally mounted growler badge.
- Xenon headlights with side light and indicator units sculptured into front wing areas.
- Standard-fit insert fog lights.
- One-piece forward-hinged bonnet with pronounced power-bulge in centre.
- One-piece bonded windscreen with twin wipers.

Rear view
- Severely tapering rear-end styling.
- Rear-hinged boot lid terminating at tonneau panel on convertible model.
- Rear-hinged tailgate incorporating rear screen on coupé model.
- Number plate surround indent in boot with Jaguar 'signature' chromed panel incorporating illumination and boot lock control.
- Rear-light clusters matching the front lighting moulded into the side of each rear wing, featuring digital light techniques.
- Twin chromed exhaust tailpipes, one emitting from each side below bumper/valance area.
- Chromed 'XK' and '4.2' badging each side of the boot panel.
- Pronounced and sculptured body-colour rear bumper/valance panel with reverse parking aid.

Side view
- Inset body-coloured vertical air vent 'signature' panels at rear of each front wing which also incorporate 'Jaguar' badging and indicator repeater lenses.
- Simple waist-height swage line running the length of the car.
- Pronounced sculptured sills.
- Pronouced body-colour door handle/pulls.
- Frameless door glass.
- Concealed fuel filler cap incorporated into the rear nearside wing, with flush cover.

XKR specifics

Front view
- Revised styling to front bumper/valance area with colour-keyed finish to foglight housings.
- Nose incorporates mesh insert to both the grille and under-grille areas without the chromed splitter bar of the XK and a larger, centrally-mounted growler badge.
- Louvred air vents set into bonnet top.

Rear view
- Restyling to rear bumper/valance area to accommodate:
- Four chromed exhaust tailpipes, two emitting from each side below the bumper/valance area.
- Chromed and coloured 'R' badging, on right-hand side of the boot panel.
- Alloy-finished rear 'signature' panel.
- Rear spoiler added to boot lid incorporating high-level brakelight.

Side view
- Inset alloy-finished vertical air vent 'signature' panels at rear of each front wing which also incorporate 'Jaguar' badging and indicator repeater lenses.
- Black R brake calipers visible through alloy wheels.

Above left: *The centre console area of the early new XK showing the conventional J-gate gear change system, in this case with poplar-veneer surround. Note also the red 'start' button, at the time unique to the XK.*

Above right: *Showing the alloy-finished interior. Note the sportier seating compared to the previous picture.*

The XKR interior with alloy-finish veneer, revised gear knob, and the different seat style.

Above left: *XKR Portfolio with different alloy-style finish and gear knob.*

Above right: *The revised interior of the XKR for the 2010 model year. Note the contrasting use of Piano Black finish to the alloy, the JaguarDrive control for gear changes, and the leather stitched centre spoke to the steering wheel.*

The 2012 update of the standard XK exterior.

The updated front view of the 2012-on XK.

Updated front view of the 2012-on XKR.

Rear aspect of the XK from 2012 onwards.

Portfolio specifics

Additional to R specification:
- Portfolio models only available in Celestial Black paint finish (or Liquid Silver for UK and Swiss markets). Became available as a convertible model from 2008.

Front view
- Reshaped front bumper area incorporating aluminium-finished grilles and foglight areas.
- Revised bonnet louvres.

Rear view
- Satin-finished alloy rear 'signature' panel.

Side view
- Inset polished alloy-finished vertical air vent 'signature' panels at rear of each front wing.
- 20in polished Cremona alloy wheels.
- Six-pot, red 'R' brake callipers with cross-drilled brake discs visible.

XKR-S pre-2011 specifics (additional to Portfolio models)

- Only available in Ultimate Black exterior paint finish.

Front view
- Revised frontal bumper/valance treatment with aerodynamic 'lip'.
- Contrast finish to grilles and spoiler/splitter.

Rear view
- Unique 'R-S' badging to right-hand side of boot lid.
- Revised more prominent spoiler.
- Rear diffuser panel below bumper level in contrast colour.

Side view
- 10mm ride-height reduction compared to other XKR models.
- Sill extensions in contrast colour.
- 20in Vortex forged alloy wheels.

XK60 specifics

Front view
- Revised front bumper/valance treatment with bright mesh grilles, circular inset fog lights and sculptured spoiler.
- Chrome splitter no longer featured.

Rear view
- Revised rear valance with diffuser.
- Revised tailpipe finishers.

Side view
- Chrome-finished front wing-mounted 'signature' vents.

- Sill appliqués.

2010 model year specifics

Front view
- New front-end treatment with larger under-grille area (finished in black on XK and Portfolio) with chromed detailing to different shaped inserts and upper mesh grille.
- Chrome lower mesh grille on XKR models.

Rear view
- LED rear-light clusters with integrated fog lights and twin reversing lights (only one on previous models).
- Chromed boot 'signature' panel now standard on all models.
- Revised-shape lower bumper/valance on XKR model with new-style exhaust tailpipes.
- 18in Venus alloy wheels standard on XK models.
- 19in Caravela alloy wheels standard on Portfolio models.
- 19in Tamana alloy wheels standard on XKR models.

Side view
- LED side indicator repeater lights in front wings.
- Revised colour 'signature' vents in front wings.
- LED repeater lights within the door mirrors.
- Chrome detailing on window surrounds.

XKR 75/175 mode specifics

Front view
- Front splitter bar similar to XKR-S (see below).
- Matt black mesh grille.
- Deep front spoiler.

Rear view
- Rear diffuser with larger than normal spoiler in body colour.
- Other rear trim in matt black.

Side view
- Only available in Stratus Grey paintwork.
- Option of grey signature striping around the top wing areas.
- Side sill extensions.
- 20in Vortex alloy wheels, diamond turned with dark grey finish.
- 10in lowered ride height.

XKR-S 2011-on specifics

Front view
- Slimmer combined LED lamp units.
- More compact matt black mesh grille with 'RS' insignia.
- Deep front air spoiler.
- The new bumper arrangement with near-vertical feature lines that run down from the

Rear aspect of the XKR from 2012 onwards.

The XKR-S.

Unique frontal styling for the XKR-S.

Rear styling of the XKR-S with unique spoiler treatment.

Engine bay of the XKR-S with little change noticeable to the eye.

Special interior trim for the XKR-S with heavily sculptured racing seats and dark alloy-finish trim.

The XKR-S in convertible form.

The XK Special Edition model announced in 2012.

edges of the grille.
- Vertical air direction slots at the extreme edges of the front bumper.
- Horizontal air slots in the upper edge of the front area near the bonnet.

Rear view
- Revised bumper shaping.
- Separate rear spoiler with carbon fibre insert.
- Rear apron with diffuser.
- New badging.

Side view
- Horizontal signature intakes finished in black to the rear of the front wings.
- Wider sills.
- Exterior trim finished to gloss black.
- 20in Vulcan alloy wheels.
- Brake callipers painted gunmetal or red.
- Suspension marginally lowered.

2012 XK model specifics
Front view
- The new style featured side air intakes in the bumper.
- Revised style under the grille and spoiler.

Side view
- Horizontal signature chromed intakes to the rear of the front wings.
- Smoother sculpturing to the sills.
- Slimmer door mirrors.
- 18in alloy wheels.

2012 XK Portfolio specifics
- 19in alloy wheels.

2012 XKR model specifics
Front view
- 'R' badging to mesh grille.
- XKR louvres in the bonnet sides.
- Aerodynamic pack (front splitter).

Rear view
- 'R' badging.
- Four exhaust tailpipes.

Interior of the XK Special Edition model.

- Aerodynamic pack (spoiler).

Side view
- Sculptured sills.
- Red brake callipers.
- Power-fold door mirrors.

Special Edition model specifics
Side view
- Unique palette of just three exterior paint finishes.
- 20in Orona alloy wheels.

Interior identification points

General points applicable to XK models up to 2010 model year
- Full-width dashboard area split into three areas, instrument binnacle in front of driver, pronounced centre console area with multi-media, air con, and auxiliary controls leading to console between the front seats holding the gear select, 'start' button, and handbrake control, and the passenger area with trim and glove compartment.
- Air-conditioning air vents in centre of dash area, plus auxiliary vents, one either side of dash area.
- Main instrument binnacle incorporates inset speedometer, rev counter, and auxiliary fuel bar gauge plus message centre.
- Centre console area encompasses air-conditioning controls, audio system plus touch-screen for satellite navigational system, and TV tuner (where fitted).
- Three-spoke steering wheel in a choice of finishes incorporating paddle controls for gearshift and thumb controls for audio system, telephone, and cruise control.
- Choice of wood veneer or alloy finish to dash and trim areas.
- Soft door trim areas incorporating door pulls, chromed door handles, and switch packs for windows/mirrors.

The limited edition XKR75 in Stratus Grey with optional signature striping along the bonnet and side.

One of the Jaguar's optional 'packs' for later models, in this case the Speed Pack.

A Dynamic pack equipped XK.

The most powerful XK ever produced, the race bred and road legal XKR-S GT.

Dashboard plaque of the XK66 special edition model.

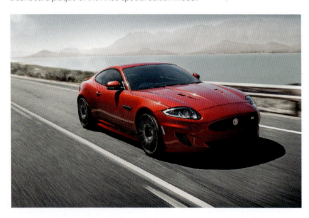
The last XKR model produced for 2014, the Dynamic R, here in coupé form but also available as a convertible.

Special diamond stitching to the seating for certain end of the line models.

- All seats trimmed in perforated leather with horizontal and vertical panel stitching.
- Each front seat contains electrically adjustable head restraints and full seat electric controls from side of seats.

XKR specifics

- XKR badging to main instruments.
- Unique alloy 'weave' finish to dash and console area as standard equipment.
- R seating with stiff bolsters and larger panels with horizontal stitching plus heavily embossed seatback side panels.
- R performance gear knob.

Portfolio specifics
Additional to XKR:

- Engine-spun alloy dash panel finish or US satin walnut alternative.
- Alloy and leather gear knob.
- Soft-grab door handles.
- Contrast leather stitching to all trim.
- Leather-edged carpet overmats.
- 'Portfolio' treadplates.
- Soft grain interior trim in choice of only two colour schemes (ivory or charcoal).
- Bowers & Wilkins hi-fi sound system.

XKR 75/175 mode specifics

- Charcoal leather seating and other trim.
- Piano black veneer.
- XKR75 or XKR175 sill tread plates.
- Commemorative plaque signed by Ian Callum and Mike Cross from Jaguar.

XKR-S pre-2011 specifics

- Piano Black veneer.
- Revised, recalibrated instrument pack.
- Alston charcoal headlining.
- Contrast-stitched leather steering wheel.
- Bright alloy foot pedals.
- XKR-S 'branded' headrests, mats, and treadplates.

XK60 specifics

- Alloy gear knob and surround.

2010 model year specifics

- Centre console now incorporates JaguarDrive gear selector control.
- Suede cloth headlining for XKR coupé model.
- Bright sill treadplates applicable to all models.
- Leather-wrapped lower spoke steering wheel.
- White instrument illumination for XK and Portfolio models.
- Red instrument pointers for XKR models.
- Heated & cooled front seats standard on all models.
- Saddle-stitched and soft padded door pulls and casings.
- Chromed highlight door pack switches.

- Soft-grain leather with contrast stitching on Portfolio and XKR models.
- Option of Ebony veneer for Portfolio model.

2012 XK model specifics

- Bond grain leather seat trim.

2012 XK Portfolio specifics

- Soft-grain leather seat trim with contrast colour stitching.
- Ten-way electrically adjustable seating.
- Heated and cooled seats.
- Bowers & Wilkins Hi-Fi audio system.
- Suedecloth headlining (coupé model).
- Heated leather-covered steering wheel.
- Heated windscreen.
- Six-disc CD player.

2012 XKR model specifics

- Bowers & Wilkins surround sound audio system.
- Suedecloth headlining (coupé model).
- Heated and cooled seats.
- Heated windscreen.
- Performance seats with carbon and soft-grain leather.
- 16-way electric seats.
- Stainless steel pedals.
- XKR-S treadplates.
- Jet leather headlining.
- Dark aluminium veneer trim.

Special Edition model specifics

- Performance seating with 16-way electric adjustment.
- Navy or truffle interior option.
- Canvas headlining.
- Scraffito-grain leather seat coverings and to door trims and instrument binnacle.
- Shadow walnut veneer or dark alloy finish to trim.
- Special edition treadplates.

XKR-S GT model specifics

Front view
- Black finish to all trim.
- Carbon fibre front splitter of race-car wrap-around type.
- Carbon fibre twin dive-planes.
- Aluminium front valance.
- Extended bonnet louvers.
- Front track widened by 52mm.
- R-S GT script on the bonnet.

Rear view
- Black finish to all trim.
- Carbon fibre diffuser.
- Elevated carbon fibre rear wing.
- R-S GT badging.

Side view
- Polaris White paintwork with black graphics.
- 20in alloy wheels in gloss black.
- Pirelli Corsa performance tyres.
- Yellow brake callipers scripted 'Jaguar Carbon Ceramic'.
- Black trim.

XKR-S GT model specifics

Front view
- Black finish to all trim.
- Carbon fibre front splitter of race-car wrap-around type.
- Carbon fibre twin dive-planes.
- Aluminium front valance.
- Extended bonnet louvers.
- Front track widened by 52mm.
- R-S GT script on the bonnet.

Rear view
- Black finish to all trim.
- Carbon fibre diffuser.
- Elevated carbon fibre rear wing.
- R-S GT badging.

Side view
- Polaris White paintwork with black graphics.
- 20in alloy wheels in gloss black.
- Pirelli Corsa performance tyres.
- Yellow brake callipers scripted 'Jaguar Carbon Ceramic'.
- Black trim.

XK66 model specifics

Rear view
- XK66 badging.

Side view
- Stratus Grey or British Racing Green paintwork only.
- Black or beige hoods (convertibles) only.
- XK66 emblem on side power vents in front wings.
- Chromed door mirror caps.
- 20in Orona alloy wheels polished with Union Jack valve caps.

XK Signature model specifics

As previous Portfolio model except:
Side view
- Limited choice of just 6 exterior paintwork colours.
- 20in Kalimnos or Takoba alloy wheels.

Dynamic R model specifics

As previous Portfolio and R models plus:

Overall view
- Aerodynamic, Speed and Black Packs standard equipment (see accessories listing).
- 20in Vortex diamond turned gloss black alloy wheels.

- Red paint brake callipers.
- Limited exterior paint finishes as XK Signature models.
- Dynamic R badging.

Final Fifty model specifics

- Fitted as standard with Jaguar's Dynamic Pack (see accessories listing)

Front view
- XK-RS GT bonnet louvers.

Rear view
- Rear wing and diffuser.

Side view
- Ultimate Black exterior paintwork.
- Black convertible hoods.
- 20in Vortex gloss black alloy wheels.
- Side sill extensions.

1: 18in Venus wheels, standard fit on XK.

2: 19in Artura wheels, an option in 2010.

3: 19in Caravela wheels, an option in 2010.

4: 19in Carelia wheels, an option to 2009.

5: 19in Jupiter wheels, available mid-2007–late 2009.

6: 19in Sabre wheels, a run-flat wheel available to 2009.

7: 19in Tamana wheels, an option from 2010 and standard on the Portfolio model.

8: 20in Cremona wheels, available mid-2007–9.

9: 20in Kalimnos wheels, standard on Portfolio and optional on XK/XKR in 2010.

10: 20in Kasuga wheels, standard fit on Speed pack models.

11: 20in Nevis R-Performance wheels from 2010.

12: 20in Orona wheels, an option from 2011 and standard on the Special Edition.

13: 20in Pegasus wheels (2007–9).

14: 20in Selena, an option from 2011.

15: 20in Senta wheels, an option to 2009.

16: 20in Takoba wheels, an option from 2011.

17. 20in Venom, an option from 2011

18: 20in Vortex, Final Fifty, XK75, Dynamic R, Dynamic Packs.

19: 20in Vulcan wheels, polished as a standard fit on Dynamic pack models. In gloss-black-finish standard on Dynamic pack black models. Both options are standard on XKR-S models.

Optional extras

Black- or Bright-finish mesh grilles.
Square stainless steel exhaust trim pipes.
Bright-finish door mirror covers.
Bright-finish front wing 'signature' vents.
Brushed aluminium or chromed gear knobs.
Tailored over-carpet mats.
Aluminium drilled pedal pads.
Wind deflector for convertible models.
18in Venus alloy wheels.
19in Carelia, Caravela, Artura, Tamana, or Saba alloy wheels.
20in Senta, Kalimnos, or Nevis alloy wheels.
20in Orona, Takoba, Kasuga, Vulcan wheels.
20in Selena, Venom and Vortex wheels.
Tyre-pressure monitoring system.
Keyless entry.
Alternative veneer dash trims.
TV tuner.
DVD audio system.
Bowers & Wilkins Premium hi-fi system.
Active front lighting.
Power fold-back door mirrors.
Front park assist system with interior touch-screen information.
Soft-grain leather seat facings.
ACC cruise control.
Premium surround sound hi-fi system.
Bowers & Wilkins hi-fi system.
Upgrade styling kit.
Garage door opener.
Heated windscreen.
Heated door mirrors.
R-Performance interior (2010 on).
Choice of veneer.
Chromed bonnet louvres.
Adaptive lighting.
Jet leather headlining.
Auto dimming exterior mirrors.
Sports steering wheel trimmed in leather.
Reverse park camera and guidance.
Stainless steel pedals.
Adaptive cruise control.
DAD radio receiver.
Performance seating.
Performance active exhaust system.
Speed pack.
Black Speed pack.
Dynamic pack.
Black Dynamic pack.
Carbon fibre engine cover.
Gunmetal or red brake callipers.
Dark-alloy trim. Carbon fibre engine cover.
Gunmetal or red brake callipers.
Dark alloy trim.
Polished exhaust tailpipe finishers.
Chromed bonnet louvers.
Growler branded wheel nuts.
Snow sock with winter traction aid.
Sport pedal covers.
3-spoke sports heated steering wheel.
Air quality sensor.
Diamond stitch interior pack.
Performance seating.

Speed Pack
Comprising for XKR models only:
Enhanced mechanical/electronic features.
Body coloured aerodynamic package, with side sill extensions and rear diffuser.
20in Kasuga alloy wheels.
Red brake callipers.
Select exterior paint finishes.

Dynamic Pack
Comprising for XKR (coupé originally) only:
As Speed Pack plus
Full machined front knuckle with unique spring and damper settings.
Revised Adaptive Dynamics.
10mm ride height reduction.
20in Vulcan alloy wheels in polished finish.

Technical specifications

	4.2-litre
cc	4196
Bore and stroke (mm)	86 x 90
Compression ratio	11:1
bhp	298
@ rpm	6000
Max torque (lb ft)	310
@ rpm	4100
Fuelling	Fuel-injection
Transmission	6-speed auto sequential
Wheel size (in)	19/20, alloy
Suspension front	Ind unequal-length wishbones, coil springs
Suspension (rear)	Ind unequal-length wishbones, coil springs
Brakes	4-wheel disc, all ventilated
Performance	
0–60mph (sec)	5.9
Top speed (mph)	155
Average mpg	25
Dimensions	
Length (in)	189
Width (in)	74
Height (in)	52
Wheelbase (in)	108
Front track (in)	61
Rear track (in)	61
Weight (lb)	3516

Technical specifications *cont ...*

	4.2-litre supercharged	5.0-litre
cc	4196	5000
Bore and stroke (mm)	86 x 90	92.5 x 93
Compression ratio	9:1	11.5:1
bhp	420	385
@ rpm	6250	6500
Max torque (lb ft)	413	385
@ rpm	4000	6500
Fuelling	Fuel-injection	Fuel-injection
Transmission	6-speed auto sequential	6-speed auto sequential
Wheel size (in)	19/20, alloy	19/20, alloy
Suspension front	Ind unequal-length wishbones, coil springs	Ind unequal-length wishbones, coil springs
Suspension (rear)	Ind unequal-length wishbones, coil springs	Ind unequal-length wishbones, coil springs
Brakes	4-wheel disc, all ventilated	4-wheel disc, all ventilated
Performance		
0–60mph (sec)	4.9	5.2
Top speed (mph)	155	155
Average mpg	22	25
Dimensions		
Length (in)	189	189
Width (in)	74	75
Height (in)	52	52
Wheelbase (in)	108	108
Front track (in)	61	61
Rear track (in)	61	63
Weight (lb)	3691	3651

Black Speed Pack

As Speed Pack plus:
Gloss black finish to upper and lower mesh grilles, side intakes, power vents and boot finisher.
Gloss black finish to window surrounds (coupé only)
20in Kalimnos alloy wheels in gloss black finish.

Black Dynamic Pack

As Dynamic Pack plus:
20in Vulcan alloy wheels in polished black finish.
Extra revisions to front suspension/steering.
Gloss black finish to upper and lower mesh grilles, side intakes, power vents and boot finisher.
Gloss black finish to window surrounds (coupé only)

5.0-litre supercharged	XKR-S	XK-RS GT
5000	5000	5000
92.5 x 93	92.5 x 93	92.5 x 93
9.5:1	9.5:1	9.5:1
510	550	550
6500	6000/6500	6500
510	680	502
6500	2300	2500
Fuel-injection	Fuel-injection	Fuel-injection
6-speed auto sequential	6-speed auto sequential	6-speed auto sequential
19/20	20	20
Ind unequal-length wishbones, coil springs	Ind unequal-length wishbones, coil springs	Ind unequal-length wishbones, coil springs (F-TYPE modified)
Ind unequal-length wishbones, coil springs	Ind unequal-length wishbones, coil springs	Ind unequal-length wishbones, coil springs (F-TYPE modified)
4-wheel disc, all ventilated	4-wheel performance ventilated discs	4-wheel high performance carbon fibre
4.6	4.2	3.9
155	186 (limited)	186 (limited)
23	21	23
189	188.7	188.7
75	74.5	79.8
52	52.2	51.9
108	108.3	108.3
61	61.4	61.4
63	63.3	63.3
3865	3865	3865

Colour schemes

Exterior	Details
British Racing Green	To 2008
Jaguar Racing Green	To 2008
White Onyx	To 2007
Porcelain	From 2007 to 2010
Seafrost	To 2007
Liquid Silver	To 2010
Lunar Grey	From 2006
Quartz	To 2007
Slate Grey	To 2008
Vapour Grey	From 2007 to 2010
Pearl Grey	From 2008 to 2010
Zircon	To 2007
Frost Blue	From 2007 to 2010
Ultraviolet Blue	To 2007
Blue Prism	2007 only

Exterior	Details
Azure Blue	From 2008 to 2009
Indigo Blue	From 2006
Midnight	To 2008
Ebony Black	From 2006
Salsa Red	To 2010
Radiance Red	To 2010
Winter Gold	To 2010
Celestial Black	From 2007 to 2008 (Portfolio only) 2012 to 2013 (SE)
Ultimate Black	From 2008 to 2012 (2008 (XKR-S Coupé only)
Claret Red	From 2009 to 2012
Spectrum Blue	From 2009 to 2012
Kyanite Blue	From 2009 to 2012 (XKR only)
Botanical Green	From 2008 to 2012

Colour schemes *cont ...*

Exterior	Details
Emerald Fire Green	From 2007 to 2009
Celestial Black	To 2009 Portfolio – From 2011 Special Edition
Polaris White	From 2011
Stratus Grey	From 2010 to 2012
Stratus Grey/Stripes	2010 (XKR75/175 only)
Rhodium Silver	From 2011 to 2012
Cashmere Gold	From 2010 (XK only)
Crystal Blue	From 2011
Caviar Brown	From 2010 (XK only)
Black Amethyst	From 2011
British Racing Green	From 2013 new shade (XKR-S/XK66/Signature/Dynamic R only)
Italian Racing Red	From 2011 (XKR-S/Dynamic R only)
French Racing Blue	From 2011 (XKR-S only)

Speed and Dynamic Pack colour options
Polaris White, British Racing Green (new shade), Ultimate Black, Liquid Silver, Stratus Grey, Satelite Grey, Rhodium Silver, Spectrum Blue, Kyanite blue, Salsa Red, Italian Racing Red.

Black and Black Dynamic Pack colour options
Polaris white, Ultimate Black, Stratus Grey, Satelite Grey, Rhodium Silver, Salsa Red, Italian Racing Red.

Hood colours (convertibles)	Details
Beige	
Dark Beige	To 2008
Blue	
Black	
Dark Grey	From 2008
Dark Brown	From 2008 Portfolio only (2010 including XKR)
Burgandy	From 2008 Portfolio only (2010 including XKR)
Dark Green	From 2008 Portfolio only (2010 including XKR)

Leather seat colours	Details
Caramel	
Ivory	
Warm Charcoal	
London Tan	From 2011
Warm Charcoal and Red	From 2011 (XKR only)
Truffle Scarfitto Grain	Special Edition only
Navy Scarfitto Grain	Special Edition only
Truffle Soft Grain	Special Edition only
Red	From 2011
Oyster	From 2012 (Portfolio only)
Warm Charcoal/London Tan	From 2012 (Portfolio/XKR only)
Warm Charcoal/Ivory	2014 (Dynamic R only)
Navy Soft Grain	Special Edition only

Trim colours	Details
Ivory	
Caramel	
Slate Blue	
Warm Charcoal	
London Tan	From 2011 (XKR only)
Red	From 2011 (XKR only)
Truffle	2012 (SE only)
Navy	2012 (SE only)
Oyster	From 2009 (Portfolio only)

Contrast stitching	Details
Ivory	
Charcoal	
Slate Blue	
London Tan	From 2011
Caramel	From 2011
Red	From 2011 (XKR/XKR-S only)
Cranberry	From 2009 (XKR only)
Carbon/Ivory	From 2012 (XKR-S only)
Reims Blue	XKR-S only

Veneers	Details
Burr Walnut	
Poplar	To 2008
Aluminium	From 2006
Weave Aluminium	To 2009 (XKR only)
Piano Black	From 2010 (Portfolio/XKR/XKR75/175 only, all cars from 2012)
Satin American Walnut	From 2008 to 2013
Rich Oak	From 2009 to 2011
Knurled Aluminium	From 2006 to 2011
Dark Mesh Aluminium	From 2009 to 2011 (XKR only)
Dark Oak	From 2009 to 2011 (XKR only)
Figured Ebony	From 2009 to 2010 (Portfolio) 2014 (Signature/Dynamic R)

Veneers	Details
Satin Rosewood	From 2011 to 2012
Satin Elm	From 2011 to 2012
Dark Linear Aluminium	From 2011 to 2012 (XKR-S only)
Shadow Walnut	Special Edition only
Dark Figured Aluminium	2012 (SE only)
Bright Knurled Aluminium	From 2001 to 2012
Gloss Rich Oak	From 2012 to 2013
Gloss Dark Oak	2012 (XKR only)
Gloss Figured Ebony	From 2012 (Portfolio) 2013 to 2014 (Signature/Dynamic R)

Prices and production volumes

NB * = Figures quoted are up to 2012. No individual figures available for remaining years, but final production figures for all XK (X-150s) was 56,415.

Model	Price (£)	2006	2007	2008	2009	2010	2011	2012	2013	2014	Total produced
XK coupé 3.5		■	■	■	–	–	–	–	–	–	630
XK convertible 3.5		■	■	■	–	–	–	–	–	–	644
XK coupé 4.2	59,232	■	■	■	–	–	–	–	–	–	9434
XK convertible 4.2	65,232	■	■	■	–	–	–	–	–	–	10,406
XKR coupé 4.2	66,732	–	■	■	–	–	–	–	–	–	6310
XKR convertible 4.2	72,732	–	■	■	–	–	–	–	–	–	5265
XKR Portfolio coupé 4.2	75,597	–	■	■	■	■	–	–	–	–	
XKR Portfolio con 42	78,232	–	–	■	■	–	–	–	–	–	
XKR-S coupé 4.2	79,995	–	–	■	■	–	–	–	–	–	
XK60 coupé 4.2	60,995	–	–	■	■	–	–	–	–	–	
XK60 convertible 4.2	66,995	–	–	■	■	–	–	–	–	–	
XK coupé 5.0	–	–	–	–	■	■	■	■	■	–	3584*
XK convertible 5.0	–	–	–	–	■	■	■	■	■	–	6792*
XKR 75/175 coupé	–	–	–	–	–	■	–	–	–	–	4412*
XKR-S coupé 5.0	97,000	–	–	–	–	–	–	■	■	■	
XKR-S convertible 5.0	–	–	–	–	–	–	–	■	■	■	7072*
Artisan SE coupé	77,350	–	–	–	–	–	–	■	–	–	
Artisan SE con	82,500	–	–	–	–	–	–	■	–	–	
XKR-S GT	135,000	–	–	–	–	–	–	–	■	■	
XK66 coupé	99,380 e	–	–	–	–	–	–	–	–	■	
XK66 convertible	107,580 e	–	–	–	–	–	–	–	–	■	
XK Signature coupé	54,950	–	–	–	–	–	–	–	–	■	
XK Signature con	–	–	–	–	–	–	–	–	–	■	
Dynamic R coupé	69,950	–	–	–	–	–	–	–	–	■	
Dynamic R con	–	–	–	–	–	–	–	–	–	■	

XF saloons and sportbrake
2007 to 2015/6

Background

The Jaguar XF (an entirely new production model identification for the company) was announced in 2007 as a direct replacement for the outgoing S-type model, which had been in production since 1999. Although initially carrying much of the S-type's architecture, including engines/transmissions, the suspension was a direct development of that used in the New XK sports cars. Although built of steel, use was made of new technology metals like high carbon, dual-phase hot-formed boron, and bake-hardened steels. New technology also allowed the use of slimmer A and B posts, not only for improved safety, but also for better visibility, and the XF incorporated the pedestrian contact system, first used on the New XK sports car.

The most striking aspects of the XF came with an entirely new body style, interior, and the sophisticated systems in the new model. Available in just one body type, a four-door saloon, but with a coupé style to the rear of the roof area, the general styling of the car owed nothing to previous Jaguar models, and provided the stimulus for all future Jaguar models designed in-house.

Introduced with the previous 2.7-litre diesel, 3.0-litre and 4.2-litre petrol engines, there was also a supercharged version of the 4.2-litre unit. The XF became the first Jaguar saloon to offer the new JaguarDrive gear-change system, as well as paddle controls on the steering wheel. With sophisticated on-board equipment levels and state-of-the-art safety aspects, the XF became an immediate class leader and success for the company.

At the beginning of 2009 a new model was announced: the XF Diesel S. The main change came in the engine, with the very latest AJ-V6D Gen III 3.0-litre unit replacing the old 2.7-litre version. Providing 275bhp with a massive 600Nm of torque punch, acceleration times and top speed were much improved, as was fuel consumption – 12% better than the previous diesel model, which this car replaced. It was also available as a more luxurious Portfolio version.

Early in 2009, for the 2010 model year, more changes took place in the XF range. Jaguar announced their new 5.0-litre AJ-V8 Gen III petrol engines (both normally aspirated and supercharged) for these cars at the same time as the New XKs, effectively replacing the old 4.2-litre V8 and 3.0-litre V6 petrol engines. Along with many visual changes, both inside and out, the XF enjoyed improvements in economy, emissions, as well as performance. Luxury Portfolio models were also added to the range.

In 2012, Jaguar equipped the XF with their 2.2-litre diesel engine in two forms: standard and

'S.' These and other XFs later adopted a new stop-start system to aid fuel economy and emissions.

Also in that year, an entirely new variant was added to the XF range: the Sportbrake (or estate car, as these vehicles are more commonly known). Only the second production estate car produced by Jaguar, although late in coming, the XF Sportbrake was the direct replacement for the previous X-type equivalent.

The XF became the most popular car ever made by Jaguar in its lifetime, finally going out of production in 2015 to be replaced by the New XF (see later chapter). It proved the success of the new design approach moving away from Jaguar's traditional styling.

Model range and development

Although of the standard three-box, four-door saloon principle, the XF provided Jaguar with a new 'house-style' with a near-coupé approach to roof design and a striking new frontal and rear aspect. With a severe sloping front end and a high rear section, this gave excellent aerodynamics with a drag coefficient of 0.29 resulting in excellent fuel economy, low wind noise levels, and high stability at speed. The high rear end also meant that the XF, for the first time in many years, provided better luggage accommodation than most of its rivals.

Models available at launch

XF Luxury 2.7-litre diesel
XF Luxury 3.0-litre petrol
XF Premium Luxury 2.7-litre diesel
XF Premium Luxury 3.0-litre petrol
XF Premium Luxury 4.2-litre petrol
SV8 4.2-litre supercharged petrol

The XF was the first Jaguar to feature the entirely new JaguarDrive system operated from a single aluminium control in the centre console, which rises when the ignition is switched on, and with a simple twist selects the gear required. The system offers different modes that interact with the engine and gearbox to change the characteristics of engine, transmission shifts, and brake interventions, depending on driving conditions and circumstances. The one gearbox fitted to the XF is the ZF six-speed with sequential change.

Technically the XF is very advanced, and standard equipment levels include emergency brake assist, electronic brakeforce distribution, anti-lock braking, traction control, dynamic stability control, cornering brake control, and engine drag torque control.

Initially available with a wide choice of 17in, 18in, 19in and 20in alloy wheels, the XF was the

The striking frontal aspect of the XF moves the company away from previous practice. Mesh grille with new growler badge, single headlights, and large under-valance air intakes.

The high back end of the XF with unique lighting, enlarged 'signature' chromed finisher and unusually styled exhaust tailpipes.

The XFR with revised, more pronounced frontal treatment incorporating chrome-finished air vents.

first car of its class to be available with the larger 20in alloys. Externally the XF was also the first Jaguar saloon to be fitted with the 'signature' front wing vents, and it saw the reintroduction of a prominent leaper mascot, although this time on the boot lid instead of the bonnet!

Internally the cars are very well appointed with a high specification regardless of model. Retaining many of the traditional features expected of a Jaguar, these have been combined with contemporary looks and feel, like the mix of wood veneer with alloy finish for example.

The range remained unchanged until the end of 2008 when a new model was announced, the XF diesel S. Effectively replacing the previous 2.7-litre diesel models, the big change came with the introduction of the new, more fuel-efficient 3.0-litre diesel engine. Providing a 10% reduction in emissions and performance of 0–60mph in under 6sec, a key feature of the new engine is the parallel sequential turbocharger system, the first of its type to be fitted to the V-formation engine. For most everyday driving a variable geometry primary turbocharger does all the work, while a smaller, fixed-geometry secondary turbo is brought on line within 30 milliseconds, boosting the engine output when necessary.

The diesel S was distinguishable from other models by the standard-fit 19in wheel, a boot spoiler and 'S' badging.

The range was not altered again until early in 2009 when Jaguar announced their revised XF range for the 2010 model year. The biggest change came in the range of engines available. Out went the 4.2-litre engine. The 3.0-litre diesel, first seen a year earlier, was retained as an 'S' model and a more standard model. To replace the 4.2-litre units, a new highly efficient 5.0-litre engine became the option in normally-aspirated or supercharged form. The model range included a choice of Luxury, Premium Luxury, Portfolio, and XFR options.

After the introduction of the new engines two 'packs' became available at extra cost. Firstly there was the Black pack, which, as the name implies, offered black finishes in various forms, giving cars an individual distinctive and edgy look. The second was an Aerodynamic pack, which offered a re-profiled front bumper, grilles and side sills.

For 2012 Jaguar added a smaller 2.2-litre diesel engine to the range, available in either standard form or as an S model with improved performance. There was also an SE model offering an improved trim package, which included items such as standard satnav. The 2.2-litre model also incorporate a stop–start facility to aid fuel economy. With the announcement of the XF Sportbrake model in 2012, this became available in all variants of the car eventually.

At the Los Angeles International Automobile Show in November 2012 Jaguar announced their new XF model, the XFR-S, at the time advertised as the most powerful Jaguar saloon the company has ever built.

The XFR-S incorporated engineering features from both the XKR-S and the all-new F-TYPE two-seater sports car to create the most driver-focused, agile and responsive iteration of Jaguar's award-winning XF saloon range. Its 5.0-litre supercharged V8 petrol engine boasted 550PS and 680Nm – up 40PS and 55Nm respectively over the XFR. Fitted with an 8-speed transmission incorporating Jaguar's 'Quickshift' technology (developed for the F-TYPE), the car could accelerate from 0 to 60mph in 4.4 seconds and on to an electronically limited top speed of 186mph (300km/h).

Airflow had been carefully managed resulting in some body changes which also created a distinctive appearance and better aerodynamics reducing overall lift by 68%.

The XFR-S utilised specially developed Pirelli tyres, had extensive suspension revisions, a recalibrated active electronic differential and Dynamic Stability Control settings, all helping to maximize the potential of the car in performance terms.

An XFR-S Sportbrake joined the saloon early in 2014 with all the characteristics of the saloon version although the aerodynamics of the Sportbrake were improved with a spoiler mounted on the top of the rear hatch to many the airflow better.

For 2014 Jaguar enhanced the trim packages for the range and introduced another derivative, the R-Sport Black, only available

The diesel S model when launched, equipped here with 20in Senta alloy wheels.

with the 2.2-litre diesel engine. This provided an additional £8770 worth of value over a standard R-Sport model.

For the existing models Jaguar improved the standard equipment with such items as the Winter Comfort and Parking Packs. The higher specification models also received Blind Spot Monitoring and upgraded alloy wheels.

Over the years the range had expanded to cover Sport, Sport LE, SE, SE Business, Luxury, Premium Luxury and Portfolio, nearly all in both saloon and Sportbrake models. For 2014 the range was streamlined discontinuing the SE, SE Business and Premium Luxury trim variants plus the 3.0-litre V6 petrol and 3.0-litre diesel engine cars, in readiness for production ceasing of all XFs to make way for the New XF (see later chapter) in 2015.

Although the saloons were replaced by the New XF in 2015, the Sportbrake continued in production for slightly longer, unitil it too was eventually replaced by the facelifted desing (see later chapter).

Exterior identification points

General points applicable to all XF models

Front view
- Curvaceous frontal aspect unique to this model.
- Bold radiator grille with chromed surround incorporating bright mesh centre with Jaguar growler badge.
- One-piece light clusters containing a single headlight, foglight, and side/indicator lenses. Bi-Xenon lighting for Luxury Premium and SV8; halogen all other models.
- Full-width bumper/under-valance incorporating central mesh area and, either side-air intakes with chromed splitter bars.
- One-piece forward-hinged bonnet with pronounced power-bulge in centre, sloping down to meet the light units and grille.
- One-piece bonded windscreen with twin wipers.

Rear view
- Much taller rear end compared to other Jaguar models, with severe sloping coupé-style roof section and wide haunches.
- One-piece, severely raked, bonded rear screen.
- Rear-hinged boot panel with reflector sections of the rear lights, illuminated number plate area, and with a Jaguar chromed leaper emblem centrally mounted.
- Chromed full-width 'signature' finisher 'Jaguar' legend.

Entirely new dash layout treatment with a contemporary mix of veneer and alloy. Unique to the XF are the air-conditioning vents that open automatically when the engine is started, and the touch-sensitive panel to open the glove box.

JaguarDrive control for gear changes, the substantial alloy knob rises when the engine is started. Also note, just ahead of this, the black 'starter button'. This interior is equipped with the rich oak veneer.

Unique phosphor-blue lighting is used in several areas of the XF, including the door panels.

XFR interior in dark oak veneer. Note the different seat style and steering wheel from other models.

- Rear bumper/valance area wraps around to form part of rear wings area, with cut-out areas for new-style square exhaust tail trims in chrome.
- Rear-light clusters wrapping around the rear wings incorporating the latest LED technology.
- Chromed 'XF' and litre-badging, each side of the boot panel.

Side view
- Coupé style roof line mated to conventional four-door arrangement forming a sloping forward wedge design.
- Pronounced styling line starting near the base of the front wing, following through the door areas, shallowing out near the rear wheelarch.
- Black window frames with one-piece chrome edging incorporated into limousine-style door frames.
- Body-coloured door mirrors encompassing indicator repeater lights.
- Front wing-mounted 'signature' vents.
- Concealed fuel filler cap integrated into the rear nearside wing, with flush cover.
- 17in Libra alloy wheels, standard fit on Luxury models.
- 18in Cygnus alloy wheels, standard fit on Premium Luxury models.
- 20in Volans alloy wheels, standard fit on SV8 model.

Diesel S specifics
- 'S' badging at rear.
- Boot spoiler.
- 19in Artura alloy wheels.

2010 model year specifics
XFR

Front view
- More pronounced bumper/under-valance incorporating a larger central mesh grille area painted black.
- Chrome surround side air ducts and lip to under-panel area.
- Painted louvres to the bonnet area like those used on the XK sports car.

Rear view
- Special enlarged aerodynamic spoiler.
- 'R' badging.
- Revised style to rear bumper/under-valance area, all now in body paint colour.
- Four exhaust pipes of revised design.

Side view
- Sill extensions.
- Aerodynamic door mirror design incorporating LED side repeaters.
- 20in alloy wheels with 'Jaguar Supercharged' wording within centre caps.

The original style of side vent in the front wings of XF models until 2011.

The later style side vent now featuring on all XF models.

The post-2011 slimmer headlight unit, incorporating daytime running LEDs.

The standard, now known as Luxury XF, with normal sills. Note the differences in the frontal view – particularly the side vents – between this and the other models.

The Diesel S model with revised frontal treatment.

- Silver-grey brake callipers with 'R' insignia.

Black pack specifics
Front view
- Gloss black grille.

Side view
- 20in Draco alloy wheels with diamond-turned rims.
- Gloss black window surrounds.

Aerodynamic pack specifics
Front view
- Re-profiled front bumper bar with deeper inserts.
- Black mesh inserts to the grille and air intakes.

Side view
- XFR side skirt sills.

SE business model specifics
Front view
- Bi-Xenon headlights as standard.

Diesel S and sports model specifics
- As Aerodynamic pack.

Other 2010 model year specifics
3.0-litre V6 diesel
- Luxury trim – 18in Venus alloy wheels (19in Artura alloy wheels on S).
- Premium Luxury trim – 19in Carelia alloy wheels (20in Senta alloy wheels on S).
- Portfolio trim – 20in Selena alloy wheels (also on S).

5.0-litre V8 petrol
- Portfolio trim – 20in Selena alloy wheels.
- XFR trim – 20in Nevis alloy wheels.

NB: All 2010 models feature digital LED rear lighting.

2012/13-on model specifics
SE model specifics
Front view
- Bi-function Xenon headlights with LED daytime running lights.

Rear view
- Twin-pipe exhaust tailpipes.

Side view
- 17in Libra alloy wheels.
- Rear parking aid.
- Revised front wing side vents and chrome trim.

The XFR with more aggressive frontal treatment.

The rear styling of the non-S and XFR models.

XFR rear styling with the distinctive four exhaust tailpipes.

The XF SE model, again another variant on frontal styling.

Luxury model specifics
As SE except:
Side view
- 17in Ursa alloy wheels.

Premium Luxury specifics
As Luxury except:
Side view
- 18in Vela alloy wheels.

Portfolio model specifics
As Premium Luxury except:
Side view
- 19in Caravela alloy wheels.
- Premium paint finishes.

Diesel S model specifics
Front view
- Deeper front bumper area with larger air intakes, sculptured chromes, deeper lower grille and black mesh.

Rear view
- Boot spoiler.
- Low-set sculptured rear valance.
- 'S' badging on boot lid.

Side view
- Sill extensions.
- 19in Aquila alloy wheels (Luxury).
- 20in Draco alloy wheels (Premium Luxury).
- 29in Hydra alloy wheels (Portfolio).

XFR model specifics
As Luxury plus:
Front view
- Unique lower-bumper-level styling with larger chromed surround side air intakes and centre under-grille with black mesh finish.
- 'F' Badging to upper grille.
- Bonnet louvres.

Rear view
- Pronounced rear spoiler.
- Quad exhaust tailpipes.
- Low-set R rear valance.

Side view
- 20in Nevis alloy wheels with R badging to centre caps.

XFR-S model specifics
- *Front view*
- Deeper front bumper incorporating large lower central and side air intakes, framed in carbon fibre.
- Carbon fibre front splitter at the lower edge of bumper.
- Gloss black trim, including grille mesh.

XF models equipped with the Black pack, including wheels.

Gloss black window frames for the Sport and Black pack models.

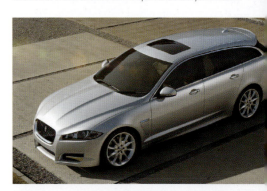

XF Sportbrake model, only available with the smaller engines.

The three-quarter rear view of the Sportbrake showing the revisions to the rear-end styling.

Rear view
- Extended rear bumper incorporating a central carbon fibre diffuser deeper than the XFR.
- Two options of bootlid mounted spoiler, a large version with carbon fibre aerofoil centre section.
- Gloss black trim.

Side view
- Extended side sills.
- Aeroblade mouldings behind the front wheels.
- Deeper side mouldings behind the rear wheels.
- Varuna alloy wheels with ceramic polished finish.
- Gloss black trim

Interior identification points

General points applicable to XF models up to 2010 model year
- Full-width dashboard area with instrument binnacle (containing speedometer, rev counter, and auxiliary gauges/read-outs) directly in front of the driver.
- Leather steering wheel with three spokes finished in alloy, containing controls for cruise control, telephone operation, and audio controls. Centre boss leather area with Jaguar growler badge. Paddle gearshift controls behind steering wheel.
- Centre dash section in alloy finish with air-conditioning vents flanking centre screen area for onboard controls/satnav, etc.
- Passenger dash area in matching alloy finish and containing concealed airbag area and air-conditioning outlet.
- Extensive centre console area featuring switchgear, ashtray, cup-holder, and JaguarDriver control.
- Wood-veneer finish to centre console area and along the edge of the dash area, full width.
- Soft-finish door trim areas incorporating door pulls, chromed door handles, speaker grilles, and switch packs for windows/mirrors. Wood-veneer inset panels and phosphor-blue subdued lighting.
- All seats trimmed in leather with horizontal and vertical panel stitching.
- Each front seat contains electrically adjustable head restraints and full seat electric controls from side of seats.

XFR specifics
- Salsa and Kyanite Blue exterior paint finishes unique to this model.
- Dark oak veneer.

The last and most powerful of the original styled of XF, the XFR-S, here in Italian Racing Red.

Revised frontal treatment for the XFR-S with the polished Varuna alloy wheels.

Unique badging front and rear for XFR-S models.

XFR-S interior with contrast stitching and carbon effect upholstery bolsters.

- Embossed 'R' logos in seats.
- Rear of front seat map pockets.
- Dark mesh alloy dash with 'R' logo.
- Instruments with red pointer dials.

Portfolio specifics
- Vented, heated, and cooled seating.
- Rear of front seat map pockets.
- Suedecloth premium headlining.
- Contrast stitching to upper door trims and instrument surround.
- Premium carpet mats with contrast piped edges and embroidered Jaguar legend.

2012/13-on model specifics
SE model specifics
- Suedecloth seating with bond-grain leather seat facings.
- Four-way electric front seat adjustment.
- Touch-screen visual rear parking display.
- Phospher-blue halo illumination and interior mood lighting.
- Bond-grain stitched instrument panel.
- Jaguar 400watt sound system.

Luxury model specifics
As SE except:
- Six-way electric front seat adjustment.
- Satnav DVD as standard.

Premium Luxury model specifics
As Luxury except:
10-/6-way electric front seat adjustment.
- Heated front seats.
- Jaguar 600watt sound system with 11 speakers.
- Front and rear carpet mat set.

Portfolio model specifics
As Premium Luxury except:
- 16-/12-way electric front seat adjustment.
- Heated and cooled front seating.
- Contrast colour stitching to instrument panel.
- Bowers & Wilkins 1,200watt sound system with 17 speakers.
- Suedecloth headlining.

Diesel S model specifics
As above by trim standard.

XFR model specifics
Trim levels as Portfolio except:
- Special sports seating.
- 18-way electric front seat adjustment.

XFR-S model specifics
- Carbon effect leather Warm Charcoal seats and door trims.
- Seats embossed with R-S logo with contrast micro-piping and stitching.
- Dark aluminium dash trim with R-S logo.

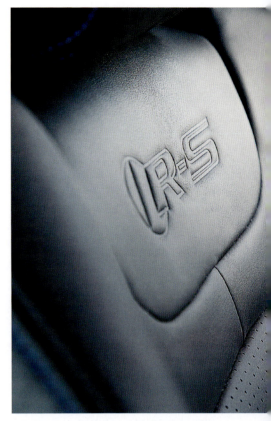

R-S embossing to the sports seating in the XFR-S model.

The XFR-S Sportbrake in French Racing Blues, showing the revised rear end bumper and exhaust treatment."

Wherever possible standard fitment to particular models is shown, but most wheels were available as an optional fit to other cars, dependent on suspension/brake specification.

1: 17in Libra, standard on Luxury models to 2010 therefore standard on SE/SE Business models.

2: 17in Ursa, standard on Luxury/Premium Luxury/Portfolio models from 2011.

3: 17in Ursa gloss anthracite grey finish, standard on R-Sport from 2011.

4: 18in Venus, standard on 3.0-litre Diesel Luxury to 2010.

5: 18in Cypnus, standard on Premium Luxury models to 2010.

6: 18in Vela, standard on Diesel Premium and Luxury models from 2011, then optioinal.

7: 18in Lyra, optional fit from 2011.

8: 18in Manra, option fit from 2012.

9: 19in Carelia, standard on Premium Luxury 3.0-litre Diesel to 2010.

10: 19in Auriga, optional fit to 2010.

11: 19in Artura, standard on Diesel S and Luxury 2009 to 2010.

12: 19in Caravela, standard on Diesel Portfolio model 2010 only, then optional.

13: 19in Aquila, standard on 3.0-litre Diesel S Luxury in 2010 to 2011.

14: 19in Aquila, satin anthracite grey finish, option from 2011.

15: 20in Volans, option fir to 2010.

16: 20in Selana, standard on Portfolio models to 2010.

17: 20in Nevis, standard on XFR models.

18: 20in Senta, standard on 3.0-litre Diesel S, Premium and Luxury, 2009 to 2010.

19: 20in Hydra, standard on 3.0-litre Diesel S and 5.0-litre Portfolio 2011.

20: 20in Draco, silver finish, standard on Diesel S Premium Luxury/Portfolio from 2012.

21: 20in Draco, dark finish, option fit Diesel S Premium Luxury/Portfolio from 2012.

22: 20in Kalimnos black finish, option fit R-Sport/Premium Luxury from 2012.

23: 20in Varuna gloss black finish, option fit XFR/XFR-S 2012 on.

24: 20in Varuna technical grey finish, option fit XFR/XFR-S 2012 on.

25: 20in Varuna dark polished finish, standard fit XFR-S.

Technical specifications

	2.2-litre diesel	2.2-litre diesel S
cc	2179	2179
Bore and stroke (mm)	85 x 96	85 x 96
Compression ratio	15.8:1	15.8:1
bhp	163	190
@ rpm	3500	3500
Torque (lb ft)	295	332
@ rpm	2000	2000
Fuelling	Fuel-injection	Fuel-injection
Transmission	8-speed auto sequential	8-speed auto sequential
Wheel size (in)	17, 18, 19, 20	17, 18, 19, 20
Suspension front	Ind unequal-length wishbones, coil springs	Ind unequal-length wishbones, coil springs
Suspension rear	Ind unequal-length wishbones, coil springs	Ind unequal-length wishbones, coil springs
Brakes	4-wheel performance ventilated discs	4-wheel performance ventilated discs
Performance		
0–60mph (sec)	9.8	8.0
Top speed (mph)	130	140
Average mpg	52.3	52.3
Dimensions		
Length (in)	195.3	195.3
Width (in)	73.8	73.8
Height (in)	57.5	57.5
Wheelbase (in)	114.5	114.5
Front track (in)	61.4	61.4
Rear track (in)	63.1	63.1
Weight (lb)	4012	4012

Optional extras

Chromed side 'signature' vents.
Boot spoiler.
Bright alloy-finished foot pedals.
Illuminated sill treadplates.
Luggage compartment finisher.
Rear screen connectivity system.
R-Performance Aerodynamic pack.
R-Performance interior trim.
Black- or bright-finish mesh grilles.
Square stainless steel exhaust trim pipes.
Bright-finish door mirror covers.
Brushed aluminium or chromed gear knobs.
Tailored over-carpet mats.
Tyre-pressure monitoring system.
Keyless entry.
Alternative veneer dash trims.
TV tuner.
DVD audio system.
B & W Premium hi-fi system.
Front park assist system with interior touch-screen information.
Soft-grain leather seat facings.
ACC cruise control.
Garage door opener.
Heated windscreen.
Adaptive cruise control.
Blind-spot mirror identification.
Adaptive front lighting.
Electrically operated sunroof.
Front and reverse park sensing aids.
Premium paints.
Auto dimming exterior mirrors.
Heated/cooled front seating.
Heated steering wheel.
Front and rear carpet mat set.
Suedecloth headlining.
Bright-metal foot pedals.
Two-tone colour seating.

Technical specifications *cont...*

	2.7-litre diesel	3.0-litre petrol
cc	2720	2967
Bore and stroke (mm)	81 x 88	89 x 79.5
Compression ratio	17:1	10.5:1
bhp	207	238
@ rpm	4000	6800
Torque (lb ft)	320	216
@ rpm	1900	4100
Fuelling	Fuel-injection	Fuel-injection
Transmission	ZF 6-speed auto sequential	ZF 6-speed auto sequential
Wheel size (in)	17, 18, 19, 20	17, 18, 19, 20
Suspension front	Ind double wishbones, alloy control arms, anti-dive, coil springs	Ind double wishbones, alloy control arms, anti-dive, coil springs
Suspension rear	Ind double wishbones, alloy control arms, co-axial coil springs (CATS)	Ind double wishbones, alloy control arms, co-axial coil springs (CATS)
Brakes	4-wheel disc, all ventilated	4-wheel disc, all ventilated
Performance		
0–60mph (sec)	7.7	7.9
Top speed (mph)	143	148
Average mpg	37.6	26.8
Dimensions		
Length (in)	195	195
Width (in)	74	74
Height (in)	57.5	57.5
Wheelbase (in)	114.5	114.5
Front track (in)	61	61
Rear track (in)	63	63
Weight (lb)	3904	3702

Optional extras *cont*

Ivory leather seating.
18in spare wheel.
Electric rear window sun blind.
Ski-hatch and fold-down rear seating.
Interactive voice control system.
Upgraded sound systems.
Black pack.
Aerodynamic pack.
Carbon fibre side power vents.
Carbon fibre mirror covers.
Carbon fibre bonnet louvers.
Polished tailpipe finishers.
Sport pedal covers.
Illuminated sill treadplates.
iPad holder.
Headrest mounted coat hanger.
Leather finished top to gear selector.
Aluminium gear shift paddles.
Splash guards.
Snow sock winder traction aid.
Black growler wheel nuts.
Stylised valve caps.
Union Jack wheel centres.

	3.0-litre diesel	3.0-litre diesel S
cc	2993	2993
Bore and stroke (mm)	84 x 90	84 x 90
Compression ratio	16:1	16:1
bhp	240	275
@ rpm	4000	4000
Torque (lb ft)	369	443
@ rpm	2000	2000
Fuelling	Fuel-injection	Fuel-injection
Transmission	ZF 6-speed auto sequential	6-speed auto sequential
Wheel size (in)	8, 19, 20	17, 18, 19, 20
Suspension front	Ind double wishbones, alloy control arms, anti-dive, coil springs	Ind unequal-length wishbones, coil springs
Suspension rear	Ind double wishbones, alloy control arms co-axial coil springs (CATS)	Ind unequal-length wishbones, coil springs
Brakes	4-wheel perf. ventilated discs	4-wheel disc, all ventilated
Performance		
0-60mph (sec)	6.7	5.9
Top speed (mph)	149	155 (limited)
Average mpg	42	44.8
Dimensions		
Length (in)	195	195.3
Width (in)	74	73.8
Height (in)	57.5	57.5
Wheelbase (in)	114.5	114.5
Front track (in)	61	61.4
Rear track (in)	63	63.1
Weight (lb)	4012	4012

Technical specifications *cont ...*

	3.0-litre V6 petrol (2013) engine	4.2-litre petrol
cc	2995	4196
Bore and stroke (mm)	84.5 x 89	86 x 90
Compression ratio	10.5:1	11:1
bhp	340	298
@ rpm	6500	6000
Torque (lb ft)	332	303
@ rpm	3500–5000	4100
Fuelling	Fuel-injection	Fuel-injection
Transmission	8-speed auto seq. (4-wheel drive)	6-speed auto sequential
Wheel size (in)	17, 18, 19, 20	19, 20
Suspension front	Ind unequal-length wishbones, coil springs	Ind unequal-length wishbones, coil springs
Suspension rear	Ind unequal-length wishbones, coil springs	Ind unequal-length wishbones, coil springs
Brakes	4-wheel performance ventilated discs	4-wheel disc, all ventilated
Performance		
0–60mph (sec)	Not stated	6.2
Top speed (mph)	Not stated	155
Average mpg	Not stated	25
Dimensions		
Length (in)	195.3	195
Width (in)	73.8	74
Height (in)	57.5	57.5
Wheelbase (in)	114.5	114.5
Front track (in)	61.4	61
Rear track (in)	63.1	63
Weight (lb)	Not stated	3856

Prices and production years

	Price new (£)	2007	2008	2009	2010
2.2-litre diesel Sportbrake	31,940	–	–	–	–
2.2-litre diesel S Sportbrake	36,440	–	–	–	–
2.7-litre diesel	33,900	■	■	■	–
3.0-litre petrol	33,900	■	■	■	■
3.0-litre diesel	33,900	–	–	■	■
3.0-litre diesel S	37,500	–	–	■	■
3.0-litre diesel SE	29,955	–	–	–	–
3.0-litre diesel Sportbrake	38,355	–	–	–	–
3.0-litre diesel S Sportbrake	44,355	–	–	–	–
3.0-litre petrol Sportbrake	Not stated	–	–	–	–
4.2-litre petrol	45,500	■	■	■	–
4.2-litre SV8	54,900	■	■	■	–
5.0-litre petrol	49,900	–	–	■	■
5.0-litre XFR	59,000	–	–	■	■
5.0-litre XFR-S	79,995	–	–	–	–
Total production figures		1430	43,972	27,236	34,396

	4.2-litre supercharged	5.0-litre
cc	4196	5000
Bore and stroke (mm)	86 x 90	92.5 x 93
Compression ratio	9:1	11.5:1
bhp	416	385
@ rpm	6250	6500
Torque (lb ft)	413	380
@ rpm	4000	3500
Fuelling	Fuel-injection	Fuel-injection
Transmission	6-speed auto sequential	6-speed auto sequential
Wheel size (in)	19, 20	19, 20
Suspension front	Ind unequal-length wishbones, coil springs	Ind unequal-length wishbones, coil springs
Suspension rear	Ind unequal-length wishbones, coil springs	Ind unequal-length wishbones, coil springs
Brakes	4-wheel disc, all ventilated	4-wheel disc, all ventilated
Performance		
0–60mph (sec)	5.1	5.5
Top speed (mph)	155	155
Average mpg	22	25
Dimensions		
Length (in)	189	189
Width (in)	74	75
Height (in)	52	52
Wheelbase (in)	108	108
Front track (in)	61	61
Rear track (in)	61	63
Weight (lb)	4061	3924

	2011	2012	2013	2014	2015
2.2-litre diesel Sportbrake	–	–		■	■
2.2-litre diesel S Sportbrake	–	–	■	■	■
2.7-litre diesel	–	–	–	–	–
3.0-litre petrol	■	■	■	–	–
3.0-litre diesel	■	■	■	–	–
3.0-litre diesel S	■	■	■	–	–
3.0-litre diesel SE	■	■	■	–	–
3.0-litre diesel Sportbrake	–	–	■	–	–
3.0-litre diesel S Sportbrake	–	–	■	–	–
3.0-litre petrol Sportbrake	–	–	■	–	–
4.2-litre petrol	–	–	–	–	–
4.2-litre SV8	–	–	–	–	–
5.0-litre petrol	■	■	■	■	■
5.0-litre XFR	■	■	■	■	■
5.0-litre XFR-S	–	–	–	■	■
Total production figures	32,910	36,840	47,341	45,119	38,912*

NB – Total production figures for all models. The 2015 figure * does include some of the New XF production (see later chapter).

Technical specifications *cont ...*

	5.0-litre supercharged	5.0-litre supercharged (XKR-S model)
cc	5000	5000
Bore and stroke (mm)	92.5 x 93	92.5 x 93
Compression ratio	9.5:1	9.5 to 1
bhp	510	550
@ rpm	6500	6500
Torque (lb ft)	461	502
@ rpm	5500	2500–5500
Fuelling	Fuel-injection	Fuel-injection
Transmission	6-speed auto sequential	8-speed sequential
Wheel size (in)	19, 20	20
Suspension front	Ind unequal-length wishbones, coil springs	Ind unequal-length wishbones, coil springs
Suspension rear	Ind unequal-length wishbones, coil springs	Ind unequal-length wishbones, coil springs
Brakes	4-wheel disc, all ventilated	Carbon fibre 4-wheel disc
Performance		
0–60mph (sec)	4.7	4.4
Top speed (mph)	155	186
Average mpg	24	24.4
Dimensions		
Length (in)	189	189
Width (in)	75	75
Height (in)	52	52
Wheelbase (in)	108	108
Front track (in)	61	61
Rear track (in)	63	63
Weight (lb)	4369	4380

Colour schemes

Exterior	Details
Porcelain	To 2011
Botanical Green	To 2010
Emerald Fire	To 2010
Vapour Grey	To 2012
Frost Blue	To 2011
Azure Blue	Until mid-2009
Indigo	To 2012)
Midnight	To 2009
Ultimate Black	To end
Ebony	To end
Pearl Grey	To 2011
Lunar Grey	To end
Liquid Silver	To 2011
Winter Gold	To 2011

Seat trim/ Upper fascia	Details	Seat/ Trim style
Spice	To 2011	Bond-grain leather
Oyster	To 2011	Soft-grain leather
Truffle	To 2011	R-Performance
Champagne	To 2011	
Navy	To 2011	
Warm Charcoal		
Warm Charcoal (carbon soft grain)	From 2013 (XFR-S only)	
Barley		
Dove		
Ivory		
London Tan	From 2010	
Red Zone	From 2010	

Exterior	Details
Radiance Red	To 2009
Spectrum Blue	To 2011
Claret	To 2012
Kyanite Blue	2009 to 2012
Salsa Red	2009 to 2011
Blue Prism	To 2011
Polaris White	2011 to end
Stratus Grey	2011 to end
Rhodium Silver	2011 to end
Cashmere	2011 to 2013
Crystal Blue	2011 to 2013
Caviar	2011 to end
Black Amethyst	2012 to end
British Racing Green	2011 to end
Italian Racing Red	2011 to end
Carnelian Red	2012
Satellite Grey	From 2012 to 2013
French Racing Blue	From 2013 to end
Ultra Blue	2014 to end
Glacier White	2014 to end
Quartzite	2014 to end
Odyssey Red	2014 to end

Contrast stitching	Details
Spice	To 2011
Oyster	To 2012
Truffle	
Navy	To 2011
Warm Charcoal	
Barley	
Ivory	
London Tan	From 2010
Red Zone	From 2010
Reims Blue	From 2013 (XFR/XFR-S only)
Red Micro Piping	From 2013 (XFR/XFR-S only)
Red Duo Tone	From 2014 (XFR/XFR-S only)

Veneers	Details	Headlinings
Satin Aluminium/Dark Oak	To 2009	Dove
Knurled Aluminium/Dark Oak	From 2009	Jet
Knurled Aluminium/Gloss Dark Oak	From 2013 (R-Sport only)	Canvas
Knurled Aluminium/Piano Black	From 2011	
Knurled Aluminium/Carbon Fibre	From 2012	
Knurled Aluminium/Satin Rosewood	From 2011	
Knurled Aluminium/Gloss Figured Ebony	From 2011	
Knurled Aluminium/Burr Walnut	From 2011	
Knurled Aluminium/Satin American Walnut	From 2011 (2013 on XFR only)	
Dark Mesh Aluminium/Gloss Dark Oak	From 2011	
Dark Mesh Aluminium/Piano Black	From 2011	
Dark Mesh Aluminium/Carbon Fibre	From 2011	
Dark Linear Aluminium/Piano Black	From 2012 (2014 on XFR-S only)	
Dark Linear Aluminium/Carbon Fibre	From 2012	

21 New XJ (X-351) saloons
2010 to 2019

Background

The Jaguar XJ flagship of the range continued with the advent of a car that had a totally different look to its predecessors. Announced in 2009, the new car, although a direct replacement for the previous XJ (X-350) models, was much more contemporary, and displayed no styling connections to earlier cars that shared the same name.

The most striking aspects of the body style incorporated some cues from the medium-sized XF model, and took things much further, with a more pronounced frontal aspect with larger grille, and a smoother shaping to the rear 'coupé' style roof panel. Key features included a panoramic glass roof, an integral part of the all-new XJ's design concept, enabling the car to have a lower, more streamlined roofline, while dramatically enhancing the feeling of light and space inside. The new bodyshell provides a drag coefficient of just 0.29, and was claimed to be 50% produced from recycled materials. For the first time in production of any XJ, the new car was available from the off in both standard and long wheelbase sizes, the latter providing an additional 125mm of legroom.

Constructed using Jaguar's aerospace-inspired aluminium body technology, the XJ was lighter than its rivals by at least 150kg. These technologies – developed into the XJ – significantly improved performance, handling and economy, while delivering increased strength, refinement and safety. Other features included air suspension, Adaptive Dynamics (continuously variable damping), Active Differential Control, and quick-ratio power steering.

Introduced with a range of three engines – 3.0-litre diesel, 5.0-litre normally aspirated, and 5.0-litre supercharged – all models incorporated the JaguarDrive gear-change system with steering wheel mounted paddle controls and sophisticated braking, suspension and steering equipment, much of which follows the practice of the XF and XK models.

The cabin, although unmistakably Jaguar, was of an entirely new design, blending elegance with contemporary design features. Three specification levels were offered at launch – Luxury, Premium Luxury and Portfolio, plus the Supersports model, which was even better equipped, but only available with the most powerful engine.

As well as an entirely new interior design and layout, the very latest technology was incorporated, including a 'virtual' instrument display, split viewing TFT screen in the centre console so that front seat passenger and driver can view different images at the same time, interactive voice control system, DVD hard drive system, and laminated glass all round. The car came equipped with a range of active safety aids including: an Anti-lock Braking System (ABS), Dynamic Stability Control (DSC), Cornering Brake Control (CBC), Understeer Control, Electronic Brakeforce Distribution (EBD), Electronic Traction Control (ETC), Emergency Brake Assist (EBA), Engine Drag Torque Control and, for vehicles fitted with Adaptive Cruise Control (ACC), Electronic Brake Pre-fill, and, not least, the Pedestrian Contact Sensing system first seen on the XK sports car, with the automatically deployable bonnet to safeguard pedestrians from injury.

Jaguar received certification from the VCA (Vehicle Certification Agency) for a comprehensive 'cradle-to-grave' study, which analysed the environmental impact of the New XJ, making Jaguar one of the few vehicle manufacturers to carry out such an assessment. Jaguar also received many other accolades for the New XJ, and after its launch it became the leading car in its sector for sales, and also benefitted from excellent reports in the US JD Power survey.

The new XJ advanced through numerous revisions, model renames and equipment levels, even in selected markets fitted with a 2.0-litre petrol or 2.2-litre diesel engine, and all-wheel-drive plus bespoke armoured vehicles produced by outside businesses. As worldwide sales of these larger luxury saloons fell, and with the demise of this car in 2019, it was the end of Jaguar XJ production.

Arguably the most luxurious interior for Jaguar yet with wrap-around wood veneer, and a strong emphasis on chrome and metal. Note the return to circular air vents and the Swiss-styled clock.

A complete departure in Jaguar styling with a much plainer rear end but with prominent 'leaper' emblem, the number plate now mounted below boot level and the 'claw-style' rear-light units.

Models available at launch:

XJ6	3.0-litre diesel	Luxury	short-wheelbase
			long-wheelbase
		Premium Luxury	short-wheelbase
			long-wheelbase
		Portfolio	short-wheelbase
			long-wheelbase
XJ8	5.0-litre (normally-aspirated)	Premium Luxury	short-wheelbase
			long-wheelbase
		Portfolio	short-wheelbase
			long-wheelbase
XJ8	5.0-litre (supercharged)	Premium Luxury	short-wheelbase
			long-wheelbase
		Portfolio	short-wheelbase
			long-wheelbase
		Supersports	short-wheelbase
			long-wheelbase

Model range and development

The basic structure of the New XJ has remained unchanged since introduction, although various models have been introduced and discontinued. Along the way, Jaguar has used the car to produce the XJ75 Platinum Concept, a one-off customised model to celebrate the 75th anniversary of Jaguar, and a hybrid model prototype.

The contemporary fontal aspect of the XJ echoes the medium-sized XF but with a more forward facing and larger grille. Note the headlights, similar to those used on the XK sports car and the tall, swept-back windscreen.

In 2010, Jaguar announced the Sentinel: a long wheelbase 5.0-litre normally aspirated XJ, incorporating the latest in armour plating technology, constructed of high-strength steels with Kevlar backing. Built to special bespoke order, the cars are produced to individual customer requirements.

For the 2012 model year new Packs were introduced to enhance the specification, which could be pre-ordered by the customer when purchasing a new car.

The rear seat Comfort Pack provided an even more luxurious appeal to the XJ providing electrically adjustable reclining seats, foot rests, etc, for the long wheelbase models.

The Sport Pack included aerodynamic and trim finish changes to the exterior, and upgrades to the interior styling.

The Sport Pack could also be specified with the Speed Pack, just for the 5.0-litre petrol supercharged models, with recalibrated engine management system, reworked software for the virtual instrument display, and adjustment to the tyre monitoring system. The combined additions to the XJR Sport/Speed model made the XJR the fastest production saloon the company had ever built up to that time.

In 2012 the 'Ultimate' model was introduced. By the nature of its name the ultimately equipped long-wheelbase XJ came with a package of interior business-class luxuries, including a champagne cabinet. Available in all engine sizes, it was the best equipped and most expensive XJ up to that time.

Optional 'packs' were introduced to enhance the exterior and interior specification of particular models.

For the 2013 model year Jaguar announced additional engines for the XJ range. The 3.0-litre V6 supercharged petrol engine producing 340 PS (developed for the F-TYPE sports car) was fitted, benefitting from the same fuel and emissions-efficient 8-speed automatic transmission and stop/start system from the XF. All models benefitted from the standard fitment of a DAB digital tuner and a more powerful Meridian Premium audio system. A new Comfort Suspension Pack was also standardised across the range.

This prompted the introduction of an All Wheel Drive (AWD) version to the XJ range, but only for selected markets like North America, China, Russia and continental Europe. The AWD was only fitted on XJs equipped with the new high-performance 3.0-litre V6 petrol engine. Jaguar was also supplying very selective markets with XJs equipped with the 2.2-litre diesel engine, although this has never been a mainstream model in the XJ range.

Finally in 2013, the best-performing XJ was announced: the XJR575 550bhp, with bespoke interior and exterior trim. Fitted with the 5.0-litre

The 'moon roof' has tinted, reflective glass and opens outwards electrically to eliminate any loss of headroom. Note also the embossed Jaguar emblems in the headrests.

Portfolio interior with jet seating, ivory contrast piping and gloss rich oak veneer.

Side elevation of an XJ long-wheelbase model finished in Indigo with privacy glass and 20in Kasuga wheels. The side-on styling has remained constant throughout production to date.

supercharged engine with suspension, brakes and steering enhancements from the F-TYPE sports car, it also featured the latest 8-speed ZF gearbox and intelligent stop/start system to aid economy. Interior and exterior trim enhancements were also carried out to differentiate this model from the other cars in the XJ range.

Between 2015 and 2016 lots more happened with the XJ range. External styling was subtly altered, many changes took place with interior trim, and some Portfolio features became available on the lesser models. All engines were upgraded in performance and economy terms.

The 'Autobiography' model was announced as the top of the range model with the 5.0-litre supercharged engine, the XJR received the 575bhp version of that engine and a new R-Sport model with two 3.0-litre power units was equipped with various sporting features.

Final XJ production from the end of 2018 revolved around just the 3.0-litre diesel models in various forms. In readiness for the end of the line, a special edition XJ50 was announced commemorating 50 years of XJs. The last XJs left production in 2019 as the final big luxury Jaguar saloons.

Exterior identification points

General points applicable to all XJ models
Front view
- Curvaceous frontal aspect, pronounced mesh radiator grille with chrome surround incorporating the new-style Jaguar growler head.
- One-piece light clusters wrapping around to the sides of the car, incorporating Xenon swivelling headlights plus fog lights and side/indicator lenses.
- Full-width bumper/under-valance moulded into the body with mesh undergrille and chromed splitter bars to air intakes.
- One-piece forward-hinged bonnet with pronounced power-bulge in centre, sloping down to the front panel of the car.
- One-piece bonded windscreen with twin wipers.

Rear view
- Coupé-style 'moon roof' area sweeping down to sharply raked rear screen meeting the boot lid.
- D-post areas of roof covered in black finish giving the effect of a 'floating' roof.
- Tall rear end with plain one-piece boot lid with little adornment except for large chromed leaper in the centre and XJ insignia to the left-hand side.

The new style of insignia featured on XJs, although this can be omitted by special order.

Rear compartment area, in this case a long-wheelbase model, depicting Heritage Tan trim with contrast stitching and business tables fitted.

Virtual instrument panel that can be altered to suit driver requirements.

Example of different interior styles, in this case a Supersport model with Bordeaux trim, gloss rich oak veneer with linear laser inlay.

- Rear bumper/valance area (incorporating the rear registration plate and lighting) wraps around to form part of rear wings area incorporating cut-out areas for new-style square exhaust tail trims in chrome. Horizontal chrome finisher to this panel.
- Rear-light clusters flow vertically over the top of the rear wings, styled to look similar to a jaguar claw and using the latest LED technology.

Side view
- Coupé-style roof line with extremely raked front and rear screens for maximum effect.
- Pronounced styling line starting at the base of the front wing, following through the door areas and tapering out at the rear.
- Black window frames with one-piece chrome edging integrated into limousine-style door frames.
- Front door mirrors incorporating indicator repeater lights.
- Front wing-mounted horizontal 'signature' vents.
- Concealed fuel filler cap incorporated into the rear nearside wing with flush cover.
- A maximum choice of six alloy wheel designs, dependent on market.

Another interior style, ivory trim with satin zebrano veneer.

2010 model year specifics

Exterior points carry through the entire range except for:

Exterior view
Luxury models: 19in Aleutian alloy wheels.
Premium Luxury: 19in Toba alloy wheels and metallic paintwork.
Portfolio: 20in Kasuga alloy wheels, metallic paintwork and rear camera aid.
Supersports: 20in Metavia alloy wheels, metallic paintwork and rear camera aid.

Conventional glovebox treatment for XJs.

2011 model year specifics

XJ Luxury model
Front view
- Bi-function Xenon headlights with LED running lights and washer system.
- Heated windscreen with timer.

Rear view
- As earlier models.

Side view
- 19in Aleutian alloy wheels.
- Heated, power-folding, self-dimming door mirrors with puddle lighting.

Special Mauveine treatment for glovebox interior, only for Supersport model.

XJ Premium Luxury model
As Luxury except:

What Jaguar term as intaglio, centre dashboard top screen rail area, which can be bespoke to owner's requirements, including a personal signature.

An XJ fitted with a Sport Pack complete with Venom alloy wheels.

All-wheel drive XJ (for selected markets only).

The Supersports model.

The XJR showing its lower stance, sculptured sills and black trim finish.

Front view
- Front parking aids.

Rear view
- 'L' badging to boot lid (LWB model).

Side view
- Smart-key locking and starting operation.
- Premium paint finish.
- Privacy glass (LWB model).
- 19in Toba alloy wheels.

XJ Portfolio model
As Premium Luxury except:
Front view
- Adaptive front lighting with cornering lamps and intelligent high beam.

Rear view
- Reverse park camera with guidance.
- Tyre-pressure monitoring system.

Side view
- 20in Kasuga alloy wheels.

XJ Supersport model
As Portfolio model except:
Side view
- Superscript front wing vents.
- 20in Mataiva alloy wheels.

XJ Ultimate model
- Special order model to Portfolio and Supersport spec, only in LWB form. Indian model with 3.0-litre engine only.
- Celestial Black paintwork or Polaris White standard, any colour by special request.
- 20in Maroa wheels.
- Sculptured lower air intakes to match the grille.
- Polished oval stainless steel tailpipes.
- 'Utimate' badging to boot and side wing vents.
- The first car to feature the 3.0-litre V6 petrol supercharged engine.

2013 model year specifics

XJR
Front view
- R badging to grille.
- Deep front splitter bar.
- Sport Pack style black mesh grille with chrome surround.
- Front bumper enlarged air intakes in black mesh with chrome surrounds.
- Louvered bonnet.

Rear view
- Quad chrome finished exhaust tailpipes.
- Rear bumper/valance styling amended to suite tailpipes.
- Boot lid mounted lip spoiler.

Jaguar All the Cars

333

XJR rear view with quad exhaust pipes, revised bumper/valance, spoiler and badging.

2016 interior, in this case an XJR. Part of the upgrade was a new virtual dash layout incorporating major improvements in the supply of driver information.

XJR rear interior showing the embossed headrests. Note all XJs feature the panoramic roof.

The R-Sport model with black trim.

- R badging.

Side view
- Unique sculptured side sills.
- 20in Farallon alloy wheels.
- Pirelli PZero Corsa tyres are 265/35 and 295/30 front/rear.
- Red brake calipers.

XJR575
- Revised front splitter bar.
- Aerodynamic sill sections.
- Unique rear spoiler.
- 'R' bonnet louvres.

2016 model year specifics
All models
Front view
- Larger, more upright grille with deeper inset.
- Sculptured chrome blades in the air intakes, of a different shape.
- Full LED headlights with twin 'J-blade' daytime running lights.

Rear view
- LED rear light units featuring J-signature tail and position light graphic.
- Rear bumper shaping
- Rear bumper gloss black valance with slender chrome insert.
- Oval exhaust tailpipe finishers.
- 'Jaguar' chrome script added below leaper on boot lid at discretion.

Luxury models
Front view
- Chromed mesh grille.

Side view
- 19in Aleutian alloy wheels.
- Non-metallic exterior paint finish.

Premium Luxury models
Front view
- Chromed mesh grille.

Side view
- 19in Toba alloy wheels.

Portfolio models
Front view
- Chromed mesh grille.

Side view
- 20in Orona alloy wheels

R-Sport models
Front view
- Three piece front splitter.
- Gloss black finish to the grille mesh.
- R-Sport badging.

The 2016 model look of the XJ in Luxury, Premium Luxury and Portfolio forms. Note the revised frontal treatment compared to earlier models depicted and the engine size badging on the front wings below the air vent.

2016 Portfolio trim style, in this case with the Premium Rear Seat Pack fitted.

XJ Ultimate rear compartment, much of which is also part of the Premium Rear Seat Pack on other models.

Frontal lighting treatment on the earlier models and later cars with 'J' daytime illumination. The pre-2012 cars did not feature any daytime illumination lighting.

Rear view
- Rear spoiler.
- Gloss black finish rear valance.
- R-Sport badging.

Side view
- Sculptured side sills.
- Revised style power vents.
- Gloss black finish to window surrounds.
- 20in Matavia alloy wheels.
- Privacy glass.

Autobiography models
Side view
- Long wheelbase chassis.
- 20in Maroa alloy wheels.

XJR models
Side view
- 20in Farallon alloy wheels.
- Other identification points as earlier XJR models.

XJR575
- Semi-aniline leather.
- Wider range of veneers with contrast stitching.

XJ Ultimate
- Herringbone/Piano Black veneer.
- Dashboard clock with brushed alloy face and embossed lozenge detailing.
- Full leather interior including headliner.
- 'Ultimate' badging.
- Bespoke headrest embroidering.
- Tailored business-class rear compartment comprising:
  » Individual rear seating in aniline leather with winged headrests, hand-stitching, powered, heated, cooled and with massaging facility.
  » Full depth centre console (front to rear) with electrically controlled table.
  » Drinks cabinet with champagne flutes and blue ambient lighting.
  » Full entertainment package with Meridan surround sound hi-fi.

XJ50
The run-out commemorative model to high specification including:
- Soft quilted leather seats, Gloss Shadow Walnut with Piano Black trim, privacy glass, illuminated treadplates, upgraded sound system plus digital TV.

Interior identification points

General points applicable to all current XJ models:
- All-leather-wrapped instrument panel sitting low across the vehicle. At the sides of the cabin,

a bold section of wood veneer sweeps forward from the doors to meet at the front of the car below screen level.
- Virtual digital instrument display in front of cover that is interactive and changes dependent on driving mode, and using phosphor-blue lighting.
- Three-spoke leather-covered steering wheel (veneer option) with centre chromed leaper, incorporating minor controls for various operations and gear change paddles.
- Circular chrome on metal eye-ball air con vents at either side of dashboard with two prominent pod-mounted vents in the centre of the dashboard area.
- Wide centre console area including operational screen, auxiliary controls and JaguarDrive control.
- Electrically locked glovebox to passenger side of dash area.
- All-leather seating with contrasting piping, electrically controlled and heated/ventilated according to model.
- Door panels with wood-veneer panels to match the rest of the car.
- Soft-finish door trim areas featuring door pulls, chromed door handles, speaker grilles and switch packs for windows/mirrors.

Subtle rear 'cats claw' lighting changes from the earlier car to the post 2015 models with 'J' effect.

Post 2015 rear end styling treatment with extra badging, oval exhaust pipes and trim.

2011 model year specifics

XJ Luxury model
- Bond-grain leather seating.
- Satellite navigational system with media hub for video and audio streaming.
- Dual-zone climate control system (four-zone climate control LWB model).
- Illuminated vanity mirrors (LWB model).
- Jaguar 400watt sound system with 12 speakers and single-slot CD/DVD.
- Panoramic roof and electric blinds.
- Privacy glass (LWB model).
- Electric rear window sun blind (LWB model).
- Manual rear side window sun blinds.

XJ Premium Luxury model
As Luxury except:
- Soft-grain leather seating, heated front and rear.
- Soft-grain leather-bound steering wheel.
- Jaguar 600watt sound system with 14 speakers and single-slot CD/DVD.

XJ Portfolio model
As Premium Luxury except:
- Soft-grain leather seating, front with massage, ventilated heated and cooled, contrast stitching and piping, plus embossed Jaguar leaper in headrests.
- Suedecloth headlining.
- Aluminium boot runners
- Bowers & Wilkins 1200watt premium sound system.
- Rear business trays (LWB only).

XJ Supersport model
As Portfolio model except:
- Semi-aniline leather seating with twin-needle tonal stitching
- Leather headlining.
- Rear seat entertainment system.
- Digital TV system.

All models
- Enhanced trim levels with new Infotainment system, higher quality audio/visual systems and driver aids.

Luxury models
- Satin Rosewood veneer.

Premium Luxury models
- Soft grain leather seating with massage, heating and air conditioning.

- Contrast colour stitching and piping to seats.
- Suedecloth headliner.
- Meridian Premium sound system
- Rear business trays (LWB only)

Portfolio models
- Quilted soft grain leather seating with diamond stitching and embossed headrests.
- Figured Ebony veneer.

R-Sport models
- Sports seating.
- R-Sport steering wheel.
- R-Sport sill treadplates.
- Jet headliner.
- Piano Black or Carbon Fibre veneer and trim.

Autobiography models
- Quilted semi-aniline leather seating with contrast stitching.
- Leather headliner.
- Rich Oak veneer with inlays.
- Illuminated sill treadplates.
- Illuminated boot finisher.
- Illuminated air vents.
- Rear individual seats with electric adjustment and massage function.
- Rear compartment entertainment system with twin HD folding screens.

XJR models
- Other identification points as earlier XJR plus 2016 revisions for other models.

The 575PS XJR575, the last 'big hitter' performance XJ.

The exquisitely finished interior of the XJR575.

The last XJ ICE car produced, the XJ50 to commemorate 50 years of the model.

Technical specifications

	2-litre LWB	2-litre SWB	2.2-litre D SWB	2.2-litre D LWB	3-litre LWB	3-litre LWB AWD
Cylinders	4	4	4		6	6
cc	1999	1999	2179	2179	2995.300	2995
Bhp	237	237	190	190	335	335
@ rpm	5500	5500	3500	3500	6500	6500
Torque (Nm)	340	340	332	332	450	450
@ rpm	1900	1900	2000	2000	3500	3500
Top Speed (mph)	150	150	150	150	155	155
0 to 62mph (secs)	7.5	7.5	7.5	7.5	5.9	5.6
Gears	8	8	8	8	8	8
Length (mm)	5248	5123	5123	5248	5248	5248
Width (mm)	2108	2108	2108	2108	2108	2108
Height (mm)	1448	1448	1448	1448	1448	1448
Track Front (mm)	1626	1626	1626	1626	1626	1626
Track Rear (mm)	1603	1603	1603	1603	1603	1603
Wheelbase (mm)	3030	3030	3030	3030	3030	3030
Weight (kg)	1698	1672	1700	1750	1799	1830
Mpg (combined)	25.3	25.3	30	30	25	24

tre B	3-litre SWB AWD	5-litre LWB	5-litre R SWB	5-litre R LWB	3-litre D SWB	3-litre D LWB
	6	8	8	8	6	6
95	2995	5000	5000	5000	2995	2995
5	335	380	503	503	271	271
00	6500	6500	6000	6000	4000	4000
0	450	505	625	625	500	500
00	3500	3500	25 3500	25 3500	2000	2000
	155	155	155	155	155	155
	5.6	5.7	4.9	4.9	6.4	6.4
	8	6	6	6	6	6
3	5123	5248	5123	5248	5123	5248
08	2108	2108	2108	2108	2108	2108
8	1448	1448	1448	1448	1448	1448
6	1626	1626	1626	1626	1626	1626
03	1603	1603	1603	1603	1603	1603
30	3030	3030	3030	3030	3030	3030
6	1806	1773	1892	1915	1796	1803
	24.2	20.6	20.6	19.4	33.6	33.6

1: 18in Meru, option wheel to 2015.
2: 19in Aleutian, standard on Luxury models.
3: 19in Toba, standard on Premium Luxury models.
4: 19in Toba polished, option wheel.
5: 19in Style 1028 Silver
6: 19in Style 7016 Silver
7: 20in Kasuga, standard on Portfolio to 2015, 2016 on option.
8: 20in Matavia, standard on Supersport model to 2015, standard on R-Sport from 2016.
9: 20in Amirante, option to 2015.
10: 20in Kasuga polished, option wheel.
11: 20in Orona, standard on Portfolio from 2015.
12: 20in Orona polished, option wheel.
13: 20in Venom, standard on XJR to 2015.
14: 20in Maroa, standard on Autobiography models.
15: 20in Farallan Technical Grey, standard on XJR from 2015.
16: 20in Farallan Silver (also available in gloss black) option wheel.
17: 20in Style 1010 Satin Grey Diamond Turned
18: 20in Style 5044 Black

16

17

18

Colour schemes

Exterior paintwork	Detail
Porcelain White	to 2010
Polaris White	to 2017
Glacier White	2015/2016
Yulong White	2018 to end
X Fuji White	2018 to end
Aurora Red	2014/2015
Italian Racing Red	to 2016
Firenze Red	2017 to end
Rosello Red	2017 to end
Odyssey Red	2014/2015
Claret	to 2011
Carnelian Red	2012 to 2014
Caviar	to 2014
Cashmere	to 2014
Quartzite Gold	2014/2015
Ingot	2014/2015
Dark Sapphire	2015/2016
Indigo	to 2012
Spectrum Blue	to 2011
Front Blue	to 2011
Crystal Blue	2011 to 2013
Loire Blue	2018 to end
Velocity Blue	2018/2019
Ammorite	to 2015
Liquid Silver	to 2010
Tempest Grey	2014/2015
Stratus Grey	to 2015
Vapour Grey	to 2010
Pearl Grey	to 2010
Satellite Grey	2012 to 2014
Rhodium Silver	to 2015
Indus Silver	2017 to end
Lunar Grey	to 2014
Storm Grey	2014/2015
Carpathian Grey	2018 to end
Corris Grey	2018 to end

Exterior paintwork	Detail
Corris Satin Grey	2018 to end
Celestial Black	2014/2015
Ultimate Black	to 2016
Ebony Black	to 2015
Narvic Black	2018 to end
Santorini Black	2018 to end
Farallan Black	2018 to end
Black Amethyst	to 2015
Black Berry	2014/2015
Botanical Green	to 2011
British Racing Green	to end

Seats	Contrast stitching/piping
Jet	Jet/Ebony
Ebony	Red/Pimento
Dove	Camel/Tan
Navy	Cirrus/Mineral
Cirrus	Ivory
Mineral	Truffle
Ivory	Oyster
Light Oyster	Navy
Parchment	Bordeaux
Cashmere	
Truffle	**Headlining**
Cashew	Jet
London Tan	Ebony
Bordeaux	Ivory
Red Zone	Canvas
	Parchment

Carpets	Upper fascia/trim
Jet	Jet/Ebony
Ebony	Navy
Cirrus	Tan
Mineral	Pimento
Camel	Mineral
Truffle	Oyster
Ivory	Truffle

Dashboard/console finishers	
Carbon Fibre	to end
Satin American Walnut	to 2012
Gloss Burr Walnut	to end
Burr Walnut Curl	to end
Gloss Shadow Walnut	2012 to 2014
Satin Elm	to 2015
Gloss Figured Ebony	to end
Gloss Figured Ebony (inlay)	to 2014
Gloss Rich Oak	to end
Gloss Rich Oak (inlay)	to 2014
Piano Black	to end
Satin Zebrano	to 2014
Satin Rosewood	2013 to 2016
Herringbone	2013 to 2015

Optional extras

Dependent on individual model specification

Driver assistance pack (forward alert, adaptive cruise control, blind-spot monitor, emergency brake assist, active seat belts).
Option to delete XJ badging from rear of car.
Privacy glass.
Air-quality monitoring system.
Front ashtray and cigar lighter.
Wood and leather heated steering wheel.
DAB radio.
Whitefire emitter and headphones.
Chromed door mirror covers.
Personalised signature.
Locking wheel nuts.
Rear number plate surround.
Wheelarch splash guards.
Boot interior finisher, illuminated.
Alloy pedal kit.
Garage door opener.
TV tuner.
Rear seat entertainment centre.
Adaptive front lighting.
Rear camera parking system.
Rear business trays.
Soft-grain leather front seating with heating/cooling system.
Soft-grain leather rear seating with heating/cooling system.
Leather heated steering wheel.
Leather and wood heated steering wheel.
Dual-view functionality centre console screen.
Bowers and Wilkins 1200 watt hi-fi system.
Tyre pressure monitoring system.
Spike spyder traction system.
Illuminated tread plates.
Parking aid kit.
Keyless entry.
600watt Premium sound system.
Premium paint finish.
Blind-spot mirror monitoring system.
Suedecloth headlining.
Tipped leather fascia.
Heated and cooled ventilated front seats.
Heated and cooled ventilated rear seats.
Ivory leather trim.
Dual-view screen technology.
Rear seat Comfort pack.
Polished chrome exhaust finishers.
Personalised intaglio (dash-mounted insignia).
Luggage compartment net.
Luggage compartment liner.
Option to delete 'Jaguar' script from boot lid (2016 models on).
Polished tailpipe finishers.
Styled valve caps.
Red centre wheels badges.
Growler wheel nuts.
Illuminated sill treadplates.
Sport pedal covers.
Leather topped gear selector.
Personalised 'intaglio'.
Illuminated boot finisher.
Headrest mounted coat hanger.
Premium infant carrier.
Child seat and with booster cushion.
iPad holder.

Speed Pack

Front aero splitter.
Rear spoiler.
Gloss black radiator grille with chrome surround.
Gloss black lower mesh panel and side intake vents.
Gloss black mesh in power vents.
Red brake calipers.
20in Venom Sparkle Finish alloy wheels or:-
20in Matavia alloy wheels.
Performance enhancements boosting top speed to 174mph.

Sport Exterior Pack

As Speed Pack but without performance enhancements or choice of Matavia wheels.

Sport Interior Pack

18-way sports seating and trim.

Sport Interior Pack (inc. Ivory leather)

As Sport Interior Pack with Ivory leather trim.

21 Prices and production years

Model	Price new	2009	2010	2011	2012	2013	2014	2015	2016	2017	2018	2019
3.0-litre Diesel SWB	£58,600	■	■	■	■	■	■	■	■	■	■	–
3.0-litre Diesel LWB	£61,690	■	■	■	■	■	■	■	■	■	■	–
3.0-litre Petrol SWB	£56,900	–	–	–	–	■	■	■	■	■	■	–
3.0-litre Petrol LWB	£60,000	–	–	–	–	■	■	■	■	■	■	–
5.0-litre SWB	£67,000	■	■	■	■	■	■	■	■	■	■	–
5.0-litre LWB	£70,000	■	■	■	■	■	■	■	■	■	■	–
5.0-litre Supercharged LWB	£90,000	■	■	■	■	■	■	–	–	–	–	–
5.0-litre Ultimate	£120,000	–	–	–	–	■	■	–	–	–	–	–
5.0-litre XJR550	£92,000	–	–	–	–	–	■	■	■	–	–	–
3.0-litre R-Sport Petrol	£76,000	–	–	–	–	–	–	■	■	■	■	–
3.0-litre R-Sport Diesel	£72,000	–	–	–	–	–	–	■	■	■	■	–
Autobiography	£100,000	–	–	–	–	–	–	–	■	■	■	–
XJR575 LWB	£94,000	–	–	–	–	–	–	–	–	■	■	–
XJ Supercharged LWB		–	–	–	–	–	–	–	–	–	■	–
XJ Portfolio LWB		–	–	–	–	–	–	–	–	–	■	–
End of line												
3.0-litre Diesel models only:		–	–	–	–	–	–	–	–	–	–	■
Luxury, Premium Luxury, Portfolio SWB/LWB		–	–	–	–	–	–	–	–	–	–	■
Autobiography, R-Sport LWB		–	–	–	–	–	–	–	–	–	–	■
XJ50 LWB		–	–	–	–	–	–	–	–	–	–	–

Rear Seat Pack (long wheelbase models only)
Individual rear seating with heating/cooling/massage and adjustment features.
Heated and cooled front seats.
Four zone air conditioning system with air filtration, humidity sensing and individual adjustment.
Rear centre armrest with cupholders, storage and rear seat control panel.
Front and rear embossed 'winged' headrests.
Drive and rear seat pack switching for front passenger seat movement.
Rear compartment footrests.
LED rear compartment reading lights.
Electric rear side window blinds.

Premium Rear Seat Pack (long wheelbase models only)
As Rear Seat Pack plus:-
Seat position memory.
Rear business tables.
Rear seat entertainment system with twin 10.2in LCD screens and rear media interface.
Remote control for entertainment system.
2 x wireless digital headphones.

Premium Rear Seat Pack – Dual View (long wheelbase models only)
As Premium Rear Seat Pack plus:-
Dual views screens.
Extra set of wireless digital headphones.

Semi-Aniline Leather Seat Pack
Semi-aniline leather seating with contrast piping and stitching.
20-way electric front seat adjustment with 4-way lumbar, 5 massage functions and intensities.
Heated and cooled front and rear seating.
Front seat 3-way memory function.
Soft grain leather on upper fascia, door top rolls, door pannier, armrests, seat valance, centre console lid and end cap with twin needle stitch.

Illumination Pack
Phosphor blue illumination to front and rear air vents, sill treadplates and boot latch finisher.

F-TYPE sports cars from 2013

Background

This entirely new type of two-seater sports car was launched at the Los Angeles International Automobile Show, in November 2012. It represented a return to Jaguar's heartland, focusing on performance, agility and driver involvement from a strictly two-seater sports car, the first produced since the demise of the E-type back in 1974.

The 2013 Jaguar F-TYPE combined low vehicle weight with high-power performance and superb aerodynamics. A true two-seater sports car, initially only available as a convertible, with a lightweight 'Z frame' soft top that, when lowered, served as its own tonneau cover that could be fully raised or lowered in just 12 seconds at speeds of up to 30mph.

The body structure was built from a special aluminum process for lightness and rigidity, although the boot lid and under-sill structures are of a high-strength polymer. Half the content of the car comes from recycled or reclaimed metals.

The F-TYPE was introduced with new supercharged Jaguar petrol engines of 3.0-litre and 5.0-litre capacity, all with the latest stop-start technology, and an active exhaust system to enhance the sound of the cars. All cars also featured an 8-speed automatic transmission with a centrally mounted Quickshift gear lever plus steering wheel mounted paddles, and certain models with a limited slip differential. Some models even featured an active exhaust system to accentuate the sound.

An entirely new style was adopted for the interior layout, including a return to conventional analogue instrumentation; special sports seating and multi-function soft-touch switchgear cutting down dashboard clutter.

Although the new F-TYPE wouldn't be available to the public until March of 2013, at the end of November that year Jaguar announced the Coupé version of the car, and publicly launched it in the UK during February 2014. With distinctive and sweeping roof line leading to a tailgate and with or without a panoramic roof, Jaguar quoted the F-TYPE Coupé as the most torsionally rigid production car they had ever produced. That tailgate gave access to a boot volume of some 407 litres – a major increase over the small boot storage area of the convertible models.

From 2015 the model range and identification system changed on numerous occasions, with continually enhanced specifications and new technology adopted. At one time there were no fewer than 14 variants, and even a manual transmission for certain models. The car underwent a face-lift in 2019 with a reduction in models, leading to the final range consisting of just four models using the V6 and V8 engines.

The final F-TYPE models left production in 2023, marking the end of Jaguar ICE (Internal Combustion Engined) sports cars.

Models available at launch
F-TYPE 3.0-litre petrol convertible.
F-TYPE S 3.0-litre petrol convertible.
F-TYPE V8 S 5.0-litre petrol convertible.

Model range and development

Initially, F-TYPEs were only available in convertible form in three models, with 340bhp 3.0-litre V6 engine, the F-TYPE S (using a 380bhp version of the same engine), and the F-TYPE V8 S which uses a developed version of Jaguar's 5.0-litre V8 engine. All used an 8-speed sequential change gearbox.

A mechanical limited-slip differential is fitted as standard for the F-TYPE S, which offers drivers the opportunity to explore the car's superb balance and outer limits of its grip. The V8 S model is fitted with an active electronic controlled differential to maximize traction and offer even greater control. Inside the differential, an electric motor acts on a multi-plate clutch to transfer torque to the wheel with the most grip.

The three F-TYPEs offered progressively more powerful braking systems, all with the high levels of pedal feedback required for accurate modulation. The Jaguar Performance system fitted to the 340hp F-TYPE has 13.9in (354mm) front and 12.8in (325mm) rear brake discs with silver painted calipers. The F-TYPE S uses the Jaguar High Performance system, gaining larger 15in (380mm) brake discs at the front. The F-TYPE V8 S uses the Super High Performance system with the largest set of brake discs fitted as standard to a Jaguar production car, including the 15in (380mm) front and 14.8in (376mm) rear. All cars are fitted as standard with ABS, Electronic Brake Force Distribution and Emergency Brake Assist.

For the suspension layout, the F-TYPE's balance favours accessible handling while still maintaining excellent ride compliance. The Dynamic Mode enables the driver – at the push of a button – to emphasise the sporting character of the car by sharpening throttle response, increasing steering weighting, performing gear changes more quickly and higher up the rev range, and also by raising the threshold for stability control intervention. Dynamic mode also prevents automatic upshifts when the gearbox is shifted into manual mode. Additionally, the F-TYPE S and V8 S models are fitted with the Jaguar Adaptive Dynamics suspension damping system that controls vertical body movement, roll and pitch rates. The system continuously monitors driver inputs and the attitude of the F-TYPE on the road, adjusting damper rates accordingly.

Differing exhaust and tailpipe designs and sounds distinguish the V6 and V8 variants of the F-TYPE. Further detail differentiation between the three variants is found in the exterior trim and wheel design.

Side elevation of the F-TYPE, much shorter than the XK models with unique styling that applies to all models, save for differences in alloy wheels – in this case 18in Vela wheels.

A good overhead view shows the overall styling and shape of the F-TYPE.

Front elevation of the F-TYPE with its unique styling compared to any other Jaguar models.

Rear view of the F-TYPE, in this case a 3.0-litre model with the twin-pipe exhaust arrangement.

The interior is of an entirely new design for Jaguar, and trim standards and types vary with each model.

With the announcement of the Coupé models, three versions were on offer alongside the existing convertibles: the F-TYPE, F-TYPE S, and F-TYPE R. The latter (only initially available in Coupé form) is powered by Jaguar's 5.0-litre supercharged V8 engine in 550PS/680Nm tune, delivering acceleration to 60mph in 4.0-seconds, and a top speed of 186mph (electronically limited). The F-TYPE S Coupé and F-TYPE Coupé are powered by Jaguar's 3.0-litre V6 supercharged petrol engines in 380PS/460Nm and 340PS/450Nm forms respectively, giving 0-60mph in 4.8/5.1 seconds, and top speeds of 171/161mph.

To accompany the above changes, the whole car's handling and drivetrain were adapted to handle the extra power of the F-TYPE R in Coupé form. This model was also available with optional carbon ceramic matrix brakes. Finally some trim changes affected all models at this time.

In 2014 the F-TYPE's appeal was broadened by the hand-building of 250 limited edition 'Project 7' cars. Built by the Special Vehicle Operations dept, this roadster (with minimal weather protection) was stylistically changed to resemble the race-winning D-type from the 1950s. Powered by what was then a new 575ps version of the V8 engine (rear-wheel-drive), this was the most powerful F-TYPE produced at the time.

Extensive changes and additions took place from 2015, with all-wheel-drive being available for all cars except the base model 3.0-litre. A 6-speed ZF manual transmission with dual-mass flywheel was available until 2019 for the V4 and V6 engined rear-wheel-drive cars. The top of the range F-TYPE R became available as a convertible (replacing the earlier 495PS V8 convertible). At the same time, Sport Design packs became available adding extra specification.

In 2016 model identification changed, the original V6, V6 S and V8 S were replaced by F-TYPE, F-TYPE S, and F-TYP R. The latter top-end model (originally a coupé only, but now also available as a convertible) received the 550ps engine and gained extra features.

Shortly after, the F-TYPE SVR was announced in both coupé and convertible options, offering 200mph performance with output increased to 575ps. This was followed by the 'British Design Editon,' only available in four paint finishes and with various standard equipment options.

Technical updates included an electrically boosted rack and pinion steering system, and there have been more trim upgrades, including the fitting of the previously optional 770-watt Meridian surround sound audio system, and the panoramic glass sunroof.

In 2017/2018 a further model, the 400 Coupé, limited to just one year's production, and later

Unique to the model, flush-mounted door handles that move outwards when the key fob is operated or when touched by hand.

Side vent arrangement, which also shows the edge panel of the forward-hinged bonnet arrangement.

5.0-litre-engined F-TYPE rear view with four-branch exhaust tailpipes.

Interior dashboard and seat area of the F-TYPE.

a 400 Sport in both convertible and coupé came along, sitting between the other two top-end F-TYPE models. This was followed by the introduction of the 4-cylinder 2.0-litre 'Ingenium' engined model at a lower price point. The model line-up now consisted of six engine options in five models.

Next, in 2019, came the 'Chequered Flag' special edition to commemorate 70 years of Jaguar sporting cars. Based on the R-Dynamic 4- and 6-cylinder models only, all the enhancements were styling and trim related.

In 2000, the F-TYPE received its first major face-lift along with a simplified range covering the base 4-cylinder coupé and convertible plus R-Dynamic versions, a 5.0-litre R in both coupé and convertible, and another limited edition 'First Edition' 2.0-litre model, also in both body styles, only available for 12 months. In total, just 8 models, all available in coupé or convertible form. The V6-engined models were discontinued, replaced by a new 450ps V8 version. All cars benefited from many technical upgrades.

The following year, yet more limited editions came on the market. First, the 'Heritage' 60', marking the 60th anniversary of the E-type sports car. Only 60 were produced in Sherwood Green (non-metallic) paintwork, with duo-tone Caraway and Ebony Windsor leather interior. Mechanically the car was based on the F-TYPE R.

The other special edition that year was the 'Reims Edition' finished in French Racing Blue. Only available to UK customers with a total build of just 150 units, it was based on the coupé RWD 300 and 450ps models, and was produced to commemorate the 1950s D-type maiden victory at the 12-hours Reims race.

More changes came mid-2021, with R-Dynamic Black models added to the range, offering enhanced specification and a more luxurious, crafted interior.

The final reduced model range included the R-Dynamic coupé and convertible, in P300, P380, P450 and R 575 engine designations. However, in 2022 Jaguar announced two end-of-line models, the F-TYPE 75 and F-TYPE R 75 (later renamed F-TYPE 75 Plus and R 75 Plus, with extra equipment), and in 2023 two more special editions, the F-TYPE ZP (of which only 150 were made with just 10 for the UK), the very last F-TYPEs available into 2024.

Mechanical identification points

F-TYPE
- 3.0-litre 340PS supercharged V6 petrol engine.
- Intelligent stop/start system.
- 8-speed sequential gearbox.

The centre air vents that normally lie flush with the dash top will extend when required.

Centre console arrangement. The finish of the alloy changes according to model.

Overall view of the F-TYPE interior showing the sports seating.

- Sports suspension with Dynamic Mode.
- Dynamic stability control.
- 13.9in/12.8in disc brake system with silver finish calipers.
- Electronic parking brake.
- Sports exhaust with twin centrally mounted exhaust tailpipes.

F-TYPE V6 S (replaced by R-Dynamic in 2018)

As F-TYPE plus:
- 3.0-litre 380PS supercharged V6 petrol engine.
- 15in/12.8in disc brake system with larger red finish calipers.
- Adaptive Dynamics suspension damping system.
- Cruise control with automatic speed limiter.
- Mechanical limited slip differential.
- Active sports exhaust.

F-TYPE V8 S (replaced by R-Dynamic in 2018)

As F-TYPE S plus:
- 5.0-litre 495Ps supercharged V8 petrol engine.
- 15"/14.8" High Performance disc brake system with red finished calipers.
- Adaptive Dynamics suspension damping system.
- Electric controlled differential.
- Quad exhaust tailpipes.

F-TYPE R (including Heritage 60 special edition)

As F-TYPE V8 S plus:
- 5.0-litre 550PS supercharged V8 petrol engine.
- 8-speed sequential gearbox (enhanced).
- 15in/14.8in High Performance disc brake system with red or black finished calipers.
- Adaptive Dynamics suspension damping system (enhanced).
- R suspension tune.
- Electric controlled differential with torque vectoring by braking.
- Switchable Active Sports Exhaust.
- Quad exhaust tailpipes.

F-TYPE (post 2015)

As F-TYPE plus:
- 6-speed Manual transmission option.
- Electronically boosted power steering.

F-TYPE S (post 2015)

As F-TYPE S plus:
- 6-speed Manual transmission option.
- Electronically boosted power steering.
- Torque vectoring by braking.
- All wheel drive option (automatic transmission only).

As F-TYPE R (post 2015)

- Electronically boosted power steering.
- All wheel drive standard fit.

The F-TYPE Coupé here seen with Black Pack.

Rear styling of the F-TYPE Coupé, in this case an R model with quad exhaust pipes and restyled under-valance.

Roof and tailgate styling of the F-TYPE Coupé, in this case with the optional panoramic roof panel. Note the style of bonnet louvre …

… The restyled bonnet louvres for all wheel drive models.

F-TYPE SVR/Project 7
- 5.0-litre 575ps supercharged engine.
- Titanium exhaust system.
- Recalibrated 8-speed transmission.
- Larger wheels and tyres.
- Electronic active differential.
- Dynamic Stability Control recalibrated.
- Carbon ceramic matrix brake system with larger discs all round.
- Thicker rear anti-roll bar/thinner front anti-roll bar.
- Uprated suspension system.

F-TYPE 2.0-litre
- 300ps 2.0-litre Ingenium engine (RWD only).
- 6-speed manual gearbox option.

F-TYPE 400 Sport
- Upgraded brakes with black calipers and '400 Sport' logos.
- 20in dark grey satin alloy wheels.
- Configurable dynamics.

Later advances applicable to most models
- Touch-Pro Entertainment System.
- ReRun GoPro App.
- Full LED adaptive headlights.
- Revised front end styling treatment.
- Lightweight slimline seating with chrome and aluminium finishers.
- Semi-automatic park assist system.
- Rear camera and front park assist fitted to all models from 2000.
- Quiet Quick-Start function (2021).

Exterior identification points

Points applicable to all models
Front view
- An entirely different 'mouth' styling to any previous Jaguar sports car with bold deep grilles leaning slightly forward, with chromed surround and black hexagonal design mesh insert with black finished splitter bar.
- Lower air intake finished to black blending into the lower bumper areas at the corners.
- Four (two per side) vertical black finished cooling ducts.
- Jaguar growler badge in the centre of the grille area.
- Xenon headlights run vertically rather than horizontally, with J-Blade LED running lights.
- Sculptured bonnet with raised centre section flanked by body coloured louvres.

All-wheel drive R car – note the restyled rear valance area and side sills.

Revised frontal treatment for the F-TYPE AWD models.

Diffuser action on the Coupé models.

Rear view
- Tapered rear end styling with deeply inset lower valance panel.
- An active rear spoiler that deploys at speed to reduce aerodynamic lift. The spoiler rises when the F-TYPE reaches 60mph and then lowers to fit flush when the speed drops below 40mph.
- Horizontal LED rear lamps, wrapping around to the sides of the car.
- F-TYPE badging to the left hand side.
- High intensity brake light incorporated into the boot panel.

Side view
- A 'heartline' begins in the blade dissecting the grilles on either side of the main grille, running up to form the sharp top crease of the wing line.
- A second 'heartline' swells out to form the muscular rear haunch before sweeping dramatically around the rear of the car.
- Horizontally mounted front wing vents forming a break between the bottom half of the front wing and closing edges of the forward hinged bonnet.
- Hidden, automatically deploying door handles.

Exterior model specific identification points

F-TYPE
- Twin centrally mounted exhaust tailpipes.
- Satin black trim to the grilles, vents, front splitter and rear valance.
- 18in Vela alloy wheels.
- Silver finish brake calipers.
- Z frame clamshell style hood.

F-TYPE S
As F-TYPE plus:
- 'S' badging to right hand side of front grille area.
- 'S' badging to the right hand side of rear panel bodywork.
- Gloss black trim to the grilles, vents, front splitter and rear valance.
- 19in Propeller alloy wheels.
- Red finish brake calipers.

F-TYPE V8 S
As S plus:
- Four (two per side) out-board mounted exhaust tailpipes.
- Front vanes beneath the vertical side grilles.
- Flat side sill extensions.
- 20in Turbine alloy wheels.

F-TYPE R
As V8 S plus:
- 'R' badging.
- 5.0-litre 550PS supercharged V8 petrol engine.

Rear luggage area on the Coupé models.

Manual transmission for many F-TYPE models from 2015.

Revised exhaust tailpipe treatment for the AWD top of the range car.

AWD badging.

The limited special edition Project 7.

The limited edition end-of-line F-TYPE ZP Coupe finished in Crystal Grey.

The ZP in convertible form in Oulton Blue.

The F-TYPE Chequered Flag model.

Interior detailing on the Chequered Flag model.

- 8-speed sequential gearbox (enhanced)
- 15in/14.8in High Performance disc brake system with red or black finished calipers.
- Adaptive Dynamics suspension damping system (enhanced).
- Electric controlled differential with torque vectoring by braking.
- Active Sports Exhaust.
- Quad exhaust tailpipes.
- 20in Gyrodyne alloy wheels.

F-TYPE Coupé exterior specific identification points

- Overall form of the coupé follows styling of the convertibles but with a third 'heartline' forms a cabin rearward sweeping roof profile, providing an unbroken silhouette.
- A tapered roof/cabin area features between the rear haunches.
- Available initially with a choice of aluminium or panoramic glass roof.
- Rear spoiler hidden within the tapered shut-line of the tailgate, rising automatically at 70mph, dropping at 50mph.
- LED 'ribbon' style stop light at the top of the tailgate.
- Tailgate made from composite materials, hinged at the top, with a choice of powered or manual open/close function.

F-TYPE R Coupé specifics

- Bright aluminium window side glass finishers.

F-TYPE SVR

- Enlarged air intakes to the front bumper.
- Front bumper extended outwards.
- Redesigned bonnet vents.
- Design pack (extended sills)
- SVR branded four-exhaust tailpipes.
- Aerodynamic rear venturi.

- Deployable rear wing.

Project 7
- Occupant rollover hoops incorporated into the rear bodywork.
- Graphics highlights to limited range of five paint finishes.
- Lowered polymer front aerodynamic spoiler with carbon fibre upper section.
- Extended side skirts.
- Rear adjustable carbon fibre spoiler and diffuser.
- Rear deck, side vents, bonnet louvres and mirror caps in carbon fibre.
- Binini tonneau weather covering (when fitted).

F-TYPE 400 Sport
- Yellow and grey satin-finished badging.
- Sport Design pack (prominent front splitter, extended sills and rear diffuser in Dark Satin Grey).

F-TYPE R-Dynamic
- Gloss black accents.

F-TYPE British Design Edition
- Body coloured exterior trim.
- 20in Cyclone alloy wheels in Satin Dark Grey.
- S badging with Union Flag detailing.

F-TYPE 2.0-litre
- Single exhaust tailpipe.
- 18in standard fit alloy wheels.

F-TYPE Chequered Flag
- Black Design Pack.
- 20in black and diamond turned alloy wheels.
- Red painted brake calipers.

F-TYPE First Edition
- Dorchester Grey.

The face-lifted frontal aspect of later F-TYPEs. (Compare with earlier models shown on pages 344-345.)

Face-lifted rear features of the later F-TYPEs.

Side-on elevation of the face-lifted F-TYPE.

F-TYPE sports cars from 2013

- 5-spoke 20in Gloss Technical Grey diamond turned wheels.
- Restricted paint schemes.

F-TYPE Heritage 60
- Sherwood Green paintwork.

F-TYPE Reims Edition
- French Racing Blue paintwork.
- Black Pack.
- 20in five-spoke Gloss Black alloy wheels.

F-TYPE R-Dynamic Black
- Gloss Black 'Style 5039' alloy wheels.
- Only three paint finishes.

F-TYPE 75
- A unique paint finish of Giola Green Metallic.
- 'R 75' badging on the front wings.
- 20in Gloss Back diamond turned alloy wheels with black centre caps.
- Black radiator badging.
- Black and grey 'R' and 'R-Dynamic' badging.

F-TYPE ZP
- Fixed panoramic roof.
- Privacy glass.
- ZP badging.
- Limited paint finishes: Oulton Blue, Crystal Grey.

Later advances applicable to most models
- From 2018 subtle differences in exterior styling to suit different models (see images).

The new F-TYPE headlights with 'J' running lights fitted to later models.

Detail showing the ZP badging

The later F-TYPE interior with the enlarged TF screen and modified controls.

The F-TYPE 75, commemorating 75 years of Jaguar sports car.

Interior identification points

- Points applicable to all models.
- Instrumentation ahead of driver with analogue gauges.
- 3-spoke steering wheel incorporating auxiliary controls.
- Finishes in the driver and passenger areas with different grain on top of the instrument panel and centre console than that found on the passenger side.
- A grab handle sweeps down the centre console on the passenger side wrapping around the centre console.
- Engine Start button, steering wheel mounted gearshift paddles and Dynamic Mode toggle highlighted in an 'Ignis' orange finish.
- Rotary dials control the heating and air conditioning for each side of the car. A display screen within the two dials indicates temperature and mode. The controls are dual-purpose: in cars fitted with heated seats.
- Toggle switches below the dials control additional climate functions.
- Air vents on top of the dashboard are hidden, and will deploy by rising out of the dashboard only when instructed to by either the driver or climate control system.
- Switches are finished in soft-feel matte black with white markings.
- Centrally mounted TFT screen for sat nav and many other driver controls.
- Sports seats with power recline and height adjustment with manual control of fore/aft movement.

Interior model specific identification points

F-TYPE
- 180watt sound system with 6 speakers.
- Single slot CD/DVD, HDD navigation enabler.
- DAB radio.
- USB connectivity.
- Light hex alloy centre console.
- Partial leather/suedecloth seating.
- 6-way electrically adjustable seats.
- Leather steering wheel with black paddles.
- Light hex aluminium console finisher.
- Single zone climate control system.
- Morzine headlining.
- Phosphor blue interior ambient lighting.

F-TYPE S
As F-TYPE plus:
- Darker finish to soft feel matte black switches.
- Ignes finished gear change paddles.
- Dark hex aluminium console finisher with S graphic.
- Ambient interior lighting (selectable palette).
- Bluetooth connectivity.
- Navigational system with route guidance.
- Leather sports seats.
- Leather steering wheel with 'Ignis' paddles.

F-TYPE V8 S
As S.

F-TYPE R
As S plus:
- Leather Performance seating with inflatable side bolsters, 'R' logo embossed in the headrests, and 'wings' for high speed cornering support.
- Premium trim leather for instrument panel and binnacle, armrests, door inserts and centre console.
- 14-way electric seat adjustment.
- Leather flat bottomed steering wheel with 'R' logo.
- Fully electrically adjustable steering column.
- Ignis gear shift paddles.
- Dark technical weave aluminium console finisher with 'R' logo.
- Bright stainless steel pedal covers.
- Sports sun visor.
- 380Watt Meridian sound system.

F-TYPE (2015 exterior changes)
- Bonnet with deeper centre power bulge with vents further apart and further forward on AWD models.
- AWD S models 19in Volution diamond turned alloy wheels standard fit.
- R models 20in Gyrodyne alloy wheels with diamond turning standard fit.
- Sport Design Pack standardised on R models.

F-TYPE (2016 exterior changes)
- Panoramic glass sunroof standardised on all Coupé models.

F-TYPE (2016 interior changes)
- 770 Watt Meridian surround sound audio system standardised on all models.
- Proximity entry and start system standardised on all models.
- 14-way electrically adjustable seating standardised on all models.
- InControl Apps system fitted to all models.
- Apple and Android smartphone integration remote control functions installed.
- R Coupé model received a power hatch.
- S model with flat-bottom steering wheel, adjustable dynamic mode and different sounding active exhaust system.
- R models revised instrument dials and gauges.

F-TYPE SVR
- Performance leather seats of a lozenge quilt pattern with contrast stitching and micro-piping, headrests incorporating the SVR logo.

- Extra-large anodised aluminium gearshift paddles
- Suedecloth instrument surround and centre panel.

Project 7
- Carbon fibre inserts to the centre console.
- Machined aluminium gearshift paddles.
- Treadplates carrying the 'Project 7' logo.

F-TYPE 400 Sport
- Branding on centre console, Steering wheel, treadplates and embroidered headrests.
- Yellow contrast stitching to all upholstery.

F-TYPE British Design Edition
- Jet Premium leather trim with twin-needle stitching on performance seats.
- S/Union Flag detailing embossed in the headrests with similar badging on the centre console and sill treadplates.

F-TYPE Chequered Flag
- Ebony Windsor leather trim in Red or Cirrus with embossed headrests.

F-TYPE First Edition
- 12-way adjustable Windsor Leather seats with contrast stitching.
- Alcantara instrument cluster wrapping with monogram embossing.
- Aluminium gearshift paddles.
- Engine spin centre console finisher with 'First Edition' branding.
- Suedecloth headliner.

F-TYPE Heritage 60
- Duo-tone Caraway and Ebony trim.
- Performance seating.
- Headrests emboss with with 'E-type 60 anniversary' logo.
- Aluminium console finisher (a la E-type).

F-TYPE Reims Edition
- Black throughout interior, including switchgear and door handles.
- Fixed panoramic roof.

F-TYPE 75
- Silhouette motif on the engine spin centre console and stainless-steel treadplates.
- Black Pack interior.
- Lightweight slimline seats either in performance or sport styles, with motifs on the headrests.
- Monogram stitching to the door trims.

F-TYPE ZP
- 150 numbered tread plates.
- Mars Red/Ebony or Navy/Ebony interior leather.

Later advances applicable to most models
- Dark brushed aluminium centre console with a chequered flag logo.
- Steering wheel with red band at the centre position and a chequered flag logo.

Alloy wheel descriptions

1 – 18in Vela (later called Style 1024) Silver.

2 – 18in Style 1036.

3 – 19in Centrifuge Silver.

4 – 19in Centrifuge (later called Style 7013) Gloss Black.

5 – 19in Orbit Silver.

6 – 19in Orbit (later called Style 1066) Gloss Black Diamond Turned.

7 – 19in Propeller (later called Style 1023).

8 – 19in Volution (later called Style 5058) Technical Grey Diamond Turned.

9 – 19in Volution Silver.

10 – 19in Style 5101 Gloss Black Diamond Turned.

11 – 20in Blade (later called Style 5042) Technical Grey/Carbon Fibre.

12 – 20in Cyclone Silver.

13 – 20in Cyclone Gloss Black.

14 – 20in Rotor Carbon Fibre.

15 – 20in Turbine Silver.

16 – 20in Tornado Silver.

17 – 20in Tornado (later called Style 5039) Gloss Black.

18 – 20in Storm Satin Anthracite Grey.

19 – 20in Storm (later called Style 5040) Black Diamond Turned.

20 – 20in Gyrodyne (later called Style 6003) Silver.

21 – 20in Gyrodyne Dark Grey Diamond Turned.

22 – 20in Maelstrom Gloss Black.

23 – 20in Style 1041 Satin Black Diamond Turned.

24 – 20in Style 5060 Silver.

25 – 20in Style 5061 Satin Grey.

26 – 20in Style 5102 Gloss Technical Grey Diamond Turned.

27 – 20in Coriolis Satin Technical Grey.

Technical specifications

Specification	2.0-litre	3.0-litre	3.0-litre	5.0-litre	5.0-litre	5.0-litre
Cylinders	4	6	6	8	8	8
cc	1997	2995	2995	5000	5000	5000
Bhp	300	340	380	450	550	575
at rpm	5500	6500	6250	6000	6500	6500
Torque (Nm)	400	450	460	580	680	700
at rpm	15 - 4500	35-5000	45-5000	25-5000	3500	35-5000
Top speed (mph)	155	162	171	177	186	192
0 to 62mph (secs)	5.7	5.7	5.1	4.4	4.1	3.6
Gears (auto)	8	8	8	8	8	8
Gears (man RWD only)		6	6			
Length (mm)	4483	4483	4483	4483	4483	4483
Width (mm)	1923	1923	1923	1923	1923	1923
Height coupé (mm)	1311	1311	1311	1311	1311	1311
Height conv (mm)	1307	1307	1307	1307	1307	1307
Track front (mm)	1598	1598	1598	1598	1598	1598
Track rear (mm)	1648	1648	1648	1648	1648	1648
Wheelbase (mm)	2621	2621	2621	2621	2621	2621
Ground clearance	100	100	100	100	100	100
Weight coupé (kg)	1628	1628	1781	1855	1855	1855
Weight conv (kt)	1646	1646	1793	1865	1865	1865
Mpg (combined)	29	24	26.4	21.4	20.8	20

Optional extras

Active Sports Exhaust.
Switchable Active Sports Exhaust.
Configurable Dynamics System with Dynamic i display.
High Performance Braking System with black calipers.
Super Performance Braking System with red or black calipers.
Carbon Ceramic Performance Braking System with yellow calipers.
Front parking aid.
Reverse park camera with guidance.
Blind spot monitoring system.
Reverse traffic detection system.
Tyre pressure monitoring system.
Panoramic glass roof.
Panoramic carbon fibre roof.
Powered open/close tailgate.
Exterior electrically controlled and heated mirrors.
Heated windscreen with timer.
Rain sensing windscreen wipers.
Adaptive front lighting with cornering lamps.
Intelligent high beam headlights.
Automatic headlights.
14 way electrically adjustable seating.
Premium leather trim.
Light hex aluminium console finisher.
Dark hex aluminium console finisher.
Heated leather steering wheel.
Premium carpet mats.
Sports carpet mats.
Dual zone climate system
Air quality sensor.
Cruise control with automatic speed limiter.
Valet mode.
Wind deflector.
Bright stainless steel pedal covers.
Heated seats.
Sports sun visor with mirror.
Illuminated tread plates.
Configurable interior ambient lighting.
Lockable interior storage.
SmartKey keyless system.
Universal garage door opener.
380 Watt Meridian audio system.
770 Watt Meridian surround sound system.
F-TYPE bonnet decals in silver or gunmetal grey.
Mirror covers in chrome, or carbon fibre.
Bonnet louvres in chrome, carbon fibre or gloss black.
Side power vents in chrome, carbon fibre or gloss black.
Roll over protection bars in chrome, carbon fibre or gloss black.

Rear diffuser in carbon fibre.
Engine cover in carbon fibre.
Exhaust finishers in chrome/black.
Stylised tyre valve caps.
Wheel badges in chrome.
Wheel nuts in black/Jaguar or chrome/Jaguar.
Locking wheel nuts.
Spare wheel cover.
Rubber floor mats.
Premium floor mats.
Sports floor mats.
Centre console in carbon fibre.
Gear shift paddles in aluminium.
Umbrella holder.
Personalised and illuminated sill treadplates.
Union Jack treadplates.
Rear mounted ski carrier.
Snow sock winter traction aid.
Snow traction system.
Five piece luggage set.
Semi-rigid load space protector.
Luggage carpet mat.
Front windscreen UV sun shade.
Child safety seat.
All weather car cover.
Battery conditioner.

Some of the following packs will be standard on certain models:

Seat Memory pack
14-way electrically adjustable seating with memory.
Electrically adjustable steering column with memory.
Auto dipping exterior door mirrors with electrical adjustment and memory.

Visibility pack
Heated windscreen with timer.
Rain sensing windscreen wipers.
Automatic headlights.
Adaptive front lighting with Bi-function HID Xenon lights with LED daytime running lights.
Intelligent high beam.

Parking pack
Front parking aid.
Reverse park camera with guidance.

Design pack
Body-coloured front bumper splitter.
Aerodynamic splitters and side sill extensions.
Body-coloured rear bumper venture.
Gloss black rear valance.

Black pack (convertible)
Gloss black finish to front grille surround, bumper beam, front splitter, front outer meshes, bonnet louvres, side power vents, rear valance and roll over protection bars.

Black pack (coupé)
As convertible plus gloss black window surrounds.

Design pack with black pack (convertible)
Body colour front bumper splitter, aerodynamic splitters, side sill extensions and rear bumper venture.
Gloss black finish to front grille surround, bumper beam, front outer meshes, side power bents, rear bumper valance and roll over protection bars.

Design pack with black pack (coupé)
As convertible plus gloss black window surrounds.

Extended leather pack (convertible)
Leather A-pillars, header, and sports sun visors with mirrors in a choice of either Jet, Stone, Red or Ivory.
Recona headlining in Jet or Stone to folding areas.

Extended leather pack (coupé)
Leather headlining and sports sun visors with mirrors in Jet, Stone or Ivory.

Extended upper environment pack (convertible)
Suedecloth A-pillars, header and suedecloth sports sun visors with mirrors in Jet.

Extended upper environment pack (coupé)
Suedecloth headlining and sports sun visors with mirrors in jet.

Interior black pack
Flat bottomed leather sports steering wheel with black trim finishers and ignis gear shift paddles.
Gloss black instrument cluster dial rings, air vent surrounds and door switch pack surrounds.
Black hex aluminium console finisher.

Carbon ceramic brake pack 1
Carbon ceramic brakes.
Yellow brake calipers.
20in Storm alloy wheels in satin anthracite grey.
Stainless steel pedal covers.

Carbon ceramic brake pack 2
As pack 1, but with:
20in Storm forged alloy wheels in black/diamond turned.

Exterior Carbon Fibre Pack
Body colour front bumper splitter, sills and rear venturi.
Gloss black to coupe side window surrounds.
Carbon fibre side vents/bonnet louvres, mirror caps and convertible roll-over bars.

Prices and production years

Model	Price New	2013	2014	201...
F-TYPE V6 Convertible	£58,520	■	■	■
F-TYPE V6 Coupé	£51,235	–	■	■
F-TYPE S Convertible	£67,520	■	■	■
F-TYPE S Convertible AWD	£72,385	–	–	■
F-TYPE Coupé S	£60,235	–	–	–
F-TYPE Coupé S AWD	£66,900	–	–	–
F-TYPE V8 S Convertible	£79,985	■	■	■
F-TYPE V8 S Coupé	£86,800	–	■	■
F-Type Coupé		–	–	–
F-TYPE Convertible		–	–	–
F-TYPE R Convertible	£92,295	–	–	–
F-TYPE R Convertible AWD	£97,135	–	–	■
F-TYPE R Coupé	£85,000	–	–	■
F-TYPE R Coupé AWD	£97,650	–	–	–
Project 7	£135,000	–	■	■
F-TYPE SVR	£126,445	–	–	–
F-TYPE British Design Edition Coupé	£75,225	–	–	–
F-TYPE British Design Edition Con	£80,390	–	–	–
F-TYPE 400 Sport Coupé	£70,115	–	–	–
F-TYE 400 Sport Convertible	£81,005	–	–	–
F-TYPE 2-litre Coupé/Convertible	£49,900	–	–	–
F-TYPE R-Dynamic 2.0-litre Coupé/Con	£53,600	–	–	–
F-TYPE V6 340 Coupé/Convertible		–	–	–
F-TYPE V6 380 Coupé/Conv RWD/AWD		–	–	–
F-TYPE R-Dynamic V6 380		–	–	–
F-TYPE R-Dynamic 340 Coupé/Con		–	–	–
F-TYPE R-Dynamic 380 Coupé/Con RWD/AWD		–	–	–
F-TYPE R 550ps Coupé/Con AWD		–	–	–
F-TYPE SVR 575ps Coupé AWD		–	–	–
F-TYPE Chequered Flag	£62,335	–	–	–
F-TYPE 300 Coupé	£54,060	–	–	–
F-TYPE 300 Convertible	£59,540	–	–	–
F-TYPE 300 R-Dynamic Coupé	£57,060	–	–	–
F-TYPE 300 R-Dynamic Convertible	£62,540	–	–	–
F-TYPE First Edition Coupé	£63,530	–	–	–
F-TYPE First Edition Convertible	£68,150	–	–	–
F-TYPE R-Dynamic 450 Coupé	£69,950	–	–	–
F-TYPE R-Dynamic 450 Convertible	£75,470	–	–	–
F-TYPE R-Dynamic 450 Coupé AWD	£74,850	–	–	–
F-TYPE R-Dynamic 450 Convertible AWD	£80,330	–	–	–
F-TYPE First Edition 450 Coupé	£75,995	–	–	–
F-TYPE First Edition 450 Convertible	£80,650	–	–	–
F-TYPE First Edition 450 Coupé AWD	£80,890	–	–	–
F-TYPE First Edition 450 Convertible AWD	£85,510	–	–	–
F-TYPE R Coupé AWD	£97,280	–	–	–
F-TYPE R Convertible AWD	£102,370	–	–	–
F-TYPE Heritage 60 Coupé	£122,500	–	–	–
F-TYPE Heritage 60 Convertible	£128,500	–	–	–
F TYPE Reims P300 Coupé	£58,950	–	–	–
F-TYPE Reims P450 Coupé	£71,450	–	–	–
F-TYPE R-Dynamic Black 300 Coupé		–	–	–
F-TYPE R-Dynamic Black 300 Convertible		–	–	–
F-TYPE R-Dynamic Black 450 Coupé		–	–	–
F-TYPE R-Dynamic Black 450 Convertible		–	–	–
F-Type R-Dynamic 300 Coupé	£62,235	–	–	–
F-TYPE R-Dynamic 300 Convertible	£67,825	–	–	–
F-TYPE 75 P450 Coupé	£78,330	–	–	–
F-TYPE 75 P450 Convertible	£83,920	–	–	–
F-TYPE 75 P450 Coupé AWD	£83,290	–	–	–
F-TYPE 75 P450 Convertible AWD	£88,880	–	–	–
F-TYPE R P575 Coupé AWD	£102,870	–	–	–
F-TYPE R P575 Convertible AWD	£108,065	–	–	–

2017	2018	2019	2020	2021	2022	2023
–	–	–	–	–	–	–
–	–	–	–	–	–	–
–	–	–	–	–	–	–
–	–	–	–	–	–	–
–	–	–	–	–	–	–
–	–	–	–	–	–	–
–	–	–	–	–	–	–
–	–	–	–	–	–	–
–	–	–	–	–	–	–
–	–	–	–	–	–	–
–	–	–	–	–	–	–
–	–	–	–	–	–	–
–	–	–	–	–	–	–
–	–	–	–	–	–	–
–	–	–	–	–	–	–
–	–	–	–	–	–	–
–	–	–	–	–	–	–
■	–	–	–	–	–	–
■	–	–	–	–	–	–
■	–	–	–	–	–	–
■	–	–	–	–	–	–
■	■	■	–	–	–	–
■	■	■	–	–	–	–
■	■	■	–	–	–	–
■	■	■	–	–	–	–
■	■	■	–	–	–	–
■	■	■	–	–	–	–
■	■	■	–	–	–	–
■	■	■	–	–	–	–
–	–	■	–	–	–	–
–	–	–	–	–	–	–
–	–	–	–	–	–	–
–	–	–	■	■	■	–
–	–	–	■	■	■	–
–	–	–	■	■	■	–
–	–	–	■	■	■	–
–	–	–	■	■	■	–
–	–	–	■	■	■	–
–	–	–	■	■	■	–
–	–	–	■	■	–	–
–	–	–	■	■	–	–
–	–	–	■	■	–	–
–	–	–	■	■	–	–
–	–	–	–	■	–	–
–	–	–	–	■	–	–
–	–	–	–	■	–	–
–	–	–	–	–	■	–
–	–	–	–	–	■	–
–	–	–	–	–	■	–
–	–	–	–	–	–	■
–	–	–	–	–	–	■
–	–	–	–	–	–	■
–	–	–	–	–	–	■
–	–	–	–	–	–	■
–	–	–	–	–	–	■
–	–	–	–	–	–	■

Jaguar All the Cars

Colour schemes

EXTERIOR PAINTWORK

Polaris White	to 2017
Glacier White	2015 to 2017
Yulong White	2018 to 2022
X Fuji White	2018 to 2022
Valloire White Pearl	2019 to 2021
Meribel White Pearl	2019 to 2021
Ice White	2020 to end
Salsa Red	to 2017
Caldera Red	from 2015 to 2020
Italian Racing Red	to 2019
Special Racing Red	2019 to 2020
Firenze Red	2020 to end
Desire Red	2019 to end
Firesand	to 2017
Madagascar Orange	2019 to 2021
Sanguinello Orange	2020 to end
Alacama Orange	2020 to end
Sorento Yellow	2020 to end
Rio Gold	2019 to 2020
Sunrise Gold	2020 to end
Tourmaline Brown	2020 to end
Constellation	2020 to end
Dark Sapphire	2015 to 2017
Indigo	to 2019
Loire Blue	2018 to 2020
Ultra Blue	2018 to 2020
Portofino Blue	2019 to end
Velocity Blue	2019 to end
Balmoral Blue	2019 to 2021
Bluefire Blue	2020 to 2022
X Petrolix Blue	2019 to end
Ammorite	2015 to 2017
Amethyst Grey/Purple	2020 to end
Corris Grey	2018 to 2019
Stratus Grey	2015 to 2017
Rhodium Silver	2017 to 2019
Indus Silver	2018 to 2020
Silicon Silver	2018 to 2020
Flux Silver	2019 to end
Verbier Silver	2019 to 2021
Ethereal Silver	2019 to end
Ionian Silver	2019 to end
Lunar Grey	2014 to 2017
Storm Grey	2015 to 2017
Carpathian Grey	2018 to end
Eiger Grey	2019 to end
Bosphorus Grey	2020 to 2020
Windward Grey	2019 to 2021
Scafell Grey	2019 to 2021
Ultimate Black	2017 to 2019
Ebony Black	to 2017 2020
Narvic Black	2018 to 2021
Santorini Black	2018 to end
Black Amethyst	2017 to 2019
Ligurian Black	2019 to end
Mescalito Black	2019 to 2020
Borealis Black	2019 to 2021
Black Berry	2015 to 2017
British Racing Green	to end
Giola Green	2022 to end
Sherwood Green	Heritage 60 only
Oulton Blue	2023/24 ZP only
Crystal Grey	2023/24 ZP only

HOOD COLOURS

Jet	to 2019
Black	2019 to end
Grey	to 2019
Red	to end
Beige	to end

SEATS

Jet	to 2018
Ebony	2018 to end
Mineral	to 2015
Cirrus	to 2019
Brogue	to 2019
Red	to 2019
Mars Red	from 2020 to end
Camel	to 2018
Ivory	to 2019
Light Oyster	from 2020 to end
Siena Tan	to 2019
Tan	from 2020 to end
Pimento	to 2019
Caraway	2022

HEADLINING

Jet	to 2018
Ebony	from 2017
Stone	to 2018
Grey	from 2017
Red	to 2018
Ivory	to 2018
Pimento	from 2017 to 2019

SEATBELTS

Jet/Ebony
Red
Camel

CONTRAST STITCHING/PIPING

Jet/Ebony
Red/Pimento
Camel/Tan
Firesand
Cirrus/Mineral
Ivory
Reims Blue
Yellow (400 Sport only)

UPPER FASCIA/TRIM

Jet/Ebony
Tan
Pimento
Mineral
Reims Blue

CARPETS

Jet	to 2019
Ebony	from 2019 to end
Cirrus	to 2019
Mineral	to 2018
Camel	to 2018

DASHBOARD/CONSOLE FINISHERS

Light Hex Aluminium
Dark Hex Aluminium
Black Hex Aluminium
Dark Technical Weave Aluminium
Delta Aluminium
Knurled Aluminium
Carbon Fibre

23 XE saloons from 2015

Background

A major move forward by Jaguar, announced in 2014 for the 2015 model year, the new model XE offered a smaller compact saloon – the eventual replacement for the X-type, which went out of production in 2007. The XE was the smallest, lightest and stiffest Jaguar saloon yet produced, introducing many unique and high tech features not seen before on a car of this class.

Following contemporary Jaguar practice, the XE's body was built intensively from aluminium (75%), utilising Jaguar's new modular vehicle architecture, which was to underpin a range of models. Parts of the body were made from aluminium RC5754 grade (the first car in the world to use this high-strength alloy), predominantly from recycled material. As well as aluminium, high-strength and dual-phase steels and cast magnesium were used in the manufacture of the bodies, which were assembled, as with other Jaguars, via a combination of self-piercing rivets and structural adhesives.

XE styling followed similar practice to the New XF (see next chapter) with a low profile and innovations like front bumper ducts channeling airflow over the surfaces of the front wheels to reduce drag, and lightweight under-floor panels for a smooth surface. At the time, the XE had the lowest drag coefficient of any Jaguar to date, at Cd 0.26.

The highly sophisticated suspension package included double front wishbones and an integral link at the rear, keeping weight to a minimum, with extensive use of aluminium for the toe links and upper control arms. Knuckles and lower control arms were hollow cast, also saving weight.

The XE was also the first Jaguar to use EPAS (electric power steering) to give better response and feel, as well as speed-dependent assistance and damping.

In addition to utilising lightweight sliding calipers and large discs (ventilated at the front), the XE's braking system incorporated enhanced cooling thanks to suspension mounted ducts and the latest electronic brake system controller. The XE also offered Torque Vectoring by braking, first seen on the F-TYPE sports car, mitigating the onset of understeer by lightly braking individual inner wheels as required to keep the car on the optimum line through corners.

The XE was powered by a range of 4- and 6-cylinder petrol and diesel engines from Jaguar's Ingenium family; all benefitting from direct injection, variable valve timing and intelligent stop-start systems. Power was transmitted to the rear wheels through 6-speed manual and 8-speed automatic transmissions. The XE also incorporated highly advanced driver enhancement and safety systems and in the interior the latest Jaguar Infotainment system, head-up displays, etc. For the 2016 model year, all-wheel drive versions were added to the XE range.

The XE range continued into 2023 with various new models, additional technology and trim, but never expanded beyond a range of three-box four-door saloons. Production in the UK was carried out at the JLR Solihull plant in the West Midlands but also expanded with cars produced in China.

With Jaguar's introduction of all-electric vehicles for 2024, XE production was phased out, being one of the last ICE and small saloons produced by the company.

Model range and development

Models available at launch

XE SE 2.0-litre turbocharged diesel
XE SE 2.0-litre turbocharged petrol
XE Prestige 2.0-litre turbocharged diesel
XE Prestige 2.0-litre turbocharged petrol
XE R-Sport 2.0-litre turbocharged diesel
XE R-Sport 2.0-litre turbocharged petrol

XE Portfolio 2.0-litre turbocharged diesel
XE Portfolio 2.0-litre turbocharged petrol
XE S 3.0-litre supercharged petrol

The 4-cylinder 2.0-litre turbocharged petrol engines were initially available in two power ratings of 200PS and 240PS. These all-aluminium engines weighed 138kg. The 4-cylinder 2.0-litre turbocharged diesel engines also offered a choice of power output, 163PS and 180PS. The 163PS version at the time making the XE the most fuel-efficient Jaguar produced, achieving up to 75mpg and a 99g/km CO_2 level on the European combined cycle.

The V6 3.0-litre supercharged petrol engine was shared with the F-TYPE sports car, another all-aluminium unit of modular design rated at 340PS. Initially fitted to the XE S model, it provided outstanding performance with a 0 to 60mph acceleration time of just 4.9 seconds and a top speed limited to 155mph.

Two transmissions for the XE were made up of a 6-speed manual gearbox with a lightweight aluminium alloy casing and a semi-dry sump system with oil spraying onto the moving parts by a compact pump. This gearbox featured on all the 2.0-litre diesel engine variants.

For the petrol engine models (and as an option on the diesel engines) there was an 8-speed ZE 8HP automatic transmission, adapted from that used on the XF and XJ saloons. Controlled by Jaguar's own Drive Control system it also includes steering wheel paddle shifts.

The XE had some of the most advanced driver assistance systems, including All Surface Progress Control (ASPC), electronically gaining traction in seconds, ideal for use on low-grip surfaces such as snow-covered roads. Laser projection technology enables the XE's optional head-up display (HUD) to generate sharp, high-contrast colour graphics (such as vehicle speed and navigation), two metres in front of the driver. A forward-facing stereo camera was mounted behind the windscreen in front of the rear view mirror, to give a 3D view of the road ahead, used for functions including autonomous emergency braking, a lane departure warning system, and even traffic sign recognition.

The XE also offered adaptive cruise control, blind spot monitoring with closing vehicle sensing, and two semi-automated park-assist functions.

Internally, a low seating position gave a more sporty feel to the car and has helped reduce the overall height of the car with its streamlined profile. Jaguar's new InControl infotainment system took centre stage with its 8in touchscreen for access to all features and functions – along with iOS and Android smartphone apps, plus Wi-Fi and premium audio systems.

Shortly after its introduction, further XE models extended the range from 2016. In addition to InControl Touch Pro, Jaguar's next-generation

The XE Prestige model with extra panoramic roof. This side-on view is applicable to the SE and Portfolio models as well, showing the chrome side vents, window surrounds and sill treatment.

An XE Portfolio with the option of the chrome radiator grille. Exterior trim otherwise as SE and Prestige models.

R-Sport model with sculptured body side sills, R-Sport badging to side vents and gloss black window surrounds.

Rear view of SE, Prestige and Portfolio models. Note the shaping of the rear door quarter window, a quick reference to the car against the larger XF model.

infotainment system, and F-TYPE-derived Configurable Dynamics, most notably torque on-demand all-wheel drive (features already identified on the New XF and F-PACE), a wider range of advanced driver assistance systems became available.

For the 2017 model year Jaguar announced all-wheel-drive 180ps versions of the XE, along with other major technical and infotainment advances. The 6-cylinder engine performance was upgraded to 380ps, but by 2018 the V6 engine was dropped in favour of a new 2.0-litre 300ps turbocharged 4-cylinder unit.

That same year the XE 'Project 8' was announced, reputably the world's fastest four-door car at the time. Just 300 of these 200mph 600PS saloon (produced by Jaguar's Special Vehicle Operations dept), powered by the 5.0-litre V8 supercharged engine, all-wheel-drive with a bespoke rear differential; even the body used bespoke panels.

For 2019 Jaguar announced a simplified model line-up, with all cars receiving a more assertive appearance, more high-tech equipment, the addition of the D180 engine with rear-wheel-drive and all cars becoming compliant with the then latest emissions levels. Amongst the model range was the first special edition, the 'Landmark' based on the other new R-Sport model with 2.0-litre engines and enhanced trim.

In 2020 another special edition arrived: the 'Reims' based on the P250 R-Sport, limited to just 200 examples, offered in the striking new-to-XE paint of French Racing Blue with a Black Pack trim.

The 2021 models featured the next generation of Ingenium engines, a new 2.0-litre 4-cylinder turbocharged 204ps diesel with rear-wheel-drive and 250ps and 300ps 4-cylinder petrol units with all-wheel-drive, all now fitted with 8-speed gearboxes. The whole range was streamlined from 24 to 13 derivatives.

The new 204ps diesel engine brought hybrid power to the XE range for the first time, using a Belt-integrated Starter Generator (BSG) situated in the engine bay to harvest energy usually lost when slowing down or braking. The energy was stored in a 48V lithium-ion battery located beneath the rear luggage space, ready to assist the ICE when accelerating.

XE production was phased out in 2023 to make way for the next generation of new Jaguars, all electric-powered.

Technical points

General aspects applicable to all models.
- ■ Torque vectoring by braking.
- ■ Stop/start system.
- ■ Jaguar Drive control.
- ■ Electric powered assisted steering.
- ■ Cruise control.

Rear view of R-Sport model.

XE S model with satin finished wide vents and unique rear trim/exhaust treatment.

Frontal view of the XE S model with unique badging and air ducts.

Interior layout of the Prestige model with brushed aluminium trim and leather seating.

- Lane departure warning.
- Automatic emergency braking.
- Traffic sign recognition.
- Dynamic stability control and track control.
- Rear parking aid.
- Hill launch assist.
- Electric park brake.
- Automatic lighting and wipers.
- Emergency brake assist.

(From early on in production, specifications and trim changed dramatically from model to model; see below and later chapter on New XF for some examples.)

Exterior identification points

General aspects applicable to all models.

Front view
- Curvaceous frontal aspect taking cues from other current Jaguar saloons.
- One-piece horizontal lighting groups with 'J-blade' running lights.
- Deep lower grille area with side vent ducts.
- Strongly sculpted low line forward hinged bonnet with raised central power bulge.
- Deeply raked front windscreen.

Rear view
- Severe slope 'coupé' style rear roof area.
- High level boot lid with pronounced spoiler type lip.
- Horizontal line rear light units intersecting a roundel similar to F-TYPE.
- Pronounced rear bumper under valance.
- Jaguar Script on boot lid with leaper motif above.

Side view
- Coupé style bodywork with slight forward sloping stance.
- Chromed front wing mounted horizontal vent.
- Neat swage line from the mid point front wing finishing at the rear door area.

SE specifics
- Black mesh radiator grille with chrome surround.
- Chrome front wing side vents.
- Chromed window surrounds.
- 17in Turbine alloy wheels
- 17in Aerodynamic alloy wheels (163PS model only).

Prestige specifics
As SE plus:
- 17in Crux alloy wheels

R-Sport specifics
- Bi-function xenon HID headlights.

Portfolio rear interior with Windsor soft grain leather seating with Herringbone perforations and tonal stitching.

R-Sport interior (manual transmission) with Taurus leather Sports seats with contrast stitching, etched aluminium veneer, and leatherette wrapped dashboard.

XE S interior with sports steering wheel, hex aluminium trim and panoramic roof.

- Gloss black mesh radiator grille with satin chrome surround.
- Gloss black window surrounds.
- Sports (slightly lowered) suspension.
- R-Sport bodykit comprising:-
- R-Sport body coloured side sills.
- Chrome front wing side vents with R-Sport badge.
- Boot lid spoiler.
- 8in Star alloy wheels.

Portfolio specifics
As SE plus:
- 18in Arm alloy wheels.
- 17in Aerodynamic alloy wheels (163PS model only).

S specifics
- Bi-function xenon HID headlights.
- Gloss black mesh radiator grille with satin chrome surround.
- Front bumper incorporates enlarged air intakes.
- Sports suspension.
  S bodykit comprising:
- S deeper front bumper bar arrangement.
- S body coloured and gloss black side sills.
- S gloss black rear valance.
- S gloss black boot lid spoiler.
- Satin chrome front wing side vents.
- Red brake calipers.
- S badging to front and rear of car.
- 19in Star S alloy wheels.

Overall face-lift from 2019
- Remodelled front and rear bumpers.
- All LED headlights (with J-blade running lights) and more slender rear light units with LED signatures.
- Larger grille and under-bumper treatment.
- Bolder graphics.

Landmark Edition
- R-Sport with Sport bumpers, 18in wheels, body coloured sills and boot spoiler.
- Gloss Black grille surround, side vents, side window surrounds and mirror caps.
- 'Landmark' badging to the side vents.
- Only available in Yulong White, Firenze Red or Santorini Black.

Reims Special Edition
- R-Dynamic S guise in French Racing Blue only.
- Black contrast roof, plus full Black Pack trim.
- De-badged.

300 Sport
- '300 Sport' branded brake calipers.
- Only available in Yulong White, Indus Silver, Santorini Black and Caldera Red.
- Dark Satin Grey Sport grille surround, side sills, mirror caps, boot spoiler and rear valance.

Example of sill treat plates, a variety of which are available for the XE.

Centre console area with Jaguar Drive control, 8in touchscreen and auxiliary controls.

Instrument and steering wheel control layout applicable to most models, in this case Prestige.

- Unique boot badge.

Interior identification points

- General aspects applicable to all models.
- Full width 'Riva hoop' style dashboard with instrument binnacle in front of driver.
- Raised central section for air-conditioning outlets and 8in touchscreen/controls.
- Passenger side glove box.
- Deep centre console area incorporating gear selection, auxiliary controls, arm rest and storage space.
- Contour hugging front seats with integral headrests and scalloped seat backs, mounted low in frame.
- Rear seat pack with scalloped seat backs, centrally mounted fold away arm rest, and three integrated headrests.
- Meridian sound system with DAB radio.
- Satellite navigation.
- Soft grain leather steering wheel with multi-functions.
- 8in touchscreen.
- Jaguar voice recognition system.
- InControl connect and protect system.
- Bluetooth connectivity.

SE specifics
- Cloth seating.
- Gloss black veneer.
- Metal sill finishers with Jaguar lettering.

Prestige specifics
- Taurus leather seating with contrast stitching.

Special Vehicle operations XE Project 8.

The bespoke interior of the Project 8.

XE 300 Sport.

XE 300 Sport interior.

The XE Reims special edition.

- Brushed aluminium veneer.
- Heated front seats.
- Metal sill finishers with Jaguar lettering.
- Phosphor blue ambient lighting.

R-Sport specifics
- Taurus leather Sports seats with contrast stitching.
- Etched aluminium veneer.
- Heated front seats.
- Leatherette wrapped dashboard.
- Metal sill finishers with Jaguar R-Sport branding.

- Heated front seats.
- Extended interior mood lighting.

Portfolio specifics
- Windsor soft grain leather seating with Herringbone perforations and tonal stitching.
- 10-way electric adjustable front seating.
- Leatherette wrapped dashboard with two colour upper and lower sections.
- Embossed aluminium veneer.
- Metal sill finishers with Jaguar lettering.
- Meridian 380watt sound system.
- Extended interior mood lighting.

S specifics
- S branded front sports seating with perforated Taurus leather and contrast stitching.
- 10-way electric adjustable front seating.
- Leatherette wrapped dashboard.
- Leather sports steering wheel with S logo.
- Dark hex aluminium veneer.
- Gloss black centre console.
- Metal sill finishers with Jaguar S branding.
- Bright stainless steel pedal covers.
- Meridian 380watt sound system.
- Jaguar smart key operation.
- Powered boot lid.
- Additional 12v sockets.
- Extended interior moor lighting.

Overall face-lift from 2019
- More soft-touch materials throughout.
- Whole interior improved ergonomically to accommodate the host of new technology and increase comfort.
- ShoftShift and JaguarDriver now redesigned as F-TYPE sports.
- Redesigned centre console area.
- New steering wheel design with 'hidden until lit' graphics and new controls for key functions.
- ClearSight 'in segment' rear view mirror.
- New infotainment system with larger screen and better controls.

Landmark Edition
- R-Sport interior specification plus:
- 'Landmark' branded treadplates.

Reims Special Edition
- Privacy glass.
- Heater windscreen.
- Cold Climate Pack.

300 Sport
- '300 Sport' badging to headrests, steering wheel, carpet mats and treadplates.
- Yellow contrast stitching on instrument panel, door casings, armrest, carpet mats, steering wheel and seats.

Interior of the XE Reims special edition.

Above: The post 2020MY front facelift treatment for the XE models; Below: rear/side views.

The revised dashboard layout of the facelifted XEs.

The facelift interior, in this instance an HSE model.

XE Landmark edition.

XE saloons from 2015

1 – 17in Aerodynamic Silver (Style 1017).

2 – Lightweight Silver (Style 1016).

3 – 17in Turbine Silver (Style 1047).

4 – 17in Crux Sparkle Silver (Style 7010).

5 – 17in Projector Sparkle Silver (Style 5032).

6 – 17in (Style 1048).

7 – 18in Star Silver Diamond Turned (Style 5030).

8 – 18in Arm Sparkle Silver (Style 6006).

9 – 18in Matrix Sparkle Silver (Style 7009).

10 – 18in Matrix Black (Style 7009).

11 – 18in Templar Silver Diamond Turned (Style 5029).

12 – 18in (Style 1049).

13 – 18in (Style 5121).

14 – 19in Star Sparkle Silver (Style 5071).

15 – 19in Radiance Sparkle Silver (Style 1015).

16 – 19in Radiance Black Diamond Turned (Style 1015).

17 – 19in Venom Silver Diamond Turned/also in Black (Style 5031).

18 – 20in Propeller Silver Diamond Turned (Style 1014).

19 – 19in (Style 1050).

Optional extras

Chrome front splitter and body coloured spoiler.
Satin chrome front splitter, body-coloured spoiler.
Sports rear valance.
Chrome grille.
Gloss black grille.
Bi-function xenon headlights.
Gloss black side vents.
Gloss black R-Sport side vents.
Carbon fibre side vents.
Carbon fibre mirror covers.
Chrome mirror covers.
Gloss black mirror covers.
Powered fold back mirrors.
Heated front windscreen.
Privacy glass.
Luxury loadspace carpet mat.
Luxury interior carpet mats.
Stainless steel Sport pedal covers.
R-Sport branded multi-function steering wheel in soft grain leather with highlights.
Leather topped gear selector.
Illuminated sill tread plates.
Personalised illuminated sill tread plates.
Union Jack sill tread plates.
Aluminium gearshift paddles.
Jaguar branded wheel nut set (black or chrome).
Stylised wheel nut sets – Union Jack/Jaguar logo/ Black Jack/R logo.
Union Jack alloy wheel centre caps.
Rear parking sensors.
Garage door opener.
Child seat.
Snow sock traction aid.
Snow traction system.
Surfboard/sailboard holder.
Ski holder.
Sport roof box.
Large sport roof box
Large sport roof box with ski inserts.
Ski bag.
Roof mounted bike carrier.
Fork mounted bike carrier.
Universal lift and load system.
Tow bar bike carrier.
iPad holder.
Sunshades.
Heated steering wheel.
Premium seatback storage.
Roof luggage box.
Roof cross bars.
Tow bar system.
Front windscreen sunshade.
Luggage compartment nets.
Collapsible boot organizer.
Centre armrest chiller.
Seatback storage.
Headrest mounted coathanger.
WhiteFire headphones.
First aid kit.
Front and rear mud flaps.
Rechargeable torch and dock.
Protective second row seat cover.
Bumper protector.
Space saver spare wheel.
Jaguar tyre repair system.
All weather car cover.
Battery conditioner.
Panoramic sunroof.
Smoker's pack
   Smoking receptacle.
   Lighter.
Dynamic Handling Kit.
Cold Climate Pack.
Technology Pack.
Convenience Pack.
Premium Interior Upgrade Pack.

Colour schemes

Exterior paintwork

Polaris White	to 2018
Glacier White Metallic	to 2018
Fuji White	2018 to end
Yulong White	2018 to end
Rhodium Silver	to 2018
Osmium	to 2016
Quartzite	to 2018
Gallium Silver	to 2018
Indus Silver	2018 to end
Silicone Silver	2018 to end
Hakuba Silver	2021 to end
Ammonite Grey	to 2018
Ingot	to 2018
Tempest Grey	to 2018
Storm Grey	to 2018
Corris Grey	2017 to end
Carpathian Grey	2018 to end
Eiger Grey	2019 to 2021

Bluefire	2017 to 2021
Dark Sapphire	to 2018
Caesium Blue	2018 to end
Loire Blue	2018 to end
Portofino Blue	2019 to end
Odyssey Red	to 2018
Italian Racing Red	to 2018
Caldera Red	2018 to end
Firenze Red	2018 to end
Black Cherry	to 2018
Ebony	to 2018
Cosmic Black	2018 to end
Norvik Black	2018 to end
Santorini Black	2018 to end
Ultimate Black	to 2018
Celestial Black	to 2018
Indus Black	2018 to end
British Racing Green	to 2018

(continued on page 370)

Technical specifications

	2.0-litre diesel (163PS)	2.0-litre diesel (180PS) 2 and AWD	2.0-litre petrol (200PS)	2.0-litre petrol (240PS)
cc	1999	1999	1997	1999
Bore and stroke (mm)	83 x 92.4	83 x 92.4	87.5 x 83.1	87.5 x 83.1
Compression ratio	15.5 to 1	15.5 to 1	10 to 1	10 to 1
bhp	163	180	200	240
@ rpm	4000	4000	5500	5500
Max torque (lb ft)	280	317	206	250
@ rpm	2500	2500	4000	4000
Fuelling	Common rail fuel-injection	Common rail fuel-injection	Common rail fuel-injection	Common fuel-injection
Transmission	6-speed manual 8-speed ZF 8HP45 automatic	6-speed manual (not AWD) 8-speed ZF 8HP45 automatic	8-speed ZF 8HP45 automatic	8-speed ZF 8HP45 automatic
Wheel size (in)	17, 20	17, 20	17 to 20	17, 20
Suspension front	Double wishbone	Double wishbone	Double wishbone	Double wishbone
Suspension rear	Integral link	Integral link	Integral link	Integral link
Brakes	4-wheel discs	4-wheel discs	4-wheel discs	4-wheel discs
Performance				
0 to 60mph (secs)	7.9 (manual) 7.7 (auto)	7.9 (manual) 7.4 (auto) 7.5 (AWD)	7.1	6.5
Top speed (mph)	132	140	147	155
Average mpg	75	67, 60.6 (AWD)	38	38
Dimensions				
Length (in)	184	184	184	184
Width (in)	81.6	81.6	81.6	81.6
Height (in)	55.7	55.7	55.7	55.7
Wheelbase (in)	111.6	111.6	111.6	111.6
Front track (in)	63.2	63.2	63.2	63.2
Rear track (in)	63.3	63.3	63.3	63.3
Weight (kg)	1475 (manual) 1500 (auto)	1550 (manual) 1565 (auto) 1660 (AWD)	1530	1535

2.0-litre petrol (250PS)	2.0-litre petrol (300PS)	3.0-litre (340PS)	3.0-litre (380PS)
1997	1997	2995	2995
83 x 92.4	83 x 92.4	84.5 x 89	84.5 x 89
10.5 to 1	9.5 to 1	10.5 to 1	10.5 to 1
250	300	340	380
5500	5500	6500	6500
269	295	332	450
4500	4500	4500	3500/5000
Common rail fuel injection	Common rail fuel injection	Fuel-injection	Fuel-injection
8-speed ZF 8HP45 automatic	8-speed ZF 8HP45 automatic	8-speed auto	8-speed auto
17 to 20	17 to 20	19, 20	19 to 20
Double wishbone	Double wishbone	Double wishbone	Double wishbone
Integral link	Integral link	Integral link	Integral link
4-wheel discs	4-wheel discs	4-wheel discs	4-wheel discs
6.2	5.4	4.9	4.8
155	155	155	155
39.2	39.2	34.9	24
184	184	184	184
81.6	81.6	81.6	81.6
55.7	55.7	55.7	55.7
111.6	111.6	111.6	111.6
63.2	63.2	63.2	63.2
63.3	63.3	63.3	63.3
1611	1690	1665	2230

Colour schemes (continued)

Seats	
Jet	Duo-tones:
Ebony	Latte/Ebony
Midnight Blue	Jet/Red
Light Oyster	Jet/Midnight Blue
Latte	Red/Might Blue
Pebble Grey	Ebony/Pimento
Sienna Tan	Light Oyster/Ebony
Brogue	Ebony/Sienna Tan
Mars Red	Light Oyster/Pimento
Pimento	Light Oyster/Pistachio

Upper fascia/trim	
Jet	Oyster/Light Oyster
Jet/Ebony	Oyster
Jet/Light Oyster	Light Oyster
Jet/Sienna Tan	Midnight Blue
Jet/Brogue	Latte
Jet/Latte	Ebony

Contrast stitching/piping
Jet/Ebony
Red/Pimento
Jet/Red
Midnight Blue
Light Oyster
Red
Sienna Tan
Pistachio
Ebony
Flame Red
Brogue
Vintage Tan
Eclipse

Carpets
Jet
Ebony
Oyster

Headlining
Jet
Ebony
Light Oyster

Dashboard/console finishers	
Carbon Fibre	2017 to end
Gloss Black	to end
Brushed Aluminium	to end
Etched Aluminium	to end
Embossed Aluminium	to end
Meshed Aluminium	to end
Monogram Aluminum	2021 to end
Satin Ash Burr	to end
Gloss Figured Ebony	to end
Satin Grey Ash	to end
Satin Grey Figured Ebony	to end
Satin Fine Line Metallic	to end

Prices and production years

Model	Price new	2015	2016	2017	2018	2019	2020	2021	2022	2023
2.0-litre D163 SE	£29,775	■	■	■	■	■	–	–	–	–
2.0-litre D163 Prestige	£30,775	■	■	■	■	■	–	–	–	–
2.0-litre D163 R-Sport	£32,325	■	■	■	■	■	–	–	–	–
2.0-litre D163 Portfolio	£32,975	■	■	■	■	■	–	–	–	–
2.0-litre D180 SE	£30,225	■	■	■	■	■	–	–	–	–
2.0-litre D180 SE AWD	£33,825	–	–	■	■	■	–	–	–	–
2.0-litre D180 Prestige	£31,275	■	■	■	■	■	–	–	–	–

Model	Price new	2015	2016	2017	2018	2019	2020	2021	2022	2023
2.0-litre D180 Prestige AWD	£34,825	–	–	■	■	■	–	–	–	–
2.0-litre D180 R-Sport	£33,025	■	■	■	■	■	–	–	–	–
2.0-litre D180 R-Sport AWD	£36,575	–	–	■	■	■	–	–	–	–
2.0-litre D180 Portfolio	£33,675	■	■	■	■	■	–	–	–	–
2.0-litre D180 Portfolio AWD	£37,225	–	–	■	■	■	–	–	–	–
2.0-litre P200 SE	£26,990	■	■	■	■	■	–	–	–	–
2.0-litre P200 Prestige	£27,990	■	■	■	■	■	–	–	–	–
2.0-litre P200 R-Sport	£29,740	■	■	■	■	■	–	–	–	–
2.0-litre P240 Presrige	£32,900	■	■	■	■	■	–	–	–	–
2.0-litre P240 R-Sport	£33,090	■	■	■	■	■	–	–	–	–
2.0-litre P240 Portfolio	£33,740	■	■	■	■	■	–	–	–	–
3.0-litre P340 S	£44,865	■	■	■	■	–	–	–	–	–
5.0-litre Project 8	£149,995	–	–	–	■	■	–	–	–	–
2.0-litre D180 S	£34,555	–	–	–	■	■	–	–	–	–
2.0-litre D180 S AWD	£36,415	–	–	–	■	■	–	–	–	–
2.0-litre D180 SE	£36,025	–	–	–	■	■	–	–	–	–
2.0-litre D180 SE AWD	£37,885	–	–	–	■	■	–	–	–	–
2.0-litre D180 HSE	£39,215	–	–	–	■	■	–	–	–	–
2.0-litre D180 HSE AWD	£41,035	–	–	–	■	■	–	–	–	–
2.0-litre D180 R-Dynamic S	£36,145	–	–	–	■	■	–	–	–	–
2.0-litre D180 R-Dynamic S AWD	£38,005	–	–	–	■	■	–	–	–	–
2.0 ltre D180 R-Dynamic SE	£37,615	–	–	–	■	■	–	–	–	–
2.0-litre D180 R-Dynamic SE AWD	£39,475	–	–	–	■	■	–	–	–	–
2.0-litre D180 R-Dynamic HSE	£41,015	–	–	–	■	■	–	–	–	–
2.0-litre D180 R-Dynamic HSE	£42,835	–	–	–	■	■	–	–	–	–
2.0-litre D200 S		–	–	–	–	–	■	–	–	–
2.0-litre D200 SE		–	–	–	–	–	■	–	–	–
2.0-litre D200 HSE		–	–	–	–	–	■	–	–	–
2.0-litre D200 HSE Black		–	–	–	–	–	■	–	–	–
2.0-litre D200 R-Sport S		–	–	–	–	–	■	–	–	–
2.0-litre P250 S	£33,915	–	–	–	■	■	■	–	–	–
2.0-litre P250 S AWD	£39,415	–	–	–	■	■	■	–	–	–
2.0-litre P250 SE	£35,385	–	–	–	■	■	■	–	–	–
2.0-litre P350 SE AWD	£40,885	–	–	–	■	■	■	–	–	–
2.0-litre P250 HSE	£38,535	–	–	–	■	■	■	–	–	–
2.0-litre P250 HSE AWD	£44,035	–	–	–	■	■	■	–	–	–
2.0-litre P250 HSE Black		–	–	–	■	■	■	–	–	–
2.0-litre P250 HSE Black AWD		–	–	–	■	■	■	–	–	–
2.0-litre P250 R-Sport S		–	–	–	■	■	■	–	–	–

Model	Price new	2015	2016	2017	2018	2019	2020	2021	2022	2023
2.0-litre P250 R-Sport S AWD		–	–	–	■	■	■	–	–	–
3.0-litre P300 S		–	–	–	–	■	■	–	–	–
3.0-litre P300 SE		–	–	–	–	■	■	–	–	–
3.0-litre P300 HSE		–	–	–	–	■	■	–	–	–
3.0-litre P300 HSE Black		–	–	–	–	■	■	–	–	–
3.0-litre P300 R-Sport S		–	–	–	–	■	■	–	–	–
2.0-litre P250 R-Dynamic S	£35,505	–	–	–	–	–	–	■	–	–
2.0-litre P250 R-Dynamic S AWD	£41,005	–	–	–	–	–	–	■	–	–
2.0-litre P250 R-Dynamic SE	£36,975	–	–	–	–	–	–	■	–	–
2.0-litre P250 R-Dynamic SE AWD	£40,885	–	–	–	–	–	–	■	–	–
2.0-litre P250 R-Dynamic HSE	£40,335	–	–	–	–	–	–	■	–	–
2.0-litre P250 R-Dynamic HSE AWD	£44,035	–	–	–	–	–	–	■	–	–
2.0-litre P300 R-Dynamic S AWD	£41,005	–	–	–	–	–	–	■	–	–
2.0-litre P300 R-Dynamic SE AWD	£42,475	–	–	–	–	–	–	■	–	–
2.0-litre P300 R-Dynamic HSE AWD	£45,835	–	–	–	–	–	–	■	–	–
3.0-litre P380 SE S AWD		–	–	–	■	■	■	–	–	–
2.0-litre 300ps AWD (all variants)		–	–	–	–	–	–	■	–	–
2.0-litre Landmark Special Edition		–	–	–	–	■	–	–	–	–
2.0-litre Reims Special Edition	£38,295	–	–	–	–	■	■	–	–	–
2.0-litre D200 SMHEV RWD	£30,205	–	–	–	–	–	–	■	■	–
2.0-litre D200 R-Dynamic S MHEV RWD	£31,160	–	–	–	–	–	–	■	■	■
2.0-litre D200 R-Dynamic SE MHEV RWD	£32,810	–	–	–	–	–	–	■	■	–
2.0-litre D200 R-Dynamic SE Black MHEV RWD	£35,590	–	–	–	–	–	–	–	–	■
2.0-litre D200 R-Dynamic HSE MHEV RWD	£35,700	–	–	–	–	–	–	■	■	–
2.0-litre D200 R-Dynamic Black MHEV RWD	£32,985	–	–	–	–	–	–	–	–	■
2.0-litre P250 S RWD	£29,635	–	–	–	–	–	–	■	■	–
2.0-litre P250 R-Dynamic S RWD		–	–	–	–	–	–	■	■	–
2.0-litre P250 R-Dynamic SE RWD	£32,235	–	–	–	–	–	–	■	■	–
2.0-litre P250 R-Dynamic HSE RWD	£36,585	–	–	–	–	–	–	■	■	–
2.0-litre P250 R-Dynamic Black RWD	£32,985	–	–	–	–	–	–	■	■	■
2.0-litre P300 R-Dynamic S AWD	£36,035	–	–	–	–	–	–	■	■	–
2.0-litre P300 R-Dynamic SE AWD	£37,285	–	–	–	–	–	–	■	■	–
2.0-litre P300 R-Dynamic HSE AWD	£40,140	–	–	–	–	–	–	■	■	–

New XF saloons and sportbrakes from 2015

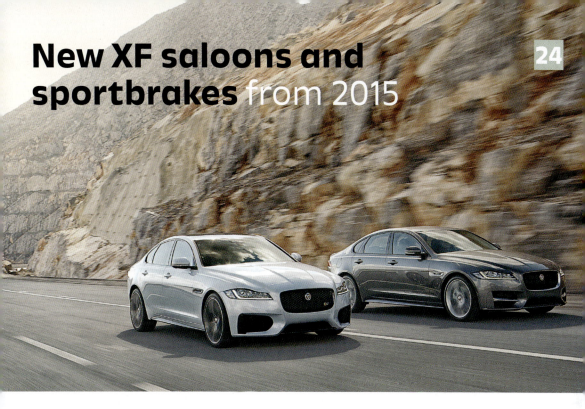

Background

The original XF, dating from 2007 to 2015, was a great success for Jaguar, increasing their sales figures dramatically as part of the new regime in styling, courtesy of Jaguar's Chief Styling Director, Ian Callum. After the launch of the XF came the New XJ, the XE, and the New XF, introduced in 2015.

Although retaining the XF insignia and some of the earlier car's looks, the New XF was just that: almost all new.

The first big change was in the production of the bodywork, now an aluminium-intensive structure following on from the XJ and XE, making the new car 80kg lighter than its competition and 28 per cent stiffer than the old XF.

With the new structure came revised styling. An even sleeker coupé style with a 51mm longer wheelbase, within a 3mm lower and 7mm shorter body, gave improved aerodynamics and interior space. The more vertical front end, shorter front overhang, longer wheelbase, and a sixth-light with characteristic daylight opening graphic signified the evolution of the Jaguar design language launched on the original XF in 2007.

The interior design was totally new, using contemporary materials in a new style following design features from the F-TYPE and XE. Technological aspects included Jaguar's highly sophisticated Infotainment and connectivity system: a multi-GB solid state hard drive for media storage for Meridian digital sound systems.

The New XF was also technically advanced, following the same principles as its smaller brother the XE, covered in the earlier chapter. Such strategic enhancements included Adopting Electric Power Steering, Advanced Passive Damper Technology, Configurable Dynamics and All-Surface Progress Control.

Only four-door coupé style saloon versions were available, while the Sportbrake continues to be produced in the original XF style with a steel body structure.

Model range and development

At first glance, one could perhaps easily confuse the New XF with the old XF, as many of the style changes are subtle, but they are important. Build quality has been improved via the attributes of Jaguar's aluminum intensive architecture and advanced manufacturing facilities. As well as for the main structure, aluminium is also used for the bonnet and front wings, while the front-end carrier and cross-car beam are cast from magnesium alloys, like the other alloy-bodied Jaguars. This presents a weight saving of 190kg over its predecessor.

Complete body sides are stamped from a single sheet of high-strength 6000-series alloy weighing less than 6kg and perfecting the deep haunches and the six-light design utilised the experience gained from the F-TYPE in terms of depth of draw and tightness of radii and a two-stage framing process was used to assemble this to the rest of the structure allowing for great joint efficiency and the optimised positioning of rivets. All this led to increased torsional rigidity of the body compared to the older car.

The New XF is more refined than its predecessor in reducing structure-borne noise. Every single part of the body was analysed to ensure that as many potential sources of noise could be designed out. In some areas, such as the crash structure behind the front bulkhead, fully-sealed, double-wall structures were used. Where sound deadening was applied, the latest spray-on materials were used due to their combination of higher performance and lower weight.

Foam baffles inside the aluminium sections were fitted during assembly so that, as the body passed through the e-coating ovens, the heat caused the foam to expand, completely filling the section. The cars therefore achieved benchmark low levels of cabin noise.

An example of the attention to detail with the New XF was the high-level brakelight fitted to the body, running all the way along the full length of the rear screen, with a seal and an acoustic barrier behind to minimise any noise leakage through to the interior.

The New XF was engineered to meet the most demanding crash test requirements in the world. As part of the intelligent material mix in the body, the rear longitudinal members and the B-pillar reinforcements were made from ultra-high strength hot-formed boron steels, providing exceptional rigidity and stability of the occupant safety cell.

Pedestrian protection benefited from the more vertical front grille and the improved energy-absorbing properties of the front bumper, enhanced further by Jaguar's latest-generation deployable bonnet technology, first seen on the New XK back in 2007.

The New XF models were engineered to provide a near 50:50 weight distribution to ensure excellent handling and balance. Double-wishbone front and integral link rear suspension systems, made entirely from lightweight aluminium, provided the inherently high levels of stiffness needed. Other refinements included lighter springs made from narrower-gauge steel, and low-friction, PTFE-lined bushes for the tubular anti-roll bar.

The new XF also utilised many technically advanced features developed for the other modern Jaguar models like a version of the Electric Power Assisted Steering, Torque Vectoring by Braking, and configurable Dynamics.

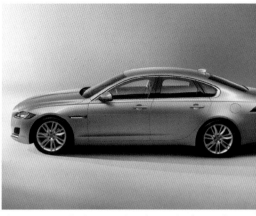

The New XF. Note the shorter overhang, longer wheelbase and swage lines compared to the previous XF in chapter 20 This is the Prestige model with Razor alloy wheels.

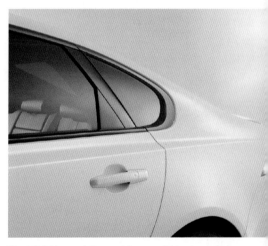

The sixth-light rear window providing more light and an instant identification feature of the New XF. This is an R-Sport model with black window finishers.

Model range at launch

XF Prestige 2.0-litre (163PS) diesel
XF R-Sport 2.0-litre (163PS) diesel
XF Portfolio 2.0-litre (163PS) diesel
XF Prestige 2.0-litre (163PS) diesel auto
XF R-Sport 2.0-litre (163PS) diesel auto
XF Portfolio 2.0-litre (163PS) diesel auto
XF Prestige 2.0-litre (180PS) diesel
XF R-Sport 2.0-litre (180PS) diesel
XF Portfolio 2.0-litre (180PS) diesel
XF Prestige 2.0-litre (180PS) diesel auto
XF R-Sport 2.0-litre (180PS) diesel auto
XF Portfolio 2.0-litre (180PS) diesel auto
XF S 3.0-litre (300PS) diesel auto
XF 3.0-litre (380PS) Supercharged petrol auto

The New XF was initially powered by a choice of Jaguar's Ingenium 4-cylinder or 6-cylinder Euro 6 diesel and petrol engines, some of which also appeared in the XE models. Details of these engines are covered in the Engines chapter at the front of this publication, and in the XE chapter previously.

The 2.0-litre 4-cylinder diesel units were rated at 163PS/380Nm and 180PS/430Nm respectively, both with 6-speed manual and 8-speed automatic transmissions.

Jaguar's 3.0-litre V6 diesel engine used in its latest generation retained the same 2993cc displacement as before, but changes to the fuel injection and boosting systems raised output from 275PS/600Nm to 300PS/700Nm.

One petrol engine was initially available, the existing 3.0-litre supercharged V6, producing 380PS, which was shared with the F-TYPE sports car as well. This was the first time the 380PS version had been used in a Jaguar saloon, reserved exclusively for the New XF S. Matched to an 8-speed automatic transmission, this model was capable of covering the 0-60mph sprint in 5.1 seconds on its way to an electronically-limited maximum speed of 155mph.

As well as the 8-speed automatic transmission this was the first XF model to be available with a light, low-friction 6-speed manual transmission developed with ZF.

In terms of styling, the front overhang was now 66mm shorter, and the mesh grille more vertical than before, with aerodynamics improved further by using apertures in the front bumper to channel air over the front wheels. The headlights – including the adaptive full-LED technology, appearing for the first time in a Jaguar – were flush with the surrounding panels. They also featured Jaguar's signature J-Blade LED daytime running lights, with the fluting running backwards from the top of the headlights. The sweeping, coupé-like profile that defined the first-generation XF had evolved, and now featured

Frontal aspects of the various models, in this case the Portfolio.

The R-Sport frontal styling pointers, including the J-blade lighting, vertical grille and pronounced vertical lines from the bonnet to under-panel.

The S model with more pronounced lower intakes.

2022 model year subtle changes to exterior styling. Note the headlight re-design.

a sixth-light. This helped to reinforce the car's status and prestige, and also allowed for a clearer view out from the rear seats. Also, the extra light flooding into the cabin created a greater sense of spaciousness, to mirror the increased leg and headroom.

Still relatively high so as to emphasise dynamics and movement through ideal proportion between the wheel, body and cabin, the waistline was now slightly more horizontal, creating a more formal, business-focused appearance. The roofline was lower and the rear deck longer and higher to reduce drag.

Running from front to back, peaking above the rear wheel in terms of height and then tapering away, was a chamfered feature line known as 'the spear of light.' The reflections made the car appear even more lithe, more agile, and more elegant.

Subtle differences between the models, this being a Portfolio.

The R-Sport – different exhaust tailpipe arrangements according to engine type.

S model.

At the rear, the LED tail lights feature the signature Jaguar graphic from F-TYPE – a line intersecting a roundel – also used on the XE. But here, the graphic is repeated, creating a clear hierarchy from XE, and an unmistakable pattern at night: everybody will know that this is the New XF.

The chrome signature blade running across the bootlid between the light clusters was now slimmer than before, emphasising the all-new XF's taut surfaces and dynamic visual balance.

To deliver the flush fit of the light clusters and perfect integration of the chrome blade, the boot lid was made from two steel pressings joined by laser brazing. As well as being highly energy-efficient, this state-of-the-art process was selected for its precision and neat, clean finish.

Advanced driver aids include Colour Laser Head-up Display, stereo camera technology enabling Autonomous Emergency Braking, Lane Departure Warning and Adaptive Cruise Control. A traffic sign recognition system introduced

2022 model year changes to the rear exterior styling.

Jaguar's first application of an intelligent speed limiter.

The interior of the New XF followed the brief for the XE with strong, simple lines and horizontal feel of the instrument panel, yet with the use of materials to enhance its position in the Jaguar chain of model hierarchy. The layered instrument panel, now with Jaguar signature 'Riva Hoop' inspired by the big brother XJ, continued into the door, enhanced by the use of veneers.

Options included the reconfigurable, 12.3in full-TFT instrument cluster and 10.2in touchscreen, four-zone climate control, ten-colour ambient lighting, Black Suedecloth headliner and fluted Windsor leather seats.

The doors were fitted with an optional soft-close shut and there was even a backlighting fade when the engine start button was pressed.

With the new layout of the architecture the New XF allowed rear seat passengers to sit further away from the rear wheels, giving an extra 15mm of legroom and 24mm of knee-room than the old model, and 27mm more headroom.

The new car also featured two state-of-the-art infotainment systems. The standard system was InControl Touch, based around an 8in capacitive touchscreen with Jaguar's new user interface, supporting gestures familiar from smartphones and tablets. There was an enhanced speech recognition engine for InControl Touch enabling the driver to make a one-shot destination entry for the navigation system.

The New XF was the first model to feature the equally new InControl Touch Pro premium infotainment system featuring state-of-the-art technologies using a 10.2in capacitive touchscreen. Like a smartphone, the home screen could be customised with wallpaper, widgets, and even to add extra home screens.

The navigation system used data stored on InControl Touch Pro's 60GB solid-state drive (SSD) accessed in a fraction of the time compared to conventional hard drive systems. It represented Jaguar's most advanced system at the time, with door-to-door route planning and guidance incorporating public transport options, a Commute Mode that learnt your daily drive so it could automatically offer alternative routes to avoid congestion, real-time traffic information, and an Approach Mode which showed a 360° interactive view of your destination from up to 200m away – it even advised on the nearest available car parking spaces.

The XFs InControl Apps allowed seamless connection to Apple and Android smartphones. For the last word in comfort and convenience, Remote Premium enabled the driver to bring the cabin to a preset temperature by remotely starting the engine (automatic transmissions only). Using an integrated SIM card and the vehicle antenna for the strongest and most reliable signal, the New XF connected to the internet, and could function as a Wi-Fi hotspot, providing a 3G connection for up to eight devices.

The new style rear lighting treatment, with 'signature' illumination strips.

The beautifully sculpted styling for the New XF.

The S model with panoramic roof and Labyrinth alloy wheels.

The R-Sport model with Star alloy wheels.

InControl Secure enhanced security by providing proactive vehicle monitoring. Should the all-new XF be stolen, the tracking service worked with law enforcement agencies to locate and recover the car as quickly as possible.

Should the worst happen and the car be involved in a collision severe enough to trigger the airbags, InControl Protect automatically notified the emergency services, and provided the GPS location of the vehicle. Occupants could also trigger an emergency call manually by pressing a button.

All Surface Progress Control (ASPC) was another advanced feature of the car, activated by pressing a button on the centre console. The driver then used the cruise control switches on the steering wheel to set the maximum speed. After that, the system provided fine control of the throttle, and used the brakes in opposition so that, from standstill, only very low engine torque was applied to the driven wheels, ensuring smooth progress with little or no wheel spin.

There was a forward facing stereo camera interpreting information via image processing software, which provided advanced driver assistance systems including: Autonomous Emergency Braking, Lane Departure Warning and Lane Keep Assist, Traffic Sign Recognition, and the Driver Condition Monitoring Systems.

In 2016 Jaguar commenced production of the XF in China, using the existing Land Rover 'Chery' facility. Only produced there as a long wheelbase model (XFL), 140mm extra length was accommodated in the new body, with the extra room added to rear occupant accommodation. This involved a modified platform, roof and rear doors. It was available with a choice of three power plans 200bhp, 204bhp or 340bhp.

The XF range developed quickly, by 2017 offering two additional petrol engines (P200 and P250) and another diesel (P240). The two larger engines were also available in all-wheel-drive form. Some of the high-technology featured was now standardised across the range, including Configurable Dynamics, and there was even a 'gesture' control for the boot lid to automatically open and close it. The infotainment system was improved, as were the electrically adjustable seats on the Portfolio model.

Jaguar's five-star EUO NCAP racing was improved with a trio of new features: Blind Spot Monitoring, Forward Traffic Detection and Forward Vehicle Guidance.

Later in 2017, another new engine was offered, a 300PS Ingenium 4-cylinder unit (P300). With twin-scroll turbos and a high-flow compressor wheel, enhanced performance considerable 400Nm of torque and mated to an 8-speed transmission.

In the same year the Sportbrake (estate car) variants of the above models became available.

The Portfolio, noticeably with more chrome trim, in this case fitted with Matrix alloy wheels.

Interior of the S model.

Interior of the Portfolio model.

The redesigned interior XF package.

Rear seating arrangement, in this case a Portfolio model.

One of several various arrangements of sill tread plates available for the cars.

For the 2018 model year, the '300 Sport' special edition was offered in both saloon and Sportbrake variants, with the option of the 2.0-litre D300 AWD or 3.0-litre P300 RWD drivetrains. Available in just three paint finishes, white, silver or black, unique badging and different finishes to exterior and interior trim set the model apart from the standard range.

In 2019/2020 the 3.0-litre P380 engine was deleted from the range and a new 'Pure' specification model became available for certain models, with a choice of 17in or 18in alloy wheels, Premium fabric seating with 10-way electric adjustment and Gloss Black veneer with Morse Code Aluminium finishing.

The extra cost digital instrument pack.

Announced in 2021 for the 2022 model year, the model names and range changed again with the introduction of the R-Dynamic S, SE HSE and Black replacing all the previous variants. The only engine variants now were the P250 2.0-litre 4-cylinder petrol with rear-wheel-drive, and P300 2.0-litre 4-cylinder all-wheel-drive, plus D204 2.9-litre 4-cylinder with the option of rear-wheel-drive or all-wheel-drive.

In line with the same engines fitted to the XE (see early chapter), both the latter models were MHEV hybrid, developing 430Nm of torque. The Best Integrated Starter Generator recoups energy usually lost during braking or deceleration, by storing it in a compact 48V lithium-ion battery. This energy is redeployed to assist the engine when accelerating.

Detail of the centre console layout.

The range for 2021 therefore amounted to 10 saloons and 8 Sportbrakes.

For production finally running down in 2023/2024 in readiness for Jaguar's new all-electric models, the range was reduced to a total of just nine models.

Exterior identification points

- General points applicable to all models compared to the old XF

The manual 6-speed transmission, available on certain models only.

Front view
- More vertical front end with shorter overhang.
- More vertical and pronounced mesh radiator grille and surround.
- Larger apertures in the lower bumper/front wing area to channel air to the front wheels.
- Flatter horizontal light units mounted flush with surrounding panels and incorporating J-blade LED running lights.

Rear view
- General style follows the current Jaguar trend set by the XE.
- LED rear light units with a signature Jaguar graphic taken from the F-TYPE – a line intersecting a roundel.
- Slimmer chrome signature blade running across the boot lid between the light clusters.
- Boot lid made from two steel pressings joined by laser brazing.
- Jaguar and leaper insignia on boot lid centre mounted.
- Separate under-bumper panel incorporating cut-outs for exhaust tailpipes.

Side view
- Front overhang 66mm shorter.
- Bonnet line 35mm lower.
- 51mm longer wheelbase.
- 3mm lower and shorter body.
- Six-light window structure.
- Waistline now slightly more horizontal.
- Roofline lower, and rear deck longer and higher to reduce drag.
- Chamfered feature swage line runs front to back, peaking above the rear wheel.

Prestige model specifics

Front view
- Bi-function xenon headlights.
- Headlight powerwash.
- Approach illumination.
- Grained black insert radiator grille with chrome surround.

Rear view
- Chromed boot lid finisher.
- Partial LED rear light units.

Side view
- Body coloured door mirrors, heated with repeater lights.
- Chromed side window finishers.
- Chromed front wing power vents.
- 17in Lightweight alloy wheels.

R-Sport model specifics

As Prestige model plus:
Front view
- Grained black insert radiator grille with satin

Luggage compartment layout of the New XF.

chrome surround.

Rear view
Satin chrome boot lid finisher.

Side view
- Gloss black side window finishers.
- R-Sport front wing power vents in satin chrome.
- R-Sport bodykit.
- 17in Turbine alloy wheels (163PS engine).
- 18in Helix alloy wheels (180PS engine).

Portfolio model specifics

As Prestige models plus:

Front view
- Heated front windscreen and screenwash jets.
- Gloss black insert radiator grille with chrome surround.

Side view
- Powerfold door mirrors.
- 17in Aerodynamic alloy wheels (163PS engine).
- 18in Fan alloy wheels (180PS engine).

S model specifics

As R-Sport plus:

Front view
- Front wing power vents in satin chrome.

Side view
- Red brake calipers.
- S bodykit.
- 19in Razor alloy wheels.

300 Sport
- Yulong White, Indus Silver and Santorini Black paintwork.
- Dark Satin Grey exterior trim.
- Satin Technical Grey alloy wheels.
- '300 Sport' badging.

R-Dynamic Black
- Gloss black finish to door mirror backs, sills and grille plus side window surrounds, roof rails and badges.

The 300 Sport, in this instance the Sportbrake version.

- Gloss Black finish to alloy wheels.
- Red brake calipers.

Interior identification points

General points applicable to all models compared to the old XF.
- Layered instrument panel with 'Riva Hoop,' similar to XJ and XE.
- General layout follows the style of the XE (see earlier chapter).
- Retention of 'disappearing' air vents at extreme corners of dash panel.
- Centrally mounted 'open' air vents set above touchscreen and controls.
- High centre console containing Jaguar rotary gear selector and other controls.
- Virtual instrument pack.

Typical enhanced interior of the XF 300 Sport model.

Last of line 2023 model year Sportbrake.

- Commonality of steering wheel with other models.
- 15mm extra knee-room for rear seat passengers.
- Overall reduced height of seating allowing 27mm more headroom in the rear compartment.

Prestige model specifics
- 8in Touchscreen.
- InControl system.
- 80 Watt Jaguar sound system with DAB radio.
- Satelite navigation.
- Voice activation.
- iPod integration.
- Bluetooth.
- Taurus leather seats with tonal stitching.
- Gloss black veneer with 'Morse Code' IP aluminium finisher.
- 8-way manually adjustable front seating with electric recline.
- Heated front seats.
- Sun visors with illuminated mirrors.
- Metal sill finishers with 'Jaguar' lettering.
- Light Oyster Morzine headlining.
- Carpet mats.
- Soft grain leather steering wheel.
- Auto-dimming rear view mirror.
- Interior mood lighting.
- Dual-zone climate control system.
- 2 x 12v power sockets.
- Cup-holders front and rear.
- Sunglasses holder.
- Gloss black veneer.
- Loadspace luggage tie-downs.

R-Sport model specifics
As Prestige model plus:
- Taurus perforated Sports seats with contrast piping.
- Metal sill finishers with 'Jaguar R-Sport' branding.
- Jet Morzine headlining.
- Bright sports pedals.
- Soft grain leather steering wheel with 'R-Sport' branding.

Portfolio model specifics
As Prestige model plus:
- 380Watt Meridian sound system.
- Windsor leather seating with tonal stitching.
- 10 way electrically adjustable front seating with power lumbar adjustment.
- 40/20/40 split rear seating.
- Premium carpet mats.
- Gloss figured ebony veneer.
- Parking pack.

S model specifics
As R-Sport model plus:
- 380Watt Meridian sound system.
- 10 way electrically adjustable front seating with power lumbar adjustment.
- 40/20/40 split rear seating.
- Metal sill finishers with 'S' branding.
- Premium carpet mats.
- Soft grain leather steering wheel with 'S' branding.
- Parking pack.

300 Sport
- Yellow stitching to the instrument panel, door casings, armrests, seating, steering wheel and gear selector.
- '300 Sport' badging on front headrests, wheel and treadplates.

R-Dynamic Black
- Satin Charcoal Ash veneer.
- Premium cabin lighting, now offering up to 30 colours.

1 – 17-inch Lightweight Silver alloy wheel (later called Style 1016).

2 – 17-inch Aerodynamic alloy wheel (later called Style 1017).

3 – 17-inch Turbine Silver alloy wheel (later called Style 9005).

4 – 18-inch Fan Silver alloy wheel (later called Style 5034).

5 – 18-inch Chalice Silver alloy wheel (later called Style 7011).

6 – 18-inch Helix Silver alloy wheel (later called Style 5033).

7 – 18-inch Helix Contrast Diamond Turned alloy wheel (later called Style 5033).

8 – 18-inch Helix Gloss Black alloy wheel (later called Style 5033).

9 – 18-inch Silver Style 5105.

10 – 19-inch Razor Silver alloy wheel (later called Style 7012).

11 – 19-inch Vortex Silver alloy wheel (later called Style 1018).

12 – 19-inch Axis Silver alloy wheel (later called Style 7013).

13 – 19-inch Axis Contrast Diamond Turned alloy wheel (later called Style 7013).

14 – 19-inch Blade Gloss Grey Diamond Turned alloy wheel (later called Style 5035).

15 – 19i-inch Blade Gloss Grey alloy wheel (later called Style 5035).

16 – 19-inch Blade Gloss Black alloy wheel (later called Style 5035).

17 – 20-inch Star Silver alloy wheel (later called 5071).

18 – 20-inch Matrix Silver alloy wheel (later called Style 9004).

19 – 20-inch Matrix Contrast Diamond Turned alloy wheel (later called Style 9004).

20 – 20-inch Silver Style 5107

21 – 20-inch Labyrinth Gloss Dark Grey Diamond Turned alloy wheel (later called Style 5036).

22 – 20-inch Venom Gloss Dark Grey Diamond Turned alloy wheel (later called Style 5031).

23 – 20-inch Venom Gloss Black alloy wheel (later called Style 5031).

Jaguar All the Cars

Technical specifications

	2.0-litre diesel (163PS)	2.0-litre diesel (180PS)	2.0-litre diesel MHEV (204PS)	2.0-litre diesel (240PS)
cc	1999	1999	1997	1,999
Bore and stroke (mm)	83 x 92.4	83 x 92.4	83 x 92.3	83 x 92.4
Compression ratio	15.5 to 1	15.5 to 1	16.5 to 1	15.3 to 1
bhp	163PS	180PS	204PS	240PS
@rpm	4000	4000	3750	4,000
Max torque (lb ft)	280	317	317	368
@rpm	2500	2500	1750/2500	1500
Fuelling	Common rail fuel injection	Common rail fuel injection	Common rail fuel injection	Common rail fuel injection
Transmission	6-speed manual 8-speed ZF 8HP45 automatic	6-speed manual 8-speed ZF 8HP45 automatic	8-speed ZF 8HP45 automatic	8-speed ZF 8HP45 automatic
Wheel size (in)	19, 20	17, 18, 19, 20	17 to 20	17 to 20
Suspension front	Double wishbone	Double wishbone	Double wishbone	Double wishbone
Suspension rear	Integral link	Integral link	Integral link	Integral link
Brakes	4-wheel discs	4-wheel discs	4-wheel discs	4-wheel discs
Performance				
0 to 60mph (secs)	8.2	7.5 (manual) 7.7 (auto)	7.1	6.7
Top speed (mph)	132	136	146	150
Average mpg	68.9 (auto) 70.6 (man)	65.7	5.04	46.3
Dimensions				
Length (in)	195	184	184	184
Width (in)	82.3	81.6	81.6	81.6
Height (in)	57.3	55.7	55.7	55.7
Wheelbase (in)	116.5	111.6	111.6	111.6
Front Track (in)	63.1	63.2	63.2	63.2
Rear Track (in)	62.7	63.3	63.3	63.3
Weight (kg)	2190	2250	1810	1875

Optional extras

This list varies according to the individual standard specification of specific models.
Adaptive damping.
Adaptive cruise control.
Sports suspension.
Space saver spare wheel.
Front parking aid.
Rear parking sensors.
Reverse park camera.
Surround camera system.
Park assist system.
Garage door opener.
Lane Change Merge Aid/Reverse Traffic Detect system.
Jaguar Smart Key with keyless entry.
Heated front windscreen.
Infra-red reflective windscreen.
Privacy glass.
Adaptive LED headlights.
Powerfold exterior mirrors.
Powered boot lid.
Soft close option.
Detachable tow bar.
Electrically deployable tow bar.
Electric sunroof.
Meridian 380W sound system.
Meridian 380W digital sound system.
Meridian 825W digital surround sound system.
12.3in TFT instrument cluster.
InControl systems.
Head-up display.
Digital television.
10 x 10 way electrically adjustable front seats.
Front power seat lumbar.
Driver seat memory.
Heated front and rear seats.
Heated and cooled front seats.
Heated and cooled front and rear seats.
40/20/40 rear seat folding.
Rear side window manual sunblinds.
Rear screen electric sunblind.
Illuminated sill finishers with 'Jaguar' lettering.
Premium carpet mats.

2.0-litre petrol (250PS)	2.0-litre diesel (300PS)	3.0-litre diesel (300PS)	3.0-litre petrol (380PS)
1,997	1,997	2993	2995
83 x 92.4	83 x 92.4	84 x 90	84.5 x 89
10.5 to 1	9.5 to 1	16 to 1	10.5 to 1
250PS	295PS	300	380
5,500	5,500	4000	6500
365	295	516	332
1300/4500	1500/4500	2000	4500
Common rail fuel injection	Common rail fuel injection	Fuel injection	Fuel injection
8-speed ZF 8HP45 automatic	8-speed ZF 8HP45 automatic	8-speed auto sequential	8-speed auto sequential
17 to 20	17 to 20	19, 20	18, 19, 20
Double wishbone	Double wishbone	Ind double wishbones, alloy control arms, anti dive, coil springs	Ind, coil springs
Integral link	Integral link	Ind double wishbones, alloy control arms, co-axial coil springs	Ind, coil springs
4-wheel discs	4-wheel discs	4-wheel ventilated discs	4-wheel discs
6.5	5.7	5.8	5
150	155	155	155
37.2	36.2	51.4	34
184	184	184	184
81.6	81.6	81.6	81.6
55.7	55.7	55.7	55.7
111.6	111.6	111.6	111.6
63.2	63.2	63.2	63.2
63.3	63.3	63.3	63.3
1775	1838	2350	2330

Bright sports pedals.
Power assisted steering wheel.
Heated steering wheel.
Air quality sensor.
Cooled glove box.
Timed climate control with remove function.
Four zone climate control system.
Configurable interior mood lighting.
Smokers pack with lighter.
Additional 12v power sockets.
Rear spoiler.
Carbon fibre front wing power vents.
Front wing power vents with British emblem.
Carbon fibre exterior door mirror covers.
Gloss black lower vent finishers.
Splash guards.
Luxury loadspace carpet mat.
Carpet sets.
Leather topped gear selector.
Sill tread plates with British emblem.
Personalised illuminated sill tread plates.
Aluminium gift shift paddles.
Roof sports and luggage boxes.
Universal lift and load system.
Cycle carrier.
Fork mounting for cycles.
Roof cross bars.
Surfboard/ski holders.
Tow bar bike carrier.
Bumper protector.
iPad holder.
WhiteFire headphones.
Front windscreen UV shield.
Luggage compartment tidies.
Centre armrest chiller/warmer.
Rechargeable torch and dock.
Headrest mounting coathanger.
Seatback storage.
Snow chains.
Snow sock.
Locking wheel nuts.
Stylished valve caps.
Union Jack centre wheel caps.
Battery conditioner.

Black pack
Gloss black insert with gloss black surround radiator grille.

Gloss black blades in front bumper area.
Gloss black front wing power vents.
Gloss black boot finisher.

Parking pack
Front parking aid and reverse park camera.

Advanced Parking Assist pack
Front parking aid.
360 degree park distance control system.
Surround camera system.

Memory (10 x 10 way seats) pack
Powerfold exterior mirrors in gloss black finish, electrically adjustable, auto dipping and heated.
Power adjustable steering column.
10 x 10 way electrically adjustable front seats with driver memory for seats, steering column and mirrors.

Memory (14 x 14 way seats) pack
As 10 x 10 pack plus:-
14 x 14 way electrically adjustable front seats with driver and passenger memory for seats, steering column and mirrors.

Power Convenience pack
Jaguar Smart Key system with keyless entry.
Powered boot lid.
Additional 12v power sockets in rear compartment and boot area.

Cold climate pack
Heated front windscreen with timer.
Heater windscreen washer jets.
Heated front and rear seats.
Heated steering wheel.

Rear Comfort pack
Heated front and rear seats.
Four zone climate control system.
Manual sun blinds for rear door windows.

Electric sun blind for rear screen.

Head-up Display pack
Head-up display and infra-red reflective windscreen.

Active Safety pack
Lane Keep Aid and Driver Condition Monitoring system.
Lane Change Merge Aid and Reverse Traffic Detect system.

InControl Touch Pro Pack with Meridian 380Watt sound system pack
InControl Touch Pro system with 12.3in TFT instrument cluster.
Meridian 380Watt digital sound system.

InControl Touch Pro Pack with Meridian 825Watt sound system pack
As above plus with:
Meridian 825Watt digital sound system.

Prices and production years

Model	Price new	2015	2016	2017	2018	2019	2020	2021	2022	2023
2.0-litre D163 Prestige	£32,300	■	■	■	■	■	■	■	—	—
2.0-litre D163 Prestige Sportbrake		—	—	■	■	■	■	■	—	—
2.0-litre D163 Portfolio	£36,400	■	■	■	■	■	■	■	—	—
2.0-litre D163 Portfolio Sportbrake		—	—	■	■	■	■	■	—	—
2.0-litre D163 R-Sport	£34,200	■	■	■	■	■	■	■	—	—
2.0-litre D163 R-Sport Sportbrake		—	—	■	■	■	■	■	—	—
2.0-litre D163 Purse		—	—	—	—	—	—	■	—	—
2.0-litre D163 Pure Sportbrake		—	—	—	—	—	—	■	—	—
2.0-litre D180 Pure		—	—	—	—	—	—	■	—	—
2.0-litre D180 Pure Sportbrake		—	—	—	—	—	—	■	—	—
2.0-litre D180 Prestige	£32,800		■	■	■	■	■	■	—	—
2.0-litre D180 Prestige AWD		—	—	—	—	■	■	■	—	—
2.0-litre D180 Prestige Sportbrake		—	—	■	■	■	■	■	—	—
2.0-litre D180 Prestige Sportbrake AWD		—	—	—	—	■	■	■	—	—
2.0-litre D180 Pottfolio	£37,300		■	■	■	■	■	■	—	—
2.0-litre D180 Pottfolio AWD		—	—	—	—	■	■	■	—	—
2.0-litre D18i0 Portfolio Sportbrake		—	—	■	■	■	■	■	—	—
2.0-litre D180 Portfolio Sportbrake AWD		—	—	—	—	■	■	■	—	—
2.0-litre D180 R-Sport	£35,100	■	■	■	■	■	■	■	—	—
2.0-litre D180 R-Sport AWD		—	—	—	—	■	■	■	—	—
2.0-litre D180 R-Sport Sportbrake		—	—	■	■	■	■	■	—	—

Jaguar All the Cars — 24

Model	Price new	2015	2016	2017	2018	2019	2020	2021	2022	2023
2.0-litre D180 R-Sport Sportbrake AWD		—	—	—	—	■	■	■	—	—
2.0-litre D240 Pure		—	—	—	—	—	■	■	—	—
2.0-litre D240 Prestige		—	—	■	■	—	■	■	—	—
2.0-litre D240 Prestige AWD		—	—	■	■	■	■	■	—	—
2.0-litre D240 Prestige Sportbrake		—	—	—	■	■	■	■	—	—
2.0-litre D240 Prestige Sportbrake AWD		—	—	■	■	■	■	■	—	—
2.0-litre D240 Portfolio		—	—	■	■	—	■	■	—	—
2.0-litre D240 Pottfolio AWD		—	—	■	■	■	■	■	—	—
2.0-litre D240 Pottfolio Sportbrake		—	—	■	■	■	■	■	—	—
2.0-litre D240 Portfolio Sportbrake AWD		—	—	■	■	■	■	■	—	—
2.0-litre D240 R-Sport		—	—	■	■	—	■	■	—	—
2.0-litre D240 R-Sport AWD		—	—	■	■	—	■	■	—	—
2.0-litre D240 R-Sport Sportbrake		—	—	■	■	—	■	■	—	—
2.0-litre D240 R-Sport Sportbrake AWD		—	—	■	■	—	■	■	—	—
3.0-litre D300 Prestige		—	—	—	—	—	■	■	—	—
3.0-litre D300 Portfolio		■	■	■	■	■	■	■	—	—
3.0-litre D300 Potfolio Sportbrake		—	—	■	■	■	■	■	—	—
3.0-litre D300 S	£49,945	■	■	■	■	■	■	■	—	—
3.0-litre D300 S Sportbrake		—	—	■	■	■	■	■	—	—
3.0-litre D300 R-Sport		—	—	—	—	—	■	■	—	—
2.0 litre P200 Prestige		—	—	■	■	■	—	■	—	—
2.0-litre P200 Portfolio		—	—	■	■	■	—	■	—	—
2.0-litre P200 R-Sport		—	—	■	■	■	—	■	—	—
2.0-litre P250 Pure		—	—	—	—	—	■	■	—	—
2.0-litre P250 Pure Sportbrake		—	—	—	—	—	■	■	—	—
2.0-litre P250 Prestige		—	—	■	■	—	■	■	—	—
2.0-litre P250 Prestige AWD		—	—	■	■	■	■	■	—	—
2.0-litre P250 Prestige Sportbrake		—	—	■	■	—	■	■	—	—
2.0-litre P250 Pretige Sportbrake AWD		—	—	■	■	■	■	■	—	—
2.0-litre P50 Pottfolio		—	—	■	■	■	■	■	—	—
2.0-litre P250 Pottfolio AWD		—	—	■	■	■	■	■	—	—
2.0-litre P250 Pottfolio Sportbrake		—	—	■	■	■	■	■	—	—
2.0-litre P250 Pottfolio Sportbrake AWD		—	—	■	■	■	■	■	—	—
2.0-litre P250 R-Sport		—	—	■	■	■	■	■	—	—
2.0-litre P250 R-Sport AWD		—	—	■	■	■	■	■	—	—
2.0-litre P250 R-Sport Sportbrake		—	—	■	■	■	■	■	—	—
2.0-litre P250 R-Sport Sportbrake AWD		—	—	■	■	■	■	■	—	—
2.0-litre P300 Pure		—	—	—	—	—	■	■	—	—
2.0-litre P300 Prestige		—	—	—	—	—	■	■	—	—
2.0-litre P300 Prestige Sportbrake		—	—	—	—	—	■	■	—	—
2.0-litre P300 Portfolio		—	—	■	■	■	■	■	—	—
2.0-litre P300 Portfolio AWD		—	—	—	—	—	■	■	—	—
2.0-litre P300 Portfolio Sportbrake AWD		—	—	—	—	—	■	■	—	—
2.0-litre P300 R-Sport		—	—	■	■	■	■	■	—	—
2.0-litre P300 R-Sport AWD		—	—	—	—	—	■	■	—	—
2.0-litre P300 R-Sport Sportbrake AWD		—	—	—	—	—	■	■	—	—
3.0-litre P380 S	£49,945	■	■	■	■	—	—	—	—	—
2.0-litre P300 300 Sport AWD	£46,525	—	—	—	■	■	—	■	■	■

New XF saloons and Sportbrakes from 2015

Model	Price new	2015	2016	2017	2018	2019	2020	2021	2022	2023
2.0-litre P300 300 Sport Sportbrake AWD	£47,800	—	—	—	—	■	—	■	■	■
2.0-litre D200 MHEV R-Dynamic S RWD	£33,975	—	—	—	—	—	—	—	■	■
2.0-litre D200 MHEV R-Dynamic SE RWD	£36,735	—	—	—	—	—	—	—	■	—
2.0-litre D200 MHEV R-Dynamic SE Sportbrake RWD	£38,590	—	—	—	—	—	—	—	■	—
2.0-litre D200 MHEV R-Dynamic SE Black RWD	£38,610	—	—	—	—	—	—	—	—	■
2.0-litre D200 MHEV R-Dynamnic SE Black Sportbrake	£40,500	—	—	—	—	—	—	—	—	■
2.0-litre D200 MHEV R-Dynamic HSE Black RWD	£40,805	—	—	—	—	—	—	—	—	■
2.0-litre D200 MHEV R-Dynamic HSE RWD	£39,650	—	—	—	—	—	—	—	■	—
2.0-litre D200 MHEV R-Dynamic HSE Sportbrake RWD	£41,500	—	—	—	—	—	—	—	■	—
2.0-litre D200 MHEV R-Dynamic Black RWD	£37,535	—	—	—	—	—	—	—	■	—
2.0-litreD200 MHEV R-Dynamic Black Sportbrake RWD	£39,395	—	—	—	—	—	—	—	■	—
2.0-litre D200 MHEV R-Dynamic S AWD	£35,620	—	—	—	—	—	—	—	■	—
2.0-litre D200 MHEV R-Dynamic SE AWD	£38,210	—	—	—	—	—	—	—	■	—
2.0-litre D200 MHEV R-Dynamic HSE AWD	£41,405	—	—	—	—	—	—	—	■	—
2.0-litre D200 MHEV R-Dynamic HSE Sportbrake AWD	£43,255	—	—	—	—	—	—	—	■	—
2.0-litre P250 R-Dynamic S Sportbrake	£37,190	—	—	—	—	—	—	—	■	—
2.0-litre P250 R-Dynamic SE	£37,860	—	—	—	—	—	—	—	■	—
2.0-litre P250 R-Dynamic SE Black RWD	£39,065	—	—	—	—	—	—	—	—	■
2.0-litre P250 R-Dynamic SE Black Sportbrake	£40,960	—	—	—	—	—	—	—	—	■
2.0-litre P250 R-Dynamic SE Sportbrake	£40,165	—	—	—	—	—	—	—	■	—
2.0-litre P250 R-Dynamic HSE	£41,225	—	—	—	—	—	—	—	■	—
2.0-litre P250 R-Dynamic HSE Black RWD	£41,265	—	—	—	—	—	—	—	—	■
2.0-litre P250 R-Dynamic HSE Sportbrake	£43,075	—	—	—	—	—	—	—	■	—
2.0-litre P300 R-Dynamic HSE AWD	£44,800	—	—	—	—	—	—	—	■	—
2.0-litre P300 R-Dynamic HSE Sportbrake AWD	£46,650	—	—	—	—	—	—	—	■	—

Colour schemes and interior trim combinations

Exterior paint
Fuji White
Yulong White
Indus Silver
Silicon Silver
Corris Grey
Eiger Grey
Carpathian Grey
Norvic Black
Santorini Black
Loire Blue
Ceasium Blue
Portofino Blue
Firenze Red
Roselle Red
British Racing Green

Veneers
Gloss Black
Glossed Figured Ebony
Satin Grey Figured Ebony
Carbon Fibre
Satin Burr Ash
Satin Fine Line Wood
Satin Rosewood
Satin Charcoal Ash
Gloss Burr Walnut
Morse Code Aluminium
Dark Hex Aluminium
Engine Spin Aluminium

Seats
Ebony
Light Oyster
Latte
Sienna Tan
Brogue
Pimento
Mars Red
Espresso
Duo-Tones:
Latte/Ebony
Ebony/Mars Red
Ebony/Pimento
Light Oyster/Ebony
Ebony/Sienna Tan
Light Oyster/Pimento

Contrast Stitching/Piping
Ebony
Red
Pimento
Light Oyster
Sienna Tan
Ebony
Brogue
Espresso

Carpets
Ebony
Morzine
Oyster
Espresso

Headlining
Ebony
Light Oyster

Upper Fascia/Trim
Ebony
Light Oyster
Sienna Tan
Brogue
Latte

25 F-PACE SUV from 2016

Background

The F-PACE represented an entirely new area of design and build for the company, brought about by two issues. First, under Tata ownership, Jaguar was now an integrated part of Land Rover (which has for years produced excellent 4 x 4s and SUVs like the Range Rover, Discovery, Freelander and more recently the Evoque). This has provided a two-way communication channel over the development of such vehicles.

Second, the worldwide popularity of the SUV has prompted most car manufacturers to introduce this type of vehicle in their range, although Jaguar has entered this market late, as it did the estate car sector back in 2004.

The F-PACE was Jaguar's first performance crossover, the first aluminium-intensive model in the class, and first among rivals for boot volume, cabin width, rear knee-room, and ease of rear access. Jaguar referred to its SUV as "A performance crossover for those who love driving, with unrivalled dynamics and everyday usability." The basis, as with any Jaguar, was styling and a design that actually looked better in the flesh than as a two-dimensional image, but still very much a Jaguar. Sharing no other chassis dimension with any other Jaguar, the F-PACE was able to provide a combination of good looks, short overhangs (ideal for this type of vehicle) and excellent interior accommodation.

Other keys features included the F-PACE body being produced in light aluminium, like all other modern Jaguar models. It obviously came with all-wheel drive, with many of the technically advanced features carried over from the later New XF and F-TYPE. One entirely new feature, seen for the first time on the F-PACE, was Activity Key: a waterproof, wearable technology allowing keys to be securely locked inside the vehicle.

The F-PACE was initially powered by the later Ingenium 2.0-litre or 3.0-litre diesel engine or a supercharged 3.0-litre petrol unit, linked to an intelligent Driveline Dynamics (IDD) enabling all-wheel drive ability with rear-wheel drive character. Due to the lightweight structure of the car and aerodynamics, with the supercharged petrol engine, the car could achieve a 0-62mph time of just 5.5 seconds.

For the launch of the car, Jaguar introduced a one-off 'First Edition' model based on the S cars, but with enhanced specifications, only 2000 of which were produced.

Model range and development

The range of F-PACE models on introduction in 2016 was as follows:
Prestige 2.0-litre (180PS) Diesel manual RWD/AWD
Prestige 2.0-litre (180PS) Diesel automatic AWD
R-Sport 2.0-litre (180PS) Diesel manual RWD/AWD
R-Sport 2.0-litre (180PS) Diesel automatic AWD
Portfolio 2.0-litre (180PS) Diesel manual RWD/AWD
Portfolio 2.0-litre (180PS) Diesel automatic AWD
S 3.0-litre (300PS) Diesel automatic AWD
S 3.0-litre (380PS) Petrol automatic AWD
First Edition 3.0-litre (300PS) Diesel automatic AWD

F-PACE Portfolio model with 22in Turbine alloy wheels.

With a length of 4731mm and a 2874mm wheelbase, the F-PACE provided an exceptionally spacious interior, with the most rear knee-room for this class of vehicle, and a large luggage compartment volume of 650 litres.

The light, stiff body structure comprised 80 per cent aluminium, with additional weight savings coming from a composite tailgate and magnesium for parts such as the cross-car beam. Because of the higher bonnet line of this crossover vehicle, the front-end carrier was designed to be stiff enough to meet all functional requirements, and durable enough to meet off-road requirements. The aluminium bonnet was also shaped with pedestrian protection in mind, with greater clearance between the bonnet surface and engine, giving more room to absorb the energy and avoid contact with hard points in the engine compartment. The bonnet edge was reshaped and windscreen wiper mechanism repositioned to improve pedestrian impact performance.

F-PACE R-Sport mode. Note the trim differences compared to the others models shown on this page.

The ground clearance of 213mm was made more effective because the underfloor was also as smooth as possible to reduce aerodynamic drag. When the architecture was developed, ECUs and other electronics modules were packaged as high up as possible to aid the all-new F-PACE's 525mm wading depth.

The body's high torsional stiffness enabled the F-TYPE sports car-derived double wishbone front suspension and integral link rear suspension to be incorporated with better overall effect. With Torque Vectoring as standard and an Electric Power Assisted Steering system tuned to give the best possible feel and response, Jaguar claimed the F-PACE was unsurpassed in this type of vehicle.

F-PACE S model (First Edition) in the special Caesium Blue exterior paintwork, with Double Helix alloy wheels.

The F-PACE was powered by a choice of three Jaguar engines, starting with the 2.0-litre (180PS) 4-cylinder diesel unit that could achieve up to 57mpg with CO_2 emissions of just 129g/km on the European combined cycle, available with a choice of 6-speed manual or 8-speed automatic transmissions.

Jaguar's latest 3.0-litre V6 diesel engine could be specified, delivering 300PS with just the 8-speed automatic transmission and all-wheel drive, with up to 47mpg and 159g/km CO_2 on the European combined cycle.

For the top of the range S model, there was the 3.0-litre supercharged V6 petrol engine, developing 380PS and a top speed limited to 155mph.

All 6-cylinder engines were paired with the 8HP70 ZF automatic transmission, while the 4-cylinders engines were matched to the lighter, more compact 8HP45 gearbox. With Jaguar's

Drive Control system, if fitted, enthusiasts could make the most of manual shift control using the steering wheel-mounted paddles.

The 6-speed manual transmission sent drive to the rear wheels only, making it the first Jaguar manual transmission compatible with all-wheel drive.

Even the entry-level model benefitted from monotube dampers as standard, but, for even better ride and handling, the electronically-controlled Adaptive Dynamics system measured body and wheel movement 100 and 500 times a second respectively, ensuring optimum damping forces in all conditions.

For the most enthusiastic drivers there was Configurable Dynamics: first used in the F-TYPE, allowing individual settings for the throttle, automatic transmission, steering, and, where fitted, the Adaptive Dynamics system.

The F-PACE used Jaguar's latest torque on-demand All-Wheel Drive (AWD) system, featuring the advanced, in-house control system first developed for the F-TYPE AWD: Intelligent Driveline Dynamics (IDD). IDD preserved rear-wheel drive agility and handling character but could transfer up to 50 per cent torque to the front wheels to exploit the performance benefits of extra traction, on all surfaces and in all weathers.

Adaptive Surface Response (ASR), developed from Land Rover's patented, award-winning Terrain Response technology, made the AWD system even more effective in challenging conditions. Integrated into Jaguar Drive Control, ASR identified the type of surface and optimised the mapping of the powertrain and Dynamic Stability Control system. First launched in the New XF, ASR was enhanced by a third mode designed for deep snow and gravel.

To make the most of the available grip, Jaguar's All Surface Progress Control (ASPC) automatically controlled the throttle and the brakes, enabling the vehicle to pull away smoothly: the driver just had to steer. ASPC functions up to 19mph, and the driver could select the desired speed using the cruise control switches.

For drivers who wanted similar results while still using the accelerator pedal, another first for Jaguar was fitted to this model: Low-Friction Launch (LFL), which used a progressive throttle map, making the vehicle easier to control.

The F-PACE also offered a Trailer Stability Assist (TSA) function that could detect if a potentially dangerous trailer sway developed, and helped the driver to regain control by gradually reducing speed through reducing engine torque and applying the brakes – individually on each side if necessary to counteract and stabilise the swaying motion.

Unique to the F-PACE was an extensive range of new wheels, including those of

Frontal view of the S and First Edition models without divided side air intakes, revised treatment to under panelling, grille and badging.

The R-Short showing the revised trim treatment compared to the S and Portfolio models.

The Prestige and Portfolio models differed only slightly, but this picture shows the plainer look to the trim compared to R-Sport and S models.

S and First Edition models rear aspect, note the trim differences with the other models.

R-Sport rear view.

Prestige and Portfolio rear view.

The later F-PACE model with facelifted interior.

Later modified front detail of the F-PACE, in this instance an R-Dynamic model.

Rear detail changes from the earlier models.

Later model side elevation to compare with earlier models.

a massive 22in diameter produced from forged aluminium, accompanied by specially developed 265/40/R22 tyres.

A stereo camera was at the heart of the Autonomous Emergency Braking system, now featuring a pedestrian detection function – another Jaguar-first. The stereo camera also enabled Lane Departure Warning, Lane Keep Assist, Traffic Sign Recognition, an Intelligent Speed Limiter, and Driver Condition Monitor systems, as seen on other models of the time.

Jaguar's premium InControl Touch Pro system, based around a 10.2in touchscreen with a powerful quad-core processor and solid-state drive, and running on the ultra-fast ethernet, was another carryover from other models. Whether you wanted to start the engine using a smartphone app, use the navigation system to tell your contacts when you'd arrive for your meeting, connect up to eight devices using the wi-fi hotspot, or just stream your favourite playlists, all this was now available with the InControl infotainment system as standard.

The F-PACE marked the world debut of Jaguar's Activity Key. A waterproof, shockproof wristband with an integrated transponder, it allowed the keyfob to be securely locked inside the vehicle – ideal for sports people. Locking the car using the Activity Key disabled any keyfobs left inside. Activity Key worked (without the need for a battery) on the same RF frequencies as the other keys and could be used to lock and unlock the vehicle by holding it in close proximity to the J of the Jaguar lettering on the tailgate.

Internally, the F-PACE used a combination of quality traditional and new materials with a high seating position, which Jaguar called 'Sports Command.' General finishes and equipment followed the same route as other Jaguar models of the time. With the longer wheelbase, rear seat accommodation was extensive, the seat base designed to allow passengers to sit further outboard. The rear seat had the usual 40/20/40 split function and to maintain headroom to the maximum, even magnetic fixings were used, which were more compact than conventional fasteners.

Space was maximised inside the car with large door pockets (that could even accommodate bottles), and storage areas scalloped into the sides of the centre console for items like smartphones. The luggage compartment of 650 litres incorporated a width of 1255mm and with the rear seats folded flat, there was an enormous 1740 litres of usable space. The luggage floor was reversible, one side carpets, the other rubberised, and the parcel shelf and/or mesh

The unique Activity Key which could be worn while leaving the keys safely secure in the car.

Interior layout applicable to all earlier F-PACE models, in this case the S/First Edition models.

Front interior of the Portfolio model.

loadguard could be stored away below the boot floor.

For the 2018 model year, Jaguar announced additional engines, all of 2.0-litre capacity: the P250 (petrol), D240 (diesel), and finally the P300 (petrol), the latter producing 400Nm of torque. The D163 engine received changes to improve its emissions rating.

Enhanced specification for the F-PACE included Configural Dynamics technology, plus safety features like Forward Vehicle Guidance, Forward Traffic Detection and dual-view screen for the Touch Pro infotainment system. Visual changes for 2018 included a revised colour palette for exterior paintwork and interior trim. The model range was expanded now to include the 'Pure' entry model.

More equipment additions came along in 2019: Adaptive Cruise Control and Lane Centring, with standard equipment now Rear Camera, Front and Rear Parking Aids, Driver Condition Monitor and Emergency Braking. There was also a larger 82-litre (replacing the 63-litre) fuel tank, and all petrol engines were fitted with particulate filters to make them cleaner.

An entirely new SUV joined the model line-up using the Jaguar supercharged 5.0-litre V8 engine developing 550PS. This high-performance model featured bespoke suspension and aerodynamic enhancements, along with a Variable Valve Active Exhaust system to create a unique 'soundtrack.'

Internally, optional slimline sports seating, a new suedecloth headliner, and illuminated treadplates were just a few of the upgrades.

For the 2020 model year various special editions were launched. First, a 'Black' model for the F-PACE R-Sport D180 AWD model, incorporating many items previously available as optional extras, the inclusive price would save buyers up to £2500. Next the F-PACE '300 Sport' and '400 Sport' fitted with both the D300 and P300 engines, with assertive sporting exterior and interior changes. Then the 'Chequered Flag,' fitted with 2.0-litre petrol and diesel engines and enhanced trim. All subsequent F-PACEs were now fitted with Apple CarPLay and Android Auto as standard.

For 2021 All F-PACEs benefited from a completely new and enhanced interior with improved materials, better sound-deadening, luxury and safety features. As well as exterior changes, model identification was also changed to match other cars in the Jaguar range, now R-Dynamic S, SE and HSE specifications.

The biggest change, however, was in the range of drivetrains. With PHEV (Plug-in Hybrid Electric Vehicle) technology, a 2.0-litre 4-cylinder P400e petrol engine was supported by a 105kW electric motor, the latter powered by a 17.1kWh lithium-ion battery located under the boot floor. When fully charged the car was capable of up to 33 miles of all-electric driving making short journeys very economical and environmentally friendly.

Other engine changes included the latest additions to the 3.0-litre 6-cylinder petrol and diesel units. Now offering 340PS and 400PS, both with MHEV (Mild Hybrid Electric Vehicle) technology, utilising an electric supercharger in combination with a twin-scroll turbocharger, the former was driven by a 48V motor, delivering virtually instant boost pressure. The MHEV system used a Belt integrated Starter Generator in the engine bay to harvest the energy lost when slowing down and braking. The energy was stored in a 48V lithium-ion battery in the rear loadspace, and then re-deployed when accelerating.

Further, there were the new advanced i4 engines, the next generation of 2.0-litre 4-cylinder Ingenium units, also incorporating MHEV technology. The 163PS produced 380Nm of torque, while the 204PS MHEV unit delivered 430Nm.

The final new model came in 2022 with the SVR 'Edition 1988' with a mere 394 examples. Produced as a tribute to Jaguar's racing success in the World Sports-Prototype Championship in 1988 with its XJR-9 racing car, it came in a unique Amethyst paint with Champagne Gold forged alloy wheels and Sunset Gold accents.

The range of F-PACE models was rationalised thereafter and remained in production during 2023/2024 until the introduction of Jaguar's all-new all-electric range.

Exterior identification points

General points applicable to all models.
Front view
- Bold more upright front grille.
- Horizontal under-grille mesh panel.
- Large air ducts either side of bumper bar.
- Full LED horizontal headlight units with 'J'-blade running light graphics.
- LED fog lights using TV screen optics and light tubes underneath the air intakes.
- Centre power bulge extends the full length of the bonnet.
- Steeply raked front windscreen.
- Approach illumination.

Rear view
- General styling form follows other current model designing.
- Steeply raked rear screen.
- Composite tailgate.
- Powered tailgate.
- LED taillights.
- Under-bumper panel contrast finisher.
- Jaguar leaper and script centrally mounted on tailgate.
- Single sided tailpipes with finishers.

Side view
- Short overhang front and rear.
- High bonnet line and general body stance.
- Sleek line to roof panel.
- Steeply raked front windscreen.
- Heat insulated glass.
- Horizontal front wing side power vents.
- Swage line from power vent through to front doors.
- Sculptured sills.
- Rakish angle of rear screen.
- Large diameter wheels/tyres.

2021 major styling changes affecting all models
- New bonnet design.
- Slim all-LED quad headlights.
- Revised design radiator grille.
- New rear lighting with double-chicane graphic.
- New rear bumper and tailgate arrangement.
- Introduction of new R-Dynamics designations with uprated trim from previous models.

Prestige model specific points
Front view
- Grained black radiator grille insert with chrome surround.
- Halogen headlights with LED daytime running lights.
- Front and rear fog lights.
- Front parking aids.

Rear view
- Rear parking aid.

Side view
- Bright chrome side window finishers.
- Bright chrome front wing power vents.
- Satin chrome roof rails.
- Electrically adjustable, heated body colour door mirrors.
- 18in Vortex silver alloy wheels.

R-Sport model specifics
As Prestige models plus:
Front view
- Grained black radiator grille insert with satin chrome surround.
- R-Sport front bumper.

Rear interior of the Portfolio model.

Taurus perforated leather upholstery option.

Sports leather upholstery option.

- Xenon headlights with LED signature daytime running lights.

Rear view
- R-Sport rear bumper.
- Dual tailpipes with finishers.

Side view
- 19in Bionic grey diamond turned alloy wheels.
- Gloss black side window finishers.
- Satin chrome R-Sport front wing power vents.
- R-Sport side sills.
- Satin black body finishers.
- Gloss black roof rails.

Portfolio model specifics
As Prestige models plus:
Front view
- Gloss black radiator grille insert with chrome surround.
- Xenon headlights with LED signature daytime running lights.
- Heated front windscreen with heated washer jets.

Rear view
- Powered tailgate.
- Rear view camera.

Side view
- 19in Razor silver alloy wheels.
- Powerfold door mirrors.
- Panoramic roof.
- Electrical adjustable, heated, memory, heated door mirrors with approach and repeater lights.

S model specifics
As R-Sport models plus:
Front view
- S style front bumper.
- Gloss black radiator grille with satin chrome surround.
- Heated front windscreen with heated washer jets.

Rear view
- S style rear bumper.
- Rear view camera.

Side view
- 20in Blade diamond turned alloy wheels.
- Red brake callipers.
- Body coloured door claddings, with satin chrome finishers.
- Gloss black window finishers.
- Powerfold door mirrors.
- Electrical adjustable, heated, memory, heated door mirrors with approach and repeater lights.

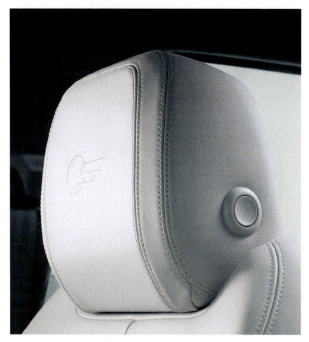

S model upholstery style with embossed branding.

First Edition Windsor leather upholstery with Houndstooth markings.

Rear luggage area of the F-PACE.

First Edition model specifics

As S models plus:
Side view
- Gloss black front wing power vents.
- 22in Double Helix alloy wheels.
- Panoramic roof.

300/400 Sport
- Dark Satin Grey exterior trim detailing, front grille, window surrounds, vents, mirror caps and door finishers plus rear valance.
- '300 Sport' badging.
- Only in Yulong White, Indus Silver or Santorini Black.

Chequered Flag
- Gloss Black trim detailing to front grille, door cladding, side vents and roof rails.
- Only in Yulong White, or Santorini Black or Eiger Grey.

SVR
- Larger front air intakes and side vents.
- Unique bonnet with air vents.
- Wheelarch extensions
- Lower body mouldings.
- Unique spoiler and bumper housing with side strakes.
- Quad tailpipe exhaust system.

SVR Edition 1988
- Midnight Amethyst paintwork.
- Gold forged alloy wheels with Sunset Gold accents.
- Laser-etched 'Edition 1988' logo to front wing panels.

Interior identification points

General points applicable to all models:
- 'Sports Command' high driving position.
- Shaped heated seats.
- Twin front cupholders.
- Sunglasses holder.
- Driver and front passenger sun visors with mirrors.
- Curving front door top rolls into the fascia.
- Large, deeply hooded analogue instrument pack.
- Sweeping centre panel incorporating 8in TFT display and auxiliary switches.
- InControl Protect, Apps, Remote Premium, WiFi
- Ambient lighting.
- Large door pockets and centre console storage areas.
- 12v supply socket in cubby box with USB ports.
- 40/20/40 split rear seating.
- Fold flat second set of seats.

The Chequered Flag model.

Interior of the F-PACE Chequered Flag

The high-performance F-PACE SVR Dynamic.

Rear elevation of the F-PACE SVR.

- Rear armrest with cupholders.
- Luggage floor covering reversible.
- Loadspace tiedowns.
- DAB radio.
- Satellite navigation.
- Jaguar Voice.
- iPod integration.
- Bluetooth.
- Auto-dimming rear view mirror.
- Jaguar Sense soft touch interior lighting.
- Dual zone climate control system.

2021 major styling changes affecting all models.

- Enlarged 11.4in HD touchscreen for infotainment, housed in a magnesium frame in Black Satin.
- Soft-touch materials with the instrument panel topper, door armrests, console side and door bins.
- New designed door casings with 360-degree grab handles.
- New range of veneer and alloy finishers.
- Full-width 'piano lid' formed across the instrument panel.
- New centre console design incorporating storage.
- Laser-etched mid-line speaker frets.
- New Drive Selector design.
- New steering wheel design with 'hidden upon lit' switches.
- Zinc alloy gearshift paddles.
- Introduction of new R-Dynamics designations with uprated trim from previous models.

Prestige model specifics

- Jaguar 80W sound system.
- Taurus leather seats with contrast stitching.
- 8 x 8 way manual front seats with electrical recline.
- Soft grain leather steering wheel.
- Metal sill finishers with 'Jaguar' lettering.
- Carpet mats.
- Gloss black veneer.

R-Sport model specifics

As Prestige models plus:

- Jaguar 80-Watt sound system.
- Taurus perforated leather Sports seats with contrast stitching.
- 8 x 8 way manual front seats with electrical recline.
- Soft grain leather steering wheel with R-Sport branding.
- Metal sill finishers with R-Sport branding.
- Carpet mats.
- Bright metal Sport pedals.
- Etched Aluminium veneer.

Portfolio model specifics

As Prestige models plus:

Details of the SVR interior.

Performance seat detailing on the SVR model.

Unique detailing on the SVR model.

The F-PACE 400 model.

- Meridian 380W sound system.
- Windsor perforated leather seats with tonal stitching.
- 10 x 10 way electric front seats with manual head adjust.
- Soft grain leather steering wheel.
- Windsor leather armrest.
- Gloss Figured Ebony veneer.
- Jaguar Smartkey system.
- Metal sill finishers with 'Jaguar' lettering.
- Premium carpet mats.

S model specifics

As R-Sport models plus:
- Meridian 380-Watt sound system.
- Taurus perforated leather Sports seats with contrast stitching.
- 10 x 10 way electric front seats with manual head adjust.
- Soft grain leather steering wheel with 'S' branding.
- Satin chrome paddles.
- Metal sill finishers with 'S' branding.
- Premium carpet mats.
- Bright metal Sport pedals.
- Jaguar Sport Key system.
- Dark Hex aluminium veneer.
- Exterior 'S' badging.

First Edition model specifics

As 'S' plus:
- Windsor leather seats with Houndstooth embossing.
- InControl Touch Pro SDD satellite navigational system.
- Illuminated sill finishers.
- Loadspace scuff plate.
- Gloss Black veneer with Houndstooth pattern.
- TFT virtual instrument cluster.
- Luxury interior lighting.
- Suedecloth headliner.
- Rear electric seat recline.
- Luggage rails to the boot floor.
- First Edition premium carpet mats.

300/400 Sport

- Yellow contrast stitching on the instrument panel, centre console and leather seats.
- '300 Sport' badging to the treadplates, carpet mats and steering wheel.
- '300 Sport' embossed into front headrests.

Chequered Flag

- Meshed aluminium detailing
- 'Chequered Flag' treadplates

SVR

- Performance front seating with lozenge quilting and embossed with 'SVR' logo.
- Heavily sculptured rear seating.
- Sport shift selector.

Edition 1988, last of the line special limited production model.

Another view of the Edition 1988 model.

The special interior finishes to the Edition 1988 model.

- 'SVR' branded steering wheel with aluminium paddle shifters.
- Duo-tone interior trim as standard.

Edition 1988

- Semi-aniline Ebony leather.
- Sunset Gold Satin detailing on dashboard, steering wheel, gearshift paddles, .
- 'Edition 1988' branding to the dashboard and treadplates.

1 - 18-inch Vortex Silver alloy wheel (later called Style 1018).
2 – 18-inch Lightweight Silver alloy wheel (later called Style 1022).
3 - 18-inch Aero Silver alloy wheel (later called Style 1021).
4 - 18-inch Fan Silver alloy wheel (later called Style 5037).
5 – 19-inch Razor Silver alloy wheel (later called Style 7012).
6 – 19-inch Bionic Grey Diamond Turned alloy wheel (later called Style 5038).
7 – 19-inch Fan Gloss Black alloy wheel (later called Style 5037).
8 – 19-inch Blade Grey Diamond Turned alloy wheel (later called Style 5035).
9 – 19-inch Blade Gloss Grey Diamond Turned alloy wheel (later called Style 5035).
10 – 19-inch alloy wheel Style 5103.
11 – 20-inch Matrix Silver alloy wheel (later called Style 1019).
12 - 20-inch Venom Gloss Dark Grey Diamond Turned alloy wheel (later called Style 5031).
13 – 20-inch Venom Gloss Black alloy wheel (later called Style 5031).
14 – 20-inch Templar Silver alloy wheel (later called Style 5036).
15 – 20-inch Turbine Grey Diamond Turned alloy wheel (later called Style 9005).
16 – 20-inch Turbine Polished Chrome alloy wheel (later called Style 9005).
17 – 20-inch Double Helix Gloss Black alloy wheel (later called Style 1020).
18 – 20-inch Double Helix Silver alloy wheel (later called Style 1020).
19 – 20-inch alloy wheel Style 1067.
20 – 20-inch alloy wheel Style 5104.
21 – 20-inch alloy wheel Style 1068.
22 – 20-inch alloy wheel Style 7024.
23 – 21-inch alloy wheel Style 5105.
24 – 21-inch alloy wheel Style 5080.
25 – 22-inch alloy wheel Style 5081 Diamond Turned Satin Grey.
26 – 22-inch alloy wheel Style 5117 Satin Black.

Optional extras

This list varies according to the individual standard specification of specific models:
Adaptive dynamics.
Adaptive cruise control.
Adaptive Surface Response.
35mm front brakes.
Space saver spare wheel.
Full sized spare wheel.
Rear view camera
Surround camera system.
Park assist system.
Park distance control.
Garage door opener.
Blind spot monitoring and traffic detection system.
Lane keep assist and drive condition monitoring system.
Jaguar Smart Key with keyless entry.
Activity key.
Panoramic roof.
Sliding panoramic roof.
Gloss black roof rails.
Heated front windscreen with heated washer jets.
Infra-red reflective windscreen.
Privacy glass.
Xenon headlights with LED signature daytime running lights.
Headlight powerwash.
Adaptive LED lighting.
Powerfold exterior door mirrors with memory and lighting.
Gesture tailgate entry/closure (only with keyless entry).
Detachable towbar.
Electrically deployable towbar.
Meridian 380-Watt sound system.
Meridian 380-Watt digital sound system.
Meridian 825-Watt digital sound system.
Full 12in TFT instrument cluster.
InControl Touch Pro.
InControl Secure.
InControl Pro Services.
Head up Display.
Digital television.
10 x 10 way electric front seats
4-way power lumbar.
Perforated Taurus leather seating.
Heated front and rear seating.
Heated/electrically adjustable/perforated Taurus seating.
Manual release for seats backs in luggage area.
Rear seat electrical recline.
Loadspace safety partition net.
Metal loadspace scuff plate with 'Jaguar' lettering.
Luggage rails to boot floor.
Illuminated metal treadplates and loadspace scuff plate with 'Jaguar' lettering.
Premium carpet mats.
Electrically adjustable steering column.
Heated steering wheel.
Air quality sensor.
Timed climate control with remote.
Four zone climate control system.
Configurable interior mood lighting.
Smoker's pack with lighter.
Carbon fibre mirror covers.
Gloss black mirror covers.
Carbon fibre front wing power vents.
Gloss black front wing power vents.
Gloss black R-Sport front wing power vents.
Deployable side steps.
Front side steps.
Bright side tubes.
Gloss black insert grille with gloss black surround.
Body side mouldings.
Dark leather gear selector.
Aluminium gear paddles.
Sport pedal covers.
R-Sport multi-function steering wheel.
Side window deflectors.
Personalised illuminated sill tread plates.
Union Flag tread plates.
Wheel centre badges (various designs)
Child seats.
Aluminium gift shift paddles.
Roof sports and luggage boxes.
Universal lift and load system.
Cycle carrier.
Fork mounting for cycles.
Roof cross bars.
Surfboard/ski holders.
Tow bar bike carrier.
Bumper protector.
iPad holder.
WhiteFire headphones.
Front windscreen UV shield.
Luggage compartment tidies.
Centre armrest chiller/warmer.
Rechargeable torch and dock.
Headrest mounting coat hanger.
Seat back storage.
Snow chains.
Snow sock.
Locking wheel nuts.
Stylised valve caps.
Union Jack centre wheel caps.
Battery conditioner.
Waterproof front and rear seat covers.

Black pack R-Sport
Gloss black insert with gloss black surround radiator grille.
Gloss black side window finishers.
Gloss black blades in front bumper area.
Gloss black front wing power vents with R-Sport branding.

Gloss black bumper blades, outer grille bezel and centre lower valance.
Grained black outer mesh grille and vertical air curtains in body colour.

Black pack S
As Black pack R-Sport (without R-Sport branding) plus:
Rear bumper gloss black diffuser and valance.
S rear fog lights.

Memory (10 x 10 way seats) pack
Powerfold exterior mirrors in body colour, electrically adjustable, auto dipping and heated, signature approach lights with black side turn indicators and memory.
Power adjustable steering column.
10 x 10 way electrically adjustable front seats with driver memory for seats, steering column and mirrors.

Memory (14 x 14 way Sports seats) pack
As 10 x 10 pack plus:
14 x 14 way electrically adjustable front seats with driver and passenger memory for seats, steering column and mirrors.

Memory (14 x 14 way Luxury seats) pack
As 14 x 14 pack plus:
Front seat upgrade with 4-way power lumbar.

Cold Climate pack
Heated front windscreen with timer.
Heater windscreen washer jets.
Heated front and rear seats.
Heated steering wheel.

Rear Seat Comfort pack
Heated front and rear seats.
Four zone climate control system.
Rear seat electric recline.
Air quality sensor.
Lockable cooled glove box.

Adaptive Dynamics pack
Adaptive Dynamics and Adaptive Surface Response (AWD only).

Practicality pack
Jaguar Smart Key system with keyless entry.
Gesture tailgate.
Remote release of second row seats in the boot.
Loadspace safety partition net.
Air quality sensor.
Lockable cooled glove box.

Advanced Parking pack
Rear view camera.
Park Assist system.
360 degree park distance control system.

Advanced Parking pack with Surround Camera
Advanced Parking pack plus:
Surround 360 degree camera.

Head-up Display pack
Head-up display and infra-red reflective windscreen.

InControl Touch Pro Pack with Meridian 380-Watt sound system pack
- InControl Touch Pro system with 12.3in TFT instrument cluster.
- Meridian 380-Watt digital sound system.

InControl Touch Pro Pack with Meridian 825-Watt sound system pack
- As above plus with:
- Meridian 825-Watt digital sound system.

Driver Assist Pack

Dynamic Pack

Extended Pet Pack

Extended Protection Pack with Dash Cam

Activity Pack

Technical specifications

	2.0-litre diesel (163PS)	2.0-litre diesel (180PS)	2.0-litre diesel MHEV (204PS)	2.0-litre diesel (240PS)	2.0-litre petrol (250PS)
cc	1999	1999	1997	1999	1997
Bore and stroke (mm)	83 x 92.3	83 x 92.4	83 x 92.3	83 x 92.4	83 x 92.4
Compression ratio	15.5 to 1	15.5 to 1	16.5 to 1	15.5 to 1	10.5 to 1
bhp	163	180	204	240	250
@rpm	4000	4000	3750	4000	5500
Max torque (lb ft)	280	318	317	368	269
@rpm	1750/2500	1750/2500	1750/2500	1500	1000/4500
Fuelling	Common rail fuel-injection	Common rail fuel-injection	Common rail fuel-injection	Common rail fuel-injection	Common rail fuel-injection
Transmission	6-speed ZF 8HP45 automatic	6-speed manual 8-speed ZF 8HP45 automatic	8-speed ZF 8HP45 automatic	8-speed ZF 8HP45 automatic	8-speed ZF 8HP45 automatic
Wheel size (in)	18 to 22	18 to 22	18 to 22	18 to 22	18 to 22
Suspension front	Double wishbone	Double wishbone arms, anti dive, coil springs	Double wishbone	Double wishbone	Double wishbone
Suspension rear	Integral link	Integral link arms, Co-axial coil springs	Integral link	Integral link	Integral link
Brakes	4-wheel discs	4-wheel discs	4-wheel discs	4-wheel discs	4-wheel discs
Performance					
0 to 60mph (secs)	9.6	8.1 (man RWD) 8.4 (man/auto AWD)	7.1	8.4	6.6
Top speed (mph)	121	129 (man RWD) 129 (man/auto AWD)	146	129	135
Average mpg	50.4	49.6 (man RWD) 47.9 (man AWD) 48.9 (auto AWD)	Dependent on electric/ICE mix	47.9	39.9
Dimensions					
Length (in)	184	186.2	184	186.2	186.2
Width (in)	81.6	85.6	81.6	85.6	85.6
Height (in)	55.7	61.5	55.7	61.5	61.5
Wheelbase (in)	111.6	113.1	111.6	113.1	113.1
Front Track (in)	63.2	64.6	63.2	64.6	64.6
Rear Track (in)	63.3	65.1	63.3	65.1	65.1
Weight (kg)	1760	1790 (RWD) 1845 (AWD)	2740	1845	1915

2.0-litre petrol (300PS)	2.0-litre diesel MHEV (400E)	3.0-litre diesel (300PS)	3.0-litre petrol (380PS)	5.0-litre petrol (550PS)
1997	1997	2993	2995	5000
83 x 92.4	83 x 92.3	84 x 90	84.5 x 89	92.5 x 93
9.5 to 1	16.5 to 1	16 to 1	10.5 to 1	9.5 to 1
300	404	300	380	550
5500	3750	4000	6500	6000/6500
295	640e	516	332	502
1500/4500	1500/4000	1500/1750	4500	2500/5500
Common rail fuel-injection	Common rail fuel-injection	Fuel-injection	Fuel-injection	Fuel injection
8-speed ZF 8HP45 automatic	8-speed ZF 8HP45 automatic	8-speed auto sequential	8-speed auto sequential	8-speed auto sequential
18 to 22	18 to 22	18 to 22	18 to 22	18 to 22
Double wishbone	Double wishbone	Ind double wishbones, alloy control	Ind coil springs	Ind coil springs
Integral link	Integral link	Ind double wishbones, alloy control	Ind coil springs	Ind coil springs
4-wheel discs	4-wheel discs	4-wheel ventilated discs	4-wheel discs	4-wheel discs
5.8	5	6.02	5.1	4.1
145	149	150	155	176
34.9	Dependent on electric/ICE mix	43.5	31.7	23.7
186.2	184	186.2	186.2	186.2
85.6	81.6	85.6	85.6	85.6
61.5	55.7	61.5	61.5	61.5
113.1	111.6	113.1	113.1	113.1
64.6	63.2	64.6	64.6	64.6
65.1	63.3	65.1	65.1	65.1
1842	2740	1954	1932	2070

Prices and production years

F-Pace SUV from 2016

Model	Price new	2016	2017	2018	2019	2020	2021	2022	2023
2.0-litre D180 Prestige RWD	£34,170	■	■	■	■	■	—	—	—
2.0-litre D180 Prestige AWD	£35,925	■	■	■	■	■	—	—	—
2.0-litre D180 Pottfolio RWD	£39,170	■	■	■	■	■	—	—	—
2.0-litre D180 Portfolio AWD		■	■	■	■	■	—	—	—
2.0-litre D180 R-Sport RWD	£36,670	■	■	■	■	■	—	—	—
2.0-litre D180 R-Sport AWD		■	■	■	■	■	—	—	—
2.0-litre D300 Prestige AWD		■	■	■	■	■	—	—	—
2.0-litre D300 Pottfolio AWD		■	■	■	■	■	—	—	—
2.0-litre D300 R-Sport AWD		■	■	■	■	■	—	—	—
2.0-litre D300 S AWD	£51,450	■	■	■	■	■	—	—	—
3.0-litre P380 S AWD	£51,450	■	■	■	■	■	—	—	—
3.0-litre D300 First Edition AWD	£65,275	■	■	■	■	■	—	—	—
2.0-litre D163 Pure RWD		—	—	■	■	■	—	—	—
2.0-litre D240 Pure AWD		—	—	■	■	■	—	—	—
5.0-litre P550 SVR AWD	£84,940	—	—	—	■	■	■	■	■
2.0-litre D180 R-Sport AWD		—	—	—	■	■	—	—	—
2.0-litre P250 Pure RWD		—	—	■	■	■	—	—	—
2.0-litre P300 300 Sport AWD	£53,980	—	—	—	—	■	—	—	—
3.0-litre D300 300 Sport AWD		—	—	—	—	■	■	■	■
2.0-litre P250 Chequered Flag AWD	£46,995	—	—	—	—	■	—	—	—
2.0-litre D180 Chequered Flag AWD		—	—	—	—	■	—	—	—
2.0-litre D240 Chequered Flag AWD		—	—	—	—	■	—	—	—
2.0-litre P163 MHEV AWD		—	—	—	—	—	■	■	—
2.0-litre D180 R-Sport Black AWD		—	—	—	—	■	■	—	—
2.0-litre D204 MHEV R-Dynamic S AWD	£48,860	—	—	—	—		■	■	■
2.0-litre D204 MHEV R-Dynamic SE Black AWD	£53,610	—	—	—	—	—	■	■	■
2.0-litre D204 MHEV R-Dynamic HSE Black AWD	£57,770	—	—	—	—	—	■	■	■
3.0-litre D300 MHEV R-Dynamic S AWD		—	—	—	—	—	■	■	—
3.0-litre D300 MHEV R-Dynamic SE Black AWD	£60,275	—	—	—	—	—	■	■	■
3.0-litre D300 MHEV R-Dynamic HSE Black AWD	£63,970	—	—	—	—	—	■	■	■
3.0-litre D300 R-Dynamic S AWD		—	—	—	—	—	■	■	—
3.0-litre D300 R-Dynamic SE AWD		—	—	—	—	—	■	■	—
3.0-litre D300 R-Dynamnic HSE AWD		—	—	—	—	—	■	■	—
2.0-litre P250 R-Dynamic S AWD	£52,415	—	—	—	—	—	■	■	■
2.0-litre P250 R-Dynamic SE Black AWD	£57,005	—	—	—	—	—	■	■	■

Model	Price new	2016	2017	2018	2019	2020	2021	2022	2023
2.0-litre P250 R-Dynamic HSE Black AWD	£61,175	—	—	—	—	—	■	■	■
2.0-litre P340 MHEV R-Dynamic S AWD		—	—	—	—	—	■	■	—
2.0-litre P340 MHEV R-Dynamic SE AWD		—	—	—	—	—	■	■	—
2.0-litre P340 MHEV R-Dynamic HSE AWD		—	—	—	—	—	■	■	—
3.0-litre P400 MHEV R-Dynamic S AWD		—	—	—	—	—	■	■	—
3.0-litre P400 MHEV R-Dynamic SE AWD		—	—	—	—	—	■	■	—
3.0-litre P400 MHEV R-Dynamic HSE AWD		—	—	—	—	—	■	■	—
3.0-litre P400 300 Sport AWD		—	—	—	—	—	—	■	—
2.0-litre P400e PHEV R-Dynamic S AWD	£60,985	—	—	—	—	—	—	—	■
2.0-litre P400e PHEV R-Dynamic SE Black AWD	£65,715	—	—	—	—	—	—	—	■
2.0-litre P400e PHEV R-Dynamic HSE Black AWD	£69,335	—	—	—	—	—	—	—	■
3.0-litre P400 400 Sport AWD	£69,280	—	—	—	—	—	—	—	■
5.0-litre P550 SVR Edition 1988 AWD	£101,500	—	—	—	—	—	—	■	■

Colour schemes and interior trim combinations

Exterior paint
Polaris White
Glacier White
Fuji White
Yulong White
Ostuni Pearl White
Rhodium Silver
Gallium Silver
Indus Silver
Silicon Silver
Quartzite
Ammonite Grey
Tempest Grey
Storm Grey
Ingot
Corris Grey
Eiger Grey
Carpathian Grey
Ebony
Ultimate Black
Cosmic Black
Norvic Black
Santorini Black
Caesium Blue
Dark Sapphire
Loire Blue
Portofino Blue
Ultra Blue
Odyssey Red
Italian Racing Red
Firenze Red
Roselle Red
British Racing Green
Midnight Amethyst (SVR Edition 1988 only)

Veneers
Ebony
Gloss Black
Gloss Figured Ebony
Satin Grey Figured Ebony
Satin Burr Ash
Satin Grey Ash
Satin Charcoal Ash
Satin Fine Line Wood
Gloss Burr Walnut
Carbon Fibre
Etched Aluminium
Engine Spin Aluminium
Meshed Aluminum

Seats
Jet
Ebony
Light Oyster
Latte
Sienna Tan
Brogue
Pimento
Mars Red
Espresso
Duo-tones:
Latte/Ebony
Ebony/Mars Red
Ebony/Pimento
Light Oyster/Ebony
Ebony/Sienna Tan
Light Oyster/Pimento

Contrast stitching/piping
Ebony
Red
Pimento
Light Oyster
Sienna Tan
Brogue
Espresso
Pistachio
Lime
Latte

Carpets
Jet
Ebony
Morzine
Oyster
Espresso

Headlining
Ebony
Light Oyster
Jet

Upper fascia/trim
Jet
Ebony
Light Oyster
Sienna Tan
Brogue
Latte
Espresso
Red
Pimento

26 E-PACE SUV from 2018

Background

A new addition to Jaguar's SUV range came in 2018 with the E-PACE, a five-seater compact model, creating a new market for Jaguar.

Having a purposeful stance with its short front and rear overhang, the fast sweep of the roofline created more space for rear seat passengers. The front grille mesh featured a 3D chamfering detail on its wide, flat hexagons. At the rear, round tailpipe finishers were integrated into the rear valance and the larger upper tailpipe spoiler was a three-piece design, tuned for optimum air flow.

From the front the E-PACE was decidedly a Jaguar with the unmistakable bold grille and the headlights that showed Jaguar's signature J-blade daytime running light style. This high-specification headlight system also featured Adaptive Matrix LED technology as an optional extra, with two slim horizontal LED modules to manage the low and high beams. Additionally, the J-blade running lights also performed the indicator function with a sweeping movement, a feature that Jaguar took up from some other manufacturers. At the rear, the slim, blade-like rear lamps featured full LED technology.

The E-PACE's profiled bonnet was produced from lightweight aluminium, saving up to 10kg over an equivalent steel part. The front wings were made from the same weight-saving material, yielding a 3kg benefit. The roof panel was also made of aluminium, reducing weight by 6kg over an equivalent steel panel, and lowering the vehicle's centre of gravity for improved handling and stability. The lightweight aluminium tailgate was 15kg lighter than a conventional steel assembly and used the riveting/bonding process that Jaguar pioneered. The thin bodysides were made from a high formability steel, only 0.7mm thick, helping to shed yet more weight.

The interior used soft-trimmed door casings with cool touch, satin chrome door handles, while the leather clad facia and seat upholstery featured twin-needle stitching to enhance the air of luxury. The interior focal point was a wraparound cockpit with the passenger grab handle forming the boundary of the driver console – a design concept directly inspired by the F-TYPE and then used on other Jaguar models.

The E-PACE broke with tradition by favouring a premium Noble Chrome treatment over traditional wood trim finishes. The understated metal finish was used on key details such as the gearshift surround, instrument panel, side vents and door pulls. Overall the interior design followed the same style and layout as other models later in their production (see earlier chapters).

There was generous passenger and luggage space, with room for five people and ingenious small item stowage solutions. The 8.42-litre centre console compartment could house four large water bottles, as well as configurable cup holders and trays; the lockable 10.07-litre glovebox offered secure storage, while 10.56-litre front and 8.26-litre rear door bins were bigger than most. The E-PACE also demonstrated versatility, with a configurable console stowage solution centred on smart device connectivity and customer experience.

Interior lighting was included for handles and stowage areas, while task lighting enabled owners to configure colour settings to their personal preference.

The seat materials were made durable with contrast stitching in vibrant colours that emphasised the E-PACE's sportiness; optional soft Windsor leathers with tonal stitching were also available.

A raft of detail also demonstrated the fun and quirky side of this Jaguar; on HSE models Jaguar 'contemporary animal print' designer labels were sewn into the shoulder hem of the front seats (in red on First Edition vehicles), and the same pattern is repeated on rubber mats in stowage areas.

Jaguar included some interesting design touches, such as the distinctive shape of a chicane that inspired elements both inside and out, most obviously in the light signature of the rear LED lamps. Tactile rotary dials found at the centre of the lower dashboard were inspired by the precise controls of a classic Leica camera lens. A fun 'Jaguar Cub' graphic in the obscuration band of the windscreen and in the puddle lamp projection were incorporated solely to put a smile on customers' faces.

The chassis was based on the rear suspension concept developed for the F-PACE. The Integral Link architecture separated lateral and longitudinal forces, providing the optimum combination of responsive steering and handling with longitudinal impact absorption and refinement. The E-PACE's rear suspension was also very compact, maximising interior space and allowing for generous wheel travel and articulation that gave the compact SUV excellent all-surface capability.

A new front suspension design further enhanced the driver's connection to the road. The front knuckle was a lightweight hollow-cast aluminium component, designed to provide additional camber for improved turn-in and to minimise understeer. A specially tuned front subframe was developed to generate a stiffer structure, including solid rear mounts to contribute to the vehicle's connected steering feel.

The new model took advantage of many features developed for other Jaguar models, such as Configurable Dynamics, All-Wheel Drive, Torque Vectoring by Braking, All Surface Progress Control and much more.

The E-PACE was originally powered by the Ingenium 2.0-litre petrol and diesel engines with a choice of 9-speed automatic transmission or a new 6-speed manual gearbox.

This was the first modern Jaguar to be produced outside of the UK, under a partnership agreement with Magna Steyre in Graz, Austria. Additionally the E-PACE would eventually also be produced for the Chinese Market at Chery Jaguar Land Rover in Changshu.

Model range at launch
E-PACE S/SE/HSE – 2.0-litre D150 FWD/AWD
E-PACE S/SE/HSE – 2.0-litre D180 AWD
E-PACE S/SE/HSE – 2.0-litre P250 AWD
E-PACE S/SE/HSE – 2.0-litre P300 AWD
E-PACE R-Dynamic S/SE/HSE – 2.0-litre D150 FWD/AWD
E-PACE R-Dynamic S/SE/HSE – 2.0-litre D180 AWD
E-PACE R-Dynamic S/SE/HSE – 2.0-litre P250 AWD
E-PACE R-Dynamic S/SE/HSE – 2.0-litre P300 AWD
E-PACE First Edition – D180 2.0-litre AWD
E-PACE First Edition – P300 AWD 2.0-litre AWD

Model range and development

In mid-2019 Jaguar announced the Chequered Flag special edition for the E-PACE. Unique, premium design touches and upgraded standard features, the model was only available in a limited range of colours. Available in a choice of four engines, the D150 and D180 AWD or P200 and P250 AWD petrol units. Prices started at £40,050.

In the same year 'Black Pack's were launched. These were models fitted with a range of options, normally at extra cost but incorporated into production models. The overall price was cheaper than individually purchasing these options for a standard car. Other new 'packs' were introduced to further enhance models.

From 2019 E-PACEs got a larger fuel tank to extend the car's range.

The most significant changes within the short lifespan of the E-PACE came with the powertrains. The introduction of the 163PS diesel unit took over from the D150 for the 2021 model year, at the same time heralding in a change of model designation with the emphasis on the enhanced R-Dynamic specifications. The D200 diesel also replaced the D180. Similarly, changes took place with enhanced petrol engines.

The biggest move, however, came with the introduction of hybrid power at the end of 2020. With PHEV (Plug-in Hybrid Electric Vehicle) technology, a 2.0-litre 4-cylinder P300e petrol engine was supported by an electric motor, the latter powered by a lithium-ion battery. When fully charged the car was capable of up to 30 miles of all-electric driving making short journeys very economical and environmentally friendly.

Mild-hybrid technology was also embraced with the introduction of MHEV (Mild Hybrid Electric Vehicle) models using revised i4 versions of both petrol and diesel 2.0-litre engines. Utilising an electric supercharger in combination with a twin-scroll turbocharger, the former was driven by a 48V motor, delivering virtually instant boost pressure. The MHEV system used a Belt integrated Starter Generator in the engine bay to harvest energy lost when slowing down and braking; the energy was stored in a lithium-ion battery, and then re-deployed when accelerating.

The introduction of new technologies and styling changes followed Jaguar's other models at the time (see earlier chapters). For the E-PACE this meant a revised, enhanced exterior trim package and a more crafted interior with many minor changes to trim.

As with Jaguar's other models in the period leading up to the introduction of its all-electric ranges, the number of E-PACE available was reduced, finally to just one model by 2024.

Exterior identification points

For broad details refer to the previous chapter on the F-PACE.

First Edition
- Based on the later R-Dynamic SE specification.
- Only available in Yulong White, Santorini Black and Caldera Red with Grey Satin Diamond Turned alloy wheels.

300 Sport
- Dark Satin Grey exterior trim detailing, front grille, window surrounds, vents, mirror caps and door finishers plus rear valance.
- '300 Sport' badging.
- Only in Yulong White, Indus Silver or Santorini Black.

Chequered Flag
- Gloss Black trim detailing to front grille, door cladding, side vents and roof rails.
- Only in Yulong White, Santorini Black or Eiger Grey.

2021 major styling changes affecting all models
- New bonnet design.
- Slim all-LED quad headlights.
- Revised design radiator grille.
- New rear lighting with double-chicane graphic.
- New rear bumper and tailgate arrangement.
- Introduction of new R-Dynamics designations with uprated trim from previous models.

Interior identification points

For broad details refer to the previous chapter on the F-PACE.

The E-PACE provided Jaguar with a compact SUV format taking styling cues from its larger brother, the F-PACE.

The E-PACE frontal aspect shows a family resemblance to the then current range of other Jaguar models.

The E-PACE's severe slope to the rear window with roof-mounted spoiler makes it instantly recognisable.

The early interior of the E-PACE with styling aspects taken from the then current other models, including the F-TYPE sports car.

First Edition
- Based on the later R-Dynamic SE specification.
- Ebony interior with red stitching.
- Ambient mood lighting.
- 'First Edition' carpet mats and treadplates.

300 Sport
- Yellow contrast stitching on the instrument panel, centre console and leather seats.
- '300 Sport' badging to the treadplates, carpet mats and steering wheel.
- '300 Sport' embossed into front headrests.

Style trim and colourways depended upon models, this being an HSE model.

Revised frontal aspect from the 2021 model year.

The rear luggage area was significantly less than the F-PACE and space below the floor was for storage, not a spare wheel.

Subtle changes from the original design to the 2021 model year.

Seating combination for the S model.

The revised interior layout from 2021. Note the enlarged infotainment screen.

The E-PACE Chequered Flag.

The E-PACE Chequered Flag interior.

The marginally simplified interior of the late hybrid E-PACE.

R-Dynamic Black model.

Late model E-PACE R-Dynamic exterior.

Left: The original headlamp treatment from 2018. Right: The later headlamp treatment from 2020.

The enhanced information display available on the later models.

Chequered Flag
- Meshed aluminium detailing
- 'Chequered Flag' treadplates

2021 major styling changes affecting all models
- Enlarged 11.4in HD touchscreen for infotainment, housed in a magnesium frame in Black Satin.
- Soft-touch materials with the instrument panel topper, door armrests, console side and door bins.
- New designed door casings with 360-degree grab handles.
- New range of veneer and alloy finishers.
- Full-width 'piano lid' formed across the instrument panel.
- New centre console design incorporating storage.
- Laser-etched mid-line speaker frets.
- New Drive Selector design.
- New steering wheel design with 'hidden upon lit' switches.
- Zinc alloy gearshift paddles.
- Introduction of new R-Dynamics designations with uprated trim from previous models.

1 - 17in Style 1005

2 – 17in Style 1037

3 – 18in Style 9008

4 – 18in Style 5048

5 – 18in Style 5118

6 - 19in Style 5119 Satin Dark Grey

7 – 19in Style 1039

8 – 19in Style 5049

9 – 20in Style 5051 Diamond Turned Gloss Black.

10 – 20in Style 5051 Diamond Turned Satin Grey

11 – 20in Style 5054

12 – 20in Style 5120 Chrome Shadow

13 – 20in Style 6014

14 – 21in Style 5053 Satin Grey Diamond Turned

15 – 21in Style 1078 Diamond Turned Gloss Black

Technical specifications

	2.0-litre diesel FWD (150PS)	2.0-litre diesel AWD (150PS)	2.0-litre diesel FWD (163PS)	2.0-litre diesel AWD (163PS)
Cc	1999	1999	1997	1997
Bore and stroke (mm)	83 x 92.3	83 x 92.4	83 x 92.3	83 x 92.3
Compression ratio	15.5 to 1	15.5 to 1	16.5 to 1	16.5 to 1
Bhp	150	150	163	163
@ rpm	3500	3500	3750	3750
Max torque (lb ft)	280	280	280	280
@ rpm	1750	1750	1500/2500	1500/2500
Fuelling	Common rail fuel injection	Common rail fuel injection	Common rail fuel injection	Common rail fuel injection
Transmission	6-speed automatic	6-speed manual/ 9-speed auto	6-speed automatic	9-speed automatic
Wheel size (in)	18 to 22	18 to 22	18 to 22	18 to 22
Suspension front	Double wishbone	Double wishbone	Double wishbone	Double wishbone
Suspension rear	Integral link	Integral link	Integral link	Integral link
Brakes	4-wheel discs	4-wheel discs	4-wheel discs	4-wheel discs
Performance				
0-60mph (secs)	9.5	9.9	9.5	9.2
Top speed (mph)	124	120	128	124
Average mpg	52.3	47.1	47.1	47.1
Dimensions				
Length (in)	4411mm	4411mm	4411mm	4411mm
Width (in)	1984mm	1984mm	1984mm	1984mm
Height (in)	1649mm	1649mm	1649mm	1649mm
Wheelbase (in)	2681mm	2681mm	2681mm	2681mm
Front track (in)	1625mm	1625mm	1625mm	1625mm
Rear track (in)	1624mm	1624mm	1624mm	1624mm
Weight (kg)	1775	1843	1809	1916

2.0-litre diesel AWD (180PS)	2.0-litre diesel MHEV AWD (204PS)	2.0-litre diesel AWD (240PS)	2.0-litre petrol AWD (200PS)	2.0-litre petrol MHEV AWD (200PS)
1999	1997	1999	1997	1997
83 x 92.4	83 x 92.4	83 x 92.4	83 x 92.4	83 x 92.4
15.5 to 1	16.5 to 1	15.3 to 1	10.5 to 1	10.5 to 1
180	204	240	200	200
4,000	3750	4000	5500	5500
317	317	368	236	236
1750	1750/2500	1500	1250/4000	1250/4000
Common rail fuel injection	Common rail fuel injection	Common rail fuel injection	Common rail fuel injection	Common rail fuel injection
6-speed manual/ 9-speed automatic	9-speed automatic	9-speed automatic	9-speed automatic	9-speed automatic
18 to 22	18 to 22	18 to 22	18 to 22	18 to 22
Double wishbone	Double wishbone	Double wishbone	Double wishbone	Double wishbone
Integral link	Integral link	Integral link	Integral link	Integral link
4-wheel discs	4-wheel discs	4-wheel discs	4-wheel discs	4-wheel discs
8.6	7.9	6.8	7.7	8
127	131	139	134	132
47.1	Dependent on electric/ ICE output	42.8	35.3	Dependent on electric/ ICE output
4411mm	4411mm	4411mm	4411mm	4411mm
1984mm	1984mm	1984mm	1984mm	1984mm
1649mm	1649mm	1649mm	1649mm	1649mm
2681mm	2681mm	2681mm	2681mm	2681mm
1625mm	1625mm	1625mm	1625mm	1625mm
1624mm	1624mm	1624mm	1624mm	1624mm
1843	1952	1926	1832	1847

(Continues overleaf ...)

Technical specifications cont ...

	2.0-litre petrol MHEV AWD (240PS)	2.0-litre petrol AWD (250PS)	2.0-litre petrol AWD (300PS)	2.0-litre diesel MHEV (300PS)	2.0-litre diesel PHEV (300e)
Cc	1997	1997	1997	1997	1498
Bore and stroke (mm)	83 x 92.4	83 x 92.4	83 x 92.4	83 x 92.3	83 x 92.3
Compression ratio	10.5 to 1	10.5 to 1	10.5 to 1	10.5 to 1	10.5 to 1
Bhp	240	249	300	300	309
@ rpm	5500	5500	5500	5500	5500
Max torque (lb ft)	296	269	295	295	398
@ rpm	1300/4400	1350	1500	1500/4500	1600/4500
Fuelling	Common rail fuel injection	Common rail fuel injection	Common rail fuel injection	Common rail fuel injection	Common rail fuel injection
Transmission	9-speed automatic	9-speed automatic	9-speed automatic	9-speed auto	8-speed ZF 8HP45 automatic
Wheel size (in)	18 to 22	18 to 22	18 to 22	18 to 22	18 to 22
Suspension front	Double wishbone	Double wishbone	Double wishbone	Double wishbone	Double wishbone
Suspension rear	Integral link	Integral link	Integral link	Integral link	Integral link
Brakes	4-wheel discs	4-wheel discs	4-wheel discs	4-wheel discs	4-wheel discs
Performance					
0-60mph (secs)	7	6.7	6.3	6.5	6.1
Top speed (mph)	142	143	149	150	134
Average mpg	Dependent on electric/ICE output	34.9	32.5	Dependent on electric/ICE mix	Dependent on electric/ICE mix
Dimensions					
Length (in)	4411mm	4411mm	4411mm	184	184
Width (in)	1984mm	1984mm	1984mm	81.6	81.6
Height (in)	1649mm	1649mm	1649mm	55.7	55.7
Wheelbase (in)	2681mm	2681mm	2681mm	111.6	111.6
Front track (in)	1625mm	1625mm	1625mm	63.2	63.2
Rear track (in)	1624mm	1624mm	1624mm	63.3	63.3
Weight (kg)	1889	1832	1894	1952	2098

Optional extras

Full length roof rails
Privacy glass
LED or Matrix headlights
Auto high-beam assist
Infrared reflective windscreen
Twin tailpipes and finishers
No badges
Auto dimming/power fold mirrors
Detachable towbar

Electrically deployable towbar
Chromed side window surrounds
Illuminated treadplates with 'Jaguar'
Bright metal pedals
Ambient lighting
Smoker's pack
Cabin air ionisation
Air quality sensors
Digital TV

Prices and production years

Model	Price new	2018	2019	2020	2021	2022	2023
2.0-litre D150 S FWD	£32,800	■	■	■	—	—	—
2.0-litre D150 S AWD	£34,740	■	■	■	—	—	—
2.0-litre D150 SE FWD	£34,950	■	■	■	—	—	—
2.0-litre D150 SE AWD	£36,890	■	■	■	—	—	—
2.0-litre D150 HSE FWD		■	■	■	—	—	—
2.0-litre D150 HSE AWD		■	■	■	—	—	—
2.0-litre D150 R-Dynamic S FWD	£34,190	■	■	■	—	—	—
2.0-litre D150 R-Dynamic S AWD	£37,120	■	■	■	—	—	—
2.0-litre D150 R-Dynamic SE AWD	£38,270	■	■	■	—	—	—
2.0-litre D150 R-Dynamic HSE AWD	£43,555	■	■	■	—	—	—
2.0-litre D180 S AWD	£35,490	■	■	■	—	—	—
2.0-litre D180 SE AWD		■	■	■	—	—	—
2.0-litre D180 HSE AWD	£42,745	■	■	■	—	—	—
2.0-litre D180 R-Dynamic S AWD	£36,870	■	■	■	—	—	—
2.0-litre D180 R-Dynamic SE AWD	£39,020	■	■	■	—	—	—
2.0-litre D180 R-Dynamic HSE AWD0	£44,305	■	■	■	—	—	—
2.0-litre P250 S AWD		■	■	■	—	—	—
2.0-litre P250 SE AWD		■	■	■	—	—	—
2.0-litre P250 HSE AWD		■	■	—	—	—	—
2.0-litre P250 R-Dynamic S AWD		■	■	—	—	—	—
2.0-litre P250 R-Dynamic SE AWD		■	■	■	—	—	—
2.0-litre P250 R-Dynamic HSE AWD		■	■	■	—	—	—
2.0-litre P300 S AWD		■	■	—	—	—	—
2.0-litre P300 SE AWD		■	■	—	—	—	—
2.0-litre P300 HSE AWD		■	■	—	—	—	—
2.0-litre P300 R-Dynamic S AWD		■	■	■	—	—	—
2.0-litre P300 R-Dynamic SE AWD		■	■	■	—	—	—
2.0-litre P300 R-Dynamic HSE AWD		■	■	■	—	—	—
2.0-litre D180 First Edition AWD		■	—	—	—	—	—
2.0-litre P300 First Editoin AWD		■	—	—	—	—	—
2.0-litre D300 Sport AWD		—	—	—	■	—	—
2.0-litre D200 MHEV AWD		—	—	—	■	—	—
2.0-litre D163 FWD	£32,590	—	—	—	■	—	—

26 Prices and production years cont ...

Model	Price new	2018	2019	2020	2021	2022	2023
2.0-litre D163 S FWD	£34,615	—	—	—	■	—	—
2.0-litre D163 SE FWD	£36,540	—	—	—	■	—	—
2.0-litre D163 R-Dynamic FWD	£33,990	—	—	—	■	—	—
2.0-litre D163 R-Dynamic S FWD	£36,015	—	—	—	■	—	—
2.0-litre D163 R-Dynamic SE FWD	£37,940	—	—	—	■	—	—
2.0-litre D163 AWD	£35,890	—	—	—	■	—	—
2.0-litre D163 S AWD	£38,255	—	—	—	■	—	—
2.0-litre D163 SE AWD	£40,180	—	—	—	■	—	—
2.0-litre D163 R-Dynamic AWD	£37,290	—	—	—	■	—	—
2.0-litre D163 R-Dynamic S AWD	£39,655	—	—	—	■	—	—
2.0-litre D163 R-Dynamic SE AWD	£41,580	—	—	—	■	—	—
2.0-litre D200 S AWD	£38,950	—	—	■	■	—	—
2.0-litre D200 SE AWD	£40,875	—	—	■	■	—	—
2.0-litre D200 R-Dynamic S AWD	£40,010	—	—	■	■	—	—
2.0-litre D200 R-Dynamic MHEV AWD	£43,125	—	—	■	■	■	—
2.0-litre D200 R-Dynamic SE AWD	£42,275	—	—	■	■	—	—
2.0-litre D200 R-Dynamic SE Black MHEV AWD	£45,705	—	—	■	—	■	—
2.0-litre D200 R-Dynamic HSE AWD	£45,215	—	—	■	■	—	—
2.0-litre D200 R-Dynamic HSE Black MHEV AWD	£48,305	—	—	■	—	■	—
2.0-litre P160 R-Dynamic SE Black MHEV FWD	£45,185	—	—	—	—	■	—
2.0-litre P160 R-Dynamic HSE Black MHEV FWD	£47,425	—	—	—	—	■	—
2.0-litre P250 R-Dynamic SE Black MHEV AWD	£47,890	—	—	—	—	■	■
2.0-litre P250 R-Dynamic HSE Black MHEV AWD	£50,130	—	—	—	—	■	—
2.0-litre P300e R-Dynamic SE Black PHEV AWD	£52,020	—	—	—	—	■	—
2.0-litre P300e R-Dynamic HSE Black PHEV AWD	£54,260	—	—	—	—	■	—

Colour schemes and interior trim combinations

Body
Fuji White
Yulong White
Ostuni White Pearl
Borasco Grey
Corris Grey
Eiger Grey
Carpathian Grey
Hakuba Silver
Indus Silver
Silicon Silver
Portofino Blue
Bluefire Blue
Caesium Blue
Caldera Red
Firenze Red
Farallon Pearl Black
Santorini Black
Norvik Black

Seat material
E-PACE – Fabric, Grained Leather or Windsor Leather
R-Dynamic – Sportsmesh, Grained Leather or Windsor Leather

Colour
Ebony
Light Oyster
Sienna Tan
Mars Red
Lunar
Eclipse

Contrast stitching/piping
Ebony
Light Oyster
Sienna Tan
Sienna Tan
Reims Blue
Mars Red

Carpets
Ebony
Lunar

Headlining
Ebony
Light Oyster

Upper fascia/trim
Ebony
Lunar

Mid roll
Ebony
Light Oyster
Sienna Tan
Mars Red
Eclipse

About Nigel Thorley

Nigel Thorley is a well-regarded motoring historian with a particular interest in the Jaguar marque. Brought up on the marque by his family, Nigel got his first Jaguar at the age of 18, and has owned over 70 models. His knowledge and expertise of these cars is widely recognised, and he has written over 20 titles on the marque, contributed to TV and radio programmes, and regularly provides talks and seminars on the cars and the company. A founder member and Director of the Jaguar Enthusiast's Club, Nigel was also Editor of the Club's prestigious Jaguar Enthusiasts magazine for nearly 40 years.

Also from Nigel Thorley

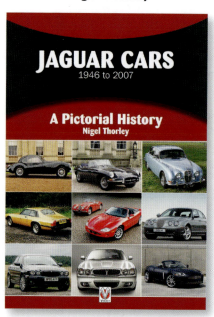

Jaguar Cars 1946-2007 – A Pictorial History

An on-the-spot information resource for all Jaguar cars from 1922 through to 2007. General model information, specifications and other production details for each model are given in chronological order, along with full colour pictures to make identification easy.

One of Veloce's popular 'A Pictorial History' series, this book will prove to be a valuable resource for any Jaguar enthusiast.

ISBN: 978-1-787117-76-1
Paperback • 21x14.8cm • 160 pages • 387 colour and b&w pictures

Thinking of buying a Jaguar?

Why not pick up one of Veloce's Essential Buyer's Guides™ – an invaluable tool to help you purchase the car of your dreams. Many other marques and models are covered in this best-selling series.

For more information and price details, visit our website at www.veloce.co.uk
email: info@veloce.co.uk • Tel: +44(0)1305 260068